S0-AGI-739

SOCIAL PSYCHOLOGY

Robert C. Williamson

Lehigh University

Paul G. Swingle

University of Ottawa

S. Stansfeld Sargent

Psychological Consultant

 **F.E. PEACOCK PUBLISHERS, INC.**
ITASCA, ILLINOIS 60143

SOCIAL PSYCHOLOGY

WILLIAMSON SWINGLE & SARGENT

Copyright © 1982
F.E. Peacock Publishers, Inc.
All rights reserved
Library of Congress
Catalog Card No. 80-52451
ISBN 0-87581-264-3
Printed in the U.S.A.

vi

PREFACE

Probably the most fundamental characteristic of this book, now in its fourth edition, is that it represents the integrated work of a sociologist and two psychologists. This collaboration is in keeping with our view that social events can be understood and analyzed only through an integrated effort among the behavioral sciences.

We approach the subject from an eclectic viewpoint. The text is related to neobehaviorism but nevertheless draws on other models in psychology and sociology; indeed, our thinking has been influenced by a number of movements, ranging from the Gestalt approach to exchange theory. We do not believe that these different perspectives are necessarily irreconcilable.

We believe social psychology as a discipline need no longer be as self-conscious as it was a generation ago. It has become a science. Social psychology has been concerned with the manipulation of variables in laboratory settings, and its findings have often seemed artificial and remote. Increasingly, however, research has moved from the confines of the laboratory on campus to the arena of life in the community. With this change the barrier between the micro approach of psychology and the macro approach of sociology has been diminished.

We are convinced that the behavioral sciences, and notably social psychology, can offer data relevant to relieving the critical tensions of contemporary society. It would be foolhardy to suggest that solutions can be found for all problems, but social psychology offers a great deal more knowledge than is currently being utilized by society. In fact, the problem seems to be to convince the politician, the manager, or the public at large to look at the wares social scientists have to offer.

The organization of the book reflects these contentions. Chapter I defines the role of the social psychologist. Part I is concerned with the relation of the individual to his or her culture and the question of socialization. In Part II we turn to fundamental psychological processes such as perception, learning, and motivation as a means of analyzing peoples' cognitions, attitudes, and communication systems. Part III focuses on group processes, which, along with attitudes, we regard as the core of social psychology. Role behavior and leadership are also analyzed in the context of the group. Part IV is concerned with the relevance of social psychology to social issues. The analysis of mass behavior, social movements, and social change is central to understanding the crises of the late 20th century. The final chapters revolve about these major dislocations, ethnic and international relations, and the more recent issues of the spatial environment and the role of the elderly in our society.

This text, as compared with previous editions, is reduced in scope but gives more attention to methodology and psychological issues. Nevertheless, we continue to be concerned with the individual's orientation to the sociocultural setting. Drawing on both a neobehaviorist and a field approach, the text stresses personality, situational variables, and the person's perception of the situation. We also are committed to the application of findings in social psychological research to the tensions and malaise besetting contemporary society.

Throughout the period of preparing this volume, all three authors have been grateful for the support of their wives and other members of their family. We also want to express our appreciation to the many teachers, colleagues, and students who have played a role in shaping our orientation to social psychology. For the editing of the manuscript we want to thank Gloria Reardon. Equally we are indebted to Ann VanDoren and Timmy Williamson for the typing of the manuscript.

June 1981

R. C. Williamson
P. G. Swingle
S. S. Sargent

INTRODUCTION

1
SOCIAL PSYCHOLOGY AS A SCIENCE

Social psychology is a unique hybrid among disciplines. As psychology, it is concerned with the motivation, attitudes, and behavior of individuals. As sociology, it investigates the structure and operation of the groups in society. In its own right as a field of study, social psychology is concerned with the reciprocal manner in which individuals and small groups influence and are influenced by one another.

Thus social psychology provides a means we can use to help us understand ourselves in our relations to others and to the society in which we live. It is a science which focuses on the interaction between individuals or between an individual and the members of a group in a social setting—workers at a workbench or students in a classroom, a family group at the dinner table or a crowd at a football game. Or the setting could be an emergency situation—a fight at a rock concert, residents fleeing from a fire or earthquake, or terrorists hijacking a plane. The social psychologist is interested in both the *overt* or evident behavior of the persons involved and in their *covert* or hidden behavior—their feelings and attitudes.

Social psychologists today have special interest in one dimension of social behavior—its rate of change. Since primitive times humans have lived in groups which have been undergoing change, usually very slowly or to a limited extent. By contrast the pace and scope of change in contemporary times, especially since World War II, have been startling. The changes produced have brought dissent and conflict, as well as massive shifts in values, attitudes, and behavior which in many cases have had bewildering effects. As a result of developments in high-speed communication, we are instantly aware of—and involved in—fundamental changes taking place all over the world. We have witnessed political attacks and assassinations and have had vivid vicarious experiences associated with acts of violence such as the takeover of the U.S. embassy and the holding of diplomatic hostages by "militants" in Iran for more than a year. As a result of the reliance of industrialized nations on increasingly scarce natural resources, the economic initiative has rapidly shifted to previously undeveloped nations who have the resources and can get them to the market.

The extent to which social psychology can help us interpret and deal with such complex and rapidly changing phenomena depends on whether it is possible to deal with them *scientifically* at all. As a scientific discipline, social psychology has existed only since the early 1900s, and it can hardly be expected to yield measurements and predictions that are as precise as those of the older physical sciences such as physics, chemistry, and astronomy. These were established fully three centuries ago, and they deal with nonliving materials and processes which are in many respects more stable and less complex than the behavior of human beings. Nevertheless, since the turn of the century social psychologists have been busily observing, getting hunches, and proposing theories—that is, using the scientific method to propose hypotheses and test them by experiment or further observation. As a result, they have amassed a sizable body of knowledge that is useful in furthering an understanding of individuals and groups under both normal and abnormal conditions.

Indeed, the research activity of social psychologists has been prodigious. Several hundred research articles appear every year in such journals as the *Journal of Personality and Social Psychology, Social Psychology Quarterly* (formerly *Sociometry*), and the *Journal of Social Issues,* not to mention the monographs, books, and other publications in the field. Most are laboratory or statistical studies which have implications for individuals and groups in real life. The ability of social researchers to offer meaningful interpretations is increasingly impressive. As with all life sciences, the goal is to predict behavior: how the individual will perform in a group setting, for example, or how children or adults can change their ethnic attitudes, or how people will react in a disaster.

This chapter introduces the many facets of social psychology. It begins by explaining the place of this discipline among the social sciences and its relevance to the problems of our time. Its history is traced from its roots in the 19th century to its emergence as a science, and its close relationship to the other behavioral sciences (such as psychology, sociology, and anthropology) is developed. An analysis of the research methods social psychologists use to study human behavior in society considers the techniques by which scientific precision can be assured and suggests which methods are appropriate for investigating certain kinds of problems. The final section discusses the broad ideas behind the principal theories in the discipline.

PRELIMINARY QUESTIONS ABOUT SOCIAL PSYCHOLOGY

What Do Social Psychologists Study?

The society we live in is complex and often frustrating. We look for explanations why we cannot find a job we want, why food and housing cost so much, or why it is not safe to be out on the streets at night. We are dismayed at its contradictions: We have a high standard of living and an advanced technology, for example, yet a sixth of the people in the United States live in poverty. The computer offers almost limitless knowledge, but it often seems to reduce human beings to mere numbers. More of the people have better educations and higher expectations, but there has been little improvement in the quality of the mass media or in the honesty or dedication of elected officials.

Every issue of a metropolitan newspaper gives further evidence of the spectrum of dissent. For years now, the peoples in most nations have been moving through a succession of crises, both domestic and international. Political leaders seem unable to find solutions for such problems as environmental pollution, deterioration of the cities, and erosion of civil liberties, not to mention the plight of the disadvantaged. The nations devote disproportionate shares of their resources to building up massive armaments in a world that has not yet found workable nonviolent ways to deal with international conflicts.

Such problems are a continuing challenge to statesmen, scientists, philosophers, and practitioners. They may be fundamentally technical, economic, or political in nature, but they all involve the interaction of human beings, and this brings the behavioral and social sciences into the picture. If we are to avoid the deterioration or even destruction of civilization, every resource for solving our major social problems must be expanded, improved, and mobilized.

Social psychologists can play a significant role in this effort. They can clarify the ways in which opinions are formed and the conditions under which attitudes and prejudices lead to overt behavior. Their research can show how groups and organizations are formed and members are galvanized into action. Their leadership studies can point out the personal qualities and situational factors that are most effective in meeting crises and solving problems.

In recent years the research methods of social psychologists have improved greatly, and their substantive knowledge has grown. They have been able to set up and test many hypotheses which have improved our understanding of social phenomena, though they fall short of predicting precisely what will happen as the result of a given course of action. Many social psychologists are impatient about the inability to provide better answers to problems. Elms (1975) points out the difficulties scientific research has in trying to keep up with the increasing demand for relevance.

How Practical Is Social Psychology?

Leaders in government and industry apparently recognize that social psychologists, along with other social scientists, can make practical contributions

Social problems surfaced well before the 20th century, though they are being more closely monitored today. Hogarth's drawing, "Gin Lane," depicts some social dislocations of 18th-century London. *Source:* Print Collection, Art, Prints and Photographs Division, The New York Public Library, Astor, Lenox and Tilden Foundations.

to their efforts. The applications of social science technology are evident in advertising and politics. In international relations, the desire to avoid using stockpiled nuclear weapons and to prevent their proliferation has placed new emphasis on finding better ways to work out conflicts than the threat of massive destruction. In labor negotiations, interracial relations, education, corrections, and many other areas, the knowledge derived from social science is being directly applied to contemporary problems.

Bruce Laingen, the senior diplomat among the 52 U.S. hostages held for 444 days in Iran by student-militarists, for example, described the attitude of Iranians in a State Department memo in 1979, shortly before the hostage seizure, in terms that could have been taken from a social psychology textbook. He spoke of a national history of instability that had given the Iranians "an almost total preoccupation with self [that] leaves little room for understanding points of view other than one's own" and described "a bazaar mentality . . . a mindset that often ignores longer term interests in favor of immediately obtainable advantages." (However, as we shall see in Chapter 2, caution must be exercised in making generaliztions about national character.)

Box 1–1
PSYCHOLOGY AND SOCIAL CRISES:
BEATING THE CLOCK

The behavioral sciences have grown out of infancy and are approaching adulthood. Social psychology has a contribution to make—provided time does not run out.

When nine leading psychologists were asked to comment on the future role of that discipline in 1978, Stuart W. Cook cited the need for more theoretical integration of research data, with emphasis on practical implications. He suggested the psychologist's input will be needed for several major problems: (1) the crisis in overpopulation, (2) the exhaustion of nonrenewable energy sources, (3) the economic and social deterioration of major urban centers, (4) the role of the aged in society and (5) domestic and international conflict.*

Besides these tensions, there are others that psychology, and particularly social psychology, can help defuse. The depersonalization of human beings caught in a bureaucratic, automated system; the persistence of violence and crime; the barriers to full participation in society that individuals may face due to their sex, race, economic disadvantage, or unconventional lifestyle are some examples.

*M. Wertheimer et al., "Psychology and the Future," *American Psychologist*, 1978, *33*, 631–647.

As social psychologists became accepted as scientists, they developed more responsibility and confidence in offering interpretations and making recommendations for solutions to crises and problems (see Box 1–1). Behavioral scientists have been employed in a number of government agencies, occasionally in a policymaking role but usually to provide information on research findings which could affect planned programs. Governments typically call in social scientists for consultation, not decisions. In the early 1970s, the recommendations of the U.S. presidential commissions on civil disorders, obscenity, and violence received at best lip service and at worst outright disapproval from former President Richard Nixon and many members of Congress. When governmental bodies have welcomed recommendations by social scientists, the problems of implementation are often not resolved. A few national governments, notably in Scandinavia, have begun to use social scientists extensively in an advisory capacity.

Speaking of the role of social scientists in current affairs, Kelman (1968) says: "We still have a long way to go before becoming truly influential and we may find the road rather bumpy. Nevertheless, we must anticipate the possibility that social scientists will meet with a serious interest in their ideas." The findings of social psychology and related disciplines are in fact being taken into account in government and industry—a notable difference from the days when executives based their decisions on hunches and guesses. The degree to which behavioral scientists' conclusions are accepted depends on the social and political climate.

If the extent to which government in particular and society in general will accept the validity of the behavioral sciences is measured by the amount of research funded by federal agencies, the evidence is discouraging. Psychologists represent about 8 percent of all research scientists in U.S. universities, but in 1974, for example, they received only 3 percent of research funds. Psychology and the social sciences together were granted a seventh of the funds allotted to the physical sciences, not including engineering. Correcting for the differing ratios of scientists in given disciplines and comparing the funds per full-time scientist, the physical scientists received almost twice as much as the psychologists and more than four times what the social scientists were awarded (Kiesler, 1977). The prospect for the behavioral sciences has become even more discouraging since the election of Ronald Reagan in 1980.

Within the social sciences, of course, there are differing orientations whose value to society varies with the times. Political scientists are particularly concerned with governmental structures and the management of conflict. Legal theorists focus on the development of group sanctions associated with departures from a society's mores or norms. Behavioral geography directs attention to the effects of physical surroundings on a person's or group's behavior.

The utility of social psychologists' contributions and the demand for their services also vary greatly. They draw upon the work of psychologists, sociologists, anthropologists, and other social scientists in their efforts to understand major tensions in our society, such as ethnic and minority relations, labor conflicts, or newer problems deriving from such social forces as sexism or ageism. More important, we are seriously concerned for the first time in history with the survival of humanity. Control of nuclear war and management of the ecology of our planet involve all the subjects in the academic curriculum, and certainly all the sciences. But since war is primarily a problem of human relationships, it is particularly a challenge to social scientists, and most appropriately social psychologists, to discover solutions to this most horrible of all social tensions. (See Chapter 18.)

THE FORERUNNERS OF SOCIAL PSYCHOLOGY

The contemporary position of a field of study often bears little relation to its origin. Thus astronomy and chemistry, two of the oldest and most firmly established sciences, sprang from astrology and alchemy, respectively. Psychology, located academically between biology and the social sciences, owes its origin to philosophy and to 19th-century physiology.

Social psychology combines elements of psychology and the social sciences and has a complex genealogy which includes strains from many disciplines. It came on the scene about 1900, after the way had been prepared by at least four groups of scholars: social philosophers, pioneer anthropologists, British evolutionists, and early sociologists.

The best references on the 19th-century background of social psychology are Karpf (1972) and Watson (1977).

Social Philosophers

Ancient, medieval, and early modern philosophers speculated widely about human nature, heredity, instincts, impulses, customs, and social relations. In Plato's *Republic,* Aristotle's *Politics* and *Ethics,* and the writings of Montesquieu, Hobbes, Locke, Rousseau, and many others, the problems of social living were given considerable attention. Some of the ideas of the pre-19th-century social philosophers were original and provocative; others now seem vague, unscientific, and contradictory. It is hardly surprising that they failed to understand the subtle relationship between an individual and society—there is some doubt that we do now! But they did focus interest on many important questions later taken up by writers who were more specialized in their training and scientific in their approach.

Pioneer Anthropologists

In 1860, two German scholars, Hermann Steinthal and Moritz Lazarus, established a journal called *Folk Psychology,* with the intention of discovering the mental processes of primitive peoples by studying their language, mythology, religion, literature, and art. Their work turned toward philosophy and mysticism as they became concerned with "group minds" and "folk souls." These concepts helped set the stage for the study of culture (see Chapter 2), and they inspired Wilhelm Wundt, the father of experimental psychology, who produced a ten-volume series titled *Elements of Folk Psychology.*

Wundt felt that higher social processes could not be explored in the laboratory, but they had to be investigated by way of individual minds. This was one of the first protests against the ancient doctrine that a group may have a collective mind, soul, or psyche over and above the minds of the individuals in the group. But Wundt could not stick to this individualized approach; like most of his contemporaries, he dealt with collective minds and made grand generalizations about the evolution of culture. Nonetheless, Steinthal, Lazarus, and Wundt did bring anthropology and psychology within speaking distance of each other.

British Evolutionists

Charles Darwin made a tremendous contribution to social science as well as to biological science. His statement of the theory of evolution in *The Origin of Species* (1859) changed the course of scientific thinking. It stimulated Herbert Spencer, Karl Marx, and others to apply the laws of natural selection to social development.

Spencer, Darwin's contemporary, is even better known for applying evolutionary concepts to social life. He wrote on both psychology and sociology, stressing scientific methods in studying human behavior even though his own methods were not always strictly scientific. His principal contributions to social psychology were his insistence that life is a process of continual adjustment of internal to external relations (the latter including society) and his emphasis on study of the social environment. He foresaw a "social science" which would study how the individual becomes an organic part of a group and how the group (consisting of individuals) becomes an organic unity. Spencer did not develop these ideas very far, but his prestige helped focus the attention of others on them.

Early Sociologists

Auguste Comte, the 19th-century French author of *Positive Philosophy* (1830), a comprehensive philosophy of the sciences, is considered the founder of sociology and possibly the first genuine social scientist. He stated clearly the idea that the human mind can develop only through society; the individual must be considered always in a social setting. Comte was one of the first to discuss the existence and importance of social change, although it is now believed that he overestimated the role of reason in producing it.

Another pioneering French sociologist important to social psychology was Emile Durkheim. His well-known theory of "collective representations" stressed the significance of group experience even more than Comte had. *Collective representations* are images or memories of group experiences every individual has which give evidence of and symbolize the common social life (Durkheim, 1915).

Max Weber, a German sociologist-economist-historian, influenced later social psychologists, both directly and indirectly. His analyses of bureaucracy in the government and business organizations and the effects of Protestantism on economic processes, as well as his studies of comparative religions, have stimulated the research of contemporary social scientists (see Weber, 1946).

THE FOUNDERS OF SOCIAL PSYCHOLOGY

These and other social philosophers and social scientists helped pave the way for social psychology, but none of them, strictly speaking, can be called a social psychologist. They did not focus their primary attention on the individual and the processes that make the individual a social being, nor did they study systematically the interactions among individuals. There are four men who can be called founders of social psychology because they did one or both of these things.

Gabriel Tarde (1843–1904), a French lawyer and judge, conducted studies of crime which led him to conclude that *imitation* is the fundamental social process and the key to the mystery of social life (Tarde, 1903). "Society," he said in 1890, "is imitation." Actually he said there were two elementary social acts, invention and imitation, but the former he found quite rare. He maintained that both social intercourse and social evolution proceed by imitation, which he considered a kind of hypnotic state.

In Tarde's hands the concept of imitation was stretched too far, and his treatment was often naive and oversimplified. But his contribution is great because he explored a basic social process that is rooted in individual action. He was one of the first writers to probe exhaustively into what is often called *social interaction*.

Gustave LeBon (1841–1931) was the author of *The Crowd* (1895), the first of many studies of crowd psychology. He was greatly influenced by contemporary French psychiatry, with its concern over *suggestibility* as the leading characteristic of hysteria. In crowds, said LeBon, intelligence is overshadowed and the unconscious is dominant; suggestibility, contagion, impulsiveness, emotionality, and credulity are rampant. As noted in Chapter 16, for LeBon the crowd has a collective mind which is inferior to the minds of the individuals in it. (See LeBon, 1917.)

Like Tarde, LeBon used his terms too broadly. For him, *crowds* meant all kinds of groups, whether they were physically gathered together or not. Despite the limitations of his theory, some of his observations on crowd behavior were illuminating and have been confirmed by later students. Probably LeBon's major contribution to social psychology was to introduce the use of psychiatric concepts to explain group behavior.

In 1908 two books appeared which used the term *social psychology* in their titles: *Social Psychology* by Edward A. Ross (1866–1951) and *Introduction to Social Psychology* by William McDougall (1871–1938). Both were designed as textbooks and attempted a comprehensive treatment of the subject. Ross had already defined social psychology as "the branch of knowledge that deals with the psychic interplay between man and his environing society." He was interested in both "uniformities" in behavior, such as religion, diet, dress, pastimes and moral ideas, and in "agitations" like the spread of the lynching spirit, the contagion of panic, or epidemics of religious emotion. Following Tarde, Ross elaborated on suggestibility and imitation and attempted to interpret crowds, crazes and fads, fashions, conventionality, custom, conflict, and public opinion on the basis of these processes.

In contrast to Ross, McDougall centered his social psychology squarely on the individual. He posited a number of instincts as the basis of social life and social interaction. All human social activities, he held, have their foundation in certain deep springs and motive powers which are innate, inherited tendencies. He classified these into several principal *instincts,* each with an associated emotional state, such as flight-fear. He also discerned major instincts without clearly associated emotions, such as reproduction, gregariousness, acquisitiveness, and construction, and threw in for good measure, as "general or non-specific innate tendencies," suggestion, imitation, sympathy, and a few others.

McDougall's views appealed to many scientists, philosophers, and others who had been impressed by instinct doctrines such as those made popular by William James in his *Principles of Psychology* (1890). However, McDougall's emphasis was distasteful to a number of psychologists and educators. John Dewey, in a work entitled *Human Nature and Conduct* (1922), insisted that *habits,* not instincts, are the key to social psychology—habits which grow out of the interaction between biological aptitudes and the social environment. Similarly, the McDougall thesis was disliked by the sociologists G. H. Mead and C. H. Cooley, who emphasized development of the *social self* and noted that the maturing human personality depends on continuous social interaction rather than instinct. Probably more than anyone else, Cooley influenced American social psychology in the direction of socialization, communication, and group participation. But cycles and swings of interpretation still occur, and recently a return to biological explanations of human behavior has become popular, as in the sociobiology movement (see Box 1–2).

Box 1–2
SOCIOBIOLOGY

Social scientists seek answers to familiar questions: What determines personality—heredity or environment? How do we explain behavior—with the social or the biological sciences? Some of the answers they find are old, and some are new.

Edward Wilson of Harvard University has formulated a "new" science, sociobiology.* The final chapter of his work introducing the concept in 1975 was a refutation of the social scientist's explanation of human behavior. Sociobiology uses a neo-Darwinian evolutionary scheme to interpret social development and social change. Social behavior in human beings is said to be controlled by "facultative genes"—that is, genes over which the environment has some effect.

Wilson sees psychology and sociology as now in their infancy or, at best, adolescence. Although psychology has made slightly more progress than sociology, both are in a transitional state. According to Wilson, sociology is in "the natural history stage of its development. There have been attempts at system building, but just as in psychology, they were premature and came to little. Much of what passes for theory in sociology today is really labeling of phenomena and concepts, in the expected manner of natural history" (p. 574). In other words, the integration of the behavioral sciences into the biological sciences is a step in the evolutionary sequence of science.

More recently, in *On Human Nature,* Wilson assumed a more charitable stance toward the social sciences, admitting that most differences between human societies are based on learning and social conditioning rather than heredity.† However, he still speaks of sociology as "the systematic study of the biological basis of all social behavior" (p. 4). Sociologist T. F. Hoult insists it is useless to think of human social behavior in biological terms because "we alone, among all animals, have evolved to the point where we have tremendous adaptability but practically no significant inborn behavior patterns. Almost all of our important behaviors must—and can—therefore be learned, which gives primary significance to our individual experiences and to the era, society, and value system in terms of which we happen to be reared."‡

---

* E. O. Wilson, *Sociobiology: The New Synthesis* (Cambridge, Mass.: Belknap Press, 1975).

† E. O. Wilson, *On Human Nature* (Cambridge, Mass.: Harvard University Press, 1978).

‡ T. F. Hoult, "Sociobiology: Friends and Critics," *The Humanist,* 1980, *40,* 45.

Experimental Beginnings

About the turn of the century a very different trend was developing in social psychology, one that would have tremendous growth: experimentation. It started in a small way; for example, children's performance was compared under competitive and noncompetitive conditions (Triplett, 1898). The same investigator also studied the effects of suggestion on 10 to 12-year-old children (Triplett, 1900). A little later, in Germany, Moede (1920) found that strength of hand grip increased and more pain could be endured when boys worked against rivals than when they worked alone. Letters or figures on a printed page were canceled more rapidly but less accurately under competitive than under noncompetitive conditions. Moede called these studies "experimental group psychology."

Meanwhile American social psychologists were becoming active experimenters. Their findings were collected and published in a large volume entitled *Experimental Social Psychology* by Gardner Murphy and Lois Murphy in 1931. Experimentation was on the way to becoming a dominant trend, if not *the* dominant trend, in social psychology.

Specialized and Interdisciplinary Viewpoints

Early social psychology reflected the approaches of both contemporary psychology and sociology, but diversification soon took place. Many sociologists published books and articles in the 1920s that established a sociological brand of social psychology (e.g., W. I. Thomas, Ellsworth Faris, Robert Park, Ernest Burgess, L. L. Bernard, and Emory Bogardus). They stressed the effects of group life—through customs, mores, institutions, and social interstimulation—on human personality or "human nature." They did not overlook the presence of various innate and biological factors, but they emphasized the actual processes of socialization and discussed rather fully the part played by language and gesture, suggestion, imitation, and the like. Attitudes, values, social roles, social control, and social change were taken up at some length. In a word, the sociologists adopted a specialty, the psychosocial environment, and explored its effects on human development and human behavior.

In 1924 a psychologist, Floyd H. Allport, introduced another viewpoint. Social psychology, he said, can be dealt with only in terms of individual psychology, since it simply studies individual behavior in regard to the part of the human environment that is comprised of other humans. He vigorously attacked the "group mind fallacy"—the theory held by some philosophers and social scientists, notably LeBon, that the group has a mind of its own, apart from the minds of the individuals composing the group. Within the individual organism, insisted Allport, are all the mechanisms necessary to explain social behavior, which is primarily a means to satisfy human biological needs. These needs he interpreted not as instincts but as "prepotent reflexes," which are considerably modified through social conditioning.

Allport's views influenced other psychologists who were turning toward the field of social psychology. They also signified the growing divergence between sociological and psychological interpretations of social psychology, a distinction which has persisted to some extent to the present. The sociologist is impressed with the social heritage and its effect on the behavior of all persons within a culture. The psychologist focuses on the needs and potentialities of individuals, how they mature and are affected by learning. Actually the two viewpoints are not inconsistent; they are somewhat like the two sides of the same coin. Many social psychologists have tried to bring about a better rapprochement between them, aided by contributions from other disciplines such as cultural anthropology and psychiatry. Not all social psychologists believe that the diversity between sociological and psychological viewpoints should be minimized, however. As Sampson (1980) has pointed out, such disagreements may be beneficial in encouraging advancement in social psychology.

The relationship of social psychology to other fields of study is demonstrated in Figure 1–1, oversimplified though it is. Social psychology interacts with several social sciences and related fields, none of which has priority over any other. In each the same problem, such as the causes of war, might be studied, using appropriate techniques and approaches. The sociologist analyzes war as a custom or institution; the anthropologist and the historian compare military behavior at different times and places; the political scientist studies the roles of nationalism and patriotism; the economist explores the industrial and financial bases of war. The social psychologist's interest in motives and frustrations, and in attitudes and prejudices, is important to all of the above approaches and can help to clarify them. An early example of this kind of cooperation is Gardner Murphy's *Human Nature and Enduring Peace* (1945). In view of the complexity of such social phenomena, it is not surprising that in many institutes and universities, social research is being conducted in an interdepartmental setting.

Figure 1-1. The Interdisciplinary Nature of Social Psychology

THE SCIENTIFIC METHOD AND SOCIAL PSYCHOLOGY

One thing all behavioral and social sciences have in common is reliance on the scientific method. Science can be distinguished from common sense and other nonscientific approaches in several ways.

First, science is concerned primarily with *verifiable statements about causal relationships*. Novelists and administrators may analyze and predict human responses, and their conclusions may be correct and frequently insightful, but they are largely guesses (sophisticated though they be), and it is seldom possible to test or verify their data, at least with any accuracy. Scientists, on the other hand, must submit their theories and findings, no matter how trivial or obvious, to rigid tests. The need to conduct their research in problem areas which are sometimes hoary with tradition tends to limit their objectivity and scientific rigor, however. A social psychologist, for example, may be called on for an immediate "solution" to problems of community leadership or racial relations. Scientists regard their findings as provisional until they have been confirmed through further research by themselves and others. This means that science essentially represents an approach rather than a finished body comprised of factual data and theory.

Second, science requires the building of a *systematic, coherent theoretical structure* through the formulation and testing of *hypotheses*. The body of science grows as the hypotheses that are found to be valid are accepted and progressively knit together into meaningful sequences. In the social sciences this development of theory has been relatively slow. In the last few decades, however, there has been a steady advance toward the development of clusters of hypotheses that permit valid predictions. As a result, we can predict that delinquent behavior is extremely probable when an individual with a given psychological structure is situated in a certain social setting. And hundreds of studies of preelection polls correlated with actual voting behavior have enabled social scientists to predict the results of most elections, within a very small margin of error.

Third, scientists are primarily concerned with *facts* and generally seek to *avoid value statements* and judgments. But they are human and can hardly pretend to be value-free, nor should they desire to be. The methodological framework within which they operate, the subjects or areas they select for study, the settings they choose for their observations or experiments, and even the sources of their research funds all reflect choices and value judgments. In their methods and reports, however, scientists typically avoid terms like *good* or *bad, desirable* or *undesirable, beautiful* or *ugly.* At least they realize that when they make evaluative statements, they are venturing into the realm of the philosopher, the artist, and the theologian.

In recent decades, as the scientists' role as citizens has been emphasized, it has become increasingly difficult for them to avoid making value judgments or being evaluated by the public. Since the dropping of the bomb on Hiroshima brought an end to World War II, atomic physicists have manifested a heightened obligation to society. Chemists who developed the napalm and defoliants which devastated Vietnam have made defensive statements and even apologized for their activities. Social psychologists are also vulnerable to public demands for accountability. Their responsibility to society demands free, objective inquiry into whatever they are investigating—persuasion, suggestibility, obedience, deprogramming. What they study and the use that is made of their results can have far-reaching effects on people, and their work rightfully is subject to public scrutiny.

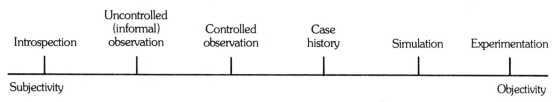

Figure 1–2. A Suggested Continuum of Research Methods

RESEARCH METHODS

A number of the research methods used by social psychologists in following the scientific method are shared with physical and other behavioral scientists, and a few are unique to social psychology. With the exception of informal observation and introspection, the basic methods were formulated during this century and have become highly sophisticated during the last decade or two. In the suggested continuum of research methods illustrated in Figure 1–2, the principal methods are located in part according to their historical development (introspection and observation appeared before simulation and experimentation) and in part on the basis of their preciseness and objectivity. To no small extent, however, the choice of research method depends on the type of problem under study. The diversity of the research methods reflects the range of phenomena with which it deals—the reasons for popularity of the leaders in senior high school, analysis of decision making by a corporate board, the direction of public opinion in an election campaign, or the dynamics of a food riot in a developing nation, to mention only a few possibilities.

Early social psychologists such as Tarde, LeBon, Ross, and McDougall showed little concern with method, and, like most early social scientists, they could hardly be considered research oriented. Their generalizations about imitation, suggestion, instinct, and the like actually were based on speculation and more or less uncontrolled observation. Their findings have naturally been questioned by those using more careful methods of investigation. The procedures used by social psychologists today are described and evaluated in Carlsmith, Ellsworth, and Aronson (1976), Orenstein and Phillips (1978), Kidder et al. (1981), and other works on research methodology in the field.

The research methods used by any scientist depend on the nature of the research problem. Techniques employed by psychologists differ according to what they are studying, such as imagination, speed of muscular reaction, or the origins of emotional crises. Sociologists' methods also vary according to what they are investigating, such as the effects of urbanization on personality, the causes of crime and delinquency, or comparative trends in divorce rates.

Thus the research methods selected must be appropriate for investigating the questions to be answered. The fact that a research technique works well in one area does not mean that it is best or even suitable for another. Further, as Boulding (1980) points out, scientific methods are not limited to science; in medieval times, alchemists used experimentation, astrologers were adept at careful observation, and diviners applied measurement techniques.

There are many ways of classifying research methods. They may, for example, be divided into *subjective* and *objective*, or *qualitative* and *quantitative*, or sorted into categories such as case history, field study, experiment, or type of statistical technique. In our classification there are five broad categories of method which differ in degree of objectivity and the investigator's relative control of variables. These categories are: introspection; observation; case history, or the developmental method; simulation; and the experimental method.

Introspection

Introspection means "looking within" and reporting on some aspect of one's own present or past experience. We may introspect about our aches and pains, our feelings, our attitudes, or our reasons for joining a certain social group. Whenever we report on our subjective experiences, we are introspecting. Rating scales, questionnaires, and public opinion polls are to some degree based on introspection, since the respondents are asked to describe their private views.

There are both advantages and disadvantages to the use of introspection in research. The method obviously yields data on thoughts, feelings, hopes, wishes, and attitudes which are peculiarly private and cannot be easily studied by other methods. But the data thus obtained may be inaccurate if the respondents are careless or ignorant or have reason to conceal their true reactions.

Although the utility of introspection in research has been questioned for over half a century, its use when combined with behavior study has recently been defended. If nothing else, it connotes the existence of mind and suggests the possibility of studying it experimentally. Introspection is, after all, the origin of many of the hypotheses in psychology, as well as most of the theorizing. Nevertheless, it must be recognized that in some instances the individual has a limited ability to discriminate among internal states and forgetting or even dishonesty may occur (Lieberman, 1979).

Observation: Informal and Systematic

Observing people's behavior is generally a more objective procedure than asking them what they think or feel. Objectivity is hard to define, but it ultimately depends upon agreement among observers. Everyone, including scholars and scientists, draws on personal observations of people to answer psychological questions. If they observe carefully and avoid generalizations without sufficient data to back them up, their conclusions may be exceedingly valuable. The defect of much observation, however, is its unsystematic nature. The persons observed may be an unrepresentative group, observed at irregular periods and in random situations. Generalizations based on casual contacts are susceptible to error. In addition, such reports may be affected by inaccuracies of memory and by the reporter's unconscious bias.

Uncontrolled, naturalistic, or informal observation is not necessarily capricious and without value, however. News reporting, for example, precludes control by its very nature. So does participant observation, in which the researcher is intimately involved with a group and its activities, such as a member of Alcoholics Anonymous who records personal impressions and experiences. The analysis of many critical social situations, like the concentration camps of World War II or the Jonestown, Guyana, murder-suicide of some 900 cult members in 1978 (see Box 15–2 in Chapter 15), largely depends on interviewing and uncontrolled observation of the surviving participants. In addition, informal observation may bring forth hypotheses which direct the scientist to further, more systematic observations.

Systematic observation differs in degree rather than in kind from the more informal type. The principal difference is that more precise techniques are used. Researchers studying the social behavior of children, for example, observe them systematically in a variety of situations. Usually they sit behind a one-way screen or window so their presence will not affect the naturalness of the children's behavior, and photograph or tape record the sessions. In field studies anthropologists or other behavioral scientists use a variety of techniques to examine and record the lifestyles and problems of groups such as a tribe, village, or urban community. Similarly, participant-observers use photographs, recordings, and interviews to study the behavior, attitudes, and backgrounds of a group's members and leaders.

Some kinds of events do not lend themselves to experimentation. When social phenomena involve extremist groups, even controlled observation is questionable. *Source:* Wide World Photos, Inc.

Case History, or the Developmental Method

The longitudinal, developmental, or case study method is widely favored in clinical psychology and social work, and it has some applicability in social psychology. These types of study (earlier called *genetic*) focus on changes occurring in an individual over a period of time. The aim is to discover the significant influences, past and present, which operate upon the individual. All kinds of data—objective and subjective, qualitative and quantitative—are used.

In social psychology a developmental study usually involves assembling the life histories of all the persons in a given sample in order to determine the formation of attitudes or other behaviors related to the phenomenon under investigation. The study may take the form of analyzing several hundred autobiographical essays or performing an in-depth analysis of ten individuals. The purpose is to discover underlying motives and personality dynamics that would be difficult to ferret out by other procedures. Among the disadvantages are possible unrepresentativeness of the sample, and the possibility that subjectivity may affect either the construction of the case histories or their interpretation. Some educators and practitioners favor making personality study or clinical experience an integral part of the social psychologist's research training.

Simulation

Since the 1950s the frontiers of social psychology have been extended as new research techniques have emerged. One of these is simulation, which involves imitating or duplicating a selected social situation so it can be analyzed and studied. Simulation techniques have been greatly facilitated by the use of electronic computers and by recently developed applications of mathematical and statistical techniques in the social sciences.

Within the context of the social sciences, simulation assumes at least three different forms. In one, an investigator may focus on some aspect of an individual or small-group process, using a computer to work out the options in, say, verbal learning or playing chess. In another, a social system may be simulated for a specific purpose, such as to test the efficiency of a proposed air defense organization and discover its bottlenecks or weak linkages. The third, which is of particular significance to social psychology, involves placing subjects in a laboratory setting to simulate episodes such as decision-making efforts to resolve a hypothetical crisis in international affairs (Abelson, 1968). A computer may be used to coordinate the elements of the simulation, and in this context it can arbitrate differences, introduce chance events, calculate payoffs to group or individual members, retain large quantities of background information, and so on.

Such *laboratory simulations* do not necessarily utilize computers, however. They can resemble a multidisciplinary experimental approach to solving problems which involves trade-offs, alliances, threats, and counterthreats as enacted by individuals or groups in a laboratory (Goetzkow, 1970). This type of simulation can be applied to relatively structured situations, as when team members are asked to make choices so as to maximize gains and minimize losses for their team in simulations involving such diverse situations as international conflict or student organization.

The Experimental Method

Experimentation represents the opposite end of the continuum of research methods from introspection, and social psychologists differ greatly in their enthusiasm for it. At one extreme are those who insist the experiment represents the ultimate technique in precision and control. At the other extreme are those who maintain that experiments are artificial and typically deal with trivia. In between are the majority of social psychologists, who believe the experimental method has yielded important data, but it is only one of several possible procedures that can be used. Generally, social psychologists trained in a department of psychology (as compared with those from sociology) tend to give special significance to the experimental approach.

The distinction between observation and experimentation is more than a difference in degree. In an experiment, variables are controlled in a way that is not possible when social phenomena are merely observed. The essence of experimentation in any field is to set the stage so that whatever happens can be interpreted meaningfully. All variables, except the one under consideration, must be kept constant. A valid experiment is hard to perform; indeed, in many areas of social psychology (as, for example, in studying riots or panics), it is impossible. However, where it is feasible and properly carried out, experimentation yields accurate data and has high predictability. Some researchers would say it is the most likely means to determine "what causes what." (Different types of variables and the concepts of validity and reliability are defined in the following section on research terms and concepts.)

Many experiments in social psychology are carried out in the laboratory, where the variables are relatively easy to control. A classic example is Sherif's (1935) study of social influence, or how the presence of others influences subjects to alter their perception of a visual stimulus. Other investigators use real-life situations into which they introduce influences or variables in order to assess their effects. Some social psychologists insist that only the laboratory offers adequate control of variables. Others maintain that real-life situations cannot be brought into the laboratory for study, and it is better to work in the natural setting even though some variables are not pinned down.

A hypothetical experiment might be designed to determine whether increased contacts between blacks and whites in a certain locale would improve intergroup relations and lessen prejudice. For purposes of the study residents of an interracial housing development might be divided into two *equal groups,* each having both black and white members. The persons in one part, the *experimental group,* would be brought together frequently to hear lectures and music, have discussions, and participate in a variety of recreational programs. Those in the other part, the *control group,* would be untouched by the experimenters; no effort would be made to influence the interaction within this group in any way. The effects, if any, of the increased contact and participation within the experimental group could be measured by noting the number of friendships made, the spontaneous visits, small-group activities, and evidence of other interrelationships. If any significant differences in attitude are discovered between the experimental group and the control group, they could reasonably be attributed to the increased contacts brought about by the experimenters. In addition, an attitude scale could be administered to both groups to see whether changes in attitude (i.e., prejudice) had occurred, and to what extent they correlated with increased contacts between blacks and whites. More important, a follow-up study should be conducted to determine whether any change in initial attitude persisted over a period of time.

Research Terms and Concepts

The various research methods used by social psychologists employ the special vocabulary scientists have devised to convey the meanings of the terms and concepts they use in describing the various steps in the research process. Familiarity with these expressions will help you understand their use in the myriad examples of research studies which illustrate the ideas forming the substantive content of this text. In addition to the essential research terms and concepts considered in this section, others are defined in the "Words to Remember" section at the end of every chapter, and all concepts used in the text are introduced in a context which gives clues to their meaning.

Preliminary Considerations

Basic to all scientific inquiry is the need for *operational definitions;* that is, the requirements that scientific concepts and findings must be presented in an observable or testable form. Thus intelligence is defined in terms of a score on an intelligence test, attitudes are measured on an attitude scale, and a lie detector is a possible index of verbal integrity. These instruments may not provide the ultimate answers to specific research problems, but they do attempt to give an objective finding, and an investigator who falls short of this goal of objectivity should be honest enough to admit the inadequacy. Even if, as often happens, the findings must nevertheless be used—or published—the problematic nature of the study will at least be evident.

Operationalism or the operational definition also requires the investigator to frame the *hypothesis,* or the tentative assumption underlying the research effort, in a testable manner. Whether oriented to observational, experimental, or some other research method, the hypothesis should appear as an "if . . ., then . . ." statement. As will be noted in future chapters, the hypothesis (in some instances, competing hypotheses) is based on the premise that certain variables will be controlled and others, usually only one, will be manipulated.

Another critical preliminary consideration is the selection of the *sample.* In order to assure objectivity or neutrality, it is essential to have a *random* sample of the universe, or *population,* which is the target of the study. Randomness theoretically allows every member of the population an equal probability of appearing in the sample; to ensure this, the experimenter would choose every seventh student in the directory or every *n*th house in the community, for example. Practical considerations sometimes make it impossible to achieve this ideal, and the researcher must settle for a *representative* sample. It is important to be aware of the limitations of this procedure, also, because conclusions can only be based on the sample selected and cannot be validated for the entire population. This is particularly relevant in attitude sampling (see Chapter 8).

Effects of Variables

The factor under study in the interracial experiment described above, the degree of contact or interaction, is called the *independent variable*. The result or effect of manipulating this factor is the *dependent variable*. Frequently, in experiments there is only one independent variable (although with certain kinds of statistical manipulation it is possible to have several), but the dependent variable—the findings or results—is often plural. In this experiment, the dependent variable may be not only higher tolerance scores but also lower turnover of renters and better physical maintenance in the housing project.

In any experiment such as this one, there are problems with the influence of unwanted or *extraneous* variables, such as unknown interracial contacts among participants outside the housing development. The experiment itself produces the *Hawthorne effect*—the ways that participation in the experiment affect the behavior of subjects. In the classic scientific management study at the Western Electric Hawthorne plant in Cicero, Illinois, the experimental group nearly always performed better or showed greater change than did the control group, probably because the subjects in the former group received more attention and thus were motivated to produce more than those in the control group (Roethlisberger & Dickson, 1939).

A cardinal requirement for scientific acceptability of results is their ability to predict future events with reasonable accuracy. The problem in achieving this is the need to isolate variables which can be identified as *causative factors*. Human social behavior is very difficult to analyze in this fashion because it involves multiple causes. To be rigorously scientific, it is necessary to strive to isolate and study a single causative factor, even though other possible causes or influences upon the person's behavior may be overlooked. Furthermore, it is possible to err in assuming a cause-effect relationship. The correlation of two variables does not necessarily imply causation; the relationship may be due to their mere proximity in time or may result because both are effects of the same underlying cause.

To understand human behavior in the social order requires more sophisticated analysis of variables. This can be secured with statistical techniques such as *cluster analysis* and *path analysis* which make it possible to manipulate patterns of variables with the aid of a computer. But many insights also can be gained through procedures which do not lend themselves to statistical or quantitative treatment. Subjective studies describing the worlds of carnival people, drug addicts, prostitutes, terminal cancer patients, or swinging couples, or self-descriptions written by emotionally troubled patients, also can provide information which contributes to the data of social psychology.

Quantification

Statistical treatment of the data is important in experimentation, however. Most experimental procedures are built around the concept of quantification, and the results usually depend on relationships which have quantified dimensions. For example, attitudes are often measured on a seven-point scale (see Chapter 8), and inferences if not conclusions are drawn from the fact that the average score on the scale for one group of subjects is statistically different from that of another group. Statistics enable researchers to communicate to others their confidence that the reported findings are, or are not, the result of error or chance. Thus the magnitude of a statistical measure is crucial for testing a hypothesis, and the development of high-speed, large-memory computers has made new kinds of statistical techniques possible which can result in breakthroughs in our understanding of social behavior (McGuire, 1973).

There are two important criteria for judging the results of research involving tests and experimentation: *reliability* and *validity*. Repetition of an experiment must produce substantially the same results, or the data are suspected of being unreliable. Even more crucial is the question whether the test or experiment is valid—that is, whether it really measures what it purports to measure. Does the intelligence test really measure intelligence, for example, or might it be sampling rote memory or school knowledge? Does an experiment actually assess personality, or might the result be some kind of superficial verbal response? Unless the researcher can satisfy the criteria of reliability and validity, the investigation is on shaky ground.

More subtle and difficult to detect is *bias* on the part of either the investigator or the subjects. Researchers have theories or hypotheses to guide them, which is natural and proper; the trouble is that the hypotheses may also influence the way they observe and interpret the data. It has been noted, for example, that researchers who believe there is a relationship between IQ and skin color tend to find positive results when these variables are measured experimentally, whereas those who hold the opposite belief usually come up with neutral or negative findings (Kamin, 1974). The subtle and often unintentional aspects of the experiment or the laboratory setting that may influence people to respond in a given way are labeled *demand bias*.

The subjects' biases are of a different sort. In all probability the participants will wonder about an investigation, make guesses about it, and interpret it in some fashion. For example, they may resent being treated like guinea pigs, or they may go all out to help the experimenter arrive at positive results. Either of these attitudes would be prejudicial to the accuracy and objectivity of the data obtained. Such biases are usually unconscious and constitute a real problem in research; they are very difficult to identify and eliminate.

Controversies over Methods

The Search for New Concepts and Procedures

Social psychology has generally followed psychology and the other behavioral sciences in cleaving to the natural science model and its mechanistic frame of reference. This course may not be the best one, however. Years ago a famous physicist, Robert Oppenheimer (1956), warned that the worst thing psychology could do would be to "model itself after a physics which is not there anymore and which has been outdated." As Carl Rogers (1973) has pointed out, "We have determinedly tied ourselves to this old Newtonian concept of science, seemingly unaware of the changes and the view of science that have been taking place in theoretical physics and in various other hard as well as soft sciences."

Only very recently have the social sciences begun to pay heed to the need for newer conceptualizations and procedures. Buss (1975) argues that a holistic and humanistic approach should be considered at least an option for psychology. Gergen (1973) asserts that it is a mistake to consider the processes in social psychology as pure or basic as they are in the natural sciences, and it would be better to think of them as the psychological counterpart of cultural norms. Similarly, Pepitone (1976) suggests social psychologists should be less bound by the methods used by general psychologists, whose primary subject matter is the individual in a nonsocial setting. They should focus on normative or role behavior and the value-belief systems of groups. Gergen (1978) further cautions that excessive concern with precise laboratory techniques, desire for ethical neutrality, and avoidance of value statements have become barriers to more creative thinking in social psychology. The time is ripe for inclusive or *generative theories* that might provide a more imaginative approach to social phenomena.

Ethical Questions

Public demand and scientific standards have recently caused psychologists to give more attention to the ethical questions inherent in observation and experimentation. The manipulative and deceptive aspects of certain kinds of investigations have come in for special scrutiny. The American Psychological Association has issued *APA Ethical Principles in the Conduct of Research with Human Participants* (1973), based on the proposition that the "psychologist is committed to a belief in the dignity and worth of the individual human being." Social scientists now are reluctant to obtain information without the consent of subjects. Studies that may cause psychological damage to participants or violate their civil liberties are no longer acceptable to social psychologists.

A questionable type of study would be one in which the experimenter creates anxiety by telling the subjects that it involves use of an electric shock (although shock is not actually used) in order to study their reactions to a fear stimulus. In a number of these experiments (which will be discussed in Chapter 11), subjects were willing to inflict considerable pain on one another as a means of testing obedience and conformity. Other experiments have asked people to tell lies, arrive at anxiety-provoking moral decisions, or eat grasshoppers (see Box 9–6 in Chapter 9). As Carlsmith, Ellsworth, and Aronson (1976) point out, "when stress is an integral part of one of the experimenter's conceptual variables, it may be extremely difficult or impossible to remove the stress without losing the whole phenomenon."

Besides creating an unfavorable emotional condition, the experimenter who conducts such studies is guilty of deception. Although the manipulative nature of experiments may demand this kind of ploy, the result is an unfavorable public image of scientific research. *Debriefing* (i.e., explaining the rationale of the experiment at its end) is one solution to the problem, but the fact remains that no one enjoys being victimized, and even when they are debriefed subjects who have been duped may be embarrassed and resentful. Debriefing actually includes *dehoaxing,* or clarifying false information, and, even more important, *desensitizing,* or removing any negative feelings that remain after the experiment. A number of the experiments to be described in later chapters proved to be highly traumatic and required fairly elaborate forms of debriefing, to teach subjects that their behavior was a product of the experimental situation and could not be considered abnormal or extreme (Holmes, 1976). It cannot be assumed that debriefing is always effective, however.

Some researchers suggest that such questionable practices can be justified because the subjects usually have volunteered for the "contractual relationship" implied in the laboratory setting. Deception in the naturalistic setting is more open to criticism. However, the consensus seems to be that in both the laboratory and the field, experimenters should consider alternative means of studying a problem or isolating the variables to avoid jeopardizing the integrity and self-esteem of participants.

THEORIES OF SOCIAL PSYCHOLOGY

The contributions that social psychology can make through scientific research to enhance our understanding of society and its problems have been generally acknowledged. But there are different viewpoints about the methods that should be employed to obtain information. Various social psychologists look at the same or different events in their world differently, and there is a certain distance between social psychologists trained in psychology departments and those trained in sociology departments. These differences are expressed in various theories within the discipline. The broad ideas in the more salient theories are discussed in this section, with a focus on how they are similar rather than how they differ.

Behaviorism, Reinforcement, and Social Learning

The psychological theory labeled *behaviorism* (see Chapter 5) developed near the turn of the century as an outgrowth of learning experiments, notably those of Ivan Pavlov on a dog's salivation in response to various stimuli presented in the laboratory. While these series of experiments, known as *conditioning,* were underway, other psychologists were conducting trial-and-error learning experiments with both animals and human beings. John B. Watson's *Behaviorism,* originally published in 1912, brought these together and called for a clear-cut break with several of the older psychological traditions. Watson was convinced that the subject matter of psychology should be as scientifically "pure" as it was for chemistry and physics. The goal of psychology, he said, should be the study of specific *responses* to specific *stimuli* in the laboratory.

Since Watson's original statement, behaviorism has adopted a more sophisticated approach, especially in the work of B. F. Skinner. But the idea remains fundamental that almost no interpretation about behavior can be made that goes beyond what is observable in the laboratory. The basic position is that people learn through *reinforcement:* They acquire responses that are rewarded, and they eliminate responses that are either punished or not rewarded.

Variations of the *stimulus-response model* have been suggested by several theorists. Neal Miller and John Dollard, for example, stressed the importance of motives and cues in the learning process. Because they were concerned with intricate social learnings, they turned to factors beyond the mechanistic confines of the laboratory. Highly complex sets of stimuli and responses are involved, for instance, when we learn to repair a car, acquire a foreign language, or fall in love.

According to *social learning theory* as presented by Albert Bandura (1977), human behavior brings into play a continuous interaction among learning, perception, and input from the environment (see Chapter 5). Like other social learning theorists, he borrows from conditioning concepts. But he insists that learning depends on a number of symbols and models that cannot readily be explained in terms of the usual laboratory equipment, because people never cease selecting and organizing the stimuli they are presented with.

Gestalt and Field Approaches

In the same years behaviorism was emerging, a new theory identified as *Gestalt,* a German word which can be translated as *configuration* or *pattern,* became accepted by a number of psychologists. Whereas behaviorism tends to be very specific or discrete in its linkage of stimuli and responses, the Gestalt position is that a person's experience and behavior are more totalistic and represent a kind of wholeness. This recognizes that when you are solving a puzzle, viewing a movie, or spending your first day on a new job, you are responding to many stimuli that are organized in dominant and subordinate cues, images, or themes. Instead of focusing on a rat in a maze (as Skinner did) or studying the substitute stimuli that would arouse salivation in a dog (as Pavlov did), the Gestalt psychologist Wolfgang Köhler studied the whole pattern of complex behavior by using a chimpanzee learning to find a solution to a problem. Thus in experimentation, the choice of organism to be studied and the structuring of the experiment may elicit different kinds of learning and different kinds of theory to explain the learning.

In social psychology Kurt Lewin broadened the Gestalt principles and combined them with other ideas to formulate *field theory.* Field theory differs fundamentally from behaviorism. Because it is aimed at resolving certain social problems, it takes a viewpoint which is much more *dynamic,* Lewin's term for the tendency of organisms to be constantly undergoing change. Whereas behaviorism accepts only directly observable responses, Lewin thinks of the field approach as including also the person's subjective interpretation of the situation along with salient personality characteristics. The field approach also places more emphasis on the complexity of motivation, maintaining that people are driven by a number of impulses which are not easily observed by the experimenter. And, for

Lewin, behavior is significantly shaped by the group, which is itself constantly undergoing change (see Chapter 12).

Social Interactionism and Role Theory

While behaviorism and field theory primarily grew out of the work of psychologists, two other ideas, interactionism and role theory, have traditionally but not exclusively been the province of sociology. The authors of this text do not see any necessary conflict between the sociological and psychological perspectives, however.

The focal point in *social interactionism* is the importance of the self and its development (see Chapter 4). Like field theory, it focuses on the influence of the group. George Herbert Mead set the stage for this theory in *Mind, Self, and Society* (1934), in which he analyzed the infant's and child's relations with others. Even more than Gestalt and field theory, this viewpoint conceives of the mind as continually growing through the use of symbols. Moreover, it maintains that human beings are interpreting or defining "each other's actions instead of reacting to each other's actions" (Blumer, 1967), which is a far cry from the experimental stance of behaviorism. Thus people acquire a self and identity through their interactions with others, and the self and personality are always subject to change. This concept is reminiscent of field theory, but the interactionist tends to use different labels or concepts and is more concerned with the changes within the individual, while Lewin was especially sensitive to how changes in the group produce differing behaviors. Field theory is more a laboratory product than interactionism, although not to the degree that behaviorism is. This is consistent with the fact that the psychologist generally relies on experimental techniques, whereas the sociologist is more likely to use observation in a natural or relatively controlled setting.

Interactionism is strongly identified with *role behavior* (see Chapter 14). Both psychologists and sociologists are concerned with how people define and enact the various roles they fill, such as boy or girl friend, son or daughter, fraternity officer or summer camp counselor, student or club member. On the whole, the study of role behavior is more a body of subject matter than a tight theoretical system (Deutsch & Krauss, 1965; Shaw & Costanzo, 1970). Among the questions raised are: What groups do people look to for cues in deciding how to express a given role? What are the standards or norms of behavior attached to role? How does one role conflict with another?

Adopting a Theoretical Stance

The three broad traditions of behaviorism, Gestalt and field theory, and interactionism form only part of the theoretical background in behavioral sciences. While these traditions are not neatly united, as is evident in the contrast between the behaviorist and social learning positions, they have been fundamental in the unfolding of the discipline of social psychology. This text borrows in part from all three. We suggest that some learnings in everyday life do follow the conditioning model, but most complex social or interpersonal learnings cannot be adequately interpreted in behaviorist terms. Field theory is more appropriate to the study of group interaction or social problems such as explaining what processes occur in a riot or how junior managers can compete for the chief executive office. Even the learning behavior of a worker on an assembly line would not be greatly illuminated by a rigid behaviorist or conditioning theory.

Behaviorism, as exemplified in conditioning, may be relevant to improving understanding of how people acquire attitudes. But it is the field theorist who is most helpful in analyzing conflicts in attitudes, goals, and rewards, or in explaining the processes of cognition and motivation. The symbolic interactionist may have the most to offer in investigating the question of conflicting identities, the consciousness of groups, and the individual's ever-shifting feelings about self.

Recently there has been increasing collaboration between the two branches of social psychology: theory and methods as conceived and practiced by social psychologists who are trained in either a department of psychology or a department of sociology. Within each approach there has been disagreement as to both the aims of the science and the means by which social phenomena can be studied. In general, however, psychologically oriented social psychologists have traditionally been concerned with the study of attitudes and group processes and have tended to be more insistent on experimentation. The sociological wing has focused on concepts like the self and role behavior (or what is known as symbolic interaction), using various forms of observation as the means of studying these behaviors.

A comparison of the two principal journals—the *Journal of Personality and Social Psychology* for the psychology oriented and the *Social Psychology Quarterly* for the sociology oriented—reveals a large degree of convergence as compared to a decade or two ago. According to Stryker (1981), "psychological social psychology is becoming more social in its stress on interpersonal behavior, and the sociological social psychologist more and more insisting on the use of measurement." The compatibility of the two approaches is represented by this text, in which authors from both traditions have collaborated.

Many other theoretical developments will be noted in the chapters to follow. Some of these are outgrowths or modifications of the three principal positions described here, and others are reactions against them. The most influential and sweeping movement is *psychoanalysis* (see Chapters 4 and 7), which is based on the work of Sigmund Freud. This examination of unconscious strivings and conflicts has had an enormous impact on certain areas of social psychology, ranging from attitude formation to leadership and crowd behavior. Because of its concern with the unconscious, psychoanalysis is most hostile to behaviorism but is less in conflict with social learning, field theory, and symbolic interactionism.

Another theoretical position is taken by *exchange theory*, which is concerned with the individual's search for reward at minimum cost. This viewpoint reflects economic theory, but in part it grows out of reinforcement and the general relation of learning and indeed of all behavior to motivation. *Attribution theory*, or how the individual perceives persons and objects in the environment has standing as a separate theory but has indirect ties to interactionism through its analysis of the relation of the self to others. On the sociological side of social psychology is *ethnomethodology,* another outlook which is not too distant from symbolic interactionism but investigates even more deeply how the individual processes reality, placing the most minute behaviors under scrutiny.

In this text some chapters may stress certain theories more than others, but a thoroughgoing social psychology would sooner or later tap all these viewpoints for one or another explanation they offer. They all can contribute to our understanding of the relation of the human being to society.

SUMMARY

Social psychology describes and interprets social behavior in terms of the individual participating in it. As a scientist the social psychologist seeks to describe and to understand social behavior, with the ultimate aims of predicting behavior, clarifying social issues, and helping to solve social problems.

Social psychology emerged as a separate discipline early in the 20th century, largely through the contributions of Tarde, LeBon, Ross, and McDougall. By the 1920s somewhat differing sociological and psychological emphases became apparent, and this trend has continued to the present. Interrelations with cultural anthropology, political science, economics, psychiatry, and other disciplines have developed and proven to be mutually beneficial.

In their research, social psychologists are concerned with discovering causal relationships and evolving a theoretical system which, it is hoped, will prove to be of practical value. Research methods include introspection, both informal and systematic observation, developmental or case study, simulation, and experimentation. Quantitative data are treated statistically, often with the aid of computers. Problems of bias sometimes arise on the part of subjects or experimenters.

The question of the proper scientific model for social psychology is open to arguments favoring new concepts and methods. Certain ethical matters involving deception and manipulation of subjects in research studies also invite controversy. A new consensus seems to be emerging in these areas, however.

The major theories or approaches to social psychology include behaviorism (which involves several viewpoints), field theory, and symbolic interactionism. Each of these ideas has relevance to social psychology, but this text is most compatible with the interactionist and, especially, the field explanations. A number of other theoretical positions will be discussed in the topics to be analyzed in the chapters to follow.

WORDS TO REMEMBER

Bias. Tendency toward a nonrepresentative sample in research because all the relevant population or variables are not accounted for; errors in perception, cognition, attitudes, etc., due to some subjective or environmental factor.

Control group. Experimental condition which provides a comparison for the experimental group. Usually subjects in a control group are identical as nearly as possible to those in the experimental group, except they do not respond to or express the independent variable. Comparison of the two groups often is the core of the experiment. Also referred to as *comparison group.* (See *experimental group; independent variable.*)

Correlation. Relationship between two variables as expressed in a number or measure between 0 and +1.00 (or 0 and −1.00). When the correlation is "plus" or positive, the two variables (abilities, traits, or behaviors) go together; when it is "minus" or negative, the presence of one indicates the absence of the other. The strength of the relation, either positive or negative, is increased as the measure approaches 1.00 or −1.00.

Debriefing. Neutralization of the emotional atmosphere or related effects of an experiment. Generally, after an experiment the investigator reveals to the subjects any necessary deception or explains the rationale of the investigation.

Demand bias. Influence of implicit or unintentional cues in an experiment or its setting which may cause subjects to respond in a given direction, often eliciting results compatible with the hypothesis.

Dependent variables. End-product effect or consequent results of a controlled experiment which provides measures of the independent variable. An example of a dependent variable is the amount of aggression (as measured on a relevant say, test) after exposure to a display of violence on TV (the independent variable).

Depersonalization. Dehumanization of the individual, as in a mass setting, bureaucracy, or totalitarian regime; occasionally can be the result of an experiment.

Experimental group. Subjects in an experiment who are the focus of the experiment or the independent variable, in contrast to the control group.

Independent variable. Variable controlled by the experimenter, or major factor under study in an experiment. Also referred to as *antecedent variable.* (See *dependent variable.*)

Introspection. Analysis of one's inner processes (feelings, perceptions, images, cognitions). Early in the 20th century, introspection constituted a major technique of psychological research, but it has been less emphasized recently.

Methodology. Analysis or study of research methods, or research design of a given investigation.

Model. Representation or structure underlying the analysis of a process or theory; person from whom one derives standards of behavior, as in imitation or simulation.

Observation. Method of social and psychological research which permits little or no manipulation of subjects, in contrast to experimentation.

Reliability. Degree of consistency in two measures (as in attitude or other psychological tests) to yield nearly identical scores on retest.

Sample. A limited part of a larger group chosen for study in order to gain information about the *population,* or the universe being studied.

Validity. Degree to which a test actually represents what it purports to identify or measure.

Variable. Factor or attribute that varies. In experimentation or controlled observation, a variable could refer to age, amount of food, pain stimuli, type of government, or other attribute. (See *dependent variable; independent variable.*)

QUESTIONS FOR DISCUSSION

1. Why should you study social psychology?

2. What purposes does social research serve?

3. What is the role of social scientists, and particularly social psychologists, in today's society?

4. What contributions did the pre-19th-century social philosophers make?

5. How did the founders of social psychology approach their problems?

6. How have the social-psychological approaches of sociology and psychology differed?

7. Explain the "group mind fallacy," as expressed by Wundt and LeBon, for example, and attacked by Allport.

8. From a scientific viewpoint, what are the proper units of analysis for social psychology?

9. What distinguishes the scientific method from common sense?

10. What is the relation between the research methodology used and what the social psychologist is studying? Give some examples.

11. Why are so many areas of human experience not extensively studied?

12. Define the experimental method and its special considerations.

13. Evaluate the advantages and disadvantages of the categories of research methods discussed in this chapter.

14. Discuss the ethical problems social psychologists may face when they conduct research.

15. Name and define the three broad traditions in the theoretical background of social psychology.

READINGS

Bohrnstedt, G., and Knoke, D. *Statistics for Social Data Analysis.* Itasca, Ill.: F. E. Peacock Publishers, 1982.

A readable presentation of the statistical variables in survey research.

Carlsmith, J. M., Ellsworth, P. C., and Aronson, E. *Methods of Research in Social Psychology.* Reading, Mass.: Addison-Wesley Publishing Co., 1976.

A readable textbook on the major methods of inquiry.

Karpf, F. B. *American Social Psychology.* New York: McGraw-Hill Book Co., 1932. Reissued in 1972 by Russell & Russell, New York.

An exhaustive presentation of the subject and its European antecedents.

Kidder, L. H., Selltiz, C., Wrightsman, L. S., and Cook, S. W. *Research Methods in Social Relations.* 4th. ed. New York: Holt, Rinehart & Winston, 1981.

Popular text provides a very complete presentation of specific research methods.

Olsen, S. *Ideas and Data: The Process and Practice of Social Research.* Homewood, Ill.: Dorsey Press, 1976.

An analysis of the why and how of research, or translating ideas into action.

Orenstein, A., and Phillips, W. R. *Understanding Social Research.* Boston: Allyn & Bacon. 1978.

Excellent chapters on experimentation, survey, and field research.

Philliber, S. G., Schwab, M. R., and Sloss, G. S. *Social Research: Guides to a Decision-Making Process.* Itasca, Ill.: F. E. Peacock Publishers, 1980.

A clear presentation of the problems of measurement, study design, data collection, and analysis.

Phillips, B. S. *Social Research: Strategy and Tactics.* New York: Macmillan Co., 1976.

Chapters 1–5 are most relevant for their presentation of the logic of research.

Stouffer, S. A. *Social Research to Test Ideas.* New York: Free Press, 1962.

Collection of studies by an eminent methodologist on the testing of hypotheses about attitudes and behavior.

Yinger, J. M. *Toward a Field Theory of Behavior: Personality and Social Structure.* New York: McGraw-Hill Book Co., 1965.

A readable, analytical treatment of the applications of field theory.

PART 1

The cultural pattern of the society in which people participate structures their personalities. Their basic orientation is fashioned by the culture into which they are born, and the formation of their personalities is conditioned in nearly every respect by the social environment.

Behavioral scientists have leaned rather heavily on anthropology for information on how the culture affects personality. This science has had almost as much influence in our understanding of personality dynamics as psychoanalysis. Chapter 2 shows how these two approaches have been used together in investigations of culture and personality in both simple and advanced cultures.

Various subcultures within the social environment, such as social class, give texture and direction to individual personalities. The gestalt, or totality, of social influences that emerge from subcultures like the family and the school is also important in shaping a person's beliefs, values, and motives. Such subcultures are examined in Chapter 3.

A unique structure that gives integration and focus to individual personalities is the self. The ways in which the self merges with the organizing principle of the ego in the personality are examined in Chapter 4.

CULTURE AND THE INDIVIDUAL

THE IMPACT OF CULTURE

A person's personality and behavior are affected by numerous social influences. The broadest of these is culture, which has been studied extensively—and intensively—by anthropologists. Culture can be defined as the way of life of a group of people, an integrated pattern of responses that are learned and passed on from one generation to the next. It is the special product of humans, incorporating what we learn from others and what we add to that knowledge. The culture of any people is a unique set of solutions to what they perceive to be their biological and social needs.

A culture consists of institutions like state, church, and family; standards and customs of all sorts, and ideas about right and wrong. Often it is referred to as a people's *social heritage*. A culture is not passed on intact, like an heirloom, from one generation to another. It changes constantly, but the basic features generally remain constant for at least a generation, and usually much longer; eventually, it becomes standardized and taken for granted. The ways in which biological needs and social demands are satisfied—a choice of clothing, marriage customs, or forms of religious worship—are all aspects of culture.

To study culture as an explanatory concept, many anthropologists and social psychologists are turning to cross-cultural studies. These studies monitor the measurement of human behavior in the context of a given culture or in the comparisons of different ethnic, regional, or national groups (Olmedo, 1979). Implicit in this approach is an awareness of the extensive borrowing or *acculturation* that has occurred in nearly all cultures. This process takes place both between total cultures, such as Western and non-Western, and within the diverse parts of a given society, such as minority groups and the host community.

As an introduction to the topic of how culture and the individual interact, this chapter examines the nature of culture and the relationship of culture and personality in the socialization process. The role of culture patterns in shaping behavior is developed in sections on anthropological study of the personality variable in preliterate cultures, the concept of a basic personality, and psychologically oriented studies of North American Indians. The understanding of this relationship that can be derived from such study serves as a basis for current attempts to define the national character of various contemporary societies.

THE NATURE OF CULTURE

One way to describe the concept of culture more precisely is by examining its unique characteristics. The first distinguishing characteristic cultures have in common is that they tend to be integrated. Every culture has a certain unit or wholeness, whether American or Tibetan, in ancient Athens or present-day Ghana. Despite inconsistencies and conflicts, all cultures have a *gestalt,* or wholeness, in which the component parts are integrated to some degree. In North American culture, for example, a striving toward unity is evident in the distaste of many individuals for war or capital punishment, since these institutions conflict with the more basic cultural trait of humanitarianism. Cultural unity is preserved by the insistence that the president (in the United States) or prime minister (in Canada) incorporate the prevailing values of the society—sobriety, reverence, hard work, optimism, a sense of humor, honesty, and so on. If they fail to extol or personify these virtues to the expected degree, criticism is likely, since cultural integrity is believed to be threatened. The Watergate crisis of the 1970s dramatized this belief more strongly than any other event of this century.

The second characteristic of cultures is that they are essentially conservative and resistant to change, in part because of the human needs for security and conformity. For example, the basic pattern of male and female roles has been altered little in hundreds of years, though it is now being vigorously challenged by women's rights groups. Such efforts as the 1975 International Women's Year and the 1980 World Conference on Women brought attention to the traditional roles of men and women, and the subject is now talked about—but a true redress of grievances will take generations. The difficulties encountered by American blacks in their attempts to alter a tradition of over 300 years of slavery and underprivileged status are another example of how perpetuation of the status quo assures security for the dominant sectors of American society. The concept of national sovereignty which emerged in the 16th and 17th centuries has never been basically tampered with, even though the idea of the independence of nations has had a fairly hollow sound since so many nations have had access to nuclear weapons.

Nevertheless, *some* change does occur in even the most static cultures. Patterns of change, particularly in technological innovations, are awesomely rapid in today's world (Toffler, 1970), as Chapter 17 will demonstrate.

Third, cultures are coercive. Individuals cannot escape their own cultural patterns; even if they were to retreat to an isolated commune or the most remote atoll off Tahiti, they would continue to be imprisoned in the thought of the culture in which they were originally socialized. In the West, for example, the culture continues to rely on the norm of monogamy to regulate sex and marital relations, despite the sexual freedom of the eighties, widespread public and private deviance from the ideal, and the existence of different standards in many parts of the world. Social scientists themselves find it difficult to understand the viewpoints of others, whether they be Black Muslims or unreconstructed Southerners, Shinto priests or Soviet officials. How can we comprehend a New Guinea tribe, for example, that has no personal possession pronouns in its language?

A fourth characteristic of cultures is their *diversity* or variability. The difference between a French citizen and a Britisher, or the infinitely wider cultural gulf separating a Zulu and an American or, for that matter, a Zulu and a Watusi, documents the heterogeneity of culture.

It is true that the industrial revolution and international trade and travel have reduced cultural differences. Coca-Cola and rock music, for example, can be found in almost all parts of the world. But nationalism, particularly as developing nations such as Tanzania, Zaire, and Sri Lanka have been freed from their colonial yokes, has accentuated certain cultural differences. Apparently a fair amount of cultural variability will persist, but certain cultural products and values seem to be more universal than others. Thus, we tend to identify with Chinese art, notably ceramics, of a thousand years ago, but have little concern for China's literature or music, past or present (Hsu, 1977).

Fifth, as open systems which interact with their environments, cultures operate within a *physical* framework. Hence they are limited and to some extent structured by their geographical and biological surroundings (Honigmann, 1967). If the human species had not developed a cerebral cortex, a mechanism for speech, bipedal locomotion, and digital manipulation, our culture might never have moved from the simple food-gathering stage. Despite technical refinements, we are still limited by our own biology and our particular geography. The ceiling may have been raised a little—as witness space exploration—but biological and geographical limits persist.

Finally, culture is not a single, simple concept but an *abstraction* which differs among peoples (Spiro, 1965). A Maine fisherman and a Texas oilworker have a common culture, but they may well perceive its political and religious values very differently. In a sense, culture exists at different layers. Some social scientists distinguish between *explicit* and *implicit* culture—that is, between a society's perceivable materials, customs, and institutions on the one hand, and its intangible, nonverbalized ideals and values on the other. A Masonic Temple and the elaborate ceremonies of the order would be part of the explicit culture, and the friendliness, gregariousness, shared beliefs, and possible mysticism of the members would contribute to the implicit culture. It is the cognitive or belief systems that anthropologists are currently emphasizing in culture (Loflin & Winogrond, 1976). Some anthropologists, in fact, think of culture as shared ideas

Status and roles based on gender are strictly assigned in some cultures. *Source:* American Friends Service Committee.

and meanings (Geertz, 1973). Certainly this aspect of culture is most important to social psychologists.

To some extent the differentiation between implicit and explicit depends on the context in which the culture is taken, that is, whether an individual chooses conventional or nonconventional behavior. Moreover, people tend to indulge in *masking,* a kind of refashioning or rationalization of the natural world. Western culture is especially marked by masking, since the natural order has been almost completely transformed. Whereas in primitive society (as in Greek drama) masks are used to communicate a symbol, we have movies, TV, and other mass media with their blatant advertising as a different kind of transformation of the world.

Some authorities also contrast the *ideal* and the *manifest* culture—that is, the prescribed standards of behavior and the behavior actually observed (Honigmann, 1959). The Kinsey, Pomeroy, and Martin (1948) and Hunt (1974) reports on American sexual behavior demonstrated dramatically the divergence between these two levels of performance. During the Third Reich, German churches slipped into the contradictory position of enunciating the teachings of Christianity and at the same time subscribing to, or at least not opposing, the dictates of the National Socialists, which meant persecuting other Christians—Lutherans and Roman Catholics, not to mention the fatal consequences for Jews. Such disparities between the ideal and the manifest are to be found in almost every culture.

The various groupings or kinds of social background within a culture—sex, age, education, occupation, class, and region, for example—comprise *subcultures* which influence the personalities of those in them. Men and women, adults and children, to name only a few categories, live in different cultural worlds and literally speak different languages. The effects on personality of several of these subcultures will be explored in Chapter 3.

CULTURE AND PERSONALITY IN THE SOCIALIZATION PROCESS

Every aspect of people's behavior is affected by their personalities. Their mental alertness, motivation, interest, and experience are particularly important. Often one or another of these variables seems to be the most salient determinant of behavior. At other times the immediate social situation in which individuals find themselves (for instance, conforming on the job so they won't get fired) may be a more critical influence. But over and above both of these factors, culture enters every category of people's experience, whether directly or indirectly—even thought processes and the texture of mental development as shown by psychological tests (DeVos & Hippler, 1969). Culture affects motives, attitudes, and values, and it prescribes the norms of such social behavior as child rearing and the assignment of statuses and roles.

Put in other terms, there are certain biological needs to which all human beings must make cultural responses (Malinowski, 1944). On this point the similarities among cultures and among individuals are almost as impressive as the differences. Moreover, since both culture and personality are abstractions, Malinowski suggests that culture may be as much an extension of personality as the reverse.

Culture is transmitted from adults to their young in a process known as *enculturation*. This cultural learning is conscious, and it operates as "the control that the older generation exercises over the means of rewarding and punishing children" (M. Harris, 1980, p. 108). Frequently the term *socialization* is used to define this kind of sociocultural learning, but more accurately this term refers to a humanization process (i.e., we learn to speak), while learning the distinct cultural object (e.g., Chinese or English language) is called enculturation. The term *socialization* is popularly used even though to some degree enculturation is implied, since the distinction between the two is an arbitrary one.

Socialization derives from a dynamic relationship between individuals and their culture. It depends on three basic variables: (1) the specific environment, (2) the sociocultural institutions as they have developed over the past generations, and (3) the psychological needs which grow out of the individual's adaptation to the environment.

An example of how these variables interact can be seen in the case of the inhabitants of the island of St. Kitts in the West Indies (Aronoff, 1967). The geographic environment, characterized by a scarcity of land and the presence of the sea, determines the kinds of living available: cutting sugar cane or fishing. The sociocultural institutions determine how the men respond to their occupations. The cane cutters are trapped by a feudalistic land ownership pattern which permits a meager living and little sense of self-gratification. The gap between aspiration and achievement is wide. Fishing offers a far different way of life. Although fishermen are little better off than cutters are, they have a greater sense of autonomy because their market is less restricted, and the organization of group tasks encourages independence and initiative. (Another example of how the means of making a living offered in an environment affect the personality is given in Box 2–1.) The psychological needs and satisfaction grow out of the physical milieu, the inherited institutions, the individual's totality of experience, and his or her definition of the situation at a given moment. The basic pattern repeats itself through socialization and enculturation with each generation.

There are various layers or levels of behavior in the socialization process which to some extent reflect the basic variables in the individual-culture relationship. At the first level is behavior that is *biologically determined*. Certain actions are innate, such as eating, defecating, or breathing. These acts are organic and hardly of serious interest to the social psychologist, although the environment may play some part in the satisfaction of these needs. Some of these behaviors—possibly as many as 50—are labeled *reflexes,* such as the knee-jerk reaction, sneezing, or breathing. Walking, smiling, touching (see Box 2–2), and similar responses are not properly called reflexes but instead are termed *quasi reflexes* because the reaction is to some degree social. At a higher level is a universal type of learning behavior called *sociogenic learning*. A principal example is speech; all human beings emit sounds, and almost all learn to talk, but the particular language a person learns to speak is culturally determined. Most

Box 2–1
WORKING AS A WAY OF LIFE

In our society there has traditionally been a distinction between the rural and urban ways of life which cannot be explained solely on the basis of geographical considerations. Study of cultures which are predominantly rural, however, has shown that specific types of occupations influence personality development among members of groups with the same geographic environment.

Robert Edgerton and colleagues studied four African tribes (Hehe, Kamba, Pokot, and Sebei), each of which contained both pastoralists (shepherds) and farmers.* On the basis of field research and comparisons with other preliterate societies, several working hypotheses were formulated as to how their livelihood might condition their approach to life situations. It was anticipated that, because of the pastoralists' more mobile existence, they would be more militant, more ready to take direct action, more able to endure hardships and not lose face. They would also show greater sexuality and a concern for physical attractiveness. The values of farmers, however, were expected to stress manipulative skills, industriousness, and chastity. They would tend to suppress their emotionality and be less likely to enter into direct action.

Various attitudinal and projective tests, notably the Rorschach, as well as impressionistic data were used to test these hypotheses. Although the findings from the two groups studied were overlapping, the pastoralists did show greater sexuality (possibly a reflection of less attachment to property inheritance), direct rather than indirect aggressiveness, and bravery and self-control. The farmers displayed a higher level of anxiety, more conflict avoidance, emotional constraint, and a tendency toward indirect action, along with disrespect for central authority (p. 275).

Although the use of projective techniques in such studies is debatable, the findings suggest that the means of making a living and the relation between individual and the environment do influence the development of personality. While there were more differences between individuals than between the two groups, pastoralists and farmers reflected different personality needs.

_____

* R. B. Edgerton, *The Individual in Cultural Adaptation: A Study of Four East African Peoples* (Berkeley: University of California Press, 1971).

behavior in the socialization process consists of action patterns at the third level, which have a *cultural origin*. These include the worship of a certain deity or deities, the marriage ceremony, and the textbook you are reading.

Box 2–2
HANDSHAKING AS A CULTURAL MESSAGE

Touching can convey not only the need for personal contact and an expression of personality but a cultural orientation as well. Harry Harlow demonstrated how monkeys depend emotionally on the feel of the mother's skin, for example (see Chapter 7). Preliterate societies differ markedly in the degree of bodily contact they tolerate or encourage. The Netsilik Eskimos, who communicate extensively through touching and skin exploration, are at one extreme.

In Western culture, Ashley Montagu found a wide gap between Anglo-Saxons and the Latin and Slavic peoples in the amount of touching tolerated, with the Scandinavians coming somewhere between.* The English manage to keep some distance apart, even within the nuclear family; only the Germans are more restrained. The United States represents a variant of Anglo-Saxon culture. Montagu observes that "While waiting for a bus Americans will space themselves like sparrows on a telephone wire, in contrast to Mediterranean peoples who will push and crowd together" (pp. 264–265).

How we shake hands can indicate how we feel or our value orientation: compare the swift, offhand touch of the official with the iron grasp of the salesperson. Culture also decrees the scope of handshaking. A generation ago, Europeans shook hands with their colleagues each morning and at the end of the day; a few even did so before and after lunch. Americans may be missing some of the texture of interpersonal relations with their casual "Hi!" to one and all which avoids touching.

---

* Ashley Montagu, *Touching: The Human Significance of the Skin* (New York: Columbia University Press, 1971).

ANTHROPOLOGICAL STUDY OF PRELITERATE CULTURES

The traditional concern of anthropologists (particularly cultural anthropologists) with the customs, institutions, and behavior of primitive or preliterate peoples was first extended to the concept of personality by such pioneers as Franz Boas, Bronislaw Malinowski, and Edward Sapir. Following these leads, several investigators set out in the late 1920s to study and compare the personalities of members of different preliterate cultures. Perhaps the best known are Margaret Mead and Ruth Benedict, both former students of Boas.

Mead's studies in Samoa and New Guinea have been frequently described and are now well known. Briefly, she found that adolescence in Samoa was not a period of stress (as it is in our society), and that Samoans were well-adjusted individuals, which she attributed to the large family groups, the liberal attitude toward sex, and freedom from pressure upon youth (Mead, 1928). Among the Manus of New Guinea, by contrast, she found personality was marked by strong ego drive and self-assertiveness, and industry, physical prowess, and respect for authority were primary goals (Mead, 1930). In a later study (1956), she found that sex was repressed among the Manus, and adolescence involved more strain than in Samoa. In this study she described the effects of recent social changes on the Manus, who had gone from the Stone Age to the Atomic Age in 25 years. She reported they were more relaxed and happy, largely as a result of contacts with Australians, Americans, and others during and after World War II—a spectacular example of successful cultural change.

In another study Mead (1935) investigated sex differences in three primitive societies to find out to what degree "temperamental" differences between the sexes were innate or culturally determined and what kinds of childhood training took place. In her study of three groups in New Guinea—the Arapesh, Mundugumor, and Tchambuli—who were racially similar and lived in the same general area, she found differing acceptable or "modal" personalities for both sexes.

For the Arapesh the ideal was essentially "feminine" (cooperative, unaggressive, and responsive) for both sexes: the mild, responsive man married to the mild, responsive woman. The Mundugumor expected both men and women to be ruthless, aggressive, and "positively sexed"; this conception was of a violent "masculine" character. The Tchambuli, said Mead, exhibited a "genuine reversal of the sex-attitudes of our own culture, with the woman the dominant, impersonal managing partner, the man the less responsible and emotionally dependent person."

Mead's characterization of essentially masculine and feminine personalities reflected the attitudes of the thirties, but it has brought her findings under fire from feminists of the seventies and eighties. Actually, in this work she concluded that our beliefs about innate male and female characteristics are erroneous. Human nature, in this as in other respects, is extremely malleable, primarily affected by cultural molding during early infancy. (This idea will be examined further in Chapter 3.) But in a later work, *Male and Female* (1949), Mead concluded that the basically different physical characteristics of men and women *must* affect the personalities of the two sexes (Chafetz, 1978). The study of sex roles is explored in more detail in Chapter 14.

Like Mead, Ruth Benedict stressed the role of culture in shaping personality and social behavior. Though cultures are amazingly diverse, she said, each has a certain pattern of integration. Each human society has somehow selected certain segments of the great range of possible interests and types of behavior. This is its culture pattern, which represents a coherent organization of behavior or personality. In *Patterns of Culture* (1934), Benedict analyzed in detail three cultures—the Zuñi of New Mexico, the Dobu of New Guinea, and the Kwakiutl of

Vancouver Island on the Pacific Coast—to illustrate the power of culture to shape human behavior.

The Zuñi, a Pueblo Indian group which stressed ritualistic ceremony, were found to be conventional to the point of suppressing individual initiative. Their ideal was a dignified, affable, conventional person who avoided deviation, or even leadership. Moderation, mildness, and sobriety were the order of the day, according to Benedict, and there was little overt conflict or sense of guilt. Benedict characterized the Zuñi as an *Apollonian* culture, in contrast to the neighboring *Dionysian* Indian cultures with their violence and sanctioned sensual excesses. Formality, sobriety, and "nothing to excess" were Zuñi watchwords and the outstanding characteristics of that group.

The Dobu of New Guinea, on the other hand, were found to be violent, competitive, suspicious, and treacherous. They cheated, and they believed in magic. Each person and each village seemed to be hostile to the others. A girl's mother arranged her daughter's marriage by trapping a boy she found sleeping with her daughter. A husband had to spend alternate years in the village of his wife, during which time he was humiliated as an outsider. The wife suffered similarly the next year when she resided in the husband's village. Economic activities were highly competitive. According to Benedict, "All existence is cut-throat competition, and every advantage is gained at the expense of a defeated rival." The culture was secret and treacherous: "the good man, the successful man, is he who has cheated another out of his place." There was widespread belief in incantations, passwords, and malevolent charms. Suspicion attached to practically all social relations, including those between husband and wife. Puritanical ideas and promiscuity went together in this society.

Like the Dobu, the Kwakiutl Indians of the Pacific Northwest were termed by Benedict a Dionysian culture. These former cannibals were found to be highly individualistic and competitive. They carried private ownership to the extreme of dividing up not only the land but also the shore, deep sea areas, and even songs, myths, and titles. Acquiring status and shaming rivals were primary aims in this society, as signified by a "potlatch" or feast at which blankets, canoes, copper, and valuable oils were distributed or destroyed. If the goods were distributed, it was understood that they were to be returned later with interest, often at a rate too high for the recipient to manage. Both distribution and destruction of goods added to the prestige of the host. In a word, the main theme of Kwakiutl culture was the will to superiority or self-glorification.

Benedict emphasized that cultures are not heterogeneous assortments of acts and beliefs but are organized and patterned around goals that their institutions are designed to further. The Kwakiutl pattern was bent to the service of an obsession. We would consider it abnormal, a megalomanic, paranoid manifestation, yet it was made the essential attribute of the ideal man in Kwakiutl society.

Neither Mead nor Benedict denied the presence of individual differences within a society, but they did insist that the psychological approach alone is insufficient for an understanding. They have both been criticized for overgeneralizing and oversimplifying, as with Mead's sharp contrasts among the Arapesh, Mundugumor, and Tchambuli, or Benedict's dichotomy between Apollonian and Dionysian cultures (Barnouw, 1973). In fact, to use the term *sobriety* for the Zuñi is questionable, in view of the history of alcoholic indulgence in that tribe for nearly a century.

Psychologists have suggested that better sampling methods could reveal interesting and significant variations in attitudes and behavior within a given culture pattern. Anthropologists generally have been interested primarily in obtaining a composite picture of personality in each culture so that cross-cultural comparisons can be made. Some anthropologists, however, have applied new investigative techniques to obtain more explicit findings. Mead's impressionistic approach to New Guinea tribes, for example, can be compared to the more rigorous research on the socialization experiences for the same cultural area by a contemporary anthropologist, E. R. Sorenson (1976), which included detailed filming.

Although interest in the interface between culture and personality continues, anthropologists have shifted their attention to more specific topics such as the cultural basis of cognition, including perception and beliefs. This multifaceted approach (which is reflected in the articles appearing in the *Journal of Cross-Cultural Psychology*) is generally identified as *psychological anthropology* (T. R. Williams, 1975; Honigmann, 1976). There is also continuing concern with the effects of culture on mental disorders. Thus concern with the association of personality and culture has not been abandoned in recent years; rather it has been broadened.

THE CONCEPT OF A BASIC PERSONALITY

The concept of a basic personality structure which became evident in the study of preliterate cultures was formally proposed by Ralph Linton, a cultural anthropologist, and Abram Kardiner, a psychoanalyst, as a "basic personality configuration—found in any society, which is shared by the bulk of the society's members as a result of the early experiences which they have in common" (Linton & Kardiner, 1945). The term *basic personality structure* refers to the characteristics which individuals have in common with others of the same culture and which distinguish them from the members of a different culture.

Study of several cultures convinced Kardiner (1945) that basic personality structure grows out of the child-care disciplines found in a society—the kind of maternal care, affectional relations with parents, discipline or lack of it, and relationships with siblings. These influences were said to determine the child's basic attitudes, which, through the process of projection, account for secondary institutions like religions, folklore, and art. These in turn determine beliefs about cause-and-effect relationships, interpretations of the universe, and the like.

Kardiner (1945) found his theories supported by a study of Alor, an island in the Indian Ocean, done by Cora DuBois, who had obtained field data and eight rather detailed biographies, a number of Porteus intelligence test results, children's drawings, and 37 Rorschach inkblot test records. Kardiner found that the biographies, test data, and field reports agreed in depicting the basic personality structure in Alor as insecure, anxious, suspicious, lacking in confidence, and with no interest in the outer world. Tensions had no adequate means of discharge; no ways existed for manifesting mastery and constructiveness. The basic cause for this kind of personality structure, according to Kardiner, was the maternal neglect fostered by a system in which the mother worked in the fields all day and the child was left in the hands of older siblings, relatives, or friends.

Critics of Kardiner's work object to his emphasis on child-rearing practices as the main determinant of personality structure, since family behavior patterns themselves result from complex cultural influences. Other studies have indicated that other social factors besides the family influence personality formation, such as roles assigned according to age, sex, and status (D'Andrade, 1961). Erich Fromm (1970) was one who insisted that basic personality, which he called *social character,* derives from more than child-rearing practices. A society's way of life, said Fromm, results from a complex of historical, economic, social, and psychological factors which manifest themselves in ideas and attitudes that shape the child's personality via the family and education. The personalities and behavior of parents and teachers and their treatment of the child reflect the dominant ideas of the society, modified by their social class or other subculture status. Thus the family is "the psychological agent of society" and is the effect as well as the cause of social character.

Karen Horney (1937) was interested in neuroses, or serious personality maladjustment, and she found them rooted in the culture pattern. Individuals *introject,* or adopt, the conflicting values found in a culture. We tell children to be generous, sympathetic, and cooperative, but they may learn from experience that success depends on their being competitive, assertive, and aggressive. For Horney, as for Fromm, basic personality derives from many individual and social factors, not just family discipline.

The term *modal personality* is a more recent expression of the idea of basic personality or social character which refers to the characteristic patterns appearing most frequently among members of a cultural group. Thus it introduces a quantitative element to the definition. The modal personality is largely socially derived and represents the shared elements of personality, ranging from activities like eating, smoking, or games to highly generalized views of life (Honigmann, 1954).

PSYCHOLOGICALLY ORIENTED STUDIES OF NORTH AMERICAN INDIANS

In our own society, opportunities to study specific cultures and their modal personalities have been found most often among the North American Indians. Until recently, the isolated socialization processes of reservation life provided an appropriate milieu for studying the distinctive personalities of members of Indian tribes. As some of their members have become absorbed in the dominant culture, these characteristics have at times carried over to affect their adaptation to contemporary life. Among Indians who have remained on reservations, particularly, cultural practices are often zealously maintained in order to safeguard their heritage.

The Hopi and Anxiety

Several studies made in the 1940s of the Hopi, a Pueblo Indian group living in the semiarid mesas of northern Arizona (Thompson & Joseph, 1947; Dennis, 1940), described them as agricultural and pastoral, governed by a strict code of life called "the Hopi way." Individuals were induced to conform through sanctions like gossip and ridicule, and typical Hopi behavior lacked aggressiveness and prestige seeking.

Thompson and Joseph gave various kinds of tests to many Hopi children and compared the results with those from a group of midwestern white youngsters. Several clear-cut differences emerged. The Hopi children found more pleasure in meeting social expectations than did the white children, and much less pleasure in individual achievement. The Hopi were more likely to be ashamed of being embarrassed or aggressive but much less ashamed of "bad behavior." Hopi fears centered on supernatural or subjective dangers rather than objective dangers. The typical Hopi child, the investigators concluded, was intelligent (average IQ 110–117 on performance scales—which suggests an atypical sample), industrious, and considerate. Hopi children became sad and angry at aggression and condemned individual efforts to rise above the group by bullying or fighting. While aware of their abilities, they did not admit or openly desire outstanding personal achievement that would separate them from the group. This personality pattern came about largely through the permissive training by which they gradually learned the group purposes and became indoctrinated with the Hopi way. A price was paid in repression of spontaneity and a tendency toward rigidity, but this kind of training and its resultant personality pattern apparently facilitated the survival of the Hopi in a rather unfavorable environment.

The rigidity and anxiety found more recently among individuals of certain Pueblo cultures are apparently attributable to the strictness of their socialization (Dozier, 1961). The first two years are generally fairly permissive, but swaddling in a cradle board traditionally restricted spontaneity of movement, and the effects of this are not clear. At the age when the child begins to walk, perhaps two years, a somewhat stricter tone is adopted in socialization. Admonitions are meted out, often with the verbalized threat that ogres will carry the nonconforming children out of the home. Throughout childhood there may be continued threats of masked bogeymen armed with whips, although no violence occurs. The initiation of boys and girls into a kiva group, especially for the boys, introduces severe physical restrictions.

Evidence indicates that the Hopi may have some degree of introjected aggression, though on the whole members of the culture have acquired a balance between duress and flexibility (Eggan, 1953; Thompson, 1950). No doubt the distinction between the biological mother, who gives birth to the child, and the social mother (the mother's sister) could cause some conflict in the child's affection. In addition, the older sister may also play the role of mother. Whatever conflicts in loyalty may exist, the tightly knit family group has provided the individual with a sense of security. Furthermore, minimal sex repression has allowed some freedom for both heterosexual and homosexual play, from childhood through adolescence, and this probably has reduced Hopi anxiety.

It is significant that in these studies the personality differences were revealed by emotional and attitude tests given at different parts of the reservation. The First Mesa boys were relatively spontaneous and outgoing, while those of Oraibi were definitely constricted and troubled by vague anxiety (Thompson, 1950), and the girls of the First Mesa appeared more constricted than those of the Third Mesa. These findings point to the dangers of overgeneralization about a cultural group, as noted by the earlier students of personality and culture.

Despite what may be an anxiety-provoking socialization, Pueblo Indians seldom have been known to have mental breakdowns (Thompson, 1950). Generally the Hopi have adjusted to contemporary American culture without serious personality disorganization, although they are usually employed in skilled and semiskilled labor and consequently have low status (Madigan, 1956).

The Hopi personality of today may be due as much to broad environmental determinants as to infantile sexual components or affectional relations within the family. The Hopi have gradually adapted to the harsh desert environment of sand, heat, drought, and wind. Their ability to grow crops in a setting that had baffled representatives from the Department of Agriculture gave them a sense of achievement that has contributed to their security and interpersonal cooperation. In recent decades this pride has been threatened by government agencies whose well-meant programs have reduced many Hopi to a relation of dependency. The same problem has been encountered by their neighbors, the Navaho (Lamphere, 1979).

As the traditional male-dominated ceremonials of the Hopi have been disrupted, the survival of "the Hopi way" has become problematic. Anxieties have particularly affected the male as his institutional life has been jeopardized by an overwhelming alien culture. Moreover, the agricultural order is threatened by Western technology. The Hopi are able to perform only a limited role in the contemporary economy, yet on various mental tests they can perceive stimuli of surprising complexity. At least, they view their world in complex images and have an ability to differentiate and synthesize to a degree not found in most preliterate societies. Whatever their ability to conceptualize, adjustment to the new demands made on their culture has been difficult (Thompson, 1969).

The Ojibwa and Isolation

Another psychologically oriented study of North Americn Indians was Hallowell's (1955) investigations of the Ojibwa and the related Saulteaux of the American and Canadian Midwest. Here was a culture that exhibited a considerable degree of anxiety. It was Hallowell's hypothesis that the mild and stoical outward personality was a facade beneath which existed hostility and ambivalence in interpersonal relations. As with other cultures, the taboo on overt aggression meant that other outlets had to be found, such as gossip, sorcery, and magic. Illness and misfortune were explained by magic performed by another individual. Dreams, folklore, and other aspects of fantasy life were caught up in suspicion and belief in the aggression of others.

Another study of Wisconsin Ojibwa children which used the Thematic Apperception Test revealed their inability to identify with any member of their own group (Caudill, 1949). Each individual appeared to be completely self-sufficient and disinterested in any personal ties, whether affectionate or hostile. (Even 17th-century observers had noted this tendency toward isolation.) The anxiety of these people may be due in part to their physical isolation. Close social ties were prevented in winter, and only the fleeting contacts of the trading post occurred in summer. Even at the trading post, individuals frequently appeared withdrawn and seclusive. The principal occupation of the Ojibwa, hunting, required isolation from social contacts, for each hunter was expected to exert supernatural influences over other hunters and warriors.

One consequence of this social isolation was a relatively higher incidence of mental disturbances. Anthropologists have described the *windigo psychosis* among the Ojibwa and related tribes; among its other symptoms is attempted cannibalism, or at least a desire for human flesh (Landes, 1938). Since this kind of illness is almost unique to the Ojibwas and a few related tribes, the phenomenon has intrigued psychiatrists and anthropologists. There appears to be no rigid pattern of windigo. In some instances it is a full-blown psychosis, or it may appear as an anxiety neurosis. In either instance it exhibits a variety of symptoms, from brooding and fantasies to witchcraft and actual violence. It is difficult to apply the causational categories traditionally used by Western psychiatrists (Fogelson, 1965). A more recent interpretation is that windigo and the accompanying cannibalism are simply the result of acute starvation and can be considered "normal" behavior under stressful circumstances (Bishop, 1975). At the very least, there seems to be a connection linking social isolation, sorcery, and strongly deviant behavior.

Acculturation among these Indians has hardly had a beneficial effect. Introduction to Western culture has deprived the Ojibwa men of their older, traditional motivating values (Hallowell, 1955). As with the Hopi, the economic activities that once sustained them are no longer available. The return of the men from the armed services signified a dependence on such government aids as unemployment insurance, while Ojibwa women (like women in general) could secure employment more easily than ever before. This has affected the psychological welfare of both husbands and children. Interpersonal aggression is more acute than under aboriginal conditions, as the only means of effective social control have become the legal and penal institutions of the dominant white group.

Further study of the Ojibwa suggests that some of their pent-up aggression can be explained as the absence of an overt outlet for their hostility toward whites (Doob, 1960). This kind of introversion is in contrast to the Indians of the Plains, where warfare was once prevalent. The Ojibwa were never forced to undergo the degree of cultural change experienced by some societies. They accepted the

Anglo-American culture without a struggle, and yet they never really integrated their own culture with the more dynamic society that surrounded them. Another interpretation turns to environmental problems, especially during the 19th century, when a dwindling food supply and an intense fear of starvation occurred at the same time as their growing dependence on outsiders. As a consequence, interpersonal bonds were weakened in their own society (Bishop, 1975).

THE SEARCH FOR NATIONAL CHARACTER

The anthropological and psychologically oriented studies of various groups have lent substance to our comprehension of the relation between personality and culture. Current efforts to define the national character of contemporary societies, so we can understand other peoples and live peacefully together, are based on this understanding.

It is more difficult to investigate the dynamics of personality in nations than in preliterate cultures, because the variables are much more numerous and intricate. Nevertheless, the effort has been made, and many volumes have been written on the value structures of the Chinese, Japanese, Russians, Germans, Americans, and other nations. Inquiry into the ethos of world powers became a priority during World War II, when the need to understand other nations as enemies and allies was considered crucial to winning the war.

Behavioral scientists are hardly enthusiastic about taking on the nearly impossible task of analyzing national character, but they are aware of the human dimension in international relations (Klineberg, 1964). Our literature and conversation abound with references to the "fighting Irish," "emotional Italians," "stolid Swedes," "inscrutable Orientals," "shiftless Negroes," "grasping Jews," and the like. Such stereotyped ideas are not only inaccurate, they are much less than half-truths. Worse, they are usually based on the false assumption that the various characteristics are innate, inherited tendencies in certain nationalities or races.

Stereotypes do change, but in the interests of the dominant group. When, in the late 19th century, Chinese laborers were needed in California, they were described as thrifty, sober, and law-abiding. Later, when the Chinese were no longer needed, they became regarded as "filthy and loathsome in their habits, unassimilable, clannish, dangerous, inferior mentally and morally" (Schrieke, 1936). In a study made in 1935, Americans described the Japanese as intelligent and industrious; in 1942, after World War II had started, they judged the Japanese to be sly and treacherous—adjectives that had not even appeared among the first dozen in the earlier study (Meenes, 1943).

Attempts to delineate the modal personality of a given national culture raise a number of questions: Is personality development related to contemporary national groupings, and if so, how? Does each culture group produce a distinct personality pattern? Do scientific data exist for newly emerging areas of the world in respect to personality and its expression? Can historical materials be used, or must contemporary analyses be undertaken in order to treat the basic problem of change in societies? Even more fundamental is the question of how personality variables are related to the many subcultures of a society. Within any national grouping, are certain traits and roles required, or simply expected?

The approach to studies of national character has varied historically. For some centuries impressionistic approaches to the study of national character were popular (see Box 2–3). In the 18th century Montesquieu drew on geographic determinism in order to construct the profile of given nations.

In this century, it was fashionable during the 1940s and 1950s for sociologists and anthropologists to construct broad theoretical treatments of a national character. Several countries were especially popular targets for analysis: Germany, Japan, Russia, and the United States. One of the more systematic studies was made of the Soviet Union by the Harvard Research Center, but inevitably it was based on interviews with refugees and expellees. This raises questions of bias—the perception of one who has fled from a country is not likely to be the same as one who has chosen to stay.

More recently, national characterizations have taken even broader perspectives. Since the introduction of behavioral science, examinations of national character have been based on family structure (particularly child-rearing patterns), folklore and mythology, literature, arts, mass communications media, and the institutional fabric, including political and economic processes. As an example, on the basis of these indices Hsu (1963) describes the Chinese as being nonindividualistic, conservative, morally relativistic, competitive but oriented to family rather than individualistic goals, and lacking interest in abstraction. These traits have, of course, undergone marked readjustment to the social changes in China during this century.

Another current approach to national character is through major *value orientations*. R. M. Williams (1970) describes the value system of American society as being characterized by personal achievement, activity and work, moral orientation, humanitarianism, efficiency and practicality, progress, material comfort, equality, freedom, and external conformity among other standards. Although these concepts are not altogether consistent, they do express the complexity of the American personality. Americans, Williams says, are directed toward active mastery rather than passive acceptance and show a restlessness and unwillingness to accept the status quo as unalterable. They tend to be oriented toward the external world rather than the contemplative. They also tend to view other individuals in a horizontal manner (peer relations) rather than a vertical way (superordinates and subordinates); they are more comfortable with equality than with hierarchy.

Cross-National Comparisons

On the whole, total studies of a given society are less popular today. More often, indirect methods are used to assess behavioral and personality differences in cross-national samples. These include self-ratings on personality measures and ratings of other persons, which pose problems of validity. In this context, Triandis (1977) compares the findings of researchers on samples of British and Japanese. The investigators had overlapping approaches in their definitions of certain traits

Box 2–3
FAIR PLAY, LE DROIT, AND EL HONOR

When travelers, journalists, and essayists try to describe the national character of peoples, their insights may be keen, but they usually have some personal bias that colors their impressions. Their acquaintance with all the various classes and sections of a country may not be adequate, and they may have little knowledge of social science. This can make their contributions of doubtful value.

One writer who frankly acknowledged that his 1928 study of Englishmen, Frenchmen, and Spaniards was based on firsthand knowledge and intuition and was not a "scientific" work based on statistics, comparative study of sources, or "facts," was the Spanish statesman Salvador de Madariaga.* He says he observed the three peoples to note "their instinctive attitudes towards everyday life" and concluded that the psychological keynote of the Englishman is fair play; of the Frenchman, *le droit;* and of the Spaniard, *el honor.* Admitting that he is oversimplifying, he presents the "hypothesis" that:

> The psychological center of gravity of each of our three peoples is placed respectively:
>
> > for the English people, in the body-will;
> > for the French people, in the intellect;
> > for the Spanish people, in the soul;
>
> and that the natural reaction toward life in each of these three people is:
>
> > for the Englishman, action;
> > for the Frenchman, thought;
> > for the Spaniard, passion. (p. 8)

De Madariaga discusses with great skill the social and political structure, historical development, language, and literature of the three nations. But his introductory remarks distress the social scientist, for he says: "The main lines of this parallel between the English, French and Spanish characters once established, it is possible to verify the conclusions thus reached a priori by direct observation of the individual and collective life of our three peoples" (p. 123).

De Madariaga openly rejects the empirical approach and relies on impressionistic, intuitive methods. Other writers are impressionistic without being so frank about it. Social scientists can only regard conclusions reached in this way as interesting hunches, which must be redefined as hypotheses to be checked by scientific procedures.

_____

* S. de Madariaga, *Englishmen, Frenchmen and Spaniards* (New York: Oxford University Press, 1928).

(honesty and cooperativeness, among others) for the two national samples, but there was a large gap between their approaches to traits like rationality and ambition.

Comparisons on fairly specific behaviors can usually be made between cross-national samples, notably between cultures that are not radically different from each other. For example, in a questionnaire study of the degree of distress elicited by social change (see Chapter 17), English subjects were found to react with more anxiety to "undesirable" social change, whereas Americans felt they were more in control of it and consequently it produced less anxiety for them (Lauer & Thomas, 1976). This kind of micro, or limited, comparison (see Box 2–4) offers a more realistic basis for studying national character than a sweeping analysis does.

Cross-national research into personality and behavior usually involves many more variables than do studies of a single culture. A notable example is the comparison of samples from Mexico City and Austin, Texas, in which a number of personality and cognitive scales were used. Among the differences found was the tendency of Americans to be more active in coping with life's problems. They were also found to be more competitive and individualistic, whereas Mexicans were generally more cooperative and family-centered, as well as more fatalistic in their outlook on life (Holtzman, Diaz-Guerrero, & Swartz, 1975).

The Need for Precise Terms

In assessing the role of national character studies, it can be concluded that the present tendency is to examine personality within social systems. The research tools available are more equipped to analyze personality in family, school, or occupational roles than to attempt to find connections between historical traditions and a modal personality. Such studies of national character require serious consideration, however, particularly in the definition of terms.

The terms *modal personality* or *basic personality structure,* as we have noted, refer to the personality pattern or the core of attitudes and values found in a majority, or at least a sizable minority, of the population. But the concept is open to question because it may imply that there is an ideal personality or that norms of efficient functioning exist within a given culture. The term *national character* has been subject to the same type of question. A more modest term, *national characteristics,* which implies a diffuse plurality rather than a completed unity, has been suggested (Klineberg, 1954).

It is important to remember that nationality is a highly arbitrary concept which changes with shifts in history. The concept of German nationality is entirely different for 1870, 1919, 1933, 1945, or the present, as a result of changes due to war, politics, or economics. In many nations, also, there are different ethnic subgroups, and in some instances the movement of boundaries is significant (Farber, 1963). Class subcultures are especially likely to produce marked differences within a national sample.

The problem of definition also applies to both personality and culture. Personality is based on a varied set of learning experiences as well as hereditary

Box 2–4
IS MAÑANA SOON ENOUGH?

Part of the excitement of traveling abroad is discovering the subtle and obvious differences in the ways people do things—their cultural norms. Foreigners in Latin America, for example, learn not to be surprised when people speaking to them get very close. There also seems to be a questionable correspondence between speech and reality in Latin Americans—even casual visitors soon notice the divergent answers they receive when they ask several people which corner a bus stops at or how often it runs. Apparently the residents consider it better to give some kind of answer to a stranger than to give no answer at all. The most obvious difference to a North American, however, is the tendency of Latin Americans to put off the fulfillment of obligations until *mañana*.

Many of the observed characteristics of other cultures are casually arrived at and misleading, but perceptions of the time dimension have been investigated. In survey samples of Californians and Brazilians, it was found that Brazilians had fewer clocks and watches, and those they had access to were less accurate than those in North America.* Brazilians more often reported being late for appointments and social affairs, and they were less inclined to make apologies for it. They were more likely to blame lateness on external factors, whereas Americans would see the cause as internal, or due to their own miscalculations. The Brazilians also felt that a person of status could afford to ignore time, while the Californians tended to perceive a punctual person as being more successful. Thus the socioeconomic situation within a culture can have implications for such norms as the perception of time.

---

* R. V. Levine, L. J. West, and H. T. Reis, "Perceptions of Time and Punctuality in the United States and Brazil," *Journal of Personality and Social Psychology,* 1980, *38,* 541–550.

factors, which are relevant to individual differences in personality but presumably are the same throughout a single culture. In the social-psychological context, individual personality also involves a number of statuses or roles, depending on specific situations. One of the problems in national character studies is to determine to what degree these personality variables are influenced by national belongingness. In these studies, the term *multimodal personality* would be more appropriate than *modal personality*. In other words, the study of national cultures ought to include examination of the several subcultures in them, such as social class, educational level, and regional variations. In certain cultures, like Japan and Germany, bimodal differences exist because of age or generational differences, and sex differences would be found in almost any national culture. A multimodal conception of national character is desirable because no single personality type or mode is likely to be found in up to 60 or 70 percent of the population of a nation (Inkeles & Levinson, 1968). Whenever the term *modal personality* is used to speak of Beijing, Seattle, Guadalajara, or Milano, for example, it refers to a mode of personality expression in given segments of the national society or urban/rural culture.

A number of studies also suggest that the differences in traits and attitudes found between individuals tested within a single culture are greater than those found between cultures. This, of course, is consistent with the finding that traits and attitudes as well as physical characteristics show as great or greater differences within a race as between races.

Another problem is the tendency to fuse personality with culture. The two constructs, culture and personality, refer to distinct phenomena. Culture is a changing but continuous totality in which the individual personality is functioning in a given direction for a limited period of time. The individual rejects as well as accepts certain traits or aspects of culture. All terms—*personality, culture, institutions, the social structure*—are convenient conceptualizations. As scientific data (or models), they must be treated with care.

Inkeles and Levinson (1969) point out the importance of the concept of modal personality in studying large groups such as nations:

> The concept of modal personality holds much promise for increasing our understanding of large-scale systems as it is brought to bear in the study of institutional functioning. The role of modal personality in the operation of social sanctions is only beginning to be understood. Its influence in rendering effective or hindering the functioning of the major institutional complexes of society—kinship structure, social stratification, the economic order, the political system—is yet to be explored in detail. Movements of protest, the rise of elite groups, and major programs of social change represent but a few of the major problem areas in which the causal influence of modal personality patterns should be more fully described and assessed (p. 492).*

---

*Lindzey/Aronson, *The Handbook of Social Psychology,* 1969, 2/E, vol. 4, Addison-Wesley Publishing Company, Inc., Chapter 31, page 270, "Leadership," by C. A. Gibb, (Chapter 34, pages 418-492, "National Character,") by A. Inkeles and D. Levinson. Reprinted with permission.

PROBLEMS IN RESEARCH ON CULTURE AND PERSONALITY

The need for precision in the use of such terms as *personality* and *culture* applies to all study of these concepts, whether it is concerned with a single culture or national character or with cross-cultural or cross-national comparisons. Several basic problems, largely of a methodological nature, are evident in this research.

The first concerns the conceptual framework in which the study is approached. Whereas much of the research of the past was based on psychoanalytical techniques, a more recent tendency has been to approach the behavior itself rather than to use projective tests or similar tools (Honigmann, 1975). Moreover, *cultural symbol systems*—beliefs, attitudes, and values—are assuming priority over unconscious needs (Spiro, 1979). As in all research, the orientation of the investigator determines what is studied and how it is studied.

The second problem is the representativeness of the events of the culture that have been selected for study. Facts must be meticulously selected, and if the study concerns a whole culture, primitive or modern, the data used should be generally true of that culture. If variations occur (as they usually do) in section, class, caste, and the like, they should be specified. The degree to which the members of the society conform to a given behavior pattern should also be determined.

The third problem is how rigorously the research procedures are followed. The population sample must be selected carefully to be of the proper size and appropriate age, sex, or social class. Cross-cultural comparisons are more meaningful if there are similar groups of informants for each culture and the same kind of information is requested of both. Reports of informants must be cross-checked.

Fourth, the investigators must be precise in framing the hypotheses of the study and must guard against being unduly influenced by them as they collect their data. Questions to be considered are: Will the data be derived chiefly from impressions and intuition, or will direct observation be used? If tests or other relatively objective techniques are to be used, to what extent are they valid for the culture to be studied?

The fifth problem concerns the researcher's determination of what bases of evidence are to be accepted and how they are to be interpreted. There has been some controversy about the possible interpretations of Pueblo cultures, for example. This disagreement is reducible to two basic observations: Pueblo society is highly integrated and Apollonian in character, but there are individuals who do not conform. The ideal personality type is directed toward the virtues of gentleness, cooperation, and modesty, but Pueblo culture is marked by *covert* tension and anxiety. Both of these observations are encountered in reports of research teams investigating the Hopi and Zuñi cultures, where they are offered to "explain" discontinuities in the functioning of personalities in those societies (Bennett, 1956). Another problem is evident in the study of Russian and American personality variations, where test and interview items may not have identical meanings for individuals of both cultures—or even within a given national culture—and all observers would not make identical interpretations of the responses. It is probably premature to expect unanimity among observers on the norms and values of cultures, but their inability to agree indicates the complexity of culture and personality studies.

Sixth, determining the cause-and-effect relationship is subject to a number of special difficulties in investigating the relationship of culture and socialization. For example, in the case of the Kutchin Indians, anxiety might be interpreted as attributable to "scaring techniques" in child-rearing, or the hostile Northern environment might be the more relevant factor, along with disease and hunger (Slobodin, 1960).

Social researchers should represent the characteristics of the culture they are investigating. The fit is seldom perfect, however, as in this UN project in Ethiopia. *Source:* United Nations.

The Search for More Precise Measures

The search for more precise measures of the variables studied in research on culture and personality is constantly underway. Anthropologists and other researchers must be alert to the problems of sampling, isolating and refining variables, and data collection and analysis, as well as other considerations of quality control. Only in this way will investigators avoid the overgeneralizations and the more facile cause-and-effect relationships which have characterized the reports of research of the past.

It is to be hoped that cross-cultural research will reach the point where "scientific laws governing humans and their behavior can be established" (Whiting, 1968). Two approaches have generally been used (Bourguignon, 1973). One is field studies such as those carried out decades ago by anthropologists like Mead and Benedict, which infer the psychological traits of persons from the institutions in their societies. The other is painstaking analysis of behavior, notably childhood training, using statistical and audiovisual techniques. The merging of these two approaches remains a possible development.

SUMMARY

Cultures demonstrate almost infinite variability, and it would be presumptuous to determine to what degree any culture provides satisfaction, not to speak of happiness, to its members. Cultures differ, too, in the degree to which they permit flexibility in the functioning of personality within the prescribed channels of behavior of the society.

The variability of cultures might be hypothesized as having a probability of normal distribution, so that we could visualize a certain characteristic as being distributed on a normal curve (two equal sides) in a diagram of the cultures of the world. An example would be the cooperativeness-competitiveness continuum, or, as a comparable trait comparison, passivity-aggression. An imaginary curve on which various cultures might be placed would be diagrammed as shown in Figure 2–1. Since situations and norms are so totally different from one culture to the next, this curve must be hypothetical. At least for some observers it is hazardous to imply that a cultural trait can be quantified in this way.

In addition to a distribution curve hypothesizing the range of cooperativeness within the potentiality of "human nature," for each culture there might be a curve indicating the extent of personality flexibility. There is considerable variability in the permissive limits within a culture. In most preliterate societies, the range of choice in personality functioning is distinctly limited, and the norms of conduct are generally ascribed and stereotyped. Maximum variation is permitted in certain advanced cultures. In present-day American culture, for example, in some quarters there is a competitiveness which is vaguely reminiscent of the Kwakiutl—as witness debutante parties that cost $30,000 or more—and at the other end of the continuum there is the ideal of selfless service in the Peace Corps.

The world's complex societies are sufficiently flexible to include both militarists and pacifists!

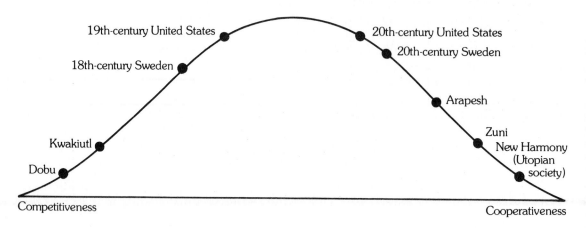

Figure 2-1. Distribution of Cultures on the Competitiveness-Cooperativeness Continuum

WORDS TO REMEMBER

Acculturation. A process of borrowing in which the (migrant) individual or group acquires the cultural traits of a new or foreign culture.

Basic personality. A constellation of personality traits identified with a given culture, as based primarily on the early experiences of the child (see *modal personality*).

Cross-cultural studies. The examination and comparison of personality and social institutions between or across preliterate or advanced societies. *Cross-national studies* are a variation of the cross-cultural approach.

Cultural conflict. Conflict or strain caused by a juxtaposition of two cultures. An example is the Navajo, who find their original culture and the Anglo-American culture are not always in harmony. The conflict may appear in social institutions and value systems as well as in individuals.

Culture. The totality of language, knowledge, and technology passed on from one generation to the next, as defined by a given society. For example, sidewalks, Bibles, wearing makeup, and democracy are a few of the thousands of elements or traits comprising Western culture.

Institution. Societal structure or organization which is indispensable in a culture. Examples are work or the economic institution, the family, the church, the school, the state. In more complex societies, science and the military might also be institutions.

Modal personality. The personality identified with a given culture on a statistical or frequency basis.

Socialization. Acquisition by the individual of the appropriate norms and behaviors expected by society; whereas sociocultural learning; is sometimes referred to as *enculturation.*

Subculture. A division of the culture or kind of social background, such as social class, ethnicity, religion, sex, or age; often referred to as a special grouping or regional variation, such as the youth, Appalachian, or Sicilian subculture.

QUESTIONS FOR DISCUSSION

1. What does the term *culture* mean? What generalizations can be made about culture, and how universally do they apply?

2. What distinctions have proven useful in the cultural approach to personality, and how might they apply to, say, North America?

3. How does geography impose certain conditions on a given culture such as our own?

4. What was Margaret Mead's contribution to our understanding of the innate nature of male and female characteristics?

5. What did Ruth Benedict mean by *patterns of culture?* How might this approach apply to the East African cultures studied by Edgerton (Box 2–1).

6. What is meant by the *basic personality structure?* How does the term differ from *modal personality?*

7. How does Hopi society demonstrate cultural conflict? Do you see any comparisons with other simpler or advanced societies?

8. How is the problem of personality and cultural change reflected in the Ojibwa?

9. In what ways has the acculturation of North American Indians probably affected their personalities?

10. How might a social psychologist treat scientifically the question of national character? What are the crucial problems in this inquiry?

11. What value orientations did Williams find in the United States? How can these generalizations be tested?

12. What are the special problems of research in cross-national studies?

READINGS

Edgerton, R. B. *The Individual in Cultural Adaptation.* Berkeley: University of California Press, 1971.

    A study of culture and personality in four East African tribal areas.

Holtzman, W. H., Diaz-Guerrero, R., and Swartz, J. D. *Personality Development in Two Cultures.* Austin: University of Texas Press, 1975.

    A depth analysis of the values of school

children in a Mexican and an American sample.

Honigmann, J. J. *Culture and Personality.* New York: Harper and Row Publishers, 1954.

Still a classic text on theory and research in this area.

Honigmann, J. J. (Ed.). *Handbook of Social and Cultural Anthropology.* Chicago: Rand McNally Company, 1973.

Chapters 25–27 are an account of the relationships among culture, psychology, and psychiatry.

Hunt, R. (Ed.). *Personalities and Cultures.* Austin: University of Texas Press, 1967.

Readings focus on a variety of problems in Old and New World cultures.

Sargent, S. S., and Smith, M. W. (Eds.). *Culture and Personality.* New York: Wenner-Gren Foundation for Anthropological Research, 1949 (reissued 1974).

Proceedings of an interdisciplinary conference of leaders of the field.

Segall, M. H. *Cross-Cultural Psychology.* Monterey, Calif.: Brooks/Cole Publishing Co., 1979.

A most readable textbook on motivation, cognition, and other psychological processes in the cross-cultural context.

Triandis, H. C., and Brislin, Richard W. (Eds.). *Handbook of Cross-Cultural Psychology* (5 vols.). Boston: Allyn & Bacon, 1980.

Volume 5, *Social Psychology,* is an excellent collection of articles on the various ways that social psychology and cultural anthropology interface.

Williams, T. R. *Psychological Anthropology.* The Hague: Mouton, 1975.

Introduction and Part Six are especially pertinent to the study of culture and personality; some 20 research studies are reported.

PERSONALITY AND THE SOCIAL ENVIRONMENT

The broad-range effects of culture on people's personality and behavior result from the more limited influences of a variety of subcultures or kinds of social backgrounds in the social environment. The most important of these is social class, or socioeconomic status, which operates to mold our beliefs, values, and motives. The relation of social class to personality and people's attitudes and behavior is relevant to many of the facets of social psychology to be explored throughout this text.

Other subcultures particularly affect the emerging personality of the child. The social psychology of the family and the basic patterns of socialization it provides are largely responsible for the social setting of early childhood. The school enhances socialization in the formative years, and peer groups comprise subcultures which form significant social settings for childhood and adolescence.

This chapter is at best an introduction to the question of how the individual is shaped by the environment. People today are subject to many other kinds of influence, such as the mass media, technological change, and religion. Later chapters will explore how our social backgrounds—social class, family, school, and the like—determine how we perceive the universe, how we speak, what groups we join, and to those interested in making a better world, how plans can be laid for social change.

This chapter first examines the concept of social class and how class systems in a society are determined. The effects of social class on behavior, particularly in the United States, are considered in various areas, including child-rearing practices. Then social mobility, which results from the effects of status inconsistency brought on by changes in society or in the person's environment, is examined.

The other significant subcultures discussed in this chapter are largely responsible for the socialization of the child. There are sections on the family, with emphasis on the parental relationship; on the school, with emphasis on educational equality; and on peer groups, with emphasis on the diversity and alienation of youth cultures.

THE CONCEPT OF SOCIAL CLASS

All behavioral scientists do not agree on the importance of the concept of social class. Some observers believe it was a significant factor in the more stable society of the 19th century but is of marginal relevance in the mobile, urban social order of the United States and Canada today. Class boundaries seem to be more fluid than ever, due to rising educational standards, attainment of higher levels of education, increased vertical and horizontal mobility, the upgrading of occupations, the effects of unionization, and a rising standard of living (at least until it was slowed down by inflation). Whereas only 35 percent of people surveyed identified themselves as middle class in 1952, 49 percent did so in 1975, and nearly all of the remainder placed themselves in the working class (Beeghley, 1978). Even the relationship of social class to ideology is getting fuzzy; in the civil rights push of the 1960s, for example, the strongest support for equality came from affluent college students.

Despite the upheaval of the 1960s aimed at assuring racial and ethnic equality (see Chapter 17), the existence of social class has never been challenged effectively (Westergaard, 1966). In a nation such as the United States, where the upper 5 percent of the population enjoys 20 percent of the nation's income and the bottom 20 percent receives only 5 percent, a class system in inevitable (Gans, 1972). These different economic strata mean vastly unequal consumption levels and educational opportunities, and basically different attitudes toward the status quo.

The reluctance of some sociologists to agree on class lines is an indication of the complexities of class. Social class functions differently in a small town and a large city, in Texas and Vermont, with professionals in a campus community and managers in an industrial complex, with those who came of age in the Great Depression and those who grew up after World War II.

Occupational Status as a Basis for the Class System

The existence of social classes and a stratified society has often been questioned. Utopian societies which attempt to abolish class systems have not lasted long, however. Even when the Soviet Union attempted to abolish classes in its early days it allowed for stratification, which can serve the same functions.

The persistence of social class, particularly in North America, is largely attributable to its basis in the status ranking of occupations. There are both

In the 18th century, social class functioned as caste as expressed in dress, lifestyle, and privileges. Court painters like George Romney immortalized members of the nobility. *Source:* Huntington Library and Art Gallery.

agreements and disagreements among different cultures about given occupational roles. The Soviet Union esteems an accountant higher than the United States does; the United States places a farmer higher than the Soviet Union does; and Japan rates a newspaper reporter or a street sweeper higher than either of the other two countries do. The military officer is highly rated in Central America, which is not surprising in view of the persistent upheavals in that area. There would be universal agreement, however, that a surgeon, cabinet minister, or university professor would outrank an accountant, pastry cook, or newspaper reporter, who in turn could lord it over several dozen lower-status occupations. The reasons that physicians and government officials rank higher are not hard to find: service to humanity, high income, lengthy education required, and symbolic nature of the work. Manual labor generally ranks lower than white-collar employment. Still, these more obvious variables do not tell the whole story.

The agreement on ranking occupations is fairly consistent in all complex societies (Marsh, 1971). Since most samples used in cross-national comparisons are university students, this consistency is not surprising. Less developed societies may have other bases for status, such as the religious symbols and concepts deriving from the caste system in India. In nearly all societies, however, occupation is the primary criterion of social position.

In explaining social stratification, sociologists generally take either the functionalist or the conflict approach. The *functionalist* view is that occupational status is assigned on the basis of its function or utility to society. The problem is that this does not take into account the notion of replaceability. For instance, trash collection provides an important service to society, possibly more than many higher-status occupations, but the training required is so minor that almost anyone could do the job. Therefore the garbage collector is usually held in low esteem. This inconsistency has been recognized in a number of communal groups, where tasks are rewarded on the basis of their importance to the commune. Some require work rotation whereby all members of the community acquire a prescribed number of work credits in a variety of tasks. Another problem with the functionalist view is that stratification is often unharmonious or *dysfunctional* (Barber, 1957). Some occupations are probably underrated and some are overrated, depending on the value systems of a society.

The *conflict* school, proposed originally by Karl Marx and represented academically by Ralph Dahrendorf (1959), views status rankings as the result of competition over scarce resources. In this context, status may be based on power over the behavior of individuals (Caplow, 1954). Thus the doctor, the government official, and the bank president are high-status individuals. But somehow police officers and clerics, who enjoy a somewhat regulatory role, do not necessarily have high status ascribed to their positions.

Another approach, which is probably closer to the functional than the conflict school, is represented by the *ambivalence hypothesis* (Cohn, 1960). According to this idea, status depends partly on standards of occupation and income, education, and the like, but it is also accorded to those who meet the criterion of *charisma*, whose basis is in the Judeo-Christian concept of extraordinary power granted to certain individuals. The physician who saves lives fulfills both criteria through both occupational prestige and a superhuman role. A Supreme Court justice and a cabinet member also represent the norms of both prestige and servant of the people. The judge, like the physician, has been credited with almost divine powers.

Thus to some degree social class represents a constellation of occupational status positions. Related factors such as the level of education necessary for placement in an occupation or the income derived from it also operate, however, and it is sometimes difficult to differentiate between them. For example, survey data from a large suburban community revealed no satisfactory means of disentangling the relative contributions of occupational status and level of education (Hodge, 1970). Persons with limited education may acquire good incomes, and those from below-average income backgrounds can land in status occupations. The educational channel itself is a major avenue of achieving status, but while the average number of years completed in school has increased greatly in recent years, this has not resulted in comparable gains in social class. The specific contribution of education to upward mobility has not yet been ascertained.

The occupational basis for the class system is reflected in substitution of the term *working class* as the label for *lower class,* as that term came into disfavor with sociologists. In a study of the American perception of class and status, Vanneman and Pampel (1977) made a basic distinction between *manual and nonmanual* employees. Prestige factors associated with the white-collar sector, such as the manipulation of persons and symbols, have little appeal to blue-collar (manual) workers (see Box 3–1).

Classification of Social Class Systems

Although there is no absolute agreement as to the proper definition of social class, all the criteria can be used to classify a given population into meaningful strata or, to use the social-psychological term, *classes.* There are at least four methods for identifying the class system of a given society. To obtain the most complete analysis of a community, these methods can be combined. They are:

1. The *subjective* or self-classification method—simply asking persons to which class or category they belong.
2. The *statistical* method—classifying individuals into strata according to income level or other measurable criteria.
3. The *objective* method—using specific criteria like lineage, occupation, and residence.
4. The *reputational* method—using local informants to assign ratings to the subjects.

Each of these methods for determining social class has advantages and disadvantages, although the objective and reputational methods are probably burdened with the least methodological difficulty.

Until the coming of age of sociology in the 1930s, scant attention was given to evidence of social class in the United States. Then researchers began to examine

Box 3–1
THE BLUE-COLLAR WORKER'S WORLD

We tend to view others in the context of our own class culture, which for students and professors has traditionally been middle class. But the class system incorporates a variety of lifestyles. An example is the informal group of skilled workers in a Wisconsin town who frequented a local tavern, as described by a participant-observer, E. E. LeMasters, in *Blue-Collar Aristocrats.**

The attitudes of these blue-collar workers on work, family, sex, politics and the like were often hard line, but they were not always consistent. LeMasters found little upward mobility, but middle-class values were often evident. They upheld separation of the sexes, to the extent of believing that only fathers could make men out of their sons but the rearing of daughters is best left to mothers. They tolerated the idea of their wives working, yet they ridiculed "women's lib." They upheld a code of freedom in sexual conduct but were repulsed at the thought of homosexuality: "Those bastards better stay away from me. I'd rather fight than switch" (p. 108). Younger workers and most women were somewhat more tolerant of deviation.

There was rigidity in other kinds of attitudes. Most of the workers were descendants of German Catholics, but they were suspicious of foreigners (notably Poles) and were anti Jew and anti black, even though they respected Martin Luther King. On the night of King's assassination in 1968, one bricklayer said: "Why in the hell did they shoot King? That crazy bastard should have shot Rap Brown—then we could have given the guy a medal" (p. 188). They were also cynical about politics (a growing attitude in all classes) and were especially critical of the then-raging Vietnam war.

---

*E. E. LeMasters, *Blue-Collar Aristocrats; Life Styles in a Working-Class Tavern* (Madison: University of Wisconsin Press, 1975).

the nature of the class system and its effects, usually choosing smaller towns and cities to study because of their more manageable size.

W. Lloyd Warner, an anthropologist and sociologist at the University of Chicago, was most responsible for stimulating research on social class in America. He formulated a scale of social class status which has become widely known and used. The sixfold classification was devised as a means to indicate class structure in an old New England community, Newburyport, Massachusetts, which Warner and Lunt (1941) called "Yankee City." The classes, shown in Figure 3–1, ranged from the upper upper, with stress on tradition and lineage, to the lower lower, marked by economic insecurity and ethnic differentiation.

One reason blue-collar workers have a set of values and attitudes that are different from those of the middle class is their necessary subordination to the machine or the assembly line. *Source:* © Theodore Anderson, 1981.

The Coleman and Neugarten (1971) analysis of Kansas City, Missouri, found five classes as the bases of that status system, but with some probing 13 layers could be discerned (see Table 3–1). As with Yankee City, an immense gulf was found between the two ends of the class continuum. At one extreme was the "capital-S society," the 45 men and women who "reigned over High Society" and whose fortunes were based on manufacturing, commerce, and the like. At the other extreme were the "people at the bottom": the "poor" of the shacks and slums, the quasi delinquents, and the "different," who were minority-group members "not assimilated into the mainstream of Kansas City life." Between these two levels were the working and middle classes, who were characterized by

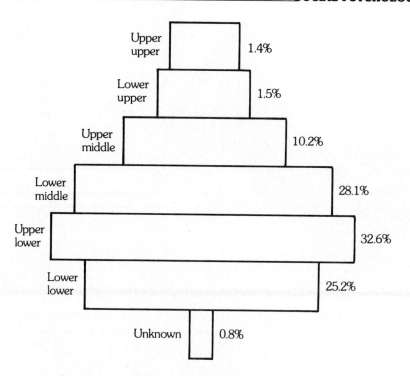

Figure 3-1. Warner's Scale of Social Class Status

Source: W. L. Warner and P. S. Lunt, *The Social Life of a Modern Community* (New Haven, Conn.: Yale University Press, 1941).

responsibility and upward striving. The gap between the lower and the working class was the most visible. Skin color and other sensory information (i.e., physical deformities) were harder to alter than the limits set by where one worked or lived.

A more recent analysis of 900 residents of Boston and Kansas City (Coleman & Rainwater, 1978) revealed seven essential strata: (1) the traditional wealthy, (2) a new "success elite," (3) the professional and managerial, who are mobile because of their education, (4) the comfortable middle class, (5) a lower and not so comfortable middle class, (6) those working, and (7) those on welfare or nonworking.

EFFECTS OF SOCIAL CLASS ON BEHAVIOR

Assignment to a given social class position on the basis of occupation and to some extent education and income determines to a remarkable degree a person's life chances. The amount of money available from employment or less often from inheritance usually sets the educational potential, the living conditions, and even

Table 3–1. **Class Structure of Kansas City, Missouri (1971)**

	Percentage of Sample
Upper Class:	
Capital-S society	0.4%
Noncapital-S, upper class	1.4
Upper Middle Class	
Upper middle elite	1.3
Upper middle core	5.3
Upper middle marginals	5.0
Lower Middle Class	
Lower middle elite	5.8
Lower middle core	17.2
Lower middle marginals	10.3
Working Class	
Working-class elite	5.0
Working-class core	25.5
Working-class marginals	9.7
Lower Class	
Lower class, but not quite the lowest	6.4
"Slumdwellers" and other "disreputables"	6.7

Note: Sample drawn from adults 40 to 69 years old in 2,300 households.

Source: Adapted from R. P. Coleman and B. L. Neugarten, *Social Status in the City* (San Francisco: Jossey-Bass, Publishers, 1971), p. 59.

the quality of medical care, which itself may assure longevity. Beyond these parameters, the lifestyle is derived from status or prestige conferred by occupation or such social factors as choice of the "right" school and membership in the proper clubs. As the German sociologist Max Weber suggested, life chances are mainly economic; lifestyles are a matter of social acceptance.

The consequences of class membership have been studied in a variety of situations—state of physical and mental health, sexual behavior, marriage patterns, and the image people have of themselves and others.

A study of mortality in Western countries found a correlation between class position and longevity, though the relationship has been weakened over the years by advancing health standards. Class differences also were found to be lowest for cultures with either very high or very low mortality (Antonovsky, 1967).

On the psychological side, differences in security are revealed in findings from the Rorschach inkblot and other tests. Workers in a blue-collar sample, compared to the middle class, had higher scores on powerlessness, feeling of deprivation, pessimism, and extrapunitiveness, and a distaste for the unfamiliar, among other characteristics (Cohen & Hodges, 1963). In another study, more lower-class than middle- or upper-class persons reported stress symptoms on a checklist of depressive and psychosomatic symptoms. It was evident that the middle class and the upwardly mobile population have been socialized to develop mechanisms to counteract stress (Kessler & Cleary, 1980).

Mental health is related to a person's choice of values and definition of success. The middle and working classes may approach both means and end values differently. For example, for the middle class a college education is not only a means value but an ends value, which implies that a member of that class is more likely to achieve that end (Abrahamson, Mizruchi, & Hornung, 1976). However, symbols of success are always complex, and the aspiration level is differently perceived by both classes. Consequently, in some cases the degree of *anomie,* or disorientation and alienation from society, is greater for members of the middle class than for those of the lower class—after all, they have farther to fall! (The concept of anomie is discussed further in Chapter 12 in the section on primary and secondary groups.)

The pioneer Kinsey studies of sexual habits of the American male in the 1940s found a more direct approach to sex among lower-class subjects, compared to a middle-class tendency to defer coitus until marriage. Between the ages of 16 and 20, masturbation and petting to climax were reported much more frequently in upper-class than in lower-class males, while premarital intercourse and homosexual outlet were reported much less frequently. Marked differences were also found in attitudes toward nudity and in patterns of erotic arousal. Kinsey commented succinctly: "Each social level is convinced that its pattern is the best of all patterns; but each level rationalizes its behavior in its own way" (Kinsey, Pomeroy, & Martin, 1948). Subsequent research has shown a decline in the influence of social class in sexual behavior (Hunt, 1974), but differences still exist. The middle classes have moved closer to the freer sexual code of the working class, which in turn has learned to defer present wants for future goals. In addition, "the pill" has made it possible for members of all social classes to control their fertility.

Komarovsky's (1962) study of marriage patterns among lower-class husbands and wives pointed to the limits that a low educational level imposes on intimacy, companionship, and communication. Those husbands who had not completed high school felt especially reluctant about sharing their feelings and seemed conscious of a necessity to preserve their masculine image. The wives felt constrained to find their satisfactions and social contacts outside the marriage, particularly with their own kin. There is evidence that lower-class persons perceive themselves as becoming angry toward their spouses more often than middle-class husbands and wives do (Scanzoni, 1970). Also, for lower-status married couples, communication or speech is more defensive, emotional, and closed, whereas in middle-class couples it tends to be more supportive, tentative, and open (Hawkins, Weisberg, & Ray, 1977).

While these reports characterizing members of different classes on various dimensions are interesting, we must be careful to avoid stereotyped outlooks regarding given social classes. Even social scientists occasionally indulge unwittingly in research studies in order to vindicate their upper-middle-class position (Lerner, 1971). Studies of mobility suggest that class lines are becoming blurred, as noted below, and others have found that such associations as equating delinquency with the lower class can no longer be supported (Tittle & Villemez, 1977).

Sometimes the similarities in values among members of different classes are more striking than the differences, especially in newer communities. In one survey no class differences were found in answer to the question: "If someone made you a gift of $10,000 tomorrow, what would you do with it?" The same held true for descriptions of greatest worries, favorite radio and TV programs, newspaper and magazine preferences, hobbies, and extension courses (Sargent, 1953, 1957).

On the whole, however, class differences do emerge. There is no evidence to dispute Barber's (1961) summary of various surveys: lower-class people participate in fewer community activities and voluntary associations (PTA, civic affairs, lodges, etc.). They are less verbal, that is, they read less and are exposed to "less serious" television material. They are less informed politically and more hesitant to express their opinions to interviewers; they often give "don't know" answers. Their mobility aspirations are lower, and they are less future oriented.

Child-Rearing Practices in Social Classes

Many researchers have examined the effects of social class on child-rearing practices. For example, A. Davis (1943), using data from samples of both whites and blacks, showed how behavior is defined according to class standards—modified, of course, by the interpretation given by the child's own family.

In studies carried out before World War II, middle-class parents were found to be more insistent on children reaching early maturity, as in toilet training, whereas lower-class parents were more relaxed in their approach to these skills and more permissive about the child's behavior in general. But in the postwar years the evidence on patterns of child rearing as determined by class lines underwent considerable change. For one thing, postwar prosperity hastened the blurring of class lines noted above.

In a study of postwar Detroit families, for example, a more relaxed atmosphere was shown to prevail in the urban middle-class home (Miller & Swanson, 1958). Other results indicate the family situation was characterized by indulgence, permissive enjoyment, and fun orientation, in contrast to the more compulsive, conformity-conscious child-rearing patterns of the 1930s and early 1940s (Davis & Havighurst, 1946). Kohn (1963) found there was more of a tendency to differentiate between the conduct of boys and girls in the working class than in the middle class, and parents in the working class were more inclined to judge the immediate consequences of a child's act, whereas those in the middle class stressed the long-range effects. A more recent interpretation of the Kohn data (Wright & Wright, 1976) confirms the emphasis in the middle class on deferred gratification—the tendency to subordinate present desires to future goals. However, the difference found between the two classes was often fairly subtle. Primarily it appeared to be one of educational level. More highly educated persons were found to stress self-direction, to participate more in community affairs, and to marry later, all of which may bring greater maturity to the task of child rearing.

On the whole, studies have shown that the middle class tends to emphasize the motivation underlying the behavior, whereas the working class is more concerned with the behavior itself. It has been assumed that parents in the lower class are more apt to use physical punishment, but Erlanger (1974), in summarizing several surveys, found the relation of physical punishment to social class to be ambiguous. The problem of time and place, definition, choice of samples, and other methodological questions leaves open questions of the effects of class on behaviors like spanking.

Still, the two classes presumably have different styles in parent-child relations. In a cross-national study of groups in Washington, D.C., and Turin, Italy, Kohn (1969) found that class is a more fundamental influence on child-rearing patterns than ethnicity, religion, or region and more important than all of these combined. Middle-class mothers appeared to be more supportive of their children and to place more emphasis on psychological satisfaction: happiness, consideration, self-control, and curiosity. Working-class mothers were more demanding of conformity, that is, obedience and neatness. The extension of Kohn's general thesis by Wright and Wright (1976) again supported the data. However, other factors (for example, region and size of city) also favored the socialization of self-direction. Certain bases of social class, like the parents' educational level, were more important than the class variable itself.

Certainly any analysis of the effects of class must consider the complexity of factors that enter into interpersonal situations, and the consciousness of class in parents and children is relevant. A child totally surrounded by a working-class culture will not have the same relations with parents as a child who lives in a neighborhood or school setting which includes both working-class and middle-class families (M. Rosenberg, 1979).

The Emergence of Class Awareness

While it might be presumed that children become conscious of the class differences between their own family and others, in fact they are often isolated from direct contact with members of other classes because of the selective effects of the neighborhood or even the school. High school students in "Elmtown," a community studied by Hollingshead (1949), selected companions or dates within their own social class or the immediately adjacent one, even though five classes were represented in the school.

On the whole, relatively little attention has been given to the process by which children accept the notion in society of differential reward according to social class and how this affects their motivation. A study of Baltimore children in grades 3 to 12, (Simmons & Rosenberg, 1971), however, found that class consciousness appears by the early school years. For instance, 59 percent of the elementary school children did not know what a Supreme Court justice is, yet those who did know placed the justice along with a doctor in the highest occupational level. Similarly, they placed at the bottom the truck driver, the garbage collector, and the shoe shiner—the three lowest occupations in a well-known scale of socioeconomic status. Upper-class children seemed to learn the realities of the pecking order more rapidly, but the lower-class adolescents placed themselves higher than their parents did. Class consciousness also seemed to arrive sooner for the advantaged than for the disadvantaged, perhaps a reflection of the desire to perceive what for them is a favorable universe.

On the whole, adolescents shield themselves somewhat from the reality of social class, though their attitudes may change when they encounter job barriers on the threshold of adulthood. Typical American adults seem to reject or minimize the notion of class and class distinctions, although they are aware of the power of the elite and the wealthy in society (Baltzell, 1964).

SOCIAL MOBILITY AND STATUS CONSISTENCY

Most people retain their original class positions for their entire lifetimes, but in the modern industrial order many changes in status occur with relative ease. Mobility can be *horizontal* or *vertical*. We move horizontally when we change location within a class, if, for example, we change our geographical location, attach ourselves to another similar kin group, or move from one office to another. We can change our status vertically by such actions as receiving a job promotion or demotion, leaving one church for another, or marrying into a different class of family. Mobility can also be *upward* or *downward*. Education and occupation, the two bases of social stratification discussed in the first section of this chapter, are the major channels of upward mobility. Downward mobility occurs because of personal factors such as an obsolescent work skill, a faulty marriage, a health reversal, a destructive habit, or a personality defect, and because of such environmental factors as an economic depression, massive changes in technology, or a decline in the profitability of particular industries.

In *intergenerational* mobility, there is a difference in the status positions of parents and children. This has been measured for a number of countries. Upward exceeded downward mobility in only about a third of the advanced nations studied by S. M. Miller (1960). Hauser et al. (1975) found an increase in intergenerational upward mobility between 1952 and 1972; that is, sons were rising above fathers in occupational status.

A path diagram by which mobility was analyzed for an American sample is shown in Figure 3–2. The thickness of the arrows reflects the relative strength of correlation between the relevant variables. The path of the father's education to the son's occupation is an indirect one; the correlation between the father's and son's occupations is direct, but weak. The strength of the correlation between the son's education and his first occupation is nearly twice as high as any other single factor (Blau & Duncan, 1967).

A later study (J. Kelley, 1973) confirmed this model. It found that favorable family background helps children secure a satisfactory education and occupation, but a number of factors determines the probability that they will follow their fathers' occupations. Once launched on a career, their current occupations are the best index to future status and income.

Social psychologists are concerned about the effects of mobility, both upward and downward, on ideology. Summarizing the not altogether consistent findings regarding class mobility and political attitudes, Lopreato and Hazelrigg

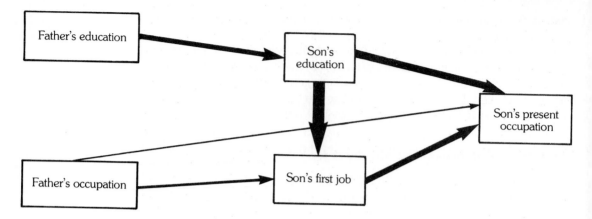

Figure 3–2. Model of Intergenerational Mobility

Source: P. M. Blau and O. D. Duncan, *The American Occupational Structure* (New York: John Wiley & Sons, 1967), p. 17.

(1972) concluded that people are more influenced by upper-status than by lower-status persons and groups. Both the upwardly and downwardly mobile tend to assume the usual conservative political consciousness of the upper and middle classes. The political ideology of the middle class becomes less attractive because of the relative unacceptability of newcomers to old-timers in the middle class, as well as the inability of "skidders"—those with inconsistent status due to a decline in status—to retain their previously high status. Consequently, the more easily the upwardly mobile are accepted by the middle class, the greater the tendency to take on the attitudes of the new social class. Also, to the degree that skidders perceive a possibility of readmittance to their class, they are more likely to assume the attitudes of their class of origin.

Effects of Status Inconsistency

Every family or individual enjoys some kind of status position within the community. Any index of these positions is a simplification of a complex set of variables, however, and it may reveal abstract rather than real status (T. E. Lasswell, 1965). Inevitably there are inconsistencies, particularly in a heterogeneous and rapidly changing social order. Since World War II, for example, there has been a growth in income of the working class and a relative impoverishment of the middle class. The findings of a recent study point to the arbitrariness of class lines and proletarization of the lower white-collar class (Vanneman, 1977).

Among the more obvious instances of status inconsistency are the real estate tycoon or the dealer in scrap metal who becomes a millionaire, the movie actor who amasses fame and fortune but whose lifestyle is not acceptable to the local aristocracy, or the gossip columnist who moves in high circles without the requisite class background. People aspiring to upper status try to arrange their affairs to meet the norms of the new class, as Joseph Kennedy did when he transferred his liquor interests to more acceptable securities in order to maintain a consistent elite position and an appropriate launching pad for his sons' entry into political office.

Status inconsistency can elicit personality strain. In a sample of 2,460 Americans (E. Jackson, 1962), those with evidence of status inconsistency had a higher incidence of physical symptoms (dizziness, upset stomach, weight loss, nervousness, heart palpitations). Especially acute rates were reported for (1) persons with ethnic rank above their occupational or educational rank as, for instance, whites holding lower-status positions, (2) males with occupational rank above their educational rank, and (3) females with an educational rank above their husband's occupational rank.

Another factor which can lead to stress is the perception of being in a "mobility trap." Hornung (1977), for example, found that "clerical workers who have attained the expected level of education and earn the expected income for their occupation are likely to lack the financial resources and security to enter the ranks of the self-employed." They also do not have the educational attainment expected of professionals.

Until recently, status inconsistency marked any member of a minority group who reached a position of wealth or power. Since the civil rights movement of the 1960s, blacks, for example, have been accepted as bank presidents, orchestra conductors, and personnel managers. Previously, a minority member who aspired to such positions would face problems of self-identity as well as hostility from others. A black colonel might receive only perfunctory support from a white lieutenant, or a Hispanic high school principal would find Anglo parents uncooperative. Today women in executive positions often have similar problems of self-identity and must cope with discrimination from the men at the top of the hierarchy in almost all organizations.

Status inconsistency can be expected to affect a person's attitudes and values (see Chapters 8 and 9). Surveys in greater Detroit (Lenski, 1966) found that people with discrepant statuses, especially those whose ethnic status was inconsistent with their occupational status, expressed liberal attitudes on political issues. Another study (E. W. Goffman, 1957) found that those who are inconsistent in occupation, education, and income are more accepting of changes in the power distribution in American society than those with relatively consistent statuses. These data have been corroborated in recent years by the tendency of well-educated ethnic minority members to play a significant role in reform movements. The offspring of the wealthy also have supported radical causes, their dress and mode of life being further evidence of inconsistent status. More often, however, a person at the bottom of the pecking order is reluctant to buck the system or prefers to rationalize the status quo (Wiley, 1967). The tendency for skidders to turn to an ultraconservative ideology was noted above. Thus it may be that the rapidity of change and the status inconsistencies engendered by a mobile society have been a factor in discouraging a more radical American political society comparable to those in several other countries.

THE FAMILY AND SOCIALIZATION

It would be impossible to consider the psychological unfolding of individuals, especially their perceptions and aspirations, without understanding the agencies that shape them. The identifications a child makes within the home are critical determinants of how the personality emerges as the socialization process unfolds, first in the family and later in the school and peer group. It is through these subcultures and groupings that personal values and beliefs are fashioned. Although socialization never really ends, the childhood and adolescent years are the most crucial ones. This development is critical in the social behavior of the individual, helping to determine attitudes and values, attraction or repulsion, to the group and receptivity to social change.

Specialists in many fields—psychologists, psychiatrists, sociologists, anthropologists, and social workers—agree that children's earliest family experiences are the most important formative social influences in their personality development. The family first of all provides security or emotional stability, and directly related to this are self-esteem and ego development, both of which are close to the core of personality (see Chapter 4). Specialists do not agree so well on the specific traits—attitudes, values, and habits—that are most affected by the family or the aspects of home and family that are most significant, as we will demonstrate. Children's behavior is primarily shaped by the interaction with their parents and successively greater involvement with peer groups. Their social world becomes meaningful at ever-more sophisticated levels as they pick up the cues from those about them.

The Social Setting of Childhood

From the standpoint of society, childhood is a process of socialization. In fact, childhood is the period during which the culture becomes part of a person's consciousness and habit systems. An extensive statistical study of a Kansas town called "Midwest" by Barker and Wright (1954) examined some of the mechanisms by which this process takes place. One fourth of all observed social behaviors were performed by children, and their *territorial range* included 60 percent of the town's *behavior settings,* gradually increasing to 79 percent in adolescence. The behavioral context of the children's lives was primarily sociability, play, eating and drinking, religion, and art. In adolescence and adulthood sociability, work, play, and government dominated. (The significance of territorial range and behavior settings to the ecology is considered in Chapter 19.)

Barker and Wright analyzed the ratio of time that children and adults taking part in the study devoted to given behavior patterns. They estimated that 60 to 80 percent of the behavior episodes of the Midwest children concerned active relationships with mothers, fathers, teachers, neighbors, peers, pets, and certain other behavioral objects. The reactions to these social stimuli could be analyzed into given relationships such as dominance, in which a child might seek to exert social pressure over others by either motor responses (beckoning, pushing, holding) or verbal responses (commands such as "sit down," "come here"). In aggression, children might strike, kick, or use language belittling or censuring other persons; in resistance, they might hold out against certain social pressures; in submission, they might give in or attempt to eliminate stress between themselves and other persons; in nurturance, they might want to give aid to others. Thus children learn to react in given directions.

In the same way culture determines the modal personality within a society or nation, as explained in Chapter 2. Children's behavior depends on the cultural context or social learning they experience, within the limitations of their own personality development as determined by the organism itself and by the set of experiences they acquire. (The emergence of the personality through application of the organizing principle of the self to the ego is described in Chapter 4.) The reaction of a child to the behavior of a sibling, for example, would depend on current social norms, the conduct observed in others, the child's personality (depending upon both heredity and environment), and the particular situation.

Figure 3–3 illustrates the myriad factors that operate in the child's personality development. The family subculture is a product of all the various subcultures to which the participants belong. The parents have their separate backgrounds of experience, colored by class, ethnic, religious, or school subcultures. Through trial and error they establish an emotional climate, discipline regime, and methods of decision making in the home. Children have their own physical and mental capacities, as well as varied experiences since birth. From these diverse influences the child's personality emerges.

In analyzing the influence of the home on personality development, the enormous changes that have been taking place in the family subculture must be taken into account. According to a U.S. Census Bureau report in the March 1978

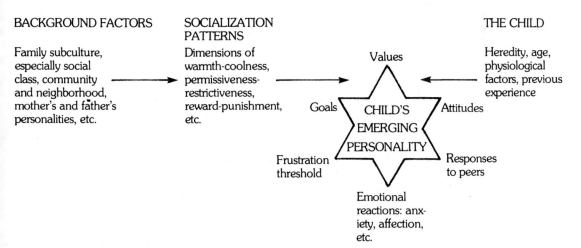

Figure 3–3. Personality Formation in the Child

Source: Adapted from J. J. Honigmann, *Personality in Culture* (New York: Harper & Row, Publishers, 1967), p. 290.

Statistical Abstract, only 13 percent of U.S. households consisted of the "ideal nuclear family"—father, mother, and child or children, with the father as breadwinner (see Figure 3–4). The others were households where both parents worked (21 percent), childless couples (30 percent), single parents (8 percent), single persons (21 percent), cohabiting couples (1.5 percent), and others (5.5 percent).

The average family shrank in size from 4.9 members in 1890 to 3.3 in 1979, and the increased employment of wives and mothers, widespread availability of birth control, and the cost of raising children in inflationary times all point to the continuance of small families. Industrialization and urbanization also have caused the family to shift from being a unit for economic production in a rural agricultural order to adopting a structure based on psychological or affectional bonds.

As a result of these developments, a more intensive interaction among family members might be expected. But parents and children alike have basic obligations outside the family. Nearly half of all wives are employed outside the home, and youth is involved in an almost endless pursuit of educational goals, peer group acceptance, and recreation.

Despite the changes brought on by industrialization, urbanization, secularism, and mobility, the family remains the primary institution for socialization of the child. The term *socialization,* as defined in Chapter 2, refers to the acquisition by the individual of the norms and behaviors expected of a member of the society. By this process, the child acquires basic personality traits and becomes a functioning member of society. As with other changes in the family, socialization itself is in a state of transition. Children no longer have the completely subordinate role they once had. Where there is only one sibling, or perhaps none, children are relatively more self-aware, though it is less likely they will have the opportunity to identify with other children. Moreover, public awareness of the rights of women and ethnic minorities is gradually being extended to children. In a scale administered to a high school and adult sample it was found that younger people and women more than men were sensitive to the rights of children to self-determination (Rogers & Wrightsman, 1978). Studies of attitudes toward children's rights among the aged, whose rights also are being recognized (see Chapter 19), would produce interesting results. The family's continued strong influence on the child's personality is all the more important in view of the continuing attacks on the contemporary family. Among the most recent bombasts is Christopher Lasch's *Haven in a Heartless World: The Family Besieged* (1977). His criticisms, such as the transfer of basic family functions to outside agencies, are of some validity; but the family nevertheless retains the critical role in socialization. There are no hard data to suggest that its inadequacy is greater today than in the past.

The Parental Relationship: Identification

In the interaction between parent and child, the child's awareness of the self emerges. Various roles also are acquired, notably as regards sex and age norms. Even without being explicitly taught, infants and young children acquire response tendencies which later become personality traits. These response patterns are

Figure 3–4.   Composition of U.S. Households

Source of data: U.S. Census Bureau, *Statistical Abstract,* March 1978.

fashioned by the process of *identification.* In identifying with their parents, children respond to cues from both the parents' own behaviors and from the parents' expectations of and reactions to the children's behaviors, and these cues guide the children's earliest *modeling,* or imitative behaviors based on identification (see Chapter 5). The reactions the parents have to each other, or the role patterns of mother and father in the basic family structure, help shape the children's emotional health (see Box 3–2). Children also become acutely sensitive to the way their parents respond to them.

Box 3–2
IS FATHER'S PLACE IN THE HOME?

Participation of the father in family tasks can be said to be beneficial for children and adolescents, but the father must maintain his role as an authoritarian and cannot be as active in household management as the mother. This was a finding in a 1969 study by W. A. Westley and N. B. Epstein which classified a sample of 96 students in a Canadian university according to basic family structure.* The classification included four basic types:

1. *Balanced*—the father assumes responsibility for a significant portion of the tasks within the home. In these families the father took over the traditional male tasks, while the mother was in charge of most household chores.
2. *Sharing*—the father enters into tasks, but in no predictable fashion. These families were characterized by role confusion or a lack of role differentiation. The father might share responsibility for the wife's usual task, such as making beds and cooking meals.
3. *Traditional*—the father participates in relatively few tasks. For these families the pattern was strict role segregation.
4. *Unconventional*—the father is equally active or more active than the mother in household management. These were cases of role reversal.

Interviews and projective tests like the TAT and Rorschach were used to identify students with satisfactory emotional health. The percentage in this category dropped off perceptibly between the balanced and the unconventional types of family. Significantly, the adjustment of the married couples declined in the same direction. Besides a balanced division of labor, other positive factors were the father being of higher socioeconomic status than the mother, and a father-led system of authority within the home.

_____

*W. A. Westley and N. B. Epstein, *The Silent Majority* (San Francisco: Jossey-Bass, Publishers, 1969), pp. 129, 166.

The socialization process unfolds through such feelings as the ten-year-old son's pride when his father wins at baseball, or the daughter's enhanced status when she puts on her mother's jewelry. Identification takes place in a broad range of feelings, perceptions, and attitudes. The learning and motivation which underlie these will be described in Part II.

In the process of socialization, the child's motives and emotions become more specific during interaction with the parent. The generalized aggressive response the child makes to frustration, for example, becomes structured. Psychologists view aggression from different perspectives (see Chapter 7), but some, like Walters (1966), see it basically as an undifferentiated response to stress. Others, like Berkowitz (1969a), consider aggression as having an indirectly innate basis but as being triggered by frustrating situations (see Chapter 7). Bandura, Ross, and Ross (1961, 1963) conducted experiments to show that children learn aggression by observing aggressive models and the reinforcement the models may receive for their acts (see Chapter 5). Probably most would agree that a specific situation eliciting aggression is influenced by the interaction of parent and child.

Most research on aggression with both children and adults has been carried out in the laboratory, but the findings appear to be corroborated by parental reports of what occurs in the home setting. If aggression is punished by the parent, fear and anxiety become attached to hostile responses, and the child begins to inhibit this type of behavior. For instance, R. R. Sears (1953) reported the pattern of aggression in three groups of nursery school children. One group of children who had nonpunitive mothers showed a low level of aggression, possibly because they were relatively unfrustrated at home. The second group, with relatively punitive mothers, tended to be the most aggressive. Children in the third group, who had the most punitive mothers, were the least aggressive, presumably because they had learned to inhibit a number of basic reactions, including hostility. In this context aggression is in part a response to a universal born need, but its level is affected by the learning experiences of the individual (Zigler & Child, 1973).

Though the learning mechanisms are very complex and the underlying theory is not settled, most psychologists agree that the child's reaction tendencies are at least indirectly influenced by the parental disciplinary regime. Competition, which is related to aggression, is encouraged or discouraged by parental expectations in regard to sex roles (see Box 3–3 and Chapter 14). Similarly, cooperativeness, achievement, dependency, and negativism become part of the response repertory the child adopts as a reaction to signs of approval and disapproval by the parents and later by a host of influences outside the home.

Effects of the Emotional Climate of the Home

A lively controversy has focused on the quality of the parental disciplinary regime, involving the relative merits of permissiveness and expression of affection versus firmness and strict discipline.

After World War II there was a swing from the scheduled conditioning of the behaviorists (see Chapter 1) to less regimented and more permissive methods, as popularized in Dr. Benjamin Spock's popular *Pocket Book of Baby and Child*

Family ties are often strained or even absent in the urban environment. This contributes to the personal and social disorganization of the city. *Source:* K. Scott
Danoff.

Box 3-3
PARENTAL EXPECTATIONS AND SEX TYPING

The child's acquisition of a sex identity is guided by the models observed in mothers and fathers and the cues received from their reactions to the child's behavior. If the parents have traditional sex-role expectations, a male child is strongly encouraged to show aggressive behavior and a female child is socialized to take a passive role. In later childhood, rewards and punishments may be stringently applied to ensure these goals, although a son who shows signs of being a "sissy" is likely to be subjected to more censure than a daughter who is accused of being a "tomboy"—two terms which are seldom used by parents with less rigid expectations.

Through play situations and interviews with parents, R. R. Sears and colleagues studied the process of identification in sex typing.* They reached the following conclusions:

1. Children of both sexes first identify with the mother, adopting feminine-maternal modes of behavior. The mother may use direct teaching or modeling.
2. By the end of the first three or four years, the boy works out a "cognitive map" of the male role as he interacts with the father. It is not certain how critical the father's responsiveness to the son's dependency is for the development of masculinity.
3. Masculinity and femininity appear to be influenced more by the parents' attitude toward verbal and physical aggression than by any other kind of interaction. Masculinity is correlated with freer expression and parental nonpunitiveness, whereas femininity is associated with parental restrictiveness.

All parents do not agree on specific norms which guide their expectations as regards sex roles for their children or how they are to achieve these goals. Identification is both conscious and unconscious, involving motives that go well beyond sex norms. Today's parents are probably less anxiety-ridden about sex typing, since attitudes toward sex roles have become more flexible, but contemporary research offers no corroboration. In any event, sex identity is only one of several parental concerns in the socialization of children.

---

*R. R. Sears, L. Rau, and R. Alpert, *Identification and Child Rearing* (Stanford, Calif.: Stanford University Press, 1965), pp. 261–269.

Care. The child-rearing best-sellers of Haim Ginott also gave parents direction in combining discipline with an understanding of the child's developing self-esteem.

In determining the emotional climate of the home, parents adopt a pattern based on their preferences in several dichotomies: restrictiveness-permissiveness, warmth-hostility, authoritarianism-indulgence (Becker, 1964). Their feelings and motives and the family circumstances will determine this pattern. As one instance, overprotection can be the unconscious reaction when a child arrives late in the parents' lives. If the child was initially unwanted, the parents may lean further in the direction of overprotection and indulgence to compensate for guilt feelings they may experience.

Parents have to console themselves that they are going to make mistakes in their child-rearing practices. The child can accommodate to either a democratic or an essentially autocratic environment. The emotional climate is probably more important than the degree of control or the style of decision making. The extensive research of Robert Sears and his colleagues on child-rearing practices underscores the importance of warmth on the part of parents. Coldness and lack of affection were found to lead to feeding problems, enuresis (bed-wetting), and aggressiveness. They also found that permissiveness, if continued, could encourage aggressiveness and other undesired traits, but punishment is ineffectual as a long-term technique (Sears, Maccoby, & Levin, 1957).

Several investigations have been made into the family settings in which rejection and other unfavorable parental reactions occur, as recorded in a number of family texts (Reiss, 1980; Williamson, 1972). Studies of marital adjustment have indicated that, contrary to expectations, merely having children does not contribute to marital happiness, although the parents' desire for children may be a positive factor. Unconscious, if not conscious, rejection of the child may grow out of the frustrations associated with child rearing. Research into the backgrounds of delinquents reports a pattern of disturbed and inconsistent parent-child relations, as compared with control groups of youngsters (Rodman & Grams, 1967).

The most important factor in the emotional climate is the predictability of the parental regime, whether directive or permissive. A totally uneven climate in which the child has no means of knowing what to expect seems to be catastrophic. A constantly shifting discipline or a grossly uneven emotional milieu, in which the parents move back and forth between indulgence and punitiveness, warmth and hostility, is wearing to the child. This ambivalence produces confusion, insecurity, and anxiety.

That the emotional climate within the family is relevant to later personality development should be no surprise. The quality of marriage, success on the job, vulnerability to alcohol or drugs, general level of life satisfaction—all are to some extent rooted in the interaction between parents and child during the early years of life. But the relationship or predictability of the early home environment to the person's later beliefs and attitudes, types of group affiliation, and participation in social movements, for example, is less clear. The question of how personality and socialization affect these and other behaviors will be a recurrent theme in this book.

THE SCHOOL AS A "SUBCULTURE"

Every society relies on its educational institutions, whether formal or informal, to supplement the family in socializing the young. The school provides academic training as well as appropriate cultural values and vocational skills. Moreover, the educational institution serves as a status-shifting (or in many instances a status-perpetuating) device. Economic elites have access to the advantageous schools, and the schools shape their lifestyles from childhood to adulthood. No less important are the latent functions of the school, such as preventing juvenile delinquency, protecting the labor force from competition, or serving as a mate selection agency. The effects of the school on personality, through the continual interaction of students with administrators, teachers, and especially with their peers, are far-reaching.

Cultural Systems in the School Setting

The school is a major means of indoctrinating the child into the existing culture. In most communities, school personnel (especially teachers) must honor the commitment of the school board, which officially represents the public, to traditional values (Scimecca, 1980). Furthermore, the educational plant is highly systematized, and those who do not conform are punished, if only through not being rewarded. The particular kind of conformity may vary with the culture, however. Studies comparing Soviet and American systems depict the American approach to conformity as linked to individual competition, whereas "group competition and collective responsibility" are emphasized in the Soviet Union (R. M. Williams, 1970).

P. W. Jackson (1968) sees the control environment as dominated by three key concepts: crowds, praise, and power. The first is due to the press of numbers; the child must learn to live in a *crowd*. In interacting with some 30 children the teacher may engage in as many as a thousand interpersonal exchanges in a day. The teacher acts as a controller of classroom communication, as supply dispatcher in determining the use of space and material, and as timekeeper. One essential thing children learn in school is how to wait—and to tolerate being denied or frustrated—as the teacher controls the dialogue. Pupils are constantly distracted because the messages are limited, and, when rigid time schedules are followed, one activity may begin even if another has not ended. They may be called from reading, leaving some questions unanswered, to go on to arithmetic, for example. In the pressure of numbers and schedules, Jackson observes, they often are required to "behave as if they were in solitude, when in point of fact they are not."

The second concept, *praise* or its absence, means that the child is introduced to a more structured evaluation by teacher, peers, and self than is usual in the home. The range of this testing and scrutiny varies widely in classrooms, from scorn and ridicule to covert and overt forms of praise. Until recently, the children (and sometimes even their parents) were often uninformed of the total evaluation, as with confidential IQ test results or evaluations discussed by teachers and administrators among themselves.

Power relationships in the school setting mean the child must learn to take orders from a more distant authority than his or her parents. Democratization of the school environment began with the reforms of John Dewey early in this century, but even though children today may find a more cooperative school environment than their grandparents knew, they are soon made aware of the need to subordinate themselves to authority within the school. In certain school districts and at different times the existing balance between permissiveness and regimentation have been found to change, however.

Educational Inequality and the Culturally Disadvantaged

The disadvantage of ethnic minorities in a society begins with the inadequate attention the child receives in an impoverished home and continues with the restricted resources in an underdeveloped school. This inequality is manifested in several ways: Society's resources are unequally distributed; some persons have more opportunity than others to attend school with the kinds of peers they or their parents prefer; and some students are not offered the curriculum of their choice (Jencks, 1972). As members of the upper and middle classes have deserted the inner city, the result has been a growing gap between the accomplishments of inner-city students and those in suburban schools, where often twice the funds per capita are spent on the school system. Even within a given school preferential treatment in terms of curriculum and activities often is provided for students who receive higher scores on intelligence and other standardized tests, which have proven to be of questionable validity when applied to minorities. New tests are being devised which relate less to the child's cultural background, but they are not yet in general use in the schools. *Tracking,* or segregation of students in the classroom according to ability, is an accepted method of attempting to individualize instruction in the elementary school and receives added momentum in the secondary program, by which time many of the disadvantaged have dropped out. Data indicate that the tracking system results in an accelerated learning loss to the minority school population.

This situation is largely attributable to the traditionally middle-class domination of both inner and outer-city school systems. Although many teachers in lower-class schools come from minorities or blue-collar families, they reflect a comparatively middle-class outlook (Lightfoot, 1972). Federal requirements to integrate faculties in inner-city schools are limited by a lack of nonminority teachers in these districts. And despite efforts to include minority representatives on urban school boards, as in the Chicago Board of Education appointed in 1980 to replace an ineffective, predominantly upper-class white group, the minority members considered qualified to serve also represent the socioeconomic status quo.

Beyond the question of faculty or curriculum is the kind of interpersonal relations children find within the school. Among other problems is the impact of the fatherless home which has come to predominate in the black lower-class subculture, largely as a result of limited employment opportunities for poorly educated black males and welfare requirements that no able-bodied adult males be present in families receiving benefits. The lack of an adult male model has serious implications for personality formation. Boys deprived of their fathers have been found to be immature, submissive, insecure, and effeminate as compared to other boys. This frustration leads to compulsive and exaggerated masculinity. The socialization pattern in the mother-dominated home also suffers from a lack of positive incentive; the child is told not to do this or that, to stay out of trouble, and not to ask questions. The school often is also quite matriarchal in orientation, and it continues this inhibitory climate. Little wonder that poor achievement scores result, even among children with very high IQs.

Bronfenbrenner (1967) suggested that more male teachers, especially blacks, should be brought into the classroom, and out-of-school contacts with male adults and adolescents of more than one race should be expanded. In the United States, the Head Start program, initiated in the 1960s as part of Lyndon Johnson's War on Poverty, focused on broadening both verbal and nonverbal experiences early in the child's life. These interactions provide reinforcement for self-identity and self-confidence, as well as a basis for beginning the acquisition of academic skills. Unfortunately, because of financial and other limitations, the project has never been able to realize its potential.

According to most observers, a dual educational system is costly for both the majority and the minority. In a sample of 2,300 students in 14 Pennsylvania high schools, blacks and whites had similar career aims, particularly when matched by social class (Williamson, 1977b.) Irrespective of class, the students perceived their parents as having almost the same aspirations for them as they did themselves.

The first step in replacing this dual system, and one that is far from completion, is integration within school systems to prevent overt differentiation in the learning environment. An influential report titled *Equality of Educational Opportunity* by J. S. Coleman et al. (1966) found a positive correlation between the black-white student ratio in a U.S. school and the performance of blacks and other minorities on standard tests. Subsequent research has substantiated this finding. In a study of 1,600 adult blacks in northern American urban areas, the probability of high school graduation and attendance at college was found to be higher for those who had attended integrated schools (Crain, 1971). The association of black students with white students was also found to contribute to higher self-esteem for blacks and a greater desire for achievement (Persell, 1977). This holds true for any minority in association with an achievement-oriented majority. Aside from scholastic attainments, integration expands the possibility of interaction within and outside the school. Beyond the school, the community resources—recreational or religious, governmental or private—must be involved in the long-term socialization of disadvantaged children and adolescents.

In a comparison study conducted in Columbus, Ohio, teachers in both inner-city and outer-city schools were inclined to fall back on rationalizations about the slow progress of their students (Corwin & Schmidt, 1972). Most important of these was a self-fulfilling prophecy—the expected poor ability or motivation of the child was the explanation for the lack of progress. Teachers in the inner-city schools were more likely to explain the deficiency as a product of the environment, however, whereas outer-city teachers placed the problem more within the child. Not surprisingly, neither perceived the fault as being a result of the kind of education taking place in the classroom. The black teachers generally were more hopeful of eventual success for minority students.

The solution to the problem of achieving school integration that has been tried most often is voluntary or involuntary busing of students. By the early 1970s student busing—that is, busing of black students to schools in white or racially mixed districts and, to some extent, vice versa—was being carried out by federal court order in numerous communities. Impetus for this practice came from the Supreme Court's call for "all deliberate speed" to achieve integration in the classroom in the 1954 *Brown* v. *Board of Education* decision. In most communities it seemed to work reasonably well; Charlotte, North Carolina, and San Diego, California, for example, reported no difficulties. But trouble developed in several cities, notably Louisville, Detroit, and Boston, which in the fall of 1975 was practically in a state of siege. In 1980 the practice was extended to entire metropolitan areas, including suburbs, because white families were leaving the cities in such numbers there were not enough nonminority students left in city schools to allow any degree of integration.

In the 1980–81 school year, Los Angeles, the nation's second largest school district in number of pupils (550,000 students), was busing 23,000 elementary and junior high students on trips which sometimes lasted more than an hour in the sprawling, 600-square-mile district. Mandatory busing was officially ended there in March 1981 when the state supreme court upheld the constitutionality of Proposition 1, a voter-approved initiative to forbid it unless it could be shown that past discrimination had been deliberate. The only member of the school board to oppose ending the program, Rita Walters, said the action "constitutes a gross denial of equal educational opportunity to minority students now participating in the plan," according to Associated Press reports. A suit to keep mandatory busing alive brought by the National Association for the Advancement of Colored People was denied by U.S. Supreme Court Justice William Rehnquist.

Evidence of "white flight" eventually led James Coleman, principal author of the Coleman et al. 1966 report which had found that black students tend to learn more in integrated classrooms, to conclude that busing could not work as a means to achieve integration because it was driving whites out of the city public schools (Coleman, Kelley, & Moore, 1975). In the 125 largest cities he analyzed, there was a continuous loss of white students from the schools between 1968 and 1973, and the loss was greater in the larger cities, in school systems with a higher proportion of black students, and where racial disparity was great between the city and its suburbs. Coleman then proposed a kind of partial desegregation by which all schools would be required to accept up to 15 percent of their student body from outside their own school districts. With this limitation, presumably only children who wanted to be bused would be included.

It is difficult to determine the cause-and-effect relation between busing and population changes. In both the North and South, busing has been found to enormously increase transfers to school districts outside the city. In a study of 22 of the largest metropolitan areas in the United States, however, it was found that while the effect of the flight of whites to the suburbs was not to be discounted, other factors such as the aging of the whites in central cities and differences in birth rates were also important (Sly & Pol, 1978). Other critics of Coleman's later findings pointed out that white flight is as much a function of social class as it is of racism, and desegregation is only one of several reasons why whites were moving out of cities (Farley, 1975).

PEER GROUPS

Along with the family and the school, peer groups, or constellations of associates of similar age and interests, account for a large share of the child's social, emotional, and attitudinal development. They are perhaps the most effective determinant of attitudes in children and adolescents, which may or may not correspond with those held by the parents. Peer groups become effective at an early age; according to Havighurst and Neugarten (1975) they help children learn to get along with age-mates, develop sensitivity to cultural values, acquire appropriate social attitudes and roles, and arrive at a level of personal independence. They also encourage social mobility in the society or community. Children's play contacts markedly influence their ability to attain sociability; achieve normality by avoiding behavior that might be labeled eccentric; and acquire attitudes on religion, ethnic relations, economic values, and various social issues.

The Search for Identity

Adolescence constitutes a type of minority group; about a tenth of the population in North America is in the teen years, neither children nor adults. In this transitional period it is difficult for young people to find a self-identity, and they may undergo an *identity crisis* as they try to develop an adequate set of behaviors for their age and sex status (Erikson, 1968). In other societies, a more mature blending process appears to take place during this transitional period from child to adult.

The search for identity is compounded if the adolescent is a member of a racial or religious minority. In addition to frustrations encountered in a deprived home situation and an unrewarding school environment, minority youths must cope with dependence on a peer group which is caught up in the same circumstances and which seethes with all the restlessness of normal teenagers but has few of the normal outlets for their energy. A study of U.S. Job Corps enrollees showed that the urban poor have the same success goals as do middle-class youth, for example, but the means are not usually available (Gottlieb, 1969). The highest incidence of crime and delinquency in society is usually found among young people, and those who feel rejected by their society may see no alternative to using illegitimate means to achieve the goals they seek. Most minority-group adolescents are relatively conventional in their behavior, but even more than the majority adolescents, they suffer from a lack of clear-cut goals. More accurately, society denies them the likelihood of realizing positive goals.

In an intensive study of 23 lower-class boys in New Haven, Connecticut, Hauser (1971) investigated the problem of black and white *identity formation*. The heroes with whom the blacks could identify—Joe Louis, Jackie Robinson, Sidney Poitier—were limited in number and remote from their own experience. Consequently, for these blacks, fantasy was distinct from school and social failures, and they suffered from a "foreclosure" far more than the upwardly mobile whites did. Whereas the whites were consumed with problems of conscience and guilt, the blacks' emotional conflicts centered on rejection and inferiority. This devaluation was reinforced by the black's inability to find even part-time jobs. The end result is *negative identity*—an unfavorable self-image.

The Generation Gap

In most Western cultures considerable attention has been paid to the existence of a *generation gap,* or the rift between the young people and older adults in the population. The occasional excursions of American youths into varied lifestyles—casual dress and long hair, rock music, drugs, and less restrictive sex mores—have reinforced the idea. There is little doubt that a rapidly changing culture has hastened the rate of socialization for young and old alike. In earlier times the older generation often found it difficult to adjust to shifts in values, especially in long-cherished institutions such as church and politics. Today time-honored ways of life are considered passé by many adults, as well as most young people. Changes have occurred in every facet of life and often have drastically changed priorities.

Whether the present gap between adult and adolescent is greater than it was for previous generations is open to debate. A survey study which compared 95 students with their parents and grandparents showed a significant difference between the generations in areas of "conventional morality, personal failure, embarrassment, and social irresponsibility," but the differences varied widely for the particular situation or behavior (Payne, Summers, & Stewart, 1973). A 1972 study of high school students disclosed no serious rift with parents; when asked what their greatest problem was, only 10 percent mentioned home or parents (Williamson, 1977b). Another study revealed that the influence parents had on the political attitudes of adolescents considerably outweighed the effects of peers and teachers (Woelfel, 1978).

Traditionally, adolescents, whose frame of reference is the standards of their peers, protest the values of an older generation. Yet it would be difficult to prove that today's teenagers are any more opposed to their elders than they were in previous periods such as the 1920s or 1950s. Only a minority of youth ever displays deviant lifestyles and radical social protest, and many adults themselves resist the traditional norms of their society. For both generations, conformity to age cohorts takes precedence over innovation or rebellion. That young people accept social changes such as the new sex mores is unquestionably true, but the older generation also has a more liberal position than it did a half-century ago. Young people do give more dramatic evidence of the alternation of revolt and conformity than those who are caught in the slower tempo of the middle years (Lidz, 1969).

Alienation in the Youth Culture

For most of this century, and perhaps as early as the 18th-century romantic movement, there has been discussion as to whether a youth culture (or subculture) exists. The development of a strong student counterculture on American campuses in the 1960s suggests that a fairly definite youth ideology and norm of behavior had come into being (see Box 3–4), and from American campuses, it spread with rapidity around the globe. One difficulty with this generalization is the *diversity* of youth subcultures, which may be centered around motorcyclists, rock devotees, student activists, "Jesus people," Black Panthers, or scuba divers, to name a few. One unifying principle for these divergent groups has been *alienation*. For the college generation, dissent was expressed in two directions: the political activists or protestors; and the withdrawn, culturally alienated students (Keniston, 1967). Activists no longer characterize many campus settings; one study comparing college and noncollege samples found little difference in awareness of political issues, except for students in the social sciences (Rich, 1976). The alienated may still retreat into themselves, into drugs and alcohol, and into unconventional dress, entertainment, and beliefs that are markedly different from those of their parents, but these types of escape are less evident than they were in the 1960s.

Beyond diversity and alienation, the youth culture would have to be characterized by a *lack of commitment*. The rapid change in Western culture, "the loss of a sense of historical relatedness, the loss of traditional community and intact task, and, perhaps most important, the loss of a compelling positive vision of the individual and collective future" are all factors (Keniston, 1960). Moreover, Western society has not yet offered a meaningful adult status to individuals who are ready for it. Some belated acknowledgment came in 1971 in the form of the 26th Amendment to the U.S. Constitution, which gave the right to vote to 18-year-olds. The same thing happened, from province to province, across Canada. But the young person still finds confusion in status and role as to when legal adulthood is attained. Even within the same area or region, authorities do not always agree on when a youth may drive a car, order a drink at a bar, or sign a contract. If there is a youth culture, therefore, society is hardly willing to acknowledge its existence.

The problem of the young may constitute an area of emphasis rather than a distinct culture. An analysis of 2,220 boys in seven Wisconsin high schools (Grinder, 1969) found three dominant areas of concern:

1. *Status seeking*—desire for association with socially approved peers; being part of the in-group; interacting on dates, at parties, and the like in order to improve interpersonal skills.

BOX 3–4
COLLEGE SUBCULTURES

In the midsixties there were four different subcultures within the North American college and university environment, according to one study.* Though the researchers considered these subcultures more as an organizational context than as distinct typings of students, the distinctions were strong enough to persist as categories which still apply to some extent today. The types are:

1. The *collegiate,* oriented to the enjoyment of campus social life as embodied in sports, fraternities and sororities, and campus fun. Although academic and intellectual pursuits are not rejected, these interests are of lower priority. Vocational goals are present, but football, dates, cars, and drinking are more immediate.

2. The *vocational,* found in the large public colleges and universities where most students, often commuters, are of lower-class and lower-middle-class backgrounds. Usually these students come from homes in which neither parent has ever attended college. The main object of the future degree is occupational success, and identification with the institution is minimal. All colleges and universities have a vocational aspect, but the institutions with the highest academic standing have the least vocational interest. Nevertheless, their graduates usually manage to get better jobs and make more money.†

3. The *academic,* which focuses on the search for ideas and in which students are closely identified with faculty. With a strong orientation to postgraduate study and a commitment to making high grades, the academic subculture is most evident in the Ivy League and junior Ivy League institutions, but it is found on nearly every campus.

4. The *nonconformist,* which has presumably always existed among students but became most visible and salient in the 1960s. By the 1980s it appeared to be melding into other groups and had all but disappeared. The alienated, the radicals, and the bohemians are characterized by a deviant ideology, unconventional appearance, and marginal commitment to the institution or the Establishment generally. Conflict between the generations has led to an increasing desire for autonomy throughout university life as a whole. At the University of California in Berkeley, a sample of nonconforming students—or more accurately, nonstudents—showed a need for self-gratification, an experimental attitude toward life situations, strong intellectual interests, aesthetic pursuits, and a marked degree of self-expression, compared to more conventional peers.‡

By 1971 the nonconformist and dissenting subculture was on the wane. The gradual phasing out of the war in Southeast Asia, the achievement of student self-government, and the worsening job situation were all factors in their return to the vocational and collegiate subcultures.

All four subcultures can be found in the same environment, and a student can participate in more than one subculture. Many institutions are oriented toward one or two of these patterns, however. A given subculture may be prevalent for a given era—the collegiate during the 1920s; the vocational during the 1930s and 1940s; a new version of the collegiate—the "silent generation"—during the 1950s, and the nonconformist in the 1960s. Career orientations again became acceptable in the 1970s, and the worsening economic conditions of the late 1970s and early 1980s brought them to the fore. Still, time and place are usually overshadowed by the student's own attitudes and values.

---

*B. R. Clark and M. Troy, "The Organizational Context," in T. M. Newcomb and E. K. Wilson (Eds.), *College Peer Groups* (Chicago: Aldine, 1966).

†M. Milner, Jr., *The Illusion of Equality* (San Francisco: Jossey-Bass, Publishers, 1972), pp. 51–33.

‡D. Whitaker and W. A. Watts, "Personality Characteristics of a Nonconformist Youth Subculture: A Study of the Berkeley Non-Student," *Journal of Social Issues*, 1969, *25*, 65–90.

2. *Independence assertion*—concern with achieving independence from adult authority and traditional social norms, as in breaking school rules or indifference to complaints of adults about raucous behavior in public.
3. *Sex gratification*—interest in making physical contact, as in necking and petting with members of the opposite sex, in addition to reading drugstore literature or perusing pornographic materials.

These characteristics suggest that contemporary adolescents are propelled by the same fundamental motives as adolescents have been for a half-century or more. If youth is alienated, it is because of its traditional opposition to adult norms. More fundamental than alienation is *role confusion,* as the adolescent attempts to organize experiences in this transition to adulthood. The search for identity described above, and educational and career choices which elicit intermittent strain, are primarily individual decisions, however, and do not necessarily constitute a youth culture.

Perhaps a society is always seeking to fashion its youth culture through education, preaching, social agencies, and the like. C. S. Smith (1968), a Britisher, could be describing the United States accurately when he points to "pressures exerted by the entertainment and clothing industries to create a demand for what they wish to sell" to an adolescent market. Advertising and publicity are used to manipulate the perceived needs and wants of 30 million North American adolescents and young adults who have considerable cash in their pockets. In such areas as music, automobiles, dress, and tastes, Western youth culture may well emanate from the advertising agencies and media centers.

SUMMARY)

   Of all the environmental influences on people's personality development, the social class subculture has perhaps had the most far-reaching effects on attitudes and behavior. There can be important differences in the amount and the type of class stratification in different parts of a country and at different times in history, however. A number of questions must be considered about the nature of social class: To what degree is it measurable? Are class differences disappearing? How does the class concept shift from region to region, from nation to nation? And, most fundamentally, to what degree is intergenerational mobility increasing the distance between parents and children?

   Study of the characteristics of social class has become more precise at the same time that changes in class belongingness have made for some degree of confusion. Socioeconomic status changes have made it difficult to mark the boundary between lower and middle class, for example, and the problem of status inconsistency constantly arises as people shift their involvements. The complexity of social and institutional life in the urban environment makes for a less than coherent ideology or lifestyle for many persons. There is also the question of whether zeal in applying measurement techniques to determine social class composition results in "a 'scientism' or a concern with the forms of investigation at the expense of significance" (Grey, 1969). Extensive research on the effects of class differences on personality has revealed some linkages (Lundberg, 1974), but association of personality traits with given social classes remains at best a set of hypotheses.

   The family is the most significant "subculture" in shaping the child's personality and behavior. Relations between parents and between parents and children are particularly important for emotional security in the family, and parents serve as models for the children's early learning of information, habits, skills, and attitudes. The many recent changes in family life have altered our ideas of child rearing, as the style of childhood socialization has swung from the strict disciplinarian attitudes of the turn of the century to the more relaxed outlook of the 1930s, reversing again toward less permissiveness in the 1970s. Currently parents are seeking a middle course between permissiveness or overindulgence on the one hand and rigidity (resulting in either overprotection or rejection) on the other. The 1980s may see a movement toward more parental authority or greater autonomy for children. Individual differences being what they are, however, parents can be expected to vary considerably in how they treat their children. The social climate, whether permissive or disciplinarian in style, has less influence than the general attitude of the parents toward rearing children.

   The impact of the school on the child is generally less far-reaching than that of the family, but it can be crucial at certain stages of development and with certain children. Efforts have been made to lessen the difficulties disadvantaged children face in public schools.

   The peer group is another subculture which has a very powerful socializing influence on the child. It particularly affects the values and attitudes of adolescents at a critical period of their lives. More than many social institutions, college subcultures were influenced by the dislocations of the 1960s. The impact of international tensions, domestic problems, and the state of the economy has brought a sobering return to the vocational subculture model and movement away from nonconformist attitudes.

WORDS TO REMEMBER

Blue collar. General label for the working class. Although this group does not necessarily have a lower income than the lower middle class, it traditionally represents a different lifestyle.

College subculture. Lifestyle taken on by a college or university because of a long-standing tradition, or the goals and values of the students, or a combination of factors in the administration, faculty, student body, and alumni. Examples may be designated as collegiate, vocational, academic, or nonconformist, but most large institutions have more than one style.

Identification. Process of assuming the characteristics of (or becoming involved with) another person, group, or ideology.

Mobility. Process of moving vertically, upward or downward, in the status system; geographic or horizontal mobility within a class, as in change of residence or workplace. *Intergenerational mobility* describes a change in status positions of children as compared to parents.

Parental regime. Quality and direction of emotional relationships within the home, notably those of the parents and their style of child rearing, as, for example, permissive or restrictive, protective or encouraging autonomy.

Peer. Person of equivalent age or status. Peers are a major frame of reference for individuals, particularly during adolescence or youth.

Social class. Strata or levels into which all societies are probably divided. Most often the criteria for class are occupation, education, residence, income, and lifestyle. The classification can be approached objectively or subjectively, statistically or historically.

Socialization. Acquisition by the individual of the appropriate norms and behavior expected by the society or group.

Subculture. A division of the culture, such as social class, ethnicity, religion, region, or other kind of social background (such as income, sex, age), or a special grouping such as the drug subculture.

QUESTIONS FOR DISCUSSION

1. Why is the study of social class important for the social psychologist? Why is it so difficult to define the concept of social class?

2. What are the different approaches to explaining social stratification? What are the objective and subjective criteria of class?

3. What personality correlates have been found for social class? Give some examples from people you know.

4. How do marriage patterns and socialization differ among classes? What changes have taken place over the past few decades?

5. Name specific changes in the lifestyles and consumption habits of the American social classes that have occurred over the past 10 or 20 years.

6. Describe the different kinds of social mobility. How does social mobility relate to ideology?

7. Explain the concept status inconsistency and give some examples.

8. How do status inconsistencies affect values? How has the American family changed since the turn of the century?

9. Describe the factors that shape the personality and behavior of the child in American society. Describe the process whereby children identify with their parents.

10. What is the principal distinction between types of family disciplinary regimes? How do they relate to the development of aggression in children?

11. What is meant by sex roles or typing? What social changes have you observed in this phenomenon during your lifetime?

12. How would you characterize the school as a "subculture?" How did Jackson describe the school environment?

13. What have been some major findings regarding the culturally disadvantaged child?

14. What is meant by the term, *a dual educational system?* What changes would you suggest to improve this situation?

15. Describe the different types of college subcultures identified in Box 3–4. Is this kind of classification valid and useful?

16. What are the problems of identity and alienation in adolescence? Why do they occur?

READINGS)

Beeghley, L. *Social Stratification in America.* Santa Monica, Calif.: Goodyear Publishing Co., 1978.
A searching account of classical and recent theories of the class system, with profiles of the various strata.

Bredemeier, M. E., and Bredemeier, H. C. *Social Forces in Education.* Sherman Oaks, Calif.: Alfred Publishing Co., 1978.
A highly analytic presentation of the socialization process in the school.
Goslin, D. A. (Ed.). *Handbook of Socialization*

Theory and Research. Chicago: Rand McNally & Co., 1969.

  The standard compendium on nearly all phases of the subject, written by psychologists and sociologists.

Kohn, M. L. *Class and Conformity: A Study in Values* (2nd ed.). Chicago: University of Chicago Press, 1977.

  A cross-national research study of child rearing and roles in Washington, D.C., and Turin, Italy.

LeMasters, E. E. *Blue-Collar Aristocrats.* Madison: University of Wisconsin Press, 1975.

  A participant-observation study of the values and attitudes in a working class tavern.

Rose, P. I. (Ed). *Socialization and the Life Cycle.* New York: St. Martin's Press, 1979.

  A selection of articles on socialization from childhood to upper age.

Scimecca, J. A. *Education and Society.* New York: Holt, Rinehart & Winston, 1980.

  Textbook on the options and conflicts facing students, teachers, and the public.

Skolnick, A., and Skolnick, J. (Eds.). *Family in Transition* (2nd ed.). Boston: Little, Brown, 1977.

  Articles deal with a range of questions regarding changing standards in lifestyle, marriage, and parent-child relations.

PERSONALITY
AND THE
SELF

The concepts of personality and self are inextricably linked, although they have received varying emphasis in the study of psychology. Personality has consistently been a legitimate concern, but the concept of the self has had a more checkered history. While it was an important construct in the early days of social psychology, in the behaviorist viewpoint of the 1920s and the 1930s it was relegated to a borderline philosophical status. Since that time, however, and particularly in the second half of the 20th century, problems of self-identity and self-control have come to be regarded as critical avenues of research.

The relationship between personality and behavior is one of the most complex matters for which social psychologists must find explanations. Not only is personality intricately related to social and cultural influences, but there is considerable disagreement as to its exact nature. Some social psychologists believe that personality is an inner cause of behavior, and so, if personality can be measured with some degree of accuracy, behavior is predictable. Others have argued that personality is a set or a constellation of enduring traits, or that personality is nothing more than observable behavior, although often labels are attributed to some observed consistencies in behavior. Those espousing the hereditary viewpoint received support in studies of identical twins reared apart suggesting rather strong genetic effects on personality.

One basic disagreement among social psychologists centers on the differences between the psychoanalytic and behaviorist views of personality. This argument stems from their different conceptions of personality as either a cause or an effect of behavior. There have been many interesting attempts to develop a meaningful theory of personality and to blend these two points of view.

Another area of disagreement is the extent to which personality is situational in origin. It is generally recognized, however, that the structure of the social situation can render personality differences inconsequential. For example, if when a door is opened it reveals an adversary poised in a fighting stance with a fist thrust forward, everyone who approaches the doorway, regardless of their personality differences, would move to protect themselves—they would back off or throw their hands up to their faces, or make some attempt to avoid being harmed. Under such threat conditions, personality differences do not seem to account for very much (Terhune, 1970). In other social circumstances, however, individual differences are easily observable.

Because the relationships found in attempts to relate behavior to personality tend to be consistent but small, many feel that personality is "transituational." However, a specific trait may be related to a person's behavior in a given situation, but when there is change in the social system of which personality is a part, the personality changes also.

Newcomb (1950) took the position that personality involves both "common and unique factors." In this view, individual personalities differ within a society and among societies, depending on the situations, but there is no small degree of similarity among human beings in a large part of the world.

Throughout this text we examine how personality factors influence various forms of social behavior. The reciprocal effects between personality structure and culture and the social environment have been examined in Chapters 2 and 3, and the relationship of personality to social influence (imitation, conformity, and the like) is considered in Chapter 11. The effects of personality are also reflected in the consideration of role expectations and behavior in Chapter 14 and of leadership behavior in Chapter 15. The development of the personality factor in these and other relationships is examined in this chapter, in which the theoretical debates regarding the structure and function of personality and its relation to the self are analyzed.

The chapter starts by examining the nature of personality, the different approaches to studying it, and its various dimensions. Then the emergence of the concepts of self and ego is investigated in a historical context, and the role of the self-concept in personality development is explored further to establish the social interaction view of personality. The alternate view is presented in a section on Freud's use of the concept of ego in psychoanalysis and personality theory. Attempts to integrate these two views are then described in a section which presents the idea that the development of a self-image or self-concept makes for some degree of self-esteem and self-identity in the personality. The conclusions topic in this section draws together the social interaction and psychoanalytic ideas on the self to focus on the social-psychological concepts of ego structure and ego involvement.

THE NATURE OF PERSONALITY

There are many areas of disagreement about the nature of personality, as evidenced by the different approaches to its study. But there are several general concepts about which many, if not most, social psychologists would agree.

First, there is an organizing principle, or *gestalt,* to personality. Personality traits or dimensions interact with one another, and this interaction results in an organized, unique personality complex for each individual.

Second, personality is most easily understood in terms of traits or patterns. A personality is often described in terms of *profiles;* a person might be said to be high on a scale of dominance, low on gregariousness, high on ego strength, and so on. The interrelationships among such personality dimensions are being recognized as critical to an understanding of individual differences among persons with apparently similar profiles.

Third, personality reflects the influence of both biological (inherent) and social (learned) factors. People differ in biological terms; some are short and fat, others tall and thin. They also have different responses and varying degrees of sensitivity to various forms of stimulation. The influence of biological factors is generally believed to be modified by social learning.

Fourth, the principal influence on personality is social learning (see Chapter 5). Personality modification is slow but persistent, and the new habit patterns depend on many learning trials. Such learning is intricate and cumulative. A child learns various simple skills which then serve as the basis for the learning of more complicated skills.

Fifth, personality is very complex. It has many dimensions, and they are highly interactive. Each dimension or trait is likewise composed of many behavioral patterns. A strong ego, for example, reflects language behaviors, social behaviors, and the individual's emotional-motivational system.

Sixth, personality factors interact with environmental factors. Most social psychologists agree that a person behaves differently in different social situations, but there is a consistency to a person's behavior across various situations. There is disagreement, however, as to the exact nature of the personality-social environment relationship.

Conceptually, much of the disagreement about the nature of personality has revolved around the issues of the stability of personality and the extent to which personality is a cause of behavior. The contemporary view, and one which promises to bring together the divergent approaches of psychoanalysis and behaviorism, is that personality is both a cause and effect. Our personalities influence the manner in which we behave in social situations and, depending on the rewards and punishments we receive, they are influenced by the learning which occurs in such situations (Staats, 1971).

Is there such a thing as personality? Some social psychologists maintain that personality *is* behavior. A person learns to act in certain ways. If the situation changes so that certain forms of behavior are extinguished, personality changes. In essence, then, according to this view personality is a label we use to describe repertories of behaviors.

Many who reject the concept of personality do so because of the inherent circularity of personality theory. For example, a person may be said to have an aggressive personality because he or she behaves in an aggressive manner. This suggests that the aggressive behavior can be explained by attaching a label to a set of behaviors. In one sense, personality shapes behavior, and yet personality "is synonymous with the pattern of behavior itself" (Marlowe & Gergen, 1969).

Approaches to the Study of Personality

Personality is conceptualized and measured from different viewpoints. In the *experimental* approach, psychologists are concerned with testing the responses of individuals to various stimuli: How does the presence of other persons affect an individual's reactions? What is the subject's threshold for pleasant or unpleasant stimuli such as flattery, drugs, or noise? The *statistical* approach utilizes personality inventories or paper-and-pencil tests which are usually oriented to traits such as neurotic tendencies, introversion-extroversion, and the like. *Projective* techniques like the Rorschach inkblot tests probe the structure of personality. *Clinical* psychology focuses on achieving personality change in desired directions through counseling or psychotherapy. Closely related to the clinical approach is the *case study,* which examines the individual's life history. Social workers, psychiatrists, and developmental and social psychologists may all turn to this longitudinal method as a means of studying the individual's problems or causative factors in personality dynamics. Biographies and fiction can be used as relevant clinical materials in this type of research.

Behaviorism examines basic learning systems by which behavior patterns develop. It is a means for determining the bases of a wide range of behavior, such as the conditions which give rise to killer behavior in mice or, on the human level, how social behaviors are learned. Advocates of this approach maintain that there is nothing more to personality than observable behavior and the biological and environmental stimuli which control a person's behavior. Indeed, the behaviorist school in psychology has approached personality in the context of testable hypotheses in the laboratory. Most contemporary psychologists researching personality avoid this rather rigid framework, and their methods run the gamut from experiments on learning, perception, and motivation all the way to intensive individual case studies. A number of behavioral scientists are committed to integrating the experimental and clinical approaches. Methodologically sophisticated techniques can be used to analyze and complement the data produced by informal observation and clinical materials. Staats (1971) expresses the hope that "the resolution of the age-old 'objective' versus 'subjective' schism helps join the very important contributions of the two heretofore separate traditions in psychology and the social sciences, leading toward the unity of science that harbors such great potentiality in the study of man" (p. 336).

The concept of personality presents the psychologists with a paradox. Such a term is needed to denote the total, or gestalt, quality of a person's characteristics and tendencies, but it is very difficult to maintain the wholeness of personality and to deal meaningfully and consistently with such a complex concept. The result is that, while paying lip service to the wholeness of personality, biologists, psychologists, psychiatrists, social scientists, and others have developed their own favorite meanings of the term. To some the word seems to mean underlying emotional tone or energy level; to others, characteristic traits or habit patterns; to still others, moral and ethical qualities, "ego structure," attitudes and values, or the pattern of typical social behavior. Much more than most psychological terms, *personality* has connotations which are disconcertingly variable.

These issues are examined in detail in a stimulating book by Arthur W. Staats, *Social Behaviorism* (1975). Other useful references include Mischel (1976), Alker (1972), and Cattell and Dreger (1977).

Dimensions of Personality

Probably the most conventional definition of personality sees it as an integration of traits. Traits are usually considered as aspects of *temperament,* or the constitutional, emotional substrata of personality. But, in a more general sense, the term *trait* implies a basic orientation to the world or one of a set of social and emotional habit systems. Stagner (1961) refers to a trait as a "consistent feature of personality which has some emotional or ideational content." Traits are often conceived as more or less quantitative abstractions based on factor analysis or statistical findings derived from tests or schedules.

Sargent and Smith (1974) contrast the relation of traits to temperament and to attitudes and values (to be examined in Chapters 8 and 9), which, along with other factors, help influence and determine personality. Figure 4–1 depicts some of the major components of personality which act together.

A similar distinction has been made between the *style* of personality and the traits that compose it. Style refers to the gestalt of reaction patterns characterizing a given person, ranging from certain perceptual and cognitive habits to types of expressive behavior (G. W. Allport, 1961). The person's particular style of cognition and perception (to be examined in Chapters 5 and 6) is a critical dimension of personality (Hamachek, 1971). Some persons approach the world in fairly rigid categories, while others easily adjust to a varying range of stimuli.

Personality styles or attitudes, as compared to personality traits, are considerably more modified by experience and the passage of time. When the concern is with causation or change (as it is throughout this text), it makes a great deal of difference what aspect of personality is being considered.

Personality style is only meaningful in the context of the world outside the self. Altman and Taylor (1973) suggest the term *social penetration* to account for the interpersonal behaviors that take place in social interaction and the internal subjective processes that precede, accompany, and follow an exchange with others. This process of interaction includes verbal, nonverbal, and environmentally oriented behaviors. Personality exchange, or interaction with others, is mostly of a dyadic nature, that is, a communication between two persons. Our personality is in constant change as we act toward ourselves, toward others, and toward objects according to the meaning they have for us (Wilmot, 1975).

Because Altman and Taylor see personality as a juncture between the outside

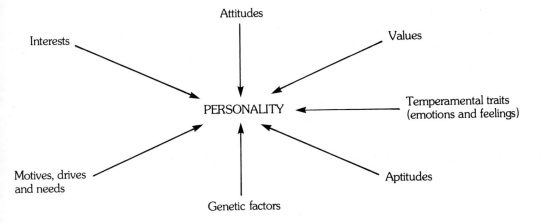

Figure 4–1. Major Components of Personality

universe and the events that occur within the self, they conceive of it as a structure of successive layers. In studying personality one moves from the external, social interactions and the surface traits into the deeper layers, somewhat like the peeling of an onion.

Social interactions may be reflected in personality as either coping or expressive behavior. *Coping* refers to the more cautious, tentative, and controlled kinds of responses, whereas *expressive* behavior tends to be spontaneous and draws out deeper motives (G. W. Allport, 1961). People differ in their ability to keep their behavior in control, and some may only express their feelings under rather unusual circumstances, such as a life crisis, an alcoholic binge, or a fit of anger. Other people are rarely inhibited and appear to remain their open selves in almost any situation.

Mischel (1976) urges a multifaceted approach to personality. He observes that research is reflecting

> . . . an emerging image of the human being that seems to reflect a growing synthesis of several theoretical influences in current personality psychology. . . . This image is one of the human being as an active, aware problem-solver, capable of profiting from an enormous range of experiences and cognitive capacities, possessing great potential for good or ill, actively constructing his or her psychological world, and influencing the environment but also being influenced by it in lawful ways—even if the laws are difficult to discover and hard to generalize. (p. 253)

EMERGENCE OF THE CONCEPTS OF SELF AND EGO

Any treatment of personality or socialization would be incomplete without consideration of the self or ego. The terms are often used interchangeably, as they are here, to represent the inner nature or the essence of personality in the person. In the historical survey in this section, they are used in the special context of the psychologists who contributed to the emergence of the concepts. The somewhat arbitrary distinction between *self* and *ego* is examined later in the section titled "The Self: Concept and Identity."

However one defines it, the ego comes close to being the essence, the organizing principle, of personality. Our ego is involved in our most intense motives and purposes, most poignant frustrations, most consistent attitudes and values. It includes our estimate of ourself and our major roles in relation to others.

In order to understand and predict a person's social behavior, the psychologist must have some knowledge about the person's ego. It is much easier to study motor abilities, language, memory, emotions, and intelligence than to deal with a complex synthesis like the ego. Between about 1910 and 1940, most psychologists avoided using the terms *ego* or *self* in their work. When it became clear that the subject is a proper concern for them, they found that certain early psychologists and sociologists had already worked out a number of productive ideas about the self and its development. Sigmund Freud, of course, postulated the ego as an integral part of psychoanalytic theory. Others also contributed to the concepts before they were subjected to the present social-psychological interpretation.

Theories of the Social Self

A famous, once widely used text, *Principles of Psychology* by William James (1890), stressed the social self: *"In its widest possible sense, a man's Self is the sum of all that he CAN call his,* not only his body and his psychic powers, but . . . *a man has as many social selves as there are individuals who recognize him. . . ."* To James and the philosophers and psychologists of the late 19th century, *self* was the closest approximation to what we now call *personality.* James saw the significance of social components in the broad and complex self and realized the importance of what later came to be called *role-playing* or *role-taking.* He did not, however, devote much attention to how the self had its origin and development.

James Mark Baldwin, a pioneer developmental psychologist and contemporary of James, asserted emphatically that the self is a social product. "My sense of myself grows by imitation of you," wrote Baldwin (1913) "and my sense of yourself grows in terms of my sense of myself." Baldwin was one of the first to use terms like *social environment* and *culture* to designate the social milieu with which the child constantly interacts. He felt that the main task of social psychology is to trace out the development of the individual in the constant give-and-take relation with the social environment.

Charles Horton Cooley and George Herbert Mead, two early American sociologists whose contributions focused on the origin and development of the social self, had many ideas in common. Mead was identified in Chapter 1 as the founder of the social interaction school of thought, which conceives of the mind as continually growing.

For Cooley (1902, 1956), the social self is a system of ideas, based on communication with others, which the mind cherishes as its own. Hence, an individual's idea of self depends on the way she or he is treated by others. Cooley's famous theory of *the looking-glass self* describes succinctly how the self develops out of social interaction. In this concept, children gradually acquire the ability to imagine how they appear to other persons and how other persons judge them, and they have a resulting feeling such as pride or mortification. Thus our self-estimates depend on interaction with others; we become socialized by understanding the reactions we produce in others.

The most significant "others" for Cooley are the *primary groups,* or intimate, face-to-face social units to which every child belongs: family, play group, and neighborhood. He regards these groups as the nursery of human nature and social life, in which the fundamental virtues and ideals that are the real basis of human nature are developed. Contacts with the more impersonal *secondary groups,* such as social institutions, are more casual and superficial, and so they are less significant to human development. In the primary groups, according to Cooley (1909), "human nature comes into existence. Man does not have it at birth; he cannot acquire it except through fellowship, and it decays in isolation." Cooley's views on the significance of primary groups have been verified by many empirical studies, such as those on the family which are described in Chapter 3. The emphasis on secondary groups in modern society is cited as a reason for the growth of anomie, or alienation from society, in Chapter 12.

Mead (1934) considered *role-taking* as an essential aspect of the child's development. He noted that the young child identifies with the mother, brother or sister, and others and is soon playing at being mama, daddy, big brother, postman, policeman, Indian, and so on. The child acts out the roles and talks out the parts imaginatively. This role-taking, with its internalized conversation or "conversation in the inner forum," to use Mead's own term, is the essence of socialization, since through it children learn to make the speech, habits, attitudes, and behavior of others a part of themselves.

Out of a kind of synthesis or distillation from all the role-taking experiences emerges what Mead calls the *generalized other.* This refers to the child's own general role, which arises from hundreds of social contacts. A significant part of this role is the child's conception of self, or *self-image,* a concept on which several sociologists and psychologists have placed great emphasis.

The self is not, however, merely an integration of roles the child has learned from others. These make up the "me," according to Mead; in addition there develops the "I," which is the self as actor and gives the personality its dynamic and unique character. The I and me are always closely related. The ever-changing and unpredictable I is modified by the me. Much of the time they fuse and operate together, especially in intense and interesting activities such as athletics. At other times they are in some degree of opposition, as during moments of indecision and conflict.

Thus, according to Mead, the I and the me are both integral parts of self or personality. The me, based on role-taking, reflects social experience and represents the more permanent aspect of the self. The more intangible and unpredictable I is the emergent factor that makes a person unique (or endows one

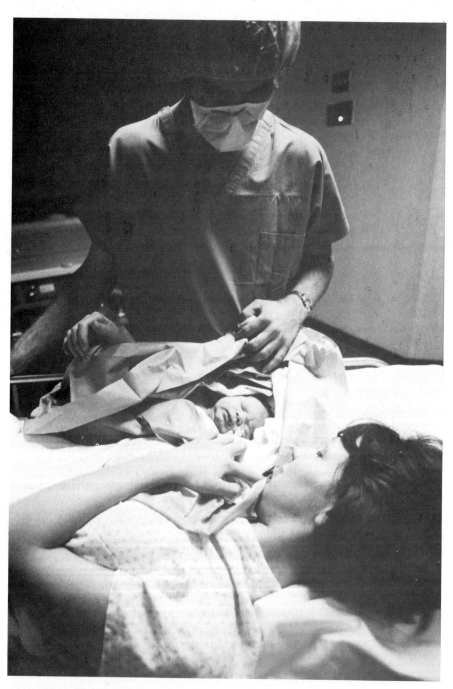

At birth the infant has neither self nor personality. The early months are critical in shaping the responses the individual will later make to the environment. *Source:* © Theodore Anderson, 1981.

with *ego strength,* a term that developed later). Contrasted with these dynamic, strong-willed persons are the conventional, timid types in whom the me far outweighs the I.

According to Mead (1934), the birth and rise of the self depend on the ability of individuals to be an object to themselves. Through communication with others, first by gestures and later by symbolic speech, children learn what reactions their words produce in others. They learn to introject or imitate other people's responses to them; that is, they learn to take the role of others. They come to see themselves as others do; they perceive themselves only after they have perceived others. (The intricacies of perception are developed in Chapter 6.)

Despite some vagueness in his theory, Mead made a lasting contribution in his emphasis on the spontaneity that emerges from the dialogue between the I and the me. As an "emergent social product," the self is something more than a passive reflection of social conventions and pressures (M. B. Smith, 1974). Mead also laid the groundwork for our understanding of communication and feedback, concepts which will be analyzed in Chapter 10. Although his viewpoint was opposed to the orthodox behaviorism of John B. Watson, it paved the way for a more modified position, what has come to be known as *social behaviorism* (J. D. Lewis, 1979).

Rediscovery of the Ego

On the whole, the self was considered outside the concern of the experimentally oriented, behaviorist psychology of the early 20th century. Clinically minded psychologists began to get interested in Freud, but more for his therapy than for his theories about the ego (see the following section). A few, particularly the Gestalt psychologists Kurt Koffka and Kurt Lewin, did give the ego, or self, a place in their systematic formulations. But by and large, from the time of James and Baldwin until the late 1940s, the ego (or self) was a lost concept in behavioral science.

Muzafer Sherif and Hadley Cantril's *Psychology of Ego-Involvement* (1947) was the first book devoted to a psychological treatment of the ego. It defined the ego as a cluster or constellation of attitudes related to what the individual considers to be me, I, my, or mine. Later Sherif described a person's ego or self as consisting of interrelated attitudes that are acquired in relation to one's own body and to objects, family, persons, groups, social values, and institutions (Sherif & Sherif, 1956). When *ego attitudes* are aroused, the individual's experience and behavior become *ego-involved.* Social values and norms of many kinds enter into the formation of the ego. (These relate in part to the Freudian superego, which is thus included in the psychologist's conception of ego.) These values "serve the individual as frames of reference by means of which he makes those judgments that affect *him;* that define *for him* success and failure; that determine *his* loyalties and allegiances; that spell out what he conceives to be *his* role, *his* status, *his* class" (Sherif & Cantril, 1947). Our ego involvements are seen as significant in determining our goals, loyalties, responsibilities, identifications with persons and groups, and even our hobbies and entertainment.

Sherif and Cantril emphasized that the ego develops gradually, its basic pattern being determined through the child's primary social contacts in the family, play group, school, and religious activities. The ego is modified or reformed at adolescence as the individual becomes identified with new groups and assimilates adult values and norms. As a result of environmental pressure or of certain organic disturbances, the ego may break down, as shown in studies of war neurosis and other pathological conditions.

Development of the Concept of Self

The concept of the self assumed a major role in the social interaction view of personality. In this view, the *self-concept* shapes new experiences to conform to its already established pattern, and much of behavior can be understood as a person's attempt to maintain the consistency of his or her self-concept, to reach a kind of homeostasis at a higher psychological level (Shaffer & Shoben, 1956). The adjustment potential of the self can be defined in at least three directions: (1) the felt and introspected self, (2) the cognitive or thinking behavior of the individual, including a wide range of values and attitudes, and (3) the self as a "controlling, coordinate structure inferred from observed behavior, where it is understood as that which accounts for integration of behavior" (Gorsuch & Cattell, 1977, p. 706).

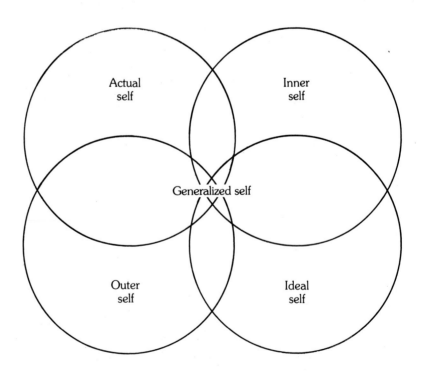

Figure 4-2. The Self-concept and Subselves

A person has many models and may acquire more than one self. The clown model offers an alternative, or at least a different kind of reality. *Source:* © Theodore Anderson, 1981.

As a person enters childhood, the self becomes progressively elaborated. For one thing, there is the distinction between the *ideal self* and the *actual self* (Wylie, 1968). In making this distinction, evaluative decisions are made. As we discover various social selves which depend on the awareness of roles, we become conscious of two selves, private and public. We also know that our own ideal self is not the same as what others hold as an ideal for us.

This division of the self is shown in Figure 4-2. There is always the problem of the congruence between the actual self and the ideal self, or between the inner self (what we know of our self) and outer self (what others know). The generalized or total self is made up of overlapping spheres, each growing out of the various self-concepts—subjective or objective, individual or social, imaginary or real. The spatial or physical means by which we can give some reality to the self are described in Box 4-1 on the territories of the self, a concept which is further examined in Chapter 19.

The Concept of Ego as a Basis for Research

As a theory of modest proportions from which hypothetical statements can be formulated and tested, ego involvement has become useful in motivation research (see Chapter 7), and it is a crucial concept in the study of communication (Chapter 10) and attitude change (Chapter 9). Because the ego establishes the person's limits of acceptance or rejection, it is useful in studying beliefs, attitudes, and values (Sherif, Sherif, & Neberhall, 1965). The concept also has provided one means of understanding the process of decision making in the small group, notably in the two-person dyad.

The significance of the self or ego in personality is now generally recognized. The term *self-consistency* refers to the unitary function of the self that gives purpose and continuity to living (Lecky, 1945). *Self-reference* is implied in defense mechanisms; whether they are considered to be warding off anxiety or bolstering self-esteem, the existence of a self is implied. The personality theory of A. H. Maslow (1954 and 1962) centers around achieving *self-actualization* as the highest need in a hierarchy of needs.

BOX 4–1
THE TERRITORIES OF THE SELF

The self carves out its own prerogatives within spatial boundaries. According to Erving Goffman, the territories of the self are *fixed,* as with the books you own, or they are *situational,* as with the table you occupy at a restaurant. Similar to the situational is the *egocentric* territory, which can be spatial but generally represents a vague kind of personal focus.*

Among the situational and egocentric territories are:

1. *Personal space*—a seat you share on a bus, where you claim more or less space depending on the size of your seatmate.
2. *The stall*—a somewhat more definitive preserve, as when you spread a towel out on the beach.
3. *Use space*—the territory immediately around or in front of you when you are viewing a work of art in a museum, implying that other viewers are not to block out your line of vision.
4. *The turn*—lining up gives you the privilege to be right *after* the person ahead of you and right *before* the person behind you. (This tradition varies markedly according to cultural norms, as travelers discover in comparing Great Britain and Latin America, for example.)
5. *The sheath*—your skin and clothing protect your self. Goffman observes that among "the American middle class, for example, little effort is made to keep the elbow inviolate, whereas orifice areas are of concern."
6. *Possessional territory*—the objects identified with you, such as your hat, cigarettes, or parcels.
7. *Information preserve*—your letters or biographical data such as age, income, or Goffman says, any "content of the claimant's mind, control over which is threatened when queries are made that he sees as intrusive, nosy, or untactful."

All these extensions of the self are conditioned by the situation and especially by the subculture. Social class (see Chapter 3) is a major determinant: the higher the status, the greater the control over space and its boundaries.

There is always the risk of violating the territory of another, and the violations show as much variability as the territories themselves do. Goffman classifies these as follows:

1. The "ecological placement of the body relative to a claimed territory." For instance, the Indian social system decrees a measurable distance between persons of different castes.
2. Physical invasion of the other person. The use of hands or any body contact is precarious; military officers and enlisted men may not touch each other at all, for example. Staring violates another person's territory; even the topless waitress is not to be too closely viewed as she serves drinks at a table.
3. Sound and speech. We avoid noise or conversation that interferes with the right or others.
4. A broad range of bodily excreta, from sweat and spit to odor or body heat. Another dimension of bodily excreta is suggested by the food left on a plate after eating, not to speak of the teeth markings an untutored child leaves in a cake or loaf of bread. Often these physical manifestations of the self are treated with subtle distinction. The most intimate lovers might be reluctant to use each other's toothbrushes.

Thus the individual defines the territory of the self. The position or stance of our body and how we move our arms, torsos, or legs may signal to another person the extent to which we will tolerate an invasion of our territory.† Body contact with strangers is generally avoided, but cultures permit a gamut of exceptions, from shaking hands to karate.

---

*E. Goffman, *Relations in Public: Microstudies of the Public Order* (New York: Basic Books, 1971), pp. 28-61.

†A. E. Scheflen and M. Ashcraft, *Human Territories: How We Behave in Space-Time* (Englewood Cliffs, N.J.: Prentice-Hall, 1976), p. 208.

THE EGO IN PSYCHOANALYSIS

A psychoanalytically inclined psychologist might say that thus far we have been more concerned with the self than with the ego. Symonds (1951) maintained that the two terms should be kept distinct, since *ego* refers to the self as object, while *self* is subjective. *Self* "refers to the body and mind and to bodily and mental processes as they are observed and reacted to by the individual," and *ego* denotes "that phase of personality which determines adjustments to the outside world in the interest of satisfying inner needs." It is in this sense that the term *ego* is used in the psychoanalytic literature.

Good personality adjustment, according to Freud, consists of a harmonious relationship between the id, ego, and superego. The *id* is our primitive or animal nature, embodying the instinctual or unconscious urges and desires that operate entirely according to the *pleasure principle.* The *ego* is the rational self, which functions according to the *reality principle,* a kind of rule of expediency which permits some expression of id impulses if they are not morally or socially dangerous. The *superego* is a tyrannical agent, equivalent to conscience, which consists of moral ideas and prohibitions. It constantly acts to force the ego to repress all expression of id impulses, under penalty of strong feelings of guilt. Thus the ego is definitely on the spot, having to mediate not only the insatiable desires of the id and the rigid requirements of the superego but the continuous demands and limitations of the environment as well. When the ego cracks under the strain, it must be built up and strengthened, which is precisely the goal of psychoanalytic therapy.

From the many years Freud spent working with neurotic patients there emerged not only his system of therapy but also his highly influential theory of personality. In his schema of psychosexual development, the ego replaces the id and develops in three stages—infantile (oral, anal, and phallic), latent, and adolescent (genital).

During the *infantile stage,* which lasts until about five or six years of age, the child's *libido* (energy or drive) is said to be directed toward biological needs or immediate satisfactions. The most significant developments in personality are assumed to take place in this period, in which there are three distinguishable but overlapping substages or phases. The *oral phase* lasts until the end of the first year or the beginning of the second. During this time the baby's activity centers about sucking, swallowing, and (later) teething, biting, and the beginnings of speech. During the *anal phase* (in the second part of the third year), the child is more active and responsive to the external world. Major demands are made in the area of bowel and bladder training, with such associated activities as learning to keep clean, to dress unaided, and to respond to parental wishes. The last phase of the infantile stage, the *phallic phase,* lasts from about age two or three to age five or six. In this phase the child's interests go to the world beyond, and growing curiosity centers around sex and reproduction.

Gradually the libido gives way to control by the superego. The *Oedipal conflict,* which arises when the child becomes attached to the parent of the opposite sex in the phallic phase, is resolved. From about seven years of age until puberty, the child is said to be in the *latency stage,* which Freud viewed as uneventful in terms of personality development. With the onset of puberty the final phase of psychosexual development, the *adolescent or genital stage,* is reached. At this point the normal person's interest is dominantly heterosexual, and the ego is said to be fully developed.

At any stage there may be (and usually are) conflicts that can predispose a child toward later neurosis if they are serious enough. One common reaction to conflict is fixation or stoppage at one stage and failure to progress in a normal way. Another common reaction is for the ego to adopt a mechanism such as repression, displacement, regression, or rationalization in an attempt to eliminate or reduce the conflict.

Assessment of Freud's Theory

Freud's theory has been criticized on many counts by psychologists and social scientists. Among other things, psychoanalytic theory is said to oversimplify parent-child relationships in the Oedipus complex and, in general, to stress instinctual forces to the neglect of social and cultural influences. Other criticisms have focused on the lack of empirical testing and quantification, the tendency to reify certain concepts like the pleasure and reality principles, and the lack of a coherent structure to accommodate Freud's many changes in his formulations over several decades (Shaw & Costanzo, 1970).

Without debating the pros and cons of these criticisms, we can answer the question of whether psychological phenomena are "overdetermined" in Freudian theory by pointing to the complex of causes involved in personality. Whether every male passes through an Oedipal stage (to use one of the more controversial Freudian concepts), for example, cannot be known, as only a small minority ever undergoes psychoanalysis. According to one anthropologist, the Oedipal tendency appears in every male child, but in varying form (LaBarre, 1968). Whatever the interpretation, the generalizations of Freud must be viewed in the perspective of individual differences.

We can also assert that the *neo-Freudians,* such as Karen Horney and Erich Fromm, can hardly be accused of overlooking cultural factors. These revisionists of Freudian thought rejected the emphasis on sexual and instinctual causes of behavior, and instead took a sociocultural direction. Erik Erikson (1950) formulated a theory of libidinal development in which he classifies the *psychosocial crises,* or the kinds of dilemmas or problems faced by the ego, at each of several "stages of man." At the oral-sensory stage early feeding experiences can lead to basic trust or to mistrust; at the "muscular-anal" stage, bowel training may increase autonomy or develop feelings of shame and doubt. The latency period is concerned with the dilemma of industry versus inferiority, and in puberty the issue is strengthened individual identity versus role diffusion. Erikson sees these and the other stages of ego development as an orderly sequence that is nevertheless much affected by the child's social experience.

To some degree the theories of Freud complement the Mead and Cooley focus on the social self. Whereas Freud provided an individualized conception, the two Americans developed a more socialized definition of personality and the self (Swanson, 1961). Freud's theories were based on his observations of a given set of middle-class Viennese patients and were limited by his bias toward biological or inherent structures. Testing of his hypotheses has met with only partial validation. Mead's theories of the self and the generalized other were the product of his introspections and have been more plausible and more generally accepted than some of Freud's assertions, but, with some exceptions, they have not received empirical verification.

In the context of a theory of the self, possibly the most important contribution made by Freud was the idea that the ego must be responsive to the reality principle. According to Shaw and Costanzo (1970), "in development the individual must progress from the primary process modes of thought characteristic of the id system to the secondary process mode of thought of the ego." The relationship between the ego and reality is clearly a reciprocal one.

Freud may be faulted for some inadequacy in his empirical and theoretical approach. Still, psychoanalysis, at least as corrected by several of his followers, seems less remote from the mainstream of academic psychology than it did a half-century ago (N. Sanford, 1970). The point of bringing Freudian theory into a social psychology textbook is that it is relevant to an understanding of how the concept of the self developed into the constructs being used in social psychology to examine the relations of individuals and groups in society. It is particularly helpful in investigating social phenomena such as rigidity in attitudes, power needs and leadership, and certain kinds of mass behavior, as future chapters will show.

THE SELF: CONCEPT AND IDENTITY

The concept of self which developed from the early American social psychologists, and reemerged after the behaviorists' wave of the 1920s and 1930s had passed took its place in personality theory and social psychology as an approach which sees the self as the product of *social interaction*. This approach, which has been called *symbolic interactionism* (Blumer, 1969), differs in significant ways from the use of the concept of ego in psychoanalytic theory. A few of the attempts that have been made to integrate the two approaches and to develop them in both experimental and clinical directions will be described in this section.

Self, Ego, and Personality

The distinction between concepts of the self and the ego is to some extent an arbitrary one. The self is not only more personal and subtle but expresses a sense of identity, a subjective awareness, the "I-ness" and "me-ness." The ego represents the self in a wider context of behavior, a sort of organizing principle, the ordering of behavior and experiences. The terms *self* and *ego* are often used interchangeably. They also overlap with personality, but personality is even more inclusive, incorporating as it does all of a person's reaction tendencies.

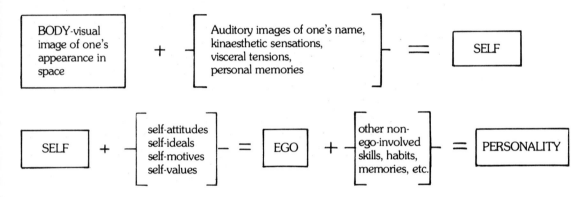

Figure 4–3.   Relations among Body, Self, Ego, and Personality

Source: D. P. Ausubel, *Ego Development and the Personality Disorders* (New York: Grune & Stratton, 1952), p. 13. Reprinted by permission.

For Ausubel (1952), the ego is an abstraction representing a complex set of experiences, perceptions, attitudes, motives, and values. Figure 4–3 depicts his idea of how the self and the ego merge in the personality. Early in life, the self is localized (or focused) in the body. Organic sensations, such as hunger or pain, mediate the meaning of the self for the infant or child. Later, personal experiences of childhood, adolescence, and adulthood shape the self, and this expansion of the self becomes the ego, which is both more cognitive and expressive of the aspirations of the individual.

In this text, however, we do not adhere to the notion that relegates the self to mere self-awareness in the early years. We prefer to view it in a wider perspective, whereby the ego is regarded as the self fortified with certain control aspects. Socialization and maturity account for the development of the self, but even more so of the ego. The self is more relevant to the problem of image and identity and the ego to the operation of certain personality components, particularly motives and values. The ego is more complete in its functions than is the self, and both are encompassed in the concept of personality.

Self-Perception

Each of us has many selves. One person can be both winner and loser, lover and hater, worker and playboy, father and son, mother and wife. We can accept the Freudian thesis that we both love and hate ourselves and Mead's idea that the self may be both subject and object suggest the ambivalence in our notion of the self.

The *self-image* (or the *self-concept*—the terms have only a slight connotative difference) is hardly a constant. To expect consistency would remove much of the color and spontaneity from behavior (Gergen, 1971). Interaction with others and the demands of specific situations call for varying self-concepts: We are sympathetic and cooperative with one person, for example, and rejecting and overbearing with another. We usually try to resolve dissonance in our self-concept, however, and to project an image of self-consistency to the outside world, even though the self may change in response to such changes as Erickson's psychosocial crises in the life cycle (see Box 4–2). We also are more satisfied and comfortable if we can maintain some degree of self-integrity.

According to Daryl Bem's *Self-Perception Theory* (1972), we become aware of the self by observing our own behavior as opposed to the behavior of others. This kind of self-perception has come to be known as *attribution,* or the "process of inferring or perceiving the dispositional properties of entities in the environment" (H. H. Kelley, 1967, p. 193). The judgments we make of others we can also make of ourselves. Often we are more aware of our outer behavior than of our inner processes—thoughts, feelings, and so on. Bem (1972) says that "to the extent that internal cues are weak, ambiguous, or uninterpretable, the individual is functionally in the position as an outside observer, an observer who must necessarily rely upon those same external cues to infer the individual's inner states" (p. 2). Thus you may prefer Pepsi-Cola to Seven-Up because you have observed yourself drinking Pepsi-Cola. We don't know what we think about an issue until we talk about it. Our self takes on meaning as its contents—beliefs and values—emerge. The concept of attribution is explored in relation to others and objects, as well as the self, in Chapter 6.

Self-awareness can be viewed as both looking inward and looking outward (Wicklund, 1975). When we are tuned in to our feelings and aspirations we may fall short of our ideals. The more outward or objective our behavior, the greater is the likelihood of self-correction. Wicklund and his colleagues have shown that subjects who carry out a task before a mirror or whose actions are recorded on tape or film tend to make either positive or negative judgments about themselves, depending on the favorability or unfavorability of the feedback. In one study, subjects were directed to write essays supporting viewpoints contrary to their own. Those who were recorded by a television camera, as opposed to those who were not, changed their attitudes so as to be consistent with their viewpoints (Wicklund & Duval, 1971). We prefer the stimuli and give the responses that are positive to our objective self-awareness. We try to reduce the discontinuity or dissonance in situations in which there is a negative balance between what we observe about ourselves and our aspirations, and we can find no way out of this objective self-awareness.

Box 4–2
THE NEW RITES OF PASSAGE

The significant changes in our self-concept which result from crises or developmental changes in the life cycle are marked by what Barney Glaser and Anselm Strauss call *status passage.** Unlike the rigid ceremonial rites of passage of primitive societies, status passage in present-day Western cultures can take numerous forms. The passage can be *inevitable,* as in going from child to adolescent, or *reversible,* as in going from being well to being sick to being well again, or *repeatable*—election to an office does not preclude reelection, for example. A passage may be voluntary or involuntary, legitimate or illegitimate.

The concept of the self tends to be freer as a result of the more spontaneous nature of status passage in our rapidly changing, less rigid society. The individual has a number of options in shaping them. The process can be dependent on the choice of agent; attending a military academy provides a different self-concept than enrollment in a free-wheeling experimental school, for example. A passage may mark a revolt, as when a priest leaves the church and marries, or a student drops out of school or the established society. The drug trip which originated in the youth subculture demonstrates how casual or precarious the passage can be.

Gail Sheehy popularized the notion of passages in a best-seller subtitled "Predictable Crises of Adult Life."† On the basis of 115 "life stories" collected mostly from middle-aged people in the American middle class, she suggested that periods of stress such as the "trying twenties and the forlorn forties" should be understood as valid stages unfolding in a sequence of growth, rather than the result of our own inadequacies. Her observations are suggested as a "guide to the inner changes on the way to full adulthood" which extends the period of personality development past adolescence into the midlife passages and on to the renewal period of maturity.

_____
*B. G. Glaser and A. L. Strauss, *Status Passage* (Chicago: Aldine-Atherton, 1971).
†Gail Sheehy, *Passages: Predictable Crises of Adult Life* (New York: E. P. Dutton & Co., 1976; paperback edition, Bantam Books, 1977).

Individuals differ markedly in their need for and ability to achieve self-perception, or what Snyder (1979) calls *self-monitoring.* The degree of personal security, the desire for affiliation with others, and the need for self aggrandizement or self-abasement are all relevant.

In our relations with others, too, we may reveal much or little about ourselves. Using a questionnaire technique with some 300 college and university students, Jourard (1971) found large individual differences in willingness to reveal intimate experiences and feelings to others. The validity of this type of report is always risky, but the findings did show that females tend to disclose more than males (and receive more disclosures than do males), and whites revealed more than blacks, Jewish (especially males) more than non-Jewish students, nursing students more than students in general. The ability to disclose was correlated with interpersonal attraction, which is not surprising in view of the inclination to be more confidential with close associates.

Most persons reveal relatively little of their inner selves. The use of a *mask* serves as "a regulating screen, a sort of censory (and sensory) apparatus" (Tiryakin, 1968). To most people we offer a "stereotyped personality." The discrepancy between the mask presented in dating and courtship and the realities of married life after the honeymoon, for example, contributes to the statistics on broken marriages. Often even the subject is only partially aware of the relationship between the mask and inner self.

Self-Evaluation and Self-Esteem

The self-concept, like the personality, is learned as we interact with others, and it changes according to the setting in which we find ourselves. The quality of the way we view ourselves, or our *self-evaluation,* reflects a balance between our own and others' positive and negative reactions to our self (Videbeck, 1960).

Self-evaluation reveals a person's degree of self-esteem, which largely shapes the self-concept. *Self-esteem* has been defined as "the degree of correspondence between the individual's ideal and actual concepts of himself" (A. R. Cohen, 1968). In Freud's analysis, the ego organization functions mainly to protect self-esteem. Laboratory experiments and clinical records have both given evidence of a process of "selective inattention" whereby we fail to respond to stimuli that can be injurious to the self (Swensen, 1973). In one study, persons of high esteem were found to be likely to accept only favorable reports on their performance. They interpreted failure less negatively than subjects with low self-esteem, who filtered experience in a fashion that made it difficult for them to better their self-image. Subjects with high self-esteem had built up a repertoire of avoidance defenses with which to insulate their self-concept (A. R. Cohen, 1968).

Self-esteem reflects changes in the life cycle and probably reaches a peak in the young adult years. For the upwardly mobile, this positive self-image remains into the middle years, but inevitably it becomes restrictive in old age. Usually we attempt to bolster our self-image as a means of bettering our reactions to others, or to increase our effectiveness on the job, or simply to cope with the vicissitudes of life.

Self-esteem is conditioned by the resources of the individual. We use numerous means to enhance our self-concept, from working for a college degree to getting married, from becoming a bridge expert to exerting our sexual prowess. There is evidence that persons low in self-esteem are usually more open to social influence (defined as suggestibility, persuasibility, or similar terms), but the degree to which these data are translatable to situations in real life is not certain (Marlowe & Gergen, 1969). In any case, it has been demonstrated that the person's self-esteem or the lack of it can be modified by the experimental setting. By means

The self is challenged by severe crisis. Abuse or rape cause violence to a woman's sense of personal identity. *Source:* Allentown Call-Chronicle.

of a perceptual test of the relations of the self to others in a given spatial arrangement, it was found that low self-esteem, when combined with limited concern for others, could produce an *alienation syndrome*, in a situation of low self-centrality (Ziller, 1969). This pattern of alienation as measured by the inadequacy of the self-concept appeared more frequently among psychiatric patients, among persons over 40 years of age, and in a sample of black children. Ziller concludes from this study that:

> Persons with low self-esteem have no recourse to a stable guidance system in social situations. They are incapable of imposing a personal structure on social situations. Persons with low social interest have no recourse to a social guidance system such as group norms. The self-centered person is presumed to reflect withdrawal from social contacts (p. 298).

Some experiments have explored the importance of others in the formation of the self-concept. An investigation by Bramel (1962), for example, illustrated how others can alter our self-esteem. In a procedure which raises some questions about ethical practices in experimental studies, male student subjects were divided into "favorable" and "unfavorable" groups on the basis of falsified personality test results. The experimenter then used a galvanometer to test pairs of subjects' reactions to pictures of male nudes but altered the needle reading so that the subjects could easily misread their own and their partners' ratings. By labeling the reactions an indication of homosexual tendencies, he created a situation of strong dissonance or anxiety. High self-esteem subjects projected homosexual attributes to their partners more than those with low self-esteem did; they seemed to secure their own self-esteem by shunting off any unacceptable traits to their peers.

An extreme case of altering the self-concept is *brainwashing*. In a laboratory experiment (Hewitt & Rule, 1968), 32 male students changed their self-concept after four hours of sensory deprivation. The discrepancy between their real and ideal self-ratings decreased when they were presented with a communication designed to improve their self-concept. The message was less critically received by the control group, which was not subjected to the sensory deprivation.

The pattern of self-evaluation relates to the person's definition of role, as Mead pointed out. The level of performance is also critical. In a study of medical students (Preiss, 1968), as the students moved through the four years of medical school, high performance and commitment to the role of doctor enhanced their self-image. For some students with high self-image, even low performance did not shake their confidence as to the career choice. The relationship of self and role is a complex one (see Box 4–3), and some persons can separate the two variables more easily than others can.

Control: External versus Internal

A recent critical issue in psychology is the degree of control we feel we exercise in our own behavior: Do we act as free agents, or do forces act upon us? In the rationalist viewpoint of philosophers from the 17th to 19th centuries, it was assumed that free will exists and all people have the power to motivate themselves. Today the tendency is to think of an individual's behavior as a

BOX 4-3
DISCOVERING WHO YOU ARE

The relation of self and role is evident in studies of the categories and attributes people ascribe to themselves. In the "Who Am I?" approach, subjects are asked to write down their responses to this question in various categories as if they were answering only to themselves, and then rate the importance of each of the attributes with which they identified themselves. For example, in a study of high school students, sex, age, and student roles were rated as of maximum importance by three fourths of the subjects. Racial or national heritage, religious affiliation, and place of residence were important to less than a fifth of the sample.

In a comparison of the responses to the "Who Am I?" test in an Ivy League university (Harvard-Radcliffe) and a large community college (Los Angeles City College), Chad Gordon found marked differences in the style of the self-concept.* The Ivy League student stressed social status, political affiliation, and ideology. Competence and the occupational roles were also important, which is hardly surprising in view of the competitive spirit in a high-level academic institution. The city college student was more likely to refer to physical qualities, material possessions, and personal likes. A major difference was the greater number of attributes assigned themselves by Ivy Leaguers, which suggests an extension of the self in an intellectually or artistically oriented environment.

In other applications of the test, schizophrenics showed a low self-concept, alcoholics had still a lower one, and university students had the highest.

These findings support the conclusion that the self-concept is more process than structure; it assumes the social, emotional, and cognitive relationships that evolve in the interaction between the person, others, and the environment.

_____

*C. Gordon, "Self-conception: Configurations of Content," in C. Gordon and K. J. Gergen (Eds.), *The Self in Social Interaction* (New York: John Wiley & Sons, 1968), Vol. 1, pp. 115–136.

response to genetics, the environment, and the responses of others. The individual does not possess free will so much as a *perception* of freedom from external control, a concept which will be developed in Chapter 6.

The issue of external versus internal control has motivational as well as perceptual aspects. In essence, the problem is whether, and to what degree, individuals can look at themselves as they would look at other persons and so determine their own responses. In psychological terms, we attempt to resolve whatever dissonance or internal conflict we may have about ourselves as we seek cognitive consistency in our self-perception, as noted above. *Dissonance,* which will be considered further in Chapters 6 and 9, is defined by Zimbardo (1969) as "a general tension state which motivates behavior, the terminal response of which results in a reduction in the level of tension."

We may seem to be acting on our own volition when in fact we are responding to others' behavior. We also may have the illusion of freedom because we do not understand the variables in our environment. A number of experiments have shown how errors in self-perception occur when the experimenter manipulates the subjects' internal and external stimuli (Bem, 1972).

The degree to which we initiate behavior or are passively responsive to the influence of others has been labeled by Julian Rotter (1966) the *locus of control*. In his *expectancy value theory*, he asserts that our probability of choosing a given behavior is a product of two factors: the anticipation that our action will be followed by the rewards implied by the situation, and the value of these rewards in our motivational system. The motivation of the athlete, for example, may depend on a belief in personal ability and a willingness to engage in the discipline and the training required for success. Another person with the same strength and dexterity might not have the drive and self-organization needed to implement similar skills. In pointing to the locus of control, Rotter refers to the tendency of individuals to believe in their own efficacy in shaping their behavior. He designed the *Internal-External Control Scale* as a means of differentiating or measuring one's sense of control over one's actions.

An investigation by Jones and Nisbett (1971) found that students tend to explain poor grades in terms of environmental factors such as an unhappy home situation, a noisy dormitory, or extracurricular involvement, whereas faculty advisors perceive the same problems as due to faulty intellectual ability, insufficient motivation, or poor organization. Much of the controversy about the achievement potential of minority groups focuses on the relative influence of environment and native ability.

Cultural factors can affect the degree to which a person perceives success as internally or externally caused. For example, in a cross-cultural study of attitudes toward social change Williamson (1970) found class and national differences in the answers to the question: "Would you say that success in life is to be attained by 'being lucky' or by 'working hard'?" In most countries the middle-class sample considered hard work as the reason for success more than did the lower class. Similarly, among advanced nations (such as the United States and Germany), success was internally "caused," or attributable to one's own efforts, whereas in developing countries like Colombia, for one, the answer was more often "being lucky."

Reference to internal and external causes appears to be related to self-esteem. An experiment based on estimates of the number of dots in a series of slides found that the students who were most accurate ascribed their success to ability and effort, and failure was more likely to be explained by external factors like chance or one's physical or mental condition. Students who were low in self-esteem (as measured by low scores on a self-concept scale) were more willing to point to internal factors, and the high-self-esteem group preferred to ignore any feedback on failure (Fitch, 1970).

We are of course influenced by our successes—or failures—in the past, which condition our perceived sense of control and autonomy. That is, we gain in ego strength as we build up a favorable self-image based on what others think of us.

Another dimension of control is the relation of the self-concept to intimacy and autonomy, or the person's ability to find meaningful and intimate relationships with others. One study showed that subjects with a high sense of autonomy were the least likely to experience an identity crisis (Olofsky, Marcia, & Lesser, 1973). For some persons the problem of self and identity reaches a crisis and therapy is sought as a solution.

Self-Identity

One means by which the individual creates and retains a self-image and self-identity is outer appearance. Self-identity refers to our ability to maintain a degree of continuity and integrity in our personalities, in response to our relations with others and the ever-changing events in our lives. A person's identity depends on a certain social class (see Chapter 3), as evidenced by, among other things, titles, dress, style of language, and hobbies. Certain symbols or cues are associated with a given person, ranging from the cigar and V-sign of Winston Churchill or the cardigan sweater and toothy smile of Jimmy Carter, to the face and figure of a currently popular model like Cheryl Tiegs in the early 1980s. The self is established, maintained, and transformed in our social relationships by a variety of communications based on physical appearances, as well as by direct verbal language (Stone, 1962).

One type of identity which is fairly easy to change is a name. Children do not always like the names their parents choose, and ethnic prejudice or a desire for easier spelling and pronunciation can lead some people to change their names legally. Moreover, because of the need for rapid speech or to show closeness or affection, it is not unusual to give people nicknames. In an investigation of American students living in Denmark, it was found that many had informally adopted a new first name, often one suggested by their Danish hosts (Drury & McCarthy, 1980). Students who showed an increase in self-esteem while in Denmark were nearly twice as likely to change their names as those whose self-esteem decreased. Relevant factors include the tendency of persons to change their self-image while living in a foreign culture and enjoying the esteem the host culture gives to the home country.

Erving Goffman (1959) introduced the idea of the self as a form of manipulation or *management*. We all need to impress others, no matter how limited our resources. Efforts to impress the other party through the manipulation of images have become a major preoccupation in all societies in which other-directedness operates and the mass media are firmly established. With the help of skillful imagery, an obscure individual can quickly rise from office boy to the board of directors, or from local politics to national leadership. Nations are so concerned with the impressions they are making on other nations that international relations are taking on the semblance of a cold war being fought by public relations experts.

We manage our self-images not only by the expressions (or impressions) we *give,* Goffman says, but by the expressions we *give off.* The former are verbal symbols intended to convey a given meaning, usually in keeping with our demands and expectations. The latter may be the kinds of impressions we cultivate, fabrications that the speaker or actor believes the other person wants to hear, even if they are not in keeping with the intent of the speaker. A woman student living in a dormitory may let the telephone ring several times before she answers in order to create an impression of being busy. She may make intriguing references to her dating experience in order to convey an idea, fictional or true, which is consciously or unconsciously designed to maintain her position in an area society considers important. According to Goffman, we operate between a "back region" in which the "performance of a routine" is planned, and a "front region" in which the performance takes place. The identity of the self is managed, even though the success of the strategy may remain in doubt.

The Life Situation and Defense of the Self

The self or ego serves at the disposition of the individual. However much the self may resist change consciously (or more likely unconsciously), alterations occur in response to environmental changes and the responses of others, as well as in the individual's efforts to achieve coherence and consistency. The biological and social order requires the self-identity to pass through certain critical stages in order for the person to assume the proper image for his or her sex, age, class, or profession (Strauss, 1962).

Psychotherapy may offer the most dramatic instances of changes in the self, which are changes in personality. The nondirective approach employed by Carl Rogers particularly stresses the strength of the self-image as a major criterion of the success of therapy (Rogers, 1942, 1951). In validating this theory, it was found that negative and ambivalent self-references shifted to positive ones during the course of therapy and were correlated with other criteria of its success (Raimy, 1948). A positive self-concept can also improve the chances for physical recovery. In a sample of paraplegic and related types of patients, individuals expressing a positive self-conception showed a significantly higher rate of progress in rehabilitation. The question of self-concept was especially critical because the prognosis for recovery was generally weak (Litman, 1962).

As Sarnoff (1962) points out, the ego functions to remove obstacles in the way of fulfillment of the individual's goals. It enables the person to cope with dangers in ways that can involve increasing or decreasing anxiety. A minimum level of anxiety is necessary in order to make the self aware of possible threats, but an excessive amount can be incapacitating. By not only handling anxiety but providing a locus for other variables such as motivation and learning, the self supports and encourages growth of the personality.

Conclusions: The Ego and the Self

The introspective approaches to the self conceptualized in the social interaction viewpoint and the psychoanalytically based interpretations of the ego and the self-concept are not always in agreement. Nevertheless, they both hold that the development of a self-image or self-concept makes for some degree of self-esteem and self-identity, although mental stress or traumatic events can lower evaluation of the self or impair the achievement of identity.

Some theorists have used the term *ego* to refer to a dynamic, patterned system within the personality consisting of those attitudes, values, beliefs, and purposes that the individual's life experiences have made most essential. In our interpretation, the difference between self and ego is one of degree. The self emerges in early childhood, whereas the ego is acquired in later childhood and adolescence. Therefore the ego is slightly more explicit, more structural, and more sharply defined or verbalized. But for many observers the difference is practically nonexistent.

The development of a self-image begins in infancy, and its growth depends in large part on an increasing command of language and acquisition of the ability to conceptualize. Children become cognizant of major social roles—child or adolescent, boy or girl, big brother or little sister, pupil, or perhaps athlete or leader. These are incorporated into a self-image which helps to channel or pattern interests and ego involvements. The adolescent's desire for independence from the family leads to identification with age-mate groups, which provides belongingness and status. In young adults, the self, or to use a roughly equivalent term, the *ego structure,* becomes more stable and consistent as their understanding of roles increases and they accept the dominant values and norms of the groups with which they affiliate.

A person's ego structure or self-image is not solely a product of socialization, however. It is also affected by the person's unique physique, temperament, and intelligence. Together these result in *ego attitudes* which are reflected in the person's interaction with others in the social milieu and with the environment.

These interactions or *ego involvements* affect the course and intensity of much social behavior at all levels, from the small group to the community and national and international affairs. Ego involvement is evidenced in the boy who is wild about football, the subteen who adores a popular singer, or the adult who is dedicated to a cult or social movement. But ego involvement is also exemplified in the social behavior of a mother who is logical and dispassionate about most subjects but becomes defensive and emotional when a family friend hints that she has brought up her child improperly, or a manager who cannot accept suggestions from subordinates. On a larger scale, national grief occasioned by the assassination of Martin Luther King or the murder of John Lennon suggests the degree to which millions of people can become identified with public figures. We believe this concept of the self or ego is meaningful and useful to the social psychologist. Our interpretation is admittedly oversimplified and tentative, but, like any definitions that can be formulated at the present time, it ought to be subjected to continual testing and reformulation.

SUMMARY

Personality has been defined in this chapter as a complex gestalt of traits. In our view, biological or genetic factors may influence personality, but it is the myriad of social influences that produces the traits that are relevant to social psychology.

The other concept considered in this chapter, the self, has had a more complicated history in psychology. A number of American social psychologists, especially Cooley and G. H. Mead, made important contributions to our understanding of the self, notably its subjective "I" and objective "me" aspects. The strong influence of behaviorism initiated by Watson discouraged a concept as intangible as the self, however.

The term *ego* became known in part through the work of Freud, who conceived of the self or personality as being constituted of the ego, id, and superego. Although criticism of Freud and psychoanalysis has been extensive, revisions by neo-Freudians have brought respectability to the concept of ego as analogous to the self.

New interest in the self and ego—which have different connotations but are often used interchangeably—was initiated in the 1940s by Sherif and Cantril. Today psychologists (Bem, for example) as well as sociologists (Goffman among others) are concerned empirically with many aspects of the self: the perception of the self as based on our own behavior, the means by which we can validate the self, and the never-ending search for self-esteem, in which problems of identity management and maintaining face are relevant. Other concerns are autonomy and personal freedom in the context of external and inner control, and the problem of defending the self and the role of psychotherapy in this effort.

The understanding of the concepts of personality and the self presented in this chapter has psychological underpinnings in the central processes of learning and motivation. An analysis of these processes and the nature of attitudes, values, and communication will be undertaken in Part II, which focuses on the dynamics of social behavior.

WORDS TO REMEMBER

Alienation. Situation of detachment, isolation, or negative response to the group, community, or total society, especially its norms and values.

Attribution. Assignment of behavioral tendencies or personality traits to ourselves or another person, on the basis of observed responses.

Behaviorism. Viewpoint in psychology (beginning with J. B. Watson before 1920 and continuing with B. F. Skinner) that the legitimate subject matter of psychology is responses that can be observed. A more complete statement will be found in later chapters, especially Chapter 5.

Ego. The conscious aspect of the self. In

Freudian theory, the ego, together with the superego, holds the id in check. (See *id; superego.*)

Ego involvement. Emotional identification of the self with another person, an organization, an attitude, etc.

Egocentrism. Perception of stimuli as directed toward the self; tendency to live in one's own world; in the child, inability to discriminate between the self and non-self.

Empathy. The capacity for identification with others.

Generalized other. Term formulated by G. H. Mead to represent a child's impression of how others respond to him or her.

Gestalt. German word for pattern, form, or configuration; used in Gestalt psychology to represent the wholeness of responses and of psychological phenomena in general. The gestalt of personality, behavior, or culture refers to the whole as being greater than the sum of its parts or implies that too-specific analysis of a given response or experience may fail to reveal the totality. The Gestalt school was an early 20th-century reaction against the narrow confines of introspectionism (see Chapter 1) on one side and behaviorism on the other.

Id. Freudian term for the deep-seated, unconscious, pleasure-seeking part of the self. It is also the seat of the *libido,* the ever-driving sexual impulse.

Identification. Process of assuming the characteristics of another person, group, nation, etc. (*see empathy*).

Looking-glass self. Term coined by C. H. Cooley to represent a phase of socialization in which people are influenced by others, or how others shape the way people perceive themselves.

Neo-Freudian. Term applied to disciples or revisionists of Freudian thought who disagree with the stress on sexual and instinctual causes of behavior and em-

phasize cultural and related factors in explaining personality and its conflicts.

Norms. Implicit or explicit standards or patterns of behavior. Although norms are defined by society, most are open to subjective interpretation.

Personality. The organized sum or totality of a person's behavior, inner and outer. (See *gestalt; trait.*)

Primary group. Small group characterized by intimacy and face-to-face relations, such as the family, in which members are considered as ends in themselves rather than as a means to an end, in contrast to a more impersonal *secondary group* such as a social institution.

Psychoanalysis. Use of Freudian and neo-Freudian techniques to seek understanding of the personality, especially its unconscious elements, as a system of psychotherapy.

Self. The individual's awareness of her or his experience, cognitions, and identity. (See *ego.*)

Self-concept. The intricate perceptions people have of themselves, including their beliefs, feelings, and relationships with others. The term is closely related to *self-esteem, self-evaluation,* and *self-monitoring.*

Self-perception theory. Term coined by D. J. Bem to represent the idea that people judge themselves the same way they judge others; that is, they become aware of their selves through their outer behavior.

Social interaction. The explanation of personality development through interpersonal relations, primarily the family and one's peers; contrasts with psychoanalysis.

Status passage. Series of roles or statuses a person encounters throughout the life cycle, especially in conditions of rapid mobility.

Superego. In Freudian jargon, the controlling aspect, both conscious and unconscious, of the self in its conflict with the *id* (or libido); comparable to but more dynamic than the conscience.

Symbolic interactionism. Viewpoint in social psychology that consciousness of the self and roles are central to an understanding of behavior. The *Chicago school* depends mainly on qualitative methods, whereas the *Iowa school* stresses the use of quantifiable techniques.

Temperament. A cluster of deep-seated personality traits, primarily oriented to emotional behavior.

Trait. Basic orientation or one of a set of social and emotional habit systems. *Trait theory* expresses the viewpoint that personality can be measured by evaluating traits on various scales.

QUESTIONS FOR DISCUSSION

1. Give your own definition of personality.
2. What different professional approaches have been taken to the study of personality?
3. What are the differences between the psychoanalytic and social interaction views of personality?
4. Describe some studies that have been published on the style of personality. How would you assess them?
5. What were the contributions of Baldwin and Cooley to the understanding of the self?
6. What do Mead's concepts, such as role playing and the generalized other, mean to developmental psychology?
7. Why did psychology turn away, at least temporarily, from the study of the self and ego? How and when did psychology return to interest in these concepts?
8. What is meant by the generalized self?
9. Of what significance is the ego to psychoanalysis? How is Freud's theory assessed today?
10. How do contemporary psychologists such as Bem or Wicklund think of the self?
11. In what ways does self-esteem affect the self-concept?
12. What factors have been shown to affect people's perception of how much control they have over their own actions?
13. What does Goffman mean by the idea of identity management? Do you agree with his appraisal?
14. What causes the self to undergo change? When, if ever, does it become static, in the social interaction view?

READINGS

Cattell, R. B., and Dreger, R. M. (Eds.). *Handbook of Modern Personality Theory.* New York: Hemisphere, 1977.
    A selection of theoretical and research statements on personality structure and development.

Corsini, R. J. *Readings in Current Personality Theories.* Itasca, Ill.: F. E. Peacock, Publishers, 1978.
    A well-selected set of readings on classic and contemporary approaches to the structure and dynamics of personality.

Erikson, E. H. *Childhood and Society.* New York: W. W. Norton, 1950.
    A highly influential presentation of the emergence of the ego is childhood.

Magnusson, D., and Endler, N. S. (Eds.). *Personality at the Crossroads.* Hillsdale, N. J.: Lawrence Erlbaum Associates, 1977.
    Series of papers analyzing the methodological and substantive issues in personality research.

Manis, J. G., and Meltzer, B. N. *Symbolic Interaction: A Reader in Social Psychology.* Boston: Allyn & Bacon, 1967.
    Articles from both the Chicago and Iowa schools of symbolic interaction: Blumer, Cooley, Kuhn, among others.

Mischel, W. *Introduction to Personality.* 2d ed. New York: Holt, Rinehart & Winston, 1975.
    A readable and penetrating analysis on the many facets of personality.

Rosenberg, M. *Conceiving the Self.* New York: Basic Books, 1979.
    A clear and insightful interpretation, from both the sociological and psychological viewpoints of the self-concept and its development.

Staats, A. W. *Social Behaviorism.* Homewood, Ill.: Dorsey Press, 1975.
    Chapters 3, 4, and 8 are especially relevant to the topics of self-concept and personality.

Stryker, S. *Symbolic Interactionism.* Menlo Park, Calif.: Benjamin-Cummings, 1980.
    Considers the functioning of the self and role in the social structure.

Zurcher, L. A. *The Mutable Self: A Self-Concept for Social Change.* Beverly Hills, Calif.: Sage Publications, 1977.
    A well-documented study of how personality and the self can function in a changing society.

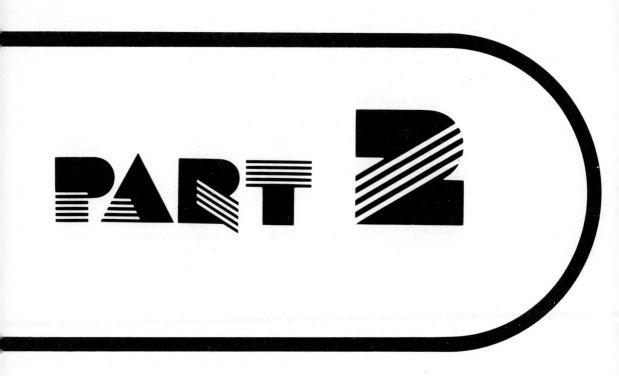

PART 2

The analysis of the cultural and psychological bases of the concepts of personality and the self in Part I provides the basis for examination of the dynamics of social behavior in Part II. Motivation and cognition are the central processes in determining how people act in social situations.

Cognition includes learning, perceiving, and symbolizing, but these functions cannot be detached from motives; indeed, no one aspect of human behavior can be isolated from any other. Each individual represents a gestalt of motives and cognitions which interact in a dynamic fashion to determine constantly changing behavior. Chapters 5 and 6 examine learning and perception and attribution, and Chapter 7 is concerned with the theories of social motivation.

Attitudes and values (Chapters 8 and 9), are both the product and the determinant of the interplay of cognition and motivation. Attitudes influence the direction of social and political life, and they provide feeling, tone, consistency, and meaning to behavior. The theory and measurement of attitudes and an understanding of their formation, persistence, and change comprise a major focal point in social psychology.

Attitudinal structures and other bases of cognition and motivation become conditioned by the language people acquire and modify for the next generation. Chapter 10 considers language as a symbolic means of communication which conditions the interaction of the culture and the individual.

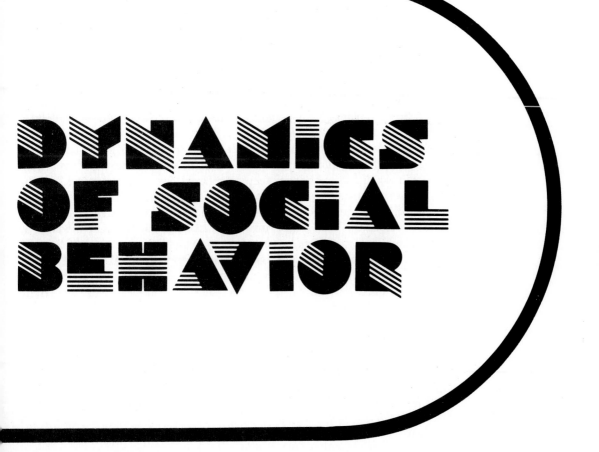

DYNAMICS OF SOCIAL BEHAVIOR

THE SOCIAL CONTEXT OF LEARNING

As one of the principal components of cognition, learning plays an important role in the dynamics of social behavior. Indeed, learning has been simply defined as being the modification of behavior through experience (Thorndike, 1911; Maples & Webster, 1980). In this sense, most social behavior is learned. All *changes* in behavior, however, are not necessarily learned; those that result from maturation or innate responses such as reflexes, for example, should not be considered learning (Hilgard & Bower, 1975). As children mature they crawl, stand, and walk, and pigeons peck at things and fly, but no one teaches a child to crawl or a pigeon to peck. These are innate responses which can be modified by influencing the environment in some fashion. A child's innate fear of falling, for example, is overcome when parents provide support as a toddler learns to walk.

Considerable controversy surrounds the issue of the extent to which human behavior is innate or learned. Ethologists such as Konrad Lorenz, who study animal behavior in evolutionary terms, agree with behaviorists that the learning process is quite similar in various species but disagree on the extent of the influence of innate behavior. Learning itself may be considered a biological process which interacts with, modifies, and is modfied by innate processes. This does not mean that genetics determines certain behaviors but rather that within certain environmental limits the influence of innate processes can be quite strong. Recent evidence, in fact, is encouraging the idea that genetics may have a considerably greater influence on social behaviors than has been generally assumed (Ho, Foch, & Plomin, 1980).

One way to analyze social behavior utilizes the stimulus-response (S–R) model identified in Chapter 1 as the basis of behaviorism. In this research process it is necessary first to isolate the relevant individual or group behaviors, as opposed to other behaviors. Then efforts are made to identify, isolate, and where possible, measure the rewards (or the fear of punishments) in the social situation that are reinforcing, or maintaining the social behavior.

It is difficult to identify and isolate the reinforcers in social situations because the number of potential reinforcers is legion, and any stimulus can have reinforcing properties for different reasons for different people. For example, members of a group may try hard to avoid ostracism from it because it offers various kinds of reinforcement. The group may be attractive to some members because they like the people in it and to others because of the social activities it provides. Different members might be afraid of being left out by not belonging, need the group's expertise to evaluate their own performance, find group membership necessary in order to engage in other desired activities (such as membership in a union), or feel the group provides the only security in a time of personal danger. (The attraction these reinforcements lend to group membership is examined in Chapter 13.)

It is also difficult to interpret the cause and the purpose of many social behaviors. For instance, you may laugh in a certain situation, not because you are amused but because you are attempting to placate a friend or ingratiate an influential person, or simply to release tension in an emotionally taxing situation.

The difficulties in interpreting complex human behavior with the stimulus-response model have led to the development of variations such as social learning. This social-psychological approach to learning utilizes conditioning concepts but stresses the importance of the person's internal processes of cognition and motivation in selecting and organizing the stimuli with which he or she is presented.

This chapter begins by describing the classical and instrumental conditioning approaches to learning. It explains the principles of reinforcement through rewards and punishments and points out the difficulties in applying them to higher-level learning in complex human events. The social-psychological approach to learning is described in terms of social learning theory, and modeling is suggested as an alternative to the use of either type of conditioning as a learning mechanism.

APPROACHES TO LEARNING: CONDITIONING AND PURPOSIVE

Psychologists have traditionally taken one of two viewpoints on learning. One is *behavioristic,* centering on the conditioned response, in which learning is regarded as fundamentally a mechanistic type of habit formation. The other view makes learning a *purposive* process involving cognition and understanding, rather than a mechanical behavior sequence.

Behavioristic approaches to learning were originated by E. L. Thorndike and John B. Watson and extended by theorists such as B. F. Skinner, who are sometimes referred to as neobehaviorists. The *stimulus response (S–R) model* evolved from the doctrine that all mental processes consist of connections between situations or stimuli presented to an organism (living being) and the organism's responses to them, which was described by Thorndike as *connectionism.* The broadened approach of neobehaviorists such as Clark Hull and Edwin Guthrie has been termed *associationism* (Maples & Webster, 1980).

Behavioristic learning draws heavily on the salivary studies of Ivan Pavlov. Several of his basic concepts should be familiar to any student of psychology—conditioning, extinction, generalization, discrimination, and reinforcement, for example. Skinner (1974) and his followers have distinguished between classical, or Pavlovian, and operant, or instrumental, conditioning. *Classical conditioning* treats the organism as relatively passive, responding involuntarily in terms of inborn or reflexive responses (salivation, withdrawal from shock). *Operant or instrumental conditioning* deals with the organism as it makes, or emits, active responses, such as a hungry rat striking a lever in order to receive food in an experimental box, or a child who learns to say "please" when asking for a cookie.

The purposive learning theorists, such as Wolfgang Köhler, E. C. Tolman, and Kurt Lewin, have taken the Gestalt theory position that learning is *molar,* or totalistic, rather than *molecular,* or segmental. They are concerned with the purposive and cognitive character of learning and view it in its relation to perception. They believe genuine learning is entirely different from mere conditioning and relies instead on the learner's own insight, understanding, organization, and reorganization to achieve meaning and transfer to other situations (Wertheimer, 1980).

Despite the advances that have been made in learning theory based on conditioning, social psychologists have had difficulty in applying it to the explanation of complex human social behavior. As Gibson (1951) pointed out, much of our knowledge of learning principles is derived from animals, often studied in isolation under precisely controlled laboratory conditions. In comparison, he maintained, human beings are motivated by a less primitive hedonism, or self-centered pleasure seeking (see Chapter 7). In many instances our learning is not in the direction of economy but rather the reverse: We learn to put on clothes in the summer to satisfy social norms, or we go out of our way to help other people. In the analysis of social motives, many needs are found to be in opposition to biological urges. In this sense, the importance some theorists have attached to the animal's search for the shortest path between two points within a maze does not apply to social behavior. Human responses are usually deferred, symbolic, and in the nature of detours, or what might be termed reaching a higher level, in the search for economy of action. Nevertheless, the concepts of conditioning have been influential in the analysis of social interaction (Stryker, 1977), as this chapter will demonstrate.

Learning Models

For the purposes of analyzing social behavior in behavioristic terms, two learning models have been devised which are oriented to the two types of conditioning defined above: classical and operant or instrumental. The *classical conditioning model* is used to examine the acquisition of behaviors which are mostly involuntary, such as withdrawal of an arm or leg which comes in contact with a painful stimulus. In the analysis of social behavior, however, this model is useful in studying the involuntary acquisition of emotions, attitudes, and values such as love, hate, fear, discomfort, and so on (see Chapter 8).

When a stimulus gives rise to a response, it is said to have *control* over the response. If you touch a hot stove you automatically withdraw your hand. Classical conditioning refers to the process by which a stimulus which does not naturally have control over a response gains some control by being paired with the

Theories of learning recognize that parents provide both the major stimulus and the model for the child's development. *Source:* © Theodore Anderson, 1981.

controlling stimulus. A little girl who is afraid of a doctor because she remembers the pain of inoculations, for example, may become fearful of all white coats similar to the one worn by the doctor and cry whenever someone approaches wearing one.

Classical conditioning can be involved in the large proportion of our behavior which is innate but modified by learning. For example, a response may become more prominent or occur more frequently because other expectancies or responses which are not useful to the organism have been eliminated. This might give the impression that a response is being learned when in fact the reverse is occurring; the response was always there, but other competing and interfering behaviors are being eliminated. This would be *zero-trial learning,* in which the learning is immediate and unavoidable (Burstein, 1977). Burstein points out that any species which required several trials to develop a fear response to the sight of a dinosaur would soon be extinct.

The learning model which is appropriate to voluntary behaviors is the *operant* or *instrumental conditioning model.* This model is very straightforward: Responses that are followed by positive states are more likely to be repeated, and responses that are followed by negative states are less likely to be repeated. For the purpose of understanding social behavior we will, of course, be most concerned with voluntary behaviors, which include any response a person can refuse to make. The distinction between voluntary and involuntary responses is arbitrary, however, and it is difficult at times to decide whether a particular response is in fact under voluntary control.

The existence of these two types of learning has led to controversy. The voluntary versus involuntary response distinction is not universally accepted; many scientists prefer to consider all learning as governed by the same set of processes. For our purposes, the distinction is appropriate for the forms of social behavior we are examining. Further, because we recognize the contributions of the Gestalt theorists, we will be more concerned with the cognitive and perceptual aspects of behavior change than is usual in strictly behavioristic accounts. People often find themselves attempting to understand and explain their actions after they have occurred. An observable response might be explained by means of one model, whereas the covert change in attitude or belief which might underlie the observable response could be best explained with the other.

While we will maintain the classical and instrumental distinction as primarily associated with involuntary and voluntary responses, respectively, we also recognize that voluntary is not a fixed category, and the person involved in the learning situation can observe responses which others cannot. In a persuasion situation, for example, a person may say things which lead us to believe that attitude change has occurred, when in fact the person's true attitude has not changed (Romer, 1979). True attitude change may eventually result from the reinforcement the person receives for saying what is expected.

We will deal with these issues in much greater detail in later chapters. The purpose here is to develop an understanding of how the principles of conditioning are applied in reinforcement as a learning mechanism.

LEARNING THROUGH REINFORCEMENT

The behaviorist theory of learning focuses on the process of reinforcement, which uses reward and punishment to bring about the repetition of responses. Most theorists would agree with Reynolds (1968) that reinforcers, or reinforcing stimuli, are "composed of environmental events which follow responses." Reinforcers assure or make probable the *recurrence* of a given response. As noted above, it is often difficult for the behavioral scientist attempting to analyze social behavior such as learning to isolate the reinforcer in the situation. In our present society, few human behaviors are concerned with primary (physiologically necessary) reinforcers, such as obtaining food or avoiding pain. Rather, human behavior is characteristically shaped and maintained by higher-order reinforcers such as the need for social support provided by the family and the school subcultures discussed in Chapter 3.

Stimuli, or environmental events, act as reinforcers when they increase the probability of future occurrence of a behavior, whenever the opportunity for such behavior exists. Such stimuli are said to be *rewards.* In contrast, the term for stimuli which act to suppress ongoing behavior and decrease the probability of future occurrence of that behavior is *punishers* or *punishments.*

Reinforcers also can be said to be positive or negative. When the reinforcer is positive, its presentation is an effective reinforcement for a response. When the reinforcer is negative, its *removal* or prevention works the same way. In this sense, rewards are not necessarily positive and punishments are not necessarily negative, depending on their use in the schedule of reinforcement.

Reinforcement Schedules

Many qualities of behavior have been found to be directly related to the nature of the schedule of reinforcement under which the behavior is established and maintained. A reinforcement schedule is a rule which specifies when and how often a given response will be reinforced.

A person's characteristic way of dealing with the environment, for example, may be described with such adjectives as hard-working, persevering, emotional, mature, or pigheaded—terms which usually refer to methods for handling situations where reinforcement is either absent or sparse. The behavior of a person who is superstitious, who cannot tolerate frustration, or who is able to postpone immediate gratification for delayed, presumably superior rewards is in each case responding to reinforcement which has been in some way restricted.

Reinforcement schedules are one way people vary their reinforcement of the behavior of those around them—or their own behavior, such as executives who reward themselves with a drink after a successful day in the marketplace (or, for that matter, after an unsuccessful day). The schedule may be *fixed,* as when parents give a child a dollar for each A received at the end of each grading period, or it may be *variable,* as when they give rewards for As one period but not another. Box 5–1 describes how two Hollywood stars administered reinforcements to a director on a fixed-interval schedule. Probably most rewards are given on a

Box 5–1
LIGHTS, CAMERA, REINFORCEMENT

When Peter Lorre and Humphrey Bogart were making the movie *Passage to Marseilles*, they decided that the director, Michael Curtiz, did not have a sense of humor. Lorre described how they undertook to "blackmail Curtiz into a sense of humor" in these terms:

> Curtiz has no sense of humor, particularly when shooting. He eats pictures and excretes pictures. Bogey and I are one-take people. In addition to that, we were not supposed to waste any film during the war. We came in from a horrible night. Bogey apologized to Warner. Then we went on the deck of a big boat set. Bogey was in the first shot. Mike says to Bogey, "You do this," and Bogey says, "I heard the most wonderful story," and tells some stupid, square joke, endless. Bogey gets through and Mike says, "Now we shoot." He made nineteen takes and didn't get it. He almost went out of his mind. Then I started to tell a long story. It took him (Curtiz) about two days to find out whenever he laughed he got the scene in one take and whenever he didn't laugh he didn't get a take. Two mornings later, Bogey and I, two staggering little figures, arrived on the big set. Mike saw us a block away on the set and he started laughing like crazy in advance.*

_____
*Ezra Godman, *The Fifty-Year Decline and Fall of Hollywood* (New York: Simon & Schuster, 1961), pp. 260–261.

variable-interval basis, whether the payoff is in terms of coins fed into a slot machine or sales made by a used car salesman in a month.

Generally, a reward reinforces behavior and a punishment suppresses it. But the *effect* of either kind of stimulus depends on whether it is being applied or being terminated. For example, electric shock may be considered punishment and will in fact suppress ongoing behavior. The termination of shock, however, is positive, and any response that was instrumental in terminating the punishment will be reinforced.

The application of a schedule of reward and punishment to complex human events is more complicated. For one thing, the effects of punishment are less readily predictable than are those of reward. An ex-convict may not find a better way of life because of either the negative reinforcement of confinement (being deprived of freedom) or the positive reinforcement of being released from prison. On the whole, obtaining rewards is positive. That is, a reinforcing event will increase the probability of repeating any responses associated with acquiring the reward.

Rather dramatic influences on behavior can be related to the type of reinforcement schedule a person has been exposed to. Depression, for example, has been found to be linked to the degree to which people *perceive* that their behavior results in given consequences. Those who consider that success or failure occurs independently of their efforts or by chance may develop an expectancy of having only limited control over events which influence their well-being.

In the laboratory, *learned helplessness,* a state in which later acquisition of a response shows a decrease because of previous exposure to uncontrollable stimuli with negative effects, has been proposed as a model for depression (Maier & Seligman, 1976). For example, persons who are exposed to aversive or negative outcomes such as unpleasant noises or failure at a task which was beyond their control have a generalized expectancy to do poorly on future tasks. Clinically depressed persons have shown improvement when they are given experience according to reinforcement schedules designed to increase persistence (Nation & Massad, 1978). Another procedure is to induce them to get angry and attempt to do something to change their environment, but such efforts must be reinforced so that patients perceive their behavior as being responsible for the change. Considerable research effort is being directed at discovering training procedures for treatment of forms of depression that appear to be similar to laboratory-induced helplessness. The related issue of the perception of control is discussed in the following chapter.

Response Interference, Suppression, and Extinction

Response *interference* refers to a situation in which one response interferes with another during ongoing behavior. The ongoing behavior is not weakened, but the probability that a particular response will be elicited falls. Response interference is often observed in a high state of arousal. Students who have crammed for important exams, for example, often "go blank" when their level of anxiety reaches a critical point. The probability that the material newly learned for the test will be recalled falls as the anxiety increases in taking the test.

In response *suppression,* a punishing stimulus is applied during the occurrence of a response one wishes to eliminate. A boy may find that making a hat out of a cutglass bowl has the effect of forcing his mother to direct her attention away from a younger sister and onto himself; he discovers that this behavior will be reinforced with the attention of his mother. The mother applies punishment every time she sees the boy touch the bowl and discovers that yelling at him has no effect but a slap will make him stop.

Punishing a response, however, does not extinguish it. In this case the boy must choose between not getting the positive reinforcement of attention or getting the reinforcement of being noticed but also being punished. The response remains suppressed only as long as the probability of punishment remains high. As soon as the child discovers that the mother no longer applies punishment for his behavior but does notice it, the suppressed behavior will return to its original strength.

Termination of the reinforcement which has established and maintained a conditioned response results in its *extinction.* The response is weakened when it is no longer followed by a positive state of affairs for a person, and its strength falls below that of some other response in the person's repertoire. At that time, the person's behavior changes; that is, he or she responds to a different aspect of the environment. Most people's performance becomes less eager or impressive when they no longer receive a reward, whether it is verbal, monetary, or of some other form.

Extinction may induce aggression against another organism, much as aversive or punishing stimulation will induce an aggressive attack by an animal upon another animal housed in the same cage. One experiment (Azrin, Hutchinson, & Hake, 1966) found that termination of food reinforcement elicits aggressive attack against another organism placed in the same experimental environment. Pigeons which had access to food and then experienced deprivation attacked a target pigeon, whereas pigeons which were satiated and had food accessible, or which were deprived but did not have food accessible, were far less likely to attack the target bird. In the same way, deprivation can trigger human beings to take aggressive or irrational action.

How strongly the person is reinforced and the frequency and predictability of reinforcement in the reinforcement schedule will determine the course of extinction. A student who expects to be regularly tested, and therefore rewarded or punished, will in most instances find some motivation in learning. Some students, however, find learning more challenging when they set their own reinforcement. For them, the reinforcement is in the learning itself. They are responding to the internal reinforcement which characterizes much higher-level learning.

HIGHER-LEVEL LEARNING

The principles of reinforcement as applied by the behaviorists have enhanced our understanding of how learning takes place. They fall short, however, when they are applied in efforts to account for complex human events, such as why a person chooses a given stimulus or a given response rather than another. A principal defect in behaviorist theory is the overemphasis on overt rewards and punishments, without sufficient attention to internal and external variables (Harré & Secord, 1972).

The relation of reward and punishment is very complex, as the preceding section demonstrated. If you think about it, it should not be difficult to give a half-dozen reasons for reading this book at the present moment. Students who enroll in a course with no interest in either the subject matter or the grades can find that their interest develops in spite of themselves. Their participation in the course is being reinforced in some way.

There are in fact two types of reinforcement: (1) *internal,* which the individual specifically experiences as having value, and (2) *external,* in which society or the cultural pattern assures a predictable value (see Box 5–2). The former is reinforcement as interpreted by the self; the latter, a more objective form, is reinforcement as judged by others. There is a close but not inescapable similarity between the two (Rotter, Chance, & Phares, 1972). A child may enjoy painting for its own sake, for example, but receive fuller satisfaction from parental praise.

It is not always certain whether the social stimuli that act as reinforcers for many aspects of our lives should be considered conditioned or unconditioned. Regardless, they at least act as "conditioned generalized reinforcers" (Ulrich & Mountjoy, 1972). Money is a good example of a *generalized reinforcer* because it is exceedingly resistant to extinction, and, like other powerful social stimuli, it functions independently of the unconditioned (naturally capable) reinforcers to which it was originally attached. Thus money, which was introduced as a means to acquire goods for consumption, can come to be enjoyed and valued for its own sake.

Box 5–2
REWARDS: NOW OR LATER?

One of the norms of Western society is that present pleasure should be postponed for future gratification. Millions of college students are motivated to plug away at books, exams, and term papers for four or more years instead of enjoying a youthful fling at independence, because they have been convinced that a college education will bring them later financial and social rewards. This aspect of the Protestant ethic is not accepted by all young people, however, as the number of high school and university dropouts indicates.

In order to analyze the cognitive and learning factors determining "self-imposed delay of reward," Walter Mischel had subjects select among alternatives varying in delay time and the perceived value of the object; that is, they had to choose immediate or remote rewards.* He found that the choice often rested on the individual's toleration of waiting and the degree to which promises or expectations in past experience had been met. Children shifted from immediate to future gratification as they grew older, becoming less apt to choose a smaller immediate reward over a larger one that would be delayed, for example.

Cultural differences are evident in the pattern of deferred gratification. Blacks in Trinidad were inclined to choose a smaller piece of candy on demand, whereas the East Indians living on the island would elect to wait for a larger piece of candy at a later time. In this case, research supported the cultural stereotype on the meaning of reward.

_____

*W. Mischel, *Introduction to Personality,* 2nd ed. (New York: Holt, Rinehart & Winston, 1976), pp. 155, 381–382.

In any case, learning is motivated by a number of rewards: social approval, status, money, and power, as well as the person's own sense of creativity and of

The skill of a race driver is acquired through a complex learning process, colored by social factors and innate abilities. *Source:* Allentown Call-Chronicle.

accomplishment. Social responses which relieve anxiety or tension also function as rewards. The average person engages in behavior that is approved by society at large. The approval acts as a positive reinforcer or reward, and the fear of loss of approval acts as a potential negative reinforcer or punishment.

Generally, punishments have been found to be less effective than rewards as motivations. In child psychology, for example, the superiority of positive reinforcement as an approach to training is stressed for several reasons. Punishment can introduce emotional conflicts into the learning situation, and in the resulting confusion or anxiety the wrong response may be acquired. A child who is penalized by a teacher for failing to memorize a verse, for example, may begin to dislike school, develop inferiority feelings, and become hostile toward more successful competitors. Most teachers (and most parents), through trial and error, reach an equilibrium between reward and punishment in their disciplinary regimes (see Chapter 3).

THE SOCIAL PSYCHOLOGY OF LEARNING

Psychologists and social scientists emphasize different aspects of learning. Psychologists are more interested in the processes of learning than the content—in how the individual learns rather than what is learned. Their work is involved with such concepts as conditioning, reinforcement, and generalization. Sociologists and ethnologists are more concerned with the product or content of learning than with how the learning takes place. They emphasize the mores, conventions, roles, and other aspects of the social heritage that pattern and modify a person's behavior in any society. Social psychologists believe both these emphases are essential to understanding learning or socialization. The two aspects are like the warp and woof of a fabric.

The social-psychological approach to learning has currently taken two prominent directions, in both of which learning is viewed as dependent to some extent on an intricate system of rewards and punishments. One is *social behaviorism,* a behavioral approach developed by Arthur Staats as an extension of the principles of conditioning in behaviorism and learning theory. Staats's carefully developed statement of principles (1975) is presented as a scientific paradigm whose body is to be fleshed out by further empirical and theoretical work. The other is the conceptualization of *social learning theory* by Albert Bandura (1977) as a means of studying how learning occurs in social situations through modeling and observation.

Principles of Social Learning Theory: Miller and Dollard

When Neal Miller, a psychologist, and John Dollard, a social anthropologist, introduced their concept of social learning in *Social Learning and Imitation* (1941), it was presented as a straightforward stimulus-response formulation in which learning occurs when a habit or S-R connection is formed. Their principal contribution to development of the theory was to synthesize and elaborate the learning concepts proposed by the neobehaviorist Clark Hull to fit the requirements of social psychology. In their analysis, the learning process consists of four basic factors: drive, cue, response, and reward, whereby an organism wants something, sees something, does something, and gets something.

Drive means "a strong stimulus which impels action." It may be *primary,* or innate, such as pain, hunger, or thirst, or *secondary,* or acquired, like ambition and desire for approval or money. Drive impels a person to respond, and *cues* determine when and where the person will respond and which response will be made. The cues of social stimuli vary quantitatively and qualitatively. They have a certain drive value, according to Miller and Dollard, depending on their strength, and a certain cue value, depending on their distinctiveness.

The Social Learning Sequence

The individual's motives, the stimulus situation, and how the response is made and reinforced are all involved in the learning process, according to Miller and Dollard. All behavior results from a functional relationship between the individual and the situation, whether in learning a new game, surviving the first day on a new job, or acquiring sexual responses (see Box 5–3). A stimulus does not itself lead automatically to a predictable response, nor does a person's drive, goal, or internal state, by itself, determine behavior.

The first steps in learning behavior, according to Miller and Dollard, are *perceiving the situation* and *initiating action.* At a party a boy stays away from the dance floor because he does not know how to dance. A girl comes up and says, "Come on, George; I'll teach you." He hesitates for a few seconds, then starts out on the dance floor with her.

Here is a social learning situation of medium complexity. On the organismic side is George's desire to learn to dance and thus conform to the accepted pattern of his social group, along with the fear that he may make a fool of himself. His perception of the situation includes awareness of the rhythm of the music and the ease with which others are dancing, a feeling that he is being regarded as a wallflower, and a favorable reaction toward the girl who offers to teach him—all of which contribute to his decision to enter the dance floor. A difference in any of these salient features might alter his behavior. The next step is learning to dance.

Making a new social response involves motor, verbal, emotional, and ideational components, as in learning to speak in public or to behave properly at a formal social function. Much of our learning difficulty, Miller and Dollard point out, focuses on making the first correct response. The initial tendency for a stimulus situation to evoke a response is very important. They therefore posit an initial hierarchy of responses, in which some responses are high up, or dominant, and others are weaker and less likely to occur. As a result of the learning process, which rewards certain responses and does not reward or punishes others, a new, revised hierarchy of responses is produced. After learning, a different reaction to a given stimulus situation occurs, since new responses have become dominant.

In the Miller and Dollard view, the final step in the learning sequence is *reinforcing the new response.* Once rewarded, the response must be reinforced or strengthened to some extent, and continued reinforcements produce a

Box 5–3
LEARNING THE SEXUAL SCRIPT

Scripts are symbolic plans or coordinators of behavior. Because they are separable from actual behavior, they can be modified without the need for overt responses by an individual. As responses are modified in moving from childhood through adolescence to adulthood, the specific meanings of given stimuli and responses change.

In sexual scripts, for example, the use of fantasy, the sense of detachment from or involvement with the other person, the distinction between sexual and nonsexual responses go beyond the situation at hand. Up to the first sexual encounter the script is manipulable within certain limits, as determined by the specific situation and the cultural setting. The capacity to use responses in a new situation that have been learned in another situation or at other moments in the life cycle is important in the process of human adaptation.

A man or woman's first coital experience may draw on models from literature, the mass media, or prior petting experiences, but the script for an encounter is adjusted to the tentative, exciting coordination of responses as the couple proceeds from kissing and petting to the removal of clothing to the more delicate operation of intercourse itself, all against the demands of timing as well as both internal and external stimuli. The cognitive processes of the couple include a number of subplans or "script elements" that have to be integrated and reassessed. Later, as new scripts emerge, a "connoisseurship" develops, and earlier skills must be removed from the contexts of the original learning. The therapeutic approach to sexual dysfunctions is a form of behavior modification which focuses on coordination of the sexual excitement cycles of both the man and the woman. The process of learning new sexual scripts can continue throughout the life cycle.

References: J. H. Gagnon, *Human Sexualities* (Glenview, Ill.: Scott, Foresman, & Co., 1977), pp. 185–189, and R. Gagnon, "The Meaning of Scripts in Sexual Responses," in *Nebraska Symposium on Motivation,* 1973 (Lincoln: University of Nebraska Press, 1973), p. 30, 54.

well-integrated habit. If, instead of reward, punishment occurs, the response tends to disappear or at least to remain latent.

The Miller and Dollard social learning theory implies that imitation is a form of instrumental conditioning, whereby parents and teachers furnish models for children to follow and reward them when they make a desired response. For example, parents teach children to say thank you by helping them perceive the appropriate situation: "When someone gives you a present . . ." and specifying the appropriate response: "Say thank you." When children size up the situation and respond correctly, the parents offer praise or otherwise reinforce the response. Much of a child's learning is unconscious, as in picking up new words, gestures, knowledge, attitudes and habits, but the basic principles of reinforcement apply.

Extensions of the Theory

Applied to psychotherapy, the Miller and Dollard theory considers therapy as a learning experience in which substitute responses are acquired (Dollard & Miller, 1950). The theory has also been applied to problems in education (Miller et al., 1958).

The approach has been criticized for failing to explain adequately imitative behavior in which the observer lacks the opportunity to acquire the response during the acquisition process, or "for which reinforcers are not delivered either to the models or the observers" (Bandura & Walters, 1963). Bandura and Walters analyzed a number of experiments in order to determine how social learning occurs in the course of socialization. Various models (aggressive, achievement-oriented, etc.) were imitated if rewards were administered to the models; models who were punished were not imitated. The observer, for example, might identify with an aggressor and thus reduce the fear of attack by becoming a perpetrator rather than an object of aggression. Some inmates in Nazi concentration camps tried to identify with the aggressor by imitating their guards, apparently to appear as tough as the Nazis and to secure certain benefits, but primarily to preserve their identities as individual human beings. A more familiar example is the child who plays at being a police officer or imitates an aggressive father figure.

Social Learning through Observation and Modeling

Bandura's concept of modeling might be thought of as a *third* type of learning, along with classical and instrumental conditioning. All three types have contributed to what has been called *behavior modification* (Bandura, 1969), a set of principles which emphasizes the means by which individuals can be helped to change their habit systems and even some aspects of their personalities (see Box 5–4).

The term *modeling* implies that more complex psychological events are taking place than in imitation. Modeling influences learning in at least three ways. First, the learner can acquire new response patterns simply by *observing* the actions of others. This kind of learning is most effective in the acquisition of novel kinds of behavior as yet unknown to the observer. Second, modeling may include the *inhibition* of previously acquired responses. Inhibition occurs when the learner fails to come through with the appropriate behavior or receives punishment for a wrong performance or failure to perform. To put the matter in other terms, there can be a "stimulus intensity reduction" (deCharms, 1968), when the person's drives are reduced by a punishment (or there can be the opposite, i.e., an increase of stimulus intensity by application of a reward). *Disinhibitory effects* are a third possibility. If the model makes a threatening or prohibited response and nothing

Box 5–4
ON CHANGING UNCHANGEABLE BEHAVIOR

Behavior modification is a psychological technique which has been popularly misunderstood as a way to make a person behave to serve dubious purposes. The grim effects on people to whom this technique has been applied were depicted in films like *A Clockwork Orange* and *The Manchurian Candidate,* which were once popular on campuses.

A more accurate description of behavior modification is a synthesis of techniques based on principles derived from experimental psychology which recognize that humans are influenced by the consequences of their behavior. The purpose is to alleviate the suffering of people and enhance their functioning.* Mental health workers, for example, use it to analyze a client's problems and determine the kinds of behavioral changes that could improve the client's family, social, or vocational life. Then they seek a means to encourage the client to adopt the change.

The approach is based on reinforcement through both rewards and punishments, as well as modeling. Aversive controls, such as electric shock or a distasteful drug, may be used cautiously as a means of eliminating a destructive behavior pattern like alcoholism or drug addiction. Fines, "time out," and loss of privileges are other means.

Systematic desensitization in order to eliminate or reduce anxiety is another form of behavior modification. Patients may be taught to relax and then introduced to increasingly disturbing situations until they can handle them. In punitive settings such as prison, the use of behavior modification is limited by the conditions of the institution.

_____

*S. S. Stolz, L. A. Wienckowski, and B. S. Brown, "Behavior Modification: A Perspective on Critical Issues," *American Psychologist,* 1975, *30,* 1027–1048.

adverse occurs (i.e., the model receives no punishment), the observer or learner may turn to what was formerly inhibited behavior. A teenager who was once punished for using vulgar words may later find a parent accepting this response.

Without going into a discussion of the technical aspects of these processes, which would go beyond the scope of this book, the simplest way to describe how modeling works is that it brings into play a wide range of cues, usually on a person-to-person basis. In the learning sequence "the actions of others acquire predictive value through their consequences" (Bandura, 1977, p. 87). We are especially sensitive to cues that have been seen as a means of reward, but these cues can have varying effects depending on whether or not they are given off by a model and whether or not they are reinforced. Generally we choose a response that is of proven value—imitating someone who is successful is safer than following the long, drawn-out, unpredictable process of trial and error.

For Bandura, modeling can occur without reinforcement. In complex, higher-level learning, it usually involves *symbolic processes* in which some degree of self-evaluation occurs. And, like most interpersonal behaviors, modeling implies input of the self (see Chapter 4). A related aspect of modeling is what Bandura (1977) calls "response consequences," that is, what a response means for later behavior. Thus, although conditioning theory is appropriate to social learning, it is not sufficient. The various anticipatory behaviors made by the person, the feedback from the environment, and the range of consequences a given response has for the learner also must be considered.

Symbolic learning is not explained by the *principle of contiguity,* or nearness in time or place of both stimulus and response (Guthrie, 1952), which underlies both classical and instrumental conditioning. Indeed, in modeling, conditioning is largely considered a descriptive concept of learning. Bandura (1974) points out that "So-called conditioned reactions are largely self-activated on the basis of learned expectations rather than automatically evoked. The critical factor, therefore, is not that events occur together in time, but that people learn to predict them and to summon up appropriate anticipatory reactions."

Learning Social Norms

In experiments using the principles of modeling to investigate the learning of social norms, some sequence of rewards and punishments, or both, is used, and the experimenter often serves as a model. Aronfreed (1968) devised an experiment in which fourth- and fifth-grade boys were asked to choose between two toys for a show-and-tell session. Boys who chose the more attractive of the toys were told by the experimenter, who served as a model, that it was for older boys, and boys who handled a toy were punished by being told they could not have it. The latter situation had the most inhibiting effects on the boys' tendency to play with the toy later (as checked by a covert observer). Punishment was less inhibiting for boys who merely touched the toy, and least inhibiting for those who were simply told the rules before they had a chance to touch it. This suggests that if norms are to be imposed on behavior there should be some overt "punishment," if only verbal. Moreover, transgressions are least likely if the subject is given a reason for the restriction.

In arriving at the learning theory underpinning this and related investigations of conduct and conscience, Aronfreed conceived of internal and external controls as providing the internal and external reinforcement of higher-level learning. The two types of controls allow for *internal* reinforcement, that is, stimuli having an interiorized value for inhibiting behavior, and for *external* reinforcement, or the reprimand received from the model. Without these reinforcements, the behavior is extinguished.

Studies of the acquisition of the social norm of conformity in the laboratory also depend on a system of rewards, especially feedback from the experimenter or model (Walker & Heyns, 1962). Like children, adults find that accepting the beliefs of others is a source of reward. We are not too likely to stand up for our own beliefs if it endangers a promotion, or we may no longer be welcome in our neighbor's house if we express attitudes contrary to the prejudices of the local community. Modeling is considered as a form of conformity in Chapter 11.

The process of reinforcement in social norms is even more complex when options are weighed as to the advantages and disadvantages of a given course of action. Learning is modifiable, but people differ in their capacity to change a mode of response. The flexibility of learning depends on the substitution of internal for external reinforcement. According to Bandura (1974), much of human behavior is regulated by "covert self-reinforcement."

According to Bandura's concept of *vicarious reinforcement,* we learn by observing the actions of others and the situations in which they are rewarded, ignored, or punished. Moreover, perceiving other people's outcomes can shape the nature and effectiveness of internal reinforcement by helping establish a norm for judging whether the treatment we usually receive is fair or unfair, or whether the consequences are to be considered a reward or a punishment. Our course of aggressiveness, for example, may be determined by what happens to others who are aggressive. The pattern of reinforcement will depend on the characteristics of the aggressor and those who are attacked, the kind and intensity of consequences and their justification, and the situations in which the aggressive act and its outcome occur.

Modeling and Aggression

Bandura's work on the effects of modeling on aggressive behavior bear out the research on socialization and aggression reported in Chapter 3. The choice of the authority or autonomy approach in the parental disciplinary regime is reflected in the choice between reward and punishment described above in the section on higher-level learning. The effects of punishment are especially uncertain and risky in training a child to avoid aggression, since a parent who physically punishes a child for aggressive activity may in fact provide a model of combativeness.

Bandura, Ross, and Ross (1961) found that aggression can be acquired by a child simply by witnessing an adult model responding in an aggressive way. Nursery school children were invited to join in a game during which half of the children were exposed to an adult model who spent nine minutes out of a ten-minute session in aggressive play with a 5-foot "Bobo" doll. The model kicked and threw the doll while making such verbal responses as "Sock him in the nose!" The other half of the children were exposed to a model who assembled Tinkertoys quietly and did not approach the Bobo doll. Following the modeling experience each child was given a frustrating experience to increase the likelihood of aggressive action. The method used to frustrate the children was to interrupt them shortly after they started playing with favored toys and forbidding further play with these toys.

The question investigated was: what type of play the children would engage in during a later 20-minute session. Toys available included dart guns, a mallet, and a three-foot Bobo doll, as well as crayons and coloring books, dolls, toy bears,

Contact sports like rugby violate our norms about touching another person yet provide an outlet for aggression. They also permit other emotions, like the mutual hugging that occurs after victory. *Source:* Lehigh University.

plastic farm animals, cars, and trucks. It was found that children who had observed the aggressive model made, on the average, 18 aggressive responses with the mallet, as compared with an average 0.5 response with the mallet for children who had observed the nonaggressive model.

Other studies (Bandura, Ross, & Ross, 1963) found that the model need not be physically present. Children watching an aggressive adult model on film became more aggressive in later play situations. Children are also affected by the consequences of the behavior for the adult model. If they witness the adult model being rewarded for aggressive responses, they will imitate that behavior more than if the adult is shown being punished for aggressiveness. More recent research also suggests that the model need not be visible as long as his or her behavior is known to be reinforced through reward. However, this kind of vicarious reinforcement has little effect unless the model has positive value because of his or her prestige or competence (Kuznicki & Greenfield, 1977).

Although the evidence indicates that models on films or television can serve as important influences on behavior (Bandura, 1967), further studies have shown that the effects differ depending on such factors as the sex, age, social class, and aggressiveness of children who view the programs. Preschoolers high in aggression were found to become more aggressive after watching aggressive films, whereas children who were initially less aggressive appeared relatively unaffected (Friedrich & Stein, 1973). Eron (1980) found that boys are more affected by TV violence because they tend to perceive television as expressing reality, whereas girls are more likely to perceive it as fantasy (see Box 14–1 in Chapter 14). Other investigators have found that *repeated* exposure to filmed material of either an aggressive or prosocial nature gives rise to reduced influence at some times and more persistent influence at others.

SUMMARY

Many social psychologists regard learning as the single most important variable in cognition, motivation, and behavior. Much of the scientific knowledge of learning has grown out of the concepts of classical and instrumental conditioning, particularly the latter. Experimental research on reinforcement and extinction has contributed much to the theories of learning, and rewards and punishments have been found to function as important conditioners of learning.

Analysis of the essential aspects of social learning provides a common ground for psychologists, who are primarily interested in the processes of learning, and sociologists and anthropologists, who are oriented to the content or product of learning. Difficulties encountered in attempts to apply the principles of conditioning to higher-level and social learning have led to the development of such concepts as internal and external reinforcement, imitation, observational learning, and modeling.

WORDS TO REMEMBER

Aggression. Responses indicating anger, often motivated by some thwarting or frustration; aggressiveness is a deep-seated social motive, possibly with an indirect biological basis.

Behavior modification. The viewpoint according to which responses can be changed through conditioning and related theories of reinforcement.

Behaviorism. In learning theory, behaviorism assumes that conditioning or the *stimulus-response model* can account for all learning. Whereas behaviorism stems from J. B. Watson, *neobehaviorism* is linked to the more sophisticated concepts of B. F. Skinner.

Classical conditioning. Theory of conditioning (originally presented by Ivan Pavlov) which maintains that the organism responds "passively" to a substitute stimulus, rather than making a "new" response. Classical conditioning refers to the original Pavlovian experiments in which the organism passively or involuntarily accepted a stimulus (e.g., the ringing of a bell) to elicit a response (salivation).

Conditioning. Theory of learning explained in terms of stimulus-response associations. (See *behaviorism; classical conditioning; instrumental conditioning; operant conditioning.*)

Contiguity. The principle of nearness; that is, people acquire, by conditioning, responses that are linked in time or space with a given stimulus, or, more accurately, associate a substitute stimulus for the natural stimulus. Examples are Pavlov's dog's salivation in response to the bell that had been presented at the time food was given, or the word *light* taking

on a negative meaning because it was formerly preceded by an electric shock.

Extinction. In learning theory, the disappearance of a given response because of the lack of reinforcement or reward.

Implicit/explicit response. A covert, private, or suspended response (implicit), in contrast to an open or direct response (explicit); a thought, feeling, or nerve impulse (implicit), as compared to speaking a word or twitching a muscle (explicit).

Instrumental conditioning. Process by which an organism makes an active or voluntary response in order to avoid punishment or to secure a reward.

Internal/external reinforcement. The process of reinforcement as viewed from the reward being an end in itself (intrinsic) in contrast to a material (extrinsic) reward such as receiving a higher wage.

Intrinsic/extrinsic reward. A reward that is an end in itself, such as finding satisfaction in the job itself (intrinsic), in contrast to a material reward, such as receiving a higher wage (extrinsic).

Model. Person from whom others derive their standards of behavior, as in imitation; for children, most often a parent, teacher, or sibling.

Modeling. Imitating another person in the socialization process, or the complex learning behavior by which people pick up cues from a significant person (model) in the environment.

Operant conditioning. Process by which the individual becomes more likely to make a given response because a reward is expected; the probability a response will be increased through the availability of reinforcement or decreased by its absence.

Reinforcement. Any stimulus or response, usually a reward, that facilitates or makes more probable the retention or repetition of a specific behavior. A *reinforcement schedule* is a rule which specifies when and how often a given response will be reinforced.

Social learning theory. An approach to individual development and socialization which stresses imitation, observational learning, and modeling.

QUESTIONS FOR DISCUSSION

1. How are the different learning models related to the types of conditioning? What are the principal uses of these models in social psychology?
2. Explain how the principles of conditioning are applied in using reinforcement as a learning mechanism.
3. What functions do reinforcement schedules serve?
4. How and why does extinction occur? How can resistance to extinction be promoted?
5. What difficulties are encountered in extending the behaviorist concepts of conditioning to higher-level learning?
6. Explain the differences between external and internal reinforcement.
7. How did Miller and Dollard explain the sequence of social learning? Give an example from your own experience.
8. What are the differences between imitation (Dollard and Miller) and modeling (Bandura)?
9. In what ways does modeling influence learning?
10. In your opinion, is behavior modification an ethical application of social psychology?
11. How might self-reinforcement enter into learning?

READINGS

Bandura, A. *Social Learning Theory.* Englewood Cliffs, N. J.: Prentice-Hall, 1977.
    A readable and yet highly analytical explanation of modeling and observational learning.
Bartlett, F. C. *Remembering.* Cambridge, England: Cambridge University Press, 1932.
    Classic study of experiments on the social factors in memory.
Gazda, G. M., and Corsini, R. J. (Eds.). *Theories of Learning: A Comparative Approach.* Itasca, Ill.: F. E. Peacock, Publishers, 1980.
    Analyses of the leading learning theories in modern psychology. Most pertinent to this chapter are operant (Skinner), Gestalt (Wertheimer), observational (Bandura), and social learning (Rotter).
Miller, N. E., and Dollard, J. *Social Learning and Imitation.* New Haven, Conn.: Yale University Press, 1941.
    One of the more insightful approaches to

learning in social settings.

Mowrer, O. H. *Learning Theory and Personality Dynamics.* New York: Ronald Press, 1950. A work for the more advanced student; among the more interesting analyses is one of Edgar Allan Poe from a semi-Freudian viewpoint.

Rotter, J. B. *Social Learning and Clinical Psychology.* Englewood Cliffs, N. J.: Prentice-Hall, 1954. A systematic work that attempts to integrate cognitive theory with the psychology of personality.

Skinner, B. F. *About Behaviorism.* New York: Alfred A. Knopf, 1974. Chapters 1–6 present in simple language the neobehavioristic outlook on innate and operant behavior, along with related topics.

Staats, A. W. *Social Behaviorism.* Homewood, Ill.: Dorsey Press, 1975. One of the more complete studies of conditioning as an explanatory principle in social behaviorism.

SOCIAL PERCEPTION AND ATTRIBUTION

In the social interaction viewpoint developed in Chapter 4, our personality structure and the sociocultural framework in which we live and interact with others guide our behavior. And in the behavioristic and social learning viewpoints developed in Chapter 5, we learn through experience that when we behave in a manner others approve of, our behavior is positively reinforced with rewards in the form of acceptance, praise, and the like; when they disapprove of our behavior it is negatively reinforced, or punished, by the withdrawal of these same rewards.

Our behavior is also regulated by another of the principal components of cognition, our perceptions about ourselves and others. We act differently toward a person we think is brilliant than we do toward one we consider stupid. When we interact with someone who we think has some power over the rewards we are to receive, we carefully monitor and control our behavior. If our perceptions of others are inaccurate, prejudice, fear, hate, distrust, and similar social errors can result.

In interpreting the stimulus-response model described in Chapter 5, it is often assumed that a stimulus situation has an objective existence which different individuals will interpret or perceive in identical ways, although they may respond to it differently. But a given situation, particularly a social one, is never *psychologically* identical for various people. Each individual perceives and interprets a situation via her or his own sensory capacities, attention, past experience, motives, attitudes, expectations, and the like—that is, in terms of a unique pattern of experience and personality. A comic's patter, for example, may seem amusing to one person, boring to another, crude to another, and insulting to a fourth person. A newcomer to a social group may be considered very attractive by one member, rather conventional by another, and actually obnoxious by a third.

This subjective, or *phenomenological,* view does not mean that the objective, or observable, properties of stimulus situations or interactions with others are not also important. The appearance and behavior of the people present—their actions, speech, laughter, and so on—significantly affect the way a phenomenon will be perceived. As Bem's (1972) self-perception theory described in Chapter 4 points out, people judge themselves and others the same way—by observing behavior. But objective actions (objective in the sense that they could be recorded on film and tape) never completely determine an observer's interpretation. They always are perceived in a context of the observer's personal experiences and tendencies, past and present.

Whether the situation, the traits of the person, or the interaction between the two is the stable determiner of behavior is a question which has a long history (Epstein, 1979). As Chapter 4 points out, *trait theorists* argue that in the world at large people determine their own environment to a great extent, and this maintains the stability of their personalities. *Situationists* maintain that individuals primarily respond to the situation itself, and their personality and behavior, including their perceptions, change as the situation demands. *Behaviorists* are prone to believe that behavior is predictable, and they typically classify behavior by people rather than by situations. *Interactionists* argue that the question of person versus situation is a meaningless one, as behavior is always a joint function of both the person and the situation. The relation between personality factors and the socioeconomic setting, or between predispositional and situational factors, is recognized throughout this text.

These issues are complicated by the fact that the procedures used to study a social question may presuppose the answers that are reached. If the idea that people generally select their own environments is accepted, for example, studying the problem in artificial environments set up in ways to facilitate observation would be useless. Similarly, focusing on a few behaviors or personality variables may give the impression that behavior is less stable than it actually is, because each is a part of a complex whole.

The stability of personality and the environment as effects on behavior is a major concern of this chapter. The importance an individual attributes to any particular variable or class of variables is itself a function of the factors which encourage his or her observation of phenomena in particular ways. In some instances the environment may have an overwhelming effect, and in others the personality structure operates more strongly. All perceptual experiences have in common a social interaction between the individual and the socioeconomic setting.

The chapter begins by defining the terms used in examining the basic concepts of perception and attribution. Then the personal characteristics of the perceiver which affect her or his perception of self and others are described: physical characteristics and personality, wants and needs, and sets and expectations. The environmental influences which affect the perceiver's interpretation of behavior are also described. The section on interpersonal relationships describes characteristics of social interactions which influence the perceiver's evaluations of the other person; these include affective bonds and status differentials, physical characteristics and expressions of the other person, and the order and amount of information communicated in the interaction. Where attribution of emotions is concerned, manipulation of this information can lead to misattribution, and attempts to achieve cognitive consistency are related, as the next section points out. The perception of two basic concepts in attribution theory—causality and freedom—is explored in the final sections of the chapter.

BASIC CONCEPTS OF PERCEPTION AND ATTRIBUTION

The Individual and the Stimulus World

Perception is the process whereby the individual structures the stimuli received from the environment and gives them meaning in terms of his or her own personality and socialization. Because the perceptual world is so massive and complex, each person can select only a limited number of stimuli. A person's perceptual orientation or readiness to perceive a given event or a certain range of stimuli is called a *set* (Bruner, 1958). This set or expectancy is influenced, as in all behavior, by: (1) the neurological state and physiological need at a given moment, (2) relevant previous learning, (3) an incentive or goal, and (4) the environmental situation in which individuals find themselves.

People's perceptions are constantly being incorporated into their knowledge of the world. The term *cognition,* which signifies a combination of perception, learning, thinking, and belief, can be considered as perception in a wider frame of reference. Perceivers must superimpose meaning on their universe by organizing their perceptions into what are for them logical structures. In social psychology, it is impossible to detach perception from cognition.

Each environmental event, or stimulus, is perceived in the context of a specific stimulus situation. But, as Rock (1975) says, the individual constantly reorganizes "potentially familiar configurations" in order to arrive at some kind of equilibrium or cognitive consistency, and this reorganization depends on verbal events which occur after the stimulus has been perceived. In other words, as pointed out in the topic of self-perception in Chapter 4, we do not know what we think about an issue until we talk about it.

Thus the individual integrates information about a stimulus object in order to form an impression of it. There are several ideas about how this is accomplished. One idea is that the information is added together, so that, for example, if "patient" is considered a moderately favorable trait and "well-spoken" is considered highly favorable, the description "patient, well-spoken" creates a more favorable impression than simply "well-spoken." Another theory is that stimulus information is averaged rather than added. In this example, adding the moderately favorable trait to the highly favorable trait would give a less favorable rating than the highly favorable trait alone would provide.

Even simple behaviors are subject to numerous revised attributions. Depending on what is known of the situation when one person touches another, for example, the touch could be interpreted as conveying love, caring, power, dominance, defense, decision, and so on. Gergen (1980) argues that the action itself tells very little. In fact as we will point out in later chapters, the people involved in a stimulus situation often have little understanding of the meaning of the behavior. When the behavior of two persons involved in an incident is observed by two other people, four different attributions may be made, all of which will influence future behavior.

Interpersonal Perception

In the same way self-perception is achieved by observing our own behavior as opposed to the behaviors of others and attributing thoughts and feelings to it (see Chapter 4), our perception of others is achieved by observing their behavior and attributing intentions, feelings, motivations, and so on to them, although we cannot actually observe these things. Thus we do not simply perceive people as being heavy or slight, fair or dark, tall or short; we make *inferences* about people with these characteristics and conclude they must be pleasant or nasty, aggressive or altruistic, according to our own standards.

The observer influences the person who is perceived, but the perceived person also responds to the observer. What is being evaluated, then, is an interaction and not, strictly speaking, a person, as the label *interpersonal perception* would imply. Perceivers not only interact with the perceived but project something of themselves into the situation. The person being perceived is communicating to the perceiver and is responding to the latter's behavior. It is a dynamic system that changes whenever change occurs in either or both persons in the situation.

The perception of another person can involve judgment based upon ever-increasing levels of abstraction and numbers of cues. Judgments of *physical characteristics* represent the lowest level (e.g., skin color, weight, height, length of nose). *Behavioral traits* or dispositions represent the next highest level of interpersonal perception. Judgments as to a person's kindness, shyness, or aggressiveness bring into play the consideration of many cues in the interpersonal situation. The third and highest level of interpersonal perception involves *attribution,* or the perceiver's assignment of behavioral tendencies or personality traits to the perceived person. There are few specific cues to justify perceptions of others' purposes, intentions, motivations, and emotions, but they are of primary importance to the perceivers because they serve as guides for her or his own behavior. We are usually very concerned about such judgments.

An experimenter may obtain from several subjects consistent descriptions of the physical or even personality traits they observe in another person. The responses the subjects make to the perceived person, however, will vary with their inferences about that person's intention. In this sense interpersonal perception is

In highly formalized settings like the United Nations, interpersonal perception usually assumes a stereotyped approach, as influenced by protocol. However, in the heat of debate personality as well as ideology shape the attribution process. Members perceive each other in the context of their cultural background and power struggles between states. *Source:* United Nations.

an instrumental conditioning, or voluntary, response which influences the probability of reinforcement in a social situation. Perceivers make judgments of other persons which serve as a guide for their own behavior in the interpersonal situation.

Research on the integration of stimulus information in interpersonal perception has attempted to find agreement between the observed results and the predictions made by either the additive or the averaging model of stimulus combination.

Anderson (1965) presented subjects with a combination of two or four adjectives describing a person and had them indicate by a rating between 0 and 100 how much they would like or dislike such a person. It was found that the liking was greater when four rather than two highly favorable adjectives were used, and dislike was greater when four rather than two highly unfavorable terms were used. This suggests an additive explanation. However, when two moderately favorable adjectives were added to two highly favorable adjectives, the result was less favorable; and when two moderately unfavorable adjectives were added to two highly unfavorable adjectives, the results depressed the unfavorability. In both of these cases, the rating change suggests averaging. Thus neither the adding nor the averaging theory was found to be entirely correct as an explanation.

Anderson (1968) later proposed that a *weighted* averaging model is most appropriate, since two people tend to give relatively high weights to highly positive or highly negative traits. Negative traits have been found to affect impressions more than positive traits (Warr, 1974), which implies that a positive impression is easier to change than a negative one.

FACTORS AFFECTING THE PERCEIVER

The ways people perceive themselves, other people, and objects and events are influenced by their own personal characteristics: physical appearance and personality, wants and needs, and sets and expectations. The environment in which the evaluation is made also affects the interpretation of behavior.

Physical Characteristics and Personality

A person who is 6 feet tall would probably not perceive "average height" in the same way a person 5 feet tall would. In the same way, robust and frail people could be expected to perceive bodily cues differently.

Some research has been directed at determining the effects of individual differences on perception. Sarbin (1954), for example, found that the sex of the perceiver influences the categories used in describing another person. Females tended to use personality variables such as "aggressive" or "pleasant" in describing people, whereas males tended to use role categories such as "chairman" or "doctor." In another study (Tagiuri, 1969), females' descriptions focused on physical appearance, social skills, nurturant behavior, and happiness, whereas males emphasized aggression, nonconformity, and physical skills.

Females also tended to be more intuitive, to stereotype others, and to seek out more information about other people than males did.

Basic personality differences also have been found to influence a person's perceptions of others. Sanford (1952) selected a sample of people who scored very high and very low on an authoritarian scale (representing roughly the top and bottom 5 percent of 963 subjects) and asked them to state why Franklin D. Roosevelt was a good leader. Authoritarians at the top of the scale emphasized Roosevelt's ability to secure material benefits for citizens, and equalitarians (at the bottom) emphasized his democratic leadership, warmth, and humanitarian qualities. Thus, though both groups admired Roosevelt, they had different reasons for doing so, and it can be assumed that they perceived him differently.

Wants and Needs

Experiments also have demonstrated the effects of the perceiver's needs and values on perception. When both hungry and satiated subjects were shown ambiguous figures and asked to identify them, those who were hungry perceived significantly more items of food among the figures than those who were satiated (Levine, Chein, & Murphy, 1942). Children from poor American homes were found to overestimate the physical size of a quarter coin, and 30 percent of black American children identified a rat as a bear (Hampden-Turner, 1974). Perceptual accentuation, or the overestimation of the size of a stimulus, seems to occur primarily when the stimulus is valuable and when its value is directly related to its physical size (Tajfel, 1969).

In interpersonal perception, perceptual distortions have been found to result from the emotional state of the perceiver. In one experiment (Bramel, 1962), some of the subjects were given several painful shocks while watching a film. When the subjects were asked to rate the anxiousness of the characters in the film, those who had received the shocks rated the characters as significantly more anxious than subjects who had not been shocked.

Studies such as this one indicate that people project onto others emotional states that are similar to their own, as well as complementary states (if one is fearful, for example, perceiving another person to be ominous complements that fear). The attributive projection of one's own emotional state onto other persons or properties of the environment can be *defensive;* when we see others as possessing our own negative characteristics, the seriousness of our imperfections is reduced, and we generally attribute more unfavorable than favorable characteristics to others (Chalus, 1978). It also can be *egotistical;* when we are successful we are more likely to attribute the cause to ourselves, and when we fail we are more likely to attribute the cause to some other person or condition. Rosenfield and Stephan (1978) found this type of attribution to be equally prevalent for males and females.

Defensive attribution can assume different directions. For instance, among hospital patients who had been paralyzed in accidents, those who tended to blame another individual were identified as "poor copers," and those who blamed themselves or attributed their situations to fate, chance, or predestination were identified as "good copers" (Bulman & Wortman, 1977). The coping was rated by a social worker or nurse familiar with each victim's adjustment.

The tendency to attribute failure to external causes may also take the form of emotional attribution, in which people evaluate as disturbing or arousing certain features of the environment which were present when they failed. In one study (Averill, DeWitt, & Zimmer, 1978), subjects worked on puzzles in the presence of disturbing photographs of mutilated corpses and arousing photographs of nudes. Subjects rated the nudes more attractive and the corpses more disturbing after they failed to solve the puzzles, apparently to find an environmental cause of their failure.

Defensive attribution is shaped by the needs of the perceiver. An experiment which tested differential social perception and attribution of violence (Duncan, 1976) found that whites labeled a shoving scene as violent more frequently when a black person was shown doing the shoving than when a white person was portrayed in this role. News events—a bombing in Belfast, a Palestinian or Israeli raid, the seizure of hostages in an embassy—are perceived differently according to each person's ethnic background, geographic location, and personality.

Recent work on the effects of arousal on attribution indicates that people often do not attribute the cause of arousal accurately. Zillman (1980) asked subjects to perform vigorous exercise and indicate when they thought their blood pressure had returned to normal. If they were presented with erotic or aggressive stimuli before their blood pressure had actually normalized but after they *said* they had recovered from the exertion, their arousal appeared to summate, and they reacted more to the stimuli. They attribute all their arousal, part of which resulted from the physical exercise, to the erotic or aggressive stimuli.

This adding of arousal from different sources is consistent with the additive model of impression formation described above, and it may offer a simple explanation for some other effects we have discussed. For example, the increase in aggression for initially aggressive children who watch violent TV programs may be due to the summation of arousal. Similarly, the influence of frustration on aggression may be the result of added arousal. This interesting area of research indicates that people's attributions may be grossly in error. It is important to note, however, that even though many attributions are objectively wrong, they are perceived as true for the person and strongly influence behavior. The topic of attribution and the perception of causality is examined further in a later section of this chapter.

Sets and Expectations

An interpersonal situation is complex in the sense that the cues available to the perceiver are almost legion. The degree of attention paid to these cues is not a hit-or-miss proposition but is a function of the perceiver's goals, sets, and expectations, as suggested in Box 6–1. Jones and Thibaut (1958) suggest that situations and goals establish *mental sets,* which in turn influence attention to certain cues.

Box 6–1
DANGEROUS BUT BEAUTIFUL

The attractiveness of another person affects how we view his or her transgressions. In experiments, a judge in a laboratory setting is likely to go easier on attractive defendants. In real life, too, law enforcement officers are more prone to arrest physically unappealing persons. Class considerations also are relevant as shown in the treatment of the accused in criminal justice proceedings.

In one study, 60 male and 60 female undergraduates were presented with an account of a criminal violation, and each was asked to sentence the defendant to a term of imprisonment.* One third of the subjects were led to think that the defendant was physically attractive, another third were told that the defendant was unattractive, and the remaining third received no information on physical appearance. Cutting across the attractiveness factor, half of the subjects were given a written account of an attractiveness-unrelated crime (a burglary), and the remainder were given an account of an attractiveness-related crime (a swindle). The hypothesis of the investigators was that the judges would be more lenient toward the attractive defendant if the crime was unrelated to the attractiveness, and harsher judgments would be meted out when the attractiveness of the defendant was involved. The hypothesis was confirmed.

_____

*H. Sigall and N. Ostrove, "Beautiful but Dangerous: Effects of Offender Attribution," *Journal of Personality and Social Psychology,* 1975, *31,* 410-44.

According to the Chalus (1978) defensive attribution study cited above, people tend to attribute more unfavorable than favorable characteristics to others. But Gage and Cronbach (1955) found that because people attend to the information about others which is consistent with their own personal orientations, they differ in their tendency to rate other persons favorably or unfavorably. People who expect to like others emphasize positive traits or evaluate traits positively. Those who expect to dislike others, or perhaps expect to be disliked, emphasize anything negative or unattractive in others. On the average, D. O. Sears (1976) found that people tend to evaluate others favorably; a *positivity bias* was found more often in evaluations of people than of objects.

Judgment of failure is one mental set which has been investigated. In one experiment, failure due to factors beyond the control of the individual was judged less negatively than failure attributable to disinterest or negligence (Jones & deCharms, 1958b). When a task depends on the contribution of all the members of a team, the individual who fails will have a greater "negative halo" than when the failure is in an individual task, such as performance on an intelligence test (Jones & deCharms, 1958a). And in a group setting a person who fails is perceived as even less dependable when the failure prevents others from attaining rewards.

When a person relies on sets or expectations and ignores the actual cues received from a stimulus object, inadequate or false perceptions, or *misattributions,* are likely to result. In interpersonal perception, a *stereotype,* or standardized, uncritical response to another person leads to erroneous perception largely by magnifying or depreciating the information about the other person that the cues in the interaction provide.

As research in interpersonal perception has shifted to interest in how perceivers actively process stimuli to create meaning (Hastorf et al., 1970), two types of stability in perceptions have been differentiated. *Inferential* stability provides a basis for making predictions with minimal infomation. The stereotype, therefore, is an inferential device which is used in making predictions about various persons on the basis of the groups to which they belong or the categories they represent. (Stereotypes are considered further in Chapter 8.) *Attributional* stability provides a basis for predicting the kind of behavior the perceiver can expect from a given person, judged by a sample of responses that have already been witnessed. The latter basis is less risky than inferential stability, but it is still problematical. Whatever its basis, attribution is a means of imposing order or meaning on our world. In this connection, perceptual defense is one phase of the struggle for perceptual clarity on the part of the individual (Postman, Bruner, & McGinnies, 1948). For probably all human beings, but especially for the neurotically inclined, there exists the necessity of integrating one's feelings of insecurity into a more stable structure. Homeostasis is demonstrated in perceptual processes as it is in other psychological functions.

Environmental Influences and Labeling

The environment can have an overwhelming effect on the perceiver's interpretation of behavior. In some environments perceptions of behavior can be determined by the social context and the labels within which the behavior occurs.

In one interesting experiment (Rosenhan, 1973), eight pseudopatients who were experimental confederates admitted themselves to mental hospitals complaining they had been hearing voices. They offered true accounts of their life histories during the admitting interview but falsified their names, present symptoms, and occupations, so the histories were not seriously pathological in any way. After being admitted to the psychiatric ward, the pseudopatients "ceased simulating *any* symptoms of abnormality," although some had brief periods of nervousness and anxiety resulting from the unique experience. They acted normally, talked with other patients, and recorded observations. About one third of the bona fide patients in one sample voiced suspicion that the pseudopatients were sane, but the hospital staff diagnosed all but one as schizophrenic, and upon discharge the diagnosis was "schizophrenia, in remission."

A second study was conducted in which hospital staff were told that pseudopatients would be admitting themselves, although none actually did.

The importance the crowd attributes to the personal appearance of a political candidate is affected by the show of force from police and the rebel flag. *Source:* Magnum Photos, Inc.

Evaluations on 193 bona fide patients were obtained from every staff member with whom the patients had come in contact. About 10 percent of the patients were judged to be pseudopatients by at least one psychiatrist, and about 20 percent were considered pseudopatients by at least one member of the staff. Rosenhan concludes, "We cannot distinguish the sane from the insane in psychiatric hospitals. The hospital itself imposes a special environment in which the meaning of the behavior can easily be misunderstood." Thus the behavior of the pseudopatients was perceived in a manner which was consistent with the environmental context in which it was taking place.

It has been suggested that many psychiatric institutions are structured to "manufacture madness" (Szasz, 1970). When patients are expected to be insane and act crazy, they accept that perception of themselves. When they act in a manner which is consistent with the expectations of the hospital staff, they are reinforced with attention, treatment, and understanding. This can create a situation in which patients must behave in an expected manner to be considered as responding to treatment. They must get sick to be considered cured.

Another kind of experiment also demonstrated that the social context in which behavior occurs can markedly affect the way the behavior is perceived (Naftolin, Ware, & Donnelly, 1973). Psychiatrists, psychologists, and social worker-educators at a teaching conference heard a "Doctor Fox" lecture the group on "Mathematical Game Theory as Applied to Physical Education." Dr. Fox, introduced as an authority on the application of mathematics to human behavior, was in fact an actor instructed to talk enthusiastically and nonsubstantively on a topic about which he knew nothing. During the lecture and the question-and-answer period which followed, the actor made ample use of double-talk, contradictory statements, and humor. When the audience was asked to evaluate the lecturer, the results clearly showed that an audience of highly trained subjects had been fooled. They evaluated the lecturer favorably and said that the lecture had stimulated their thinking. Thus they attributed competence and knowledge to a person who happened to be in a social context in which knowledge and competence were expected.

INTERPERSONAL PERCEPTION

In interpersonal perception, the perceiver's evaluation of the other person is affected by certain factors in the stimulus situation, such as affective bonds and status differentials. The physical characteristics and expressions of the other person and the order and amount of information transmitted in the interaction also influence perception.

Affective Bonds

Certain types of affective bonds between persons seem to be easily recognized by the perceiver. For example, a "liking relationship" is more accurately perceived than a "disliking bond," according to a study by Tagiuri, Bruner, & Blake (1958) in which groups of subjects met for 12 sessions to discuss general topics. Each subject was then asked to state which participants they liked most and least and to indicate those who they thought liked or disliked them. According to the findings, these judgments were not mere guesses; rather they significantly exceeded chance accuracy. In addition, liking was significantly more accurately perceived than was disliking. This suggests that cues necessary for the perception of dislike may either be denied by the perceiver or politely masked by the other person.

Many factors can operate on the perceiver to influence the perception of an affective bond. Members of small groups working on common tasks tend to feel influenced by, and feel that they influence, people they like (Tagiuri & Kogan, 1960). The reverse also holds; that is, people tend to like those whom they influence and by whom they feel influenced, as the evidence on interpersonal attraction and group cohesion in Chapter 13 will show. In a study of the acquaintance process, Newcomb (1961, 1978) found a high probability that people will like and feel liked by those whose attitudes are similar to their own. Thus the perception of liking seems to be influenced by interpersonal bonds or relationships which are compatible with a liking relationship.

The perception and development of a positive interpersonal relationship is a complex process influenced by the perceiver, the perceived, and the environment. In a study of first impressions, Clore (1977) had groups of six women students hold five-minute get-acquainted conversations, after which each one was asked about the conversation and the other participants. Women who were taller, richer (measured by father's occupation), and more sociable (drinkers), and those who made many positive but few negative statements were most liked. Perceivers who said they liked others also enjoyed the conversation, talked a lot about themselves, made few negative statements, and did not ask many questions.

The perception of physical characteristics of people as influenced by affective bonds between the perceiver and the other person has been considered in a number of studies. The method used in some of these is to gradually distort the physical perception of the perceiver by such devices as a trapezoidal room, and then determine if and when the perceiver notices it. Ittelson and Slack (1958) found that the perceived distortion is inversely related to the significance of the relationship between the perceiver and the perceived. Thus an authority figure or a newlywed partner (see the Honi study in Box 6–2) does not appear to become distorted to the same degree as a less significant person. In ambiguous situations, persons important to the observer may serve as frames of reference and thus appear less distorted than others. Other factors, including familiarity and emotional loading, have also been found to influence the degree of perceived distortion.

Status Differentials

Perception is more complex when it involves inferences about the unseen characteristics of the other person. Status differentials can cause different interpretations about these, as Thibaut and Riecken (1955) found when they asked subjects to read a prepared appeal for a Red Cross blood donation to two people who were experimental plants. One was dressed and introduced as a high-status person, and the second was presented as a lower-status person. After hearing the statement read to them, both agreed to donate blood. The subjects were then asked to rate the two persons according to whom they had influenced most by their appeals and who would have donated blood anyway. The results indicated that the subjects perceived the high-status person's compliance as being internally caused, while the lower-status person was perceived as having been persuaded by external means. Pepitone (1958) found that the higher the status of perceived persons, the more they were perceived as being responsible, acting justifiably, and having good intentions, and the greater their attraction to the perceiver.

Box 6–2
DID YOU SEE *THAT?*

Two distorted rooms designed by Adelbert Ames were used to examine the effects of social factors on perception. In both rooms, the floors were tilted, the windows were trapezoidal in shape and of different sizes, and the rear walls were slanted so that the rooms were deeper on one side than on the other. Nevertheless, to the normal observer looking at the rooms monocularly (i.e., with one eye only) from a particular point, each room appeared to be much like any other room seen in perspective—the floor was level, the rear wall was perpendicular to the side walls, and the windows were rectangular and of equal size.

One room was large enough for a person to walk around in. The typical observer saw persons in the room "grow larger" as they walked from the observer's left to right, and smaller when they walked in the opposite direction. In a smaller model of the room, hands or faces could be seen through the windows. As in the large room, they would be seen as abnormally large or abnormally small, depending upon which window was used.

In a 1949 study using this apparatus, a woman subject named Honi reported that a stranger she saw in the large room was distorted in the usual manner, but when she saw her husband there he was of normal size in all cases. This became known as the *Honi phenomenon.* *

Experiments were conducted to determine whether the phenomenon could be reproduced with other individuals. The subjects were ten couples who had been married varying lengths of time up to ten years. They viewed both the large and the small rooms monocularly. In the small rooms, they were asked first to describe the room, the experimenter's hands in the window, and a marble rolled across the room, apparently uphill, in order to check if they saw the room in the usual manner. Then they were asked to describe two strangers with their heads through the window, and then one stranger and their spouse. In the large room, the subjects were asked to describe two people standing in separate corners. In one condition these were two strangers, and in the other condition they were a stranger and the spouse. Finally, the subjects were requested to describe a stranger and their spouse walking separately across the room.

Results showed that the Honi phenomenon could be reproduced, but with an interesting qualification. The original Honi couple had been married 25 years. In the later experiment, most of the couples married *less* than a year showed the effect, but only one of those married *more* than a year showed it.

Another experiment was designed involving six couples, all married for about one year. The hypothesis was that if the spouse and a stranger walked across the large room, the stranger would have to walk further from the corner to appear of normal size. Sometimes there was just one person in the room, either the spouse or a stranger, and sometimes two persons. The results confirmed the hypothesis that the spouse would have to walk a shorter distance from the corner than either of the two strangers in order to appear normal in size.

It would seem that familiarity has some effect upon perception, but the causation is not simple since a negative correlation was found between length of the marriage and intensity of the effect. More recent investigation of the Honi effect found the strength rather than the length of the relationship to be the critical factor. It also found that men tend to distort more than women; the investigators concluded that because of greater visual orientation, men possibly take spatial cues for granted.†

---

*W. J. Wittreich, "The Honi Phenomenon: A Case of Selective Perceptual Distortion," *Journal of Abnormal and Social Psychology*, 1952, 47, 705–712.

†K. L. Dion and K. K. Dion, "The Honi Phenomenon Revisited: Factors Underlying the Resistance to Perceptual Distortion of One's Partner," *Journal of Personality and Social Psychology*, 1976, *33*, 170–177.

Perception of high status is comparable to perception of power, which can be seen in terms of granting or prohibiting rewards. M. Horowitz (1963) told students they had a vote in determining how class time could be spent. They were led to believe that at certain times their vote was more significant than at others, but the instructor always managed to conduct the class in a manner opposite to the students' wishes. Their dislike of the instructor was found to be greatest when he was arbitrary, that is, when he disobeyed the votes they thought were most significant, thus robbing them of their power. (Social power is investigated further in Chapter 11.)

Many other variables—physical surroundings, dress, grooming, and behavior toward others—also contribute to attributions of interpersonal power. Scroggs (1980), for example, asked college students to rate photographs of people in dyads in office settings where one person was shown touching the other one. Nonmutual touch was found to increase the rating of power of the touchers, particularly when they were female.

Physical Characteristics of the Perceived Person

The effects of the physical appearance of the stimulus object (the perceived person) on interpersonal perception have been widely investigated. Secord (1958) found that various personality characteristics are often associated with specific facial or physiognomic appearances. In describing women, for example, men tended to associate bow-shaped lips with conceit and the amount of lipstick used with sexuality. Generally, upward curvature of the mouth is associated with smiling, which in Western culture is interpreted as friendly; wrinkles at eye corners convey an impression of a sense of humor. Many facial features, such as narrow or slanted eyes, high foreheads, and thin lips, impart predictable impressions which result in erroneous interpersonal perception, since the other person has little or no control over the perceiver's interpretation of these cues. In two-way interaction, however, perceptual responses to physiognomic features may be corrected by the presence of many other cues.

There is no question that, in any culture, physical appearance is the basis of generalizations based on race, sex, physical beauty, and the like. Americans have a negative stereotype of obesity, for example, and they consistently rank overweight persons as least likable (Maddox, Back, & Liederman, 1968).

Height is another source of influence on interpersonal perception. In general, tall men are associated with higher status; they are considered more likely to be hired, to receive higher starting salaries, and to achieve top-level positions. When a lecturer was introduced to a class as either a visiting professor or a graduate student, class members to whom he was introduced as a professor estimated his height as a full 5 inches taller than those to whom he was introduced as a graduate student (P. R. Wilson, 1968).

In another study, however, women asked to rate a person's attractiveness and likeability rated those of medium height as more attractive and likeable than either tall or short persons. Men actually found shorter men to be more likeable than tall men (Graziano, Brothen, & Berscheid, 1978). Perhaps men expect tall men to be more aggressive and to have higher status, and so they regard shorter men as probably more likeable.

Both perceived attitude similarity and physical attractiveness also were found by Berscheid and Walster (1974) to enhance interpersonal attraction. What's more, Mashman (1978) found that physical attractiveness enhances both interpersonal attraction and perceived attitude similarity. Hence the relationship among these variables is bidirectional. Attitude similarity enhances attraction, as Newcomb (1961, 1978) reported, and physical attractiveness enhances both of these variables. We expect to like people who are attractive and share our attitudes.

We also tend to associate attractiveness with goodness and happiness. In a study directly focused on the relation of physical beauty to attributed personality traits (Dion, Berscheid, & Walster, 1972), subjects were shown photographs of three persons of high-average or low-average physical attractiveness and asked to give their impressions of these persons. Physically attractive persons were rated as possessing more socially desirable personality characteristics and experiencing greater personal happiness than those who were less attractive.

Ability is also related to what is considered physically attractive. Sixth-through eighth-grade school children showed a striking similarity between the peers they rated as possessing athletic and scholastic ability and those they considered most good looking (Felson & Bohrnstedt, 1979). The reverse did not hold, however; that is, the perception of physical attractiveness did not carry over to perceived abilities.

Expressive Communications

In addition to relatively fixed physical characteristics such as facial features, height, and attractiveness, the perceived person's appearance is also affected by a range of postures and expressions over which the individual has some degree of control. Consciously or unconsciously, these typically are used to communicate intentions and feelings, and attention to the cues they present can improve the perceiver's accuracy in judging others. Such nonverbal communication is discussed further in Chapter 10.

The way people move, hold, and position their bodies is a form of communication which Fast (1972) calls *body language*. Research on the relation between posture and emotions goes back to William T. James (1932), who photographed a manikin in 350 different positions and found that certain postures were considered expressive of inner states or attitudes. Once we learn the language of the body, according to Lowen (1958), the way we position ourselves and move reflects our every trait and attitude.

Eyes convey so much meaning they are popularly called "the mirror of the soul." Looking directly at others when speaking to them communicates a positive state, and an evasive gaze indicates a negative mood, hostility, or guilt. The interpretation of such eye contact, however, is influenced by the content of the verbal communication (Ellsworth & Carlsmith, 1968).

Experiments have shown that the size of eye pupils increases markedly when people gaze at something they like and decreases in anticipation of an unpleasant stimulus. Oriental jade dealers have the reputation of being particularly astute readers of eye reactions. They watch the pupils of their customers' eyes, and when they observe them widening they bargain more relentlessly, for they know the customer finds the piece attractive and desirable.

Many facial expressions are typically used to communicate with other people, and unless deception is involved, taking them into account can improve perceptual accuracy. Charles Darwin maintained that facial expressions universally convey the same emotional state, and Ekman and Friesen (1971) found that this was generally true across a number of different cultures.

Some people reveal their emotions more openly in the facial expressions than others do. In a study by Notarius and Levenson (1979), subjects who observed a stressing film were divided into those who showed high facial expressiveness and those who showed little facial expressiveness. These two groups were then exposed to a threat of electric shock while various physiological measures were taken. The results indicated that natural inhibitors (those with low facial expression of emotion) were more physiologically reactive, as measured by heart rate, respiration rate, and skin conductance, than those who let their emotions show in their expressions. The perceiver's ability to assess the emotional state of another person is of course influenced by that person's tendency to express emotions in a manner in which they can be perceived. We may conclude that a person is "calm, cool, and collected" in the face of a stressful situation because we cannot "see" the person's internal reactions.

Early work with a related variable, voice quality, was done by Allport and Cantril (1934). Their subjects listened to recorded speeches and then attempted to judge various characteristics of the speaker. Voice qualities were found to provide some accurate information about other characteristics, such as age and sex, as well as some of the more dynamic inner characteristics, such as ascendancy. The most interesting research finding, however, was that perception of the voice arouses fairly consistent personality impressions of the speaker, whether they are correct or incorrect. Allport and Cantril suggested that the listener identifies the voice with a cultural stereotype that serves as a basis for personality judgments and thus produces a fairly uniform, even if inaccurate, impression.

The meaning of communications can be altered by changing the emphasis given to specific words. Rosten (1970) studied Yiddish expressions and found that shifting the emphasis can markedly change the meaning of a sentence. In the example, "Two tickets for *her concert* I should *buy?*" three different meanings are achieved if a different one of the italicized words is emphasized each time the question is asked.

Other studies have shown that vocal expression accurately communicates emotional meaning. Even letters of the alphabet can be read with voice qualities that communicate fear, anger, love, happiness, and so on (Davitz & Davitz, 1959).

There is also persuasive evidence that voice quality can reliably indicate the stress of the speaker and can indicate when the speaker is lying. Krauss, Geller, & Olson (1976) found, for example, that people could detect lying better when they only heard the speaker's voice than when they both heard and saw the speaker.

Order and Amount of Information

Interpersonal perception can be thought of as a communication system (as described in Chapter 10); in a one-way system the perceived person is providing cues from which the perceiver extracts information and from which various inferences and judgments can be made. In a two-way system, the perceiver also receives cues from which inferences can be made, but the perceiver's influence on these cues must also be considered. The order and quantity of cues or information the perceiver receives are important considerations. It has been fairly well established, for example, that first impressions may predispose the perceiver to make erroneous judgments of another person. Bruner and Tagiuri (1954) offered an illustration of the effect of prior information on the judgments of photographed facial expressions. When told in advance that the person photographed was watching a hanging, the perceiver saw a grimacing face as expressing disgust; if the prior information was that the subject was running a race, the same expression was seen as determination. In short, the perception complemented the impression provided by the previous information.

The relative influence of primacy and recency of information upon impression formation was investigated by Luchins (1957). Four groups of subjects were given two descriptions of a fictitious person, one stressing introversion and the other extroversion. Each of the groups received a different combination of information presented in a different time order. After reading the descriptions provided, the subjects were asked to write short paragraphs describing the fictitious person's probable behavior in social situations. The first information presented had greater influence upon the formed impression than later information, a finding which has been supported frequently by other experimenters. However, when the information about a perceived person is complex, the order of the information does not seem to matter (Rosenkrantz & Crockett, 1965).

Perceptions of personality traits also are affected by the *amount* of information available about such factors as length of acquaintance. The accuracy of personality judgments, however, is not directly related to length of acquaintance but appears instead to have a curvilinear profile (Hollander, 1956); that is, accuracy increases rapidly early in the acquaintanceship, reaches its limit, and then declines. Apparently the necessary information is obtained quite early in the association; with prolonged acquaintanceship, accuracy tends to decrease. This suggests that the perceiver is seeking cognitive consistency by disregarding cues which are incompatible with positive impressions of long-time acquaintances. Accuracy of emotional perception also is greatly influenced by the amount of information available regarding the context in which the emotions might be expected.

EMOTIONS AND MISATTRIBUTION

The perception of emotional states in ourselves and others is one area of perception in which attribution can easily turn to misattribution. Considerable research has been directed to the question of how a person identifies emotions in others. Thompson and Meltzer (1964), for example, showed that some emotional states, like happiness, love, and fear, are relatively easy to identify, whereas others, like disgust, contempt, and suffering, are more difficult. Unless the stimulus situation is known, labels attached to emotional behaviors on the basis of facial expression alone can be misleading. In self-perception, too, factors like one's feelings, the situation, and the behavior itself come into play, and both physiological changes and overt reactions are relevant.

An interesting aspect of self-perception of emotions is the interrelationship of

Box 6–3

THE INFORMED, THE MISINFORMED, AND THE IGNORANT

"You just *think* you're sick" is a comment many a reluctant scholar, huddled under the blankets on a frosty Monday morning, has heard. It doesn't take much to convince yourself you don't *feel* good under some circumstances.

In the same way the emotions can affect perception or cognition about physiological processes, these processes and cognition can affect the emotional state, as Stanley Schachter and J. E. Singer found in an experiment on determinants of emotional state.* They administered epinephrine (a variant of adrenalin) to experimental subjects and a placebo to subjects in a control group. In effect, there were three experimental groups: (1) the *informed,* who learned precisely what the effects of the drug would be, (2) the *misinformed,* who were given false information about the effects of the drug (the feet will feel numb, itching sensations will be felt in parts of the body, etc.) and (3) the *ignorant,* who were told that the injection was mild and harmless, with no side effects, and who would have no real explanation for their physiological state. Those who were given a placebo were told nothing, and like the misinformed and the ignorant, would not be able to account for their experience.

Following the injection, half of the subjects were led back to a waiting room where a confederate of the experimenter was engaging in carefree, childish behavior—playing basketball with crumpled paper, making and throwing paper airplanes. As the drug took effect the misinformed and the ignorant imitated to some degree the euphoric state of the confederate. The informed were less inclined to enter into the fun, and the placebo group behaved somewhere between the two extremes. The other half of the subjects were led into a room where a confederate displayed states of anger, and here the reactions of the various groups were less clear-cut than for those exposed to euphoria. In general, however, awareness of the physiological cause of their feelings made the informed group less suggestible to the stimulus situation.

---

*S. Schachter & J. E. Singer, "Cognitive, Social, and Physiological Determinants of Emotional State," *Psychological Review,* 1962, *69,* 379–399.

a physiological process with the cognition about it (see Box 6–3). According to Schachter (1971), there are three propositions related to the experimental analysis of emotions:

1. Given a condition of physiological arousal, we will apply a label to this state and describe our feelings on the basis of what cognitions are available to us. We speak of pleasure or anger according to the information present.
2. If there is a physical explanation ("I feel this way because I have just had an injection of adrenalin"), we do not need to turn to a cognitive explanation.
3. If we are in an emotion-provoking situation but for some reason are not activated physiologically, we experience no emotion even though the stimulus or cognition would warrant otherwise.

H. H. Kelley (1967) points out that the attribution the person "makes on any given occasion depends on some sampling of the information available . . . , both from . . . present and recent experience and from social sources." When this information is manipulated, misattribution is the probable result.

An experiment by Storms and Nisbett (1970) concerning the effects of a placebo (a pill containing a chemically inert substance) given to insomniac patients demonstrates the effect of misattribution due to emotional states. One group was told that the pill would cause arousal, whereas the others were told that it would have a relaxing effect. Those expecting arousal fell asleep more quickly than they had on previous nights, possibly because they attributed their wakefulness to the placebo rather than to their emotional state and consequently were less conscious of their anxiety. Those expecting relaxation got to sleep less rapidly than usual. Apparently they assumed their emotional state was unusually stressful, since their level of arousal was high even after taking a relaxant. The findings are the opposite of what might be expected, and the study underlines the potential of experimental manipulation for misattribution.

Another investigation focusing on misattribution by the use of cognition and derived emotional states involved male volunteers from an introductory psychology class (Valins, 1966). The experimental group was administered bogus heartbeat recordings while viewing illustrations of seminudes in *Playboy* magazine. It was hypothesized that the cognition ("That girl has affected my heart rate") would change the preferences, as well as biasing the emotional reaction toward given pictures. A follow-up showed that the choice preferences lasted over four to five weeks, and such feedback was absent for the control group, who were told that the sound stimulus they received was merely extraneous. Valins comments, "Internal events are a source of cognitive information, and as Schachter has proposed, individuals will want to evaluate and understand this kind of information. When an emotional explanation is prepotent, they will label their reactions accordingly."

Cognitive Consistency in Feeling States

The concepts of cognitive consistency and dissonance have found their way into the area of self-perception (Bem, 1972). Whereas in the early 1960s the emphasis was on the drive toward cognitive consistency, by the 1970s it had shifted to consistency in self-perception and the analysis of feeling states. The question of how information is processed and qualities are attributed to ourselves and others has become a central concern. As we manipulate our emotions and the related cognitions in pursuit of cognitive consistency, our attributions can easily turn into misattributions. Bem's (1967) idea that our attitudes may be derived from our behavior, rather than the reverse, is to the point (see Chapter 9).

Many of the studies discussed in this chapter lend support to the contention of cognitive compatibility theorists that cognitions within a specific system, or gestalt, tend toward consistency. Individuals attempt to evaluate others so that their overall perceptions are consistent, and they evaluate themselves to project an image of self-consistency (see Chapter 4). Their attributions are revised and reorganized as necessary to achieve cognitive consistency and remove sources of cognitive dissonance, concepts which are examined in Chapter 9.

People appear to have preconceived notions as to cognitions that do or do not go well together. According to their expectations, bad acts are performed by bad people; liked people perform better on tasks than those who are not liked (Sherif, White, & Harvey, 1955). When judging someone's personality, for example, the perceiver tends to organize the various characteristics consistently in order to achieve the feeling of equilibrium produced by a unified impression. When the characteristics are contradictory, the perceiver has difficulty organizing an impression and may disregard or distort those traits that do not seem to be consistent (Gollin, 1954). This process is often referred to as *implicit personality theory*. After receiving certain cues from a person, the perceiver's further judgments of personality are based more on preconceptions or expectations than on characteristics actually perceived (Kelley & Volkart, 1952). This kind of evaluation can result in stereotyped perceptions, as noted at the beginning of the chapter.

A similar phenomenon is *generalizing from the self.* Bender and Hastorf (1953) found that social sensitivity depends on empathic ability; high-accuracy scores in judging another person may often be the result of attributing to others what one sees in oneself. Once a cue suggests a similarity of some common characteristics in the perceiver and the perceived, other personal characteristics of the perceiver are also attributed to the other person.

On a broader scale, cognitive consistency also is sought in evaluations of national character, both our own and others.' Bronfenbrenner (1961) has proposed a *mirror image phenomenon* (see Box 6–4), whereby people in the United States and the Soviet Union perceive themselves in similar positive ways and each other in similar negative ways, perceptions which may have more to do with emotions than cognitions. This hypothesis has been corroborated for other pairs of countries, such as Japan–United States, India-Pakistan, and Colombia-Venezuela (Salazar & Marin, 1977), but not as impressively as Bronfenbrenner does for the two superpowers. As Box 6–4 suggests, political leaders also strive for cognitive consistency in their perceptions of other nations and other leaders, and dissonance is probably more of a strain for them than it is for the average person.

Thus the involvement of emotions in interpersonal perception is a principal reason why it has peculiarities which differentiate it from object or event perception. A perceiver may alter the stimulus to confirm a judgment or expectancy. If the perceiver dislikes a person, for example, and acts accordingly (i.e., in a hostile or unfriendly manner), it is very likely that the other person will respond in kind and thus confirm the perceivers' preconception.

THE PERCEPTION OF CAUSALITY: ATTRIBUTION THEORY

Another type of misattribution—misattribution of causality—has been called one of the major causes of anxiety, stress, and neurotic behavior in people today.

Box 6–4
THE MIRROR IMAGE

John F. Kennedy and Nikita Khrushchev were recognized by both Americans and Russians as the spokesmen for U.S.–U.S.S.R. confrontations during the Cold War of the fifties and sixties. From the American point of view, Kennedy represented the American aims of world peace and freedom from communist domination, while Khrushchev's boast that "we will bury you" was interpreted as an expression of the communists' intention of conquering the world, militarily if necessary. Uri Bronfenbrenner has suggested that the distorted American picture of the Russians as communist aggressors is identical to the Soviet view of capitalists as imperialist aggressors. In other words, he says there is a mirror image in the reciprocal perceptions of Russian and American people.*

One way the prevalent attitudes in a country are publicly aired is through the pronouncements of its political leaders. Another study examined Bronfenbrenner's mirror image hypothesis further with an analysis of the public speeches of Kennedy and Khrushchev.† Six speeches given by each man were selected as being most representative of the views of their respective nations. The speeches were scanned for clearly stated value judgments (i.e., goals which a society refers to as being obviously desirable), and these judgments were classified into 31 value categories.

As shown in the accompanying figure, several important values were expressed by Kennedy and Khrushchev in their speeches. Both advocated peace and nonaggression quite often, and both mentioned aggression infrequently. The values of practicality, dominance, and generosity were mentioned by both to about the same extent. Kennedy placed greater emphasis on military strength but did so in connection with the defense of peace and freedom, while Khrushchev emphasized economic welfare more often.

In the speeches by Khrushchev, the values of peace and freedom were combined in the concept of "peaceful coexistence," in which war was not to be used to solve international disagreements, and the internal affairs of other countries were not to be interfered with. In Kennedy's speeches, the United States was always pictured on the side of peace and freedom (exactly where the Russians placed themselves), and the communists were considered the enemy of these values. Khrushchev maintained that socialism operates for the good of the people and capitalism is the antithesis of peace and freedom. Communists, according to Kennedy, were bent on world destruction; the Russians viewed the Western powers as having "nightmarish plans for world domination."

The reciprocal perceptions of the two countries were almost identical mirror images.

---

*U. Bronfenbrenner, "The Mirror Image in Soviet-American Relations," *Journal of Social Issues,* 1961, *17,* 45.

†W. Eckhardt and R. White, "A Test of the Mirror-Image Hypothesis: Kennedy and Khrushchev," *Conflict Resolution,* 1967, *11,* 325–332.

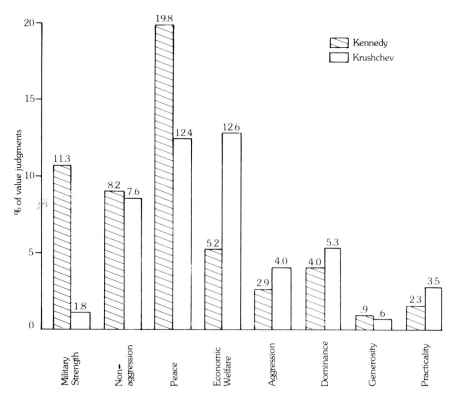

Values Mentioned in Political Speeches by U.S. and U.S.S.R. Leaders

Ellis (1973) maintains that people think in a completely distorted fashion—"magical thinking," he calls it—whereby those who are angry or frightened or insecure attribute the cause to the stimulus rather than to themselves. He cites Epictetus: "Men are disturbed not by things but by the views which they take of them," and Shakespeare in *Hamlet:* "There's nothing either good or bad but thinking makes it so."

One of the pioneers in the development of attribution theory was Fritz Heider, who argued in the 1920s that social psychologists could greatly benefit from a systematic analysis of the commonsense explanations of everyday persons. People naturally attribute cause and intention, they blame themselves and others, they perceive others to be competent or incompetent. Following publication of Heider's *Psychology of Interpersonal Relations* (1958), social psychologists began taking his theorizing seriously. Today attribution theory, based on Heider's conceptualizations, is one of the most important research areas in social psychology.

The perception of causality is related to the issue of internal versus external control introduced in Chapter 4. We conclude that we have internal control and our behavior causes or influences a change in our environment if an action of ours is more or less directly followed by a change. If we cannot relate an action of ours to a change, we conclude that its cause is external. The rapidity of the environmental change following a behavioral response influences our perception of control. Heider (1958) described some of this thinking about causal attribution as *naive psychology*—that is, the psychology of the ordinary person. Attribution theory was later elaborated and refined by Harold Kelley (1973), whose work forms a basis for the following discussion.

We expect social events to occur in orderly and consistent fashion. Friendly people are nice and kind, and unfriendly people are the opposite. We become distressed if someone we do not like does something nice for us or someone we do like does something harmful to our well-being. We tend to be suspicious and look for ulterior motives or for situational causes which could explain the inconsistent behavior.

Most people have done things which seem inconsistent or foolish. Rather than attributing stupidity or rudeness or social ineptitude to themselves, they reason that they were tired at the time or under the influence of an intoxicant or responding to a severely taxing or frustrating event. Bem's contention that people achieve self-perception by observing their own behavior (see Chapter 4) was borne out by research in which subjects were asked to write essays contrary to their own attitudes, for either trivial or substantial rewards. Bem (1967) found that the subjects themselves acted very much as observers did. If an observer saw another person writing an essay on a subject which was opposed to that person's attitude, the observer would look for causes to which to attribute this behavior. If the inducement was large, for example, if a person was paid $5 for writing a ten-minute essay, the observer would conclude that the person was writing the essay to obtain the money. If the inducement was inadequate, such as responding to the simple request of an experimenter, the observer often concluded that the subject was writing the essay because the position advocated was consistent with personal thinking. Bem suggests that under some circumstances people engage in exactly the same sort of self-attribution process and do not perceive themselves as changing their attitudes. Bem prefers to analyze attribution in the framework of self-perception rather than cognitive dissonance theory. Perception does not function exclusively as a means of reducing inconsistency in our environment and behavior.

Kelley (1973) has pointed to several basic concepts underlying the process of causal attribution in social situations. Probably most important is the concept of *covariation;* people tend to attribute causal properties to anything which has a mathematical relation to occurrence of an event over time. They also feel that the event which occurs first is most likely to be the cause and that effects should occur shortly after their causes. Certain primitive peoples do not attribute the cause of childbirth to sexual intercourse because of the long time between cause and effect! Attribution theory is concerned with how ordinary persons order their world; Kelley calls it "an attempt to analyze, refine and enlarge on common sense." There is an expected relationship between causal attribution and the person's subsequent behavior, and many causal attributions are incorrect.

People seek causes for events. Being subjected to events they cannot control is psychologically and physically deleterious, as noted in the discussion of depression and learned helplessness in Chapter 5 and the final section of this chapter. We feel a greater sense of control if we can attribute our failures to factors such as our intentions or motivations, other than our physical or mental incompetence or the environment (Kelley, 1971).

The desire to perceive oneself in control is also said to be responsible for the *just world principle.* Observers tend to blame or credit those to whom events happen, even if they happen accidentally. The notion that people get what they deserve and deserve what they get satisfies a just world notion which does not threaten a person's sense of control (Lerner, 1975).

A related concept is blaming oneself for being a *victim.* Lifton (1963) found that many victims of the Hiroshima nuclear bombing were caught up in feelings of guilt and self-blame, and Medea and Thompson (1974) report that many female rape victims feel guilty and blame themselves for having had rape fantasies and secretly wanting the assault to happen. The need to feel a sense of control is a strong motive, and being deprived of that perception can have serious consequences.

The tendency for people to take credit for success but attribute failure to the environment or others when they can (Wortman, 1976) was pointed out above as an aspect of egotistical attribution (Rosenfield & Stephen, 1976). Generally, positive behaviors are attributed more to the characteristics of the person, such as personality, whereas negative behaviors are more likely to be attributed to the environment. Our own behavior is more likely to be perceived as being influenced by the situation, while others' behavior is attributed to their personalities, and these tendencies are further influenced by the degree of intimacy between the perceiver and the perceived (Taylor & Koivumaki, 1976).

Even gambling behavior is influenced by perception of the opponent. In a chance-determined card game of drawing the highest card, subjects who played against a well-dressed, confident-acting person bet less than those who played against an awkward, poorly dressed "schnook" (Langer, 1975). They may have felt that an awkward, unconfident person did not deserve to win, and they were willing to bet that he would lose.

There is some question as to just how rational attributions are, as some of the studies cited in this chapter have indicated. People make attributions in situations which contain very little information (Gergen, 1980), and they attribute bodily arousal to the wrong source (Zillman, 1980), for example. The controversy is reflected in the distinctions among the various theories of attribution. Some, like Kelley's (1972) model, emphasize greater rationality and the weighing of information about the covariation of effects with possible causes. Others have prepared attribution models which stress the prominence or salience of probable causes (Pryor & Kriss, 1977; Taylor & Fiske, 1978), suggesting that possible causes which are most noticeable or most easily recalled are likely to be perceived as the causes of events.

Current research in the area of causal attribution is extensive, and the findings are leading to the conclusions that attribution is a complex process in which rationality as well as salience figure. The nature of the entire situation the person is involved in must be considered, as well as the importance or significance of the event for the person. Concern about the accuracy of causal attributions is not likely in situations of trivial interest or importance.

THE PERCEPTION OF FREEDOM

The other side of the coin of internal control reflected in the perception of causality is external control reflected in the perception of freedom. The idea that all citizens are free to pursue their own interests is embedded in Western culture. But if a society tries to assure complete freedom of action, the quality of life will deteriorate rapidly, because certain segments or society as a whole will pursue short-term reinforcement of special interests at the expense of long-term, more continuous reinforcement of the social good (see Box 6–5). To prevent such social traps, which can give rise to the destruction of the environment, the erosion of social life, and the depletion of the earth's resources, it has been suggested that the perception of freedom must be tempered in some way.

B. F. Skinner points out, in *Beyond Freedom and Dignity* (1971), that in Western society the tendency is to conceive of freedom as an inner state. That is, we are free if we *feel* free. But people are never free from control. The problem, he maintains, is not to free people from control but rather to apply behavioral technology for the purposes of analyzing and then altering the kinds of controls to which people are exposed. Skinner concludes that if Western culture is to survive, it can no longer afford freedom.

One aspect of this broad and controversial issue is the deleterious effect of the loss of the perception (or illusion) of freedom. Inmates of institutions, for example, can exercise very little control over their condition. Few of the decisions they make influence the rewards and punishments they receive in the system. In mental

Box 6–5
WITH LIBERTY AND JUSTICE FOR ALL

In the free world, where the individual's freedom of choice is considered a constitutional right, there is a possibility that short-term reinforcement (or goals) will interfere or be inconsistent with long-term reinforcement (or benefits). When public policy supports an activity which provides immediate rewards but proves in the long run to be unprofitable or even destructive, the result is said to be a *social trap.**

An example of a social trap is the commons, in old New England villages, public grasslands where anyone's cows could graze freely. The townspeople tried to make more money faster by simply increasing the number of cows grazed on the commons. Of course, as the number of cows was increased, the grass became scarcer. Finally it was destroyed entirely, and the owners wound up with a loss rather than a gain.

A similar example is the decline of commuter railroads as the use of automobiles increased. As more people used their cars to commute to work, railroad service began to deteriorate, which encouraged an ever-increasing number of people to use their automobiles. The process, which is self-accelerating, results in exceptionally poor or nonexistent railway service, traffic jams on the highways, and commuters wishing they could use rail transportation.

The solution to the problem of social traps was recognized by the Founding Fathers: Freedom and justice go hand in hand, and it is a purpose of government to provide the amount of regulation needed to assure that immediate gratification is postponed in order to achieve long-term benefits. Today it is recognized that rewards which are deferred are more attractive in the sense that they do not lead to destruction of the source of the reinforcement. How to accomplish long-term social goals without violating individuals' perceptions of their rights and freedom continues to be the subject of vigorous debate.

---

*J. Platt, "Social Traps," *American Psychologist*, 1973, *28*, 641-651.

institutions, for example, if patients follow a simple routine and remain quiet and nondisruptive, they are well cared for, well fed, and offered such privileges as walking on the grounds or seeing a movie. The effects of such loss of control give rise to what has been called the "institutionalized patient," one who is unable to make decisions and hence becomes more and more dependent on hospital routine. Lack of internal control and decision-making prerogatives also has curious effects on children and welfare recipients and various marginal members of society.

Several ingenious experiments have demonstrated the serious debilitating effects of loss of personal control over potentially harmful events. One of these explored the effects of having a "panic button" available (Glass, Singer, & Friedman, 1969). As subjects worked on simple tasks, such as adding sets of numbers and finding letters embedded in columns of words, highly aversive noise (110 decibels) was presented at random intervals. Half of the subjects were provided with a button with which they could terminate the noise; the others had no means for stopping it. Subjects with the button were encouraged to use it only if the noise became too much for them to bear.

In the preliminary session the simpler tasks were to be completed in the presence of the randomly occurring noise. Then the subjects were instructed to complete a second set of tasks without noise; these included proofreading tasks and tracing problems, some of which were unsolvable. One important measure was how many times the subjects tackled the unsolvable problems. The results were quite startling. Subjects who had had access to the off switch on the preliminary task did much better on the proofreading and made five times as many attempts at solving the unsolvable tracing problems as those who had not had a switch to stop the noise, even though those with the off switch did not actually use it. This finding suggests that it is the perception of the ability to terminate a situation which might become unendurable that makes the difference. Similar results have been found in studies of learned helplessness in humans (see Chapter 5).

The same kind of effect appears when positive reinforcement is not controlled. Many cases of depression have been directly related to situations in which rewards occur independently of the individual's efforts, such as the "success depression" prominent people may experience when they receive rewards because of who they are rather than what they are doing. One therapy that has proved its worth with hospitalized depressed patients is exposure to anger-producing abuse (Taulbee & Wright, 1971). After the patients are forced to express anger they are immediately reinforced by being taken out of the anger-producing situation; they also receive apologies from their abusers. This treatment places patients in a situation in which their behavior affects the reinforcements received.

Thus, as Lefcourt (1973) points out, "the illusion that one can exercise personal choice has a definite and positive role in sustaining life." To dismiss the illusion of freedom can bring some undesirable consequences. To submit to a master planner, however wise the planner may be, "is to surrender an illusion that may be the bedrock on which life flourishes."

SUMMARY)

Perceiving, a major cognitive process in social behavior, depends on the senses and certain structural processes, although its content is determined largely by social experience. That is, we react to a number of physical cues, but these are interlaced with constantly changing needs. It is through perception that the world takes on meaning for the individual and a consistent frame of reference is achieved. Misinterpretations, misattributions, and disruptions in perception produce stereotypes and maladaptive social attitudes.

The term *perceptual defense* suggests that we arrange our perceptions to protect the self. By defensive attribution, the individual can gain ego expansion and reduce inner tensions. Attempts to achieve cognitive consistency all are affected by the emotions and can easily result in misattribution. Extensive research in interpersonal perception has been directed to examining the means by which people judge others in a complex world. Both internal and external control are rooted in the perceptual process. Moreover, as our individual or social situations change in time, we tend to perceive ourselves as either more free or more limited by the options we have—whom we may marry, what kind of job we may have, or to what degree we can enjoy our civil liberties.

As an integral part of cognition, perception is one of the two concepts which provide a basis for determining the dynamics of social behavior. The other concept, motivation, is the topic of the following chapter.

WORDS TO REMEMBER

Attribution. Assignment of behavioral tendencies or personality traits to ourselves or another person, on the basis of observed responses.

Attribution theory. Theory regarding the tests or procedures by which people gauge the motives and traits of others. It includes the use of tests to determine the genuineness of responses to others.

Authoritarian personality. An individual characterized by intolerance toward minorities and social inferiors, marked ethnocentrism (belief that one's own group is superior), and deference to authority. Rigidity in perception and inflexibility in beliefs, attitudes, and possibly personality are indices of *authoritarianism,* which can be measured by a test or scale.

Cognition. Psychological process of perceiving, learning, thinking, and believing.

Just world phenomenon. Tendency to rationalize reality as basically just or logical, as a means of eliminating personal obligations or the need for control.

Misattribution. Misinterpretation of cues, often because of a mental set that predisposes the individual to infer false information.

Perception. Process by which people monitor outside stimuli. The sensations transmitted by the sense organs are processed according to the person's socialization and needs.

Perceptual defense. Selection and working over of outside stimuli in order to maintain one's cognitive balance.

Set. Predisposition to perceive or respond in a given fashion or to accept a given attitude; often called a *mental set* or *mind set.*

Stereotype. Reduction of information about a stimulus object to a simplistic or abbreviated perception or attitude, as with the image of a member of a political party or ethnic group.

QUESTIONS FOR DISCUSSION

1. From what you recall from Chapter 4, how does perception serve the individual in maintaining self-identity?
2. Describe the process by which we arrive at perceptions.
3. How is perception related to cognition?
4. What is meant by the concept of set? How is it related to the concept of stereotype?
5. Describe some studies of perception which have been made in atypical settings like mental hospitals.
6. What is the Honi phenomenon, and what is its significance?
7. How do physical appearance and expressions relate to interpersonal perception?
8. How does the order and amount of information affect *impression formation*? What are some of the more important studies in this area? What meaning does the term have for you?
9. Give an example of how the relation of emotions, physiological processes, and cognition can result in misattribution.
10. What is meant by the term *cognitive consistency*? Give some examples of cognitive dissonance from your own experience.
11. How are the perceptions of causality and freedom related? What is the significance of Bem's research on the attribution process?
12. What are Skinner's thoughts on freedom? How is this concept related to perception?

READINGS

Allport, F. H. *Theories of Perception and the Concept of Structure.* New York: John Wiley & Sons, 1955.

A far-reaching report of the major theories of perception in psychology and their supporting evidence.

Berkowitz, L. (Ed.). *Advances in Experimental Social Psychology* (Vol. 12). New York: Academic Press, 1979.

Part I presents studies in social cognition—person perception and the attributional analysis of stereotyping—which will be of interest to the advanced student.

Hastorf, A. H., Schneider, D., and Polefka, J. *Person Perception.* Reading, Mass.: Addison-Wesley, 1970.

Well-documented textbook on the subject.

Lindzey, G., and Aronson, E. (Eds.). *Handbook of Social Psychology* (Vol. 3). Reading, Mass.: Addison-Wesley Publishing Co., 1969.

Chapters 22 and 23 (by Tajfel and Tagiuri, respectively) offer a clear if academic analysis of the social factors in perception.

Miller, G. A., and Johnson-Laird, P. N. *Language and Perception.* Cambridge,

Mass.: Harvard University Press, 1976.
A major contribution to the theory of information processing; Chapters 1 and 2 are most relevant.

Shaver, K. G. *An Introduction to Attribution Processes.* Cambridge, Mass.: Winthrop Publishers, 1975.
A highly readable text in this multifaceted area.

Tagiuri, R., and Petrullo, L. (Eds.). *Person Perception and Interpersonal Behavior.* Stanford, Calif.: Stanford University Press, 1958.
A variety of papers on such topics as causality, cognition, trait perception, and the group setting.

Toch, H., and Smith, H. C. (Eds.). *Social Perception.* New York: D. Van Nostrand Co., 1968.
A compilation of interesting studies in interpersonal perception.

THE ROLE OF MOTIVES IN SOCIAL BEHAVIOR

Because motives are not directly observable or measurable, it is hard to determine why people behave as they do in their relations with one another. An inquiry into motivation is an inquiry into the basic nature of causes, a problem philosophers have wrestled with for over two thousand years. De Charms (1968) tried to analyze individual causation and found the concept wanting. He could find no satisfactory operational definition or empirical statement of it, and so he decided there were two alternatives: "Either we pursue the goal of a completely objective science of behavior and renounce the concept of motivation, or we pursue the concept of motivation and renounce the goal of complete objectivity."

This text considers motivation and cognition as the two central processes in the dynamics of social behavior. While they are interrelated to the extent that neither can be completely detached from the other, they are easier to comprehend if they are studied separately. In this chapter we will outline several theoretical efforts to explain motivation and analyze some critical social motives, such as aggression and how it is acquired. The concepts of affiliation and attraction, which can serve as social motives, are discussed in relation to group behavior in Chapter 13. Other concepts with motivating properties are dealt with in other chapters, such as cognitive dissonance in Chapter 9.

Motivation, like all social motives, is understandable only in terms of social systems, however. An overall view of social systems is necessary in order to understand fully the development and stability of socially determined motives and how they can energize and direct individual and group behaviors. This overall view is contributed by the Gestalt and functionalist schools of thought.

Since motivation is concerned with causation, in a sense motives can be regarded as causes. Why you eat, why you read this book, why you do or do not get married—these are all types of questions that are concerned with the determination or causation of behavior. The search for causes is difficult and baffling, but it is the central task of any science and can hardly be ignored in social psychology. Our major concerns in this text, such as attitudes, leadership, social change, and group dynamics, are all related to this quest for motives or causes.

This chapter reviews some of the ideas that have been learned about how certain motives develop, how they are influenced by a person's environment, and the conditions under which they affect observable behavior, particularly social behavior. It begins by noting the problems encountered in studying motives and then presents an overview of historical approaches to the investigation of motivation. The Gestalt-oriented cognitive approaches of E. C. Tolman, Kurt Lewin, and Gordon Allport are described, and theories of a central motive or a plurality of motives are contrasted. The focus of mechanistic theories on goals and reinforcers and the distinction between primary and secondary motivation are examined, and emotions are compared to instincts or drives as a motivating factor. The special difficulties in explaining sociogenic motives are explored in the final section, which suggests a classification of types of social motives and describes efforts to establish a motivational basis for an important antisocial motive—aggression.

PROBLEMS IN STUDYING MOTIVES

The complexities of motivation have made the study of the role of motives in behavior particularly difficult. One problem is that investigation into motivation is primarily concerned with the whys rather than the hows or whats of behavior. That is, it is concerned with explanation rather than description.

Another difficulty is that motives are never directly observable in the ways that emotions, learning, memory, or even intelligence are. Motives are always inferred or hypothesized from behavior. If individuals seek out other people and seem to enjoy being with them, they are said to have a sociability or affiliation motive. If they persistently amass goods and wealth, they are characterized as having an acquisitive drive.

The trouble is that people sometimes do the same things for different reasons. Of five people attending church, one may be devoutly religious, one may wish to show off new clothes, one may hope to make good business connections, one may be escaping from a noisy household, and the fifth may enjoy the music. Conversely, persons similarly motivated may behave differently. Two individuals who are intent on recognition may seek it in widely different ways—one through boasting, and the other through writing or scientific research.

Studying motivation is also difficult because psychologists and other students of motivation do not agree about the meaning of terms they use. Is a motive an "inner push," like an instinct? Do motives operate all the time, or do they come into play only at certain times or in certain situations? Should motives be thought of as broad, dynamic tendencies like prestige seeking and gregariousness, or are they more specific, like "seeking prestige in my community" and "wanting to be with my old friends"? Are motives separate from attitudes, habits, interests, emotions, and other processes, or do they overlap? Agreement will have to be reached on such questions before real progress can be made in the study of motivation.

One of the perplexing questions in motivation is whether a motive is *intrinsic* (originating within the person) or *extrinsic* (originating in external situations). Is a certain act performed because it is good or pleasurable in itself or because it is a means of obtaining another goal? Perhaps the answer can be found in the theory of de Charms (1968), who sees motivation as personal: People want the primary cause of their behavior to be in themselves, and so they resist being the pawn or victim of other forces. Notz (1975) suggests that people derive satisfaction when the behavior involves both internal, personal causation (the intrinsic dimension) and external rewards (the extrinsic dimension).

On the whole, the relation between intrinsic and extrinsic motivation is elusive. Blockages in extrinsic motivation likely enhance the intrinsic dimension, and negative feedback or punishment probably inhibits intrinsic motives. According to de Charms, personality factors are critical in determining the relative influence of the intrinsic or extrinsic factors. Some persons have more capacity for intrinsic motivation than others do.

A basic reason why the study of motivation is difficult and exciting is that we generally are not aware of the stimuli which influence our behavior (Brody, 1980). Many studies have shown that people cannot give accurate reports of their motivational states. Zimbardo (1969) found, for example, that even though physiological and behavioral response to pain could be altered by manipulation of justification for enduring the pain, verbal reports of level of pain experienced were not consistent with other indicators. In an attribution study (Nisbett & Schachter, 1966), some of the subjects were given a placebo but were told that the pill would produce bodily feelings similar to those experienced with electric shock. These subjects were able to tolerate higher levels of shock than other subjects who took the pill but were not misinformed about its effects. This appears to be a straightforward attribution situation (such as those described in Chapter 6), in which the first group of subjects attributed their physiological arousal to the pill rather than to the effect of the electric shock and hence could tolerate more shock. They were unaware of any such process, however, and when informed of the experimental procedures they denied that it explained their behavior. Psychoanalytic theory (discussed below) suggests that the unconscious serves a function in motivation, and the psychological processes responsible for verbal responses may not be the same as those that determine behavioral responses.

Motives are dispositions in the person which involve *incentives*, usually in the environment, and there is considerable individual variation as to how these two aspects are to be brought together (Atkinson, 1981).

There are other problems with the concept of social motivation. Just as evidence has indicated rather weak relationships between personality traits in different situations (see Chapter 4), there is some question about the stability of motives. A child of eight may demonstrate a high need for achievement, but as an adolescent or an adult the same individual may demonstrate markedly different levels of such motivation. Furthermore, there is a problem of whether to consider such motives as energetic or homeostatic systems. A drive is an *energizing system,* as when a person becomes anxious and behaves in a manner which is described as a function of his or her level of anxiety. Normally, however, anxiety does not necessarily lead to a particular type of behavior. A *homeostatic system* is built on an equilibrium position, so that any time one part of the system changes, another part must change in a predictable, well-defined manner—for example, when you get too hot you perspire, which has the effect of cooling you off and maintaining your bodily temperature. Ideas about concepts like aggression are based on homeostatic principles. The frustration-aggression hypothesis evaluated in the final section of this chapter, for example, proposes that people can tolerate a certain amount of frustration, but once a critical level is exceeded they will reduce their frustration by acts of aggression.

HISTORICAL APPROACHES TO MOTIVATION

Historically, motivation has been considered a matter of reward and punishment, like learning, to which it is closely related. The ancient Greeks and Romans proposed that people select behaviors that give pleasure and avoid behaviors that mean pain. This theory of *hedonism* was refined by the 19th-century utilitarians, who attempted to distinguish between the quantitative and qualitative aspects of a "calculus of happiness." The approach was ingenious, but it provided no scientific explanation as to why individuals behave as they do. The problem of unconscious motivation was ignored, as was the occasional selection of behaviors that bring pain.

Theories of Instinct

Aristotle approached human behavior as a matter of inborn action tendencies or appetites, and at the turn of the century William McDougall revived this viewpoint with an elaborate theory of instincts. Until about 1920 it was easy to answer "why" questions in psychology. The answer to such questions as why people are sociable or why people seek the company of others seemed obvious: because they are instinctively gregarious. Instincts of acquisitiveness, competitiveness, and pugnacity were invoked to explain possession of goods, business practices, and war. Theorists, including William James and E. L. Thorndike as well as McDougall, drew up long lists of instincts that purported to explain practically every human activity from abortion to zealotry. In 1924, the sociologist L. L. Bernard reported a survey of some 400 instinct theories and found that together they had identified almost 6,000 human urges or activities as "instincts" or "instinctive"!

After 1920, the instinct theories were badly discredited. For one thing, it was becoming clear that positing instincts was like arguing in a circle: People are sociable because they have an innate tendency to be sociable. At best, this represents dubious reasoning. More important, anthropologists were accumulat-

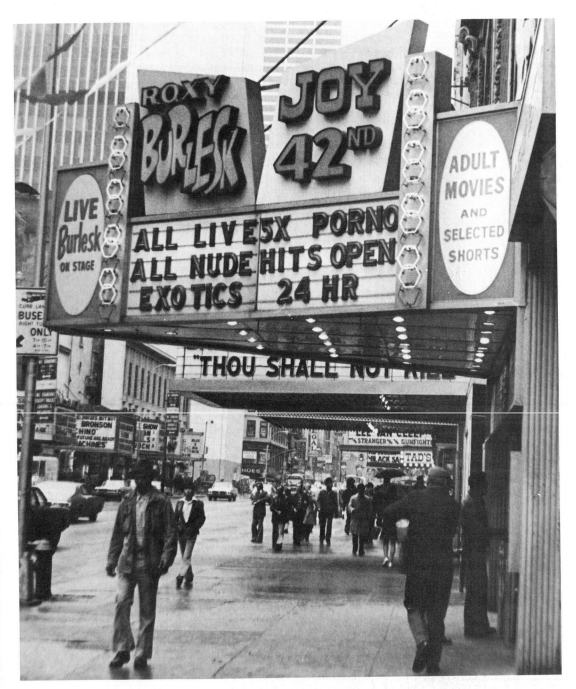

Sexual needs find many forms of expression. In this case perception and motivation are closely related as the blatancy of the sexual scene demonstrates. *Source:* Eric C. Williamson.

ing considerable data to show that different culture patterns produce great variations in human behavior, or "human nature," and psychologists and sociologists were demonstrating that much of the behavior that is considered innate is actually learned. Since from its derivation the word *instinct* has to mean innate or inherited, it is a misnomer when applied to behaviors or behavioral tendencies that are based on experience. So little human behavior is clearly inherited, unaffected by training, or universal to the human species that the term *instinct* was generally dropped from the vocabulary of the psychologist and social scientist.

Instinct is correctly used, of course, to describe fairly complex patterns of animal behavior that are clearly innate, unlearned, and universal to a species, such as the web spinning of spiders, nest building of birds, or honeycomb construction of bees. Hypotheses have been offered to explain the instinctive behavior of lower organisms as attributable to neural energy released in response to certain types of stimuli. Courting and parental behaviors, for example, are apparently controlled by different mechanisms, and the former can be directed with no effect on the latter. Instincts are highly specific to the organism and are controlled by specific types of neural and inborn releasing mechanisms. Except for the lowest organisms, however, it is doubtful whether any behavior is truly innate, since environmental stimuli can affect even the most elemental responses (Verplanck, 1955). Box 7–1 points to such an instance.

Drive Theory

An alternative to the instinct theories was proposed by physiologists and comparative psychologists who conceived of the idea of physiological tensions like hunger, thirst, and sex as *drives* that impel the organism toward satisfaction of its tissue needs. Some theorists included play, avoidance of danger, maternal, and aesthetic drives in the classification. Edward C. Tolman (1942) divided drives into appetites (e.g., hunger, thirst, sex) and aversions (e.g., injury avoidance). All interpreters agree that these drives are essentially biological and are found in all human beings, irrespective of training, though the way they are aroused and their mode of expression are affected by experience.

To a great extent drive theory depends on the concept of *reinforcement*, which was examined in Chapter 5. Neobehaviorists such as B. F. Skinner defined a reinforcer as anything that strengthens the probability that a response will recur, and they maintained that any response which is reinforced will in all probability recur. Because, for the human being, many responses persist which are not related to primary need reduction, a distinction was made between *primary* reinforcement, in which the stimulus satisfies primary needs, and *secondary* reinforcement, whereby a stimulus present when primary reinforcement occurs tends to take on reinforcing qualities.

Reinforcement theory still has great difficulty explaining the more intricate motives, such as creativity or achievement, however. The behavior of human beings is dynamic in the sense that it takes place within an orbit of freedom and responsibility. Zimbardo (1969) has pointed out that the most critical motivation

Box 7–1
ARE YOU HUNGRY?

Some people eat out of habit, and others eat because they are hungry. The discrepancies in what people accept or reject as food and in their attitudes toward eating as pleasure or nourishment can mean the difference between being well fed and being fat.

Stanley Schachter was intrigued with the question of how hunger is determined and set out to compare the eating habits of normal people with those of the obese.* He found that, as compared to people of normal weight, obese persons were less sensitive to internal and external clues. They were less conscious of the physiological distress accompanying food deprivation (more technically, they did not experience to the same degree states like gastric motility and hypoglycemia), for example, and eating crackers was less effective in reducing appetite for them. The obese also were less affected by shifts in the time of meals, either in the laboratory setting or in real life. The food presented also affected appetite; the obese were less likely to reject inferior ice cream, whereas the normals were quite sensitive to the quality of any dish. Overindulgence was observed among the obese; if three sandwiches were offered, they ate on average 2.3, as opposed to 1.6 for the underweight and 1.9 for the normal person. The obese also ate more irregularly than the normals during weekends.

The research begs the question of the more obscure factors underlying excessive eating, such as anxiety or compulsiveness. It also should not be suggested that all obese people eat in an identical fashion. Recent medical research has found support for a physiological basis for abnormal appetite in excess insulin in the blood. Nevertheless, Schachter's study does imply that the hunger drive is highly subject to conditioning and is influenced by what occurs both inside and outside the organism.

---

* S. Schachter, *Emotion, Obesity, and Crime* (New York: Academic Press, 1971).

---

stems not from appetite or aversion but from the tensions felt by all the higher organisms in their search for autonomy and control.

Freudian Theory and Revision

Sigmund Freud's well-known theories had something in common with both the instinctual and the drive approaches. In his view, motivation depends primarily on internal stress. Its basis is found in the various instincts—hunger, thirst, aggressiveness, and, most important, the sex instinct, which derives its energy from the *libido* (see Box 7–2). Freud believed that practically all social and emotional behaviors and experiences are rooted in this striving, pulsating, amorphous force, which is largely unconscious in origin, and that most motivation for these behaviors also is directly or indirectly connected with the sex libido. Every act, every idea, every dream, "slips of the tongue"—all are somehow caused by this unconscious impulse. (In his later writings Freud did shift his emphasis somewhat to repression and ego defense.)

The strategic force in motivation and conflict, Freud said, is ambivalence. There is the *life instinct* (which is identified largely with the sex libido) and the *death instinct*. The life instinct represents positive, constructive tendencies which are in opposition to the destructive forces of the death instinct. The struggle is love against hate, life against death, and the individual is constantly caught in the warfare of these vast, instinctual forces.

Freud also had a unique concept of the conservation or transformation of energy, maintaining that what he called *psychic energy* could be changed into muscular or mechanical energy. This shift in the form of energy takes place as a process of thinking (psychic energy) followed by action (muscular energy).

Thus the libido expresses itself in a number of distinct fashions and will find devious ways of controlling thought and behavior. In fact, for Freud, the major problem in motives is the concealment of the genuine urges.

Perhaps the most interesting aspect of psychoanalytic theory from the standpoint of motivation is the role of the unconscious or the *id* (see Chapter 4). The concept of unconscious motivation has not enjoyed popularity among social scientists, but recent evidence and a reconsideration of earlier work is leading to a reassessment of its value. There are many examples of alterations in a person's behavior or self-reported mental states that have been brought about by manipulation of stimuli of which people are unaware. Silverman (1976) has shown, for example, that stimuli people are unaware of influence their behavior in a predictable manner which is different from the way the same stimuli would influence their behavior if they were aware of them. In the case of pathology such as depression and stuttering, stimulation of unconscious fantasies was found to increase pathology, but only if the subjects were unaware of the motivational influence. Swingle (1979) reported that verbal messages presented at a volume lower than that which is audible to a person (subliminal) can influence behavior in a predictable fashion.

Thus it appears that behavior is influenced both by motives about which the person is aware and those that operate outside his or her awareness. In the case of some pathological states, lack of awareness may even be a necessary condition for the motivational influence to become manifest. In some cases, a person's awareness of the motive state enhances the influence of the motive (Scheier et al., 1978). And a belief that one can do something, the belief in one's own capability, can enhance the influence of a motive-modifying procedure (Bandura, 1977).

In evaluating Freud's theory from the standpoint of motivation, it is difficult to overestimate the enormous contribution he made in opening up a forbidden territory. Until his time, sex as a motivational factor had been ignored, or more exactly, had been driven underground. Even more important was his discovery of the unconscious as a potent force in the dynamics of adjustment. There are

Box 7–2
GAYS, STRAIGHTS, AND BISEXUALS

What constitutes, or what causes, a person's sexual orientation has been subject to inquiry ever since Freud first presented his theory of sexual stages. Many observers have reservations about his theory that homosexuality results from an unresolved Oedipal complex, that is, the son "transforms himself" into the mother. It is possible, in fact, that homosexuality arises in two opposite situations: when a person either strongly identifies with the characteristics of his or her own sex or has a minimum of identification with it.*

In examining the question of sexual identification, Michael Storms administered questionnaires on personal attributes and erotic fantasies to 186 men and women selected from a social psychology class and from gay student organizations and gay friendship networks.† He found little difference in the scores for masculinity or femininity between subjects who identified themselves as straight, gay, or bisexual. He found the gays did have more erotic fantasies toward their own sex than the straights, but they also had some fantasies toward the opposite sex. The bisexuals (those who reported an orientation toward both sexes) reported as many same-sex fantasies as the homosexuals and as many opposite-sex fantasies as the heterosexual.

In view of the sensitivity about sexual orientation, the methodology of any research in this area can be questioned. Yet the Storms study at least shows the complexity of sexual motivation. According to a number of investigations, the adjustment of the homosexual is not radically different from that of the heterosexual.‡ These findings are related to the growing tolerance of deviant lifestyles and the absurdity of stereotyping individuals with a given sexual preference, as Storms's research shows.

---

* C. A. Tripp, *Homosexual Matrix* (New York: McGraw-Hill Book Co., 1975).

† M. D. Storms, "Theories of Sexual Orientation," *Journal of Personality and Social Psychology*, 1980, *38*, 783–792.

‡ E. Hooker, "The Adjustment of the Overt Homosexual," *Journal of Projective Techniques*, 1957, *21*, 18–31.

---

weaknesses, however, in his system. His terminology was vague and not verified empirically, although some misunderstanding was due to problems of translation. The term *instinct* (as the German word *Trieb*, or *drive*, was translated) had come into disfavor in American psychology by the 1920s.

In addition, his single-cause viewpoint and dogmatism were not altogether scientific and led to considerable revision by later psychoanalysts. It is unlikely that any one factor, such as sex in classical psychoanalysis or economics in Marxian theory, can be the central cause of complex human behavior.

Instinctivism still haunts psychoanalysis (Berkowitz, 1969b). Nonetheless, from a social-psychological viewpoint, the movement is of considerable significance in focusing on drives like aggression and sex. Moreover, various defense or adjustment mechanisms—such as repression, rationalization, and sublimation—are important in explaining the equilibrium people maintain for themselves and their behavior toward others with whom they interact.

Current Conceptualization

Currently, motivation is usually conceptualized according to two basic viewpoints, similar to those on learning described in Chapter 5. *Mechanistic theories* of motivation, which approach behavior in terms of the behaviorists' stimulus-response (S-R) model, come closest to the traditional reward-and-punishment concept. *Cognitive or purposive theories* of motivation look at the sequence of behavior as initiated by a cognitive process rather than a mere stimulus. Weiner (1972) says we are motivated to act when "External or internal events are endowed, categorized, and transformed into a belief, such as 'I am hungry.' " These cognitive theories have assumed many forms, but for all of them behavior is purposive. Gestalt psychology has contributed to this viewpoint of motivation by various avenues.

COGNITIVE APPROACHES

Purpose, Behavior, and Conflict: Tolman and Lewin

Edward C. Tolman demonstrated the intimate relationship between learning and motivation and rejected the viewpoint of the behaviorists that motivation involves a specific response to a specific stimulus. As a Gestalt theorist, he maintained that behavior, like other psychological phenomena, must be viewed in a molar (the whole) rather than a molecular (the parts) perspective. The organism is said to select its stimuli as well as its responses.

Tolman (1932) regarded "stimuli, heredity, past training, and momentary initiating physiological states" as the four irreducible "causes" of behavior. This position was substantially adhered to in his later work. Tolman (1951) considers motives as "hypothetical constructs," as explained in Chapter 1. The stimulus situation, the physical drive, and various individual differences (such as age or sex) constitute the independent variables which produce the dependent variable, namely, behavior. The basic problem in understanding motivation is seen as isolating the intervening variable, or the specific cause of the behavior.

Kurt Lewin, identified in Chapter 1 as the originator of a broadened view of Gestalt principles known as *field theory,* distinguishes between the physical field, or objective stimulus situation, and the psychological field. He refers to the stimulus situation as perceived, interpreted, and given meaning by the individual.

Objects, persons, and activities have positive *valence,* or incentive value, for the individual if they are attractive and negative valence if they are repellent (Lewin, 1935, 1976). The main determinant of valence for a person is his or her favorable or unfavorable experience with the stimulus in question. Thus to a hungry American a hamburger has positive valence and seal blubber does not; to a hungry Eskimo, the reverse might be true.

Valences, Lewin says, change as tension states change in the individual. After a person has eaten heartily, food temporarily loses its positive valence. This seems fairly simple, but actually, the relationship between tension states and incentives is rather complicated. Not only does a tension state influence the valence of an incentive, but the incentive affects the tension state. This can be seen best when the need or tension state is *latent,* or not conscious or operating to produce overt activity. Though you are not consciously hungry, you can suddenly get hungry if you happen to smell freshly popped popcorn. There is a reciprocal relation between the motive (internal) and the goal (external) of behavior; a change in either one will affect the other. If a young man finds that the woman he wants to marry does not share his rhapsodic affections, his whole motivational structure—his sexual and emotional needs—will undergo change. That is, he may present a new image of himself or try to change some aspect of his personality. But if his marital ardor cools, the object of his affections will seem less attractive.

Both Tolman and Lewin performed a service in removing motivation from the mechanistic framework that behaviorists and various other psychologists had erected. The breadth of their conceptualizations derives in part from their use of constructs from physics and certain new branches of mathematics, notably topology.

Functional Autonomy: Allport

Another interpretation of motivation is that behaviors once acquired in order to serve some purpose become an end in themselves and, consequently, act as motives. This is Gordon Allport's (1961) theory of functional autonomy, which proposes that adult motives are "infinitely varied . . . self-sustaining, contemporary systems, growing out of antecedent systems, but functionally independent of them." That is to say, purposive activities proceed under their own steam, no matter how they originate. Thus, says Allport, the ex-sailor yearns for the sea, or a businessman "long since secure economically, works himself into ill health, and sometimes even back into poverty, for the sake of carrying on his plans. What was once an instrumental technique becomes a master motive."

One of the criticisms that can be made of Allport's theory is that autonomous motives may actually be latent rather than active, or, if they are active, they may be serving other motives. Thus, the businessman's devotion to his work may serve primarily to keep him with his friends and get him away from the dreary environment of his home—an escape his wife probably did not have access to until recently. Another objection is that this approach is more descriptive than explanatory (Hall, 1961). Allport's reply is that motivation must be related to the lifestyle of the individual. The potential of motives to become functional has been demonstrated in experiments regarding sexual arousal and exposure to erotic films (see Box 7–3).

In assessing the functional autonomy theory, J. P. Seward (1963) suggests a modification to explain social motives as patterns of behavior acquired by an organism that were not part of its inborn motivation but have developed out of the context of given situations. In his view, organisms have different preferences; so that, for instance, curiosity emerges as a "function of learning the environment," and cats prefer soft cushions to hard floors. These preferences can be interpreted as exogenous, or externally caused, motives that are functionally autonomous. Seward regards the theory of functional autonomy as secondary to the tendency of organisms to select behaviors in order to deal with the environment.

BOX 7–3
EROTIC FILMS AND SEX AROUSAL: ENOUGH IS ENOUGH

Efforts to determine the motivational effects of exposure to erotic materials have produced somewhat inconsistent results. Viewing erotic materials stimulates immediately subsequent sex activity, as noted in a University of Hamburg study.* Male subjects showed a significant rise in frequency of masturbation during the 24 hours following the viewing of erotic slides and motion pictures, and females reported an increase in petting and sexual intercourse. These results were generally supported by a California study in which 77 percent of the males and 63 percent of the females who viewed sex films reported greater sexual activity during the night, as compared to only 41 percent of the males and 35 percent of the females who were shown nonerotic materials.†

Repetitive exposure to sexual stimuli can weaken its impact, however, and satiation (or erosion of the motive) can be the result. This is because motivation for which there is little or no new learning is most vulnerable to attrition, or weakening, and learning is most efficient when a novel response is involved. The stimulating effects of erotic materials were found to be transitory in a study of the effects of sexual stimuli viewed on a screen over several weeks by a sample of middle-class men and women, who reported that their sexual arousal eventually declined.‡

---

* G. Schmidt and V. Sigusch, "Sex Differences in Response to Psychosexual Stimulation by Films and Slides," *Journal of Sex Research*, 1970, *6*, 268–283.

† J. L. Howard et al., "Effects of Exposure to Pornography," in *Technical Report of the Commission on Obscenity and Pornography* (Vol. 8), (Washington, D.C.: Government Printing Office, 1971), p. 206.

‡ J. Mann et al., "Satiation of the Transient Stimulating Effect of Erotic Films," *Journal of Personality and Social Psychology*, 1974, *30*, 729–735.

Human beings have complex patterns for making these selections. Needs may be integrated into more intricate motives, or *quasi needs,* which become functionally autonomous and die away when the situation changes (Vernon, 1969). An underlying concept of functional autonomy is the changing character of motivation, in contrast to the sterility of a purely associative principle of drive reduction.

The Search for a Central Motive

The existence of a "central motive state" based on neural and physiological grounds was suggested by Clifford Morgan (1959). Few psychologists seem to support such a concept, but the search for a primary, all-embracing motive continues. The *self-actualization theory* of Kurt Goldstein (1939) is an early example of the holistic, or unitary, approach to motivation. According to Goldstein, the basic drive or motive of the organism is to "actualize itself, to actualize its nature." This theory developed from his study of brain-injured patients and their attempts at recovery. Goldstein saw the protection and enhancement of the self and the reduction of anxiety as the major preoccupations of the individual.

From the economists of the 18th century to the psychologists of the 20th, most motivation theorists have presumed that the individual strives to maximize gains and minimize losses. This approach underlines the focus of motivation on the self. Yet each person is geared to other persons, and the affiliative motive (to be discussed in a later section) bears this out. Our motivations are rooted in cognitions, and so we process incoming informatiion from interactions with others and use it to relieve tensions and obtain goals (Wyer, 1974).

Motivation is inevitably geared to the learning system, and external as well as internal rewards are central in this process. As one instance, a problem of management in modern organizations is to create work situations for employees that they can link to intrinsic rewards. In repetitive work, often the most that can be hoped for is that the rewards can somehow be related to the task and made proportionate to the effort expended (Katz & Kahn, 1978).

Classificatory Systems of Motives

In contrast to the conceptualization of a central motive are theories of a plurality of motives. A number of classifications have been made. Perhaps the best-known list is Murray's (1938) 20-odd "viscerogenic" and "psychogenic" needs, including activity, nurturance, succorance, harm avoidance, autonomy, acquisition, affiliation, cognizance, construction, deference, dominance, recognition, achievement, and blame avoidance. The classification suggested in this text, which is described in the section titled "Social and Cultural Factors in Motivation," is based on the satisfaction of certain social needs: security, achievement, affiliation and status, and integration and creativity.

Rather than classifying motives according to their nature or content, as Murray did, Klineberg (1954) devised a different method based on four broad categories of motives according to origin. These categories are:

1. Motives which are absolutely dependable, have a definite physiological basis, and allow no exceptions. These include hunger, thirst, the need for rest and sleep, the elimination of waste products from the body, as well as activity and aesthetic drives.
2. Motives which have a definite physiological basis. These are found in all societies, but there are individual exceptions. These include sex, postmaternal behavior, and possibly also self-preservation.
3. Motives which have an indirect physiological basis and occur with great frequency but allow exceptions in both groups and individuals. These include aggressiveness, flight, and probably also self-assertiveness.
4. Motives which have no known physiological basis and which occur with some frequency. These include gregariousness, the paternal motive, the premater-nal motive, the filial motive, acquisitiveness, and self-submission.

MECHANISTIC THEORIES: FOCUS ON GOALS AND REINFORCERS

When motivation is considered in behaviorist terms, as it is in the drive theory described above, the difficulty of identifying the variables intervening between stimulus and response often directs attention to the *goals* of behavior. For instance, much of our understanding of the nature of conflict is gained from an analysis of the *resource pool* which is the object or goal the parties in conflict are attempting to attain. There are many behaviorally oriented psychologists who feel that the only way to understand motivational behavior objectively is to ignore the traditional concepts of motivation and focus on *reinforcers* (Reynolds, 1968). They argue that observed behavior can be explained by examining the conditions that make reinforcers effective, although at times the goals underlying certain behaviors may seem incomprehensible.

An attractive feature of this focus is that such concepts or goals, resource pools, and reinforcers are likely to be objective and therefore able to be somewhat accurately measured. This does not hold for many goals, however. Conflict, for example, often revolves around the resource pool of personal freedom, a perceived state which interacts with actual restrictions against one's self-determi-nation, which perhaps can be objectively measured, as well as with one's need for and perception of one's own independence, which is difficult to measure. In Jean-Paul Sartre's statement that "we were never more free than under the Nazis" (during the German occupation of France in World War II), for example, the term *free* is being used in a special existentialist sense as "the discrepancy between . . . tyrannical pressures . . . and . . . capacity to generate meanings which contradicted this environment" (Hampden-Turner, 1971).

Social behavior is enormously complex, circular, and replete with reciprocal phenomena, and it seems to be explicable only in terms of total systems. Nevertheless, a firm understanding of social phenomena requires an under-standing of the ways the phenomena operate, in conditioning terms. Classically, the term *goal* has been defined as "any object or event that terminates an ongoing activity of the organism"; in other words, a goal is "an incentive that is chosen by the investigator as a reference point for describing observed behavior." (Bindra, 1959). The food pellet for the rat in the maze and the completion of a symphony for the composer are both goals. In social psychology, of course, we are more concerned with the complex goals of human beings in their social settings.

Goals can be positive or negative, conscious or unconscious. They may be patterns of action we are attempting to attain, or situations or actions we are trying to avoid. Many goals remain unverbalized—attitudes and emotions, for example—and still function as motives. Conflict often arises because a goal is not appropriate to the situation confronting us, or our capacity for achieving it is limited.

Primary and Secondary Motivation

Behavior serves motives in various ways, depending on the variety of behavioral response in a situation (Kimble, Garmezy, & Zigler, 1974). First, there is tension reduction, most frequently obtained by *consummatory* behavior which terminates a drive. Thirst drives you to drink, curiosity leads you to the library or laboratory. Second, there is *instrumental* behavior, or activities performed in order to realize certain goals. You attend class in order to obtain grades, which give you academic standing and may be useful in a future career. Third, there is *substitute* behavior. Masturbation may be the outlet for the sexual urge when heterosexual channels are blocked. Both instrumental and substitute activities may become motives in themselves, as the theory of functional autonomy demonstrates.

Like the terms *primary and secondary reinforcement* defined above, *primary motivation* applies to physical drives like thirst and hunger, while *secondary motivation* applies to behavior derived from the basic drives that come to have motivational character. For example, if you work in order to obtain a means of securing the necessities of life, work is for you a secondary motive. However, the motives involved in most activities are so complex that the distinction between primary and secondary motivation is extremely difficult. For instance, getting married or seeking a job encompasses a variety of motives, both physical and psychological.

In daily living, most motives are of the acquired or secondary type, and learning is the major means of motive acquisition. More basic motives, such as maternal love, may be influenced by a number of related motives, including those based on physical needs. The research of Harlow (1958, 1962) suggests that higher-level motives develop from lower-level ones. Substitute stimuli may come to elicit such responses as maternal-filial behavior. Harlow experimented with two groups of monkeys reared by different types of artificial "mothers"—one made of wire mesh, with nipples to dispense milk, and another made of soft terry cloth with no nipples. The infant monkeys came to prefer the terry-cloth "mothers" to the wire ones, even though milk was given by the latter. They displayed close affectional bonds toward these mother substitutes, and disorganized behavior appeared when they were isolated from them for a lengthy period. Their social

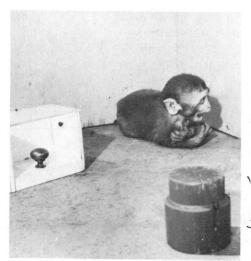

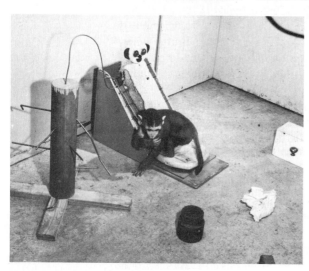

Harry Harlow's experiments on different forms of mothering are classic. 1. When no surrogate mother was present the monkey showed fear and withdrawal. 2. Introduction of the cloth mother immediately attracted the infant. 3. After contact with the cloth surrogate, the infant regained some security and was able to turn its attention to play objects in the room. 4. Infants fed on a wire mother usually left it right after feeding. *Source:* Harry F. Harlow.

development was less complete than when they were reared with their real mothers, however.

Caution is in order when making comparisons of animal and human behavior, but Harlow's experiments strongly suggest the modifiability and manipulability of primary motives. Studies of institutionalized human infants also point to the extreme effects of parental deprivation, notably the loss of the affection for parents (Spitz, 1945). Nevertheless, substitute stimuli and responses can enormously extend the range of motivation for humans.

Emotions as Motivators

It has been suggested that emotions, like drives, have motivational character and also originate in the lower or subcortical areas of the brain and are accompanied by hormonal or endocrine stimulation (Wong, 1976). It may be, however, that neither emotions nor organic drives directly control behavior; rather both may serve the purpose of alerting or energizing the cognitive processes that initiate behavior (Leeper, 1965). Emotional processes are complex responses which develop out of intricate stimulus patterns and which can have a number of motivational consequences for a person who, for example, falls in love, goes to a funeral, or watches violent programs on TV (see Box 7–4).

Fear, anger, elation, and other emotional states serve as motives in the sense that they can arouse (or serve as a form of arousal for) activity, organize it, and channel it in a particular direction. McClelland (1951) defines a motive as a "strong affective association, characterized by an anticipatory goal reaction and based on past association of certain cues with pleasure or pain."

In learning to organize the stimulus situations in the environment, the individual acquires a number of emotional patterns and the appropriate emotional responses to given cues. Anxiety, for example, may be a major factor in determining with whom a person prefers to interact and to whom she or he turns for support (Schachter, 1959). Because much of motivation is conflict oriented, emotions such as anger, anxiety, and love often operate to direct behavior. Fundamentally, emotions act as energizers, as in anger, or as deenergizers, as in mild disgust (Rethlingshafer, 1963).

A number of emotions can be manipulated in studying central motives in adult and child behavior; for example, five-year-old children could be observed playing with dolls in order to determine the experimental conditions that favor aggression or affiliation (Gordon & Cohn, 1963). The differential effects of anxiety and fear on motivation were studied in an ingenious experiment with 72 Yale undergraduates by Sarnoff and Zimbardo (1961). Subjects were divided into four groups. In the "high fear" group the subjects anticipated painful shocks; in the "low fear" group the word *pain* was never used, and they were told they would experience only harmless shocks. Subjects in the "high anxiety" group were told to suck on such objects as baby bottles and pacifiers (objects of oral significance, according to Freud) while their physiological reactions were being tested. For the "low anxiety" group more neutral objects, like balloons and whistles, were used. The findings indicate that the desire to be with others increased from the low fear

Box 7–4
VIOLENCE: VIEWING AND DOING

Whether or not watching violence on TV leads to aggression has been the subject of considerable research. In the late sixties, for example, a study was made of 625 boys residing in three private and four public schools who were assigned to watch for six weeks either "aggressive" programs ("FBI," "The Untouchables," among others) or "nonaggressive" programs ("Gilligan's Island," "Lucy Show," and "Yogi Bear").* The boys in the public schools who viewed the violent fare actually showed less aggressiveness, as determined by tests, peer ratings, and supervisor reports. They were also involved in only about half as many fights as were the control group. One possible explanation would be the stimulation or working out of their own aggressiveness that watching violence on the screen provided.

Most research, however, has found a relationship between exposure to TV violence and aggressiveness. Typical is a study comparing children watching "The Untouchables" with those watching a sporting event.† After the TV experience the children went to a play area with other children, and those who had been exposed to the violent program were markedly more combative with their peers.

In 1977 the National Citizens Committee for Broadcasting estimated that by the age of 14 the average American child had witnessed 11,000 murders on TV! This interest group and others such as the Parents-Teachers Association have brought pressure to bear on advertisers, networks, and the Federal Communications Commission to limit violent programs and promote other types. L. D. Eron points to the need for more intervention on the part of parents as well as reforms in the media. His suggestion that boys should be socialized as girls traditionally have been is based on his observation that viewing TV violence increased aggressive behavior in boys but not girls, until girls began to be socialized as boys are.‡

---

* S. Feshbach and R. Singer, *Television and Violence* (San Francisco: Jossey-Bass Publishers, 1970).
† R. Liebert and R. Baron, "Some Immediate Effects of Televised Violence on Children's Behavior," *Developmental Psychology,* 1972, *6,* 469–75.
‡ L. D. Eron, "Prescription for Reduction of Aggression," *American Psychologist,* 1980, *35,* 244–252. Eron's studies are described in Chapter 14 (Box 14–1).

to the high fear group, but the desire to be alone increased from the low anxiety to high anxiety group. Fear seems to induce the need for affiliation, but when forced into inappropriate behavior, the anxious person is "loath to communicate his anxieties to others."

SOCIAL AND CULTURAL FACTORS IN MOTIVATION

Despite certain unanswered questions about the motivating character of physiological drives, or *biogenic motives,* this basis of motivation is relatively easy to understand. The real difficulty in explaining motivation comes in relation to the learned, or *sociogenic motives.* Here we can find no evidence of bodily needs, but motives that have been identified by such terms as *prestige-seeking, sociability, mastery, conformity,* and the like often are more significant than the basic physiological drives.

Actually, the patterning of motives in a society is always social. Whether the behavior is directed at satisfaction of the hunger drive, choice of a friend or an occupation, or purchase of furniture or an automobile, cultural conditioning plays a major role in the selective process. In Western culture, for example, our preference is for certain foods; only when faced with acute starvation would most Americans conceivably eat grasshoppers or worms. While members of a few subcultures may favor rattlesnake meat over hamburger or filet mignon, this only demonstrates the power and sanctity of the cultural norms. Moreover, there are prescribed types of foods for various levels of the life cycle, and people do not eat merely to satisfy hunger; status needs determine culinary taste in many cultures. Thus even a primary drive like hunger is conditioned by culture.

In prehistoric times and early history, when culture changed slowly, motives may have remained fairly constant, but as cultural change has accelerated in the 20th century, patterns of social motivation have been subjected to rapid change and have become widely diversified. Some motives may become practically inoperative when other needs have not been met, as suggested in Maslow's (1954) hierarchical theory of lower-order needs which must be satisfied before the next higher-order need is effective as a motivator. For some people, some motives take priority over others. In any case, status, social approval, and even sex hardly matter to a person who is threatened with starvation, for example.

In Western society, however, drives and basic physical needs are seldom critical, because members are protected against the rigors and depredations of nature and inadequate socialization that characterize more primitive societies. In American society, therefore, the role of *social motives* is highlighted, and the major choices are between motives such as achievement versus fear of failure or security versus new experience, rather than priorities in satisfying drives such as hunger or thirst or keeping warm.

Many classificatory systems such as Maslow's have been proposed to designate the various kinds of social motives. The one suggested in this section is based on the individual's needs for security, achievement, affiliation and status, and integration and creativity.

Security Needs

There are several forms of security. The most important is physical security, since it requires satisfaction of biogenic needs like food and temperature maintenance. Financial or economic security, which is derived from the socioeconomic order, also is instrumental to physical security. (In a sense, then, financial security is a secondary drive.) Psychological security, based on the other two types, rests on other personality needs. It is basically a feeling of well-being which may or may not harmonize with the relatively objective criteria of personality stability and tension reduction.

There is a close connection between psychological and physical security. Failure to receive adequate nutrition and the fulfillment of other biogenic needs in the early years promotes anxiety in adolescents and adults. Material deprivation can be a crucial reason for this result, but in Western culture a different kind of situation—material gratification in lieu of affectional warmth though parental attention—is more serious and more prevalent. Rejection, whether physical or affectional, is the greatest enemy of psychological security.

The Achievement Motive

Achievement deserves special attention, if only because of the volume of research that has been concerned with this motive. This research, much of which was done over several decades by David McClelland and his colleagues (1961, 1978), has had three principal purposes:

1. To test the various kinds of methodologies in the study of the achievement motive.
2. To determine its psychological variables and its relationship to other social motives.
3. To obtain material for cross-cultural comparisons (see Chapter 2).

Achievement motives have been studied in experimental situations where results in certain tasks were compared with the findings of projective tests, which present neutral stimuli to be interpreted by the individual. According to Atkinson (1964), achievement is related to the "expectancy that certain actions will lead to success which may be inferred from the instructions and other situational cues" (p. 233). Success or failure in a task can determine the degree of achievement drive for an individual.

Individuals with a high need for achievement can be expected to aspire to positions of prestige. One study showed that a person with a strong need to achieve and low fear of failure is the most likely candidate for high political office, such as circuit judge or state governor (Burnstein, 1963).

The presence of anxiety can affect the need for achievement positively or negatively (Feather, 1965). In a mobile, industrial society, people must continually strive for better positions or struggle merely to hold on to what they have. Glaser and Strauss (1971) describe this as *juggling*. American movies, they say, "often show the hero caught between crossfires of motivation," as when the choice is between success in business and an ideal family life. Transitional positions between career crisis points are especially likely to produce anxiety and frustration. When there are blockages in what Glaser and Strauss call *status passage* (see Box 4–2 in Chapter 4), the careerist must weigh the options carefully. In every organization, sooner or later there are power struggles for position and prestige. The decision of moving from specialist to generalist, or vice versa, often faces professionals, and athletes, entertainers, and artists are particularly vulnerable to reversal.

The complexities of the development of a social motive are nicely illustrated by recent research on the achievement motive. It has been found, for example, that achievement motivation and university grades are related only if the student perceives good grades as being instrumental to future career success (Raynor, 1970). It would seem to be obvious that a strong motive to succeed or to avoid failure is related only to goals that the individual considers meaningful. Nevertheless, researchers frequently make such judgments as evaluating the internal motivational states of schoolchildren on the basis of achievement scores. The achievement score represents a measure of success of importance to the school system, parents, and so on, but it can mean little or nothing to the child. The strength of the motive to succeed is a function of both parental training and peer-group influences, although the relationship is not at all simple. It has been found, for example (as pointed out in Chapter 3), that the performance of schoolchildren from disadvantaged backgrounds is influenced by the background and aspirations of the other students in the schools they attend (Coleman et al., 1966). Parental influence seems to be most important when children are very young; one study found that eight- to ten-year-olds with strong motives to succeed had parents who rewarded independent accomplishment and expected accomplishment at an early age (Winterbottom, 1958). Another study found, however, that mothers who encourage independence at an early age tend to encourage it less later (Feld, 1967). Strong emphasis on independence at an early age can encourage children to be too independent in adolescence, a more troublesome time.

A critical investigation of the achievement motive has been carried out by John W. Atkinson at the University of Michigan. With his colleagues and students, he has been concerned with both the intrinsic and extrinsic factors surrounding the tendency to avoid failure and to strive toward achievement, and they have tested these components in a number of tasks in varied settings. In one of these studies Matina Horner (1974) focused on the achievement aspirations of women. On the basis of TAT scores, she found that women had a greater fear of success, and women honor students had more fear of it than other women students. The pattern of fear was affected by the curriculum, the size of the competitive groups, the number of male competitors, and the anticipation of success in a given course. Subsequent research on fear of success in women was more ambiguous in its results, but Chafetz (1978) observed that "it is probably still safe to say that there is pressure on adolescent females to dampen or minimize their achievement strivings in areas other than popularity." The social climate in recent years has generally encouraged women to be more assertive, however. A study comparing the shift of social motives over a 20-year period, from 1957 to 1976, revealed an increase in achievement motivation among women, whereas there was no change in the scores for men. The two intervening decades gave women more opportunity to realize their career ambitions (Veroff et al., 1980).

Power is another motive that is related to achievement needs. McClelland (1975) also has played a major role in this research area, outlining how it varies for subcultures like age, sex, and social background. The power motive is a complex one which emerges from our desire to manipulate others and is also related to the needs for leadership and social status. An excessive power drive may spring from unsatisfactory or insufficient emotional ties to other people; alcoholics, for example, may have been frustrated in trying to satisfy their power needs. With training in power motivation, the rehabilitation rate in a sample of alcoholics was increased in one year by nearly 50 percent (McClelland, 1978).

Affiliative and Status Needs

The cluster of motives that surround gregariousness, sociability, or the "wish for response," as W. I. Thomas (1936) called it, encompasses an enormous range of affiliative behavior. At one end are such mild social tendencies as enjoying the knowledge that other people are living in the house down the road, even though we are not acquainted with them, or the greater responsiveness we feel in attending a movie rather than sitting alone before a television set. At the other end of the range of affiliative needs is the deep relationship of affection, love, and sexual response. Somewhere between these extremes are the tendencies to association and friendship that operate in most of social contacts. These sociable tendencies are very greatly affected, if not determined, by social experience.

Extensive research has demonstrated the complexity of affiliative needs. In a study of friendship formation in a campus residential house, T. M. Newcomb (1961) found that the friendships were based on agreement and congeniality regarding a number of values, attitudes, and opinions on topics such as sports, campus politics, or religious outlook. Perceived consensus and shared attitudes were reported as the foundation of friendships with one or two others. Indiscriminate friendships occurred less frequently, as did attempts at conversion. Thus affiliation is in part the product of congenial belief systems. Considerable strain can result from attempts to balance one's friendships and loyalties with one's beliefs and values, as further discussion of this study in the balance theory topic in Chapter 13 will demonstrate.

A number of variables also determined affiliative relationships in Schachter's (1959) study of a sample of American university women. Anxiety was one: When confronted with an anxiety type of situation, the students preferred to be with others who were simultaneously experiencing anxiety. Ordinal position in the family also affected the level of anxiety and affiliation; firstborn children were more anxiety prone than those with older siblings. Even with anxiety held constant, the earlier born were more dependent, less self-reliant, and formed more friendships. (It may be that firstborn children are comparatively more overprotected and less consistently treated.) In addition, hunger was found to be related positively to both anxiety and affiliation, though under extreme hunger the affiliative tendency is less marked.

Both the Newcomb and Schachter studies indicate the possibilities of empirical exploration of social motivation. The distance between this contemporary approach and the older instinctual doctrine should be evident. Although individual variations were noted in these studies, the interrelation of behavior and social motivation was emphasized.

Integrative and Creative Needs

For most people in every society, motivation involves more than the need for security, achievement, affiliation, and status or approval. The urge to work and play with other human beings, to enter into deep affectional relationships, to marry and have children, and to create things of lasting value, whether building a house, writing a poem, or organizing a charity drive—all these are characteristically human. The various forms of prosocial behavior seem to develop from a complex sequence of learnings, concerned with (1) change from a state of unawareness to one of awareness of the other person's needs, (2) the decision whether to do something about the situation, and (3) the degree of reciprocity that the behavior elicits in the recipient (Bar-Tal, 1976). A similar sequence occurs in negative or antisocial behaviors like competition or aggression, although the specific interaction differs.

The integrative motive, or cooperation, is universal; social life would not be possible without some degree of interdependence. There are even biological bases for this social motive, such as sex relations, the nursing of the infant, and symbiosis (biological interdependence) among animals. The basis of integrative behavior or altruism depends on the development of empathy in the organism, and this responsiveness to the needs of others is rooted in deep neural structures or the lower brain of many animals (M. L. Hoffman, 1981). However, there also is conclusive evidence that cooperation depends on learning. The dependence of the infant on the adult is one of the initiating phases of cooperation, and play with peers (siblings and neighborhood children) helps it along. Conditioning and other mechanisms of learning account for the development of this motive.

Considerable variation in the need for cooperation or its opposite, competition, has been found among and within cultures. Study of Utopian colonies has produced evidence both for and against cooperation as an inherent drive. The enduring desire through the ages for a community based on brotherhood and equality has raised the question whether cooperativeness is a primary drive that has been socially repressed. Since nearly all of these Utopian experiments have been short-lived, however, this evidence suggests that humans are basically competitive and aggressive. Arguments about the inherent nature of both of these motives rest on hypotheses that have not been critically tested, however.

Parental needs seem to be one of the clearest of the integrative motives. The maternal drive, particularly, has been found to have a hormonal basis, but wide variations in both the prematernal (the desire for children) and the postmaternal (the desire to protect and care for one's offspring) drives argue against a simple inborn determination. In the United States, for example, a substantial number of

The street carnival offers a momentary escape from the search to satisfy security needs and provides a chance for new experiences. *Source:* Courtesy of the French Tourist Office.

married women of child-bearing age have decided against motherhood for themselves. Since rejection occurs in mothers of legitimate as well as illegitimate children, the existence of a maternal instinct is questionable. Other social motives and a number of economic and psychological considerations also are involved in the decision to have—or not to have—children.

A Motivational Basis for Aggression

If cooperation represents the positive side of the integrative motive, competition represents the negative side. When competition is carried to an extreme, the result is aggression, which has been identified as the cause of many of society's problems but which can occasionally be positive. Various aspects of aggression have been investigated, and the research is examined at several points in this text. From a motivational standpoint, the concern is with the genesis of aggression as an inherent drive or learned behavior.

One controversial concept in this research is the *frustration-aggression hypothesis,* which was first proposed by John Dollard and his colleagues (1939). Its basic thesis is that when a motive is blocked, frustration is experienced; this frustration inevitably gives rise to aggression, and the occurrence of aggression presupposes frustration. These conclusions are hard to defend, as several critics have pointed out. Leonard Berkowitz (1969b), for example, disagrees with the originally stated hypothesis that frustration always leads to aggression, though frustration under certain circumstances may indeed enhance the probability of aggression.

Another difficulty with the frustration-aggression hypothesis is that aggression does not always have identifiable antecedents (Berkowitz, 1965). Aggressive responding in children, for example, is encouraged by their identification with parental behavior, as noted in Chapter 3. Other evidence has also indicated that certain frustrating experiences may actually decrease aggression (Taylor & Pisano, 1971).

The frustration-aggression hypothesis has been widely used as an explanation for *scapegoating* behavior, particularly in regard to racial-ethnic prejudice (see Chapter 18). Racial violence has frequently been attributed to displaced aggression resulting from social or economic frustration, and this aggression may be enhanced when a particular person or group is identified as responsible for blocking goal attainment. Katz and Cohen (1962) found greater antiblack prejudice among lower-class than middle-class whites, in part because the former were competing with blacks for the same jobs.

Berkowitz (1965) proposed a modified frustration-aggression hypothesis: Frustration creates a readiness for aggression, but aggression does not occur unless suitable cues are present. These releaser-type cues are stimuli that have been associated in the past with aggression. In one study (Berkowitz & LePage, 1967), experimental subjects administered significantly stronger electric shocks to other people when a pistol and a rifle were displayed than they did in the presence of neutral or irrelevant objects. Schuck and Pisor (1974) replicated the experiment but concluded the stronger shocks administered in the presence of firearms may have reflected the subjects' belief that the experimenters expected or wanted strong shocks to be administered, rather than the effects of the guns as releaser stimuli. In another study (Berkowitz & Alioto, 1973), university students who had been angered frequently displayed more aggression toward their tormentors after viewing film of either a prizefight or a football game which had been identified as an aggressive encounter. Another experiment was built around showing male subjects three kinds of films—neutral, erotic, or aggressive-erotic—and then giving them an opportunity to express aggressiveness by delivering electric shocks to their partners. Exposure to the aggressive-erotic film was followed by increased aggression to members of both sexes, but especially to females (Donnerstein, 1980).

The learned-behavior basis of aggression is supported by findings that it can be reduced by favorable stimuli. In one study automobile drivers engaged in less honking of their horns, as compared with a control group, when the stimulus for the honking evoked *empathy* (the driver was a girl on crutches with a bandaged leg), *humor* (the driver was wearing an outlandish clown mask), or *sexual arousal* (an attractive, scantily clad female driver). When the temperature was above normal, however, horn honking increased (Baron, 1976).

In groups, aggression can be *a response to blocked needs,* as the militancy of minority groups in South Africa demonstrates. A culture also may sanction or encourage aggressiveness. According to Loewenberg (1976), the aggressiveness of the Nazi youth movement in Germany in the 1930s appealed to a generation of adults who as children themselves had undergone a series of traumatic episodes in World War I. The absence of their fathers at the front encouraged an Oedipal fixation on their mothers, and the return of these fathers in defeat and the abdication of the Kaiser caused further loss of father figures. After undergoing postwar conditions which included acute food deprivation, massive inflation, and severe economic depression, they saw in Adolf Hitler a new father symbol, and he provided them not only with a mechanism for identity but a springboard to ritualized aggression as well.

Aggression also can serve as an instrumental response, providing rewards of money, advantage, prestige, and the like. Revolutionaries, for example, have demonstrated that acts of violence perpetrated against a repressive society can have a soul-cleansing effect, a kind of *catharsis.* The Iranian militants who took U.S. diplomats hostage capitalized on this effect by using them as a target for the people's wrath againt the Shah, who had been supported by American foreign policy. When important models such as the family or peer groups behave in an aggressive manner, children and adolescents tend to imitate that behavior, especially if they are rewarded for it (Bandura, 1971), an aspect of aggression that was investigated in Chapter 5.

Anger can also induce aggression, though the perpetrators may not be aware of their anger; that is, it does not appear to be necessary for people to interpret their emotional state as anger in order to behave aggressively (Berkowitz, 1978). Thus, as noted at the beginning of the chapter, people may not be conscious of the cause of their behavior or may not behave in a manner which appears to be consistent with their emotional and psychological state.

SUMMARY

Motivation is one of the most complex problems in social psychology. It is difficult to explain motives in a way that will satisfy social scientists, though considerable progress has been made in this effort since the instinct theories at the turn of the century. Psychologists are reasonably agreed about how the primary biological or biogenic needs function in eliciting behavior, but the bases of the secondary, social or sociogenic motives like security, status seeking, and aggressiveness have been variously interpreted. One difficulty is that secondary motives are not directly observable and are subject to more diverse interpretations. Study of the primary motives, particularly, has followed the distinction between behaviorist and Gestalt principles that applies to learning.

In addition to need satisfaction, motivation is also determined by other sectors of the personality and self; the role of emotions is especially critical. Moreover, the motives operating in our daily lives appear to be generally latent rather than internally compelling.

Because of the complicated chain of cause and effect in behavior it is doubtful whether any adequate classification of human motives can be made. The classification suggested in this chapter is based on the individual's need for security, achievement, affiliation and status, and integration and creativity.

Among the perennial controversies in motivation is the relation between frustration and aggression. Like other motives, aggression has a basis in social learning, and theorists differ about whether it also has an instinctual basis. Many of the tensions in contemporary society, particularly in national politics, international affairs, and ethnic relations, are complicated by interpersonal rivalries and vested interests which find their expression in some form of aggressiveness rationalization. This aspect of social motivation is a function of a society's attitudes and values, which will be examined in the next two chapters.

WORDS TO REMEMBER

Achievement motivation. Behavior associated with (or the process of acquiring aspirations toward) mobility and sometimes creativity, often as related to the status needs of the individual. Explored by David McClelland, the concept is subject to cross-cultural differences.

Affiliation. Tendency or need to be with others—a fundamental social motive.

Biogenic motives. Initiation of behavior as based on underlying tissue needs such as hunger or thirst; often identified as *drives.*

Catharsis. Reduction of aggression (or some other pent-up emotion or motivation) through a substitute form of behavior, as in confession, fantasy, or work. For instance, people who enjoy books or movies about violence may be releasing their aggressiveness.

Frustration-aggression hypothesis. Assumption that the major factor in aggression is frustration. Initially the theory, as presented by a group of psychologists, stated that frustration could account for all aggression, but it is presently considered as a hypothesis to account for certain kinds of aggression.

Functional autonomy. Concept developed by Gordon Allport that habit systems become a motive in themselves, often latent or relatively unconscious. For instance, personal attachment to a given region is due to a set of experiences and may become a driving force which is more or less independent of other motives.

Instinct. Inherited or inborn mode of behavior found among lower animals, such as nest building in birds. The concept played a central role historically in explaining motivation, but it is rarely used today in reference to human behavior.

Intervening variable. In motivational theory, the critical factor or "cause" in the organism which "explains" the relevant behavior of the organism. This internal event or process which connects the stimulus and the response occurs in the nervous system, so it cannot be observed by the experimenter.

Intrinsic/extrinsic motivation. *Intrinsic* motives arise within the person, without reference to rewards in the environment. *Extrinsic* motivation implies behavior based on reward or punishment from the outside.

Latent/overt motives. *Latent* motivation is unconscious or not immediately apparent or readily analyzable, in contrast to *overt* motivation.

Molar. Examination of behavior according to totalistic or Gestalt principles.

Molecular. Analysis of behavior through minutely analytical or particularistic methods.

Primary/secondary motivation. The term *primary* motivation usually points to biogenic motives or physical drives. *Secondary* motivation is acquired or learned, frequently explained by some form of conditioning, as when the infant learns to love the mother because she administers food, dry clothing, etc.

Projective tests. Personality measuring techniques utilizing neutral or unstructured stimuli, such as the Rorschach Inkblot Test or the TAT (Thematic Apperception Test), to which the subject gives an individual interpretation. Projective tests can be contrasted to standardized paper-and-pencil or verbal tests of personality.

Social motives. Fairly universal motives, at least within a given culture, such as achievement or aggression. These motives are learned and are subject to individual variation.

Sociogenic motives. Motives that are based on the involvement of other persons or are learned in an interpersonal setting, in contrast to *biogenic* motives. Whereas *social* motives imply universality, as with affiliation or competition, *sociogenic* motives are usually more limited in scope, such as joining a club, going to a band concert, or becoming a homosexual. Social motives are sociogenic motives which appear to some degree in all societies, but sociogenic motives may involve relatively few people or subcultures.

Valence. In motivational theory, the attraction or repulsion arising from a specific object, goal, or situation which gives it incentive value.

QUESTIONS FOR DISCUSSION

1. What are some of the reasons for the difficulties in explaining motivation?

2. Explain the differences between the functions of internal and external motivation.

3. How would you describe the rise and the fall of the instinct theory?

4. How did Schachter go about investigating the motives surrounding obesity?

5. How is Lewin's theory of positive and negative valence related to motivation?

6. What is meant by functional autonomy? What objections to this theory have been expressed by researchers?

7. Is it possible to think in terms of a central motive? What kind of a cluster can you suggest to account for the most important motives?

8. Suggest a workable classification of social motives.

9. Distinguish between primary and secondary motives. To what degree is this distinction a tenable one? Which motives seem most critical in your life? Why? In what ways does drive-theory differ from it?

10. How did Harlow contribute to the explanation of secondary motives?

11. How do the emotions serve as motives?

12. How does society affect biogenic and sociogenic motives? How are these types related to primary and secondary motives?

13. What are the difficulties with the frustration-aggression hypothesis?

14. How does Berkowitz approach the role of cues in the acquisition of aggression?

READINGS

Antaki, C. (Ed.) *The Psychology of Ordinary Explanation of Social Behavior.* New York: Academic Press, 1981.
  Contributors analyze the relation of motivation to attribution and other aspects of cognition.

Atkinson, J. W., and Raynor, J. O. *Motivation and Achievement.* Washington, D.C.: V. H. Winston & Sons, 1974.
  Large compendium of research on achievement motivation.

Cofer, C. N., and Appley, M. H. *Motivation: Theory and Research.* New York: John Wiley & Sons, 1964.

One of the more complete discussions of motivation; Chapters 9, 13, 14, and especially 15 are most relevant.

De Charms, R. *Personal Causation: The Internal Affective Determinants of Behavior.* New York: Academic Press, 1968.

Well-written theoretical account of emotions, attribution, motivation, and related issues.

Deci, E. L. *Intrinsic Motivation.* New York: Plenum Publishing Corp., 1975.

Integrates a number of research studies into a coherent theory.

Geen, R. G., and O'Neal, E. C. (Eds.). *Perspectives on Aggression.* New York: Academic Press, 1976.

Theory and research on a variety of questions: the relation of motivation to personality and environment, and other aspects.

Lewin, K. *Field Theory in Social Science,* ed. D. Cartwright. New York: Harper and Row Publishers, 1951.

Review of some of Lewin's provocative work in motivation and related areas.

McClelland, D. C. *The Achieving Society.* New York: D. Van Nostrand Co., 1961.

Appealing historical and cross-cultural approach to the achievement motive and its economic ramifications.

Schachter, S. *Emotion, Obesity, and Crime.* New York: Academic Press, 1971.

Considers the relationship of emotional states, the nervous system, metabolism, eating habits, and antisocial behavior.

Stotland, E. *The Psychology of Hope.* San Francisco: Jossey-Bass Publishers, 1969.

Considers the coping activities of mental patients and others in a world of anxiety.

THE NATURE OF ATTITUDES AND VALUES

One of the most complex and significant areas in the study of social psychology is attitudes, which are both derived from and help determine the central processes in social behavior—motivation and cognition. Knowledge of how attitudes are acquired, the processes that maintain them, and the effects they have on behavior is necessary to an understanding of the field. Social progress, especially, requires an awareness of what causes attitudes to be changed and what factors make them resistant to change. Attitude formation and change and the effects of attitudes on social behavior are examined in this and the following chapter.

Several years ago the flyer shown in Figure 8-1 was found under the windshield wiper of a car in a university parking lot. There is, of course, nothing unique about this example of bigotry and irrational hate directed at members of a group. Such derisive social attitudes are encountered so frequently that it seems society is making no progress at all in the search for tolerance, and one form of prejudice is simply being exchanged for another.

When we consider the vastness of the problem and the impotence of philosophical attempts to encourage tolerance, brotherhood, and equality, we are forced to conclude that social action or specific reforms, rather than rational persuasion, is the most effective way to change society in this direction. We may delude ourselves into thinking that our society has made some progress toward tolerance in attitudes and values, but then we must face the reality of McCarthyism, Watergate, and failure to ratify the Equal Rights Amendment.

Discrimination and intolerance take many forms. Just one example is the popularity of book and record burnings by the Moral Majority, who took the conservative victory in the 1980 presidential election as a signal to follow the lead of the government-supervised burning of Wilhelm Reich's books in New York City in 1960 and a North Dakota town's suspension of a teacher in 1975 for classroom use of classics in American literature. In most countries there have been similar examples of intolerance directed at some object or another.

It is possible to have an attitude toward anything, but for our purposes the more highly charged social attitudes such as racial prejudice are most relevant. This chapter first examines various dimensions and components of attitudes and suggests a working definition. Attitudes and values are compared to other cognitive constructs—knowledge, opinions, faith, and interest—on the basis of six components and characteristics. Then attitude scales and other techniques that have been designed to measure certain properties of attitudes are described and evaluated. The central role played by attitudes in personality development and social behavior is examined in relation to the processes by which they are formed as the individual interacts with the sociocultural setting and is influenced by various reference groups. Another section on attitudes examines the problem of consistency between expressed attitudes and overt behavior. The final section briefly explores some of the dimensions of values as differentiated from attitudes and suggests how values change, laying the foundation for consideration of attitude change and persuasibility in Chapter 9.

DIMENSIONS OF ATTITUDES

In its broadest sense, an attitude can be defined as a hypothetical cognitive construct which reflects the organization of beliefs, opinions, values, and behaviors within an individual. Because an attitude is inferential and cannot be directly observed, the study of attitudes is subject to many of the same methodological and theoretical problems that are encountered in the study of motives, as described in the first section of Chapter 7.

Attitudes can be simple or complex. A statement like "That's a nice painting" reflects a simple attitude, and so does the leaflet reproduced in Figure 8–1. Simple attitudes usually are derived from a unilateral understanding of a situation, often in association with an erroneous conception of causality. Complex attitudes may reflect many interrelated concepts, colored with nuances and limited by logical exceptions.

Because attitudes do not represent separate, distinct objects, like books on a shelf, it is important to consider how they are interrelated or interconnected in an organized structure. Theories of attitude organization are discussed in the following chapter, but an example of an attitudinal structure could be evidenced by xenophobic persons, who fear strangers or foreigners and react against anything unknown, new, or strange. They are likely to have egocentric attitudes which cause them to view other racial, linguistic, ethnic, and cultural groups as unpleasant or potentially threatening to their own lifestyle. They also are likely to view social change as threatening and to have conservative attitudes which cause

SPECIAL BULLETIN
By World Service

We do not say every Jew is a Communist, but that the majority of the Communist leaders and spies were and are Jews. Therefore:

COMMUNISM IS JEWISH.

At present we have no means of bringing the truth to the people, except our leaflets etc. To expose ourselves now would be suicide. We would be smeared or even assassinated as countless other patriots were: The Czar and his family; Count Folke Bernadotte (1st U.N. Secretary); and the British Governor of Palestine — all murdered by Jews; Moise Tshombe, Katangan Christian leader — also martyred!

Over 1000 British officers and men blown to pieces, knifed or hanged by Jewish terrorists in Palestine. Thousands of defenseless Arab women and children! Through the Jewish stranglehold on money, business and press, the German, Italian, Hungarian and Slavic peoples are blamed for alleged war crimes. The Jews should take action against the criminal and communistic elements in their midst before crying persecution. Are they trying to divert attention from their own atrocities?

Instead of producing anti-communist films, Jew-controlled Hollywood continues to pour forth anti-nazi and anti-christian films (e.g. the latest "Cardinal" by Otto Preminger, another Zionist Jew).

Christians unite, boycott Jewish filth. Nazism is dead, but Communism lives.

FIGHT COMMUNISM OR DIE A SLAVE.

Figure 8-1. Example of a Simplistic Attitude Structure

them to reject tendencies toward informal dress, freer sexual relationships, or relaxed family roles. Their untrusting attitude toward others may be reflected in beliefs that society needs strong law-enforcement agencies, that war is the only method for settling international disputes, and that if given the opportunity, "everybody will screw you." Such a degree of consistency between attitudes as well as within the attitude structure could be characterized as a personality trait or variable, in experimental terms.

Components of Attitudes

Three components of attitudes can be differentiated. The first is the *cognitive component*, or the facts or assumed facts about an object. A concrete object (e.g., paper) is associated with facts about it (e.g., paper has a certain kindling temperature) which are to a great extent objectively verifiable. The less concrete the object, the fewer facts are available, and the more we must depend on beliefs.

The second component of attitudes is the *emotional* or *visceral component*. People tend to have an emotional reaction to a person, object, or situation; they like or dislike it, are pleased or unhappy with it, love or loathe it, and so forth—all visceral, emotional reactions.

The third is the *action component*, which consists of two elements. The first is a general action element, that is, the tendency to do something or not do it. The second is a general attraction-repulsion element, that is, the tendency to move toward or away from a particular object or person. An example is the rigid nature of the attitude of white Americans toward black Americans. Most middle-class, middle-aged whites who grew up in a typical American city or suburb in the 1940s and 1950s have a simplistic, negative attitude toward blacks. Their homes and schools were segregated from the black community, and they rarely saw blacks except in highly ritualized circumstances, serving as entertainers or service personnel (bus drivers, mail carriers, laborers) in predominantly white settings. As a result, most of the information about blacks they received as children came from parents, friends, and neighbors, and because of their limited contacts with black people, the negative attitudes expressed to them were not subject to correction or modification. The observations they were able to make served to support the negative conceptions: They were told that black people are not intelligent, and they only saw blacks in service or menial jobs, for example.

Since the civil rights push of the 1960s, representative blacks, particularly in the cities, have assumed virtually all the roles in the community. The federal government requires affirmative action procedures to provide equal employment opportunities, and school integration is minimizing the impact of negative attitudes by bringing black and white children, as well as those of other backgrounds, into long-term contact. Nevertheless, the dominant Americans, white Anglo-Saxon Protestants, are a long way from changing their attitudes toward other racial and ethnic groups, as the evidence investigated in Chapter 18 indicates.

A Working Definition of Attitudes

A mechanically inclined theorist might describe attitudes as the flywheel of social psychology, the thing that makes it work. Probably no other single area of the discipline has been subject to so much experimentaion. Emphasis on the individual as a member of society is reflected in the social-psychological view of attitudes as indicating how people feel and think about their social situation. Attitudes are one of the most important factors in the dynamics of social behavior by virtue of their links with the key processes of motivation, learning, and perception. Together with values and norms, attitudes structure our orientation to the social world, and their dynamic nature is expressed in a tendency to cross over into behavior. The range of attitudes is practically limitless, since no person, object, or situation can be removed from its social and cultural context. Primarily, however, social psychology is concerned with *social attitudes*—those directed at interpersonal relations, politics, international and ethnic relations, and social programs.

As a starting point in arriving at a definition of an attitude, we can think of it as a fairly consistent learned tendency to behave in a certain way (generally, positively or negatively) toward persons, objects, or situations. A definition frequently cited over the years is that of Gordon Allport (1935): "An attitude is a mental and neural state of readiness, organized through experience, exerting a directive or dynamic influence upon the individual's response to all objects and situations with which it is related."

There are certain implications in this definition of attitudes that should be clarified. First, an attitude defines a person's *position* toward a given aspect of the perceptual world. An attitude is either *for* or *against* an object, situation, person, or group. It is doubtful that a neutral position can correctly be called an attitude. You are not likely to have an attitude toward a certain mathematical concept ($2 \times 2 = 4$, for example), for these constructs are inherent in the universe, and, being remote from human events, are hardly subject to controversy. The mere sight of numbers and equations can make some people feel uneasy and incompetent, however, and they may summarize a personal dislike in the statement, "I hate mathematics." You probably do have an attitude toward certain foods, like potatoes or rice. You may be fond of one or another, or both, although you may try to avoid them because of their high caloric content. To a person in another culture, the only relevant fact may be that they are a cheap source of food. Unusual experiences also can influence attitudes toward things. A person might have been forced by famine to live on rice for an extended period, or a family fortune might be attributed to successful growing or marketing of potatoes.

Thus attitudes can be formed about relatively neutral objects, like potatoes or rice, although the attitudes themselves are not neutral. In social and emotional situations, which may call for attitudes on what one thinks of other people or the possibility of nuclear war, for example, the cognitive processes and results are much more complicated.

Second, attitudes are rooted in motivation as well as cognition, and they are often colored by emotion. They provide a continual impetus to behavior, as implied by Allport's term *state of readiness*. A teacher's favorable or unfavorable attitude toward foreigners will affect (probably unconsciously) the teacher's grading of essay tests written by foreign students. Attitudes provide the emotional basis of most of a person's relations with others and identification with groups and

Buttons may or may not reflect a particular person's attitudes accurately, but they do offer a partial index to prevailing attitudes in a society. *Source:* K. Scott Danoff.

social movements. They have a driving force which impels people toward action, leading them to vote, fight wars, engage in labor strikes, or help alleviate suffering, for example. Whether attitudes are explicit and well verbalized or implicit and unexpressed, they can operate as motives and initiators of behavior.

Third, attitudes are integrated into an organized system, although this does not exclude the possibility of inconsistency in attitudes, opinions, and behavior. They are one of the major components of personality, as noted in Chapter 4. They are relatively persistent and enduring, yet like any aspect of the self, they are subject to change. This problem of persistence and change, which is central to the measurement of attitudes, is the subject of the following chapter.

Fourth, as a part of personality, attitudes help define the individual's ego structure. Belief in civil liberties, for example, is positively correlated with various personality traits such as independence, self-reliance, and flexibility (as well as with a higher educational level and socioeconomic status), and negatively correlated with anomie and anxiety (Zalkind, Gaugler, & Schwartz, 1975). An individual who is deeply ego involved in what he or she believes may be extremely sensitive, so that others can approach that person's attitudinal world only with caution, especially with regard to religion, politics, and social issues.

Attitudes and Other Cognitive Constructs

Confusion persists regarding distinctions among such concepts as facts, beliefs, attitudes, and values. In terms of conditioning (see Chapter 5), it has been suggested, for example, that knowledge differs from attitudes in that the stimulus feedback of knowledge has only cue value (i.e., it directs behavior), whereas attitudes may be considered to have, in addition to cue value, a drive aspect (Doob, 1947). Others point out the differences between opinions and attitudes, arguing that opinions deal with matters which are, theoretically at least, empirically verifiable, whereas attitudes deal with matters of taste (Osgood, Suci, & Tannenbaum, 1957). Opinions are also said to refer to one's expectation of future events; beliefs to theoretically verifiable facts; and attitudes to one's wants and desires with respect to facts or events. Others have argued that beliefs do not have drive properties, whereas attitudes do; or that opinions are single beliefs, whereas attitudes incorporate many beliefs.

It is simpler and more helpful to search for the elements underlying the cognitive constructs of knowledge, opinions, faith, and interests, as well as attitudes and values. If independent cognitive elements could be isolated, the components and characteristics of the various cognitive constructs might be identified as follows:

1. *Facts*—the given, immediately verifiable.
2. *Beliefs*—relatively neutral and unemotional, verifiable in theory.
3. *Wants*—needs or motives.
4. *Valence*—direction of feeling toward the object: liking or disliking, positive or negative.
5. *Action*—degree to which behavior is directed toward or away from the object.
6. *Intensity*—magnitude of feeling or behavior.

Various combinations of these components and characteristics can be considered as producing the various cognitive constructs. *Knowledge* might be considered to be facts alone or a combination of facts and beliefs; *opinions,* a combination of beliefs of some intensity; and *faith,* a combination of beliefs, wants, and valence, in addition to a strong emotional component (DeVito, 1976). *Interest* might be considered principally as composed of valence and action components which in turn increase the person's attentiveness toward the object in question, presumably to gather more facts. *Values,* as they are identified in the final section of this chapter, reflect individual wants projected onto other people, objects, or situations. *Attitudes,* considered in this sense, can be regarded as combinations of values and beliefs (Rosenberg, 1960; Jones & Gerard, 1967).

These and other concepts may in fact be derived from almost infinite combinations of the elements, and the lines between them are indistinctly drawn. For example, attitudes often pass into beliefs, and vice versa. Fishbein and Ajzen (1975) have identified three methods of belief formation, based on a theoretical linkage of fact 0 and fact X. The linkage can be established through direct observation (descriptive belief) or rely on the report of some other belief (inferential belief) or some outside source (informational belief). Most beliefs, and consequently most attitudes, rest on more than empirical knowledge alone.

This relation of cognitive elements and constructs is subject to numerous problems faced by attitude theorists in attempts to refine the conceptual framework. All such conceptualizations are to some extent artificial, since virtually all behavior is affected by intricate combinations of cognitions which themselves vary from simple facts to highly complex attitudes.

THE MEASUREMENT OF ATTITUDES

In order to study and evaluate attitudes, some method of measuring them must be devised. This is difficult because attitudes cannot be observed, but they do have dimensions or properties that are measurable to some degree. These six dimensions include direction, degree, and strength (the valence, action, and intensity characteristics of cognitive constructs described above), as well as salience, coherence, and consistency.

Direction. The positive or negative aspects of an attitude (its "for" or "against" quality in regard to an object) indicate its direction. This is relatively easy to determine because every attitude—on quiz shows, a school bond issue, disarmament, mercy killing, or interplanetary travel, for example—takes one direction or the other.

Degree. This dimension is concerned with the *amount* of favorableness or unfavorableness an attitude possesses. A person does, or does not, like politicians, proletarians, or Poles—but to what extent? The assumption is that attitudes can be placed on a continuum along which the degree of positive or negative feeling can be measured.

Strength or intensity. Attitudes are at different levels of intensity; a tourist may like the French but prefer the English, for example. It is possible to determine to what extent an attitude can become a basis of action, or how strong a belief is compared to other beliefs. The motivational and emotional aspects of attitudes dominate this dimension.

Salience. The circumstances which give a person freedom to express an attitude determine its salience, which is closely related to intensity. For example, antiblack feelings might be more overtly expressed in the southern parts of the United States than in Canada. The reactions of Germans to Jews demonstrated more salience under Hitler than it had previously, although the attitude may have been of approximately equal strength. Salience is difficult to measure because in a sense it refers to the centrality the attitude has within the individual, as well as the spontaneity with which it is manifested, and it is affected not only by cultural permissiveness but by many internal factors which can condition the behavior of the individual. Some people find it difficult to give expression to their attitudes, and many are unaware of exactly what their attitudes are.

Coherence or consistency. The ordering or integration of attitudes determines how an individual maintains an attitude under different situations. Measurement of this dimension is concerned with such questions as whether a person who believes in civil rights extends the belief to all races, both sexes, and every social class. Consistency among attitudes or between attitudes and behavior often is an impetus to attitude change, the focus of Chapter 9.

Measurement of all these characteristics of attitudes cannot be equally satisfactory. The first three—direction, degree, and strength—are more conveniently incorporated into a measurement scale, the quantitative device used most often to evaluate attitudes. The measurement of salience and consistency, as well as other dimensions of attitudes, is a challenging area for future research.

Attitude Scales

Scales for the measurement of attitude have been developed by psychologists and social scientists who generally have conceived of an attitude as a fairly broad or generalized tendency to respond in a characteristic way (favorably or unfavorably) toward certain classes of objects, persons, or situations. Scales designed to test radicalism-conservatism, pacifism-militarism, and international-ism-prejudice toward foreign and minority groups are examples. Most of the early scales were little more than collections of statements which were presumably related to the attitude being studied. Respondents noted their approval or disapproval of the statements or checked the item most nearly approximating their own attitude. Each item was scored in some fashion (e.g., strong disapproval = -2, mild disapproval = -1, no opinion = 0, some approval = $+1$, strong approval = $+2$), and a total for the scale was computed.

Thurstone Equal-Appearing Interval Scale

Objecting to these crude methods, L. L. Thurstone set about devising a more scientific procedure for the construction of attitude measures. He maintained that an attitude score could have meaning only if the weight given each item were empirically determined. In one study (Thurstone & Chave, 1929), 300 judges were asked to sort 130 miscellaneous opinions about the church into 11 piles, representing opinions ranging from extremely favorable to extremely unfavorable. The median position judged for each item determined its scale value. Only those items on which the judges' agreement was fairly close were selected for the final attitude scale, and the 45 items chosen represented the entire range of gradations along the scale, from 1 to 11. A few illustrative items are:

Scale Value

  .5 I feel the church is the greatest agency for the uplift of the world.
3.0 There is much wrong in my church, but I feel it is so important that it is my duty to help improve it.
4.2 I am sympathetic toward the church, but I am not active in its work.
5.5 Sometimes I feel the church is worthwhile, and sometimes I doubt it.
7.2 I believe that the church is losing ground as education advances.
8.6 The church deals in platitudes and is afraid to follow the logic of truth.
10.6 I regard the church as a parasite on society.

In such scales the items are presented in random order, and subjects are asked to check every statement with which they agree. An average or median of the scale values of the items checked yields a person's score for the test. Thurstone and various associates prepared attitude scales in a number of areas to judge attitudes toward war, prohibition, birth control, minorities, censorship, treatment of criminals, and the like.

Likert Summated Rating Scale

Rensis Likert found the Thurstone judging technique laborious and suggested that an arbitrary assignment of scores to the questionnaire items is just as satisfactory. He proposed an alternative method (Likert, 1932) in which a large number of statements relating to a subject (e.g., internationalism, religions) are collected. These are presented to groups of persons who are instructed to indicate their approval or disapproval on a five-point scale on which strong approval counts 5, approval 4, undecided 3, disapproval 2, and strong disapproval 1. The value of a given item is determined by discovering whether or not it correlates highly with the rest of the items on the list. For example, if those who favor segregating blacks receive consistently higher scores on the rest of the list, and those who favor nonsegregation receive consistently lower scores, the segregation question is considered a good one for inclusion.

Disagreement as to the relative merits of the Thurstone and Likert methods has been rather technical (Edwards & Kenney, 1946). One problem with the Thurstone scale, as Edwards (1957) points out, is the difficulty of selecting the most sensitive or discriminating item among those having roughly the same scale value. The objectivity or validity of the scale depends on the panel of judges, which may be biased in its ratings. In the Likert scale, there is no means by which the five different scale values for any given item can be equated with other items in the scale. It also has the disadvantage of having no zero point, and it cannot include items that are not constructed as positive or negative (Fishbein & Ajzen, 1975). The major advantage of the Likert scale is the convenience it provides in arranging measurements of various attitudes, either in the same scale or in different scales. The five-point scale from strongly agree to strongly disagree is relatively convenient to construct and to administer. Yet if this scale is developed rigorously, it can, like the Thurstone, be a very time-consuming process.

Various improved procedures have been suggested. Guttman (1944), for example, developed a *scale analysis* technique which is based on selection of about 10 to 12 consistent items, which are then arranged along a single dimension. A person's rank on the continuum shows fairly accurately how he or she answered the questions both above and below. Edwards and Kilpatrick (1948) proposed a somewhat complicated *scale discrimination* method that attempts to combine the better points of the Thurstone, Likert, and Guttman techniques. Lazarsfeld (1957) contributed a rather complex *latent structure analysis* which was used, along with the Guttman method, in studying the attitudes of service personnel during World War II.

Still another variant is the *plausibility scale* applied by Waly and Cook (1965). Subjects rated the plausibility of each of a set of arguments labeled as "prosegregation" or "prointegration" on an 11-point scale, ranging from very ineffective (-5) to very effective ($+5$). The sum of the scores is the measure of the attitude; that is, a statement is considered more effective or plausible by subjects who agree with the viewpoint than by subjects who take issue with it. This indirect approach appears to be more valid than the self-report measures ("do you agree or disagree with . . . ") called for in many scales.

Some attitude scales have used more than one of these methods. An example is the F scale, which measures authoritarianism with such components as rigidity, submissiveness, aggressiveness, stereotyping, power needs, and punitiveness. The scale appeared shortly after World War II and, in order to make it sensitive to personality needs in a changing sociopolitical order, it has been revised at least twice (Cherry & Byrne, 1977). A variety of such scales, including the *Mach Scale* (Box 8–1), have been developed recently.

Other Measuring Techniques

The *Semantic Differential Scale* developed by Charles Osgood and colleagues (1957) is an attempt to discover the dimension of meaning of the attitude object. The individual's reaction is measured by a seven-point scale on: (1) *evaluation of favorableness-unfavorableness*—good-bad, beautiful-ugly; (2) perception of *potency or power* of the object—large-small, strong-weak; and (3) perception of the *activity* of the object—fast-slow, active-passive. These three dimensions are used with adjective pairs to measure quite diverse objects or concepts. Roosevelt and Hitler might be considered somewhat similar on the potency and activity dimensions but very different on the evaluative dimensions, for example.

The scale employs many different items in relation to the attitude object, and each item is measured in the three dimensions, as illustrated in Figure 10–2 in Chapter 10.

Box 8–1

MACHIAVELLI LIVES!

The directions a person's attitudes take depend on both the individual and the culture. A treatise written in the 16th century to instruct Italy's monarch on how to increase and consolidate power (Machiavelli's *The Prince*) is still relevant as a portrait of the politician or opportunist. In fact, it may have wider applications today than it did in the Renaissance.

The attitude of Machiavellianism is popularly characterized as the belief that in political affairs, at least, the end justifies the means. A cluster of responses associated with Machiavellianism was incorporated into the Mach Scale by Richard Christie and Florence Geis, who adopted it from *The Prince* but adapted it to the contemporary college setting.* Among the more discriminating items (both pro- and anti-Machiavellianism) are:

The best way to handle people is to tell them what they want to hear.

Anyone who completely trusts anyone else is asking for trouble.

One should take action only when sure it is morally right.

It is wise to flatter important people.

All in all, it is better to be humble and honest than important and dishonest.

Barnum was very wrong when he said there's a sucker born every minute.

The scale allows a wide range of views of human nature. What most characterizes Machiavellians is an emotional detachment from other persons.

Among the experiments to compare the high and low Mach scorers was a con game which used specially designed playing cards. One variation offered a stake of $10 to be divided between any two of three players in any way that could be worked out. In the bargaining and coalitions, the split might be 5 and 5 or 8 and 2 between two partners, with the third person making some kind of deal. The pattern of coalition partnerships by Mach classification of the members was found to be far from random. Overwhelmingly, high Machs were successful at outbargaining low Machs.

The social characteristic underlying the Mach component is complex. It is not too closely correlated with intelligence or social status, but it increases from childhood into early adulthood and then becomes stabilized. The score differed for samples of Washington lobbyists as well as college militants. In some instances, as with student revolutionaries, respondents were low on one part of the scale, such as Mach Tactics, but high in another, like Disbelief in People.

_____

*R. Christie and F. L. Geis, *Studies in Machiavellianism* (New York: Academic Press, 1970).

The semantic differential technique can be combined with other approaches. A combination with Guttman scale analysis (Brinton, 1961), for example, proved successful in the measurement of attitudes toward capital punishment.

A variety of attitude scales have been devised to tap various feelings and attitudes of individuals toward their social world. One of the early methods was the *Social Distance Scale* devised by Bogardus (1925), on which individuals were to indicate their attitudes toward various national, racial, and religious groups, in these terms:

1. Would admit to close kinship by marriage.
2. Would admit to my club as personal chums.
3. Would admit to my street as neighbors.
4. Would admit to employment in my occupation.
5. Would admit to citizenship in my country.
6. Would admit as visitors only to my country.
7. Would exclude from my country.

This scale has been used for years to locate various ethnic groups along an acceptance-rejection continuum (Bogardus, 1958). Although there is an increased tendency toward acceptance, the relative position of the various groups has not basically changed—most Americans still prefer western Europeans to eastern Europeans or Asians and reject racially different groups. The scale cannot be considered to have equidistant intervals, nor is it certain that acceptance at one level precludes rejection at another: A person who accepts a member of an ethnic group as a co-worker might reject the same person as a neighbor, for example. Still, investigations indicate that the scale is a valid and reliable one (Dodd & Griffiths, 1958).

Another technique utilizes an *open-end questionnaire* or free response, in which an interviewer attempts to elicit spontaneous verbal responses from individuals on various social issues or attitudinal clusters. Interviews are held with the on-the-job employees, persons waiting for buses, and so on, with the interviewer deliberately attempting to bring forth freer and franker statements than would be made with a more conventional interviewing technique. In any open-end technique, however, difficulty arises in tabulating the findings because the responses are unstandardized.

BOX 8–2
THE EYE OF THE BEHOLDER

Interest in certain social attitudes varies with the times. An example is organized labor: In the 1940s, the push toward labor unionization was strong in certain industries, and people took opposite sides in the arguments favoring or rejecting labor unions, particularly in a wartime economy. Harold Proshansky used a projective technique to assess these attitudes in which he presented subjects with ambiguous pictures and asked them to identify the people in the picture, tell what they were doing, imagine what had led up to the situation, and suggest what might follow.*

The following descriptions of the same picture indicate opposite attitudes toward laborers in the 1943 study:

> Home of a man on relief—shabby—dresses poorly. Scene is probably of a shack down South. Also might be the home of some *unemployed* laborer. Horrible housing conditions. Why don't the government provide for these people? The ordinary worker is always forgotten and allowed to rot.

> Picture of one room, very messy, stove in center, woman on the left, man standing next to stove, couple of children near them. This is a room of what we call "poor people." They seem to be messy, sloppy people, who seem to enjoy dwelling in their own trash.

As these responses indicate, a shortcoming of this technique is that much of the response may be only partially relevant to the attitude being investigated. It is useful, however, when the attitude is particularly sensitive, as this issue was at the time.

---

*H. M. Proshansky, "A Projective Method for the Study of Attitudes," *Journal of Abnormal and Social Psychology*, 1943, *38*, 393–395.

A more indirect approach to attitude measurement is the *behavioral test,* or observing such behavior as what an individual does in taking a seat on a bus (whether or not a white person sits next to a black, for example) or what kinds of complaints reach the personnel department from employees of a factory that employs ethnic minorities. A variation of this technique was used in selecting personnel for the Office of Strategic Services during World War II, among a variety of behavioral personality tests which were tried.

Some investigators prefer indirect approaches for measuring attitudes because they recognize the possible inconsistencies between verbalized attitudes or cognitive states and actual behavior. One interesting version is the *projective* technique in which Proshansky (1943) used pictures which could be variously interpreted in terms of social conflict (see Box 8–2). Another is Hammond's (1948) *error choice test,* which presents alternative items, all equally erroneous, on a given social attitude. Subjects are asked to mark which of two equally distorted statements is "correct," and the direction of the error reveals the individual's attitude compared to a judge's rating or a control group.

Selecting a Measurement Technique

All the approaches to the measurement of attitudes described in this section have some degree of *validity*—that is, they do measure what they purport to measure. They have varying degrees of success in predicting whether the respondents genuinely feel and will demonstrate in their action the characteristics indicated by their performance on the measuring instrument, however.

The discrepancy between attitude and action is a somewhat broader concern than test validity alone, as suggested by evidence that a person can have a verbalized hostile feeling toward a minority group and yet not display it when dealing with members of that group. Years before the Civil Rights Act made the question irrelevant, a sociologist and his wife traveled across the country with a young Chinese couple and tested whether they would be accepted for lodging (LaPiere, 1934). With only one or two exceptions, hotel managers and innkeepers allowed them to register, but some months later when they were queried by mail whether they would accept Oriental guests, their responses were overwhelmingly negative. In a later study (Kutner, Wilkings, & Yarrow, 1952), a letter was sent to restaurants asking whether a small dinner party of whites and blacks would be permitted to dine in the establishment. Practically all proprietors refused, were evasive, or did not respond. Some who replied said that they did not accept reservations, apparently as a means of avoiding the issue, yet they accepted the reservations when a member of the party made them without identifying the nature of the group. In any case, the group was allowed to dine when it appeared at the restaurant.

In general, validity is improved by combining several scales or developing projective and other indirect techniques. Since it is usually difficult to provide for behavioral tests, in fact, the best way of dealing with the complexity of measuring and analyzing social attitudes may be a combination of conventional verbal scales with projective techniques, which attempt to measure aspects of personality with neutral stimuli such as Proshansky's pictures described in Box 8–2. Although projective tests have the advantage of depth and can tap unconscious factors to some degree, they do have problems of irrelevant responses and lack of standardization in the measurement instrument.

Evaluating Measurement Instruments

An important consideration in testing attitudes is the type of scale or questionnaire used and the kinds of items selected for the instrument. Items are of two general types: *open-end* questions, which are usually used to assess the climate of attitude or opinion (respondents provide their own answers), and *scaled* or *predetermined* responses. Instruments using the latter type can run the gamut from the simple yes-no questionnaires to the more sophisticated types of Thurstone and Likert scales and other variations.

Items in an attitude scale must represent a "proper sampling of content" (Robinson, Rusk, & Head, 1968). To determine this, there should be an extensive survey of potential opinion and attitudes in the relevant cognitive area. An attitude scale on busing students, for example, should include the goals the public perceives in education, the range of feeling about racial interaction, respondents' concerns with civil rights, and their ideology concerning means and ends.

The wording of the items must be clear and precise, and the scale should be adequately pretested and analyzed to prevent the presence of bias. Ideally, the study sample will be representative of the total population of possible subjects (see Chapter 1). If, as is more likely, the sample is a biased or nonrepresentative one, no interpretation can be made beyond the results found in the groups tested. A representative sample is particularly important in studying attitudes because the population of possible subjects with a particular attitude is usually very large. In addition to the random sample described in Chapter 1, studies on attitudes often use *quota* samples (specified numbers or ratios based on age, ethnicity, or other subcultures) or *area* samples (based on geographical or residential areas).

In order to secure validity and reliability in the use of an attitude scale, the subjects must have verbal integrity, be within the range of average intelligence or above, and have some knowledge of the cognitive area to which the test applies. As noted in Chapter 1, *validity* refers to the ability of the scale to measure what it purports to measure, and *reliability* refers to the degree to which the scale would secure the same results on retest. A valid test will tend to be high in reliability, but a reliable test is not necessarily valid. As pointed out above, there are difficulties in achieving validity in attitude scales because verbalized reactions may be very different from deep-seated feelings or actual responses in a behavioral situation.

THE FORMATION OF ATTITUDES

Study of the nature of attitudes requires even more than knowledge of the meaning of the term in its various dimensions and provisions for a means of measurement, as described in the preceding sections of this chapter. It also calls for an understanding of how attitudes are formed and the central role they play in personality development and social functioning. This role has been considered in relation to motivation, perception, and learning (Chapters 5 to 7), and its significance will be observed in regard to communication (Chapter 10), group processes (Chapter 12), and role patterns (Chapter 14). The bases of attitude formation also must be established in order to investigate persuasibility and change in attitudes, the subject of the following chapter. An example of how attitudes are formed through a series of perceptual and cognitive steps in P. A.

Katz's (1976) study of the acquisition of racial attitudes in children, which is described in Chapter 18.

Attitudes as Conditioned Responses

From a behaviorist viewpoint, attitude formation is a matter of involuntary and voluntary responses to stimuli. While all attitudes are learned rather than inherent, many behavioral reactions are in fact involuntary, as noted in the discussion on classical conditioning in Chapter 5.

Imagine a situation in which a child is being disciplined for violating certain household rules. Every time a violation is noticed the parent administers a punishment, which gives rise to an *unconditioned response* of pain or an unpleasant or unhappy feeling, as noted in Figure 8–2. As a result of the contiguous relationship between rule violation and punishment, the violation itself becomes capable of eliciting the *conditioned response* of fear or unpleasantness. Now, to go one step further, assume that while punishing the child the parent uses such terms as *bad, dirty, not nice, disgusting,* or *selfish.* These words will soon have negative connotations for the child, and if the parent then associates them with a racial, linguistic, or cultural group, as shown in Figure 8–3, part of the emotional reaction to the word will be transferred to the *label.* After prolonged training of this sort, the stimulus object of a member of the racial or cultural group will probably be sufficient to elicit the emotional state of unpleasantness in the child.

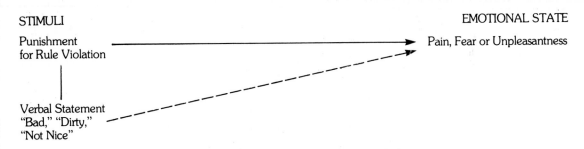

Figure 8–2. Basis of Emotional Conditioning

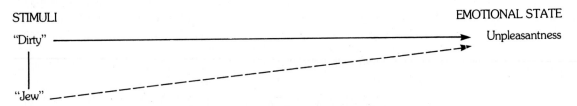

Figure 8–3. Example of Verbal Conditioning

Since many emotional states are physiologically similar, people experiencing them often have difficulty defining them, and they typically depend on environmental conditions to dictate their appropriate interpretation. If close association with members of another racial or cultural group is sufficient to give rise to an unpleasant feeling, most people will carefully avoid such contacts, except in the most ritualized circumstances; they find interracial interactions awkward and unpleasant.

Involuntary responses such as these emotional states are difficult to extinguish (see Chapter 5) because people simply avoid situations which produce them. What is more, they frequently have difficulty understanding why they are experiencing such reactions. If they interpret the reaction as fear they may develop an attitude about a group to justify this fear (maintaining, for example, that members of the group are dangerous, cannot be trusted, and the like).

All involuntary emotional reactions are not negative, of course. Love, attraction, and other positive feelings are involuntarily elicited emotional responses to situations which a person interprets positively rather than negatively.

Attitudes also can represent voluntary responses in instrumental or operant conditioning (see Chapter 5). The operant conditioning of the voluntary component of an attitude is very straightforward, since people naturally find certain beliefs and attitudes rewarding. Children learn to hold and express the beliefs of their parents, because this often brings reinforcement in terms of praise, affection, and attention. Adults find that the expression of certain attitudes helps them to be accepted in some groups and to enjoy vicarious identification with certain people.

It may well be that people develop the verbal component of an attitude by learning what expressions are appropriate and under what conditions certain statements should be made, and then they develop a set of attitudes and beliefs which are wholly consistent with these verbal expressions. Thus the overt responses may be operantly conditioned, whereas the development of attitudes or beliefs may derive from the individual's need for consistency and harmony between attitudes and behaviors. Such attitudinal adjustments can take place without awareness (A. S. Tannenbaum, 1968), and attitude change to make behavior and attitudes consistent can occur without being able to recall the initial attitude. The problem of consistency is examined later in the chapter.

Attitude Formation as Social Interaction

As an aspect of behavior, attitude formation is derived from the reciprocal relation between the sociocultural setting and personality factors, which was identified as the principal influence on behavior in Part I. The formal and informal groups with which a person identifies constitute a part of this interaction. Together, these elements comprise the *frame of reference,* or the relevant situation—considering both past experiences and the present social environment—in which a person finds herself or himself. It is in this frame of reference that the person's attitudes are acquired.

The Sociocultural Setting

The crystallization of a person's attitudes is determined to a large extent by the cultural pattern in the social environment and its various institutional groupings. The sociocultural setting defines and limits the shaping and expression of attitudes; for example, the rigidity of thinking and speech in a totalitarian regime can be contrasted with the freedom of expression allowed in a democracy, and within these two general forms of government there are almost infinite gradations.

Although it is possible to distinguish basic differences in the national character of such groups as Russians and Americans or Scandinavians and Chinese (see Chapter 2), dependable continuities between cultural patterns and the individual's social attitudes have not been discovered. Yet there is little reason to doubt that attitudes are related in various ways to the cultural framework. Socialization or enculturation, the process by which the individual accepts the norms of society, can be accomplished by formal or informal means, as noted in Chapters 2 and 3. Attitudes may be deliberately cultivated, as in the school or church, or acquired in noninstitutionalized fashion through primary groups such as the family. The greater part of a teenager's attitudes probably develops from contact with peer groups, for example.

Personality Factors

It is the way a person functions within the sociocultural setting that puts the individual stamp on his or her attitudes. Study of the specific effects of personality factors on attitude formation has centered on such topics as the satisfaction of ego motives, open-mindedness, cognitive dissonance, and authoritarianism.

One reason attitudes inevitably assume the stamp of individual personality is that they are strongly affective in nature. When attitudes are charged with emotion, the self becomes an anchorage point for them. The term *ego instrumental* applies to attitudes (or the object to which they refer) which become instrumental in the satisfaction of ego motives (Katz & Stotland, 1959). An example is the bigot whose self-perception is enhanced by devaluing others.

Open-mindedness is one personality trait or characteristic which has been investigated in relation to attitude formation. The critical role of rigidity and dogmatism in determining belief systems was demonstrated by Ehrlich (1973). Rokeach (1960) found that an open mind enhances the person's ability to distinguish the source of a message from the information itself. The use of a dogmatism scale among subjects reacting to the two major American presidential candidates in the 1960 election, for example, confirmed that open-minded voters could distinguish between the content and the source of a message and judge each on its own merits (Powell, 1962). Closed-minded people were less able to make this differentiation and so were less tolerant when the incongruity between the two was perceived.

Open-mindedness is related to the studies on cognitive dissonance described in Chapter 9. According to Brehm and Cohen (1962), personality traits may operate to determine:

1. Readiness to change on a given variable, such as accepting the idea of fluoridation in water systems.
2. Resistance to change on a given variable, such as reluctance to vote for a candidate because of family tradition.
3. Preference for one mode of dissonance reduction rather than another, such as rationalizing the shortcomings of public officials or repressing the fact of having voted for them.

The authoritarian personality.   A good example of the effects of personality on attitude formation is found in the study of authoritarian characteristics, which can result from the insecurity and ego defensiveness of an individual. An early, far-reaching investigation of the effects of authoritarianism on attitudes was reported in *The Authoritarian Personality,* by T. W. Adorno and collaborators (1950). Using the personality correlates of a sample of California men and women, the study identified the authoritarian personality structure with antidemocratic, intolerant tendencies and related it to *ethnocentrism,* or belief in the superiority of one's own group.

In the Adorno study, neurotic tendencies were found to be relatively prevalent among the prejudiced (ethnocentric) subjects, on the basis of scores on the Minnesota Multiphasic Inventory, Rorschach inkblot test, and Thematic Apperception Test (TAT), a projective instrument which requires subjects to compose stories about a series of pictures. Anxiety states, particularly among women subjects, were in fact identified with prejudice. On the TAT, for instance, ethnocentric subjects attributed to the protagonists in the pictures less enjoyment of sensual pleasures, less creativity, and less congenial relations with other individuals than unprejudiced subjects did. Aggression was expressed in more direct form, and the individual was interpreted as being caught up with impersonal forces over which he or she had minimum control. The less prejudiced subjects sublimated aggression into more constructive channels in their interpretations and were more likely to suggest "inner rational decision" by the heroes in the pictures.

The Adorno study introduced the F scale as a measure of personality and attitudinal traits associated with authoritarianism. This instrument has helped make it a key area of research, and the underlying factors have been found to be complex and multidimensional. For example, various components of *anomie,* such as anxiety, hostility, and intolerance for ambiguity, have been associated with ultraconservative attitudes (McClosky & Schaar, 1965). Ego defensiveness was also found among subjects who were negative about civil liberties (Gaugler & Zalkind, 1975).

Authoritarianism is related not only to the insecurity and ego defensiveness of the individual but to motivation as well. Sarnoff (1962) says, "an individual's attitude toward a class of objects is determined by the particular role these objects have come to play in facilitating responses that reduce the tension of particular conflicts among motives." These attitudes may apply to religion, politics, ethnic relations, or other cognitive areas. In an elaborate study of reactions among military and naval cadets in Norway to problems in international relations, Christensen (1959) compared individuals who approached situations or problems to be solved logically or by trial and error with those who were largely aggressive in their approach. The beliefs of individuals who were threat oriented or "destructive" in their thinking about foreign affairs (rather than being problem oriented) were not an "isolated aspect of the individual personality," Christensen says, but were the result of various "dynamic and cognitive aspects."

Reference Groups

The proliferation of groups to which the average individual belongs in modern urban life has brought strong pressure to conform to group roles, statuses, and norms, as Chapters 11 and 14 will demonstrate. All of the attitudes group members are expected to accept are not in agreement, however, and each person must select those he or she finds most congenial. These are the ones that promise the highest rewards or the least dissonance for the individual.

Both formal groups, such as a school or church, and informal groups, such as the family, peers, and opinion leaders, form the reference groups (Newcomb, 1957) with which a person identifies and from which many of a person's attitudes, values, and norms emerge (see Chapter 12). Sherif and Sherif (1964) studied the formation of reference groups and their impact on members. Other research studies have shown the effects of group influence in determining readiness to accept a given attitude. In one instance (Menzel & Katz, 1955), the diffusion of new medical techniques and drugs was found to be most pronounced among physicians who formed a professional community, as determined by the number of contacts each had with other doctors. Other factors than the group influence were also present, such as the mass media, professional journals, and drug sales representatives. In this case as in others, however, the major impact on attitudes comes from peers and opinion leaders; it is through the group that the individual's own attitudes are reinforced.

There have been numerous studies on how the influence of reference groups causes people to change their attitudes. A longitudinal study of women as students in the freshman class at Bennington College in 1935 and as adults in 1960 (Newcomb et al., 1967) showed that their attitudes moved from conformity to their parents' conservative stance to an enduring acceptance of the more liberal standards of their professors and the older students at the college. Similar results were found for the topic of the original study, political attitudes, and in the drift from religious orthodoxy and traditional sexual practices to a far freer ethical stance. Such shifts are even more predictable if the parents themselves are ambivalent or are in disagreement between themselves (Bem, 1970). These findings support the viewpoint that attitudes emerge from interpersonal influence, particularly that of peers.

Thus people's attitudes are a product of the sociocultural setting, their personality structure, and the institutional and group influences in their own frame of reference. This affects their cognitions in specific situations and directs their predisposition to react in a given fashion. In a political context, this process may be as shown in Figure 8–4, although the interaction of the variables is usually more complex than the arrows suggest.

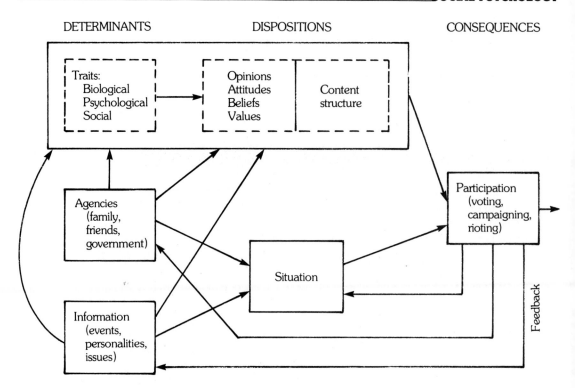

Figure 8–4. Relations between Personal Frame of Reference, Attitude Formation, and Political Participation

Source: A. R. Wilcox, *Public Opinion and Political Attitudes* (New York: John Wiley & Sons, 1974), p. 2.

ATTITUDES AND BEHAVIOR: THE PROBLEM OF CONSISTENCY

The complex problem of consistency in attitudes and behavior (which is explored further in Chapter 9) involves several dimensions, as Fishbein and Ajzen (1975) have pointed out. In behavioristic terms, the first is *stimulus-response consistency,* that is, whether the attitude is consistently favorable or unfavorable toward its object. The second, *response-response consistency,* refers to the consistency of behavior in respect to a given object. This problem is complicated because most objects represent clusters of events. For example, a person who has moderately militarist attitudes may oppose action in Southeast Asia but support U.S. commitments in Europe, since the two involvements represent different definitions of collective security. The increase of ticket splitting in recent U.S.

national elections shows that conventional *Republican* and *Democratic* labels have lost much of their original meaning. The third dimension, *attitudinal consistency,* may break down for multiple behaviors at different times. A person who supports a cause like abortion may contribute financially to the campaign, attend meetings, and picket an antiabortion organization, but will not write letters or give speeches. This kind of inconsistency relates to such personality dimensions as ego strength, aggressiveness, and ascendance-submission rather than merely reflecting favorability or even liberalism-conservatism.

Few ideological decisions escape problems of consistency; for example, attitudes associated with belief in a divinity may not be altogether consistent with day-to-day ethical practices or faith in the scientific method. And a decision to buy a car may be related to attitudes about one's place in the community, attitudes toward foreign and U.S.–made automobiles, or perception of how much one can afford to spend. The same individuals who question the government's deficit spending may have a different attitude to their own financial planning. They may publicly reject a government spending program and yet privately enjoy it as a means of justifying their own expenditures in view of inflationary tendencies in the economy. We are not suggesting, however, that attitudes are *necessarily* inconsistent with or divorced from behavior.

Inconsistency between attitudes and behavior can also be observed in the election booth. How a person votes depends on the cross-pressures between his or her various attitudes and how public opinion is manipulated. Gun control, for example, has been an emotional issue since the assassination of President John Kennedy in 1963, followed by Martin Luther King, Robert Kennedy, the folk hero John Lennon, and the near assassination of President Ronald Reagan in 1981. In a 1980 Gallup poll, 62 percent of the American people favored stricter laws regulating handgun sales, yet the failure of many U.S. representatives and senators to support handgun control legislation has been attributable largely to the powerful lobbying efforts of the National Rifle Association. This curious inability of a democracy to achieve what its electorate seemingly desires points to the danger that powerful single-interest groups can block the public will. At the same time, it implies that many persons do not hold their attitudes with sufficient strength to transmit them into action, and they have difficulty in achieving consistency or establishing priorities among their attitudes.

Verbalized Attitudes and Overt Behavior

Considerable discrepancy has been found between attitudes and behavior or between publicly expressed and privately held attitudes. When the inconsistency can be perceived the person expressing the inaccurate attitude may be accused of lying (see Box 8–3). As M. B. Smith (1974) puts it, "What people *say* and what they *do* are surely governed in part by different contingencies, different positive and negative sanctions" (p. 34).

In measuring attitudes, it is assumed that they will predict later behavior. Generally, the results of studies of this dimension of attitudes have borne this out, as in Stouffer's (1962) studies of American combat trainees' self-reports of attitudes and subsequent behavior on the battlefield. The men who rated

Box 8–3
GETTING AWAY WITH LIES

If someone calls you a liar, the severity of the charge depends on the kind of lie you seem to have told: the white lies you tell to avoid divulging your true attitudes, in order to save face or protect a friend's feelings; or what you say to an enemy compared to what you say to a friend; or outright lies you tell purposively in order to serve your own interests. Some people are more successful liars than others, and some can tell whether other people are lying more easily than others can.

A decade of research on lying has had not altogether consistent findings. In one study, experimenters posing as actors were either very good or very bad at convincing observers they were lying. Observers showed more variability in their ability to *detect* a lie, as there were a number of conflicting cues to choose from.* Other research has shown the effectiveness of visual over auditory cues in making a lie convincing to an observer.

In order to shed light on the art of deception, Bella M. DePaulo and Robert Rosenthal videotaped 20 men and 20 women while describing someone they liked, someone they disliked, someone they felt ambivalent about, someone they were indifferent about, someone they pretended to like but didn't, and someone they pretended to dislike but didn't.†

On the whole, the subjects were better able to uncover the lie itself than the underlying feeling of the speaker. However, those subjects who were able to identify deception in another person were also better at interpreting the underlying affect. The performers who were more easily identified when lying were also those whose feelings were somewhat more discernible.

An interesting aspect of this investigation was *hamming,* or an exaggerated pretense of liking someone one dislikes more than a person one really likes, or the reverse—pretending to dislike a person one likes and coming on stronger than with a person one really dislikes. Subjects who were most successful in hamming had above-average scores in the Mach Scale (power needs and manipulative skills in interpersonal relations; see Box 8–1).

The findings point to fairly complex factors that determine both deception and its detection. There was little relationship between the ability to get away with one's own lies and the ability to catch other people in their lies. There also was no significant difference between men and women in these abilities.

---

*R. E. Kraut, "Verbal and Nonverbal Cues in the Perception of Lying," *Journal of Personality and Social Psychology,* 1978, *36,* 380–391.
†B. M. DePaulo and R. Rosenthal, "Telling Lies," *Journal of Personality and Social Psychology,* 1979, *37,* 1713–1722.

themselves highest in (1) willingness for combat, (2) combat stamina, and (3) combat skills had the lowest casualty rates once in action. There were significant differences between highly seasoned GIs and neophytes in the battle situation, however. The veterans had higher confidence in their combat skills, whereas the fresh soldiers rated themselves higher in their enthusiasm and stamina, yet all three factors were significant in assuring survival on the battlefield.

There is evidence that the more specific the attitude, the more likely it is to have an effect on behavior. In one study (Heberlein & Black, 1976), different types of questionnaires were used to determine beliefs and attitudes about the relation of auto emissions and air pollution. At the same time, subjects were observed as to whether they bought lead-free or regular gasoline. The recipients of questionnaires containing the most specific information were more likely to purchase the lead-free gasoline, at a time when new automobiles did not require lead-free fuel and the choice was voluntary.

The effects of attitudes on behavior in regard to dating, studying, and physical exercise were studied by Bentler and Speckart (1981). For dating, for example, "indicator behaviors" were going out on a date, visiting a friend of the opposite sex, and making out or necking. The findings support the hypothesis that there is a linkage from attitude, to intention, to behavior. Thus attitudes can be said to "cause" behaviors, and behavior may also have an effect on attitude.

Certain inconsistencies in regard to people's verbalized prejudices and their more accepting behavior, such as permitting a black person to dine in a restaurant, were noted in the section on attitude measurements. Other studies have probed into the relationship of ethnic attitude and "overt action opportunity." On one American campus, white women students were requested to permit themselves to be photographed with a black man and to authorize use of the photographs in various ways, from display in the laboratory or classroom to national publicity campaigns for integration (DeFleur & Westie, 1958). The responses indicated an inverse correlation between degree of prejudice shown on a test and willingness to be photographed for this purpose; 30 percent of the subjects behaved differently, usually less tolerantly, in the photographing situation as compared to the position their verbal attitudes had indicated.

In a variation of the experiment with more careful controls (Linn, 1965), more than half of the subjects departed from their verbalized attitude of willingness to be photographed with a black person. These differences operated in both directions: prejudiced attitude but nonprejudiced performance, as well as the reverse. These disparities were the result mainly of the contrast between the climate of the society at large and that of the university subcultures. These two environments had different norms, and the strength or weakness of the liberalism expressed by a person depended on the degree of involvement with both of them. Discrepant behavior (i.e., not living up to the expressed tolerance) appeared when the tolerant attitudes were unstable. Two relevant variables were high pressure to conform to the group and lack of interracial experience. Movement from a negative attitude to a tolerant behavior, which was relatively less frequent, occurred with strong social involvement (if the subject believed that only a university audience would view the picture, for example).

Thus the stability of attitudes and their predictability in overt behavior are related to the total value structure of the individual and to the groups to which he or she belongs (see Box 8–4). For instance, in a Cornell University study it was found that students who were directly involved in a housing shortage showed greater consistency between their attitudes and behaviors in attempting to resolve the crisis (Regan & Fazio, 1977).

Box 8–4
HELP FOR A STRANGER IN THE NIGHT

The difficulty of predicting an individual's behavior from an attitude or an attitude from behavior is complicated by the person's entire attitude structure. In an ingenious experiment, Samuel Gaertner studied the willingness of liberal and conservative subjects to help others in distress who seem to be black or white and male or female.* The subjects represented relatively matched samples of 230 Liberal and 238 Conservative party members in New York City. The only essential difference between the two samples was age; the liberals were on the average 37 and the conservatives, 27.

The subjects were approached in the evening at home, by telephone, as follows:

Caller: Hello. . . . Ralph's Garage? This is George Williams. . . . Listen I'm stuck out here on the parkway, and I'm wondering if you'd be able to come out here and take a look at my car.

Subject's expected response: This isn't Ralph's Garage. You have the wrong number.

Caller: This isn't Ralph's Garage! Listen I'm terribly sorry to have disturbed you, but listen—I'm stuck out here on the highway, and that was the last dime I had! I have bills in my pocket, but no more change to make another phone call. Now I'm really stuck out here. What am I going to do now?

(Subject might volunteer to call the garage.)

Caller: Listen . . . do you think you could do me the favor of calling the garage and letting them know where I am? I'll give you the number. They know me over there.

Prod A: Oh brother . . . listen I'm stuck out here. Couldn't you please help me out by simply calling the garage for me? (Pleadingly)

Prod B: Listen . . . if you were in my situation, wouldn't you want someone to help you?

If after Prod B subjects refused to help, they were relieved of any concern they may have had for the stranded motorist when the caller reported: "Oh, one second. Here comes a police car. I think he will be able to give me a hand."

The caller was racially identifiable largely through his or her diction. The taping of the phone conversation revealed that the Liberals tended to hang up sooner than the Conservatives, but if they did remain on the phone the Liberals more often phoned the garage. (The call actually reached an outside source that promised to follow through.)

About four fifths of the total sample actually helped by making the phone call, but the Conservatives were decidedly more likely to respond to a white than a black, whereas an ethnic preference was less apparent for the Liberals. Also, the Conservatives came to the aid of either race more frequently if it was a female caller.

The Liberals were not without prejudice but seemed to use universalistic criteria when a person was in trouble. Gaertner suggested, "Apparently the Liberal's sense of social responsibility, ability to sympathize, or sense of justice ignores the personal characteristics of *who* requires assistance and is guided more strictly by the general principle involved. Liberals would thus apply such a *principle* in an egalitarian manner" (p. 339).

_____

*S. L. A. Gaertner, "Helping Behavior and Racial Discrimination among Liberals and Conservatives," *Journal of Personality and Social Psychology,* 1973, 25, 335–341.

Stereotypes

Attitudes and opinions about an object (or person or situation) can become stereotyped about it when there is a perceived inconsistency among an individual's attitudes or between attitudes and behavior, as noted in Chapter 6. The perceiver disregards the actual stimuli received from the object and substitutes preconceived notions which support cognitive consistency.

The term *stereotype* was introduced in the 1920s by Walter Lippmann, who used it in the sense of a rigid and standardized "picture in the head." Modern life, Lippmann (1922) said, is hurried and often impersonal, so it affords little time or opportunity for intimate acquaintance. It contains "so much subtlety, so much variety, so many permutations and combinations . . . we have to reconstruct it on a simpler model before we can manage with it" (p. 16). Thus stereotypes often persist because they provide a consistent picture of the world in which we come to feel at home. Any disturbance of a person's stereotypes becomes an attack on his or her social foundations, particularly because stereotypes tend to become emotionally charged. People strongly resist any threat to their stereotypes.

The stereotype usually functions as a convenient generalized attitude for the purpose of specifying a feeling of prejudice. So blacks are dubbed lazy, stupid, unclean, musical, athletic, or oversexed; Germans are called hardworking, meticulous, overpowering, rigid or dull. In most instances these group attributes are learned by children in the socialization process in the home, school, playground, or on the job. Others may be based on personal experiences which are filtered through a person's selective perception process, in which the treatment of cues can be extremely complex (see Chapter 6). An example of the intricacy of this process was given in the report of an investigation of 44 university students in which the stereotyping of attributes was found to be differentiated more by occupation than by race (Feldman, 1972). The stereotype directed to blacks appeared to relate primarily to their lower-class background rather than to skin color or other attributes. Positive attitudes were more attached to black professionals than to white professionals, giving evidence of an awareness of greater mobility barriers for blacks than for whites. For these students, race was not a central trait. Stereotyping seems to be a more subtle and uneven process than it was a generation or two ago.

A classic example of the early experiments on stereotypes was a study which showed the consistency of students' stereotyped notions about the characteristics of people in various occupations. Rice (1926) cut out newspaper pictures which showed a bootlegger (appropriate for the times), a European prime minister, the Soviet envoy, a U.S. senator, a labor leader, an editor-politician, two manufacturers, and a financier. The pictures and the occupational titles were presented in mixed order to a large number of university students, who were asked to match pictures and occupations. Over half the students identified the bootlegger correctly; his attire and cigar seemed to fit the stereotype. But over half also identified the European premier as a "Bolshevik" or communist, and almost as many thought the Soviet envoy was the European premier. In these cases the subjects had stereotyped concepts that led them astray.

In a much later study (Hamilton & Rose, 1980), in which subjects were asked to recall given traits as linked to given occupations, they were more likely to retain the linkage when it was harmonious with their stereotypes (as with "helpful-doctor") than when the trait was neutral or unrelated to the occupation. Efforts at attitude change (see Chapter 9) thus must recognize that new information is retrieved from memory more easily when it is congruent rather than opposed to a person's stereotypes.

Confusion as to the meaning of the term led Edwards (1940) to propose that as types of attitudes, stereotypes have several aspects. He researched political stereotypes and found these four dimensions:

1. *Uniformity*—the extent to which an individual's response agrees with responses of others.
2. *Direction*—whether a response is favorable or unfavorable.
3. *Intensity*—the degree of favorableness and unfavorableness.
4. *Quality*—the content of the response.

Edwards found a correlation between uniformity and intensity. In his experiments, those who strongly opposed communism agreed better on the characteristics of democracy than those who favored communism; those who favored communism agreed better as to its nature than did those who opposed it. Other researchers have not all found this relationship, but there is a tendency for a stereotype to act as a halo in reverse. As noted in the discussion of perception in Chapter 6, white people interpret behavior such as shoving as accidental when performed by whites but aggressive when performed by blacks. According to Duncan (1976), the "threshold for labeling an act as violent is lower when viewing a black committing the same act."

Studies of stereotypes demonstrate how attitudes and opinions, based on varying individual experience, come to form rigid attitude patterns which are often highly standardized in application to all members of a group. The existence of stereotypes facilitates the formation of a consensus, which is basic to public opinion and forms a basis for social influence and group pressure (see Chapter 11).

DIMENSIONS OF VALUES

Values represent a type of societal norm, or standard, which is closely related to attitudes. Rokeach (1972) differentiates between attitudes and values by noting that both are "widely assumed to be determinants of social behavior," but a value is also a determinant of attitude, as well as behavior. Both also are types of motives, since they represent orientation or striving toward a given goal.

In the broadest sense, *values* can be considered attitude-related attributes that are projected onto people, objects, and situations. They also are considered "inclusive attitudes" or dominant clusters of attitudes (Newcomb, Turner, & Converse, 1965). Dodd (1951) defines values as "desiderata, i.e. anything desired or chosen by someone sometimes." In polling behavior, this would mean that any item in a questionnaire that the respondent selects is a value for that person. Generally, however, values are thought of as the more enduring clusters of wants a given individual or group works toward fairly consistently, though the values may shift in time (see Box 8–5). Like attitudes, they are basic to personality, and yet they can be distinguished from traits (see Chapter 4). Values resemble attitudes—and differ from traits—in that they are general reactions toward persons, situations, and objects in a positive or negative direction. The distinction is that values tend to be in the nature of general life themes or goals, whereas attitudes are somewhat more content oriented.

Classificatory Systems

Various systems have been devised for distinguishing between types of values. Philosophers have distinguished between higher and lower, mental and physical, permanent and transient values. Intrinsic values, which are an inseparable part of the object or situation, and extrinsic values, which are supplemental, have also been differentiated. Another distinction is between instrumental values, which are related to the accomplishment of certain goals, and inherent values, which like intrinsic values are an essential part of the object or situation. This is familiarly known as the distinction between means and ends—what is done in order to reach a given result. From a psychological viewpoint it is also important to distinguish between implicit and explicit values (Kluckhohn, 1951). Implicit values are known only to the individual, and explicit values are sufficiently verbalized so an outside observer can make judgments about them. This distinction is highly arbitrary, however.

Box 8–5
HOW VALUES CHANGE

The values you hold today probably will change as you mature, according to D. R. Hoge and I. E. Bender. In a study titled "Factors Influencing Value Change among College Graduates in Adult Life," they considered values as embodying deep-seated response tendencies, different psychological needs arising during the life cycle, and developments in the environment.*

In line with this distinction, three models of value change have been designated by T. M. Newcomb and associates.† In the *current experience model,* values change in response to experiences. In the *cohort model,* values are structured and restructured during critical periods, such as the university years; Newcomb et al. found a profound resocialization of values and attitudes in a sample of Bennington College students studied in the 1930s and 25 years later. In the *standard life cycle model,* change accompanies growth, such as the tendency to conservatism accompanying middle age, even though in the Bennington sample, liberal attitudes persisted beyond the college years.

In the Hoge and Bender study, samples of Dartmouth students taken between 1931 and 1956 and again as alumni between 1952 and 1960 found that the profiles on the Allport-Vernon scale (especially the theoretical, aesthetic, and religious values) showed aspects of all three models. Particularly critical was the effect of the social climate of a given period. Liberal values were salient in the 1930s; a conservative tide began about 1939, peaking in the early 1950s in the McCarthy (anticommunism) era; and the late 1960s were marked by strong dissent, at least among those who were still of university age.

---

*D. R. Hoge and I. E. Bender, "Factors Influencing Value Change among College Graduates in Adult Life," *Journal of Personality and Social Psychology,* 1974, *29,* 572–585.
†T. M. Newcomb et al., *Persistence and Change: Bennington College and Its Students after 25 Years* (New York: John Wiley & Sons, 1967).

Personality and interest inventories with a psychological orientation have been used in attempts to arrive at a system of human motives which can be identified as values. A most influential classification of values was made by Edouard Spranger (1928), who proposed six basic value attitudes which produce six personality types: theoretic, economic, aesthetic, social, political, and religious. Using Spranger's six types, Gordon Allport and Phillip Vernon prepared a scale of values to indicate which major areas of endeavor are most important to specific individuals (Allport, Vernon, & Lindzey, 1960). Typical findings were as expected: theological students rate high on religious values and business students rate high on economic values.

Using the Allport-Vernon scale, other researchers found, for instance, that friendship patterns were correlated with value scores in a sample of university women; friends were selected on the basis of corresponding values (Richardson, 1940). Value systems based on the scale have proved to be useful in the analysis of certain social attitudes in the past, such as anti-Semitism and its correlates. In one study (R. I. Evans, 1952), persons high in political and economic values were also anti-Semitic, while those high in aesthetic and social values were less so. Those high in theoretical and religious values proved to be slightly anti-Semitic, although the relationship was not statistically significant.

Values and Personality Systems

Values are not only complex structures which are interrelated with other cognitive constructs, as noted earlier in this chapter. They also are incorporated in the personality system. In an attempt to account for political ideology, Eysenck (1954) posited two dimensions, radicalism-conservatism and religious-humanitarianism, or tender-mindedness. A study of these dimensions by DeFronzo (1972) found that the scores of 118 university students on an attitude scale showed a positive relationship between conservative values and traditional religious orientation, whereas scores in the tender-minded or humanitarian orientation were associated with political radicalism. A slightly negative correlation appeared between the religious and humanitarian values.

Like other values, formal religious orientation represents an intricate patterning; attendance at church has low predictability for the other components of the religious value. Allport and Ross (1967) found irregular attendance was positively correlated with ethnic prejudice, but persons with either no attendance or regular attendance had relatively little prejudice—a curvilinear relationship.

A number of other attempts to determine the strength of certain values have centered on the types of projective responses to story-completion tests. In these tests, for example, individuals will take risks, but under slightly varying conditions they will remain cautious. Does this mean that Americans in general are inclined to be adventuresome or self-restrained? Or are they more adventuresome in an individual or a group setting? Such questions about the relation of individual values and attitudes to group conformity will be discussed in Part III.

SUMMARY

The concept of attitude, a central one in social psychology, represents a learned tendency to behave positively or negatively toward persons and situations. Attitudes are dynamic cognitive constructs which have several dimensions and components and are basic to personality structure. Several types of scales have been devised for measuring attitudes or aspects of them, supplemented recently by more indirect techniques.

Attitudes play a central role in personality development and social behavior. They can act as involuntary responses in emotional or verbal conditioning or as operant-conditioned voluntary responses designed to secure rewards. Attitudes are culturally conditioned but are also influenced by personality factors, and they are particularly affected by the reference groups to which an individual belongs. Like almost all cognitions, attitudes must be arranged to fit in with a person's motives, as authoritarianism has been found to do. They also must satisfy standards of cognitive consistency; the stereotype—a kind of standardized concept or response—can grow out of a cognitive dissonance problem.

Values are related to attitudes but they represent attributes projected unto people, objects, and situations. They can be considered as generalized goal symbols that people work toward fairly consistently, though they may change over time. Value classifications differentiate between those that are intrinsic or extrinsic, implicit or explicit, and instrumental or inherent, among other distinctions.

WORDS TO REMEMBER

Area sample. Choosing a study sample on the basis of geographical or residential area.

Attitude. A response tendency, positive or negative, toward a given object, situation, person, or group; a learned predisposition to react or respond preferentially. Attitudes can be explicit or implicit, conscious or unconscious, latent or manifest, and can be defined as complexes related to both belief and feeling. They resemble values but are less diffuse.

Attitude measurement. Various means used in attempts to ascertain and quantify a person's attitudes. A number of ingenuous approaches have been used, such as equal-appearing interval, summated ratings and the use of projective or behavioral tests. (See *scale.*)

Belief. A cognitive structure that is relatively neutral and unemotional, as compared to an attitude; a cognitive element that is theoretically verifiable.

Bias. Errors in perception, cognition, attitudes, etc. due to some subjective factor; errors which occur in a sample or experiment because all the relevant population or variables are not accounted for.

Cognitive constructs. Intellectual or mental functions as compared to emotional or motivational functions, such as thinking, beliefs, or attitudes.

F scale. A test or inventory of personality and attitudinal traits associated with authoritarianism, such as ultra conservative political ideology or anti-Semitism.

Frame of reference. Total relevant situations in which people find themselves and in which attitudes are acquired. The concept includes past experiences as well as the present environment.

Halo effect. The tendency to exaggerate either the positive or negative aspects of a given object (person, group, etc.) in order to reduce cognitive dissonance. If the limited knowledge about an object or person is favorable, people tend to rate other characteristics as favorable, or if the few traits known are negative, they assume that the other traits also are negative.

Mach scale. Test designed by Richard Christie and Florence Geis to measure opportunism, manipulativeness, and relativistic ethics or norms. (See *Machiavellianism.*)

Machiavellianism. Use of opportunism, cunning, dishonesty, or arbitrary force in order to reach a given end. A Machiavellian attitude would support the use of deceit or any means in order to gain political or related ends.

Norms. Standards of behavior or belief which are generally agreed on by society, but in some instances are subject to individual interpretation.

Quota sample. A study sample with specified numbers or ratios based on age, ethnicity or other characteristics, as closely as possible in the same proportion as these attributes exist in the general population. (See *sample.*)

Random sample. A study sample in which every member of the population has an equal chance of being included. In a very large universe, complete randomization is very difficult or impossible to achieve. (See *sample.*)

Sample. A limited part of a larger group chosen for study in order to gain information about the population or the universe being studied. (See *area sample; random sample; quota sample.*)

Scale. Pretested instrument for measuring attitudes, personality traits, or other behaviors.

Semantic Differential Scale. Measurement instrument which uses different words or verbal symbols (usually adjectives) to measure the direction or strength of attitudes or, posssibly, personality traits.

Valence. The positive feeling or affect one invests in an object, belief, attitude, or goal.

Value. Deep-seated feelings and beliefs about given objects or goals in life. Values are generally more pervasive and permanent than attitudes, but the two are usually interrelated.

QUESTIONS FOR DISCUSSION

1. Why is the study of attitudes traditionally believed to be the central preoccupation of social psychologists?
2. How would you define an attitude? How does it differ from a fact, an opinion, and a belief? How would you define a value?
3. What are the components of attitudes? Why are attitudes described as being dynamic?
4. What dimensions of attitudes can be measured?
5. What are some of the more important tests of attitudes? Which ones would you use to study an attitude of classmates?
6. What are the principal approaches to the study of attitude formation? How do they relate to learning theory?
7. How do attitudes differ as involuntary and voluntary responses? Give examples of each kind.
8. What personality factors are involved in attitude formation?

9. Of what relevance are reference groups to attitude formation?
10. Describe some of the studies that have been carried out on the relation of verbalized attitudes and overt behavior?
11. What is the basis of the term *stereotype?* For what purpose do people use stereotypes?
12. What are the principal differences between values and attitudes?

READINGS

Fishbein, M., and Ajzen, I. *Belief, Attitude, Intention and Behavior.* Reading, Mass.: Addison-Wesley Publishing Co., 1975.

A penetrating analysis of attitudes and their measurement.

Osgood, C. E., Suci, G. J., and Tannenbaum, P. H. *The Measurement of Meaning.* Urbana: University of Illinois Press, 1957.

The semantic differential principle as applied to attitude research.

Rokeach, M. *The Open and Closed Mind.* New York: Basic Books, 1960.

Rokeach, M. *Beliefs, Attitudes and Values.* San Francisco: Jossey-Bass, Publishers, 1972.

Both books treat the nature of attitudes and the problem of rigidity and change.

Rokeach, M. *Understanding Human Values: Individual and Societal.* New York: Free Press, 1979.

Series of empirical and interpretive studies on values in conditions of both stability and change.

Silverstein, A. (Ed.). *Human Communication: Theoretical Explorations.* Hillsdale, N.J.: Lawrence Erlbaum Associates, 1974.

Considers the questions of motivation, belief, and meaning and their relation to communication.

ATTITUDE CHANGE AND PERSUASIBILITY

Like all the cognitive constructs involved in the dynamics of social behavior, a person's attitudes constantly undergo change as the individual interacts with others in the sociocultural setting. The attitudes are interrelated or interconnected in organized structures which help determine whether the person will maintain them or be open to change about them. Lack of consistency in a person's attitudes or between attitudes and behavior is one of the principal causes of attitude change.

In the search for cognitive consistency, the individual's attitudes must be changed often to reflect the constantly changing social environment. However, because of the reciprocal relation between personality factors and the sociocultural setting in attitude formation (as noted in the preceding chapter), the impetus for change also may come from the individual. All social change depends to some degree on the ability of at least a portion of the populace to alter their attitudes and opinions. The extent to which they are willing to do this depends on their persuasibility, and the persuasiveness of those who are seeking the change and the messages they are communicating.

During the Vietnam War, for example, the proponents of the peace movement, many of whom were college students and faculty members, eventually persuaded the majority of Americans to adopt their antiwar attitude, despite the official support of the conflict by the government (see Box 9–1). The consensus of opinion became so strong that the incumbent president, Lyndon Johnson, was convinced he had lost his base of public support, and so he chose not to seek reelection for his second full term in 1968.

Box 9–1
THE ART OF PERSUASION

Attempts to persuade others can follow a very slippery road, and the strategy of conversion can take on opportunistic overtones. Philip Zimbardo speculated on the methods of attitudinal change which might have more than routine influence, among those who overheard communications.

During the Vietnam War students took various roles in trying to convince voters to support the peace movement. For example, a woman student might go into a busy laundromat, and, while her clothes were in the washer, phone another person she called "Mom." As she described her busy, productive life, the other women would smile in approval. Then she could tell her "mother" of the need to end the war in Vietnam and suggest that a vote for candidate X would be a move in that direction.

The two-person approach was even more effective. A student and an older person (presumably an "uncle" or "Dad") on a bus made ideal partners. They would hold a loud spirited discussion about the mood of campus youth, not necessarily agreeing but showing some respect for each other. The student might describe how "when I was fixing the sink last night I was thinking down the drain, down the drain, boy, all the money we're spending on war is just going down the drain, totally wasted." "Dad" might complain that students were not working as hard as they did in his day, and the son would explain that anxiety over the war is the reason. After more talk "Dad" would agree to write his political representative about the war.

*P. G. Zimbardo, "The Tactics and Ethics of Persuasion," in B. T. King and E. McGinnies (Eds.), *Attitudes, Conflict and Social Change* (New York: Academic Press, 1972), p. 98.

At present a number of attitudes are striving for public acceptance. The abortion issue, for example, has become highly polarized between those labeled *pro life,* who would limit or forbid abortions, and those who believe the woman should have a personal choice. The issue is surrounded by emotional intensity, which discourages rational judgments. Moreover, the abortion question illustrates the inconsistencies in attitude structures. Pro lifers believe all human life is sacred, but they often oppose gun control, favor capital punishment, and advocate heavy military spending. On the opposite side, those who assert that the choice should rest with the individual usually limit this choice to the woman and permit little or no participation by the husband or father in the decision making. In this case, as in

Strongly held attitudes can become the sole basis of judging a political candidate. Few attitudes in recent years have been as salient as those of the "pro-lifers" in the continuing debate over abortion. *Source:* Wide World Photos, Inc.

others, the very emotional and motivational character of salient attitudes can keep people from making objective appraisals of what they believe.

This chapter examines the major theories of attitude structure and change, which focus on various components of or processes in attitudes: functional or motivational, cognitive or affective, and compliance, identification, or internalization. A central concept in all these theories, cognitive consistency, is investigated in a separate section which discusses the balance and congruity theories and introduces cognitive dissonance theory. The determinants of attitude change are considered in terms of social background, intergroup relations, and personality structure.

Persuasibility, or openness to change, is the second principal topic in this chapter. It is affected by such factors as the credibility of the source and the content of a persuasive message, the order of presentation of the information, and the nature of the message, or how the information is presented. The latter topic is concerned with questions of impartiality, cognitive consistency and selective exposure, and emotional appeal.

THEORIES OF ATTITUDE ORGANIZATION

The cognitive and motivational functions of attitudes are derived from their position as organized, interrelated attitude structures. To varying degrees, the theories which have been developed to account for the way a person's attitudes are organized, both in relation to one another and within the larger structure of personality and the self, represent the cognitive, procedural approach to the study of attitudes which is based on the purposive principles of Gestalt psychology (see Chapters 5 and 7). The major theories, which will be considered in this section, focus on both the structure of attitudes and their dynamic nature. Like other psychological processes and properties, attitudes are constantly undergoing change.

Functional or Motivational Theory of Attitudes

The functional view of the structure of attitudes devised by Daniel Katz (1960) is similar to many of the theoretical approaches in social psychology in that it includes elements of several theories: behaviorism, psychoanalysis, and Gestalt psychology. This theory is based on the assumptions that attitudes have both cognitive and affective (emotional or feeling) components, they are related to a given value system, and they have *centrality* because they are identified with the individual's self-concept. In this context, attitudes have four major functions.

1. *The instrumental, adjustive, or utilitarian function,* on which Jeremy Bentham constructed the utilitarian model of humans. A modern expression of this approach can be found in behavioristic learning theory.
2. *The ego-defensive function,* in which the individual protects the self from acknowledging the basic truths about it or the harsh realities of the external

world. Freudian psychology and neo-Freudian thinking have been preoccupied with this type of motivation and its outcomes.

3. *The value-expressive function,* in which the individual derives satisfaction from expressing attitudes appropriate to personal values and the self-concept. This function is central to doctrines of ego psychology which stress the importance of self-expression, self-development, and self-realization.

4. *The knowledge function*, based on the individual's need to give adequate structure to the universe. The search for meaning, the need to understand, the trend toward better organization of perceptions and beliefs to provide clarity and consistency for the individual are other descriptions of this function.

These functions may be involved in a given set of attitudes or even a single attitude. For example, some people may have strongly negative attitudes about an alleged communist conspiracy in the United States. Aside from information they have received about the threat, the basis for holding this belief may be that it pleases their employers, stands them in good stead with peers, or provides leverage in running for political office. The ego-defensive function of hating communism is that it provides an out-group they can blame for their own inadequacies or defects of society or culture that they cannot accept. The value-expressive function can be stated in terms of antagonism toward communist activities which may incorporate basic authoritarian values, avoidance of deviancy, and esteem for traditionalism. Communism can be cited as an explanation of lawlessness, high taxes, or some other troubling event. Internal communist factions can be regarded as "explaining" group phenomena that might be otherwise unexplainable, as in social movements, the intricacies of social legislation, or even the antics of teenagers.

As Rokeach (1972) points out, social psychology still lacks the sophistication in theories and methods which would make it possible to determine objectively what function a specific attitude serves for a given individual and to what degree. He notes that beliefs such as faith in one's country also can have similar functions; in fact, when a belief becomes the basis of action, it takes on the character of an attitude.

Attitudes as Cognition and Affect

An elaboration of the theory of attitudes as relationships between cognition and affect (or emotions or feeling states, the terms used in reference to the affective dimensions of perception in Chapter 6 and of motivation in Chapter 7) has been suggested by Rosenberg and Hovland (1960). This theory, which is related to the concept of *cognitive consistency* introduced in Chapter 6, suggests that people seek a congruence between their beliefs and their feelings toward objects, and modification of their attitudes depends on changing either the feelings or the beliefs. A noteworthy feature of this theory is that changed feeling states are said to have an effect on later attitudes, rather than changed attitudes being followed by a change in feeling, as had been previously demonstrated. He assumes the existence of an attitude structure composed of various affective and cognitive components so interrelated that a change in one will set in motion a change in another. When the components are sufficiently inconsistent to exceed the individual's *tolerance limit,* instability results. This instability may be resolved in three possible ways: (1) disavowal of the communication about the inconsistency, (2) fragmentation of the attitude or isolation of the given components from each other, or (3) acceptance of the inconsistency so that a new attitude is formed. All attitude change does not emerge from instability, any more than inconsistency inevitably leads to attitude change, but attitude change basically results from the relationship of affect and cognition.

Thus Rosenberg suggests that cognition, affect, and behavior are determinants of attitudes, and attitudes in turn may determine affect, cognition, and behavior. In behaviorist terms, they can all be regarded as intervening variables between a stimulus and a response as shown in Figure 9–1. The term *intervening variable* is used as in motivational theory (see Chapter 7), to represent the critical factor or "cause" which explains relevant behavior. In this sense, attitudes are considered as hypothetical constructs which are motivational in character. The term *behavior* represents neutral events—namely, what the

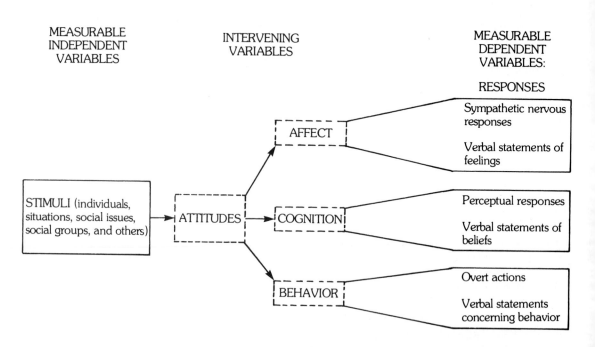

Figure 9–1. Schematic Conception of Attitude Organization and Change

Source: M. J. Rosenberg and C. I. Hovland, "Cognitive, Affective, and Behavioral Components of Attitudes," in M. J. Rosenberg et al. (Eds.), *Attitude Organization and Change* (New Haven, Conn.: Yale University Press, 1960), p. 3.

individual does about the situation—which cannot be properly identified as either cognitive or affective.

This theory was validated in Rosenberg's (1960) experiment on the effects of hypnosis in changing a limited sample of attitudes toward U.S. aid to other nations. Subjects' attitudes were manipulated through a suggestion during hypnosis that they would have strong negative feelings toward foreign aid. Once the effects of the hypnosis session wore off, the subject's original positive feelings toward foreign aid returned, but the entire process was accompanied by feelings of guilt and discomfort. Both the affect and the cognition could be measured as subjects returned to the prehypnotic situation, but certain aspects of their beliefs did not return to the original state. An individual who previously believed in aid for the economic development of African nations, for example, might have reservations about it after the hypnotic experience.

Rosenberg (1960) also demonstrated that attitudes and beliefs are frequently composites of positive and negative components. If cognitive-affective inconsistency is sufficiently acute, the individual may really have no attitude about an object. This has been evident in a number of U.S. presidential elections in which the leading candidates aroused both negative and positive affect, making prediction of the 1980 election results extremely difficult, as it was in 1948, 1960, 1968, and 1976.

Certainly the idea that cognitive components help determine attitudes and attitude change has considerable implications for propagandists or manipulators of attitudes. Rosenberg points out that the problem is to maintain affective-cognitive inconsistency within tolerable, as opposed to intolerable, limits. A collector of funds for the Red Cross has to be able to demonstrate that the positive aspects of the cause (e.g., aid to families in disasters) outweigh the negative aspects (e.g., high overhead costs). The theory is similar to the cognitive dissonance approach (discussed below), in that attitudes are seen as means of reducing inconsistency in beliefs, but Rosenberg relates attitude change directly to the amount of motivation and reward rather than the reverse, as in cognitive dissonance theory.

Process Theory of Attitude Formation and Change

Herbert C. Kelman's (1961) *three-process theory,* which utilizes public conformity and private acceptance as criteria of attitude acquisition, is based on studies of social influence in small-group interaction and research on persuasive communication and opinion change. Kelman identifies the processes underlying attitude formation and change as compliance, identification, and internalization. In *compliance,* the individual passively accepts an attitude from another person or group in anticipation of a favorable reaction from authorities or peers. In *identification,* the individual identifies with the role of another person in order to enhance the self-image. The degree of relationship may vary; during the Korean War, brainwashed prisoners accepted their captors' negative evaluations of themselves, for example, and children normally accept their parents' attitudes as part of the socialization process. The self-concept can also be expanded through identification with others, which differs from compliance because the other persons' attitudes are believed or intellectually accepted. In *internalization,* the individual absorbs an attitude as part of his or her own value system, and it becomes a part of the personality structure, not merely a convenience in interpersonal relationships.

The significance of these three processes varies with the individual person and the situation. The distinction between the processes is arbitrary, and their relative importance may depend on the cognitive style of the person. Compliance is more important for those who have few convictions of their own and who regard attitudes as serving utilitarian purposes, for example. An ingenious experiment illustrating the three process-theory of attitude change is reported in Kelman (1958). On the eve of the 1954 Supreme Court decision regarding integration, he analyzed the process of attitude change among a sample of college blacks after different communicators (who varied in attractiveness, perceived power, and credibility) argued for the preservation of Negro colleges, even though educational facilities were about to be integrated. Compliance, identification, and internalization were all important but not to the same degree for all subjects.

THEORIES OF COGNITIVE CONSISTENCY AND DISSONANCE

The theory of congruity in attitude formation and change, one of the major recent developments in social psychology, is derived largely from the concept of cognitive dissonance, which is described later in this section. The goal of cognitive consistency, or coherence in beliefs and attitudes, is complicated by compromises in real life such as the cognitive schizophrenia in political attitudes described in Box 9-2.

From early childhood we are taught to pursue the objective of consistent attitudes, behaviors, and opinions. Our actions must make sense to us, and they must not appear irrational or erratic to others. As pointed out in Chapter 6, we expect our friends not to do things we find unpleasant, and we are suspicious if a person we dislike does something nice for us. We suspect that a person who does not believe in God but nevertheless goes to church must have some reason for doing so, such as appearing reputable in the community, meeting people, or enjoying the music.

All theories of attitudes (particularly Rosenberg's, described above) involve the problem of consistency in some way. Most studies begin with the assumption that people's behavior, opinions, and beliefs represent highly complex cognitions. Moreover, people have a certain perception of their behavior which includes how they think it appears to others, and they may be aware of the motivation underlying their actions. People's behaviors and attitudes must be perceived by both themselves and others as being reasonably consistent. Therefore, they usually will not cause physical discomfort to friends, except perhaps as part of a game, and they expect the same treatment in return (Swingle, 1966). They do not lie unless they are being well paid or expect favorable returns from being

Box 9–2
COGNITIVE SCHIZOPHRENIA

For the U.S. citizen, there is a great deal of confusion as to what constitutes liberalism or conservatism. The wide divergence of ideologies within the two major political parties is one reason. Most politicians, Democrats and Republicans alike, assume an accommodative viewpoint or some position on a sliding scale between the left (liberalism) and the right (conservatism). As president, Jimmy Carter alternated between fiscal conservatism and a commitment to social welfare, and Ronald Reagan was elected on a conservative platform laced with New Deal liberalism to broaden the base of the Republican Party.

In a 1967 poll by L. A. Free and Hadley Cantril, a large-scale sample of Americans expressed support for what might be called "operational liberalism" by favoring such social issues as Medicare, federal low-rent housing, urban renewal, and programs to reduce unemployment.* When the respondents were asked about the social and economic principles they favored, or their ideology, the responses were very different, however. The two profiles can be compared as follows:

	Operational Scale	Ideological Scale
Completely or predominantly liberal	65%	16%
Middle of the road	21%	34%
Completely or predominantly conservative	14%	50%

Thus the average American can be described as neither liberal nor conservative. Ideologically a person may honor the traditional individualistic values espoused by conservatives, but operationally the same person does not want to give up social programs devised by liberals. Daryl Bem calls this inconsistency *cognitive schizophrenia.*† He recognizes, however, that one explanation of these ambivalent findings is the tendency for respondents to say yes to whatever a pollster suggests or to give what they consider to be socially acceptable answers. Bem observes that "Many of the individuals in the Free-Cantril study who ended up being classified as both ideological conservatives and operational liberals were simply pleasant people who tended to agree with anything the nice man said that seemed reasonable" (p. 38).

*L. A. Free and Hadley Cantril, *The Political Beliefs of Americans* (New Brunswick, N.J.: Rutgers University Press, 1967).

†D. S. Bem, *Beliefs, Attitudes, and Human Affairs* (Belmont, Calif.: Brooks/Cole Publishing Co., 1970), pp. 35–38.

dishonest, with the exception of "harmless" white lies in social situations (see Box 8–3 in Chapter 8). They are careful not to express inconsistent beliefs publicly.

Cognitive consistency and dissonance grow out of the person's perception of the world, as described in Chapter 6. Although there are subtle differences among the various cognitive consistency theories, they are all based on the assumption that any two related cognitions in a person's awareness at a particular time must be consistent. Several of them are *drive theories,* which suggest that a person who is made aware of an inconsistency experiences discomfort which is not reduced until consistency is restored. Others are *homeostatic theories,* which maintain that once a person is made aware of a relationship between cognitive elements, the elements are automatically brought into a state of balance.

You know why you are bombarded with propaganda and advertising—it is intended to change your attitudes and beliefs. The interesting question is why such techniques have the effect they do. A number of the processes which give rise to changes in the structure of attitudes are discussed in this section, which considers two theories of cognitive consistency—Fritz Heider's balance theory and the congruity principle of Charles Osgood and Percy Tannenbaum—as well as Leon Festinger's cognitive dissonance theory.

Balance Theory

In Heider's balance theory (1958), attitudes represent types of equilibria in which positive and negative alternate. Individuals perceive an object in different ways—as positive, neutral, or negative—and an increase or decrease in a person's attraction to the object may be influenced by another person's perception of it. According to Heider, attitude change is in the direction of resolving the inconsistency in the cognitive organization of the positive and negative elements. Much of our attitude toward a given object depends on how we feel toward the person connected with it; for example, we often take a positive interest in activities favored by people we strongly like. If either the person or object is unappealing, the negative element predominates. Cognitive balance occurs when the relationships among the perceiver, the other person, and the object associated with the other person are all positive, or when two of the three are negative.

Although there is some difficulty in quantifying Heider's concepts about the structure of attitudes, he made a notable contribution in analyzing their dynamic interrelationships (Fishbein & Ajzen, 1975). In his view, attitudes are formed and changed by perception of the relationship of dissonant and consonant elements. Paradoxically, more indecision can be experienced with moderate dissonance; with major conflict or dissonance there may be a dramatic change in position often accompanied by some degree of selective forgetting.

The Congruity Principle

Osgood and Tannenbaum's congruity principle (1955) suggests that each person's positive, negative, and neutral perceptions of an object are organized to determine the predominant *valence,* or direction, of the person's attitude toward the object. People are constantly making judgments about other people, items,

Effective advertisements attempt to provide congruity between the target audience's perceptions and their attitudes toward the product. The macho image, the lure of the wide open spaces, and the size of the billboard are all designed to assure a favorable attitude toward the cigarettes. *Source:* © Theodore Anderson, 1981.

and situations, and these judgments represent differing degrees of congruity. Positive and negative valences are found even in simple classificatory statements such as "Butter and eggs contain cholesterol"; "The son of the president smokes pot"; and "The mayor was once a used-car salesman." At a somewhat more complex level are conceptual statements such as "Socialists favor welfare projects." The individual arranges his or her attitudes, either implicitly or explicitly, into a predominantly negative or positive grouping which produces an attitude of acceptance, rejection, or neutrality toward an object, with conflict minimal or nonexistent. Changes in this evaluation, according to Brown (1965), are always in the direction of increased congruity with the existing frame of reference. Therefore, measurement of the degree and direction of feeling makes it possible to predict the direction and amount of change in attitudes. Although other variables also affect attitude change, shifts in the positive or negative polarization of given attitudes are a principal factor which is within the limits of the cognitive structure.

In its attempts to work out a quantitative approach to attitudes, congruity theory stesses the discontinuity between the content and the source of attitudes. The congruity model, as defined by Osgood and Tannenbaum (1955), provides for placing the attitudes of individuals on a scale with dimensions which arbitrarily run from $+3$ to -3, in order to obtain an idea of the person's *cognitive system*. In Figure 9–2, for example, the placement of several cognitive elements as they might be related in one person's mind is indicated on the scale. This person feels strongly and positively (strong, positive valence) about free speech, likes dry-roasted peanuts a lot, doesn't care one way or the other about vodka, and intensely dislikes (strong negative valence) the notion of an armed forces draft. As long as there are no interrelationships between the elements, every attitude stays as it is. There is nothing disharmonious about liking John Smith less than dry-roasted peanuts, for example, if there is no relation between the concepts.

Association can lead to problems in cognitive balance, an effect often observed in politics (see Box 9–3). Interrelationships between attitudes, either negative or positive, may be *associative bonds,* as when a person says something nice about another person, or *dissociative bonds,* which express dislike or criticism. A cognitive system is said to be in equilibrium when the bonds between elements have produced *cognitive reorganization.* In congruity theory, it is the incongruities or imbalances that are responsible for attitude change. If the head of a strongly disliked nation denounces the head of a strongly favored nation, a person's attitudes toward them probably will not change because in that person's cognitive system the former has a high negative valence of -3 and the latter's valence is $+3$. Moreover, positive statements (associative bonds) between two equally negative or equally positive elements result in no cognitive incongruity. The formal rule is that an associative bond between two equally polarized elements or a dissociative bond between two mirror-image elements (with equal but opposite signs, as in the Soviet-American attitudes described in Box 6–4 in Chapter 6) does not present the problem of cognitive incongruity, and therefore no attitude change occurs.

Various kinds of movement or change are possible in the congruity model. For instance, cognitive elements move in inverse proportion to their valences. Thus, the higher the valence or prestige of one object relative to another, the greater the movement of the lower-status object, as implied in Box 9–3. If the

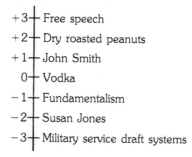

Figure 9–2. Example of a Cognitive System in the Congruity Model

president of the United States said something very favorable about Joe Nobody, a candidate for county sheriff, we would expect a greater change in our attitude toward Joe than in our attitude toward the president. The direction of the assertion is also important. We would expect our attitude toward Joe to change more if the president spoke highly of him than if he spoke highly of the president.

In most instances the cognitive elements in an attitude are fairly complex. A person may have varying negative valences for some of the attributes of President Jimmy Carter, such as peanut growers, southern accents, and evangelism, but the same person could have varying positive valences for the necessity of human rights, fiscal responsibility, and patient negotiation in international affairs. If these positive valences outweigh the negative ones, a movement from a negative to positive attitude could result. Unfortunately for Carter's second-term aspirations, this was not the case prior to the 1980 elections, but the final appraisal of Carter's presidency is still to come.

Cognitive Dissonance

More than the balance and congruity theories, Leon Festinger's *The Theory of Cognitive Dissonance* (1957) stresses behavior as much as belief or attitudes. Avoiding conflict among attitudes and maintaining consistency between inner

---

Box 9–3
COATTAIL RIDING

The coattail effect in politics refers to the desire of local candidates to be identified with prominent state or national leaders of the same party. If the leaders also are candidates—for higher office—their success at the polls can often sweep others on the ticket into office. This maneuver recognizes that a general feeling of liking for something is enhanced if it is associated with other people or things that are liked. What's more, local candidates who are perceived as being linked to an experienced official might have some ability or influence in government attributed to them by the public.

It is interesting to watch the way pictures of this interaction are taken at election campaign functions. The major nominee stands in place, with the right arm outstretched ready to shake hands and the left arm poised to encircle the other person's shoulders, to signify a warm greeting. The less well-known candidates stand in line and on cue hop into position. They grasp the nominee's hand, smile, and look at the camera. After a few shots are taken they get out of the way and the next candidate gets a turn. Edward Kennedy conveyed a reserved acceptance of Jimmy Carter as the Democractic presidential nominee in 1980 by *not* shaking hands with him in front of the television cameras on the convention platform.

Cognitive dissonance is reflected in public reaction to situations such as the refugee problem, in which Americans' humanitarian impulses to make room for displaced persons was countered by anxiety about accepting alien peoples into a nation whose resources were becoming limited. *Source:* United Nations/J. Robaton.

convictions and overt behavior can produce considerable strain in a person's cognitive systems. Should you buy a sports car you can't afford? Can you "fudge" on your income tax return without jeopardizing your value system? Should you join a sorority if you believe in social equality?

Cognitive dissonance has been described as "psychological tension having motivational characteristics" which occurs when a person has "two cognitions which are somehow discrepant with each other" (Brehm & Cohen, 1962). Festinger, the originator of the theory, stated these basic hypotheses about the existence of dissonance in a person's cognitive systems:

1. Because dissonance is psychologically uncomfortable, it motivates the person to try to reduce it and achieve consonance.
2. The person will actively avoid situations and information that are likely to increase dissonance.
3. Dissonance gives rise to pressures to eliminate it, the magnitude of the dissonance determining the strength of these pressures.

Dissonance has been created for habitual smokers, for example, by information regarding the correlation between tobacco and lung cancer. If they continue to smoke, they must interpret the data in a particular way. In a study by Feather (1963), smokers reduced their dissonance by finding good reasons for continuing their behavior, although they were interested in all relevant information, both positive and negative, about it. Relevant information is interpreted in accordance with the person's cognitions in order to minimize dissonance; thus, according to Feather, a "member of the Ku Klux Klan should be very sensitive to any information about Negroes, whether it be complimentary or hostile, but his evaluation of this information will tend to be consistent with his prejudice. In short, dissonant states seem to have more obvious effects on evaluation than on sensitivity" (p. 163).

Integrating cognitions with reality and achieving consistency between verbalized attitudes and overt behaviors is a long-standing problem in the study of attitudes, as noted in Chapter 8. The theory of cognitive dissonance offers another approach to this problem which focuses on processing information and weighing alternatives in the decision-making process, and the conflicts encountered in these efforts (Festinger, 1964). The degree to which decisions are made impulsively or painstakingly has been subjected to experimentation, as have the concepts of postdecision regret (the uneasy, uncertain feeling you have after committing yourself to a course of action) and, especially, decision reversal. An unsolved question concerns the stability and persistence of decisions.

The major means of reducing internal dissonance is some type of rationalization, or what often turns out to be insufficient justification. We blame the environment or external causes rather than ourselves, as noted in Chapter 6. For example, you know too much alcohol will make you drunk, but you blame a friend or the Christmas party when you overindulge.

Justification often involves more complex explanations, however, as in an experiment on forced compliance, or public compliance without private acceptance, by Festinger and Carlsmith (1959). They asked undergraduate students to perform repetitious, boring tasks in a laboratory setting. Then some of the subjects were paid $1 to act as assistants to the experimenter and tell other waiting students that the boring assignment was interesting and enjoyable; others were paid $20 to do the same. In an interview following the experiment, the lower-paid subjects claimed they really had enjoyed the tasks they performed before being hired. For the higher-paid assistants the cognitive rearrangement was different: They said they perceived the tasks as monotonous, but they could not resist such a large sum; they felt it gave them ample justification for misinforming others. In other words, more tension or dissonance occurred for the $1 assistants than for the $20 ones; the more narrowly opposed the two pressures, the greater is the dissonance. The lower-paid subjects had to change their cognitive systems, and the more highly paid subjects simply found a plausible argument for themselves.

The use of a control group in this study suggests that the findings were valid, although forced-compliance experiments have not generally allowed for the subjects who refuse to cooperate (Chapanis & Chapanis, 1964). In a later study, M. J. Rosenberg (1965), in contrast to Festinger and Carlsmith, found a positive relation between the amount of money given and the change in attitude toward the viewpoint advocated.

Most people can tolerate some inconsistent attitudes without feeling dissonance, but at some point the *comfort threshold,* when resolution is necessary, appears. An attempt by Gerard, Conolley, and Wilhelmy (1974) to probe this threshold suggested that either insufficient or excessive justification may force cognitive change, as illustrated in Figure 9–3. They call the point where resultant justification equals the justification for a change decision minus the justification against it the *action threshold.* When the justification for cognitive change becomes sufficiently strong that little or no conflict is perceived, the *sweetness threshold* is entered. Both intrinsic and extrinsic factors influence the justification process; for instance, you might make a speech for a cause because you perceive it as right, but if you are paid for the speech your commitment would be enhanced. The strength of the justification or its perceived importance thus produces differing curves of acceptance. The gap between the solid and broken lines in Figure 9–3 reflects the degree of strength in the justification and the cognitive change.

Criticism and Extension of the Theory

For over a decade after the publication of Festinger's *A Theory of Cognitive Dissonance* in 1957, the study of cognition and attitude was dominated by the analysis and testing of this theory. One volume alone (Abelson et al., 1968) included some 80 studies on the subject and listed over 800 references. Yet the first article (Aronson, 1968) states that the theory had still not been proven; all the theory had done was generate research.

In Aronson's view, the problem is that individuals differ greatly in their toleration of dissonance. Despite the warning on cigarette packages that tobacco is injurious to health, millions of smokers still rationalize their habit with a variety of

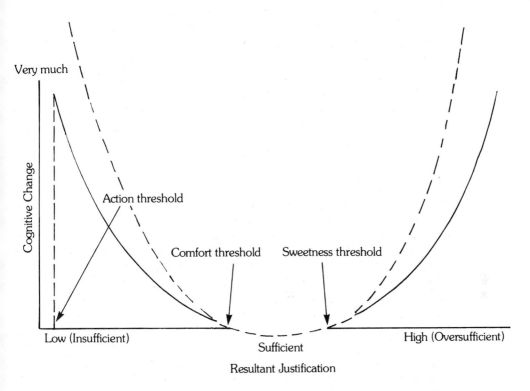

Figure 9–3. Hypothetical Relationship between Resultant Justification and Cognitive Change

Source: H. B. Gerard, E. S. Conolley, and R. A. Wilhelmy, "Compliance, Justification and Cognitive Change," in L. Berkowitz (Ed.), *Advances in Experimental Social Psychology,* Vol. 7 (New York: Academic Press, 1974), p. 231.

explanations ("I would rather live a few months less and enjoy the relaxation of a cigarette"; "My grandfather was still smoking at age 85"; or "Statistics never prove anything"). The fact is that most people can accommodate to internal conflict. They continue to make purchases they cannot afford and remain dedicated to public figures whose ideologies or lifestyles are alien to their own. People also differ in their preference for a mode of dissonance reduction, and what may be dissonant for one person may be consonant for another. The political sphere offers innumerable examples, as Box 9–4 shows.

Other hypotheses have emerged in the debate over the causes and significance of cognitive dissonance. In his theory of *self-perception,* Bem (1967) asserts that dissonance is the result of the individual's inferences about the causes of his or her own actions. Thus Bem maintains that an attitude is formed after the relevant behavior occurs; the attitude does not initiate the behavior. We shape our

Box 9–4
PRAISING CAESAR—OR BURYING HIM

Coping with a fallen hero presents a problem of dissonance to followers. When Edward Kennedy drove off a bridge at Chappaquiddick Island on a July night in 1969 and Mary Jo Kopechne drowned, his followers had to decide whether to accept his justification that because of shock and exhaustion he could not think rationally. The Senator did not seek help that might have saved her life, though he said he tried to rescue her after he had escaped from the submerged car, nor did he report the event to the authorities until almost 11 hours later. Eventually, Kennedy was tried for leaving the scene of an accident, pleaded guilty, and received a two-month suspended sentence.

When a sample of 102 University of Florida students and faculty was asked how their attitudes toward Kennedy had been affected by the incident, 84 said they had been favorable to Kennedy before the incident, and about half, or 49, remained loyal to him after the event and chose various means of resolving their dissonance.* A number felt that once he had made an effort to save the girl's life, even an unsuccessful one, it was appropriate for him to think of his political future. In regard to his sentence, they were convinced that a private citizen would have been similarly treated. The fact that Kennedy and his family had experienced a number of tragedies was another reason they did not blame him for this one. The study emphasizes the degree to which people will involve a major part of their value systems in resolving dissonance.

A no less massive assault on cognition was experienced by followers of former President Richard Nixon in their attempts to justify his involvement in the Watergate scandal. From the first revelation in April 1973 until his resignation in August 1974, when conclusive evidence as to his direct participation became known, his loyal supporters were continually shifting their attitudes. When the Judiciary Committee accepted the articles of impeachment, the Nixon loyalists still considered the accusation a partisan affair, even though 7 Republicans joined 21 Democrats in voting for impeachment on at least one count. Even after Nixon's resignation, his hard-core defenders maintained a number of rationalizations: the press was the culprit in bringing to light an affair that should not have been disclosed; Nixon's aides were incompetent; the magnitude and strain of the presidential office were too great. Some supporters questioned his wisdom or ethics but adhered to the notion that the end (national security, the need for a strong executive office) justified the means—not unlike the belief that Edward Kennedy was entitled to special treatment.

---

*Irwin Silverman, "On the Resolution and Tolerance of Cognitive Dissonance in a Natural-Occurring Event: Attitudes and Beliefs Following the Senator Edward M. Kennedy Incident," *Journal of Personality and Social Psychology,* 1971, *17,* 171-178.

view of the self through new beliefs about it which follow our actions, and we change our attitudes about the outside world accordingly.

Impression management is another approach to cognitive consistency (Tedeschi, Schlenker, & Bonoma, 1971). In this view, people arrange to give an image of consistency when confronted with incongruous attitudes because they are concerned about how others will view their inconsistency. Whether their attitudes and behaviors will give favorable or unfavorable impressions of them to others is important, because others' perceptions will largely determine the rewards and punishments they receive. They weigh the costs and benefits of leaving an inconsistent impression, and compare it to the costs and benefits of engaging in fencework to mend this image.

Another hypothesis related to the problem of consistency is *reactance theory* (Brehm, 1972). *Reactance* describes the tendency of people to do the opposite of what they are supposed to do and points to the attractiveness of alternatives that are not open to them, or which at least have apparent barriers or conflicts. If you are told that you must attend church, read a certain book, or believe a certain idea, you may well feel urged to follow a different course of action. Psychologically, the theory is concerned with the perception of freedom (see Chapter 6); if we sense a threat to our freedom from coercion by others, we attempt to counter it. In attitude formation and change, this means we may resist directives, especially if there is a negative or dissociative reaction toward the source.

DETERMINANTS OF ATTITUDE CHANGE

In the search for cognitive consistency or equilibrium, attitude structure faces a constant challenge from attitude change, as noted at the beginning of this chapter. Our society is involved in a continual, always-escalating process of change (see Chapter 17), and people's attitudes must change as rapidly if they are to continue to define their relation to an inconstant world. This section is concerned with the factors that operate to maintain stability or encourage mobility in attitude structures and the processes by which attitudes can be restructured.

In many respects, the elements determining attitude change are the same as those comprising the frame of reference in which the individual's attitudes are formed, which was described in Chapter 8. The social background topic in this chapter reflects the socioeconomic setting topic in Chapter 3; similarly, intergroup relations are concerned with reference groups, and personality structure and personality factors deal with essentially the same variables. In fact, the distinction between attitude formation and attitude change is arbitrary. An analysis of research on attitude change reveals that some of these studies actually deal with attitude formation, since they have tapped cognitive areas in which the subjects had no defined attitudes (Whittaker, 1965).

Social Background

Numerous kinds of social backgrounds (or subcultures, as the term is used in Chapter 3) affect the relative rigidity or fluidity of a person's attitudes: social class, the family, the school, and peers, which were discussed in Chapter 3, as well as demographic variables such as age, education, occupation, and geography.

An early example of the considerable research that has centered on this aspect of attitudes is a study by Newcomb and Svehla (1937) which showed high correlation coefficients between children's and parents' attitudes on war (.44), communism (.56), and religion (.63). The most decisive influence on a young child's attitudes is the parents' orientation. During the university years, however, students' attitudes shift away from the usually more conservative position of their parents, as noted in the study by Newcomb et al. (1967) of attitudes of Bennington College students described in Chapter 8. Newcomb (1957) also noted that these effects were significantly more evident for those who remained students for three or four years; those who left earlier tended to revert to their less liberal precollege attitudes. Hovland et al. (1959) found that in the presentation of orientation films such as *The Battle of Britain* and *Prelude to War* to service personnel during World War II, the training effectiveness was in part a function of the viewer's educational level. This could be a matter of intelligence; that is, those with lower IQs were less capable of understanding the lessons presented.

It is sometimes difficult to disentangle the background factors in the expression of given attitudes. Public reaction to two areas of concern in Buffalo, New York, in 1970–71—student protest at the State University of New York and the uprising at the Attica prison—was studied by Cryns (1975). The research procedure was to analyze the content of letters to the local press, along with the findings of attitude scales (the Wrightsman Philosophy of Human Nature Scale and the Srole Anomie Scale, among others) administered to the letter writers. Although there was no significant difference for sex or the kind of protest behavior addressed, writers who were critical about campus and prison disturbances tended to have a more pessimistic and simplistic view of human behavior. The two groups did differ in their evaluations of the past, present, and future for society, but authoritarianism and a tendency toward anomie did not differ significantly between them.

Intergroup Relations

The changing of attitudes in many areas of intergroup relations depends on the experience of personal contact, as well as on acquiring and evaluating information. People modify their neutral or negative attitudes toward a group in a positive direction when they have associated with members of that group over a period of time. Demonstrations of this type of change have been found in studies of the armed forces, work groups in industry, housing projects, education, and religion. It cannot be assumed, however, that familiarity with other ethnic groups will *necessarily* ensure unprejudiced attitudes toward them.

A classic study (Brophy, 1946) revealed a basic change in antiblack feeling among a study sample of merchant marines. One third of those who had never served (shipped) with blacks were rated as unprejudiced. The unprejudiced rating increased to 46 percent for those who had shipped once with blacks and to 62 and 82 percent after the second and third shippings, respectively.

In a study of New Haven suburbs undergoing racial change (Hamilton & Bishop, 1976), a symbolic racism scale (statements suggesting the possible inferiority of blacks) couched in a more general questionnaire was administered periodically over a one-year period to the residents of recently integrated neighborhoods and to a control sample in neighborhoods that had retained all-white residents. There was a progressive decline in racist scores for the integrated neighborhoods, as well as reports of increased interaction with black neighbors.

Research on the improvement of interracial attitudes has not been entirely consistent; increased contacts make a higher tolerance score likely, but they do not guarantee that attitude change will be permanent. Undoubtedly, much of the success of education and shared-experience projects in this area depends on the frame of reference of the individual. Selective perception is a critical part of this frame of reference, because we "see" in a social situation the data that are in harmony with our own attitude structures.

Furthermore, attitudes reflect the ego or self-involvement of the individual, as noted below. A person who has definite religious and political convictions and a long history of emotional conditioning is not likely to change her or his attitudes easily. Many attitudes involve cherished economic and prestige goals. A graduate who wants to become a bank manager might continue to hold liberal or even radical views acquired from a nonconformist teacher, but the prevalence of more orthodox attitudes among colleagues would probably bring the aspirant's attitudes into line. Attitude change is especially difficult when the new attitude conflicts with the individual's more deep-seated motives.

Personality Structure

The personality structure is the final determinant of the attitude-change potential of each individual. There are marked individual differences in receptivity to new attitudes and values. In an extensive discussion of the relation of personality to persuasibility (see the following section), Hovland and Janis (1959) summarized the following tentative findings about the effects of various personality factors on openness to change.

1. *Self-esteem.*   Feelings of social inferiority and self-inadequacy, at least in male subjects, were found to be related to high persuasibility. A. R. Cohen's (1964) research suggests that persons of low self-esteem are characterized by "expressive defenses," which sensitize them to environmental influences, whereas high-self-esteem subjects are apt to reject or ignore new data or challenging information arising from their environment. This relationship between high self-esteem and nonpersuasibility could imply that social change, which is based on attitude change, whether desirable or undesirable, is less likely to be accepted by psychologically secure individuals, a question which will be considered again in Chapter 17.

2. *Hostility and aggressiveness.*   At various age levels and for both "normal" and emotionally disturbed persons, hostility, aggressiveness, and

rebelliousness were found to correlate with low persuasibility, but "neurotic defensiveness" was not.

3. *Perceptual dependence.*   Subjects who depended on internal cues rather than the surrounding physical environment (as measured by a tilting room–tilting chair test) were less persuasible. Also, subjects whose attitudes were changed by a persuasive message were found to be relatively more sensitive to interferences in their total stimulus field.

4. *Authoritarianism.*   There was no clear-cut relationship between total authoritarianism scales and persuasibility. Yet certain subscores of the authoritarianism scale, such as submissiveness, were related positively to persuasibility.

5. *Inner- and other-directedness.*   Students who chose an other-directed rather than an inner-directed solution for personal dilemmas on a questionnaire were found to be more persuasible. Conformity needs, therefore, suggest receptivity to attitude change. In this connection, it has been hypothesized that one factor predisposing American prisoners of war to brainwashing during and following the Korean war was a lack of inner-directedness and commitment (Schein, 1961). Low self-identity made it easier for these men to accept ideas from the outside and also facilitated their desire to comply with the pressures from their peers (cellmates who were indoctrinated) and authority figures (the camp commanders).

6. *Social isolation.*   The degree of separation from peers was found to be related to persuasibility among classroom children. The need to find social acceptance favored persuasibility; however, the relationship was statistically significant only for the boys. Whether peer-group pressure on boys is higher than on girls is not clear.

7. *Richness of fantasy.* It was hypothesized that individuals who showed more extensive daydreaming, imagination, and fantasy would be more sensitive to the anticipation of rewards and punishments conveyed by a persuasive communication. Again, the relationship proved tenable for male but not for female subjects.

8. *Intelligence.*   There were no significant differences for various general intelligence levels and persuasibility; but there were differences for kinds of intelligence and the medium and content of the persuasive message.

In addition the degree of persuasibility was found to be related to sex-role differences only in regard to given personality traits, such as social isolation and fantasy. A few studies have shown women to be more persuasible than men, presumably because of the traditional emphasis on acquiescence in the socialization of girls.

The kind of ego involvement in a group discussion also can affect the potential of the discussion to bring about attitude change. Cialdini et al. (1973) conducted an experiment in which two topics were argued—the adoption of euthanasia and the shortening of medical training. Subjects who engaged in a face-to-face discussion were more likely to accept a moderate position than those who merely listened to the arguments. Apparently, the experience of having to make a public statement moved the speaker toward a middle position. The experimenters concluded that people feel a loss of self-esteem if they are unable to moderate their stand, and when they anticipate discussion, evaluation, and an audience, their attitudes are more subject to the influence of the reality principle.

Role-Playing and Attitude Change

The use of role-playing as an educational or therapeutic means of bringing about attitude change is based on the temperamental traits (emotions and feelings) component of personality (as shown in Figure 4–1 in Chapter 4), as well as the affective component of attitudes. The technique encourages *empathy,* or identification with another person's feelings, by having subjects assume the roles of others in various types of social interaction. For instance, recruits to the Los Angeles Police Department have been assigned such roles as spending the night in jail or being an indigent in the ghetto or a transient in a city park. In a widely studied schoolroom experiment with a third-grade class (Peters, 1971), children were placed in brown-eyed and blue-eyed groups for the purpose of exploring the experience of being a victim of discrimination, as each of the two groups took turns at playing the role of inferior.

In a study by Janis and Mann (1965) of inveterate smokers, members of the experimental group modified their smoking habits after playing the role of cancer patients. "Passively exposed controls," who listened to tapes of "doctor-patient" conversations (with the subject as the patient and the experimenter as the doctor) showed a decline in smoking, but the "marginal controls" were only moderately affected. A follow-up study (Mann & Janis, 1968) confirmed the finding that emotional role-playing produces a strong conversion effect:

> . . . eighteen months after the experimental sessions the effectiveness of the emotional role-playing procedure, as compared with the passive exposure to the same information about lung cancer could still be observed. . . . The large majority of smokers who were influenced by the [U.S. Surgeon General's] Report evidently quickly reverted to their normal smoking habits. In contrast, the emotional role-players and the passively exposed controls showed a relatively sustained decrease following exposure to the Surgeon General's Report. (p. 341)

Emotional involvement seems to be highly effective in some kinds of attitude change. In a University of Illinois study (Clare & Kefferey, 1972), three groups were set up: (1) role-players who spent an hour in a wheelchair as partially paralyzed patients, (2) vicarious role-players who walked behind the patients at a distance of 20 feet, and (3) a control group of students who went about the campus discussing the incident. On affective rating scales and other tests, an increase in empathy and in positive attitudes toward disabled people was most conspicuous for the "patients," and least, although still significant, for the controls.

FACTORS IN PERSUASIBILITY

A person's persuasibility, or openness to persuasion by others, is one of the principal influences on attitude change, as the preceding topic on personality structure indicated. The study of persuasibility has centered on problems related to communication of the persuasive message: the credibility of the source and content, the order of presentation, and the nature of the message in terms of impartiality, cognitive consistency, and emotional appeal. This emphasis on the message is indicative of the critical role communication plays in social psychology—the topic of the following chapter.

Source, Content, and Credibility

The success of persuasive efforts often depends on the approach of an audience to the communicator and the message. Using arguments about student-instructor relationships and semester length Chaiken (1980) found that the specific structuring of the experiment could predispose subjects to focus either on the attractiveness of the communicator (the *source* approach) or on the nature and method of argumentation used in the message (*content* approach). Opinion change was more durable when the emphasis was on the message. In a related experiment, Wood and Eagly (1981) found that when subjects approached the message (for instance, restrictions on the sale of pornography) as factual data rather than focusing on the communicator's credentials they tended to judge the communicator as unbiased, a situation favoring opinion change toward the message. When the communicator was immediately perceived as unbiased, however, there was poorer comprehension of message content, which in turn lessened opinion change. As Figure 9–4 shows, concentration on the message makes for persuasiveness, at least among college students, who are so frequently used for research in attitude change.

Acceptance of any communication depends both on the reputation or status of the communicator and the content of the message. The recipient may suspect that the source is not properly accredited or that the communicator's motivation reduces the validity of the message (see Box 9–5).

A number of experiments have investigated the trustworthiness of the source. For instance, Kelman and Hovland (1953) had high-school students listen to a recording in which the speaker pleaded for more understanding and leniency in the treatment of juvenile law offenders. The speaker was identified for three groups of subjects as (1) a judge in a juvenile court (positive version); (2) a member of the studio audience, with no further information (neutral version); and (3) a member of the studio audience who was a former delinquent (negative version). Arguments by the judge (the positive identification) were accepted most readily by the audience. The negative approach of the former "juvenile delinquent" was least acceptable. Although the amount of retention was not significantly different for the three approaches, the study demonstrated the importance of credibility.

The identification of the communicator was also found to be an important factor in a study where arguments for raising the legal age at which young people could be licensed to drive a car were presented to two high school groups by a speaker (Allyn & Festinger, 1961). One group was asked to judge the speaker's personality, and the attention of the other group was directed to the nature of the

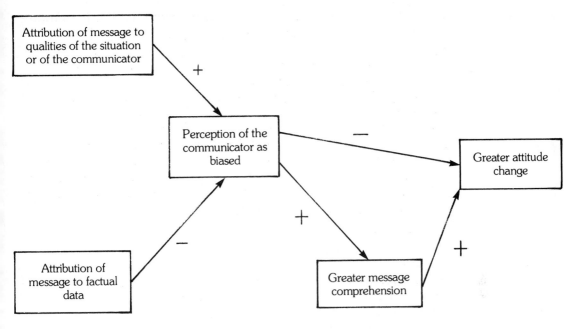

Figure 9–4. Relationships of the communicator, recipient, message, and attitude change
Source: Adapted from Wendy Wood and Alice H. Eagly, "Stages in the Analysis of Persuasive Messages: The Role of Causal Attributions and Message Comprehension," *Journal of Personality and Social Psychology,* 1981, 40, 246-259.

appeal. Approximately 80 percent of subjects who were in the personality-oriented group changed their opinions significantly, compared to 60 percent in the opinion-oriented group. However, neither group abandoned its basic opposition to the speaker's argument.

External factors in the communicator, such as dress, physical attractiveness, or looking a person straight in the eye and other demonstrations of personal style, can add to the effectiveness of an appeal (see Box 9–6). Credibility is also enhanced by the tempo of a speaker; in both laboratory and field settings a rapidly spoken message was found to be more persuasive than one spoken slowly (Miller et al., 1976). This suggests that an audience judges competence by whatever cues are available; that is, the perception is that the faster the persuader speaks, the more he or she must know.

Research also suggests that a communicator is more successful when the recipients of a message can perceive some similarity between themselves and the communicator. In an experiment by Berscheid (1966), change was most likely to occur when the advocate was recognized as having characteristics that were relevant to the message, which concerned decisions about international affairs

Box 9–5
PACKAGING INFORMATION

The categories of truth and falsehood may be irrelevant to an evaluation of a message, especially as it is treated in the communications media. Christopher Lasch notes that "Truth gives way to credibility, facts to statements that sound authoritative without conveying any authoritative information."* Lasch gives two examples:

> Statements to the effect that a given product is preferred by leading authorities without saying what it is preferred to, statements that claim a product's superiority to unspecified competitors, statements that imply that a given characteristic belongs uniquely to the product in question when in fact it belongs to its rivals as well, all serve to submerge the distinction between truth and falsehood in a blur of plausibility. Such statements are "true" while at the same time they are radically misleading.

> The Nixon administration has provided us with a celebrated instance of the political use of this technique, in the form of Ron Ziegler's admission that his previous statements on Watergate were "inoperative." Many commentators assumed that Ziegler was groping for a euphemistic way of saying that he had lied. What he was actually saying, however, was not that events had shown his earlier statements to be false but simply that they were no longer believable. Not their falsity but the fact that nobody any longer believed these statements rendered them "inoperative." The question of whether they were true or not was beside the point.

---

*Christopher Lasch, "Paranoid Presidency," _The Center Magazine,_ Vol. 7 (March 1974), p. 27.

and financial aid for students. Conversely, when there were dissimilarities between the source and the recipient, change of opinion was minimal. Consequently, a movie star or a leading political figure might be less effective as an advocate for an informed, thinking person than a friend or colleague would be.

Both the communicator and the content of the message are important as determinants of attitude change. Kelman and Eagly (1965) found a difference in results for the effects of content orientation (what the message said) and source or communicator orientation (who delivered the message). When both are high, attitude change is at its maximum. Conflict occurs when the content is acceptable but the communicator is not, and transfer occurs from the communicator to the message. The subject must be able to find a balance between these two orientations and to distinguish between source and content.

Box 9–6
GRASSHOPPERS AS A GOURMET ITEM

If you were presented with a plate of fried grasshoppers and asked to eat at least one of them, what would your reaction be? It might depend on the way the request is made.

Philip Zimbardo and his staff conducted an experiment in which college students and army reservists were ostensibly asked to evaluate the palatability of survival foods.* They were asked to eat at least one of the five fried grasshoppers on a plate placed before them and then report on how highly they would endorse eating grasshoppers as a survival food. The communicator in the experiment appeared to be friendly, mature, and tolerant for half the subjects, and for the others he assumed an unfriendly, cold, and hostile manner. Whether the communicator was friendly or unfriendly, only about half of the subjects chose to violate their norms by eating an obnoxious food.

Those subjects who actually ate grasshoppers changed their attitude toward the object of their behavior (fried grasshoppers) but not their attitude toward the communicator when they were exposed to the negative communicator who acted in a bossy and tactless manner. In essence, they decided that the grasshoppers were not as unpleasant as they had assumed. When the communicator was friendly, however, the subjects justified eating grasshoppers in terms of the attributes of the communicator, and they ate more grasshoppers because the communicator was a nice fellow.

As this study demonstrates, the attributes of a communicator who attempts to induce people to act publicly in a way contrary to their privately held attitudes can influence attitude change! This finding is consistent with predictions from cognitive dissonance theory that the greatest attitude change occurs when behavior cannot be easily justified in terms of personal characteristics, such as the friendliness of the communicator.

A more appalling but not altogether dissimilar example of cognitive dissonance is the report of B. Bettelheim that prisoners in concentration camps occasionally came to admire the Nazi officers who had induced them to carry out behaviors that were contrary to their values.†

---

*P. G. Zimbardo et al., "Communicator Effectiveness in Producing Public Conformity and Private Attitude Change," *Journal of Personality*, 1965, *23*, 233-255.
†B. Bettelheim, "Individual and Mass Behavior in Extreme Situations," *Journal of Abnormal and Social Psychology*, 1943, *38*, 417–452.

Order of Presentation

The timing in presentation of information is another important factor in the relation between persuasibility and attitude change. Much of the research on this issue has centered on primacy versus recency—that is, the comparative effectiveness of the first and last material presented. Summarizing the data of extensive experimentation on the order of presentation in persuasion, Hovland (1957) discovered that primacy is generally an advantage in attitude change. Following presentation of the favorable side of an issue, the effectiveness of a subsequent presentation of the other side is reduced. However, primacy does not always have the advantage, especially if the information is presented in two different experimental settings. The primacy effect arising from the presentation of contradictory information in the same communication can be reduced by interpolating other activities between the two blocks of information and by warning against the superficial nature of first impressions.

In Hovland's view, the problem of primacy and recency must be considered in regard to individual needs. Arousal of needs first, followed by information, is more successful than the reverse procedure. Thus order of presentation is more important in cases of low interest or need than when there is strong motivation. Presenting information that is highly desirable to the subject first and following it with more neutral statements elicits more attitude change than the other way around.

Subsequent research has not basically challenged Hovland's findings. Because of the high forgetting rate, time intervals between successive presentations of information or propaganda can be critical (Miller & Campbell, 1959). For example, the primacy advantage can be undermined if there is a long time delay between the first and second presentations. A series of communications also can diminish the primacy effect, especially if pro and con appeals are made successively (Anderson & Barrios, 1961). In an experiment with undergraduates, arguments for and against Medicare were presented over a week's time, and tested with use of the Semantic Differential Scale (see Chapter 8); the results favored recency over primacy. Yet the nature of the information—specific or general, denotative or connotative (see Chapter 10)—was more critical than the actual order of presentation (Crano, 1977).

In addition, other factors may influence primacy. For instance, when inconsistent information is given in a single communication, there is a strong tendency for the items presented first to be dominant in retention. Yet McGuire (1964) found that a respondent's reply to a questionnaire considering only one side of an issue does not necessarily reduce the appeal of the second side.

The differential effects of time or forgetting by which a communication becomes acceptable after a given period is called the *sleeper effect*. The research of Hovland, Lumsdaine, and Sheffield (1959) on filmed material with army personnel showed that retention of certain factual material decreased with time, whereas opinion change increased with time. Skepticism about negative material was forgotten at the same time that the positive aspects were reinforced. Gruder et al. (1978) have shown that the effect of the trustworthiness of the communicator on attitude change and a message which is received without reference to a communicator decay at different rates. Skepticism about the communicator decreases faster than the information contained in the message, resulting in an attitude-change effect which occurs only after a period of time. If a communicator is credible, a person's attitude might be influenced immediately, whereas if a communicator is questionable the influence on attitude may occur only after the suspicions have been forgotten. It is also possible that some of the sleeper effects are attributable to interaction among the subjects following the experiment, in which positive rather than negative aspects may be stressed (Tesser & Conlee, 1975).

Order of presentation is also related to the individual's ability to identify with the communicator and internalize or assume a proposed attitude, two of Kelman's three processes underlying attitude formation and change identified at the beginning of the chapter. Identification is a matter of feeling, but internalization depends on the influence of the communicator. Mills and Harvey (1972) tested two communicator variables, expertness and attractiveness, with a sample of 72 college women. Presentations were made to two groups, but in different order: One group was given descriptions of a number of communicators' qualifications first; and the other group was shown their photographs first. Opinion change was greater for attractiveness, whether presented before or after the qualifications, but expertness lost dramatically when it was shown after, whereas attractiveness gained. Thus empathy may be of more consequence than intellectual and professional considerations, but the aspects of timing can be most important.

The Nature of the Message

Another factor affecting persuasibility and attitude change is how the information is presented in a persuasive message. Research on this factor has been concerned with several types of questions: Should both sides of a question, pro and con, be presented, or is admission of disadvantages in a proposal likely to hamper its acceptance? How can an issue be presented so it will fit the recipient's cognitive consistency and selective exposure criteria for acceptance? To what degree can fear or anxiety be used to elicit support?

One-Sided and Two-Sided Presentations

Attitudes tend to be objective when the communication regarding them has been impartial, or *nonloaded*. Generally, recipients of the communication are more convinced by it and more inclined to accept the argument if the communicator assures them that the negative position has been considered, although the integrity of the argument and the communicator will depend on the education and other subcultural attributes of the listener. Because two-sided arguments stress the controversial aspects of an issue, however, they may set off discussion, and the effects may be less predictable than when one-sided messages are used (Festinger, 1955). The effectiveness of an argument also can depend on whether the communicator draws conclusions for the listeners or encourages them to make their own judgments. In one study (Hovland & Mandell, 1952) regarding reaction to the devaluation of currency, subjects were more convinced when the arguments were drawn out explicitly. With another more highly educated sample, however, the difference was negligible (Thistlewaite, de Haan, & Kamenetsky, 1955).

Cognitive Consistency and Selective Exposure

The recognized need for individuals to maintain or restore consistency among their cognitions (discussed above) can cause recipients of communications to disregard, deny, or distort incoming information or, when necessary, to seek out and attend to sufficient information to satisfy their requirements for cognitive consonance. Many studies have demonstrated this. Allyn and Festinger (1961), for example, found that people who had been warned of the communicator's discrepant point of view evidenced less attitude change than those who had not been warned. This suggests a selective attention or denial mechanism, which was demonstrated in an observation reported by Maccoby (1962). During the 1960 Kennedy-Nixon presidential debates, observers recorded the amounts of attention paid by TV viewers while each candidate was speaking. The results showed that people paid attention to their own candidate's arguments but tended to engage in distracting activities (conversation, drinking, eating) when the opposition candidate was speaking. Thus they effectively disregarded the communication of the unfavored candidate.

The most obvious consideration is the size of the discrepancy between the recipient's attitude toward an object, person, or situation and the one being advocated. Research indicates that the greater the initial discrepancy, the greater the attitude change (Fisher & Lubin, 1958). The explanation, in terms of *cognitive consistency* theory, is that the discomfort experienced by the recipient of such a communcation is directly related to the discrepancy, and the greater the discrepancy, the greater the likelihood of some attitude change and the greater the amount of change required to restore consistency. It should be apparent, however, that size of discrepancy interacts with many other factors in the communication, such as the *importance* of the issue, the *prestige* of the source, and the *credibility* that differences of particular magnitudes can in fact occur. Should the discrepancy be extremely large, the recipient is likely to discredit the sources or to assume that the communication is being presented for purposes other than argument or persuasion. The communicator may be attempting to be amusing, annoying, arrogant—or may simply have lost contact with reality.

It has also been found that when people are confronted with attitude-relevant information they cannot avoid, they process the information more rapidly and recall it more readily when it is either extremely consistent or extremely inconsistent with their own attitudes. Judd and Kulik (1980) had subjects rate their degree of agreement or disagreement with attitude statements and then recall as many statements as they could a day later. It was found that the more extreme the subjects' agreement or disagreement with an item, the faster they made their ratings of it, and the more likely they were to recall it later. Thus these data support the notion that attitudes serve a categorizing function for incoming information,

Studies of presidential debates have found that most viewers primarily focus on their preferred candidates. As in most campaign activities, the debate is directed to changing the opinions of the undecided. *Source:* United Press International, Inc.

and items that are more extreme are more easily categorized and recalled. It should be noted, however, that this refers only to the processing and retrieval of information relevant to attitudes, not to the effect the information has on attitudes.

On the basis of such evidence, it is tempting to assume that people are motivated to monitor incoming communications and deny attention to those that appear to be at variance with their existing attitudes, the extent of the denial being a function of the importance of the existing point of view to the person. Very important ego defenses (e.g., prejudices) would be highly guarded against opposing communications, whereas those of little significance to the person would be less highly guarded, if at all. An attempt probably would also be made to maintain support for *ego-defensive attitudes* such as prejudices. Individuals would be expected to seek out people and communications that share their prejudices in order to add support to their ego defense, and to avoid those that do not.

Nevertheless, the empirical evidence for the notion of *motivated* selective exposure is weak, although Sears (1968) found some evidence for *de facto* selective exposure. In natural settings people are more aware of sources of supportive, rather than of nonsupportive, information (meetings, TV and radio programs, books). In addition, habits based on social class, such as reading specific newspapers, tend to expose a person to more supportive than nonsupportive information. This selective exposure does not necessarily result from preference, Sears said, but rather from "long-term habits of tastes and preference, normally irrelevant to (but empirically correlated with) political and social opinions."

According to Sears, the available evidence raises doubts about the *inconsistency-avoidance hypothesis,* which suggests that people in everyday situations avoid unpleasant information. He did find they may do so in extremely stressful situations such as death or bodily injury, however. McGuire (1969) points to research which indicates that under some conditions, at least, the opposite of the selective exposure hypothesis may be the dominant tendency, in that both attitude-consistent and attitude-inconsistent information are attended to more closely than neutral or attitude-irrelevant information.

Emotional Appeal

The affective component of attitudes, particularly such emotions as fear and anxiety, often tends to take precedence over the rational component in persuasive messages. People are persuaded to accept social changes, for example, with the argument that failure to adopt them would have dire consequences: "Automation causes unemployment"; "If you don't stop smoking you'll get lung cancer"; "Birth control is necessary to prevent a population explosion."

One study of the fear motive (Janis & Feshbach, 1953) used three different messages in a college sample on dental hygiene: one emphasizing highly negative stimuli, including pictures of diseased gums; another with a less dramatic lecture on the remote possibilities of cancer; and the third with relatively neutral data. The effects of these messages were determined before and after the communications by the subjects' reports of their own dental hygiene (care of the teeth and the degree to which they followed recommendations). Students who received the most moderate messages changed the most, which suggests that anxiety-arousing communications may inhibit learning because of their distractibility, and strong emotion may have a *boomerang effect*.

These hypotheses were confirmed in a study of the effects of smoking conducted on a limited number of adult subjects (Janis & Terwilliger, 1962). The communications suggested low threat ("Smoking is bad for one's health"— and high threat ("There is a possibility of lung cancer") in their emphasis on the health hazards of smoking. In this study the subjects had the unique opportunity of expressing their reactions during the experiment. Considerably more rejection was encountered in the high threat group; the act of resistance appears to become a motivating factor in rejection of the communication.

There are individual differences in response to emotional appeal, as in any type of communication. The variables of ego-defense and self-esteem are particularly related to the success or failure of persuasion. Experimental evidence shows that threatening messages are more frequently rejected by individuals with higher self-esteem (A. R. Cohen, 1959).

Following an analysis of the research on fear as an agent of attitude change, Leventhal (1970) proposed what he calls a *parallel response model*. He believes that a fear drive has too often characterized attitude-change studies. People make both adaptive and emotional responses to the fear stimulus, and what they do with such a communication depends primarily on this vulnerability to the threat. Leventhal's interpretation of the data in research on the use of threat films, for example, was that subjects who showed in their self-reports a fear of lung cancer "tuned in" on a threat message less than those who felt invulnerable. Smokers were less inclined to accept a fear communication because they defined the situation as nonthreatening. In Leventhal's view, danger is detected on the basis of cognitive and personality factors which process the fear message, rather than the emotional appeal. Moreover, such a communication is interpreted according to the danger stimulus, emotional responses, and attempts at coping behavior such as adaptive processes like fear control used to varying degrees. A strong fear presentation has more effect than a weaker one in encouraging people to take a simple step, like having a tetanus shot. But strong fear arousal is generally not more successful with habitual smokers, who can face neither the threat of lung cancer nor the thought of giving up smoking.

In order to test Leventhal's theory that cognitive processes are more important than emotional processes in inducing attitude change, Rogers and Newborn (1976) placed 176 university students in three groups, each responding to different kinds of fear situations depicted in films on (1) cigarette smoking, (2) unsafe driving, and (3) venereal diseases. The groups were further divided into subgroups designed to test the degree of noxiousness, degree of severity, likelihood of occurrence, and the possibility of coping responses. Two factors, severity of the threat and the ability to ward off the danger, were found to be critical. Fear stimuli are apparently monitored according to the person's cognitive ability to muster a defense.

Limiting the Effectiveness of Persuasion

Various methods have been proposed which could make it possible to immunize recipients against persuasive messages. McGuire (1969) specifies the following ways to decrease vulnerabilty to persuasion:

1. *Strengthening motives* to resist persuasion, such as raising one's self-esteem or avoiding anxiety, whose effects can be dubious at best.
2. *Training* the public to adopt a *more critical approach* in handling data, even though the payoff can be very low. McGuire warns that instruction on how to analyze and assess arguments "may enhance the effective reception of the persuasive message more than it lowers the amount of yielding to what is received, thus producing a net increase in influenceability."
3. *Commitment,* or internally thinking about one's belief and then making it public and acting overtly on the basis of the belief.
4. *Anchoring,* or tying the belief to other cognitions, either by initiating new links or by making prior links salient. Testing the belief or attitudes in the framework of other cognitions means working through toward consistency or at least reducing the inconsistency. The influence of reference groups can help anchor beliefs.

The limits of persuasibility are explored in the first section of Chapter 11, which is concerned with social influence and group pressure toward conformity.

SUMMARY

This chapter has presented certain theoretical aspects of attitude structure and change: Katz's functional or motivational theory, Rosenberg's cognitive-affective theory, Kelman's process theory, Heider's balance theory, and Osgood's congruity principle. The range of theories testifies to the complexity of attitude structure and change processes, and their conceptualizations have been the point of departure for extensive research. The findings regarding cognitive consistency and dissonance particularly illustrate how deeply attitudes and beliefs are anchored in a person's cognitive and motivational systems. This dependence is illustrated in considering the conditions that influence attitude change, such as social background, intergroup relations, and ego involvement and other aspects of personality structure.

The trustworthiness of the source and the content of a persuasive communication is a basic consideration which involves the recipient's perception of and identification with the communicator. Primacy in order of presentation of information in a message has been found to be a greater advantage than recency, and presenting both sides of an argument generally increases its credibility. A person's openness to persuasive messages is affected by the need to screen out dissonant information and maintain cognitive consistency, as well as the tendency toward selective exposure to supportive sources of information. The affective basis of an appeal, particularly fear or anxiety, also can influence receptivity of the message, but cognitive processes have been found to be at least equally important by some theorists. Under certain conditions, immunization against persuasibility may be possible.

WORDS TO REMEMBER

Affect.   Feeling or emotion, as compared to intellectual or cognitive experience. Attitudes have both affective and cognitive aspects.

Balance theory.   The idea that people try to maintain some degree of cognitive consistency; that is, they attempt to hold on to consistent or compatible beliefs, especially in order to remain in harmony with peers. An example is the desire to rearrange personal beliefs into an internally satisfying equilibrium; for instance, if someone disapproves of our beliefs we may decide that this person has less than adequate judgment or does not understand our viewpoint.

Boomerang effect.   The tendency of people to change their opinions in the opposite direction of that advocated in a persuasive message. This behavior often occurs when the message is exaggerated or presented by someone who arouses negative feeling in the audience.

Cognitive consistency.   Induced integration or harmony of a person's perceptions, beliefs, attitudes, and behavior in order to avoid contradiction. For instance, a favored presidential candidate is viewed as representing the virtues considered necessary for leadership, and any traits inconsistent with this belief are dismissed or somehow repressed and forgotten.

Cognitive dissonance.   Theory devised by Leon Festinger to express the idea that holding contradictory beliefs arouses discomfort or conflict. Consequently, people tend to alter their beliefs and attitudes in order to reduce this conflict when new ones are introduced.

Cognitive system.   A balance of cognitions or of beliefs and attitudes. This equilibrium depends on the organization or reorganization of the attitudinal components.

Communication.   Transmission of information from one person or source to another.

Congruity theory.   The idea that people search for personal consistency or balance; that is, when attitudes or values are placed on a continuum from plus to minus, they tend to arrange the elements in order to achieve some kind of balance.

Empathy.   Emotional identification, or "feeling into," with another person.

Functional theory of attitudes.   The concept that attitudes have a certain utilitarian or practical value, either objective or subjective, for the individual; that is, attitudes and values serve the individual in a given direction.

Media.   The various means of communication whereby attitudes and public opinion are formed; usually refers to the press, radio, television, and motion pictures.

Persuasibility.   The capacity or ability of an

individual or group to be convinced of or manipulated toward a given attitude or belief.

Polarization. Drifting apart, or opposition, of two or more persons, groups, or ideologies, as in liberals and conservatives, or pro- and anti-integrationists.

Primacy effect. In attitude and opinion formation, the idea that what is presented first has the greatest influence.

Reactance theory. Explanation for the disturbing feeling accompanying the reduction of freedom, which leads to attempts to restore the freedom, often by disengagement from the task or group. In attitude formation, the concept refers to people's tendency to think the opposite of what they are expected to.

Role-playing. Taking the part of another person, either mentally or in real life; often an effective means of attitude change.

Selective exposure. Awareness or openness to certain kinds of information because of the person's special environment or prior attitude structure. A college professor or student is likely to receive or "tune in" certain stimuli that would not ordinarily be available to the public at large; a Republican might be more sensitive to a certain range of data than would a Democrat.

Sleeper effect. Delayed operation of a persuasive communication which can cause a later change in attitude of the recipient.

QUESTIONS FOR DISCUSSION

1. How is the study of theories of attitude organization useful?

2. Compare the functional theory with the cognitive-affect approach to the study of attitude structure.

3. Explain Kelman's process theory of attitudes. Can you give an example from your own observation?

4. What is meant by cognitive congruity and incongruity? How do these terms relate to cognitive dissonance?

5. How did Senator Edward Kennedy's experience at Chappaquiddick pose a problem of cognitive dissonance for his followers? Can you think of similar problems in political life that have caused dissonance?

6. What are the major determinants of attitude change? Under what conditions is attitude change most realistic?

7. To what extent are personality factors involved in openness to change?

8. What are the major factors to be considered in studying persuasibility?

9. What research has been carried out on sources and credibility? Has the spread of higher education and the growth of multiple mass media had any effect on this problem?

10. What is meant by "order of presentation"?

11. What are the arguments on one-sided versus two-sided presentations?

12. To what extent has selective exposure been found to influence attitude change?

13. Give the arguments favoring affective or cognitive processes—or both—as an agent of attitude change.

14. Give some examples of immunization against persuasibility. How effective is this process?

READINGS)

Bem, D. J. *Beliefs, Attitudes and Human Affairs.* Belmont, Calif.: Brooks/Cole Publishing Co., 1970.

An engaging analysis of attitudes and the question of consistency.

Greenwald, A. G., Brock, T. C., and Ostrom, T. M. (Eds.). *Psychological Foundations of Attitudes.* New York: Academic Press, 1968.

Contributions analyze the relation of learning and cognition to attitudes and attitude change.

Himmelfarb, S., and Eagly, A. H. (Eds.). *Readings in Attitude Change.* New York: John Wiley & Sons, 1974.

Intended for the research-oriented student; over 50 articles on methodology, persuasibility, types of appeals, and the message context.

Hovland, C. I., and Janis, I. L. *Personality and Persuasibility.* New Haven, Conn.: Yale University Press, 1959.

Along with Hovland's previous volumes, this became the starting point for subsequent research in attitude change.

Kiesler, C. A. *The Psychology of Commitment: Experiments Linking Behavior to Belief.* New York: Academic Press, 1971.

A clear and insightful discussion of attribution and commitment.

Swingle, P. G. (Ed.). *Social Psychology in Natural Settings.* Chicago: Aldine Publishing Co., 1973.

Chapters 3, 6, 8, and 10 deal with questions of attitude change.

Zimbardo, P., and Ebbesen, E. B. *Influencing Attitudes and Changing Behavior.* Reading, Mass.: Addison-Wesley Publishing Co., 1969.

A thoroughly readable introduction to the interface between attitudes and cognition.

LANGUAGE AND COMMUNICATION

The study of language and communication has moved to the center of the stage in the behavioral sciences. Although anthropologists have been engrossed with this area for over a half century, sociologists and social psychologists have only recently begun to emphasize the importance of language in such phenomena as national loyalties, group conflict, social class, and role enactment, in recognition of its significance to every phase of human society. In this respect, the task of the behavioral scientist is to determine the structure of language and to examine what the speaker does with it (Erde, 1973).

The development of new research areas such as psycholinguistics, metalinguistics, and information systems has broadened the concern with language, to encompass it within a virtual science of communication. While these movements are highly technical and not centrally related to the core of social psychology, they do contribute to the critical position of communication in psychology and social science today. The tendency to consider a number of other processes—such as perception, cognition, roles, and the effects of the mass media—as a part of communication may give too broad an extension to the original meaning of the term, however, so it loses some of its serviceability. In this chapter we will focus on communication between individuals and members of groups, reserving discussion of the more peripheral aspects of the concept for other chapters.

The chapter begins with an examination of the idea that language is the principal advantage humans have over animals. The communication process is then examined, and the elements of language are described in a section on language as symbolic communication. The nature of language is further developed in a section describing how the language of a culture is acquired by the child, and cultural and social influences on language are examined in a section on sociolinguistics. The discussion of language concludes with some special considerations in the relation of language to thought and the study of semantics. Various means of communicating without language, or nonverbally, are described in the final section.

IS LANGUAGE UNIQUELY HUMAN?

Until very recently, it was thought that language more than anything else distinguishes humans from animals. Studies had shown, for example, that monkeys could make and respond to a variety of cries and that bees have an elaborate system of communication, but the conclusion was that animals make use of "signaling reflexes" and are probably incapable of speech and symbolic communication.

Animals in a Human Environment

Several studies, notably those using apes and other simians, have questioned the assumption that animals cannot use language. An early experiment by the Kelloggs, who raised a young ape with their own son, was reported by Hayes (1951). They found that by the age of 16 months the ape could respond correctly to 58 verbal phrases, such as "Don't do that"; "Give it to me"; and "Show me your nose." Hayes also reported his own family's three-year experience with training a young chimp, Vicki, to respond to several dozen sounds. She also learned to utter three words, "mama," "papa," and "cup," and apparently could use them with meaning. On her third birthday, Vicki drank her cup of coffee and asked Mrs. Hayes for a refill by holding the cup up to the coffeepot and saying: "Mama!" and then "cup."

Later investigators undertook serious exploration of the symbolic ability of chimpanzees. Gardner and Gardner (1969) explored gestural rather than verbal language, using American Sign Language (ASL), a set of hand gestures corresponding to words. Washoe, a female chimp, began to learn her "signs" when about a year old, and less than a year later she started making combinations, much as young children do: "Gimme key"; "Roger tickle"; "Washoe sorry." After three years of training, she had a vocabulary of 85 signs, and she had almost doubled that by the fourth year. Because all the signs did not refer to objects or actions, she was able to use such ideas as "hurt," "sorry," and "funny" in appropriate situations (Hahn, 1971; Fleming, 1974).

Plastic chips or blocks of different shapes and colors were used by Premack (1970) to teach the names of objects, verbs, and concepts to a chimp, Sarah, through conditioning by rewards. Soon she was making combinations, such as "Mary gives apple Sarah," and she was later able to learn more complex sentences like, "Sarah insert apple red dish apple banana green dish." At the end of two and a half years of training, Sarah had mastered many language functions, including the interrogative, negation, class concepts, matching, similarities, and dissimilarities. She sometimes surprised her teachers, as when she set up a kind of sentence completion test for one of them.

A number of theorists, including Limber (1977), have questioned whether this kind of language is what is meant by communication in the human sense, however. Part of the problem is the failure to distinguish between language *function* (the ability to label objects), which both primates and young children can perform, and language *structure* (a complex capacity with a largely neural basis). While the chimpanzee seems to be at par with a human two-year-old in using a hundred or so verbal symbols, the animal apparently reaches a ceiling and cannot move on to the complex conceptualizations attainable by the older child. Others, like Meddin (1979), argue that chimpanzees are not only able to use verbal symbols but can also form abstractions. Using human beings as role models, they can even enter into creative and cooperative activities, such as hunting expeditions for meat as a variation from their vegetarian diet.

The controversy continues as to whether or not apes are capable of true language. Terrace (1980), working with a chimpanzee named Nim, concluded that the apes' apparent language is actually imitative signing in which they put together several signs which result in reinforcement. According to Terrace, the signing is largely imitative, is seldom spontaneous, and does not indicate understanding of grammatical rules or language structure so that new or expanded uses of signs in sentences can occur. Others strongly disagree, criticizing the methods Terrace used to instruct the animal and the environment in which the animal was reared.

At a minimum, it seems that with proper training, including exposure to a human environment, some animals can communicate remarkably well. Whether they are capable of true language remains in doubt, and research on this problem continues.

Human Isolates

The possibility that animals can be trained to use language is enhanced by studies of the capabilities of *feral children,* or untamed children nurtured by wild animals such as wolves or bears. Unfortunately for science, only 30 or 40 such cases have come to light, and of these only two, the Wild Boy of Aveyron and the Wolf Children of India, have been reported in any detail—and perhaps not altogether accurately. The retarded and "unhuman" characteristics of these children have been attributed to the denial of early experience (Bettelheim, 1959; Singh & Zingg, 1942), but others insist the data are too scanty to rule out the possibility of mental or organic defects in the individuals.

Somewhat more evidence exists in cases of isolated children, the best known of whom was Caspar Hauser (Wassermann, 1973). This child was kept in a small cell until he was 16 and never allowed to see his attendant. When set free, he could understand no human speech, could walk only with great difficulty, and was socially helpless. Under friendly guidance he learned rapidly and later wrote the story of his experiences.

Like all messages, graffiti have a source and a destination. The case of initials and names indicate an ego orientation. In restrooms the focus is on sexuality, and in developing areas like Latin America they tend to be political in nature. *Source:* © Theodore Anderson, 1981.

In the few rare cases where a potentially normal child who had been rendered inhuman by a socially abnormal environment was later socialized, missing language skills were easily acquired. This is hardly surprising in view of the years that parents spend training their children in language and other habits and in the forms of emotional and social behavior that are approved in their culture, as noted in Chapter 3.

THE COMMUNICATION PROCESS

Communication plays the central role in relations between individuals or groups. For example, the impasse in attempts to relieve international tensions and defuse the possibility of nuclear war are in large part due to failures in honest,

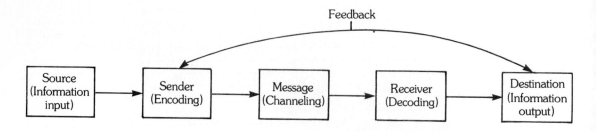

Figure 10-1. The Communication Process

effective communication. Communication barriers also help account for the inability to achieve harmony between labor and management, the generation gap between adolescents and senior citizens, and the difficulties therapists have in reaching clients, teachers have in reaching students, or ministers have in reaching congregations. There also are frictions and barriers to communication within primary groups—the family, the work group, the neighborhood gang.

Communication can be thought of as a process which enables the individual to control or adapt to the complex stimuli presented by the environment. It is also an abstraction from reality, or a symbolic process which mediates between the individual and reality (R. G. Smith, 1970). A musical note, a billboard drawing, a signal code, a gesture, as well as words and grammatical symbols, can all be units in this process.

A distinctive technical jargon and diagramming technique have been developed by students of communication to represent this process—whether it is concerned with the communication between programming and the computer, an artist and the public, or Bill and Betty. Despite the special vocabulary required for this new theory of communication, it has helped clarify our understanding of how human communication takes place. The transmittal of information from the source to the destination in this five-step input-output process is illustrated in Figure 10-1. The analysis of the developmental sequence of the sender-receiver relationship presented here is derived from a number of sources, principally Carroll (1953) and Miller and McNeill (1969).

1. *Source (information input).* Psychologically speaking, this step might be labeled the *intentive behavior* of the sender or communicator. Neural activity of some kind has produced information in some form which becomes the source, or the cognitive material (perceptions, thoughts, feelings) that is to be communicated.

2. *Sender (encoding).* This step in the process includes the decision to communicate and the choice of medium (the specific words, in language). The sender must decide what code to communicate in, such as a gesture, a song, or an oral command. There are numerous forms messages can take; in some cases, incipient responses are inhibited, and no encoding takes place. The sender may

communicate only to the self and use only a few words, or the communication might require an extremely elaborate encoding, as with a formal lecture.

3. *Message (channeling).* In this step the communication takes an objective form—the message. The message has been defined as "that part of the total output (responses) of a source unit which simultaneously may be a part of the total input (stimuli) to a destination unit" (Gardner, 1954, p. 2). It is the link between the sender and the receiver. The message can consist of a danger signal, a prehistoric cave painting (for which there have intermittently been receivers for over 25,000 years), or the words "I love you." Frequently the message has a composite form, such as speech accompanied by gestures. It provides all the behavioral information that is observable to the receiver.

In the channel of communication, there may be a number of barriers that operate to reduce the intelligibility of the message. Anything that acts as a distraction or barrier to communication is known as *noise*. To overcome it, the sender uses various means of implementing the message, such as repetition ("I love you, I love you") or increasing the size, volume, or color of the stimulus. In English (and most languages) there is a great deal of redundancy, or excess verbal material, to ensure comprehension of the message by the receiver. For instance, "He goes to the end of the road to pick up the hat" could be understood if stated "goes end road for hat." It has been estimated that perhaps 75 percent or more of English is redundant (Shannon, 1951).

4. *Receiver (decoding).* Compared to animals, humans have advantages in communication because they can respond to more complex and abstract messages, though they are at a limited disadvantage in responding to high-frequency sounds or to smells. The response potential of individuals is also determined by their unique capacity to receive and process messages, which is shaped by their level of mental functioning and such subcultures as age, sex, social class, or educational level.

The particular circumstances of the receiver determine the way a transmitted message is accepted, rejected, or altered in some fashion. In this step the receiver makes discriminations and interpretations of what has been heard (or seen or smelled, and so on); the individual's entire background of experience can affect the way the message is received. The receiver may react to only certain parts of the message, and in some cases, owing to noise or some internal condition, it may not even reach the destination. Sometimes entirely false interpretations are made; "I love you," for example, might be interpreted in diverse ways, depending on the individuals involved and the situation in which they find themselves.

5. *Destination (output).* This step might be called the *interpretive behavior* of the receiver after receipt of the information. It is "information that is not linguistically coded" by the receiver (Carroll, 1953), and there can be a multitude of resultant behaviors at this stage—cognitions, feeling, and the like. In the average conversation, there will be reciprocal activity from the receiver, who will answer the sender, and the cycle will be reopened.

Another important factor in the communication process is *feedback*—the receiver's reaction as interpreted by the sender. In the speaker-hearer relationship, particularly, it is of crucial importance to know whether one is

Pantomime can be a form of communication. Marcel Marceaux is unsurpassed in his ability to communicate mood and even personality without words. *Source:* Magnum Photos, Inc./Max Waldman.

"getting across." Generally, this is an automatic process of confirming by "yes" and "no" reactions but it can lead to varied interpretations. The receiver's own contribution can influence the message, and feedback can increase the degree of identity between the receiver's interpretation and the sender's intent (Hulett, 1962). There are a number of historical and literary accounts of the sender's misinterpretation of the feedback from the destination. For instance, Abraham Lincoln thought his delivery of the Gettysburg Address had failed to impress his audience, and it was some time before he realized that the silence that greeted it represented the highest level of appreciation.

The communication process illustrated in Figure 10–1 applies to both the formal communication channels in a group and the informal communication structures described in Chapter 15. Figure 15–2 in that chapter illustrates various types of three-, four-, and five-person communication networks.

LANGUAGE AS SYMBOLIC COMMUNICATION

Language is a form of symbolic communication because it consists of conventional *signs* or *signals* (Leach, 1976). Through usage, certain sounds and their written equivalents come to represent persons, things, and activities. With very few exceptions, these words have no inherent or necessary connection with the items to which they refer. They are conventional substitutes or symbols in the sense that their meaning is understood and agreed upon by the members of the culture group.

Psycholinguistics

Communication, like other social-psychological problems, cannot be detached from the central processes of cognition (particularly perception) and motivation. A relatively new area of study, psycholinguistics, is concerned in the broadest sense with relations between messages and the characteristics of the individuals who select and interpret them. In terms of the process illustrated in Figure 10–1 above, psycholinguistics takes two approaches: *phonetics,* which attends to the information in the source unit and the problem of sending (or transmission) and encoding it, and *psychoacoustics,* which focuses on receiving and decoding the message and the information in the destination unit (Osgood & Sebeck, 1965).

Thus individuals develop a language system out of their response to the environment. This ever-expanding representation of experience becomes a "predictive apparatus" in the building of a storehouse of what to expect in interactions with others (Underwood, 1965). Although the language vehicle is shaped by society and culture, the individual colors it with an ever-changing usage of words and other symbols. That is, each person develops some flexibility in extrapolating from experience the significant features she or he chooses to verbalize. Thus we fashion verbal habit systems to increase the efficiency of our cognitive filing systems.

According to experimental studies, the individual codes verbal units for storage purposes and, at the time of recall, decodes back the unit which is later required for the appropriate responses (Erde, 1973). Interpretation of the precise means by which a language is acquired varies in different learning theories (see Chapter 5). Whatever the theoretical explanation, however, some kind of semantic generalization—a gradual acquisition of symbols and meaning—must take place, in a process which begins in early childhood (de Villiers & de Villiers, 1978). Meanings grow through their interrelationships to other meanings or concepts. In expanding these abstractions, we increase our ability to cross-reference our perceptual and behavioral world. Eventually a rich and complex symbolic system of words and grammar enables us to describe, explain, and predict our environment.

The Elements of Language

How symbolic communication originated in the course of human evolution is an interesting but highly speculative problem, one which is more in the province of the archaeologist than the social psychologist (Tur-Sinai, 1957). All we know is that language began somehow, and because it had utility it became the most essential part of our cultural heritage. Anthropologists and philologists (students of human speech and language as used in literature) have investigated the basic forms and patterns of the languages of the world, both written and unwritten, and have found that in even the most primitive society, the language has become quite complex. As Kroeber (1948) says: "It may safely be estimated that every existing language, no matter how backward its speakers are in their general civilization, possesses a vocabulary of at least 5,000 to 10,000 words."

College students must have a much larger vocabulary, since it has been estimated that on the average they must listen to 100,000 words a day between attending lectures and conversing with fellow students, and if they spend five hours in the library, they might read 90,000 words, assuming they read 300 words per minute (Carroll, 1964). In addition, they will communicate with the world about themselves in a number of other auditory and visual symbols that can be mentally transcribed into language. As you walk across the campus, for example, you might think, "Those two on the bench are making love," or "The clock says I should go to the gym"—although you might not verbalize those experiences to yourself in those particular words. While nonverbal communication can convey meaning, as noted in the final section of this chapter, the study of language is mainly concerned with the use of verbal symbols, which were sounds or combinations of sounds before they became written symbols.

It is usual to distinguish in language between *phonemes* (speech sounds) and *morphemes* (meaningful sound forms). In English there are 45 distinguishable phonemes; other languages have more or less than this number. Phonemes can be described as a "group or variety or class of related sounds which are handled by the speaker as a discrete unit, regardless of position within the communication (Pei, 1965, p. 13) The *p* sound exists as a phoneme in *spit, pit,* or *pip,* and it sounds slightly different in each. A Britisher, Sir James Pitman, constructed an initial teaching alphabet (ITA) based on 44 phonemes, or lower-case letters representing specific sounds. It has been successful in teaching language in the schools throughout England, as well as in certain American cities where it has been adopted for the early school years.

In the same way that *phonology* refers to the science of language sounds, the term *morphology* is applied to the forms of language. Morphemes, strictly speaking, are the smallest units of meaning. In a large dictionary there are nearly a half million morphemes built from the 45 phonemes, a few of which also constitute morphemes (*a* and *I*, for instance). As with phonemes, the structure of morphemes is generally in the form of compounds: the word *stopped* is a verb with the past-tense ending. Similarly, different meanings are attached to such forms as *bull, bulls,* and *bullish.*

Morphemes are the basis of *grammar,* or the rules underlying language. For both morphemes and phonemes, an orderly arrangement is necessary in order for communication to take place. It would be difficult to interpret "If John Mary and love in are" or "He lzkes to lxve well on the hzll," which illustrate discontinuity in the use of morphemes and phonemes, respectively. *Syntax,* or the order of words and verb structure, constitutes a major area of grammar. English is especially dependent on syntax for its meaning. The order of subject-verb-object is essentially a syntactic relationship.

The dependence of the English language on an extravagance of words, or redundancy, to convey precise meanings was noted above in Step 3 of the communication process. You would not find it economical to send a telegram worded "Having lost most of my luggage in changing taxicabs, and having missed the evening train, I am wondering if you could send me some money," for example. "Dear Dad: Send money" would be a more likely message. Economy in the use of words is a sign of good writing as well as speech. Perhaps children know this since they eliminate auxiliary verbs, articles, prepositions, and conjunctions in imitating adult speech.

LANGUAGE ACQUISITION

The Neural Basis of Language

The question of the human being's potential or foundation for language remains open, and the degree to which language is innate or acquired has not been established. Chomsky (1967) asserts that humans innately possess deep, underlying neural structures which make language possible. A certain level of development of the nervous system must be reached before a child can handle the intricate speech patterns involved in syntax or grammar, semantics (meaning), and phonology (sounds), however (LaPalombara, 1976).

The precise nature of the language center in the human brain is also in dispute. According to Morton (1971), two interpretations are possible. One is that there is some general unfolding of the nervous system whereby the individual reaches a certain level of complexity at a given period of development. The other interpretation, which is more speculative, considers the innate component as especially important. Whatever the explanation, it is conceivable that circuits are available to connect the auditory recognition system and the motor speech center. Presumably there are more or less separate systems of speech perception, speech production, and speech structure. These neural systems have reciprocal relations with one another, and no system is necessarily central. Much of our cognition apparently depends on the language development within these various centers.

While the innate nature and the precise structural basis of language acquisition remain in doubt, the predisposition to speech seems to be inborn. The process whereby language makes it possible for the individual to select from and categorize the barrage of stimuli encountered in the sociocultural setting is rooted in the sensory and motor circuits of the cerebral cortex. The differentiation and classification of inputs are accomplished through many billions of synaptic (nerve) connections.

How Children Learn to Speak

All languages describe relationships and provide a system of categorization (Menyuk, 1971). Children learning any language, therefore, must learn the *syntactics* (grammar and word order), *semantics* (vocabulary and meaning), and *phonology* (pronunciation) of the language. They have to understand the complexities of verbal forms: the difference, for instance, between *I went there* and *she came here*. Later they perceive the difference between such expressions as *Mama loves Johnny* and *Johnny is loved by Mama*. They become acquainted with the parameters of tense or time, gender, case, and so on, and they learn the various verbal structures and how to modify them.

A child may understand the meaning of a sentence but not the particular way it is constructed, or may acquire morphemes without knowing how to put them together. Children seem to understand the meaning of some utterances before they try to produce them. Usually this understanding begins when a parent names certain objects. Language acquisition depends on spontaneous verbalizations as well as imitating others' nomenclature for events and objects in the day-to-day world. Children eventually learn how to order these various elements and, through making innumerable permutations and combinations, to handle the language with skill. A child's success in mastering a language depends on internal factors, notably the functioning of the cerebral cortex, and on external factors such as stimulation by parents, siblings, and peers.

Some children are deficient in verbal ability because of a motor or sensory defect. Children deprived of sight or hearing or suffering from brain damage try other means of communicating. In these deviant cases, children may be slower in learning to speak, use shorter sentences, or have difficulties in the syntactic or semantic area, or both.

In behaviorist terms, the process by which a child learns to speak is *conditioning* (see Chapter 5). Skinner (1955, 1957) interprets language as verbal behavior, whereby the child learns to talk when he or she emits a variety of sounds and some of them are reinforced with rewards. During the first year, for example, certain vocalizations such as "da" or "ma" are rewarded and encouraged by the family. Others such as "otch" or "glug" are extinguished as responses by lack of reinforcement.

Skinner is more interested in the function of language than its precise form, however. He introduced two new terms to describe language functions—the mand and the tact, which parallel the imperative and declarative moods of syntax, respectively. The *mand,* or imperative, which develops early in the child's experience, functions to secure for the speaker specific reinforcements from the hearer. In this category are commands, entreaties, and requests of all sorts which operate to satisfy the speaker's drives. The *tact* has a declarative function; its form is determined by the names of particular objects or events that have stimulated the speaker. Tacts are learned through generalized reinforcement from hearers, such as smiles, rewards, and other signs of approval when a word is used correctly.

Skinner's behaviorist approach focuses on the functions of verbal responses and the conditions determining them. In this view, meaning is not to be understood by introspection but simply by relating the act of speech to its controlling factors. The ability of this learning-centered approach to answer major questions about symbolism and symbolic communication is a subject for further research.

How Concepts Emerge

As children learn from family members and others the sound patterns which make up the language of the culture, they acquire meanings. The words become symbols for particular persons, objects, situations, and activities that have furnished certain kinds of experience, and, with time, clearly differentiated meanings for these symbols gradually emerge. As Palermo (1978) puts it, "with enough experience, the child abstracts the central tendency of the distribution of functional, perceptual, and affective characteristics of concepts to allow his or her meanings to overlap those of others to the extent which allows communication and the similar classification of a common base for communication . . ." (p. 249).

Children generally learn to distinguish between objects, persons, or events with more refinement as they disentangle the similarities and dissimilarities in their perceptual world. There is both downward and upward categorization (Church, 1961). *Downward categorization* refers to the necessity of distinguishing a dog from a cat or other animal. *Upward categorization* appears later, when children can generalize between quite different classes of objects, as, for example:

Living thing ← Animal → Dog-cat.

Conceptualizations continue throughout the entire educational process in learning. For example, that dogs and cats are mammals, insects have certain structures in common, or the church, state, and family are all social institutions.

The Sociocultural Setting

Cultural norms have much to do with the way the child perceives and conceptualizes the world. The socially transmitted meanings of things are

Language is the ultimate expression of a culture. Arabic has nearly 6,000 words for the most important animal in that culture—a term for each year of the camel's life, each month of pregnancy, the different cuts of meat, and so on. *Source:* United Nations.

commonly understood and appreciated by members of a group (see Box 10–1). For example, if the cow is held sacred in a certain society, its children will not consider the cow just another animal, along with horses or sheep, as we do. There are all kinds of interesting contrasts in the ways colors, numbers, weights, measures, and time relationships are conceptualized in different cultures.

Box 10–1
LANGUAGE AS A CULTURAL EXPRESSION

The early folk psychologists hoped to explain the group mind of primitive peoples by studying their language. They did not succeed, but clearly there is some relationship between material culture and language and between a people's language and their thinking.

Anthropologists have shown that language reflects important aspects of a culture. In English we have a few words for frozen water: *ice, snow, sleet, hail,* and *slush.* The Eskimos, in whose lives ice and snow are much more significant, have dozens of words to denote ice and snow in many different stages and conditions. Even more striking is the evidence presented by W. I. Thomas, who found several thousand words in Arabic connected with one important item, the camel.* Visitors to the United States are often impressed with the richness of our vocabulary in relation to mechanical and technical matters. When the Russians turned to industrialization after the 1917 revolution, they borrowed technological terms from English and German. The Russian language now contains hundreds of words slightly modified from terms like *automobile* and *tractor.* Under the National Socialist, or Nazi, regime in Germany, technical terms that were international cognates, like *Telefon* and *Munition,* were nationalized and turned into *Fernsprecher* and *Rüstung.* Language also reflects the culture in the interpretations given to classes of words—the feelings and needs that individuals in the cultures have toward the symbols and sounds themselves. The extensiveness and imaginativeness expressed in vocabulary are demonstrated in the jargon used to describe a primary American cultural trait: regard for money. Common words used to designate U.S. currency include: *lettuce, cabbage, green stuff, moola, lucre, shekels, jack, loot, dough, booly,* and *mazuma.* Another overwhelming vocabulary is associated with inebriation: *pickled, high, plastered, potted, oiled, tight, crocked, soused, polluted, swacked, stinking,* and the like. Undoubtedly the terms for money reflect its importance in our culture. The richness of language referring to states of intoxication may be explained more by the ambivalent status of that state: It both attracts and repels us.

_____
* W. I. Thomas, *Primitive Behavior,* New York: McGraw-Hill, 1936.

Like perceptions and attitudes, socially transmitted meanings have affective as well as cognitive components. In all cultures and the subcultures within them, there are many words and concepts that arouse feeling states which are consonant with the dominant values of the group. In the United States, for example, words like *home, mother, God* and *freedom* evoke favorable emotional reactions, while *liar, sissy, dictator,* and *traitor* arouse unpleasant feelings. This topic is considered further in relation to collective behavior (Chapter 16) and social movements (Chapter 17).

Thus our concepts and the language that symbolizes them reflect to a considerable degree the culture from which they spring. Significant aspects of the culture, such as values and ways of thinking, are expressed in verbal concepts and communicated to the child, whose development is thereby patterned. Indeed, the conceptualization of these social norms influences all the other dynamics of social behavior—learning and thinking, perception, motivation, and the formation and change of attitudes and values.

SOCIOLINGUISTICS

A functional approach to language which deals with its social and cultural usages has recently been taken by sociologists, anthropologists, and social psychologists who have an interest in language as a social vehicle. Research in this area has been concerned with a number of problems: how language can affect social interaction, how it unites and divides human groups, how it differs for subcultures, and, in the spirit of nationalism, how language can function as a force for nation building. This approach, called *sociolinguistics,* deals with social influences on language (which consists of phonology, morphology, syntax, and grammar). A related area is the *sociology of language,* or the role language plays in society, which considers such questions as the degree to which language may function as a facilitator or an obstacle to social interaction. The distinction between these terms is arbitrary, but in general terms sociolinguistics is more micro, or narrow, and the sociology of language is more macro, or broad, in interest. Another relevant term is the *social psychology of language,* which refers to the reciprocal effects between language and group cohesion, role behavior, and attitudes, among other relations.

There is a perennial debate as to which comes first: social structure or language. More fundamental than either, perhaps, is the kind of organization resulting from the individual's cognitions within the biological and cultural universe. Few observers question, however, that by the second or third year of life, language is the primary instrument of the culture the individual uses to organize experiences encountered in the environment.

Issues in Language Survival

Since the industrial revolution of the 18th and 19th centuries, large-scale migration and conflicts of national loyalties have raised the question of official language maintenance and the related problems of bilingualism and linguistic dominance. In recent years, rapid travel and communications among nations and groups have closed the distances between them and given a sense of urgency to such problems as the tension between speakers of Flemish and French in Belgium and the search in India for a national language, with the resulting tenuous status of Hindi. A variety of responses—rival movements for one language or another, decrees setting literacy standards, and official policies on dual languages—have been made to cope with these problems. Switzerland has functioned as a trilingual state for centuries, and in other countries governments have imposed one language by decree or encouraged it by education and assimilation. In the Soviet Union most of the 16 republics retain their native languages, but Russian is the official means of communication. In the United States, immigrant groups have varied in the extent to which they have retained their original languages. Pennsylvania Germans living in rural areas still speak a "home" dialect two centuries after their arrival in North America, for example.

When different national strains exist in a country, bilingualism can be a major issue. Canada is currently attempting to achieve a truly bilingual national status, although the French and English cultures have remained distinct, existing side by side. In cities like Montreal and Ottawa, where the two languages co-exist, the result is a *stable bilingualism* somewhat similar to that found on the language frontiers of Switzerland. In contrast, the bilingualism of the United States has been unstable. In the Eastern and Southern European enclaves of cities in the Northeast and Scandinavian and German "islands" in the Midwest, the first generation may never really move beyond the native language, the second generation tries to forget it, and in the third generation there may be some "haloization" of the original culture and language (Fishman, 1972).

The language problems of migrants to the United States who tend to retain their own languages, such as the Spanish-speaking Mexican Americans and Puerto Ricans, can become a matter of public controversy. For some observers, the U.S. Department of Education mandate to provide instruction in basic subjects in an immigrant child's native language threatened to impose a burden on some school districts. The regulation was lifted in the early days of the Reagan administration.

Language Integrity

The close relation of nationalism and a linguistic identity was demonstrated by Norway when, in establishing itself as a nation-state early in the 20th century, it set certain orthographic standards to distinguish its language from Swedish and Danish. More recently, all street signs in Libya appeared exclusively in Arabic to demonstrate the country's separateness from the Western world.

Worldwide concern with national language integrity has followed the trend to use English as an international language, although it is spoken by less than an eighth of the world's population. Its universality is not hard to understand. The British Empire held a dominant position at the turn of the century, and after World War II the United States in effect imposed a Pax Americana on the world, through a diffusion of arms, mass communications, and commercial methods, and movements of officials, tourists, and multinational business executives and technicians. As a result English has emerged as the *lingua franca* for much of the world—at least as the language of business. It is the official means of communication in most air traffic, and words like *drugstore, okay, weekend, coke, hot dog,* and *jazz* have penetrated nearly all Western languages.

The ascendancy of English has met with resistance from established nationalities as well as from emerging nations such as Tanzania, where Kiswahili has a tentative status as a national language. The French, whose language at one time was regarded as the international tongue, officially resent the anglicization of their vocabulary. Latin Americans also are not happy about the diluting effects of English on the Spanish langauge.

Speech, Class, and Ethnicity

Social class, identified as the major subcultural determinant of behavior in Chapter 3, imposes differences on the ways people who speak the same language communicate. English language studies in both Britain and the United States have found subtle differences in the vocabularies of the middle and upper classes, and even greater differences for the lower class (A. S. C. Ross, 1967). The effects of social class on speech socialization in Britain were studied by Bernstein (1971), who found that, compared to lower-class parents, those in the middle class stress the importance of style and propriety: "The language-use of the middle class is rich in personal, individual qualifications, and its form implies sets of advanced logical operations; volume and tone and other non-verbal means of expression, although important, take second place." The complexities of this class difference also suggest that despite the assumed greater verbal stimulation for the middle-class child, the quality of the communication is as important as the amount. In taping the conversations of mothers and children, Bernstein found that middle-class parents placed more stress on cognitive responses, and working-class parents emphasized the affective component. Middle-class children tended to use more intricate grammar in their speech, including more passive verbs, adjectives, and adverbs. They used nouns with qualifiers, whereas the working-class children were more likely to depend on pronouns, which are more vague, and to use fewer modifying words and phrases. In an earlier study, Bernstein (1962) found a working-class preference for *you* as a symbol of identity with others, as compared to the middle-class use of *I* as a means of differentiating the self from others. For instance, *I believe* or *I mean* were contrasted to *you know* or *don't you think.*

Bernstein (1971) conceives of social structure as determining modes of speech. Social class belongingness is related to given ways of describing events, means of address (see Box 10–2), and style of abstraction. Beyond the subcultural factor is the specific situation confronting the individual speaker, which may cause a drift into one of two codes: restricted or elaborated. The *restricted code* is more simplistic and is generally confined to the person's status level or the in-group. It takes the form of implicit statements emphasizing the solidarity of the group—a married couple, a children's play group, a fraternity, or a delinquent gang. The content of the dialogue, according to Bernstein, tends to be "concrete, descriptive and narrative rather than analytical and abstract." The *elaborated code* is oriented to more formal and tenuous social relationships. The speaker must weigh the differences among members of the group and cannot take others' viewpoints for granted. Meanings must be explicit, and vocabulary and phrasing must be deliberately chosen.

While the middle class apparently moves between the two codes and the working class confines itself more or less to the restricted code, individual factors like intelligence can shape a preference for one or the other. The idea that codes can be identified with social class has not always been substantiated by research, which continues in both Britain and the United States. The complex relationship of social class to language code can be illustrated in a study of a minority language (usually the restricted code) against the powerful effect of the dominant or national language (the elaborated code), as in the relationship of Gaelic to English in parts of Scotland (Williamson & Van Eerde, 1980). Middle-class subjects tended to favor English in their speech, but a number were troubled about the possible extinction of Gaelic and its ancient heritage. As a major aspect of culture, language becomes part of the self, and in bilingual areas language loyalty is often emotionally charged.

Speech can reflect the need to secure status by using a vocabulary designed to shock or subdue associates. A study of social behavior in the card room of a college dormitory found that verbal play was in part a protest against middle-class norms but more the ritualized display of a "line" (no less than 12 different forms of "bullshitting" were catalogued) (Nellis & Graziano, 1975). Generally these verbal thrusts were used to project a self-image of "coolness."

The relation of ethnic subcultures to speech has been explored by Labov (1970a, 1970b), who compares black dialect (nonstandard English) with standard English. Recordings of street conversations with adolescent males in Harlem, for instance, showed shifts in verb form. After hearing the sentence "I asked Alvin if he knows how to play basketball," the subject repeated it as "I ax Alvin do he know how to play basketball." "I don't have any" would be "I don't got none." Though the use of equivalents for nouns and other parts of speech may not be a barrier to meaning, confusion can result from the use of singular verbs, such as "the boys am."

Dialect usually gives way to standard English if the child is introduced to a "normal" classroom situation, because the language children learn is the language they hear and the language that is expected of them. In nonintegrated classrooms, however, or where black community pressure has insisted on academic acceptance of nonstandard English, this assimilation process does not occur. The degree to which the use of dialect limits logical thinking is open to question, but continued use of nonstandard English inevitably places adult blacks at a disadvantage in the business and social world. Nevertheless, peer pressure and a desire to preserve black identity may encourage adolescents to continue its use. Lower-class blacks have little incentive to emulate the speech of a majority society that has traditionally rejected them.

Similarly, Hispanics may retain an accent as a means of maintaining ethnic

Box 10–2
STATUS IN THE SECOND PERSON

Any student of a foreign language must recall the confusion in learning to distinguish between two forms of the second person. Whereas in English it is always *you,* in other languages it is *tu* and *usted, tu* and *vous, du* and *Sie,* and so on.

Presumably the Romans used *tu* for the population at large and *vos* for the emperor. So began a distinction which Roger Brown identifies as formal address, using *V (vos),* for persons of status and power, and *informal address* using *T (tu),* for family members, close friends, servants, or others to whom either solidarity or lower status would be appropriate.* English at one time had a distinction between the single *thou* and the plural *you.* (The Quakers, or Society of Friends, shocked their compatriots by using *thou*—later changed to *thee*—as a means of demonstrating the equality of all persons and at the same time expressing a feeling of group solidarity.)

As European society became more democratized, rigid distinctions based on social rank diminished. The dual usage remained as a means of demarcating those with whom one is familiar from those to whom distance and respect are due. Brown surveyed European students in the Boston area and found Germans as compared to French use the *T* form for remote relatives but are less likely to address fellow students as *T.* Italians extend the *T* to female students even on meeting them for the first time.

Gone almost completely is the nonreciprocal usage of *T* from employer to employee, master to servant, or priest to parishioner, with the lower-status person addressing the superior by *V.* This explicit institutionalization of social rank could hardly survive in a society marked by high mobility. Following World War II, the French army passed a regulation that officers should address enlisted men as *vous.* Part of the irritation encountered by the French in North Africa was due to their use of *tu* to natives, with the expectation of *vous* in return. Historical developments have an impact, as in the shift toward less formal address at the time of the French Revolution. Similarly, when Communism came to Yugoslavia the populace took to the comradely *T,* but as revolutionary zeal dwindled the distinction between *V* and *T* returned.

The English-speaking visitor may find this dual categorization baffling. One of the authors visiting his wife's relatives in Milan recalls his pain in trying to decide when to use *tu, voi,* and *Lei* (Italians use three forms of the second person). He soon learned how a sudden reversal of *T* and *V* can be a means of insult. An irate driver yells out of the window to another driver an epithet beginning with *T,* and when a wife uses *V* to her husband it is time for him either to pack his bags or mend his ways!

Although we avoid these problems in English, we often have to decide whether to use the first or last name. This choice becomes especially awkward when a friend moves from a position of equality to one of authority. On the whole, if English-speaking people aspire to the ideal of an equalitarian society, the goal may be easier because of the universal *you.*

_____

* R. Brown, *Psycholinguistics: Selected Papers* (New York: Free Press, 1970), pp. 302–335.

pride, but those who are upwardly mobile are likely to rid themselves of it. Ryan and Carranza (1975) investigated this by dividing 63 Mexican-American, black, and Anglo high school students into groups of roughly 20 members and asking them to judge the oral reading ability of their peers. Both in the school and in a simulated home setting, the standard English speakers were given more favorable ratings in personality rating scales. In neither environment did the students prefer accented English, although the ratings of users of accented English were less unfavorable in the home context. An experiment such as this can hardly demonstrate actual linguistic preference, but it does suggest that middle-class persons (as these subjects were) consider linguistic ability a means of social acceptance and mobility.

LANGUAGE AND THOUGHT

As a social vehicle, language makes possible the creation and transmission of a cultural heritage which gives us an understanding of the past and the present, as well as some ability to forecast the future. But our command of the environment is also enhanced by the role of language in our development of cognitive concepts and of thinking in general. Compared to the signaling reflexes animals are generally believed to possess (as noted in the first section of this chapter), symbolic language makes human communication infinitely richer, more subtle, and more complete.

When Klineberg (1954) reviewed evidence of the interdependence of language and thought, he concluded that it is likely that "an individual born into any particular culture will think in terms of the medium of expression current in his society and . . . the nature of his thinking will be affected thereby." Language is a device for categorizing experience. What people notice (or the stimuli they attend to) in a complex world and subsequently think and talk about is partly a function of the linguistic patterns in their sociocultural settings. The relationship between language and thought is not simple, however. It has been reported, for example, that the Trobriand language has no words to express causal relationships (Lee, 1940). Does this mean that the language reflects—or results from—the Trobrianders' lack of interest in motives, purposes, and causality in general, as Lee suggests? Or does it mean that they lack causal concepts because their language does not contain them? Or both?

Communication often breaks down between groups within the same culture, such as the struggles of black youths to function with nonstandard English in an urbanized, postindustrial society noted above (Labov, 1970a, 1970b). In Africa, certain societies have secret languages which have been institutionalized for special groups or contexts (Doob, 1961), much like the lingos in U.S. society of jazz musicians, homosexuals, truck drivers, or adolescent gangs, which use language that is intelligible only to the initiated. Between cultures with different national languages, there can be even more acute communication difficulties. Despite provisions for instantaneous translations, misunderstandings which are due to differences not so much in ideological positions as in word meanings often arise in United Nations sessions.

The Case for Linguistic Determination of Thought

There is a continuing debate concerning the degree to which the language conditions the thought structure of members of a society. More investigation of linguistic patterns is necessary before definite ideas of their relationship to systems of thought, causality, and value orientation can be formulated.

Undoubtedly, categories of space, time, movement, and various modes of perception are limited by language. Western languages are particularly oriented to time; when we say "The man is coming," the emphasis is on the present. Students of foreign languages often have difficulty learning the eight or ten verb conjugations expected in a course. The Kwakiutl, an Indian tribe of western Canada studied by Ruth Benedict (see Chapter 2), may be more interested in whether or not the subject is visible rather than in any time considerations: "The visible man is coming." For other cultures the important question is whether the subject is present or absent, animate or inanimate. A possible counterpart is the use in various Western languages of gender, whereby nouns are masculine, feminine, or neuter, although this distinction no longer has functional significance. In French, for example, the word or symbol *la constitution* does not lose its abstraction simply because it has a feminine article. Thus it cannot always be said that language structure influences abstract thinking.

Apparently there is no close correlation between the structure of a language and the type of culture represented. Primitive societies may have as complex, or even more intricate, languages as those of more advanced cultures. Undoubtedly, each language has its advantages. If there is a superiority in the Western communication system, it is the ease of symbolizing certain kinds of abstractions.

The viewpoint that people's thought structures, as well as their general culture patterns, are conditioned by the vocabulary and syntax of the language they speak was introduced by Edward Sapir (1921) and developed by Benjamin Whorf (1952, 1956). In what has become known as the *Sapir-Whorf Theory,* our whole mode of perceiving and thinking is said to be conditioned by linguistic symbols:

> . . . the linguistic system (in other words, the grammar) of each language is not merely a reproducing instrument for voicing ideas but rather is itself the shaper of ideas, the program and guide for the individual's mental activity, for his analysis of impressions, for his synthesis of his mental stock in trade. (Whorf, 1952, p. 21)

Thus science may have developed in Western culture because the languages have provided for abstractions and time consciousness—which predispose people to collect records with meticulousness and curiosity. Experimentation would unquestionably be more difficult for, say, the Hopi, who have different concepts of mathematics and time.

Whorf's *linguistic-relativity hypothesis* maintains that the individual is only in partial contact with reality because of the limitations in his or her language system. This hypothesis is probably overdrawn because Whorf studied somewhat exotic language groups, particularly those of North American Indians (Carroll, 1964). In explaining linguistic relativity, various approaches are taken in the comparison of one language with another, as well as in the study of the usefulness of a specific language in meeting the needs of individuals. Presumably most if not all languages fulfill the needs of the members of a society, even though some languages have not permitted or encouraged certain types of thought patterns. An Aristotle or an Einstein might (or might not) have found intellectual limitations in, for instance the Mayan culture or language.

Many psychologists have insisted that thought goes on in linguistic patterns. G. H. Mead, an empirically minded sociologist, was one of the first to formulate such a view. According to Mead, thinking is "inner conversation." The behaviorists emphasized from the first that thinking is subvocal speech or "talking to oneself." They saw the physical basis of talking as not so much in the tongue and larynx as in the muscular responses of the cheek, tongue, and throat, a thesis never proven experimentally.

The case for linguistic influence on thinking does not depend, however, on demonstration of muscular movements. Our best psychological information indicates that thinking goes on in terms of some combination of words, concepts, images, gestures, and feelings—but it does not necessarily depend on any of these. All of them—whether basically verbal, visual, or emotional—have arisen in a context of social communication. Hence it can be said that the form or process of thinking, as well as its content, is greatly influenced by language.

Semantics: The Study of Meaning

Along with the advantages verbal communication offers a society, there are disadvantages. These have been stressed by the semanticists, including Count Alfred Korzybski (1933), the founder of this school of thought. The scope of semantics is conveyed by Hayakawa (1941) as follows:

> From the moment Mr. Smith switches on an early morning news broadcast to the time he falls asleep at night over a novel or a magazine, he is, like all other people living under modern civilized conditions, swimming in words. . . .
>
> Whether he realizes it or not, however, Mr. Smith is affected every hour of his life not only by the words he hears and uses, *but also by his unconscious assumptions about language.* . . . Words and the way he takes them determine his beliefs, his prejudices, his ideals, his aspirations—they constitute the moral and intellectual atmosphere in which he lives, in short, his semantic environment. If he is constantly absorbing false and lying words . . . he may be constantly breathing a poisoned air without knowing it. (pp. 7–10)

Semantics deals with the general problem of meaning. Our communicative messages convey different kinds of content, and each has special problems of meaning. Doob (1961) designated these categories as:

1. *Information*—verified or verifiable facts about any object, person, or event in the universe: "The flight for Buffalo departs at 8:55 P.M."
2. *Values*—normative statements about the superiority or desirability of objects or relationships: "Shakespeare's poetry is more beautiful than Keats's is."
3. *Action*—advisory or imperative statements about "overt behavior to be initiated or completed": "Vote the straight Democratic ticket."

Each of these types of statements poses semantic problems, particularly those that make evaluations.

In their pursuit of exact meanings, semanticists are concerned with clarifying the distinction between *extensional* and *intensional* meaning, or between denotation and connotation. Extensional meaning is what words stand for or *denote;* intensional meaning is what is suggested or *connoted* inside one's head. One of the greatest pitfalls of linguistic communication is mistaking intensional meanings for extensional ones, or assuming that words with strong pleasant or unpleasant connotations reflect objective reality rather than subjective feelings.

Another way of stating the point is to say that a word refers to some person, object, or event, which is called a *referent,* much as a map symbolizes or represents a certain piece of territory. If the connotation of a word diverges greatly from its referent, the word is likely to be misleading or confusing. This is particularly true when words acquire strong emotional connotations.

Statements in the platforms of political parties make abundant use of words having pleasant and unpleasant connotations, such as *friendly firmness, cooperation, abundance, appeasement,* or *enslavement,* in efforts to win a following without making specific commitments. An important part of propaganda analysis is identifying such extensionally meaningless items and evaluating their effects on people.

One attempt to deal with the meaning of concepts, feelings, and attitudes is the *Semantic Differential Scale* described in Chapter 8 (Osgood, Suci, & Tannenbaum, 1957). This measurement instrument provides a means for rating concepts on a scale according to evaluative categories or dimensions (good-bad), potency (strong-weak), and activity (active-passive). The individual's rating of such bipolar adjectives provides a measure of individual differences in the meaning of concepts. Factor analysis (a statistical technique designed to explore the clusters or interrelationships of attributes) is applied to the *polarity* (distance from the center of semantic space, or semantic neutrality) of a concept and the *distances* between concepts. Thus the meaning of objects and concepts is determined on a tridimensional scale, as illustrated in Figure 10–2.

In recent years the semantic study of meaning has focused on the more abstract aspects of syntax or grammar. The purpose is to examine the relationships among verbal symbols and to expand Osgood's type of analysis, notably the search for semantic clusters. Another development, which began in the late 1960s, is *ethnomethodology,* which probes beneath the surface of

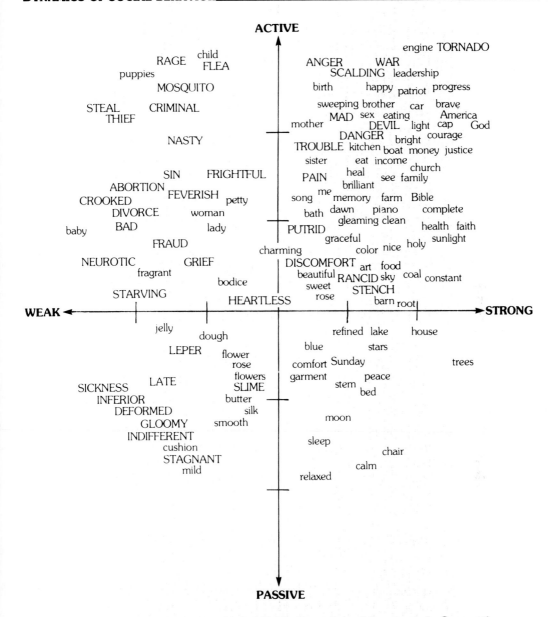

Figure 10–2. Example of an Individual's Location of Concepts in Semantic Differential Space

Locations of selected concepts in the semantic differential space defined by three scales: strong–weak, active–passive, and good–bad. Concepts rated good are in lower-case letters, concepts rated bad are in capitals.

Source: J. J. Jenkins et al., "An Atlas of Semantic Profiles for 360 Words," *American Journal of Psychology,* 1958, *71,* 688–699, reprinted in J. B. Carroll, *Language and Thought* (Englewood Cliffs, N.J.: Prentice-Hall, 1964), p. 104.

everyday reality in communicative habits and investigates minutely what lies below the surface in arriving at our norms, or how we process culture and social structure (Cicourel, 1974). According to the ethnomethodologist, much of our speech takes reality for granted. For example, when the patron tells the barber, "Cut my hair short," there may not be as much vagueness as when the politician speaks of "freedom for all Americans," but both messages ask the hearer to supply contextual information (Mehan & Wood, 1975). Words like *short* or *freedom* are defined according to the background and need system of each individual.

However different their approaches to meaning, semanticists are all engaged in the analysis of language. From Korzybski to the present, they are most sensitive to the problems of meaning in abstractions such as democracy, security, or happiness. One solution is to provide *operational definitions,* or to define these terms according to what they actually do in, say, an equation (see Chapter 1). Functional definitions of this kind are not easy to achieve, however, because of the nature of abstraction and the vested interest of the communicator.

NONVERBAL COMMUNICATION

While language is the most facile means of communication between people, nonverbal communication through gestures, facial expressions, bodily position, and movement also conveys meanings. Used alone as a substitute for language or with verbalization in interpersonal relationships, nonverbal communication is an expressive means for enhancing meaning and conveying impressions to others, as was noted in Chapter 6. Fast (1972) considers the way people move and position their bodies to be so authentic as a symbolic means of communication that he calls it *body language.* Another term for this is *kinesics,* a technique for studying both large and small muscular movements devised by Birdwhistell (1960). Using *kinegraphs,* he defines significant motions, ranging from movement of the eyelids to the hands and feet, as they function in interpersonal communication.

Some linguists and anthropologists have suggested that symbolic speech is derived from gestures (see Box 10–3). G. H. Mead (1934) attached great significance to them, considering the gesture as the basic element in communication. To Mead, a gesture is a "truncated" act, an act cut short, because it is responded to and does not need to be consummated.

Cross-cultural comparisons show variations in gestural expressions of greeting, assent, dissent, beckoning, affection, dislike, and so on. Therefore gestures cannot be considered a type of natural expression; their special meanings as symbols or abstractions of attributes are determined by historical and cultural influences. This cultural determination was brought out clearly in a study of the gestures of Italian and Jewish immigrants and their descendants by Efron and Foley (1947). Traditional Italian and Jewish gestures were found to disappear as the individuals became assimilated into American life. A recent study of nonverbal communication among Jews and Episcopalians in their respective places of worship showed few differences in gestures (although women in both groups gestured more than men) but statistically significant differences appeared in touching or tactile contact, with Jews displaying more of this behavior (Shuter, 1979).

The kiss is another means of nonverbal communication which can be considered a type of gesture. Never in recent centuries has kissing been so universal as it is today. But the meaning and the technique vary, as in the deep kisses between lovers, a presidential candidate lightly bestowing this endearment in an effort to gain votes, or two middle-aged women who meet and incline "the planes of their cheeks . . . close their eyes in a split-second transport of fraudulent bliss and smack their lips minutely upon nothing" (Morrow, 1977).

Facial expressions also function as nonverbal communication, particularly in perceptions, as noted in Chapter 6. Compared to gestures, facial expressions of emotion appear to be more standardized. Ekman (1978) found remarkable similarities among different national groups in identifying photographs depicting emotional expression (happiness, disgust, surprise, etc.). On a videotape, subjects from different cultures also showed similarities when they were alone, but a group setting encouraged the Japanese, for example, to mask their feelings more than the Americans did.

The use of bodily expression as a means of communication has been studied by Edward Hall (1959; Hall & Hall, 1972). He includes not only gestures and facial expressions but posture, gait, dress, and the person's approach to space and time. (Some of Hall's ideas on the relation between the handling of space and socialization are considered in Chapter 19, in the section on the environment.)

There are almost countless ways in which spatial relationships are used to communicate (see Box 10–4). Our sense of privacy and territoriality, which was described in Chapter 4, is largely mediated through nonverbal communication (Altman, 1975).

Various forms of nonverbal communication have been categorized as action language and object language by Ruesch and Kees (1956). *Action language* refers to all movements that are not employed directly as signals. Smiling, eating, walking, or closing a door not only serve the individual's needs but are meaningful acts to those who perceive them. *Object language* includes all material things that communicate something to the perceiver. A store display window, the type of dress one wears, debris scattered on a lawn—all make a statement for the observer. The statement may be intentional, as with the studied attractiveness of the store window, or unintentional, as with the blond hair the bald husband discovers on his brunette wife's dress. Object language may be very important in art, archaeology, or history, as it is possible to reconstruct a set of symbolic relationships from artifacts.

In some situations, however, our communication is restrained. Staring at another person generally is frowned on; at least, eye movements have to be controlled in Western cultures. A woman visiting a country with a Latin culture, such as France or Italy, is likely to find men are less inhibited about staring—and touching and pinching—than American males are.

Box 10–3
SAYING IT WITH GESTURES

Italians, Spaniards, and other Latins use gestures as a major means of communication. Americans use them much less often, but a number have come to the United States through waves of immigration. Unlike native languages, gestures are not obliterated in their new setting, although they may be changed in meaning.

Desmond Morris and his colleagues analyzed 20 gestures by comparing their use in 40 locations in western and southern Europe.* Many of these gestures could be traced back to ancient times.

The Fingertips Kiss

Like several gestures, the fingertips kiss was more ritualized in earlier times. It generally communicates praise or adoration, but in localities as far apart as Sicily and Sweden it can be a greeting. For a few, it refers to eating.

The Fingers Cross

Originally, the fingers cross gesture probably was a version of making the sign of the cross. Today the gesture has no less than six meanings, but for most people it symbolizes protection. The idea that crossing one's fingers would bring good luck or provide a defense against bad luck spread to the American colonies.

The Nose Thumb

The nose thumb usually conveys the idea of mockery. The gesture had diverse origins, all negative, such as a "deformed salute" or the idea that "something smells bad." These meanings linger on.

The Forearm Jerk

In Mediterranean areas the forearm jerk comes across as a sexual insult, a kind of "up yours." It is related to the gesture of holding up the erect middle finger (which the Romans referred to as the impudent finger, or *digitus impudicus*). In Britain the gesture is more of a sexual comment whereby males indicate to one another that a woman is physically exciting. In parts of Scandinavia and Central Europe, the display of muscle communicates the idea of masculine strength.

The Thumbs Up

In ancient Rome thumbs up (as compared to thumbs down) was supposedly used by spectators to show approval for a gladiator. But many Italians claim they picked it up from the American GIs in World War II to communicate "OK." This meaning is current for most Europeans. The gesture can also stand for the number one, or hitchhiking, and in a few spots in the Mediterranean it may be a sexual insult.

The other 15 gestures Morris et al. studied run the gamut from the specialized V for victory sign (which has sexual significance if the palm is turned *away* from the observer), to simple gestures like touching the ear, which has at least seven different meanings, depending on locale. Its most universal meaning may be found in Italy, where it signifies effeminacy.

---

* Desmond Morris et al., *Gestures: Their Origins and Distribution* (London: Jonathan Cape Ltd., 1979).

Box 10–4
INTERPRETING THE SOUNDS OF SILENCE

Edward Hall, one of the pioneers in studying nonverbal communication, has categorized American business and social relations as taking place at four main distances: intimate, personal, social and public.* Each of these distances has a near and a far phase, and the volume of the voice changes as the distance does.

Intimate distance varies from immediate contact with another person to a distance of 6 to 18 inches and characterizes most private activities, such as making love. At this distance people may be overwhelmed by sensory contact with others—body heat, tactile stimuli, the aroma of perfume, even breathing sounds all "literally envelop" the other person. Even at the far phase, people remain within touching distance. This kind of behavior is too close for strangers, and embarrassing situations can result when the spatial norms are inadvertently transgressed, as can happen on a subway train at the rush hour.

In the second zone—*personal distance*—the close phase varies from 1½ to 2½ feet. This distance usually separates husbands and wives in public. The far phase, or 2½ to 4 feet, is the distance in the usual spatial patterns in conversation.

The third zone, *social distance,* is used during most business transactions or such encounters as dealings with a clerk or repairman. Except for cocktail parties or conventions, this is the distance for conversations at social events. It also gives the effect of domination, as with the teacher over the student or the boss over the secretary. The far phase of the third zone, 7 to 12 feet, is most likely to be found in an executive office where status needs are important.

The fourth zone, or *public distance,* is for communicating impersonally. Visiting dignitaries and U.S. presidents, for whom not only status but security can be important, usually remain at this distance.

Two types of Americans who know how to exploit the unwritten, unspoken conventions of eye and distance are pitchmen and panhandlers. Both take advantage of the fact that once explicit eye contact is established it is rude to look away, because to do so means to brusquely dismiss the other person and his or her needs. Once having caught the eye of a mark the panhandler locks on, not letting go until the relation moves through the public zone, the social zone, the personal zone and, finally into the intimate sphere, where people are most vulnerable.

---

* E. T. Hall and M. R. Hall, "The Sounds of Silence," *Playboy Magazine,* 1971; reprinted in V. P. Clark, P. A. Eschholz, and A. R. Rosa (Eds.), *Language: Introductory Readings,* 2nd ed. (New York: St. Martin's Press, 1977), pp. 453–465.

SUMMARY

It is the ability to communicate symbolically, more than anything else, that differentiates humans from animals. Studies of isolates or individuals in atypical environments and of animals in human society illustrate this critical differential. A commitment of the psycholinguist is to analyze the communication process from its input or source, through the encoding of the message, to the receiver's role in determining its destination or output.

Structurally, language consists of phonemes and morphemes. The "conceptual structure" as outlined by Chomsky and others relates to both innate and learned elements.

Through language the child becomes acquainted with his or her social heritage and is introduced to the concepts and norms of the social group. Both the form and context of human thought are in large measure functions of language, which in turn reflects basic features of the culture. Relatively new areas of intensive research are sociolinguistics, and the sociology of language, in which the problems of language survival and integrity in response to nationalism and other cultural demands are salient. The influence of class and ethnicity on language has had implications for minority rights and other sociocultural issues.

For all human beings, language influences the thought structure. Even the nature of one person's relationship to another is fraught with ambiguity when *you* is the only form of address. Most European languages provide two or three forms of the pronoun to make a better distinction. Symbolic thinking and communication offer disadvantages as well as advantages to a society, as students of semantics have indicated. Words may lose touch with their referents or may become so abstract that they no longer convey meaning. There also are nonverbal ways to communicate.

This discussion of language as the means by which most social interaction is structured and communicated leads to consideration of the nature of social interaction and the influence of groups in Part III. Persuasibility, particularly, is related to the power of group pressure as an agent of social influence, the topic of Chapter 11.

WORDS TO REMEMBER

Communication. Process by which information (ideas, feelings, etc.) is exchanged through verbal and nonverbal means. The process usually involves encoding information, channeling a message, and decoding information.

Ethnomethodology. A movement or school of sociology and social psychology focusing on the meaning of behavior and its subcomponents. In communication, it investigates the meaning below conventional speech or probes into what is taken for granted.

Kinesics. Study of large and small body movements, commonly referred to as *body language.*

Language. A culturally structured and transmitted system of imparting messages, most often through the medium of sound.

Linguistic integrity. The goal (or process) of purifying a language of dialect, outmoded speech, or foreign words.

Morpheme. Minimal unit of speech which is identifiable and meaningful.

Noise. Any disturbance or barrier to communication.

Phoneme. Minimal sound unit which usually has no meaning attached.

Phonetics. The science of speech sounds, commonly referred to as the study of pronunciation and the acoustic properties of human communication.

Psycholinguistics. A basic approach to the study of language and communication; analysis of codes, messages, and speech development, including the socialization of speech.

Referent. The object in the real world to which a verbal symbol refers.

Sapir-Whorf theory. The notion that the world can be viewed through a linguistic structure (as conditioned by the culture); sometimes referred to as *linguistic relativity.*

Semantics. The study of meaning.

Sociolinguistics. The study of the cultural and social aspects of language and communication. Often the term refers to specific speech patterns (phonology, etc.), as compared to such broader issues as language and group conflict.

QUESTIONS FOR DISCUSSION

1. What studies have been made of animals in human settings? What are their implications, if any, for human speech?

2. Describe the five steps in the communication process and their functions.

3. What is the significance of approaches to language like phonetics?

4. Compare morphology and phonology.

5. What is Chomsky's contribution to linguistics? Why is his theory somewhat controversial?

6. What are the major findings on language acquisition in children, including concept development?

7. To what extent are people dependent on nonverbal communication? Give some examples that have come to your attention.

8. How does the colloquial language reflect American culture, as compared to other languages or cultures you have studied?

9. What are some of the major differences between preliterate and advanced languages? In what ways are they similar, if any?

10. What is the problem of language maintenance, or survival?

11. In what ways can dialects or minority languages become a social or political issue?

12. Does language structurally determine thought? How?

13. Explain the Sapir-Whorf hypothesis, and give some arguments for and against it.

14. What is semantics? To what degree has it been a useful contribution to the study of language? What possible social and political applications does it have?

READINGS

Brown, R. *Words and Things.* New York: Free Press, 1958.
    A classic on the social psychology of language, pleasantly written.

Carroll, J. B. *Language and Thought.* Englewood Cliffs, N.J.: Prentice Hall, 1964.
    A brief but informative treatment by a well-known linguist.

Chomsky, N. *Language and the Mind.* New York: Harcourt Brace Jovanovich, 1968.
    Not easy reading, but an eminent treatise on a controversial subject.

Cicourel, A. V. *Cognitive Sociology.* New York: Free Press, 1974.
    Language, meaning and their relation to social structure from the ethnomethodological viewpoint.

Clark, H. H., and Clark, E. V. (Eds.). *Psychology and Language.* New York: Harcourt Brace Jovanovich, 1977.
    Textbook on the psycholinguistic approach to nearly all phases of language.

Clark, V. P., Eschholz, P. A., and Rosa, A. F. (Eds.). *Language: Introductory Readings.* 3rd ed. New York: St. Martin's Press, 1981.
    Excellent set of readings on such topics as animal communication, systems of grammar, regionalism, and body language.

Fishman, J. A. *The Sociology of Language.* Rowley, Mass.: Newbury House, 1972.
    An interdisciplinary approach to language maintenance and shift, among other topics.

Forsdale, L. *Perspectives on Communication.* Reading, Mass.: Addison-Wesley Publishing Co., 1981.
    An excellent introduction to historical backgrounds and, especially, communicative models and codes.

Goodenough, W. H. *Culture, Language, and Society.* Menlo Park, Calif.: Benjamin/Cummings Publishing Co., 1981.
    An anthropologist ably presents the cross-cultural approach to language.

Hornby, P. A. (Ed.). *Bilingualism: Psychological, Social, and Educational Implications.* New York: Academic Press, 1977.
    Studies of bilingual persons and groups: advantages and disadvantages.

Miller, G. A. (Ed.). *Communication, Language and Meaning.* New York: Basic Books, 1973.
    Contributions represent a number of viewpoints on development and structure of language.

Scheflen, A. E. *Body Language and Social Order.* Englewood Cliffs, N.J.: Prentice-Hall, 1972.
    Well illustrated, this book is an engaging account of outer behavior as a communication system.

West, F. *The Way of Language.* New York: Harcourt Brace Jovanovich, 1975.
    An enjoyable introduction to the history, structure, and meaning of language.

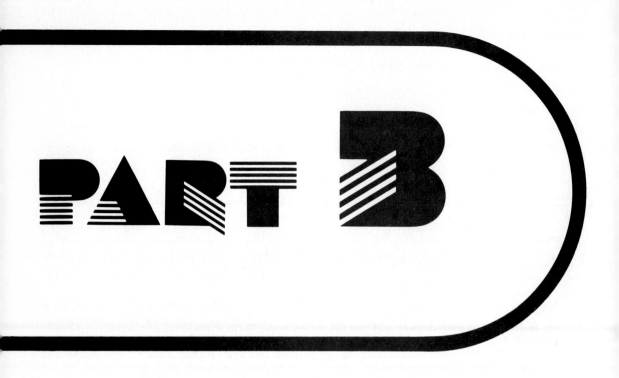

Taken together, Parts II and III represent the heart of social psychology, which has focused on group processes since its inception as a field of study. Along with an intensive study of attitudes, scores of social psychologists have been involved in investigating the nature of groups and what keeps them together or makes them fall apart. They also are concerned with how individuals are attracted to other people and the influences people have on one another.

Most social life takes place in dyads (two-person interactions), triads (three-person groups), and other primary groups. Our examination of these interactions and the processes and structure of groups starts in Chapter 11 with an overview of social influence, which exerts group pressure to encourage such behaviors as compliance, conformity, and imitation on the one hand and prosocial or helping behavior on the other.

Chapter 12 defines and classifies groups and shows how their structure and functions can be examined through such techniques as sociometry, group dynamics, interactional analysis, and game theory. A principal focus is on the rewards and costs of interactions between people, as well as group reward structures oriented to individual achievement, competition, or cooperation.

The relation between interpersonal attraction and group cohesion is spelled out in Chapter 13, which considers the factors at work in group problem solving and describes the balance and exchange theories as means of studying people's interactions in groups. Chapters 14 and 15 expand knowledge of group processes by describing how behavior in groups is channeled and patterned by the multiple social roles people take and examining the roles of followers and leaders as they are related to various interpretations of leadership.

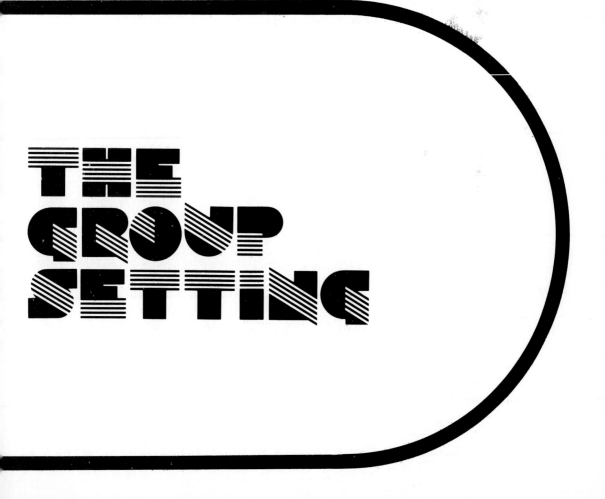

THE GROUP SETTING

SOCIAL INFLUENCE

Social influence represents a kind of power whose use and misuse are at the heart of the issue of conforming or yielding behavior in groups of all sizes: from interpersonal relationships, to organizations, to entire societies. Group pressure operates both in real life and in laboratory experiments as a potent influence on the behavior of individuals, generally encouraging conformity and compliance.

In establishing the reciprocal relation between the individual and the sociocultural setting and examining the dynamics of social behavior in the preceding parts of this text, we have indicated that the problems facing society stem from people's behavior. We have also implied that the solutions to these problems are to be found in people's cognition and motivation, and that changes in social conditions ultimately depend on change in the perceptions, attitudes, and motives of the people who make up the society. In behaviorist terms, we have demonstrated that people act in accordance with the rewards and punishments which their behavior elicits from others in any particular situation, and in social interaction terms we have shown that the behavior of people is influenced by both their environment and their personality structure. To demonstrate how these processes work, we have examined people's perceptions of themselves and others, the nature of attitudes and how they are formed and changed, and how communication utilizes language as a medium individuals can use to control selection of the stimuli they will attend to and to classify their experiences.

In this chapter we turn from emphasis on the individual to examine how larger social units influence people's attitudes and behavior. Among the processes involved in group behavior, perhaps the strongest is conflict, which generally revolves around patterns of competition. Considerable research by social psychologists has focused on the analysis of these forms of rivalry and accommodation, which account for much of our interpersonal behavior. Equally important, however, are varieties of cooperation such as the helping or prosocial behavior discussed in this chapter.

Generally the first three chapters of this part are concerned with the micro processes of interpersonal behavior as they operate in the small group, particularly primary groups (see Chapter 12). Part IV will be oriented more to the macro processes of both competition and cooperation as they apply to secondary groups and such phenomena as collective behavior, social movements, and ethnic and international tensions. An understanding of how these processes operate in the smaller social units thus provides a basis for investigating them in the larger society.

This chapter begins with a discussion of the limitations on the effects of persuasion on people's attitude structures and behavior which were described in Chapter 9. The dimensions of social power are considered as the basis for the strength of social influence and the motivating effects of group pressure. Evidence of the effects of group pressure on the individual in producing conformity or compliance, which research has shown to have negative effects on behavior and attitudes, and alternatively in producing of prosocial or helping behavior is examined. The final section, on the factors in the individual and the group (or sociocultural) setting which affect the exertion of group pressure, focuses on group size and personal characteristics such as public commitment, consistency, and status to suggest the circumstances in which social influence is most likely to have an effect on people's attitudes and behaviors.

THE LIMITS OF PERSUASION

Western societies have a tendency to rely on attitude-change procedures such as education, propaganda, or petitions to bring about social change, although change in a person's attitude does not necessarily mean that that person's behavior will be changed accordingly, and changing one person's—or many people's—behaviors may not ensure eventual change in social conditions. In fact, there is evidence to suggest that persuasion is not very effective. The U.S. government, for example, has had only minimal success in getting people to drop harmful personal habits such as smoking or drinking alcohol to excess, despite the millions that have been spent on persuasive efforts.

A study to determine the least costly way of decreasing automobile fatalities found that the cost of driver education necessary to save a single life in 1980 was approximately $135,000; it was much more efficient to make seat belts mandatory on all vehicles, at a cost of $184 per life. Certain European nations and parts of Canada have gone a step further, to require that the seat belts be worn. In many cases such as this, government regulations of actions are more effective than persuasive attempts to change attitudes.

In combating mental illness and drug addiction, also, either medical help or environmental changes have proven more effective than attempts at persuasion. Educational programs such as Head Start have been partially effective in attempting to compensate for a disadvantaged home environment, but Kamin (1974) suggests that it is necessary to restructure both that environment and the educational system in order to produce significant change in this area. Propaganda and public education also have failed to have much effect on people's attitudes regarding social issues such as women's rights or racial and ethnic equality, despite federal legislation requiring equal educational and employment opportunities and an end to discriminatory practices. Extensive advertising and promotional campaigns may change the tastes or preferences of a few, but it is difficult to change the basic habits or attitudes of the majority of the people so that their private attitudes will be reflected in their public behavior.

Even though many commonly used persuasive techniques do not work, research has demonstrated that it is possible to change attitudes measurably and to effect minor changes in behavior, as shown by the evidence reported in Chapter 9. Under highly controlled experimental conditions, people can even be encouraged to act in questionable ways. In many of the group pressure studies examined in this chapter, when subjects are directly confronted by another person making a demand, they tend to respond in a compliant manner, and once having complied their attitudes toward that behavior may change.

DIMENSIONS OF SOCIAL POWER

Threats, punishments, rewards, and the like are based on the premise that one person is able to affect the life of another. Threats, for example, are promises to do harm; their credibility depends on the threatener's past history of carrying out threats, and the sources or basis of the threatener's power.

Simplistic ideas like Mao Tse Tung's pronouncement that all power flows from the end of the gun ignore the nature of the relationship between influencer and influencee, source and target, or superior and subordinate. If a hoodlum holds a gun to your head and tells you to be silent, you will comply only as long as the gun is pointed at your head. As soon as the hoodlum is out of gunshot range, you will yell at the top of your lungs. In a master-slave relationship, the master's freedom is as restricted as the slave's in the sense that the master must always keep the slave's behavior under surveillance and administer appropriate punishments whenever the slave fails to follow the rules.

In analyzing social power, furthermore, attention cannot be focused only on the person being influenced or on the person doing the influencing; it must consider the entire social structure. All social behavior is complex and is derived from multiple causes which are intermeshed with many other factors in the situation. It is similar to the concept of relativity, by which the movement of any entity being examined is understandable only in terms of its change relative to the rest of the system; a change in a particular element is influenced by and influences many other factors in the system.

Components of Social Power

Social power is a very complex matter, although everyone wields it in some form. Many definitions of the concept have been proposed, and there is little agreement as to its components. A thorough analysis is beyond the scope of this text, but it is necessary to consider the concept of power as it applies to social influence or group pressure.

In an attempt to make sense out of social behavior, attention has been focused on linear, causal explanations, without sufficient emphasis on the circular, reciprocal nature of all interpersonal situations (Swingle, 1976). In a simple causal explanation, at the most fundamental level person A is said to have power over person B to the extent that A can get B to do something that B would not do otherwise (Dahl, 1957). Power has also been defined as potential influence: One person (the source) is considered to have power if the source can change another person's (the target's) probable behavior. This power is defined as a change in the probability of an act occurring (or of compliance with a command) following the intervention of the source. According to this view, power resides in the source by virtue of the resources—physical, monetary, informational, charismatic, or whatever—that the source can marshal. Other definitions have been more inclusive; it could be argued, for example, that any interference with autonomy is a display of power.

Of course, a source's power varies from one situation to another. The greater the number of different situations in which the source can exert influence over the target, the greater the scope of the source's power. And the more targets the source can influence, the greater is the source's dominion of power. The cost to the source for exercising influence also enters into the calculations. The greater the cost to the source to use power, either because of direct costs (e.g., loss of money) or indirect costs (e.g., reduced prestige), the less powerful is the source considered to be (Tedeschi, Schlenker, & Bonoma, 1975).

Sources of Social Power

The various sources or bases of social power have been identified by Raven and Kruglanski (1970). Informational influence refers to the source's ability to alter the target's understanding of a situation. A physician can influence your behavior by pointing out possible complications of an untreated condition, or a friend might encourage you to select a different route for a trip by providing information about a scenic view you should not miss. The ability of the source to make special appeals to accepted authorities (such as a higher ranking military officer or a traffic judge) or to mutually valued social structures (such as the integrity of a family or a social club) also is a source of potential influence. The most straightforward bases of potential influence or power are those that permit the source to make contingent promises or threats. The source's ability to give the target something of value, or to expose the target to something unpleasant or take away present satisfactions, are obvious bases of social power.

Richard Chadwick's (1971) analysis focuses on the target, suggesting that every person is being pushed and pulled by society to develop a predictable adaptive, nondisruptive lifestyle which will support or at least not threaten the status quo. The target's power is defined in terms of power to resist these forces, or how far away from the pull of society the target wants to be. Raven (cited in Swingle, 1976) summarizes this position as follows: "A powerful person is one who determines where the stream of society is pulling him or her and then swims like hell to reach a point which is against the current."

Chadwick's theory defines power as the opposite of compliance and conformity, the focus of many experiments on social power. For example, Stanley Milgram's research (to be discussed in the following section) showed that people will obey a questionable authority to a terrifying extent, and they could be persuaded to expose another person to extremely painful—if not dangerous—conditions with minimal justification. Jack Brehm's (1972) reactance theory, which suggests that when people's perception of freedom is threatened or interfered with they become aroused and motivated to regain it (as explained in Chapter 9), is also relevant. Reactance theory, the research on obedience, and recent theories of power are all based on the concept that moving against encroachments on personal freedom is a motivational state. As Chadwick suggests, a person's success in moving against these restrictions characterizes that person's power. There are, of course, realistic limits to such a conception of power.

ATTITUDINAL AND BEHAVIORAL EFFECTS OF GROUP PRESSURE

As the section in Chapter 1 on the founders of social psychology indicated, during the early decades of the discipline the topic of social influence was predominant. The early theorists, especially Gustave LeBon, were fascinated with processes like *suggestion,* or the ability of one person to influence the behavior of another, and *imitation,* or the tendency of one person to copy the behavior of another. These social influence processes later were described by the term *social facilitation,* or the facilitating effects of the presence of another person or group on an individual's responses. The opposite, the inhibiting effects of other people, is called *social inhibition* (some examples are given in the section on group effects in Chapter 12).

When social influence takes the form of group pressure, it affects the establishment, maintenance, and change of people's attitudes and behavior for various reasons. An individual's basis for being influenced by another person, a group, or society can be tradition, convention, desire to be accepted, fear of physical harm, fear of rejection, desire not to look odd or strange, a predisposition to obey (or at least not to be disruptive), and so forth. The results of this influence most often produce diverse forms of conforming or compliant behavior: conformity, yielding, obedience, compliance, or imitation.

According to our cultural norms, we try to live up to the expectancies of the members of the groups with which we voluntarily affiliate or the ascribed roles of members of groups to which we are assigned on a biological basis such as sex or age (see Chapter 14). We recognize that if others are expected to behave in a manner which protects the group's existence (working toward group goals, respecting privileged information, supporting group activities, etc.), they have the right to expect the same of us. Living up to the perceived expectations of the group is a major source of group pressure which results in conforming or compliant behavior.

Regardless of a tendency to think of conformity as a negative characteristic, with conformers acting like sheep, placidly following more outgoing, independent people, *conventional* behavior is what holds our society together. Without convention, tradition, and other societal norms and codes, organized society would break down. We accept such uniform behavior, based on convention, but if everyone thought alike and were unwilling to entertain new ideas, it would be impossible to change a social system in order to correct inequities or to progress in any way.

The opposite of conformity is counterconformity or revolt, with nonconformity or independence between the extremes. An independent or nonconforming person evaluates the appropriateness of his or her behavior and attitudes in any particular situation, regardless of group pressure.

Commitment and Conformity

Everyone tends to conform to some extent, though they may be rigid about some of their beliefs and attitudes and flexible about others. Even rugged individualists can find themselves agreeing when they do not want to. This tendency to support someone else's opinions can be given a variety of explanations, such as tact, consideration of persons' feelings, avoidance of unpleasantness, or anticipation of some reward.

In extreme cases conformity needs are rooted in an inflexible authoritarianism. Such individuals follow orders beyond all dimensions of morality, like the Nazi, Adolf Eichmann, who asserted that in murdering several million Jews he was simply obeying orders, or the Watergate politicians who claimed they were only satisfying their obligations to the White House. Thus the relation between authority and conformity can have an ethical dimension (see Box 11–1).

It has been debated whether conformity is a personality trait or a response to a situation. There are three approaches to defining the concept (Kiesler, 1973):

1. It is an enduring personal characteristic; or in other words, "organization men are essentially born, not made, so their seduction to conformity comes without strain."
2. It is a tactical agreement with others for whatever advantage can be gained without any real change in conviction.
3. It includes something of both views, but more of the second. A change, likely to be permanent, in private as well as public opinion, takes place as a result of dialogue with the group.

Conformity is considered in Chapter 14 as an aspect of role behavior, which combines both personality and situational factors.

Box 11–1
SOCIAL RESPONSIBILITY VERSUS PERSONAL CONSCIENCE

Endorsements of the ethics of social responsibility as opposed to the ethics of personal conscience were used as a measure of subjects' attitudes toward authority and conformity in a study which related these attitudes to moral judgment and personality.* The investigators used the Hogan Survey of Ethical Attitudes (SEA) with a community college sample, asking subjects to rate the concepts of mother, father, police, and government on a modified Semantic Differential Scale. Those who endorsed the ethics of *social responsibility* (impersonal or bureaucratic authority such as the government, courts, police, or the church) were found to have more favorable attitudes toward authority and to be more conforming than those who endorsed the ethics of *personal conscience* (authority vested in parents, bosses, or teachers). The conclusion is that those who support the ethics of responsibility tend to conform because they do not trust other people—including people in authority.

The link between authority and conformity depends to some extent on the attitude measurement instrument used, however. High scorers on an authoritarianism scale may also demonstrate stereotyping, restrictiveness, lack of subtlety in making moral judgments, and relatively poor adjustment. In comparison, individuals who show a need for conformity on the SEA do not necessarily show poorer adjustment or lower intelligence than nonconformers do. Their conformity emerges not from the love of their parents or respect for authorities but from a lack of confidence in other people's motives. They conform to standards rooted in an organization or a tradition that transcends individuals.

_____

*J. A. Johnson, R. Hogan, A. B. Zonderman, C. Callens, and S. Rogolsky, "Moral Judgment, Personality, and Attitudes Toward Authority," *Journal of Personality and Social Psychology,* 1981, 40, 370–373.

A person's tendency to agree with or conform to the opinions or attitudes of another person or group is related to her or his degree of attraction and commitment to that person or group. Kiesler (1973) conducted a series of experiments in which high school and university students were misinformed that the purpose of group exercises in evaluating objects like paintings was to find how groups can work together for common goals. They were asked to rank each other as members of the group and were given false versions of how others thought of them.

Kiesler found that the more the experimenter impressed on subjects the idea

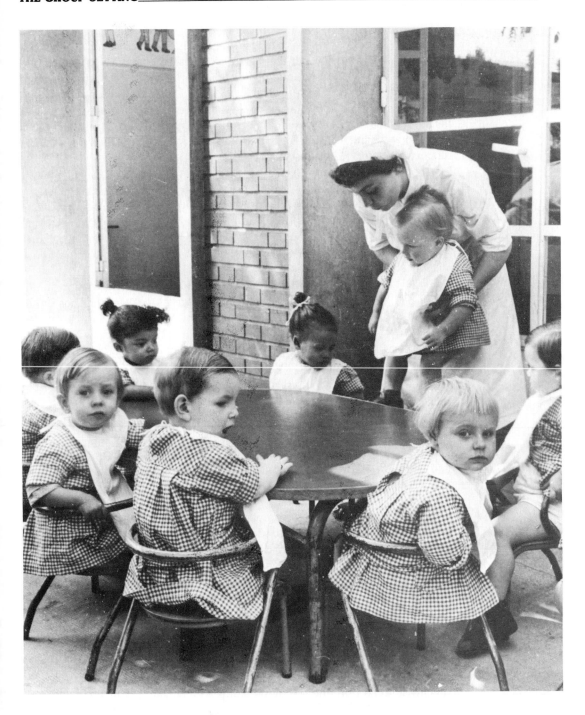

Conformity begins in the family, is formally initiated in the preschool, and assumes more elaborate forms by high school. *Source:* Courtesy of the French Tourist Office.

that they were not liked by the group, the more they insisted that they did not like the others, and the less they changed their opinions to conform to the group opinion. However, when subjects were told they were to remain with the group, which meant a kind of commitment, their opinions tended to be modified whether they thought they were liked or unliked (i.e., were attracted or unattracted). According to Kiesler, "at the extreme—when least attracted—the committed person (but not the uncommitted) changed his opinions almost as much as the highly unattracted did" (p. 89). The significance of group attraction for individual members is explored in Chapter 13.

Something akin to this occurs in real life. You might ignore a disagreement in a private conversation with a passing acquaintance, but if you are committed to a relationship with another person you would probably insist on airing disagreements between you, and you might make an issue of differences you would ignore in a stranger. In this case, insistence on frankness may well be a means of removing potential sources of conflict and achieving a more honest relationship.

The status of a person in a group is related to his or her commitment and conformity to its goals. Shaw (1976) summarized the research findings on the status factor in laboratory groups and concluded that "the high-status person, to a greater extent than the low-status person, is permitted to deviate from group norms in an attempt to aid in goal achievement, although the high-status person usually conforms more than low-status members" (p. 246).

Conformity versus Yielding

Another important consideration in group pressure is the distinction between conformity, or norm acceptance, and compliance. It is not unusual for people's attitudes and behavior to be at odds, as noted in Chapters 8 and 9, and people may behave publicly in a manner consistent with group pressure while they privately disagree with the group. V. L. Allen (1965) suggests that there are four possible dimensions of a person's response to group pressure: He or she may publicly (1) comply or (2) not comply; and at the same time may personally or privately (3) agree or (4) disagree with the group. When a person both privately accepts the group norm and publicly complies with it, the condition is referred to as *conformity versus yielding.* The conforming person accepts the norm of the group as his or her own and acts accordingly. When a person complies with group pressure but does not inwardly agree with the group, this is referred to as *yielding.*

Yielding, or public compliance, usually occurs when an individual is placed in a situation in which the group or a group spokesperson has rewarding or punishing power. In this situation it may be expedient to behave in a manner consistent with group expectancies, while inwardly holding to one's own point of view. Yielding does not imply that the yielder is keeping a private lack of agreement secret from the rest of the group. People who are trying to ingratiate themselves with a group may or may not keep secret their disagreement with the regulations with which they are complying. Disagreeing with an attractive group, or being the "odd person out," is an uncomfortable feeling and is sufficiently punishing (or conversely, agreeing with the group is sufficiently reinforcing) that people will yield simply to avoid the unpleasantness of being at odds with the group. However, a person's agreement must be instrumental to the group's regard for that person, or group attraction alone will not lead to greater public conformity or compliance (Walker & Heyns, 1962).

In a classic study of yielding behavior, Solomon Asch (1958) demonstrated that individuals yield to group pressure even with respect to undisputed facts. Subjects in this situation were asked to publicly state which of three vertical lines drawn on a card was closest in size to a comparison line—an obvious and easy discrimination. Their statements followed those of several experimental confederates who responded as the experimenter wanted them to, giving the correct answer or being unanimously inconsistent with, or contrary to, the norm. In a number of experiments using this procedure, Asch found that about one third of the subjects yielded to group pressure. The easier the discrimination (that is, the larger the differences between the lines), the fewer the subjects who yielded. Even with very large differences, however, subjects agreed with the wrong answers of the confederates about 28 percent of the time.

Special Cases of Yielding: Obedience and Compliance

Yielding experiments such as Asch's have a "gun-at-the-head" character about them: Individuals are placed in the uncomfortable situation of being evaluated in a laboratory context in which their judgment seems to be inconsistent with that of the other people involved. This kind of situation puts a premium on yielding behaviors for the sake of expediency. However, the tendency to yield to majority opinion is also quite prevalent in everyday life; we tend to agree with high-status people and feel uncomfortable when we are at variance with the groups to which we belong (see Box 11–2). Similarly, in group problem–solving situations the pressure towards consensus and uniformity is great indeed, as Chapter 13 will demonstrate.

In studying the special cases of yielding that are concerned with obedience and compliance, the extent of such behavior is measured with a request or command from another individual. In a number of experiments on compliance that have been conducted under field conditions, a surprising number of people were found to be willing to comply with some extraordinary requests. For example, about a third of those contacted by an unknown person will usually agree to a 15-to 20-minute personal interview. Other results are even more striking. Freedman and Fraser (1966), for example, found that 22 percent of their sample of housewives complied with the request of a stranger to allow five or six men to enter their homes for two hours and take an inventory of the contents. If the request for this inconvenient disruption was preceded by a preliminary telephone contact in which the women were first asked to answer a few questions about the brand of soap they used, approximately 53 percent consented. Moreover, the request specified that the survey team would "have to have full freedom in your house to go through cupboards and storage places." This study

Box 11-2
THE IRON LAW OF CONFORMITY

Clifton, Ariz. (AP)—A teenage girl whose parents were too poor to buy her a new dress was sent home in tears from her Grade 8 graduation ceremony because her clothing did not conform with school rules.

School principal McDowell said Wednesday students "had been given their instructions long before the graduation. I felt a girl who did not abide by the required dress should not participate."

The parents of 13-year-old Eleanor Stacy said their daughter was ordered to leave the graduation ceremony May 30 because of her yellow-flowered dress.

Carpenter Ed Stacy said: "We're kind of poor right now. We couldn't afford to buy a dress."

Instead, he said, the girl's aunt made a dress.

Stacy said Eleanor had left early for the graduation ceremony with friends. As he and his wife were driven to the school by relatives later "the headlights of the car caught this girl walking along the highway."

"It was Eleanor. We couldn't believe it. She was crying her eyes out."

Stacy said he took the matter before the school board June 4 but "they treated it as a joke."

William Blair, board president, said "We had 66 graduates and we couldn't have everybody different. She was defying authority."

established the *foot-in-the-door technique,* which suggests that a person can be induced to agree to a larger task by being first led to agree to a smaller one. It is similar to the low-balling technique of Cialdini et al. (1978) which is described later in the section on predispositional factors in group pressure.

In a similar experiment Freedman and Fraser (1966) found that 105 women and 7 men living in Palo Alto, California, were willing to have a large, unattractive "Drive Carefully" sign posted in their front yards. Depending on the number of preliminary, foot-in-the-door requests and the person's persuasibility, one fourth to three fourths agreed. That this many people would comply with what seems to be an unreasonable request suggests a basis for the justification of "following orders" in such situations as the Nuremberg war crimes trials following World War II. One of the principal defenses for those charged with Nazi crimes against the people was that they were "just following orders" or had been caught in situations where they had to obey. Milgram's original intention in his classic 1963 study of obedience and disobedience to authority was to compare American and German samples of subjects, to see if this was a national characteristic. He found that about two thirds of the American subjects would comply with a request which could harm or hurt another human being (Milgram, 1965).

In Milgram's experiments, naive (uninformed or unsuspecting) subjects varying in age from young to middle-aged and coming from diverse occupational backgrounds were paired with partners who they thought were also volunteers but who were actually experimental confederates. They were told by the experimenter that they would be involved in research dealing with the effects of punishment on learning. One "volunteer" was to take the role of learner and the other was to serve as an experimental assistant or teacher, but through a rigged drawing the subject was always the teacher and the confederate was always the learner. Subjects were paid $4.50 on their arrival at the laboratory and given some brief instructions, after which they were seated in front of a bogus shock generator with 30 switches which they could presumably pull to deliver electric shocks varying from 15 to 450 volts. They were instructed by the experimenter to shock the learner any time the latter made a mistake. The learner, who was strapped into a chair with electrodes attached to his body, made noises and comments consonant with the level of shock that supposedly had been delivered. At 75 volts the learner began to grunt and moan, at 150 volts he demanded to be let out of the experiment, at 180 volts he stated that he could no longer stand the pain, and at 300 volts he refused to provide more answers. The subject was instructed to consider *no answer* a wrong answer, to be followed by a shock.

The behavior of special interest is the number of sequential shocks subjects gave victims when commanded by the experimenter. The results of Milgram's experiments are extremely disturbing because over 60 percent of the subjects were willing to administer the maximum shock in compliance with the experimenter's expectation (or in some cases, command). Several conditions did weaken this response, such as the proximity of the victim—the closer the victim, the less willing the subjects were to administer the maximum voltage. The proximity of the experimenter was also found to be important; the farther away the experimenter was, the less likely the subject was to comply with his requests. When subjects were not under pressure, they would administer milder shocks. If a confederate posing as another subject defied the experimenter and refused to administer a shock, most of the subjects were encouraged to do the same. Apparently, the confederates suggested that disobedience was an acceptable response, and it may have confirmed the personal convictions of the subjects that delivering severe shocks is against social and moral values. Nevertheless, two thirds of the subjects did follow the experimenter's directions, even though they were free to abandon the experiment. Some cynics would say that orders can be used to justify *any* behavior, and Milgram's findings seem to support this thesis.

Milgram's numerous studies using this technique have had tremendous impact, and their implications are of the greatest importance. Box 11–3 gives some idea of the lengths to which compliance studies have gone, but these types of experiments have been criticized on ethical grounds because of the stress induced in the subjects and the deception involved. Milgram held a debriefing period at the end of his experiments, including a friendly reconciliation between subject and victim, and asserted that the follow-up showed no permanent harm. Yet there could be long-term effects for a subject's self-image, not to mention his or her opinion of such experiments or attitude toward the profession of

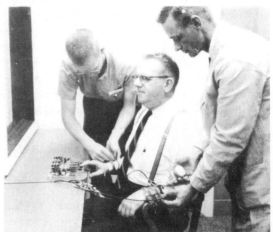

In the Milgram obedience experiment, (upper left) a shock generator is used. The learner (upper right) is strapped into a chair, electrodes are attached to his wrist, and he provides responses by depressing switches that light up the numbers on an answer box. A subject (lower left) receives a sample shock from the generator as the experimenter looks on. The subject (lower right) decides to abandon the experiment. *Source:* Copyright 1965 by Stanley Milgram. From the film OBEDIENCE, distributed by the New York University Film Library.

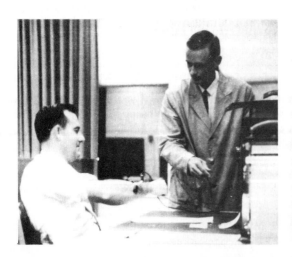

Box 11-3
PLAYING THE PART: PRISONERS AND GUARDS

Would typical American college students have different attitudes toward compliance in the role of a prison guard than in the role of a prisoner? Philip Zimbardo and his associates at Stanford University investigated the effects of stress in a simulated prison situation in an ingenious experiment which has become a classic.*

To obtain subjects for this experiment, an advertisement offered $15 a day for participation in a simulated prison. After 19 students had been chosen from an original pool of 75 (following interviews and a battery of tests to assure that the subjects had no atypical personality traits), the assignment to prisoner or guard status was determined by the toss of a coin.

The "prisoners" were rounded up in their homes, handcuffed, and taken to Stanford County Jail (an improvised section of the basement of the psychology building), fingerprinted, sprayed for lice, and ordered to stand naked outside their cells as they listened to the guards read the rules and regulations. Both prisoners and guards wore uniforms, but the guards also wore silver reflector sunglasses and carried long billy clubs, whistles, and cell keys. The prisoners were subject to any order of the guards and had to ask permission even to go to the toilet. Visitors were to be admitted only on a special day.

After a few days both sides fell all too well into their respective roles. Among other things, the prisoners were forced to answer roll call in the middle of the night and do pushups, with a guard occasionally putting his foot on a prisoner's back. As the first few days passed, sadism increasingly characterized much of the guard's behavior toward the prisoners, who soon were showing acute emotional distress. By the fifth day the prisoners wanted to be released from their experiment, despite forfeiture of their original objective, a monetary reward.

By the sixth day the investigators recognized the impossibility of continuing the experiment. Zimbardo reflects: "We witnessed sadism in men who were not sadistic, emotional breakdowns in people chosen precisely because they were stable, and the loss of objectivity in men whose professional training should have prevented it. How terrible must be the psychic costs of real prisoners in their struggle to adjust and adapt in an environment far harsher and more cruel than any we could have simulated and who, unlike our student-prisoners, live with absolute uncertainty as to their eventual deliverance from it." (p. 270).

---

*C. Haney and P. G. Zimbardo, "Social Roles and Role-Playing: Observations from the Stanford Prison Study," *Behavioral and Social Science Teacher*, 1973, *1*, 25–45. Reprinted in E. P. Hollander and R. C. Hunt (Eds.), *Current Perspectives in Social Psychology*, 4th ed. (New York: Oxford University Press, 1976), pp. 266–274.

psychology. In any event, the Milgram studies were among those which led the American Psychological Association to publish *Ethical Principles in the Conduct of Research with Human Participants* (1973), an enlightening discussion of the importance of full disclosure, honesty, responsibility, attempts to minimize distress, and the like.

Social Learning and Imitation

Many of people's ideas about compliance and conformity come from their perceptions and learning background. When people have to make judgments in ambiguous situations in which they cannot determine the accuracy of their judgments objectively, they tend to turn to group norms to guide their estimates. Sherif's (1935) study utilized the autokinetic effect, by which a fixed point of light in a completely darkened room appears to drift different distances to different observers, to demonstrate that groups establish norms which individuals follow in a sort of social learning experience (see Chapter 5).

Subjects were asked to estimate how far the point of light moved when presented for short periods. When the subjects were alone, they established a subjective standard (a norm) which they used to evaluate all their estimates. For example, a person who assumed that the dot of light moved about six inches on the first trial would match his or her perceptions of the distance moved on subsequent trials with that one. By placing several subjects together in the judgment situation and requiring them to announce their estimates aloud on every trial, Sherif could determine the extent of influence one subject or group of subjects had on another. Since the point of light did not actually move, any change in the norm would have to be due either to individual change (the subject changed his or her own norm) or social influence (the subject's norm changed in the direction of that of the other person).

In imitation or modeling, as noted in the discussion of Albert Bandura's research in Chapter 5, one or more persons (the model) provide cues for the imitator to follow in making behavioral responses. Thus imitation, which Tarde (1903) called the fundamental social process (see Chapter 1), is one kind of conforming behavior, and it is likely to result in praise or other positive reinforcement from the group—such as being granted increased access to it. Rejection by the group, or being made to feel odd or different, would be negative reinforcement which would tend to discourage the imitative or conforming behavior. "Being different," however, might have sufficient reinforcing value in some situations to overcome the negative effects of not agreeing with the group.

As noted above, the more people are attracted to a group, the more likely they are to conform to its norms, and the more likely the group is to serve as a model for their behavior. Festinger, Schachter, and Back (1950) confirmed the relation between attraction and conformity to group norms. The attractiveness of the source of the influence (as distinguished from attraction to the group) has also been found to be positively correlated with conforming behavior (French & Snyder, 1959). Interpersonal attraction and group cohesion are investigated further in Chapter 13.

For the group to have influence over an individual, it must be important as well as attractive to that person. People will agree with friends and the "right" people (or model themselves after these persons), and they will disagree with those they assess negatively. When they learn that a highly regarded person evaluates X as greater than Y, for example, they can have a vicarious association with that person by being among the first to express agreement. If you find yourself in an unfamiliar social situation where you do not know how to act, such as a ritualistic religious service, or a formal reception with established protocol, you will probably watch and imitate the behavior of someone who clearly has status and belongs in the surroundings. People model their behavior on that of high-status persons for several reasons: It is assumed that they are more likely to know what is right or correct, and if one associates oneself (by imitation) with them, even if the imitated behavior violates some rule or norm, it cannot be too bad if those of high status also do it.

Within an organizational hierarchy of positions, group members often feel under pressure not to disagree with those of higher status. Many executives do have power over the careers of lower-status subordinates and may use this power to discourage disagreement or dissension. Subordinates often want to be associated with their superiors or hope to gain tangible (a better job) or intangible (a more attractive title) rewards through pleasing high-status persons. These "yes-men" avoid disagreeing with any statement made by higher-status persons and may even attempt to anticipate the preferences and prejudices of their superiors, so that any opinion they offer is consonant with the perceived preferences of high-status persons and represents what the latter want to hear.

Conformity and compliance in any organization are extremely costly and time-consuming. No new ideas will be generated by a group whose members offer suggestions which are only mild departures from the real or *presumed* position of the high-status persons in the group. Hours are lost as conformers or compliers waste their own and others' time with restatements of well-known positions. High-level managers and supervisors who are aware of this problem are careful not to express their own points of view before subordinates have evaluated the ideas and expressed their opinions. Good chairpeople also do not allow criticism too early in a discussion, so the expression of novel ideas is not inhibited.

The principle behind modeling is that people tend to do what they observe other people doing. In a crisis situation, they might observe others hesitating to act and interpret it as an indication that others feel the situation does not warrant intervention. If they observe others assisting, they are stimulated to help too. This illustrates the concept of *prosocial* or *helping behavior,* a relatively new one in social psychology.

GROUP PRESSURE AND PROSOCIAL BEHAVIOR

When group judgment and standards are substituted for those of the individual, the effects on social behavior are often negative, as demonstrated in the studies of conformity and compliance. But the response of individuals in a group setting may also demonstrate indifference (see Box 13–2 in Chapter 13), or cooperation, helpfulness, and altruism. These responses are usually attributed to the personal qualities of the individual, but recent research indicates that to a large extent they are a function of the social context in which the behavior occurs.

While prosocial behavior is often initiated by individuals, they are influenced by the activities of other people. In a social situation they look to see what others are doing when they are unsure about their behavioral response, as shown in the experiments by Latané and Darley (1970a, 1970b) on offers of help or nonintervention by bystanders in emergencies (these are described in Chapter 13). According to a study by Piliavin, Rodin, and Piliavin (1969), when a person obviously needs help (for instance, if someone collapses), the situation appears mixed and bystanders have conflicting motives, both wanting to help and wanting to withdraw. People are much more likely to help when someone else is already offering assistance.

Petition signing is another example; a person is more likely to sign a petition that others have already signed than one that has no other signatures on it, according to Blake, Mouton, and Hain (1956). Similarly, bystanders are more likely to come to the aid of a woman rather than a man whose car has a flat tire (Bryan & Test, 1967), and subjects are more likely to volunteer for psychology experiments (Rosenbaum, 1956), when they observe others behaving in a generous or helpful manner. It is possible, of course, that the reason more people tend to offer help when they witness others being helpful is simply that attention is being focused on helping, and people are reminded of the norm of social responsibility. It is also possible that the hazards of intervention are reduced when the responsibility is shared, or that people are made to feel guilty if they do not respond to an appeal for help when they observe others responding.

The tendency to give or withhold assistance, or to react with indifference or act in a prosocial way, is influenced by many interrelated factors in the individual's personality structure and the sociocultural setting (see Box 11–4). The relationship between the donor and the recipient is obviously important (Bar-Tal, 1976), as is the method used to apply implicit rules in what is often an ambiguous situation (Mayo & LaFrance, 1977).

The effects of subcultural variables were found to be largely as expected in a study of subjects confronted by a situation in which a motorist's car supposedly had been disabled (West, Whitney, & Schnedler, 1975). It was found that helpers were more generally male, and female victims were helped more readily than male victims; black victims were given aid more quickly in a black neighborhood and whites in a white neighborhood. One exception was the effect of the educational subculture. When the situation was set up adjacent to predominantly black and predominantly white college campuses, victims of the opposite race received help faster than those of the same race. Generally, less racial bias was displayed by blacks than by whites. As in most of these types of experiments, the tendency to help was influenced by witnessing others helping.

Age differences were also found to be relevant by Stotland et al. (1978). When asked to describe events of their early years, children who described their experiences as happy tended to donate their earnings from an experiment more often than children who focused on sad experiences. For adults, adversity was found to operate in a different direction. Persons who had just watched a tragic

Box 11–4
WHEN ARE FINDERS KEEPERS?

Helping behavior was studied in a Madison, Wisconsin, experiment to determine the type of person most likely to return a "lost" letter and other material which gave the identification of the addressee.* The letter was dropped (more accurately, left when the experimenter picked up a bag after shopping), and an observer recorded the characteristics of those who picked it up. In approximately half the instances the letter was accompanied by a note with unfavorable racial remarks, and all included a form offering a prize to anyone who filled it out with a name and address.

In 72 percent of the incidents the letters were returned. The offer of the prize was a deterrent because if the letter were returned the form could not be used, but only two subjects, or 4 percent of the total sample, made such a claim. Women returned the letter more often than men did. The return rate was relatively high (80 percent) when the finder was similar to the fictitious loser of the letter—the name, Michael Erwin, indicated a white, Anglo-Saxon Protestant (WASP) male. But there was a still higher return rate (86 percent) for the letters accompanied by racist comments.

Variations of the experimental procedure also found greater helping behavior with the negative referent (the racial remarks) than with the positive referent (similarity to the loser). One explanation is the resolution of the cognitive dissonance of subjects who returned the letter together with a note indicating their disapproval of the racial attitudes the loser of the letter had expressed.

_____
*S. H. Schwartz and R. E. Ames, "Positive and Negative Referent Others as Sources of Influence: A Case of Helping," *Sociometry*, 1977, *40*, 12–20.

movie were more generous at a charity booth than those who had sat through an emotionally neutral movie. Later-born children also were found to have greater empathy or sensitivity to the needs of others than first born or only children.

Other studies have investigated whether negative or positive mood induces (or inhibits) helping behavior. A Stanford research team conducted an experiment in which the subjects listened to one of three different tapes: (1) a tape describing a friend dying, with the narration focusing on the need and feelings of the dying friend, (2) a tape describing the same situation, but focusing on the needs and feelings of the subject, and (3) a neutral tape presented to the control group (Thompson, Cowan, & Rosenhan, 1980). Affect or mood was measured by a scale of the reactions of subjects as described in their accounts of the experience. There also was a test for altruism; help was invited on an anonymous basis in completing a complex task (a series of almost unanswerable multiple-choice items) for which there was no external reward. Students who had focused on the needs of the dying person rather than their own needs volunteered to stay on for this task most frequently.

Thus it seems that negative mood can elicit helping behavior if the focus is on the other person rather than on the self. Negative moods also have been found to increase helping behavior when the cause is an important one and the cost of helping is low (Weyant, 1978). Other researchers have found that generally positive mood states brought about by success at a task (Barnett & Bryan, 1974), thinking happy thoughts or reading elation statements (Rosenhan, Underwood, & Moore, 1974), or receiving or finding something (Levin & Isen, 1975) also increase the likelihood of helpful or generous behavior.

Environmental conditions such as noise also can influence helping behavior. S. Cohen (1978) suggests that these stressors overload people's attentional processes so that their attention is focused on their own goals, to the relative exclusion of other social cues. Yinon and Bizman (1980) found that when noise is low, subjects helped more than when noise is high. Studies of the effects of environmental noise such as that produced by planes (Cohen et al., 1980) on motivational and cognitive processes indicate that children in noisy environments are more likely to fail or give up on tasks. It also appears that such stressors may reduce prosocial behavior, which leads to questions about the effects of urban noise and activity on positive interpersonal behavior.

PERSONAL AND SITUATIONAL FACTORS IN GROUP PRESSURE

As in helping behavior, a person's reaction to other types of group pressure is affected by both the individual's personality structure and the sociocultural setting of the group situation. The two types of factors in group pressure can be classified as situational and predispositional.

Situational factors are related to the characteristics of the group entity and the conditions under which it acts and communicates. Such factors as size, composition or membership, status positions, and operational procedures are in the general category of structural variables, or aspects of the group situation to which the individual is exposed.

Predispositional factors are personal characteristics which are part of the personality structure and the cultural background of the individual. Personality traits, age, sex, physiognomic characteristics, attitudes, feelings, beliefs, group attraction, and the like are examples of the types of variables which can be classified as predispositional.

These categories are not mutually exclusive, and many factors might be considered either predispositional or situational or both. Status, for example, is difficult to classify because it refers to a person's position on any dimension held to be of value by the group. Thus age, wealth, intelligence, strength, power, expertise, and skin color—among other factors—could all be status linked.

Although many of these characteristics are personal in the sense that the individual embodies them (like age), their status value is determined and therefore bestowed by the group. A person might find, for example, that age affords high status in group A but confers only low status in group B.

The two classes of factors also interact, and the influence of any particular variable on people's attitudes or behaviors depends to a great extent on its relation to other variables. This relationship should be evident if you consider the situations in which two persons of equal status—one of whom is humble and friendly and the other of whom is arrogant and hostile—would have the most influence on you.

An intriguing example of the social factors in group pressure is the tendency to avoid violating group norms, even when they are not known. This has been called *pluralistic ignorance* (or, where facts as well as values are concerned, Irving Janis's concept of *groupthink,* which is described in Box 13–3 in Chapter 13). For example, suppose a group of supervisors has to decide whether to fire a secretary who does a little work for each of them. All the supervisors may feel strongly that the secretary should be dismissed, but individually they do not know the opinions of the rest of the group. When the subject comes up everyone waits for someone else to speak, fearing that a negative opinion might be at odds with the group consensus. To break the silence, someone may express an innocuous positive sentiment such as, "Well, she is a nice person." As a result, each supervisor could develop the misperception of being the only one who wants to fire the secretary. Even though everyone privately believes the secretary should be fired, each person assumes that the opposite is the case. Consequently, the group agrees on a course of action that is contrary to the personal beliefs of the majority of the group members.

Situational Factors: Group Size

Group size is the most likely of the structural characteristics of groups to affect an individual's behavior. Large groups can reduce the actual or perceived importance of any individual's effort. The influence of individuals tends to decrease as group size increases, because controls on behavior are frequently less rigid, the effects of status discrepancy may be more severe, and so on.

In experiments on yielding behavior and group size, Asch (1956) found maximum yielding behavior when three to four people disagreed with the subject. The size of the disagreeing majority tends to increase yielding behavior up to groups of five (i.e., the subject and a discrepant majority of four persons). People seem to have a greater tendency to resist yielding when the group is larger, although the effects of very large groups of 25 or so have not been experimentally determined.

The increase of conformity with the size of the group to a maximum of four or five members is understandable: The larger the ratio of group members who give the same reaction simultaneously, the less is the individual's self-confidence and the greater is her or his adherence to the group norm (Shaw, 1976). A replication of the Asch experiment (L. A. Rosenberg, 1961) showed that even when the subject was led to believe that the other group members had performed much better (i.e., with greater accuracy) on a similar task, the maximum effect of group size on yielding behavior in five-person groups was a majority of three persons. Holding out alone against the other four members did not increase but actually decreased the amount of yielding behavior.

Another study of conformity and group size (Gerard, Wilhelmy, & Conolley, 1968) found that while maximum influence occurs in a group of four for males, it occurs in a group of seven for females. There is evidence that males are more suspicious of experimental manipulations, as noted in the section on situational factors in group pressure. Therefore they may resist the social influence as the group size increases simply because it seems less credible. In any event, generalizations based on a small number of university students are always open to criticism.

The most interesting aspect of the group-size effect is that interactions between group size and the status composition of groups can be expected. In two-person groups, conformity or compliance can be expected to be related to the relative status or power of the two persons; the person with lower status yields more frequently, and the extent of the lower-status person's yielding is directly related to the magnitude of the difference in status. In very large groups, individuals may be more influenced by the majority than the status of any one person, but there can be a complex relationship between status composition and the *nature* of a member's compliant behavior: Does the person simply yield or actually conform?

In small groups it is difficult for the individual to remain uninvolved in any issue. In a four-person group, for example, if the chairperson asks, "Does anyone disagree?" remaining silent implies agreement. In larger groups it is possible to figuratively hide in the crowd, and failure to voice disagreement does not carry the same implications of agreement.

More research on group-size effects is needed to determine how they are related to differences in conformity when responses are made either publicly or privately. Group size may be related to privacy on the assumption that large groups permit the individual to hide in the crowd. Deutsch and Gerard (1955) have collected data which show that individuals conform less when their responses are not made known to the group or when they are not in a face-to-face situation.

Predispositional Factors: Personality and Conformity

The tendency in our society to expect conformity to have negative effects is supported by personality theories which maintain that people's conforming behavior is associated with personality defects like insecurity, guilt, or anxiety. Conformity is also said to distinguish national characters; the United States, from Main Street of the 1920s to suburbia of the 1980s, has been considered to be a society which values and rewards conforming behavior. Research has produced no hard data on sociocultural differences in the tendency to conform, but there have been a number of investigations on its relation to group structure and personal characteristics. Conformity has been linked to guilt and anxiety, for example, which can lead to attempts at restitution; Carlsmith and Gross (1969) found that subjects who had shocked a victim complied more often when a favor was asked than those who had simply exposed the victim to loud buzzes.

In a study of conformity and character by Crutchfield (1955), independents, compared to conformists, showed greater intellectual and leadership ability, activity and vigor, and maturity in interpersonal relations. Conformists displayed authoritarian attitudes, submissiveness, narrow interests, excessive self-control, and a lack of self-confidence. Steiner and Vannoy (1966) found that conformers as compared with yielders had higher scores on an anxiety test, were more accepting of the other group members, and had higher aggression test scores, but no differences were found for authoritarianism.

Public Commitment and Consistency

The critical factor determining whether a person will comply with or resist a request or command is how public the requested behavior or position will be. If people do not have to make their positions known or they cannot be personally identified with them (through use of a secret ballot, for example), they are least vulnerable to group pressure and social influence.

The more anonymous a person's position, also, the less is the pressure to be consistent. Research has shown that people who yield under group pressure tend to continue to yield throughout an entire experimental session, and noncompliers early in a session tend to remain noncompliers. Possibly this consistency simply reflects the effects of personality dispositions (some people always conform, others resist) and requires no further explanation. It may be, however, that persons who do yield feel committed to publicly stated attitudes or opinions, and therefore they consistently yield to group pressure to satisfy interpersonal and psychological needs for consistency. Crutchfield (1958) found that once a public commitment has been made, subjects will continue to respond in a manner which is consistent with their initial response.

The *low-balling* sales procedure—an extension of Freedman and Fraser's (1966) foot-in-the-door technique described above—is an example of the effect of public commitment on future compliance. If you have ever bought a car from a dealer you are familiar with this one: The salesman offers to sell a particular automobile at a remarkably low price which is later adjusted upward for one of several reasons, such as "The sales manager won't let me sell at that price"; "The only available car like that has a few extras on it"; or "We made an honest mistake in calculating the price." Getting prospects to buy a high-priced item is easier when they first have been committed to the purchase at a lower cost.

One reason throwing a low ball is successful in such circumstances is that the salesperson is able to create a feeling of obligation on the part of the prospects. In one experiment subjects who agreed, but were not permitted, to carry out an initial request were later willing to comply with a more costly form of the request (Burger & Petty, 1981). The conclusion was that low-balling demands a more intricate or sustained kind of behavior than the foot-in-the-door technique because "an unfulfilled obligation to the requester, rather than a commitment to the initial target behavior, is responsible for the effectiveness of the low-ball technique."

Cialdini et al. (1978) applied this technique to secure commitments of subjects to take part in an experiment that started at 7 A.M. Not only did more low-balled subjects (who were not told of the designated time of the experiment) agree to participate in the study, but more than twice as many who said they would participate actually showed up at the designated time, as compared with subjects who were told straight away about the time of the experiment. Thus obtaining agreement to a minor request increases the likelihood of agreement to a major request.

Status and Related Dimensions

The ability of a person with high status in a group to influence other members to conform or comply was described above. A person who is at odds with another person of higher status yields more easily than when his or her private opinion differs from the position of a person of lower status (Luchins & Luchins, 1961). The question here, however, is how a person's own status position influences her or his tendency to conform to the group's norms. Status can take a variety of forms, but basically it indicates the worth, value, or position an individual has on any scale or dimension shared and valued by the group. Thus special skills, reward power (the ability to give other members something of value), popularity, highly regarded characteristics (such as height, strength, physical attractiveness, or intelligence), wealth, and psychological security are all potential sources of status within a group (Berger et al., 1977).

There is no consistent relationship between status position and the tendency to conform; it is affected by the issue and the basis of the person's status position. In a situation in which special knowledge or skill is required, a clear relationship might be expected between a person's tendency to conform to the group opinion and the person's knowledge relative to that of other group members. Shaw's (1976) finding that while high-status group members are freer to deviate than low-status members, they usually are more conformist as cited above. Ideological considerations also affect group members' consensus and conformity, but insistence on conforming to party lines does not always determine political outcomes, as Box 11–5 shows.

Gender and Birth Order

Although Cooper (1979) found a general tendency for women to show greater susceptibility to social pressure than men in face-to-face situations, this tendency has also been found to be affected by personality factors (Allen & Crutchfield, 1963). Males, for example, were more suspicious than females with regard to the purpose of a conformity study and the method of deception employed to exert group pressure. Since suspicious subjects are less conforming, the sex differences in conformity scores may reflect a difference not so much in

Box 11–5
CONFORMITY IN AN UNEASY COALITION

A dramatic case of a group struggling for consensus was the debate of the Judiciary Committee of the U.S. House of Representatives over the impeachment of former President Richard Nixon.* The committee was established in October 1973 during the Watergate revelations as a response to Nixon's firing of the special prosecutor, Archibald Cox. After months of sifting through evidence, including the tapes which were provided by the White House only on orders of the Supreme Court and the testimony of various participants and witnesses, the majority committee counsel, John Doar, urged a bill of impeachment.

The committee was composed of 21 Democrats (three of whom were from southern states) and 17 Republicans. Committee Chairman Peter Rodino knew the case for impeachment would lose out if the vote were on a purely partisan basis. Through most of the proceedings the Republican members were reluctant to consider a vote of impeachment against a man who was both the president and their party chief, and House Minority Chairman Edward Heath insisted on unanimous support for Nixon. By July 1974, Rodino's only hope was that a few Republicans and the Southern Democrats might go along with the Democrats. The conservative ranks held firm until William Cohen, with the help of Tom Railsback and Hamilton Fish, expressed personal dissonance with the evidence. Joined later by Caldwell Butler and the three Southern Democrats, this "Unholy Alliance" became a centrist group which met more or less secretly to try to muster more support. The group gained two other Republicans for a vote of 26 to 11 for impeachment on Article I on the obstruction of justice. For Article II on the abuse of executive powers, the coalition was expanded by the addition of one more Republican, but it dwindled somewhat for the vote on Article III and fell apart for votes on Articles IV and V.

Thus the pressures on Nixon supporters for conformity were not sufficient to combat the other pressures the committee members experienced, such as that from their conscience and sense of integrity as well as the effect of anti-Nixon sentiment in their home districts. The cross-pressures were devastating on the Southern Democrats, especially Walter Flowers of Alabama, whose constituents overwhelmingly favored the president.

_____

*J. A. Lukas, *Nightmare: The Underside of the Nixon Years* (New York: Viking Press, 1976), p. 511ff.

suggestibility as in each sex's tendency to develop suspicions regarding the experiments they are involved in (Stricker, Messick, & Jackson, 1967).

Males have demonstrated a linear relationship between self-esteem and conformity; the lower the male's self-esteem, the greater his conformity when subjected to group pressure (Janis & Field, 1959). Females, on the other hand, have shown a curvilinear relationship; those who are either high or low in self-esteem show less conformity than those who are moderate in this dimension (Cox & Bauer, 1964). Low-self-esteem males tended to seek social approval by agreeing with others, whereas low-self-esteem females were apt to be defensive and rigid when exposed to opinions at variance with their own.

Whatever the findings of earlier studies, it is questionable whether conformity and gender can be meaningfully related. As Chapter 14 will demonstrate, men and women have begun to assume each other's roles. Research by Locksley et al. (1980) has questioned the linkage of sex identity to either dominance or submissiveness, attributes which are related to conformity. It may be that because of women's tendency to foster harmony in a group, they are more conforming than men (Eagly, 1978). This hypothesis was not supported, however, in an experiment in which subjects of both sexes were under surveillance, that is, the opinions they expressed could be heard by others (Eagly, Wood, & Fishbaugh, 1981). Little difference was found between the women who were under surveillance and those who were not; men who were under surveillance were more independent in their opinions. The reason may be that men try to project the image of independence whether or not they embody this quality.

Birth order in a family also is related to a person's response to group pressure. Firstborns have a greater disparity between aspiration level and ability which is believed to be related to lower self-esteem. They also show less confidence, and their emotional state seems to be related more to the social environment. Gilmore and Zigler (1964) suggest that such differences result from the parents' treatment of firstborns and only children compared with later-born children. Because firstborns are likely to be continually satisfied with social reinforcers by their parents early in life, their independence training could be retarded. However, later research has found birth order to be of little influence in group pressure.

Unobtrusive Social Influence

A perceptive person can often recognize the effects of social pressure or the deliberate attempt of one person to obtain compliance from another. Witnessing a person behave in a certain way may encourage others to join in, if the behavior is praiseworthy or likely to be rewarded, or to avoid similar behavior if it is likely to be criticized or punished. Some attempts to influence behavior are hidden, however, and usually people are not aware the methods are being used. There is reason to believe, for example, that verbal messages presented below the level of conscious awareness can alter behavior (Swingle, 1979) and that manipulation of background music can affect performance (Smith & Curnow, 1966).

Shevrin and Dickman (1980) concluded that a great deal of complex mental activity can go on without the benefit of consciousness, and if it is possible to influence that unconscious activity, people's behavior and attitudes can be manipulated without their awareness. Such effects need not be extremely powerful to make them useful; if a store is losing several hundred thousands of dollars a year to pilferers and shoplifters and can use such methods to influence employees and shoppers to be more honest, even a modest decline in losses of 5 percent represents a great deal of money. Corporations often use unobtrusive methods in their advertising campaigns; if this will enhance the national market for a product by as little as a single percentage point, the profits are substantial. The ethics of manipulating behavior without the awareness of those involved, however, is open to question.

SUMMARY

The principal concern with social influence is the tendency of group pressure to encourage conformity or compliance, though it also promotes prosocial or helping behavior. While conformity is generally regarded as a negative personal characteristic compared to independence, without its regulatory and sustaining influence no society could survive for long.

The success of persuasive efforts to change people's attitudes or behaviors will be limited unless some kind of social pressure is applied. Efforts to reduce smoking or alcoholism have more often than not been failures, but experiments have shown that in certain group settings considerable reorganization of an individual's behavior can occur. A fourth to three fourths of the people contacted by a stranger were willing to have an unsightly object placed on their front lawns, and about half of those first contacted by phone were persuaded to allow five or six total strangers to come into their homes and search their cupboards. Even more amazing, numerous subjects were prepared to expose other human beings to severe electric shocks because they were ordered to do so by a person in authority. Moreover, as the self-perception research reported in Chapter 6 and the cognitive consistency research reported in Chapter 9 showed, people try to make their attitudes consistent with their behavior. When called on to do something inconsistent they rationalize that behavior; that is, they find justifications for the inconsistency.

Group pressure is affected by the interaction between situational factors like group size, composition, and status and the predispositional factors the individual brings from his or her own background. The early experiments on yielding and conformity such as Asch's demonstrated that the individual defers to the group. The implications of the Milgram experiments on obedience raise important questions as to how far a person will go in following an authoritarian leader or group.

In examining the concepts of social influence and group pressure, this chapter has used the term *group* to represent any number of people engaging in collective interaction; thus it applies to an interpersonal relationship between two or three people, an organization hierarchy, or the entire society. The following chapter further defines usage of this term and examines the research on the interactions in small groups.

WORDS TO REMEMBER

Autokinetic effect. A kind of optical illusion; as used by Muzafer Sherif in an experiment to test group influence, it referred to the appearance of movement of a small spot of light exposed in a darkened room.

Compliance. Obedience to norms or orders communicated by the group or its leader, even though this behavior is in opposition to the individual's ethics or judgment.

Conformity. Loyalty or adherence to beliefs, attitudes, norms, or expected behaviors.

"Foot-in-the-door" technique. Compliance technique based on the assumption that a subject who can be induced to agree to a minor task will agree to a major one. See *low-balling.*

Group. A collectivity of two or more individuals who interact with each other. Groups can be studied both in the laboratory and real life.

Imitation. Copying the behavior of another person. In the Tarde and LeBon theory of social contagion, the individual who is caught up in the crowd or is under the stress of emotion may follow the example of another person, even though it contradicts conventional norms.

Low-balling. A technique of compliance whereby the subject agrees to a given condition and then the requester raises the ante. The initial commitment is to the behavior to be performed. See *foot-in-the-door.*

Pluralistic ignorance. The tendency of the group to voice or agree to a norm or belief, even though the members know that the norm is invalid or inappropriate, because they are reluctant to be nonconformers.

Social power. The ability to stimulate or enforce compliance in a society. There are several types of power which can be used by leaders to promote acceptance by the group.

Social facilitation. Process by which the performance of one person is expanded by the presence or influence of another person or group; the opposite of *social inhibition.*

Suggestion. A form of *social facilitation.* In Gustav LeBon's theory, suggestion assumed special significance due to crowd anonymity.

QUESTIONS FOR DISCUSSION

1. Describe the various sources of social power. How does Chadwick's theory of social power relate to compliance and conformity?

2. What is the difference between conformity and yielding? Describe some experiments that have been concerned with these two processes.

3. Describe the classic studies of Milgram on obedience and compliance. What is their significance to our own society?

4. What is meant by *social facilitation?* How has the approach to this and related phenomena like imitation been structured in laboratory investigations?

5. What is the autokinetic effect? How does it relate to facilitation and conformity?

6. How do people with higher status in a group affect the conformity of members? Can you think of examples in private or public life?

7. In what kinds of situations are people likely to help others, and in what kinds do they avoid getting involved? What are the arguments for these behaviors?

8. Explain pluralistic ignorance and "group think." Have you ever seen these in real life?

9. In what ways does the size of a group affect members' behaviors?

10. How does public commitment affect private acceptance? Give some examples.

11. What relationships did Crutchfield find between conformity and personality factors?

12. Is birth order a relevant variable in conformity? What other personal factors may be involved?

13. How do individuals handle conflicts in their beliefs as they seek to conform to group standards?

14. Give some examples of unobtrusive social influence you have observed or heard about.

READINGS

Bickman, L. (Ed.). *Applied Social Psychology Annual.* Vol. 1. Beverly Hills, Calif.: Sage Publications, 1980.
    Several articles concern the applied aspects of cooperation and social influence.

Festinger, L., Schachter, S., and Back, K. *Social Pressures in Informal Groups.* New York: Harper and Row, Publishers, 1950.
    Classic monograph focuses on interaction within the community, especially as it relates to a housing settlement.

Milgram, S. *The Individual in a Social World:* *Essays and Experiments.* Reading, Mass.: Addison-Wesley Publishing Co., 1977.
    Parts 2 and 3 bear on the individual, authority, and the group; controversial experiments are included.

Schachter, S. *The Psychology of Affiliation.* Stanford, Calif.: Stanford University Press, 1959.
    An experimental approach to gregariousness and the determinants of affiliation.

Swingle, P. G. *The Management of Power.* Hillsdale, N.J.: Lawrence Erlbaum Associates, 1976.

The psychology of authority and power and its implications for society.

Wispe, L. (Ed.). *Altruism, Sympathy, and Helping.* New York: Academic Press, 1978. A well-selected set of studies on various theoretical issues concerning prosocial behavior.

GROUPS: STRUCTURE AND FUNCTION

What is the difference between a group and any other kind of aggregation or collection? This chapter defines the term *group* and considers different kinds of social groups, but it is primarily concerned with what happens in groups of people and how they can be studied. The focus is on the small group, specifically dyads (two persons) and triads (three persons). The structure and function of groups have most often been studied in terms of units of this size. (Larger groups, such as political factions and special-interest groups, are included in the discussion of various effects of leadership in Chapter 15.)

The distinction between a cluster of persons (such as the people standing on a street corner waiting for a bus) and a social group is somewhat arbitrary, but some distributions of people ordinarily fall outside the notion of groups. One is the *aggregation*—two or more people in proximity, such as two people walking to work who happen to be heading in the same direction on the same block at the same time. This aggregation would become social only if one or both of them became aware of the other and responded accordingly. Another is *parallel responding,* which characterizes the relation between persons who live in the same place and time and share a common resource such as a water supply. A group signifies more than mere proximity of two or more people, even when they are responding similarly. The essential characteristic of a group is that there is some degree of *interaction* between the individuals who comprise it.

The definition and classification of groups are clarified in the first section of this chapter, and then the principal methods of studying their structure and function—sociometry, group dynamics, and interactional analysis—are described. Game theory is presented as an approach to the analysis of groups in terms of behavioral options and the rewards and costs of expected outcomes. Group effects on learning and performance in the form of increased tendencies to cooperate or compete are examined as an introduction to consideration of the orientation of various types of group reward structures in individual achievement, competition, or cooperation.

DIMENSIONS OF GROUPS

Definitions of what constitutes a group are varied, but they all include the concept of interpersonal relations. An example is the definition by Sherif and Sherif (1969):

> A group is a social unit consisting of a number of individuals who stand in role and status relationships to one another, stabilized in some degree at the time, and who possess a set of values or norms of their own regulating their behavior, at least in matters of consequence to the group. (p. 131)

Burgess's (1929) briefer definition describes the group as a "unity of interacting personalities." An intermediate position is Newcomb's (1950) definition: "A group consists of two or more persons *who share norms* about certain things with one another and *whose social roles are closely interlocking.*" Newcomb, Turner, and Converse (1965), however, say that the only unambiguous meaning of *group* is "a set of persons considered as a single entity" and so groups must be specified by terms such as *formal, membership, reference, ethnic, or residential.* An implication of these definitions is that social concepts of personality, role, and status have little meaning apart from the group.

A fundamental distinction in types of groups is that between psychological groups and social organizations. According to Krech, Crutchfield, and Ballachey (1962), a *psychological group* consists of "two or more persons who meet the following conditions: (1) the relations among the members are *interdependent*—each member's behavior influences the behavior of each of the others; (2) the members *share an ideology*—a set of beliefs, values, and norms which regulates their mutual conduct." Examples are families, friendship groups, social clubs, and work groups. A *social organization* refers to "an integrated system of interrelated psychological groups formed to accomplish a stated objective." An example is a political party or a factory, with its many constituent groups, each with its own structure, ideology, and role relationships.

Social groups can be classified in many ways: according to *size*—from the simple dyad of two persons to the complex groupings in nations of millions; according to *permanence;* according to how members are *distributed* geographically; or according to certain *determinants* (such as blood relationship, similarity in bodily characteristics or in cultural interests, and so on, to name a few). Not only are there different kinds of groups to which individuals can belong, but the groups to which one person belongs can fluctuate many times during the course of even a day. Most influential is probably the family group; this primary group is actually subdivided for various purposes into husband-wife, or, say, father-son relationships, or a mother and daughter may constitute a separate group that "gangs up" on the male contingent of the family. Some members may give priority to a baseball-playing group at the corner lot or to the Missionary society at the local church. A group may simply be you and your bridge partner as you plot how to triumph in a tournament. Thus a group can emerge whenever two or more people are involved in some common activity. What's more, we are constantly imagining or projecting ourselves into group situations. Even an individual who is not in a group may be imagining a social relationship: What will my girl friend think of the roses I sent her? A group relationship can involve potential as well as overt interaction.

Some of the principal categories of social groups are defined in the following sections: primary and secondary groups, formal and informal groups, in-groups and out-groups, and membership and reference groups.

Primary and Secondary Groups

Charles H. Cooley made an observation of tremendous significance in his differentiation between primary and secondary groups—a concept introduced in Chapter 4 in relation to the development of the social self. Cooley (1909) describes a *primary group* as representing an intimate, face-to-face relationship such as that in the family, neighborhood, or play group. In a *secondary group,* such as a political party, state, or nation, contacts between persons are more impersonal, more indirect, less frequent, or more removed in space or time. Primary groups involve close physical proximity, but more important is their warm emotional tone. In the casual, fleeting contacts of modern urban culture, people have come to depend increasingly on secondary groups for their norms, their motivation, and the satisfaction of their affiliative needs (see Chapters 7 and 13). The great range of secondary-group relationships has frequently prevented them from making long-term friendships. Hence in the 20th century many people have developed a kind of *anomie* or "normlessness"—a personal disorientation or loneliness (Fromm, 1955; Bowman, 1955). The typical American is considered to be a professional joiner, but many associations are of a superficial variety, in secondary groups.

Formal and Informal Groups

The basis for the differentiation between formal and informal groups is the comparative need in the group for rigidly defined roles and statuses. Although size is a factor, it is more the type of relationship that determines the degree of formality in group structure.

The typical 20th-century administrative group in government, industry, or social organizations is a *bureaucracy,* a formalized group structure characterized by specialized functions, fixed rules, and a hierarchy of authority with a basis in positions. In most organizations, however, there is also an *informal group structure* in which an unofficial, loosely defined chain of command supplements the formal one. In this structure much of the decision process takes place at informal social gatherings such as the coffee break or cocktail party, where primary groups can communicate more easily than through formal channels. (Similarly, various informal roles are assumed by members at different levels in the formal hierarchy, as described in Box 14–4 in Chapter 14.)

In this connection it is also possible to distinguish between "real" and "ideal" groups. Ideal groups as defined by an institutional framework, such as the formal units in a hierarchy as shown on an organizational chart, are cut across by more realistically oriented informal groups built around the face-to-face relationships in the typing pool or on the assembly line (Roethlisberger & Dickson, 1939). These real groups are not the ideal production groups conceived by management, which reach or exceed the production rate, uncritically accept suggestions from authority, and interact socially only at prescribed times. Studies of military personnel in World War II showed the enormous importance of the informal primary group, which focused on loyalty to one's buddies rather than to the avowed purposes of higher echelons (Shils & Janowitz, 1948). In some cases the formal and informal group coincides; a machine-gun detail, for example, can also be the primary group to which the soldier attaches loyalties and looks for norms.

In-Groups and Out-Groups

Another fundamental differentiation is between in-groups and out-groups, or majority and minority groups. The *in-group* is socially accepted; it sets the dominant norms within a given society and tends to reject marginal or "inferior" groups. What may be the in-group in one culture or subculture may be an out-group in another; the dominant Anglo-Saxon strain in the mainstream of American culture for example, can be an out-group in some portions of Chicago or the Bronx (Baltzell, 1964). Likewise, in-groups and out-groups may be very specific; a particular team or squad may consider any adversary or deviant as the out-group. There is a kind of group ethnocentrism, whether it be centered on a nation's armed forces, or the infantry as opposed to the air force, or one particular battalion, squadron, or platoon (see Sherif & Sherif, 1953, 1956).

Membership and Reference Groups

A distinction has also been made between membership and reference groups (Hyman, 1942). Membership groups are those to which people actually belong, like the family, play group, gang, or school. Reference groups, as noted in Chapter 8, are those to which they aspire or refer themselves, which may or may not be the same as their membership groups.

A child, motivated by the desire to belong and to gain prestige among peers, learns or *introjects* the norms and standards of her or his reference groups. These in large part determine the structure of the child's ego and the nature of ego involvements, which in turn affect the child's personality and relationships to other persons and groups, as described in Chapter 4.

Thus reference groups function to determine the norms for most of our attitudes and behavior, religious, political, or social. Because of our multigroup membership, we have a complex set of norms, and not all of them are in harmony. A study of adolescents by Sherif and Sherif (1964), for example, found that status in the group depended on, among other things, conformity to group-accepted norms, which were often in conflict with the norms of other groups to which they belonged, such as family or school.

There is a gradual process by which membership groups and reference groups come to coalesce, or at least strongly overlap. Newcomb's (1958) finding of a tendency among Bennington College students over a four-year period to move from conservative positions on many social and international issues to liberal ones was noted in Chapter 8. As the family increasingly ceased to be a reference group for the girls, they assumed the attitudes of their instructors and of their peers, who, of course, were moving in the same direction. Some girls, however, continued to regard their families as the primary reference group and their peers as a negative reference group. The conclusion was that people relate themselves and their attitudes "to some reference group or groups, positively or negatively."

Reference groups—political parties, religious groups, allegiance to a cause (save the whales, bring back prayer in the schools), or a variety of others—help establish self-identity and provide a means of attachment to or separation from types of people or situations (Wicklund & Duval, 1971). A study of Cuban American students at the University of Miami found they were more likely to reject opinions which were identified with Castro than those that did not have this negative label (Carver & Humphries, 1981). As a negative reference group for Cuban residents in Florida, Castro's Cuba served mostly to promote a feeling of solidarity, rather than a means to determine opinion or define the self.

Conflict between membership and reference groups—or between in-groups and out-groups—can be lessened, particularly when members' attitudes have been polarized, by efforts to promote understanding, as Box 12–1 shows.

Because of the intense need for status in Western society, there frequently is considerable conflict between the groups people belong to and the groups they aspire to join. The expectancies by both the individual and society regarding group roles produces indecision about group loyalties. The basis for this feeling in present-day society has been labeled *multiple-group membership*. One person can belong to the Presbyterian church, the Young Republicans, the Masons, and the West End bowling league, in addition to primary group associations in the family, a neighborhood gang, or a golf foursome on Saturday morning. Often group associations linger when the original attachment no longer exists; your college friends, for example, may remain on the margin of your adult social relationships, although they may have little to do with your later life.

APPROACHES TO THE STUDY OF GROUPS

The small group was of interest even before empirical sociology was well established. Typical of early studies was George Simmel's (1908, 1950) investigation of the size of the group as a determinant of interpersonal relations.

Box 12–1
FAMILIARITY CAN ALSO BREED RESPECT

When students rioted at Stanford University in the spring of 1970, violent contacts with police aggravated an already tense campus situation. In an experimental attempt to depolarize the attitudes of police and students toward each other, 164 students (95 of whom were control subjects with no interactions with the police) and 37 local policemen were invited to participate in three forms of interaction.* In the first, students rode in police squad cars, so they could observe police officers performing their professional duties and learn their attitudes and beliefs. In the second, dinners and "rap sessions" provided opportunities to discuss such concerns as Vietnam, drugs, and civil disobedience. And in the third, encounter sessions (in triads and sextets), were led by a professional facilitator, to encourage the expression of feelings and attitudes and, in a few groups, to introduce "nonverbal sensory awareness encounter techniques."

Self-report questionnaires were used to examine the attitudes of members of each group toward the other, both before and after the interaction. Depolarization was indicated on 70 out of the 82 items; 32 reached statistically significant changes, 6 showed increased polarization, and 6 indicated no change. Although the three approaches were not formally compared, the encounter sessions appeared to be the most efficient in reducing hostility, probably due to their structured nature.

Both groups saw that beyond the commitment to nonviolent interaction, there was a vague similarity between the roles of police and students, since both were regarded as stereotyped victims of prejudice and to some extent separated from the rest of society. Both groups were conscious of the injustices of the legal system and, in fact, of society at large, and both "are similarly frustrated in the availability of responses to such problems." The police were required to enforce rather than reform the laws, and the students realized their powerlessness to change them.

The investigation was more of an exploratory study than a controlled experiment, but it does suggest how two groups can reduce their hostility when they come into intimate contact.

---

*M. J. Diamond and W. C. Lobitz, "When Familiarity Breeds Respect: The Effects of an Experimental Depolarization Program on Police and Student Attitudes toward Each Other," *Journal of Social Issues*, 1973, *29*, 295-110.

He was interested also in structural questions such as the implications of the small group to the larger social structure. On the functional side, it was Cooley who, as has been noted, pioneered in distinguishing between primary and secondary groups and in discussing the socializing aspects of the group, particularly the family.

Sociometry

Social psychologists have sought for years quantitative techniques they could use to investigate interpersonal relations. The pioneer in this effort was a socially oriented psychiatrist, J. L. Moreno, who coined the term *sociometry* to describe one such technique. The sociometrist is concerned primarily with obtaining choices in interpersonal relations, such as with whom one would like to live, work, or play. Using groups of girls at the Hudson Training School, Moreno (1934, 1953) mapped out the "spontaneous" likes and dislikes of each girl for her cottage mates. He then constructed a *sociogram* of each group to show the pattern of attractions and repulsions, the isolates and leaders, and subgroup networks of relationships. In the simplified example in Figure 12-1, there are mutual attractions between AB, AC, AD, DE, BF, and FG. Mutual rejections are shown by CD and DG. F accepts A but is rejected by her, and the same is true for BC, CF, and ID. Isolates are H, J, and I.

Moreno found the sociometric method valuable in many ways. For example, it can be used to rearrange individuals into congenial groups for purposes of living, eating, or working together. The technique has also proven useful in studying leadership and group morale, as will be indicated in Chapter 15.

In offering choices of companions to the individual with this technique, several guidelines have been suggested by Lindzey and Byrne (1968). These are:

1. Individuals should make the choices privately and in regard to specific criteria, namely, under what *conditions* one person will work with another.
2. The choices should be unlimited; as few or as many individuals should be chosen as the individual wishes.

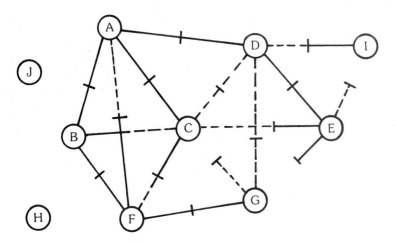

Figure 12-1. Sociometric Diagram of a Small Group

Source: Adapted from J. L. Moreno, *Who Shall Survive?* (Beacon, N. Y.: Beacon House, 1953).

3. Results of the test should be used to "restructure the group." New living arrangements or new incentives should grow out of the choices made.
4. The items should be gauged to the level of understanding of the group: In some cases the questionnaire may be used; in others, interviews or some other form of survey technique may be preferable.

In the voluminous literature on sociometry, a number of structural variables such as physical proximity, status, occupational roles, educational level, and a number of others have been found to correlate with choices.

An application of the theory of sociometric techniques is the study of organizational effectiveness by Massarik et al. (1960), which addressed such questions as:

1. To what degree are interpersonal relations in an organization defined and prescribed?
2. Do team members perceive relations as they are defined?
3. What is the climate of interaction taking place among the members?

The study examined patterns of acceptance and rejection in interpersonal relations among subjects in a naval research and development laboratory. Two social climates in style of interaction and leadership were found: democratic and restrictive. The democratically led division had higher morale, more productivity, and greater job satisfaction; the restrictively led division had greater efficiency and clearer perceptions of organizational relations.

A variation of sociometry is *network analysis* (Boissevain & Mitchell, 1973), which offers a more subtle and flexible approach to the study of friendship circles, kinship involvements, and informal relations in large organizations. Because of its innovativeness and broad range, network analysis has appealed to almost the entire gamut of behavioral scientists.

Group Dynamics

Because quantitative descriptions of group structure such as sociometry do not always reveal the meaning of a group to its members, social psychologists next began to explore the workings of group processes. Group dynamics is a technique which examines the effects of primary groups (such as the family, play groups, gangs, or clubs) and more impersonal secondary groups (like corporations and nations) on the needs, frustrations, attitudes, and values of group members and their influence in turn on people's social behavior. For example, Lewin (1948, 1965) studied how food consumption habits during World War II could be changed by group discussion, as opposed to the more traditional lecture method. Comparing experimental groups (group discussion) and control groups (lecture), it was found that 10 times as many women in the discussion groups as in the lecture groups changed their habits, on the basis of their participation and discussion.

Group dynamics developed out of Gestalt psychology, particularly through Kurt Lewin's application to groups of the *dynamics of involvement* he and his colleagues earlier had analyzed in individuals, as noted in Chapter 1 (de Rivera,

1976). The difference between group dynamics and sociometry is somewhat arbitrary, and many empirical studies of interpersonal behavior have been influenced by both techniques. Group dynamics has introduced a number of new concepts for studying the functioning of groups both as to changes within the group and relationships between groups (Cartwright & Zander, 1968). We will return to this topic later in connection with roles (Chapter 14), leadership (Chapter 15), social change (Chapter 16), and other aspects of social relations.

Interactional Analysis

One of the most promising approaches to studying interactions has been provided by Robert F. Bales, who calls it *interaction process analysis* (see Weick, 1968). After extensive experimentation with observing and recording group behavior, Bales (1950) proposed 12 categories or dimensions of behaviors which appeared to fit a range of interpersonal reactions at leadership training conferences, committee meetings, staff round tables, or many competitive situations such as games. Bales described these dimensions, which are listed in Figure 12–2 as part of an *interaction system*. Some of the problems he observed in group discussion, accommodation, and cooperation are: (1) *orientation*, finding a common definition of a situation; (2) *evaluation*, finding some means of arriving at a common value system; (3) *control*, attempts of the participants to influence each other; (4) reaching a final *decision*; (5) *problems of interpersonal tension*; and (6) *integration* and planning.

Interaction analysis is interested not in the content or results of group action and productivity but in the types and methods of interpersonal behavior; not in what is said but how it is said. A one-way screen allows the observer to be detached from the group itself; and after five or ten minutes the group is usually unaware of the psychologist's presence. This method of measuring interaction also enables the observer to compare one group with another.

An example of interaction process analysis is Bales's (1965) investigation of groups and members' interactional abilities and leadership. Three variables were measured: (1) activity, (2) problem solving or task ability, and (3) likability, and indexes such as communication, feedback, and patterns of hostility were used to identify different member-role types. These included:

1. The traditional *great-person* leader—a group member high in all three categories.
2. The *task specialist*—high in activity and task ability.
3. The *social specialist*—high likability, lower in activity and task ability.
4. The *overactive deviant*—high in activity and low in the other roles.
5. The *underactive deviant*—low in all three dimensions; rarer than all other types except the great-person leader.

A few of Bales's findings have been questioned, such as the apparent contribution of the specialist to the solidarity of the group (S. Wilson, 1978). Moreover, physical factors such as seating arrangements also can influence the degree and quality of group participation (Hare & Bales, 1963). Nevertheless,

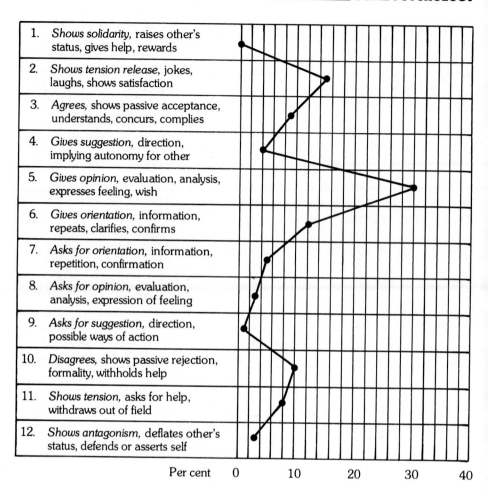

| | Per cent | 0 | 10 | 20 | 30 | 40 |

1. *Shows solidarity,* raises other's status, gives help, rewards
2. *Shows tension release,* jokes, laughs, shows satisfaction
3. *Agrees,* shows passive acceptance, understands, concurs, complies
4. *Gives suggestion,* direction, implying autonomy for other
5. *Gives opinion,* evaluation, analysis, expresses feeling, wish
6. *Gives orientation,* information, repeats, clarifies, confirms
7. *Asks for orientation,* information, repetition, confirmation
8. *Asks for opinion,* evaluation, analysis, expression of feeling
9. *Asks for suggestion,* direction, possible ways of action
10. *Disagrees,* shows passive rejection, formality, withholds help
11. *Shows tension,* asks for help, withdraws out of field
12. *Shows antagonism,* deflates other's status, defends or asserts self

Figure 12–2. Pooled Interaction Profile for Five Four-Person Groups of Ninth-Grade Boys

Source: R. F. Bales, *Interaction Process Analysis* (Reading, Mass.: Addison-Wesley Publishing Co., 1950), p. 23.

interaction analysis is valuable in differentiating styles of participation and leadership in group activities. Gibb's (1969) summary of the important aspects of interaction theory, particularly as the process is related to leadership, is reported in Chapter 15.

Interaction process analysis can be applied well beyond the usual laboratory or format setting. Wish, D'Andrade, and Goodnow (1980) showed videotapes from the television series "The American Family" and asked subjects to classify speech acts as: (1) asking versus informing, (2) initiatory versus reactive, (3)

In a small groups laboratory researchers observe an experiment in restricted communication through a one-way mirror. *Source:* Lehigh University.

dissension versus approval, (4) forceful versus forceless, and (5) judgmental versus nonjudgmental. A number of significant correlations were found between these dimensions and the characters' personality traits, which were rated independently. For instance, interactors rated as ascendant initiated forceful acts more often, and those who were less favorably evaluated were more apt to dissent, demand, or disapprove.

EXPERIMENTAL GAMING

An interesting approach to the study of the effects of group structure on behavior is experimental gaming or simulation (Greenblat & Duke, 1975). In this sense a game is a research situation in which rules and social structure can be precisely specified, so that the structure and function of groups can be studied. *Game theory* also can be applied to predict behavior and anticipate outcomes of alternative strategies; it is often used this way in business and government as a substitute for the more costly and time-consuming trial-and-error method of decision making.

The games used for research purposes vary in complexity from simple two-person, two-choice games to complex city planning or international bargaining simulations. Complex games are most often used for educational purposes such as management training and the development of decision-making and group problem-solving skills. Participants may assume the roles of leaders of countries with different degrees of wealth and armaments, for example, in order to study such behaviors as deterrence and cooperation. Simulations have also been used to develop scenarios of the future by varying the conditions of the groups to examine potential outcomes and predict trends.

In a sense most human relationships can be seen as games of strategy. That stratagems end by mutual agreement is itself a crucial aspect of the trust accorded by players to one another (Lyman & Scott, 1970). Experimental gaming provides a capsule view of social conflict and clarifies how the structural features of such problems affect their solution, as documented by such studies as Tedeschi, Schlenker, and Bonoma (1975). The findings of experimental gaming are seldom *directly* applicable to real–life conflict situations such as the activities of international terrorists or labor management disputes, but the results do provide insight into the properties of such situations that can shape the course they are likely to take.

Any classification of games is arbitrary, but four principal types have been identified:

1. *Face,* in which two players or groups are in a defensive or protective action vis-à-vis the other.
2. *Relationship,* in which one party is increasing or decreasing the social distance toward the other—there are *positive* or *negative* relationship games.
3. *Exploitation,* in which one party tries to obtain compliance from the other.
4. *Information* games, where one party desires to uncover information from another which is trying to conceal it.

Two-Person Games

The process and structure of groups are most clearly seen and have been studied most often in the two-person group, or dyad. In the simplest group situations, there are only two protagonists, and they have only two courses of action. The more strictly defined two-person games have been used most often for research in social psychology. These matrix games, which have a wide variety of structures ranging from pure cooperation to pure opposition or competition, include zero-sum games, non-zero-sum games like Prisoner's Dilemma and Chicken, and power matrices.

Zero-Sum Games

Some two person bargaining situations are structured so that the interests of the players are totally opposite, and the situation is one of pure conflict. Two-handed poker is an example—whatever one player wins, the opponent loses. In such conflict structures, we do not attempt to persuade an opponent to behave in a certain way by using threats, punishments, or rewards. Rather, we attempt to select strategies which will minimize our losses or maximize our returns. It can be assumed that our opponent is similarly motivated and will also select strategies to minimize losses.

An example is the game of matching pennies, which almost everyone has played. Any time both players show heads or tails, player A wins one cent from player B. Any time there is a mismatch, B wins one cent from A. This game can be illustrated by a matrix with single entries in each cell, as in Figure 12-3. Such matrices are always read in terms of the player on the left (A). Any positive

Player B

		Heads	Tails
	Heads	1	−1
Player A	Tails	−1	1

Figure 12–3. Zero-Sum Game of Matching Pennies

number, such as 1, indicated that A wins one of B's pennies. A minus number means that the specified amount moves from A to B.

The game situations discussed in this chapter are 2×2 games, which means that each of two players can make only one of two possible choices. In the resultant four-cell matrix, the quadrants indicate the payoffs.

Non-Zero-Sum Games

Zero-sum games are pure conflict situations in which whatever one player wins, the other must lose. In most situations, however, there is at least some scope for cooperative settlement. Such situations may be represented in matrix form by the non-zero-sum game, in which one player may win or lose, or both may win, or both may lose.

Prisoner's Dilemma. An experimental game which is characterized by partially coincident and partially divergent interests of players is the Prisoner's Dilemma. This involves the hypothetical case of two prisoners held incommunicado; each is offered, independently, the option to confess or remain silent. If both remain silent they will be charged with a lesser crime, and each will receive one year in prison. If both confess, they will be convicted of a more serious crime and will receive three years' imprisonment. If, however, one confesses while the other remains silent, the confessor goes free while the other is convicted of the most serious crime and receives imprisonment for four years. Thus, the best situation for the two prisoners taken together is for both to remain silent. However, each prisoner individually is better off if he or she could be the only confessor, and should either prisoner not feel confident in trusting the other to remain silent, confession minimizes the loss.

The Prisoner's Dilemma matrix can be transposed so that all the payoffs represent positive units (e.g., dollars). The larger the number in the matrix, the more positive the payoff (Figure 12-4) which can be in quantitative terms, i.e. cash outlay, or the situation described above as: in the upper left quadrant both confess; in the upper right A confesses and B does not, in lower left B confesses and A does not, and in lower right both remain silent. Each player is best off in the game if he or she alone defects (or confesses) and worst off if he or she alone cooperates (or remains silent). Each player faces the dilemma of sacrificing short-term gain for long-term gain (assuming the game is played for many trials), as well as the dilemma of whether or not to trust the opponent.

Chicken. An intriguing high-risk game is Chicken, which provides severe punishment for bilateral defection: One is better off being a chicken and not defecting than suffering the losses realized when both players defect. The game of chicken is preemptive, in that if one player can make it known to the other that he or she has defected, the latter must either give in or suffer substantial loss. If the punishment is very severe, there may be no option but to yield so as to avoid disaster. To make the game even more dangerous, the payoff for simple cooperative settlement can be reduced so the players must flirt with disaster in order to enjoy a high payoff in points or money (see Figure 12–5). In international

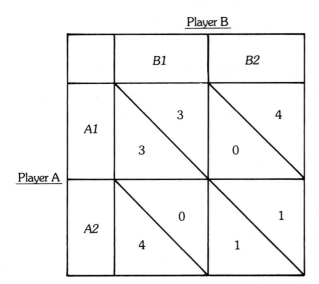

Figure 12–4. Prisoner's Dilemma Game

Player B

	B1	B2
A1	3 / 3	4 / 0
A2	0 / 4	1 / 1

Figure 12-5. Chicken Game

Player B

	B1	B2
A1	3 / 3	4 / 0
A2	0 / 4	−20 / −20

Box 12–2
BLINKING IN INTERNATIONAL RELATIONS

Heads of state seem to have an unhappy tendency to play games of Chicken, which has led S. I. Hayakawa to call the study of international relations a legitimate branch of child psychology. In conflict situations nations often seem to behave toward one another the same way children do. The tendency to resort to violence is controlled if it is known the other party is capable of violence in retaliation, and neither party wants to be labeled the aggressor.

This is also the gunslinger view which characterized the frontier: the opponents face off and dare each other to reach first for their weapons. This attitude was expressed in a remark by Dean Rusk, Secretary of State during the Kennedy administration, to John Scali, State Department correspondent for ABC, during the Cuban Missile Crisis: "Remember when you report this, that eyeball to eyeball, they (Soviet Union) blinked first."*

_____
*R. Hilsman, *To Move a Nation* (Garden City, N. Y.: Doubleday & Co., 1967), p. 219.

relations, leaders often seem to be playing Chicken (see Box 12–2), as will be demonstrated in the discussion of mutual deterrence in Chaper 18.

Both the Prisoner's Dilemma and the game of Chicken can be illustrated in the taking of hostages or other acts of terrorism (Corsi, 1981). The terrorists want to maximize the concessions, whereas governments want to minimize their losses. A number of unknowns exist for both sides. Who are the authorities willing to sacrifice? Are the terrorists ready to die? Manipulative strategies and communications increase the riskiness of the game. If terrorists are captured, the hostages may be killed; if hostages are released, concessions must be made. It can be a no-win proposition on both sides.

Power Matrices

When a punishing capability is available, a player may be tempted to threaten the use of it to persuade the opponent to behave in a desired manner. When both protagonists have this capability, threat-counterthreat spirals frequently begin, and actual use of the capability can escalate into high levels of mutual destruction. In such situations, protagonists usually lose sight of the real payoff situation and become concerned only with beating the opponent.

Power in game situations refers to either *force*, the capability of inflicting punishment (or providing reward) to one's opponent should the opponent not behave in the desired manner, or *preservation*, the ability to protect one's own payoffs by limiting or preventing the opponent from altering the payoffs. A *threat* is a statement of intent to use force in certain circumstances. The unilateral, bilateral, and no-threat conditions are described in Chapter 18 in the section on conflict and its resolution.

Areas of Research

The research on two-person matrices generally focuses on one or more of three general areas. First there is the *structure of the situation* or the mechanical features of the game, such as the relationship between payoffs (or rewards in the outcome), the amount of threat or punishment available to each player, the cost of playing, the speed of play, the number of trials, the amount of information available to each player before and during play, the extent of communication between players, and so on. Second is *strategic* research, which concentrates on the effects on subjects' behavior of various strategies and different levels of promises, warnings, and threats. Third is *predispositional variables* like the personalities of the opponents, the affective relationship between them, and various stresses and special orientations of the individuals involved.

Structural dimensions: Information and communication. The payoff or reward structure of any gaming situation is usually the most important structural-variable influence on behavior (reward structures are discussed in the final section of this chapter). Other structural factors in games also are of interest, however. In conflict situations a player often lacks complete information about the opponent's payoff schedule. The player may know that the opponent prefers one outcome to another, but precisely what each payoff is worth is not known. If a player is motivated only by the desire to maximize her or his own payoff, incomplete information about the other's payoff should increase reliance on optimal strategy solutions.

The availability of a communication channel between the two players is important because it makes bargaining possible. Communication channels allow two people to agree to play the game in a specific manner before actually making any choices, but communication channels also open the possibilities of double-crosses, threats, ultimatums, and so on. When conflict develops, protagonists frequently stop talking to each other; use of a communication channel ensures greater cooperation. As an example, in a variation of the Prisoner's Dilemma game with a laboratory group of eight West German students, coalitions were necessary for rescue from a sinking boat; that is, two passengers had to be forfeited in order for the remaining four to be saved. Group members with whom the subject could not communicate were the most likely to be left out of the coalition (Pool, 1976).

Strategy in mixed motive games. Much research effort has been directed toward determining the effectiveness of various strategies for eliciting cooperation or reducing the belligerence of subjects in conflicts. The effectiveness of a particular strategy, however, is highly dependent on the payoff structure of the

The hostage ordeal in Iran was perceived by the American people as an agonizing threat to national integrity. For the hostages themselves, it represented new kinds of group loyalties and relationships and resulted in 14 months of intensive, complex bargaining on the international scene. *Source:* United Press International, Inc.

situation. Obviously one cannot behave punitively when one has no force capability, nor can one respond cooperatively in a zero-sum game situation.

In situations which have provisions for cooperative, exploitative, punitive, competitive, or related behaviors, the effects of various contingent strategies (in which a player bases his or her strategy at least in part on the strategy choices of the opponent) and noncontingent strategies (in which the player's strategy is independent of the opponent's choices) can be determined experimentally. In experiments by Swingle (1970b), highly cooperative strategies by powerful opponents resulted in exploitative play by the subject, and a tit-for-tat strategy drastically reduced the exploitative responding of weak players. In general, in symmetrical game situations, calculated or limited cooperative strategies elicit more cooperation from an opponent than highly cooperative strategies, which tend to encourage exploitative behavior.

Predispositional variables. A player's personality and affective relationship with and attitudes toward the opponent are brought into the game situation. They can influence the player's tendency to be cooperative, trusting, or forgiving, or they could predispose the player to be exploitative

One player's predisposition to behave in a certain way in a game obviously has an effect on the other player's behavior. Thus the outcome reflects the interaction of the predispositions of both players and the structure of the situation. Frequently the effects of the game structure override the effects of personality.

Simulations in Triads and Larger Coalitions

In the dyad group relationships discussed in the preceding section, two protagonists usually have only two courses of action. In addition, each player is completely knowledgeable, which means that each is fully aware of the payoffs to both himself or herself and the opponent. In real-life situations, of course, bargainers typically have many alternative courses of action, and they often do not know the precise consequences of any particular response. Frequently, a person has only a vague indication that the other person in the situation seems to prefer one outcome over another, and it is usually not possible to be entirely sure of one's own outcomes. In most real-life situations, too, more than two people are involved in any conflict or bargaining situation, either actively (they make independent choices) or passively (they suffer only the consequences of the actions of the principal game players). In multiperson games, players usually can form temporary alliances, or *coalitions,* in which several players collaborate to their mutual advantage and to the disadvantage of other players in the situation.

Thus, in game theory, the most important difference in group size is the jump from two to three players. In a two-person game, coalitions are not possible, but as soon as there are three or more players, two of them can gang up on the third one. Much research has been devoted to the patterning of the coalitions that are formed for these purposes.

Consider, for example, a situation in which three major stockholders are attempting to gain control of a company. Stockholder A has 47 percent of the outstanding shares, shareholder B has 27 percent, and shareholder C has 24 percent. The other 2 percent of the shares is scattered among large numbers of people and institutions. Assuming that each stockholder wishes to gain as much control over the company as possible, what kinds of coalitions would be most effective?

Usually various kinds of trade-offs result. Shareholder A, for example, might think he or she is bringing the most into the coalition and therefore is entitled to the lion's share of the payoffs to be gained from it. This could encourage the smaller shareholders to form a coalition excluding A. Each member of the coalition has some power, if only to a limited degree, and thus can trade off shares for decision-making purposes.

Maximum Influence Theory

In another type of situation, each shareholder may want to gain control not only of the company but also of as many other shareholders as possible. Assume that the shareholder with the largest percentage of the shares will have the greatest influence in the direction of the company. If shareholder A has 45 percent of the outstanding shares; shareholder B, 40 percent; and shareholder C, 13 percent, maximum-influence theory indicates that the weakest shareholder (with only 13 percent of the shares) should be included in any coalition. In this two strong–one weak coalition situation, if one of the strong shareholders forms a coalition with the weak shareholder, they both gain control of the other powerful shareholder in the situation. For example, if B formed a coalition with C, they would have 53 shares together and would gain control over A, with 45 shares the most powerful single person in the situation, and B would also gain control over C.

Conflict Reduction Theory

If the shareholder with the most shares in a triadic coalition with two strong and one weak shareholders will become chairperson of the board of directors, thereby having greater influence over the other shareholders, conflict reduction theory suggest that the most powerful and the least powerful shareholders should form a coalition. In that way not only would they gain control of the company, but the division of influence would be most consistent—the most powerful member would become chairperson; the least powerful member, in return for the pivotal power, could attain board membership; and collectively they would control the other powerful shareholder. If two almost equally powerful but weak shareholders formed a coalition, they would have to resolve the conflict of who would assume control of the board, but this might be the only way either one of them could do so.

Other Coalition Theories

A number of other theories of coalition formation have been proposed. The *minimum-resource theory* is based on the idea that "any participant will expect others to demand from a coalition a share of the payoff proportional to the amount of resources that they can contribute to a coalition" (Gamson, 1961). In the *pivotal power theory,* participants as usual try to maximize their shares of the payoff, the pivotal power being determined by the potential winning coalitions as compared to potential failures by others. *Bargaining theory* essentially refers to a negotiating process. In one variant, the individual has the option to join or stay out of a coalition which offers the highest expected outcome (Komorita & Chertkoff, 1973). In a test using four-person teams and monetary rewards, Michener, Fleishman, and Vaske (1976) found that when positive choices (nonveto distributions) were made the bargaining theory was relevant, but for negative choices (veto distribution) the other two theories, minimum-resource and pivotal power, were more appropriate.

Many of the coalitions suggested by these theories depend to a great extent on the power distribution in the group being analyzed. Different coalitions are preferable when there are different power distributions, and the divisibility of the payoff derived from coalition formation also is an important consideration.

In real life, coalitions are an important factor in international relations and politics (see Box 11-5 in Chapter 11). In this sense, the term applies to alliances of groups, parties, or nations to serve mutual political interests. The principles of maximum influence, conflict reduction, and the other coalition theories described above have a basis in political science and are often applied in that discipline.

COACTION AND RIVALRY: GROUP EFFECTS ON LEARNING AND PERFORMANCE

The pervasive influence of group structures in society on people's attitudes and behavior was demonstrated in the preceding chapter, which showed how group pressure can encourage conformity to the group's norms or prosocial behavior. Whenever two or more people interact together, a group is formed which becomes a source of influence on the members. Thus an individual's performance and learning are inevitably affected by the presence of others. The interaction may take the form of *coaction,* in which the others serve cooperatively or as an audience, or *rivalry,* in which they directly compete.

In a group which consists of organisms of the same species, laboratory tests have found that the drive level of the individual organisms is increased and the performance of their basic responses is enhanced (Zajonc, 1966). Animals execute well-learned or highly probable responses with greater speed, shorter latency, or with greater efficiency when two or more organisms are together. Numerous behaviors are affected by the passive presence or coaction of other animals—copulation in rats, feeding in dogs, nest building in ants, and maze performance in fish and cockroaches, for example. When a response is only partially learned, however, the heightened drive conditions created by the presence of other organisms can result in more errors. Performance may also be inpaired when animals are distracted by the presence of other animals, of course (Jones & Gerard, 1967).

Among humans, too, the presence of others can either restrict or heighten behavior. It can make us nervous or tongue-tied, or induce us to give a better performance than usual. As with animals, the presence of other people enhances performance but inhibits learning. The other people increase a person's *arousal level,* or threshold of being activated to a given behavior, and the more directly competitive the other people are seen as being, the greater is the arousal.

The relationship between arousal and learning is curvilinear, as shown in Figure 12-6. Learning is enhanced as the arousal level rises from low to moderate, but it decreases as the arousal level rises still further. Since humans in test environments are at least moderately aroused to start with, the presence of other persons as an audience or direct competition may increase arousal above the optional level, and this in turn will reduce learning efficiency. Because arousal increases the number of mistakes in the early phases of learning, it increases the time required to learn a task. The presence of others in a learning situation can have a beneficial effect, however, if the arousal level is low to start with or if they provide some sort of instruction or model behavior.

When a task has been well learned appropriate responses are likely, and under normal circumstances performance should be enhanced by the presence of others. However, under very high arousal levels, performance has been found to be adversely affected (Swingle, 1970c). Since the level of arousal is normally not extraordinarily high, the presence of others can be expected to enhance performance but suppress learning.

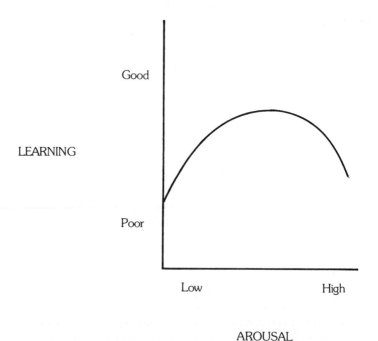

Figure 12-6. Relationship of Learning to Arousal

The other persons in a situation may be perceived as a passive audience, a critical audience, sympathetic coactors, or rivals. The performer's perception of the role of the other persons in the situation will affect the degree of arousal. If the other persons are competitors, the degree of challenge or the frequency of winning can affect performance (see Box 12–3). In sports competition, for example, athletes who perform exceeding well in practice frequently do poorly in stressful competitions. Conversely, a dramatic performer who is indifferent throughout rehearsals may give a brillant performance on opening night.

Other performers may suffer from *stage fright,* however, which also is related to the size and status of the group or audience. Using a simulated audience in a laboratory setting, Jackson and Latané (1981) found nervousness was postively correlated with the size and prestige of the audience. Subjects who sang for an audience of professors and graduate students of the music school experienced more anxiety than those who sang for a less discriminating audience. This study also examined stage fright in a university Greek Week talent show. The degree of tension reported by performers in musical, dancing, or comedy acts was inversely related to the number of participants in the act. The researchers concluded that the difference between the amateur and the professional is the ability to project "the nervous tension of stage fright into stage presence and project this energy back to the audience in the form of vivacity, depth, or intensity" (p. 84).

Group interaction can result in social inhibition not only when people are apprehensive about being evaluated but also when they fear their responses will be regarded as uncommon or unusual. Most people don't want to be considered different and avoid acting in an unconventional way without group support. If you are shaking your shoulders and tapping out a solid beat coming over your car receiver, you may be embarrassed if an unsympathetic driver in another car looks your way, for example. In one of the earliest experiments on the influence of the

Box 12–3
ON YOUR MARK

Competition has different effects on people, depending on the degeee of challenge an opponent represents. In repeated races with the same opponent, how often a person actually wins and the degree to which the person leads or lags are important.

In an experiment by Paul Swingle, using model trains, each contestant had a programmed opponent, so races could be arranged to let the contestant win 10, 50, or 90 percent of the races under conditions of high or low challenge.* Low challenge was created by arranging the programmed opponent's trains so that it led or lagged behind the contestant's train by more than one car length. In high challenge both trains were kept neck and neck by controlling the speed of the opponent's train.

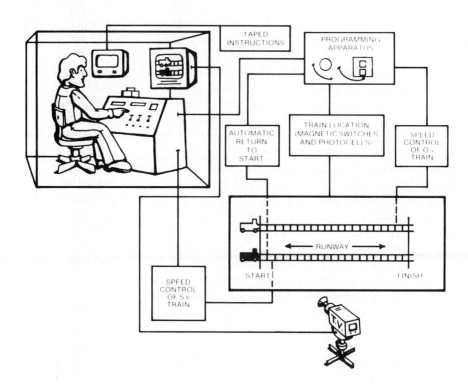

As the contestants' percentage of races won increased, there was an orderly increase in rate of responding (pressings of the control lever). Among those who won 90 percent of the races, challenge appeared to make no difference to performance. However, when trains ran neck and neck, slower performance resulted for the 10 percent winners and faster speeds for those in the 50 percent group. Subjects' speed decreased following a win, particularly in the low-challenge groups, and increased following a loss.

After the races were over each player's attitudes regarding the rival were measured. Opponents in the W50 condition were viewed most favorably as future competitors, while the victorious opponents in W10 were rated as least attractive. The rating of W90 opponents, who were consistent losers, fell between these two extremes. High-challenge opponents were generally more favorably described than those in the low-challenge situations, and the ratings of the high-challenge W50 opponents were the most positive.

It is commonly assumed that conditions of high challenge will provide the greatest motivation to perform, but these results indicate that winning a race tends to slow down performance speed, while losing a race increases it. Because this effect was most evident in the low-challenge situation, it supports the notion that the effects of either victory or defeat are more pronounced when the race's outcome is predictable (i.e., the lead or lag margin is great) than when the competitors are running neck and neck. There appears to be an important interaction between the reinforcing properties of winning and the stimulating properties of high challenge, since the most favored rivals were those in the close races, while at the same time players viewed rivals they had beaten more favorably than those who consistently beat them.

*P. G. Swingle, "Effects of the Win-Loss Ratio and Challenge on Speed in a Two-Person Lever-Pressing Race," *Journal of Experimental Psychology,* 1969, *80,* 542–547.

group on association and thought, F. H. Allport (1920) found that people involved in a word association task give fewer uncommon responses in the presence of others. For example, if the word *chair* makes you think of the words *table* and *pineapple,* you are likely to suppress the uncommon association (*pineapple*) when others can hear your response.

Another aspect of social inhibition is *social loafing,* or reduced output when performing in a group setting (Latané, Williams, & Harkins, 1979). When subjects were asked to shout and clap in an experiment, the rate decreased as the size of the group increased from a pair to a group of four or six. In a later investigation, when subjects were informed that microphones would record their individual shouting performance the scores increased (Williams, Harkins, & Latané, 1981). Individual identifiability within the group also applies to real-life settings: In football, for example, does a lineman have the same motivation to performance as a running back? The Ohio State University, like others, records each play on videotape and holds weekly press luncheons at which the lineman of the week is announced. The cliché that teamwork depends on the individual as well as the group has been proven innumerable times.

REWARD STRUCTURES: INDIVIDUALISTIC, COMPETITIVE AND COOPERATIVE

The rewards of group interaction have different types of structures which are oriented to individual achievement or varying degrees of competition or cooperation among members. To illustrate, consider a situation with which you are very familiar: grades received in a college course. If the instructor indicates that students will be marked on a curve, regardless of the actual performance of each student in the class, a small proportion will receive As, a like proportion will receive Fs, and slightly larger numbers will receive Bs or Ds. If your work represents the assumed average in the class, or that of the largest proportion of students, you will receive a grade of C. You might come out better in a grading situation in which the grades are solely based on each student's performance; then your grade would be totally independent of the grades received by other students in the class. In other circumstances your grade might depend on the communal achievement in a project by a work group you join or to which you are assigned.

The first situation illustrates *intra-group competition,* in which students compete for a restricted number of good grades. The second condition is an *individualistic reward* structure; each student's grade is independent of the grades received by others. The third example is a case of *group cooperation* in which each person shares equally in the goal obtained collectively by the group. These examples, which illustrate different types of *intragroup* reward structures, do not exhaust the possibilities. In a *second-order* reward structure, for example, groups or teams of individuals may attempt to accomplish or acquire group-desired goals. The structure may be competitive, as in team sports in which each team is attempting to be victorious.

There is also an *intergroup* reward structure, as when two groups compete or combine their efforts to attain desired goals. As an example, in pioneer American rural communities it was not unusual for several families to cooperate in building barns or bridges and clearing forests or roads. The organizational plan, or the pattern of groups in an organization, also can determine the reward structure, as Box 12–4 shows.

The orientation of a group's reward structure to individual achievement, competition, or cooperation can greatly increase the complexity of the group structure. There can be more than a single goal for which the group is striving, either collectively or individually, and care must be taken not to confuse group reward structures with individual motives. A highly competitive person entering a cooperatively structured group will still pursue an individual goal and perceive himself or herself as in competition with others in the group. People also can perceive the same reward structure in different ways. There is evidence, for example, that women tend to view three-person bargaining situations in a less competitive way than men do. Whereas women are concerned with equitable distribution of payoffs, men are more likely to define the situation in terms of conflict or competition. They see the situation as one in which they must attempt to attain a greater share of the payoff than others in the group will get.

In the individualistic structure a group member pursues a goal whose attainment is not influenced by, nor does it influence, the goal attainment of other members in the group. In the cooperative reward structure, either the participation of other people within the group is required, or the attainment of the goal is enhanced by such participation. In the competitive reward structure, the individuals in a group compete for scarce resources. To the extent that one individual acquires all or some part of the goal, the amount or quality available for other persons within the group is reduced.

Box 12–4
BOTTOM-UP AND TOP-DOWN:
FUN AND GAMES AT WORK

Specialized games and simulations have been used extensively in business and management to study and improve the effectiveness of organizations. J. A. Vaughan and B. M. Bass, for example, set up two simulated corporations patterned on different systems of organization for a sample of day and evening graduate business students.* One used the bottom-up style, in which the personnel was divided into subsystems responsible for productivity at all levels, with operators, planners, and coordinators sharing in the decision making. The other was set up in the top-down style, in which decision making is carried out in the more familiar hierarchical structure.

The simulated product was "I-beams," constructed by cutting and stapling IBM cards together in specified designs. They were "marketed" competitively with the help of advertising, but no real value was attached to the money transactions. In the bottoms-up arrangement the players had access to necessary resources, such as money and equality of reward, and they could alter and restructure the various subsystems. Almost all decision making was carried out in groups; no one person could be thought of as the overall supervisor. In the pyramidal or top-down system, management had a line organization capable of both perceiving outside needs and coordinating the production line efficiently.

In terms of both satisfaction and income, the bottoms-up system appeared to be superior. The day (or full-time) students were generally more satisfied with this system than the evening (or part-time) students, who were already entrenched in the business world and felt more comfortable with the top-down approach. In both systems, the evening students outproduced the day students, presumably because practical experience gave them a kind of know-how about production.

While group structure is an important factor in organizations, in this study the attitudes of the participants probably were more important than the organization style. The differences between the day and evening students also demonstrate the difficulty of generalizing from a limited sample, and in any case care must be taken in making inferences from simulated games to the real world.

*J. A. Vaughan and B. M. Bass, "Putting the Business World into a Test Tube," in E. Aronson and R. Helmreich (Eds.), *Social Psychology* (New York: D. Van Nostrand, Co., 1973), pp. 99–101.

Effects on Groups of Competition or Cooperation

In the same way interaction in a group affects the individual's learning and performance through coaction or rivalry, the degree of competition or cooperation in the group reward structure has effects on the structure of the group. In some circumstances, intergroup and intragroup competition have been found to have opposite effects. Research suggests that intergroup competition enhances group cohesion: for example, Sherif et al. (1961) found that teams become more cohesive when they are involved in competition with other teams. The effects of team failure also seem to be cushioned by intergroup association (Fiedler, 1970). In conditions of intragroup competition, however, there is a tendency for individuals to hoard information, and higher tension is evident. Thus groups with internal competition experience lower cohesion, but as noted above, under some circumstances competition can enhance performance. The relation between group attraction and cohesiveness is the subject of the next chapter.

The diffusion of responsibility often operates in group situations where rivalry is less influential than coaction. In the helping behavior studies described in Chapter 11, people in need were found to be less likely to receive help as the number of people observing the situation increased; a person who might offer help when alone would expect others to share the responsibility when several observers were present. There is also a tendency for groups to accept greater risk than individuals, as shown by the evidence on the risky-shift phenomenon to be described in Chapter 13.

The intragroup and intergroup reward structures of a group frequently are in conflict. Organized team sports offer the best example of a situation in which team members want their teams to win but also want the recognition accorded star players. In learning situations, both cooperative reward structures and intergroup competitive reward structures have been found to be superior to individual competitive systems. Deutsch (1949) found that groups organized according to cooperative reward structures, as compared to those with individually competitive structures, demonstrated greater coordination of efforts, achievement pressure, mutual comprehension of communication, productivity, quality of product, friendliness, and positive evaluation of the group's members and production.

SUMMARY

In all types of groups—primary groups like the family and secondary groups which comprise so much of contemporary urban life; in-groups and out-groups; reference and membership groups which function to determine norms and values—the group influences its members and is in turn influenced by the members. At the most fundamental level, the simple presence of others exerts an influence over behavior. Rivalry enhances the level of arousal, which tends to enhance performance but generally retards learning.

Several approaches to the analysis of groups have been devised. Sociometry, developed by Moreno, concentrates on the selection process in interpersonal relations, such as the people we would choose to share our activities. Group dynamics, conceived by Lewin, focuses on how groups function and the ever-changing properties of the group. Bales's interactional analysis is an ingenious process for monitoring interpersonal relations in the group. The newer techniques for studying the group are adaptations of these classic approaches.

A major topic in this chapter is the various aspects of experimental games or simulation. Gaming focuses attention on the structure of the group and its effects on cooperation, competition, and so on. Problems of power and strategies are often analyzed with game matrices illustrating interactions in dyads and simulations of coalition triads. The reward structure of the group influences the degree to which its members cooperate, compete, or hoard information and helps determine the attractiveness of the group to members. The relation between interpersonal attraction and group cohesion is examined in the following chapter.

WORDS TO REMEMBER

Coalition. An alliance, often temporary, between persons or organizations in which attempts are made to resolve differences in order to present a common front.

Dyad. Two individuals in some form of interaction.

Game theory. Analysis of groups according to behavioral options and expected outcomes in terms of rewards and costs which utilizes experimental game situations.

Group. Collectivity of two or more individuals who interact with each other. Groups can be studied in both the laboratory and real life; there are various classifications, such as formal and informal, membership and reference, primary and secondary groups.

Group dynamics. Theory of group behavior initiated by Kurt Lewin which stresses dynamics or change within the group and which approaches the group as process. Tends to overlap with *sociometry,* which is more concerned with the structure of the group.

Interaction process analysis. Approach to group processes devised by Robert Bales in which participants are monitored according to 12 categories oriented to communication and accommodation.

Matrix. A rectangular arrangement of numbers; in game or exchange theory, a table indicating the costs and rewards for each option open to the participants.

Primary group. Group characterized by intimacy and face-to-face relations, in which fellow members are considered as ends in themselves rather than as means to an end. (See *secondary group).*

Prisoner's Dilemma. Simulation technique or game for laboratory study of cooperation and competition. The game supposes two suspects have been apprehended for a crime. If both can keep silent they are likely to receive a light sentence or be released, since they cannot be found guilty. If one confesses, that person may go free for turning state's evidence. If both should confess they will both be found guilty. In the laboratory, the game is often played according to a point system.

Secondary group. Group composed of a large number of members who have relatively formalized and impersonal relations with one another, such as larger classrooms or the work force in a factory. A secondary group may break down into primary groups.

Sociometry. Study of group behavior by analyzing personal preferences or the bases of interpersonal preferences or rejections. Sociometric tests may include questionnaires which ask for names of persons with whom the subject wants to sit, live, work, or generally interact.

Triad. A three-member group, often a more unstable structure than a dyad.

Zero-sum game. A gaming situation in which the pluses balance the minuses, in contrast to the *mixed-motive* situation which results in a differential score.

QUESTIONS FOR DISCUSSION

1. Describe an *asocial* aggregation. What are the essential features of social groups?

2. Distinguish between primary and secondary groups. Give examples of how these types of groups function in your own interpersonal relationships.

3. Give some examples of possible conflicts between membership and reference groups. What kinds of people might have problems in relating the two kinds of groups?

4. Name and describe the basic approaches to the study of groups. What kinds of problems might best be studied using each approach? What are their advantages and limitations?

5. What is an experimental game? How is game theory used in social-psychological research?

6. What form do two-person games usually take? Give some examples.

7. How are the structural and predispositional variables of two-person games related?

8. Describe the various theories of coalition formation and give some examples of studies examining them.

9. How do the variables in interactional analysis affect different types of group members?

10. What are the principal types of behavior reflecting the effects of the presence of others? Describe how the presence of others affects learning and performance.

READINGS

Arnold, W. E., and Hirsch, R. O. (Eds.) *Communicating through Behavior*. St. Paul, Minn.: West Publishing, 1977.
> Part II offers several intriguing discussions of the role of communication in group settings.

Bales, R. F. *Interaction Process Analysis*. Reading, Mass.: Addison-Wesley Publishing Co., 1950.

Bales, R. F. *Personality and Interpersonal Behavior*. New York: Holt, Rinehart & Winston, 1970.
> The first volume points to the potential and the second to the actual "pay-off" in the Bales technique of probing the individual in a group setting.

Cartwright, D., and Zander, A.(Eds.). *Group Dynamics: Research and Theory*. 3rd ed. New York: Harper and Row Publishers, 1968.
> This volume remains a landmark for its contributions to methodology, goals, standards, and structure.

Crosbie, P. V. (Ed.). *Interaction in Small Groups*. New York: Macmillan Co., 1975.
> Well-edited collection of papers on group formation, group structures, and processes.

Dinkmeyer, D. C., and Muro, J. J. *Group Counseling: Theory and Practice*. 2nd ed. Itasca, Ill.: F. E. Peacock Publishers, 1979.
> Considers the applications of group dynamics in various settings for interpersonal behavior.

Fernandez, R. (Ed.). *Social Psychology Through Literature*. New York: John Wiley & Sons, 1972.
> Although this book draws from several areas of social psychology, its examples on group processes, drawn from extracts ranging from Flaubert to Koestler, are especially relevant.

Hare, A. P. *Handbook of Small Group Research*. Rev. ed. New York: Free Press, 1976.
> Analysis and integration of some hundreds of studies in group processes.

Kowitz, A. C. and Knutson, T. J. *Decision Making in Small Groups*. Boston: Allyn and Bacon, 1980.
> A well-written analysis of groups structure and its relation to tasks and resources.

Newcomb, T. M. *The Acquaintance Process*. New York: Holt, Rinehart & Winston, 1961.
> A much-cited study of interpersonal attraction among students in a University of Michigan housing unit.

Shaw, M. E. *Group Dynamics: The Psychology of Small Group Behavior*. 2nd ed. New York: McGraw-Hill Book Co., 1976.
> A comprehensive text on groups in action, with chapters on the physical and personal environment of groups, the task environment, and special topics such as children's groups.

Sherif, M., and Sherif, C. W. *Reference Groups*. New York: Harper and Row Publishers, 1964.
> A study of norms and consequent behavior among a group of adolescent boys.

13

INTERPERSONAL ATTRACTION AND GROUP COHESION

As the analysis of the nature of social influence and the structure of the group in the two preceding chapters demonstrates, the group setting encourages conformity, obedience, and yielding behavior, and the presence of others and the reward structures of groups are as likely to produce coaction or cooperation as rivalry or competition. This integrative influence of the group structure on people's attitudes and behaviors is an important consideration in the group problem-solving process to be examined in this chapter. The principal focus, however, is on bonding in the group, or what has become known as *group cohesiveness,* the attractive property a group has for each of its members.

In Western society, the time an individual spends in groups of some sort—primary or secondary, membership or reference, in-groups or out-groups—is constantly expanding. In the United States, the self-reliance of the frontier has been replaced by the need for collective effort to keep people from invading each other's territory. But the nature of collective behavior (which will be examined in Chapter 16) is not well understood, and the related idea of systems organization is a recent development. The solutions to many of the problems facing our society would be advanced by a better understanding of groups and systems. For example, we run the risk of burying ourselves in our own refuse because we have not worked out a system to dispose of the packaging for the things we use. Consumers are willing to pay a penny or two more for a product with throw-away packaging so they do not have to bother returning containers, even though in the long run they must pay more to have them collected and disposed of, and the waste of resources will have far-reaching effects.

By the nature of society, then, social scientists must be interested in groups and organizations. Effective group functioning, systems development, conflict management, and leadership are all challenging research areas. The efforts of the most creative and experimentally minded people could well be directed toward developing the social science of groups and organizations.

This chapter begins with a comparative evaluation of individual effort and group activity. Then it considers some of the characteristics of group problem solving, such as spontaneity and innovation, limitations on capacity, diffusion of responsibility, and the effects of reinforcement. Group cohesiveness and attraction are examined in relation to participation, satisfaction, and productivity, and various methods of measuring cohesiveness are described. Then interpersonal attraction is related to affiliation needs and social power, and the balance and exchange theories are discussed as means of studying people's interactions in groups.

INDIVIDUAL EFFORT VERSUS GROUP ACTIVITY

Whether a specific procedure could be handled better by an individual or a group depends to some extent on the structural characteristics of the task. The nature of a task can be defined according to a dimension ranging from very simple (such as dropping a coin into a slot machine) to extraordinarily complex (such as designing and constructing a jet plane). The complexity of the task is related to its degree of *divisibility*. The simple task of dropping a coin into a slot machine is not divisible—one person can perform the task in a single step. Other tasks, such as changing a flat tire on an automobile, are divisible because two or three people can perform the different subtasks that are required. One person could be jacking up the car while the second is removing the lugs that hold the wheel on and the third is getting the spare tire out of the trunk and placing it in position to be mounted. If more than three people attempt to help change the tire, however, a decrease in efficiency is likely because they would interfere with one another.

With most complex tasks, group performance is superior to individual performance simply because the combination of talents, expertise, and experience required to complete the task cannot be found in one person. In industrial applications where repetitive tasks can be broken down into subtasks, output is enhanced when individual workers become specialists or expert at one small part of producing a final product. This is the concept Henry Ford recognized when he introduced the automobile assembly line. Such specialization can produce dramatic increases in output; the problem, from a strictly engineering point of view, is to find the most efficient way to divide the task among individual workers through such techniques as task allocations, equipment design, and time and motion studies. This raises another problem, however. Although task specialization increases output and efficiency in the short run, repetitive, monotonous tasks can cause people to become bored and resentful, with negative effects on productivity. The broader implications of these effects are considered later under the topic of participation, satisfaction, and productivity.

The superiority of group or individual effort for a particular task can also be determined by the nature of the task. Most tasks have two components, manual and cognitive, in varying degrees. Repetitive, assembly-line types of tasks have high manual and low cognitive components; tasks such as writing, preparing an advertising campaign, or solving arithmetic problems have heavy cognitive components and relatively minor manual ones. These properties of the task may be of prime importance in determining not only when group activity would be superior to individual effort but, more importantly, what factors operate to inhibit the performance of such a task by either individuals or groups.

As in repetitive tasks, in group activity with a high cognitive component, such as problem solving or decision making, technical or procedural analysis does not tell the whole story. Here, too, social factors, such as the perception of group belongingness, can be of great significance. The human relations movement in industry and management in the 1930s and 1940s was a reaction to the mechanistic concepts of scientific management, which had prevailed in the 1920s. Interest shifted from the process of tasks to the people who performed them and the interrelations between the person, the group and the task. Roethlisberger and Dickson (1939) reported, for example, that when workers could pride themselves on being members of a special group it was reflected immediately in work of greater quantity and better quality.

The group provides for heterogeneity of ability, information, and orientation, which has been found to contribute to effective problem solving. Attacking a problem from several different points of view seems to produce a more creative and effective solution. Thus mixed-sex groups can be superior to single-sex groups, and groups representing different personalities, age grouping, and attitudes all have been shown to be more effective in problem solving than more homogeneous groups (Hoffman, 1965). A difference in attitudes can lead to better communication and more sensitive perceptions of others in groups, as Box 13–1 shows.

GROUP PROBLEM SOLVING

Few research areas in social psychology are as intriguing as the study of group problem solving. Because these processes are complex and are affected by an enormous number of variables, research in this area requires exceptional skill, ingenuity, and creativity. In exploring the effects of group variables like size, composition, structure, and communication networks (see Chapter 15), experimenters have developed such concepts as brainstorming, information overload, the risky shift, and nonintervention.

Spontaneity and Innovation

The possibilities for open, meaningful communication in groups encourage active and spontaneous participation which gives group members material to work on and stimulates the generation and refinement of ideas. In one experiment on the task of self-disclosure (J. D. Davis, 1977), dyads took turns volunteering information about themselves. For one group of subjects, free discussion was

Box 13–1
THE AGREEABLE EFFECTS OF DISAGREEMENT

Differences in opinion among group members inevitably occur, although people may not be attracted to groups in which the majority disagrees with their own points of view. When group members become aware that other members' opinions differ from theirs, they may attempt to persuade those who disagree to change their minds, or they may communicate only with others who share their ideas.

To study discussion groups in which different attitudes were expressed, Irwin Altman and Elliott McGinnies placed 500 high school students in six-member groups on the basis of their ethnocentrism, or Eth scores.* (Ethnocentrism has been defined as belief in the superiority of one's own group.) Five types of groups were set up: (1) *Low Eth Homogeneous*—all six members had low prejudice scores; (2) *Low Eth Majority*—four low Eths, two high Eths; (3) *Balanced*—an equal number of high and low Eths; (4) *High Eth Majority*—four high Eths, two low Eths; and (5) *High Eth Homogeneous*—all had high prejudice scores. An antiprejudice film was shown, after which each group discussed the film and the topic of ethnic conflict. These discussions were recorded, and a questionnaire was filled out by each subject. Finally, all subjects were retested on the ethnocentrism scale.

The pace of discussion was found to quicken in the heterogeneous groups, but not in the balanced or homogeneous groups. Among the high Eths a few persons dominated the discussion; the low Eths showed more equal individual contributions. In balanced groups most of the remarks were found to be directed to like-minded members. When in a minority, low Eths discussed actively with everybody; high Eths in a majority interacted little with those holding opposite opinions.

After all the discussions, an overall decrease in ethnocentrism was found for both high and low Eths; when group members, especially the low Eths, perceived opinions to be different from their own, they tended to communicate more with others. Members of balanced groups communicated less, were less attracted to the group, and less accurate in perceiving the attitudes of others.

In this experiment, at least, unbalanced diversity was most conducive to intragroup perception and communication.

---

*I. Altman and E. McGinnies, "Interpersonal Perception and Communication in Discussion Groups of Varied Attitudinal Composition," *Journal of Abnormal and Social Psychology,* 1960, *60,* 393–395.

permitted; for the other, only the more rigid question-answer format was allowed. Dyads who had freer discussions reached the desired "intimacy level" sooner. A highly structured situation thus appears to discourage openness and spontaneity.

Spontaneity also fosters early detection of errors, which keeps group activities oriented to the problems being studied. But evaluation of suggestions can reduce the effectiveness of the group if each proposal is subjected to long discussion, or if the group has an unrealistically high standard of acceptability for ideas.

People who are sensitive about and critical of their own ideas may have to be encouraged to try them out on the group. A technique for increasing the group's capacity to come up with ideas called *brainstorming* was originally developed in the advertising business. The procedure is quite simple, although some groups may need a little time to get used to it. Participants are encouraged to suggest as many ideas as rapidly as possible, and no idea is ever criticized; the more harebrained the idea, the better. Free-wheeling, or building upon somebody else's idea, is encouraged. The basic assumption is that if a large volume of ideas is produced, the probability of obtaining a good one is greatly increased.

The brainstorming technique enjoyed some popularity for a time, but research on it has indicated that such groups tend to produce more poor-quality ideas. Individuals working alone and free discussion groups in which criticism and evaluation are discouraged until a large number of ideas have been accumulated have been found to produce more high-quality ideas (Dunnette, Campbell, & Jaastad, 1963). Another problem with brainstorming is the tendency of the group to develop a one-track mind. Brainstorming groups come forth with a large number of ideas of a particular type, whereas people working alone or in free discussion groups initiate a greater variety of ideas (Osborn, 1963). Graham (1977) suggests that the type of problem selected is related to the success of the task, and artificially arranged groups seem to perform as well as "real" groups.

Limitations on Capacity

In considering whether enlarging the size of the suggestion pool increases the probability that a group will select a high-quality idea, it must be recognized that there are limitations on the number of ideas that can actually be considered. These limitations can be related to both social and structural group factors. If a group has a large quantity of ideas to evaluate, social influence or group pressure might operate to produce the usual results of yielding or conformity, which could reduce the effectiveness of the group's problem-solving efforts. For example, if a high-status member selects an idea out of the pool and indicates that the idea is a superb one, lower-ranking members may simply agree, with the result that other possible ideas are never submitted to group evaluation.

The structural factor is one that we have termed *information overload*. Individuals can handle just so much information in a specific period. As the amount of information they must process, abstract, and store builds up, the tendency of individuals to get confused, forget, or simply ignore information increases. A doctoral study by Springborn (1965) showed a significant *negative* correlation between the number of alternative solutions a group has available and the quality of the final solution selected. The effectiveness of the group's decisions rests to a great extent on the ability of the central person in the communication structure, as Chapter 15 will demonstrate. In another aspect, overload results when the leader or manager insists on having a hand in all decisions.

Diffusion of Responsibility

One of the most interesting group effects is the diffusion of responsibility, or the spreading of accountability. An individual who is required as a member of a group to make a decision involving some degree of risk can be convinced that other group members who participate in the decision making must also accept some of the responsibility for it. Individual accountability for decisions is much more likely to be recognized by a person working alone. This diffusion of responsibility can have at least two effects on a group: the risky-shift phenomenon and nonintervention.

The Risky Shift

A group of individuals can be encouraged to accept more risk than each individual alone would accept. Many experiments based on this risky-shift phenomenon have demonstrated that the average risk accepted by individuals working separately is less than the one they would accept as part of a group.

Several explanations have been offered for the risky-shift phenomenon. In addition to those who have argued that the shift occurs because of a diffusion of responsibility, others have considered risk taking to be a value that people like to perceive themselves as having. When individuals who have made conservative estimates are put in a group situation, they adjust the judgments toward the risky side so as not to appear overly conservative (Sanders & Baron, 1977). Persuasion may also influence group members to accept risk (Burnstein & Vinokur, 1977). Both factors help explain risky-shift behavior.

The more group members know about one another, the more likely it is that social comparison will encourage the more cautious members to accept risks like those taken by other group members who are comparable in other ways (Goethals & Zanna, 1979). It could still be argued, however, that in a group situation the shift of conservative individuals to more risky decisions is facilitated by their feeling of reduced responsibility for their actions. In one experiment it was found that when a group is oriented to the task of assessing arguments the risky shift occurs, but when it is oriented to the exchange of ideas and information there is much less shift (Clark, Crockett, & Archer, 1971).

Moreover, when there is a change in the attitudes exchanged, the participants who perceive themselves as less cautious are actually the last to change. In a study of pari-mutuel betting at a racetrack, group consensus (as compared to individual decision making) led to a shift to caution (McCauley et al., 1973), but groups placing bets in blackjack games showed shifts toward greater risk (Blascovitch, Ginsburg, & Veach, 1975). The shift toward greater risk or greater caution appears to be related to several factors, including the individual's desire not to appear overly conservative, the evaluation of other group members' attributes and abilities, and the importance of the decisions being taken.

Nonintervention

The second line of evidence of responsibility diffusion in groups is related to the research on helping behavior described in Chapter 11, which offers evidence of whether or not people take decisive actions when other people are around. Latané and Darley (1970a, 1979b) explored the disturbing phenomenon of nonintervention in the classic example of the street murder of Kitty Genovese (see Box 13–2) and in laboratory experiments in which subjects witnessed someone being victimized or in need of help. They found that people exposed to a situation in which another person needs help or in which intervention is appropriate are more likely to intervene if they are alone than with a group.

Box 13–2
GETTING INVOLVED

Shortly after 3:00 o'clock in the morning of March 13, 1964, Kitty Genovese was returning to her home in Queens, New York. As she left her car she was attacked by an assailant with a knife. Struggling, she reached the street corner and screamed "Oh my God, he stabbed me! Please help me! Please help me!" Lights went on in a number of apartments and residents peered out; one man called out, "Let that girl alone!" The attacker was frightened off, but as the lights gradually went out, he returned. The victim was stabbed again and screamed "I'm dying! I'm dying!" Again the attacker left, only to return a third time to finish the murder.

No less than 38 people testified to hearing the screams, but not one called the police, which could have saved the woman's life.* One explanation for this is that each onlooker, in a separate apartment, thought that someone else would call for help.

The Genovese episode and similar incidents of disinterest have given rise to a considerable literature on bystander indifference. Laboratory research, which was initiated by John Darley and Bibb Latané, has generally found only small correlations between personal characteristics of bystanders and the tendency to intervene. Still, there is some evidence that intervenors are comparatively more conscious of responsibility and are equipped with the skills to deal with emergencies. A bystander is more likely to take action if one of the subjects clearly states that an emergency exists, if signals of alarm are present, and if the bystander has some kind of identification with the victim.†

To analyze the intervenor, Gilbert Geis of the University of California turned to real-life emergency situations. His research was facilitated by the California Good Samaritan law, which provides compensation for persons who suffer any injury or other loss as a result of intervening in a crime, aiding an accident victim, or helping a police officer. From files on these cases Geis and his collaborators studied 32 individuals who had intervened in assults, holdups and other serious crimes.‡

The intervenors were compared with a control group matched on ethnic background, age, sex, and education. The intervenors differed little in social backgrounds and attitudes and were almost all male (31 out of the 32). But they were comparatively taller and heavier, had had training in self-defense or first aid, and revealed more aggressiveness. Moreover, they perceived themselves as more formidable physically than the offenders against whom they were taking action. It is significant that only 2 of the 32 said that they were aware of the Good Samaritan law before they intervened.

In real life, examples of willingness to intervene when someone needs help are reported as newsworthy events. A touching example was the birth of a child to a 23-year-old woman on a Chicago elevated train. Commuters acted as midwives, bystanders applauded and yelled "Praise the Lord!" and a shopper offered a newly purchased baby blanket to cover the infant. When the paramedics arrived, according to the *Chicago Tribune* for June 1, 1981, one remarked that "Everybody was working in unity, and there was a lot of harmony, and it was beautiful. People clapped afterwards, and what struck me was how people can work together in a unity when they have to."

---

*A. M. Rosenthal, *Thirty-eight Witnesses* (New York: McGraw-Hill Book Co., 1964).

†B. Latané and J. M. Darley, *The Unresponsive Bystander: Why Doesn't He Help?* (Englewood Cliffs, N. J.: Prentice-Hall, Inc., 1970).

‡T. L. Huston, M. Ruggiero, R. Conner, and G. Geis, "Bystander Intervention into Crimes: A Study Based on Naturally-Occurring Episodes," *Social Psychology Quarterly*, 1981, 44, 14–23.

The larger the size of the group, the less probable it is that any one individual will intervene. And for those who do intervene, the time taken to do so increases as the group size increases.

Studies of nonintervention suggest that group decision making and problem solving may be more sluggish in response to crisis situations. This could result from a diffusion of responsibility or from a social validation. In ambiguous situations people tend to look to those around them to determine the appropriateness of their response; Schachter's (1959) finding that those who experience a threatening or frightening event often choose to associate with others who have also experienced it in order to interpret the appropriateness of their reactions has been cited in preceding chapters, for example. When everyone in a group waits for someone else to intervene or act first, then the group may develop the pluralistically ignorant impression that no one interprets the situation as being serious enough to justify intervention. This again demonstrates the tremendous influence of the group on our behavior and attitudes.

Effects of Reinforcement

In the conditioning view described in Chapter 5, our behavior in the presence of others is affected because we gain reinforcement from their attention or praise, and we are punished when others criticize or ridicule our performance. As the preceding chapters in Part III have demonstrated, when people are apprehensive about being evaluated, they are inhibited and tend to exercise caution in expressing novel or unpopular ideas. Moreover, groups exert enormous pressure on deviates by threatening to reject people who disagree or are abusive. In fact, group sanction and censure are about the most potent reinforcers in society. By and large, people expend their efforts to gain the approval of groups of persons who have high status and groups to which they aspire to belong.

The perceived worth of group membership is simply the value of the object or purpose of membership times the perceived probability that the group will continue to satisfy the need. For example, a person may join an exclusive country club to gain the prestige associated with membership. The attractiveness of this group for that person could be altered considerably by changes in the prospects for continued prestige, as would happen if the club lifts all restrictions on membership or if several prestigious members join another club.

The task itself can provide reinforcement for an individual's participation. When a group is asked to discuss a particular issue about which a person has special knowledge, the opportunity to demonstrate this knowledge increases the person's participation. Individuals whose personal convictions are in accord with the point of view to be discussed also tend to participate readily. As we pointed out in the study described in Box 13–1, McGinnies and Altman (1959) showed groups of high school students a film which depicted irrational ethnic prejudice and asked them to discuss it. Analysis of the tape-recorded group discussions indicated that students who were very prejudiced toward ethnic minorities spoke less, responded less frequently, and required more prompting from the discussion leader than those with an attitude of tolerance toward ethnic minorities.

Several experiments have demonstrated that reinforcement of a group member's behavior by a source external to the group can also affect group participation. The method typically used in these experiments is to have a group sit around a table and discuss some assigned topic or case study. Lights in front of each member can be lit to indicate that the experimenter thinks the member is doing well (e.g., "showing insight") or doing poorly. The results of these experiments indicate that when a person receives reinforcement the frequency of participation increases (he or she talks more), and when a punishing signal is activated, it decreases (Aiken, 1965).

Reinforcement can modify interaction as well as participation in groups. In laboratory studies of the jury system, higher visibility and status seem to be accorded to those in the minority, who tend to stand out in the group and whose confidence in their convictions can be impressive. An example is the role played by Henry Fonda in the film *Twelve Angry Men*—a man of principle who holds out and convinces the other 11 members of the jury that the defendant is innocent. Research has shown that a minority holding the not-guilty position is more likely to sway the majority than the reverse (Nemeth, 1979). Usually it appears to be the behavioral style of jurors more than the number in the minority or majority that determines the outcome of jury trials.

Reinforcement can also contribute to the development of group leaders. If a group is led to believe that one of its members is correct much of the time, it perceives that person as the leader and may allow him or her special privileges such as approval for deviation from group norms and procedures (Hollander, 1960). Other aspects of the relationship between participation and leadership are discussed in Chapter 15.

GROUP COHESIVENESS AND ATTRACTION

The *cohesiveness* of a group describes its ability to attract and hold members. As Chapter 11 noted, people's tendencies to conform to group norms are shaped by the extent of their attraction and commitment to the group. A highly cohesive group is attractive for each of its members, and they all are concerned with the viability of the group and are motivated to support and contribute to it. This commitment can apply to simple interpersonal relationships as well as interactions in a complex group structure such as a presidential cabinet (see Box 13–3).

Individuals basically are attracted to a group because of the reinforcements to be found in group membership, the values of which grow out of the individual's needs as described in Chapter 5. Cartwright (1968) says that the level of the person's attraction to a particular group is a function of the person's need state, the incentive properties of the group, the subjective estimate of the probability that the group will satisfy the person's needs, and the member's estimate of the alternatives (i.e., the availability of other sources of satisfaction). There is a large number of possible incentives for membership in a particular group. Among those suggested by Cartwright are attractiveness of group members, similarities among members, activities of the group, style of leadership and opportunity to participate in decisions, various structural properties of the group, the group's atmosphere, and size of the group.

Participation, Satisfaction, and Productivity

The more a member participates in group problem solving or decision making, the greater is his or her satisfaction likely to be. This increased interaction might be due to leadership style, structural properties such as the overall size of the group or the person's position within it, or degree of group attraction.

In business groups, for example, it has been found that a person's job satisfaction and satisfaction with the organization increase as the person moves up in the organizational hierarchy (Porter & Lawler, 1965). In laboratory situations, peripheral members who simply provide information but do not participate in problem solving or decision making showed little satisfaction with the task (Shaw, 1964). A fairly consistent finding is that the larger the group, the less the job satisfaction of individual members, and greater absenteeism, turnover, and

Box 13-3
GROUPTHINK: THE FINE ART OF NOT ROCKING THE BOAT

On learning of the Bay of Pigs fiasco (an unsuccessful U.S.–backed attempt by a group of Cuban exiles to invade their homeland in 1961 and topple Castro), Irving Janis was intrigued with the reasons why this improbable suggestion of the CIA had been accepted by intelligent leaders such as John F. Kennedy and his cabinet-level advisers. He decided they had been what he called *victims of groupthink:* The president's advisers were so deeply involved in striving for unanimity in the cabinet that "their motivation to appraise realistically alternative courses of action" was overridden, and a bad decision resulted.*

Robert McNamara, secretary of defense at the time, later tried to speak up against bombing in Vietnam as a member of Lyndon Johnson's cabinet, but Johnson did not allow dissent. Janis also gave the example of a conversation at a dinner party at the Pearl Harbor home of an admiral on December 6, 1941, the very eve of the Japanese sneak attack. The focus was on the supposed invulnerability of the U.S. naval and military positions there. This was a particularly disturbing question because U.S. naval intelligence had been unable to locate the Japanese aircraft carriers for the past week. To express any doubt about our strength at Pearl Harbor would have been to imply that the bastion in which the dinner party was taking place was not impregnable.

Janis summarizes the characteristics of groupthink in these ill-fated decisions as: "(1) an illusion of invulnerability, (2) a collective effort to rationalize the decision, (3) an unquestioned belief in the group's inherent morality, (4) a stereotyped view of enemy leaders as too evil to warrant genuine attempts to negotiate, and (5) the emergence of self-appointed mind-guards."†

---

*I. L. Janis, *Victims of Groupthink: A Psychological Study of Foreign Policy and Fiascoes* (Boston: Houghton Mifflin Co., 1972).

†I. L. Janis, "Groupthink," in E. P. Hollander and R. G. Hunt (Eds.), *Current Perspectives in Social Psychology,* 4th ed. (New York: Oxford University Press, 1976).

interpersonal conflict result. The relationship between the size of the group and job dissatisfaction probably results from the individual worker's perceived loss of contact with the decision-making center. As the structure becomes larger a breakdown in communication may occur, and necessary task specialization may make individuals feel divorced from the final product or goals of the organization.

When group attraction is high, individuals can be expected to do what they can to protect the group and enhance its cohesion by increasing their level of participation. Members who are attracted to a group place a greater value on group goals, as evidenced both by their own adherence to the goals and by their tendency to exert pressure on or reject people who violate the group goals (Schachter, 1951). Highly attracted members attend and participate more in meetings, maintain membership longer, and in general, accept greater group responsibilities. Moreover, as Sakurai (1975) found, when group cohesiveness is the result of interpersonal attraction, it tends to promote conformity whether or not conforming would enhance the welfare or goals of the group, but when cohesiveness is based on the members getting together to complete a given task, conformity is apparent only when it is detrimental to the group goals. In a laboratory test of the groupthink hypothesis (see Box 13–3 above), Flowers (1977) found little relationship between cohesiveness and the ability of the subjects to find solutions to a crisis situations.

The relationship between group cohesiveness and productivity depends largely on the goals of the group. If the group endorses productivity group cohesiveness will improve it, but if productivity is not valued by the norms of the group, individuals attracted to it can be expected to have low levels of productivity. Misunderstanding of the relationship between employee satisfaction and productivity was a flaw in the human relations movement in industry and management, which eventually produced satisfied but unproductive employees. Schachter et al. (1951) found that the ability of cohesive groups to exert more influence on their members may or may not increase the overall level of productivity.

Measuring Group Cohesiveness

From a research standpoint, the most important question about group cohesion is how it is measured. On a purely intuitive level it is possible to appreciate that some groups are more attractive than others; they will provide greater payoffs in such rewards as friendship, sports, companionship, security, status, or prestige, for example. In studying group cohesion, however, it is necessary to formalize the definition of the variables and state them in precise terms, or, as defined in Chapter 1, to *operationalize* the definitions. It is also important to keep in mind the differences between measuring cohesiveness in real-life groups and in experimental groups formed for research purposes. Experimentally, a common model used to create cohesiveness is to lead each person in a group to believe that he or she will like the other members and that the others will return the liking. This is normally accomplished by collecting bogus attitude and personality data on the subjects and then telling them that their attitudes and personalities are most compatible with those of other group members. The studies reported in this chapter exemplify this type of technique.

The measurement of cohesiveness in real-life groups has been approached in s number of ways. Some of the methods for measuring group cohesiveness suggested in Cartwright and Zander's *Group Dynamics* (1968) are the following:

1. *Interpersonal attraction.* Friendship ratios of various sorts have been used, on the assumption that a group will be more attractive to its members the

The Watergate episode included various forms of illegal activity, such as break-ins, wiretapping, and cover-ups. For most of those involved in this massive conspiracy, group consensus and commitment to the leader were central factors. *Source:* Wide World Photos, Inc.

more the members like one another. Usually people are asked to list ten or so "best friends," and on this basis ratios are formed of the number of group members selected to the number selected outside the group or to the total number that could be selected from the group. Other researchers have attempted to measure interpersonal attraction by asking each group member to rate every other member on a liking or friendship scale.

2. *Group attraction.* Group members are asked to rate the attractiveness of the group as a whole. Researchers such as Good and Nelson (1971) who have used this technique in conjunction with measures of interpersonal attraction report that the two measures are similar but not identical.

3. *Group identification.* Members are asked questions designed to measure the degree to which they identify with, feel they belong to, or are involved with a group.

4. *Desire for membership.* Members are asked to rate the extent to which they desire to enter or remain in a group.

Other measures of group cohesiveness involve measuring the frequency of references to the group, such as saying *we* instead of *I* or using the group's name or label, or measuring norms and values (using scales such as those used to measure attitudes, which were described in Chapter 8), on the assumption that more cohesive groups share norms to a greater extent. In groups of long duration it is possible to measure direct consequences of cohesiveness such as turnover, absenteeism, attendance at meetings, or payment of dues, all of which have been found to vary directly with the degree of group cohesiveness.

One consequence of cohesiveness in groups is an increased in-group bias. The more highly cohesive the group, the greater is the tendency to discriminate between in-group and out-group and to favor in-group members (Tajfel, 1970). Research has supported the tendency noted in Chapter 12 for intergroup competition to heighten in-group cohesion, and it also has been found to enhance discrimination and hostility toward out-groups (Blake & Mouton, 1961). Cohesive groups were found to exhibit greater hostility toward those outside the group who are perceived to be responsible for frustrating them (Pepitone & Reichling, 1955). Dion (1973) opposed dyads with similar and dissimilar attitudes and personality in the Prisoner's Dilemma game (see Chapter 12) to investigate whether hostility and prejudice toward out-groups would be increased by attempts to increase group cohesiveness. Though cohesiveness increased throughout the experiment, there was no significant increase in hostility and exploitation of others.

INTERPERSONAL ATTRACTION

The phenomenon of interpersonal attractiveness, on which group processes and group cohesion depend, transcends the boundaries of groups. An individual's desire to affiliate with other individuals, which was described as a social motive in Chapter 7, is based on interpersonal perceptions and related positive and negative attitudes and feelings.

Affiliation Needs

After a series of experiments to test the notion that people seek affiliation with strangers for cognitive purposes or to reduce anxiety, Schachter (1959) concluded that the adage "Misery loves company" should be "Misery doesn't love just any company, only *miserable* company." An experimenter was introduced to groups of women university students as a psychiatry professor who was conducting research on the effects of electric shock. Some subjects were led to believe that the shocks would be mild and not painful; in the high-anxiety condition, however, subjects were told the shocks would be extremely painful. Subjects were informed that there would be a ten-minute delay while equipment was set up, and they could wait in private cubicles equipped with armchairs, books, and magazines or in a large room with other subjects. When the subjects were asked whether they wanted to wait alone or with others or had no preference, twice as many of those who were highly anxious preferred to wait together. Some of the subjects were given the opportunity to wait either alone or with other women students who were waiting for appointments and therefore had nothing to do with the experiment, but not one subject who was given this option chose to do so.

The desire to affiliate with people in situations similar to one's own may be attributable to a search for information. In an ambiguous or novel situation people are unsure of the meaning and purpose of the event and may seek to affiliate with others to try to gain some understanding of the situation, as was noted in regard to group status in Chapter 11.

In one experiment, subjects experiencing a vague physiological arousal showed a stronger desire to affiliate with other subjects in the same experimental situation than subjects exposed to arousal from a known source did (Mills & Mintz, 1972). The subjects were given caffeine, a stimulant, and told either that it was an analgesic or a stimulant. Those who thought it was an analgesic could not explain the physiological arousal they experienced and wanted to spend more time with others undergoing a similar experience in order to get information they could use to identify the source of their arousal.

A person becomes more anxious if she or he finds that other individuals exposed to the same threat are less anxious. Also a higher level of skill can be reached in a game or sport when one's level of skill can be compared to that of others having the same amount of training.

People also may want to affiliate with others in stressful situations in order to reduce anxiety or threat. Affiliation can decrease anxiety indirectly in the sense that talking with others can get one's mind off an impending threat.

Social Power

It is generally assumed that one person's attraction toward another derives from social power, as described in Chapter 11, or the extent to which one controls the welfare of the other. Persons perceived as responsible for periods of plenty or pleasure are rewarded with liking and social attraction, whereas those responsible for pain or deprivation are perceived as unattractive. There are many exceptions to this rule, however. A $1 Christmas present from a wealthy aunt would generate anger and hostility, whereas if a poor uncle shared his limited resources this way it would be received as an act of kindness and generosity.

Some of the same thinking has been apparent in U.S. foreign-aid programs. The simplistic assumption is that gifts build goodwill, but there are striking examples that the opposite is the case. In some situations gifts generate feelings of suspicion, hostility, and anger or a tendency to consider the benefactor as stupid or exploitable. Gergen et al. (1969) directly manipulated the conditions under which an unsolicited gift was received. A gift of ten poker chips was made to gambling subjects who were losing and had limited resources. With the gift was a note which indicated the recipient was under high, medium, or no obligation to the donor. When the subjects later rated the donors as to likability they found those who had proposed equal or medium obligation to be most attractive; those proposing either high or no obligation were not well regarded.

Reciprocity, or the ability to interact on equal terms, may be the most satisfying state, but power, by definition, upsets reciprocity. The powerful cannot simply equalize a situation by redistribution of resources, for by that very act they are exercising unique control over those resources. Reciprocity must be obtained by giving other things of value or perhaps, as Homans (1974) suggests, by exchanging behaviors, as described in a later section. Thus Ebenezer Scrooge had to pay dearly in psychological terms to partake of the Cratchit family's Christmas spirit.

A study by Morse and Gergen (1971) used a simulation technique to investigate the giving of material aid. Groups which played the roles of nations in various conditions of need applied to a donor-nation group for aid. The nations were portrayed as in states of high or low need, and the requests for aid were either denied or granted. When denied aid, high-need groups evaluated the donor group more negatively than low-need subjects did, and, as would be expected, groups who were given aid evaluated the donor as comparatively more attractive.

Bases for Liking

The bases for interpersonal attraction, or liking, rest in interpersonal perception, as described in Chapter 6, and attitudes, as described in Chapters 8 and 9 (see Box 13-4). Byrne (1969), for example, found that interpersonal attraction is directly related to perceived similarity. The more similar to ourselves we perceive another person to be, the greater is our attraction to that person, but if a similar person behaves in an obnoxious manner we dislike that person more than we would a dissimilar one who behaved the same way (Taylor & Mettee, 1971).

The most capable people in problem-solving groups are often not those who are liked best (Hollander & Webb, 1955). The same is found to be true for persons rated as the best "idea person" in discussion groups. In Bales's (1965) investigation of group members' interactional abilities described in Chapter 12, it was found that the second and third highest persons in idea activity in five-person groups are usually the most liked.

Box 13–4
IS IT LOVE—OR PROPINQUITY?

Propinquity (nearness) has sometimes been confused with love. Repeated exposures to another individual can result in increased attraction, regardless of the circumstances. One experiment designed to test the idea that contact with another person under pleasant circumstances would give rise to more interpersonal attraction than similar exposure under less pleasant conditions resulted in a finding that "the mere repeated exposure of people is a sufficient condition for enhancement of attraction, despite differences in favorability of context, and in the absence of the obvious rewards or punishments by the people."*

Female subjects were asked to taste either pleasant or noxious solutions in what was purported to be an experiment designed to study their perception of the taste of substances that differ in specific ways and are presented in different order. They were given three flavors of Kool-Aid and several noxious solutions—vinegar, quinine, and citric acid—to taste. Then they were asked to rate the taste of the solutions on several scales.

The subjects watched other subjects tasting either pleasant or noxious substances as they moved to different cubicles in which the liquids were stored in large vessels. Records were kept, and the frequency of contact with other subjects for each one was determined by who else was in the cubicle tasting a liquid at the same time. Interpersonal attraction varied as a direct function of the number of encounters in the negative as well as the positive context.

_____

*S. Saegart, W. Swap, and R. B. Zajonc, "Exposure, Context, and Interpersonal Attraction," *Journal of Personality and Social Psychology,* 1973, *25,* 234–242.

As the conformity and compliance studies cited in Chapter 11 showed, there is a tendency to evaluate high-status and high-ability persons more favorably and to yield to them more easily. Criticism received from high-status individuals is assumed to have more laudable motives than that from low-status critics (Deutsch, 1961). People with more ability are liked better, even when their ability is not relevant to the other person's well-being (Stotland & Dunn, 1962).

Loving: The Ultimate Interpersonal Attraction

In the context of Part I, theories of love have varied from the behaviorist viewpoint of John B. Watson to Freudian and neo-Freudian doctrines. Over a half century ago Watson insisted that emotions are basically physical responses; love was simply regarded as the conditioning of lust, an inborn physiological response of the same level as rage or fear. Freud's view of love as the blocking of the sex drive, or libido, was vaguely plausible (although hardly acceptable), in view of the Victorian taboo on sex expression and the detachment of romantic love from sexuality. Another psychoanalytic variation is the theory of Theodor Reik (1944), which sees love as an escape from the self. Love is regarded as a projection of the "ego ideal" onto another person, so we can remove our deficiencies by incorporating another self into our own personalities.

The Greeks used at least three words for love: *eros,* a physical attraction, as in erotic love; *philios,* the strong affection between relatives or close friends; and *agape,* the love of fellow human beings, a term which appears often in St. Paul's writings. After extensive analysis, John Alan Lee (1976) suggested a somewhat different typology. Besides *eros,* which in his definition refers to a kind of passion, often at first sight, there is *ludus,* a more casual but largely erotic affiliation, with frequent flights from one infatuation to another. *Storge* is a more stable relationship in which the physical bond is subordinate to rationality and self-control. Of lesser importance are *mania,* represented by the extremes of romantic love, with states of emotional highs and lows; *pragma,* in which love is largely a service function; and *agape,* the most idealistic type of love.

Lee constructed a 170-item self-report inventory with which individuals could classify their love relationships. Most persons reported experiences which could be described by more than one of these labels, even in the same relationship. The sixfold classification can also be applied to homosexual love (Lee, 1981).

In the United States, romantic love has characterized dating and mate selection, and the mass media, notably motion pictures, have capitalized on romanticism. The antecedents of romantic love can be found in the poetry and music of the Romantic movement, which began in the late 18th century.

The components of romantic love are:

1. Suddenness and inevitability—love at first sight.
2. Idealization and a sense of perfection—few if any flaws can be found in the partner.
3. Permanence—lovers live happily ever after.
4. The suggestion of pain and suffering—a lover is likely to experience indigestion, insomnia, etc.
5. Irreality and emotional transport—for the lovers, only their love exists.

To some degree these characteristics have been colored recently by greater flexibility in the role behaviors of women and men, freer norms of sexual behavior, and restrictions on censorship in the mass media. Unquestionably the classic treatment of romance has been revised; think of the difference between ideal lovers—Rudolf Valentino in the 1920s and Dustin Hoffman or Robert Redford more recently.

The Social-Psychological Study of Love

Social psychologists have only recently begun to study romantic love, which supposedly defies measurement. Indeed, in 1975, Senator William Proxmire of

Wisconsin gave the Golden Fleece Award—his means of ridiculing inconsequential research—to three prominent social psychologists for their National Science Foundation grant of $84,000 to investigate the differences between passionate and companionate love. Proxmire's attack was countered by a number of observers who reflected that in view of the rising divorce rate, no area was more in need of scientific analysis.

A notable contribution to the definition and validation of *loving* as opposed to merely *liking* a person was made by Zick Rubin (1970, 1973). He categorized love as (1) emotional attachment, affiliative and dependent need, (2) caring or the predisposition to help, and (3) intimacy, exclusiveness, and absorption. Liking, in comparison, is a more rational or cognitive relationship.

Rubin (1970) defined love as "an attitude held by a person toward a particular other person, involving predispositions to think, feel, and behave in certain ways toward that other person" (p. 265). His 13-item scales for love and liking includes the following examples:

Love-Scale Items

1. If _____ were feeling badly, my first duty would be to cheer him (her) up.
2. I feel that I can confide in _____ about virtually everything.
3. I find it easy to ignore _____'s faults.
4. I would do almost anything for _____ .

Liking-Scale Items

1. When I am with _____, we are almost always in the same mood.
2. I think that _____ is unusually well-adjusted.
3. I would highly recommend _____ for a responsible job.
4. In my opinion, _____ is an exceptionally mature person.

The scales were administered to 168 University of Michigan couples who were tested in pairs. Part of the measure was the amount of time the partners spent gazing at each other, as measured by observers in the laboratory. This measure was significantly correlated with scores on the love scale. The love scores were nearly identical for the partners, but the women *liked* their partners more than they were liked in return. The explanation of these results may be that some women assume a more pragmatic approach to the love relationship, since, in view of employment opportunities and child-rearing responsibilities, they have more to lose if a marriage should terminate. In a study of preferences in mate selection, the men were primarily concerned with physical attractiveness and more apt to reject a woman on basis of physical imperfections, whereas the women valued intelligence, educational level, earning capacity, and social values and were less rejecting of physical defects in a prospective mate (Williamson, 1965). Recent advances toward sexual equality are likely to diminish the differences in outlook of the two sexes toward mate selection and the quality of love.

Another experimental approach to the study of loving utilizes the concepts of exchange and equity, to be discussed in the next section. In the context of these theories which regard love as a balance of rewards and costs, the important factor is the resources each partner brings to the relationship. If a love relationship becomes inequitable the partners experience distress; as a result, they may either attempt to restore equity to the bond or move toward a breakup. Consciously or unconsciously, there is a reckoning of the benefits of maintaining the partnership as opposed to the costs of terminating it (Walster, Walster, & Berscheid, 1978).

THEORIES OF INTERACTION IN GROUPS

The dynamics of the relations between two or more people can be studied in terms of theories developed from the context of group relations, psychological concepts, and economic principles. The principal theories are balance theory, represented by Fritz Heider and T. M. Newcomb, and exchange theory, represented by George Homans and Peter Blau.

Balance Theory

The ultimate putdown in interpersonal relations—"With friends like you, who needs enemies?"—is at the heart of balance theories. As the research on interpersonal perception discussed in Chapter 6 established, people who are like-minded with respect to certain attitudes and beliefs tend to be attracted to one another. Similarly, if you discover that a friend of yours dislikes somebody you like, you probably will find the situation uncomfortable. Heider's (1958) formulation of balance theory, which was introduced in Chapter 9, attempts to formalize these simple associative structures, or as Heider put it, the nature of the psychology of the person on the street.

The theory of balance is based on triads and the bonds between the three persons in such groups, although extensions of the theory include structures with two persons and an inanimate entity such as an object, attitude, or concept. Liking is indicated by a positive bond and disliking by a negative one. The basic idea is that these systems may be balanced or unbalanced—a balanced triad has either no negative bonds or an equal number of them—and triads that are unbalanced produce a state of discomfort which creates a pressure to restore balance. Hence, if person A likes person B, B likes person C, and C likes A, a balanced triad exists. If C dislikes A, the triad is unbalanced.

The four basic configurations in balance theory are shown in Figure 13-1. In a situation in which all possible linkages are positive, as in Triad 1, there is a balanced state of affairs. A balanced state also exists when two people have a positive relationship and both dislike or have a negative relationship with the same person or thing, as in Triad 3. Triads 2 and 4, however, indicate unbalanced structures in which two people who have a positive relationship with one another have an inverse relationship to some other person or entity. In Triad 2, A likes B, B likes X, but A dislikes X. In Triad 4 all the entities are negatively related, and therefore they are considered to be out of balance.

The theory maintains that because unbalanced structures are unstable, they create tension towards balance. The resolution of the unbalanced triad could

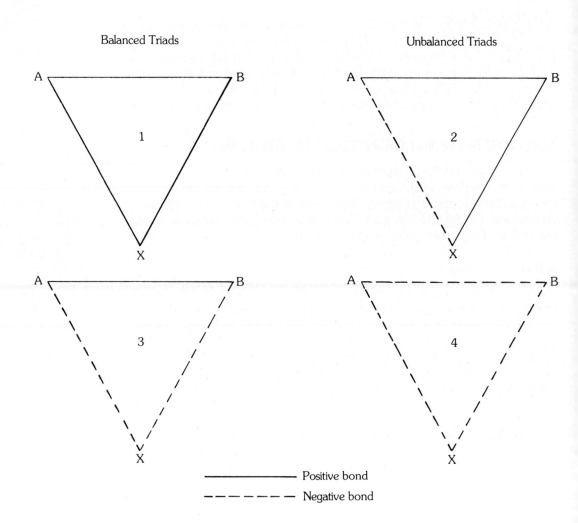

Figure 13–1. Balanced and Unbalanced Triads

involve several different processes. For example, a positive relationship could become a negative one in order to restore the system to balance: A is in favor of X, B is not in favor of X, and so A and B develop a negative relationship. Or the relationship of either A or B could change toward X. A may decide that B is in fact correct about the merit of that particular entity and change his or her attitude toward it so that it is consistent with B's attitude.

Newcomb's (1961) classic study of the effects of balance in interactions between people was cited in the affiliative needs section of Chapter 7. For purposes of this study he obtained a house at the University of Michigan campus

The triad is inherently an unstable group structure; sooner or later one member is destined to become an outsider. *Source:* © Theodore Anderson, 1981.

and arranged to have 17 new male students who were strangers to each other live there for a year, in an attempt to determine to what extent the attitudes and personalities of the individual students would affect the acquaintance process. At the start of the study each student completed a number of attitude and personality scales and inventories, estimated the attitudes of other subjects, and indicated sociometric measures of attraction (see Chapter 12). Although it is well known that friends tend to agree with each other on important issues, Newcomb demonstrated that such attitude consistency or agreement precedes interpersonal attraction and can be a predictor of it. The study also demonstrated that while forced association tends to produce changes in unbalanced systems, little change was found in the attitudes or values of the subjects. Newcomb concluded that as a component of the balance system attitudes were the least subject to change, whereas attraction toward other individuals as well as perception of the attitudes of others did tend to change to produce balance. Thus although close proximity may increase interpersonal attraction, this does not necessarily imply attitude change.

Balance theory deals with a very simple system involving only three units. In real life, however, the situations we are involved in are extraordinarily complex and involve a multiplicity of different attitudes and causes. Person A may like person B, and both may like the Republicans and dislike chocolate sodas, but with respect to a number of other entities or attitudes they will be completely at variance with one another.

To determine the degree of balance in larger, more complex systems, it is necessary to calculate the ratio of balanced to unbalanced triads within the larger system. The greater the number of unbalanced triads relative to balanced ones, the less is the system's balance and hence the weaker is its stability.

In addition, some relationships are more important than others. If we find that an important relationship is negative, for example, the relevance of the remaining relationships is reduced. As Newcomb (1968) put it, "since I dislike O (or do not respect or trust O), I have no interest in O's attitude toward X." Support for this contention is found in another study in which subjects rated hypothetical triads with positive bonds between two persons as more *involving* than those having negative PO (person-oriented) bonds (Crano & Cooper, 1973). The conclusion was that if the PO bond was negative, subjects relegated the situation to a position of subjective indifference, whereas the positive PO relationship stimulated them to investigate the remaining bonds.

The Strain toward Symmetry

People expect those they are attracted to to be attracted to them. The relationship between the evidence a person gives of attraction to others and what the person expects in return is strong (Ettinger, Norwicki, & Nelson, 1970), and mutuality of attraction does in fact exceed the chance level (Blumberg, 1969).

One explanation for both perceived as well as actual mutuality of attraction, based on the balance theory, is that of a *strain toward symmetry*. In cognitive consistency terms, a perceived imbalance in reciprocal attraction generates an unpleasant and unstable state which motivates attempts to restore balance. Thus we may offer explanations when a liked person opposes us (see Box 13–5).

Since asymmetry of interpersonal attraction is associated with discomfort, negative asymmetry (disliking someone more than they dislike you) can also be expected to be more uncomfortable than negative symmetry. Hence, we should prefer to be disliked by those whom we dislike and to be liked only as much as we like others, and Blumberg (1969) found that subjects experienced the most comfort when the attraction they gave and received was about equal. In situations of positive asymmetry (i.e., being liked more than you like), it was also found that subjects preferred reduced liking from the other person and wanted disliked others to dislike rather than to like them.

Box 13–5
I'LL BE NICE JUST TO BE NASTY

We are not surprised when people we like offer help or when people we dislike are uncooperative, but we may be suspicious when disliked people offer help. Our expectancies about people can lead to some interesting behaviors when they are not confirmed.

For example, we might expect people to respond differently when harmed by a friend than when harmed by a rival. This question was examined in a study in which groups of two males having either friendly or unfriendly relationships played a competitive game.* The subject, after experiencing cooperation from the other player, was led to perceive that the opponent was becoming highly competitive, the result of which could be the loss of a small prize.

The results indicated that when the other player was a friend, the subject *retaliated* by becoming less cooperative himself, but he maintained the friendship by stating that his friend was just goofing around. Rather than reduce liking, the subject simply perceived the situation as one in which both he and his friend were fooling around. When the other player was disliked, however, the subject *maintained* his initial level of cooperation and also maintained or intensified his dislike of the other player. Interviewed subjects indicated that they would not behave as the disliked opponent had; hence the motivation for not retaliating in such situations may be derived from a desire to see oneself as different from the disliked person.

The prize at stake in this study was small. When larger prizes were offered, the hesitancy to retaliate against disliked opponents was overridden.

_____

*P. G. Swingle, "Effects of the Emotional Relationships between Protagonists in a Two-Person Game," *Journal of Personality and Social Psychology,* 1966, 4, 270–279.

In an experiment with university students, only the women were found to be sensitive to changes in their relationships in a condition of positive asymmetry (Smith & Campbell, 1973). Neither sex, however, made an attempt to agree with their associates in negative asymmetry relationships.

Exchange Theory: Costs and Rewards

Homans (1950) based his conceptualization of exchange on the priority of the small group—a semidelinquent gang in Boston, the kinship arrangements of a Polynesian village, the workbench of a Chicago factory, or a permissive suburban family, for example. Most aspects of exchange represent investments and transactions between people in intimate group settings (Homans, 1974). These transactions include three components:

1. *Activities*—all behavior involving objects; may include transference of physical objects and materials to other people.

2. *Sentiments*—feelings, emotions, attitudes, and beliefs, or the affective or cognitive components of behavior. Sentiments, a special class of activities, are "signs of the attitudes and feelings a person takes toward another person or other persons"; in other words, they are overt behavior and are directly observable, such as desire for social approval.

3. *Interactions*—activities directly affecting the relationship of two individuals, as when a person rewards or punishes another person.

These three components, especially sentiments and interactions, are basic to exchange transactions or the bargaining negotiations in interpersonal relations. They are interrelated, and a change in one will effect a change in the other two. Our social relations are conditioned by value; we are under constant pressure to maximize our rewards at minimum cost. Moreover, the theory of value also involves rewards and costs (see Box 13–6). Value can be measured in terms of the activity required to obtain rewards, which vary in desirability and range from food and love to money and knowledge, although an individual's sense of values constantly changes. As we interact with persons whose values are similar to our own, the chances of securing a reward at minimum cost are generally greater and the bargaining process is less strained.

Homans (1961, p. 53 ff.) developed the following propositions to outline his theory:

1. "If in the past the occurrence of a particular stimulus-situation has been the occasion on which a person's activity has been rewarded, then the more similar the present stimulus-situation is to the past one, the more likely the person is to emit the activity, or some similar activity, now." In other words, we tend to retain behavior that is satisfying.

2. "The more often within a given period of time a person's activity rewards the activity of another, the more often the other will emit the activity." Activity and reward tend to be related, such as our desire to help those who appreciate it.

3. "The more valuable to a person a unit of the activity another gives to the person, the more often he or she will emit activity rewarded by the activity of the other." Value, like satisfaction, is a determinant and is measurable in the rate of exchange. When we must choose between two satisfying activities, we tend to select the one with value.

4. "The more often a person has in the recent past received a rewarding activity from another, the less valuable any further unit of that activity becomes to the

Box 13–6
EQUITY: TIT FOR TAT

How do we protect our self-integrity in our encounters with others? How does society resolve the conflict implicit in most interpersonal relations? Out of the context of exchange theory and experimental games, equity theory has emerged to seek answers to these questions.* A basic assumption is that people try to maximize their outcomes, on the basis that outcome equals rewards minus costs. Unlike individuals, groups have to share their outcomes and seek to evolve systems whereby rewards and costs can be distributed equitably among members. Groups tend to reward members who treat others equitably and to demand higher costs for those who do not.

The search for equity or compensation is seen as an inevitable goal in life. One aspect is retaliation—our wish to restore equity by getting even with wrongdoers. Another is forgiveness; in order to compensate for the harm done we begin with "I'm sorry" and hope in return for "You're forgiven." If not, we may proceed through "apologies, self-derogation, and exaltation of the victim." If that does not succeed, we move on in desperation to some form of self-justification, and if all else fails, we begin again with a "forgive and forget" appeal. Equity theory encompasses a variety of human relationships, from the administration of prisons to marriage. Most social encounters represent to some degree a market situation. Our system of justice operates on the basis of retribution, but the suggestion has been made that society might well redirect the energy and resources now used to pursue the culprit to compensate the victim instead. And prospective marital partners turn to each other for what each can bring to the encounter; beyond any romantic consideration, they tend to choose partners of approximately their own social worth.

_____

*E. Walster, E. Berscheid, and G. S. Walster, "New Directions in Equity Research," in L. Berkowitz (Ed.), *Advances in Experimental Social Psychology*, Vol. 9 (New York: Academic Press, 1976).

person." Satiation may appear, which will lower the frequency of the given activity.

In exchange relations with another individual, a person anticipates that the reward will be proportional to the cost. In psychological and economic terms alike, the greater the reward, the greater the cost; the net reward will be directly related to the investment, and the greater the investment, the greater the profit. Inability to secure reward results in emotional thwarting, both in interpersonal relations and in the larger society. The relationship of cost and reward makes for a certain predictability or rationality in the exchange relationship which Homans refers to as *distributive justice.* This principle dates back to Aristotle, who proposed that the distribution of rewards in a society should be on the basis of merit (justice). The principal alternative would be distribution on the basis of need (fairness). According to Heffernan (1979), "Neither distribution on the basis of need nor distribution on the basis of merit is the functional equivalent of distribution on the basis of equity (or equality)." The need to balance these criteria was described in Box 6–5 in the section on the perception of freedom in Chapter 6.

Often such an exchange is affected by people's status relationships; they are constantly assessing their status positions vis-à-vis other persons as they validate their cognitions of each interpersonal situation. Pepitone (1964) calls this a *cognitive validation need.* By this validating technique each person attempts to determine the threat of status loss in a relationship to another person. As Pepitone says, "the greater the reduction of threat of status loss the other person brings about, the more attractive this person becomes to the individual." When people encounter a negative evaluation they may project it to another person, but an attempt to make oneself more attractive by reducing the status of the other person may not be favorable to one's own bargaining position.

Calculating the Costs and Rewards

An analysis of interaction as an exchange relationship by Blau (1964) involves calculation of the costs and rewards of such a transaction. The rewards can be intrinsic or extrinsic, unilateral or reciprocal, and entering directly into the interaction or deferred. *Spontaneous* rewards are not generally bartered in exchange, but *calculated* actions are directly based on the reward-cost assessment.

In Blau's formulation the costs can be of at least three types: *direct cost,* with an immediate payoff; *investment cost,* with a long-range return, or *opportunity cost,* the extent to which a chosen course precludes other alternatives. These costs vary with the need for resources such as time or money. The calculation of rewards in terms of differential costs can involve such questions as: Should I attend this New Year's Eve party or that one? Should I go to the party that will pay off soonest, or should I select the one with a deferred payoff—that is, should I please my immediate supervisor, who can help me now, or the vice-president, who can help my future plans? Costs can be measured in terms of the present (direct cost), the long term (investment cost), or whether an investment in one interaction will prevent the opportunity to participate in another (opportunity cost).

In Blau's view, social exchange negotiates an intermediate position between "pure calculation of advantage and pure expression of love." In contrast to economic transactions, it often depends on trust rather than a binding contract. Each individual attempts to gain as much as possible at minimum cost, and this maneuvering provides a certain degree of conflict which is resolved by seeking intrinsic or extrinsic support from various associates.

Exchange transactions are determined by the social setting and the nature of role relationships. First, the nature of the affective relationship structures the exchange. For example, two individuals on a date represent a different bargaining position and power relationship than a husband and wife would. Love is a relationship in which bargaining is generally at a minimum, at least for the partner most emotionally involved. In fact, the more committed of the two partners is unlikely to consider the transaction as one of reward and cost. Second, norms operate in connection with other pressures to discourage manipulation. Members of a fraternity or the mayor's council cannot ignore in their own transactions the expectations associated with their loyalty to the group. In other words, there is a prevailing rate of exchange, and group standards determine what is or is not in line. Third, coalitions can form within a group to restrict the individual and the resources that can be offered. Finally, the general social situation has a bearing on the transactions and their relationships. A person may leave a large tip or make a sizable contribution to charity because of the anticipated approval of the other guests at a table or of society at large, for example, but that person's income may have been derived by exploiting a lower social class through unfair rents or inadequate wages. Our membership in many groups makes it possible for us to choose whom we will favor or disfavor, or with whom we will have the most advantage in carrying on certain transactions.

In experimental games it has been found that subjects will often continue to play even at a loss because there appears to be no other alternative, or it appears to be more profitable than other kinds of reinforcement. We may give more to a partner than we receive if there is no attractive option in this exchange situation (Burgess & Nielson, 1977). Exchange theory implies, too, that in real-life situations a person may trade present resources (time, money, or some other asset) with the risk of a future reward—or loss.

Thibaut and Kelley (1959) presented another theory of exchange which is more akin to the concept of game theory, that is, the concept of power relationships is dyads, triads, or larger social groups. They analyze interaction as composed of units of a behavior sequence, or set. Each identifiable behavior consists of a "number of specific motor and verbal acts that exhibit some degree of sequential organization directed toward the attainment of some immediate goal or end state." The term *set* suggests that the person has a fairly continuous orientation or intention throughout the behavioral sequence or task. The interaction, as in Homans' theory, is motivated by the rewards or satisfaction derived from the relationship with another individual or with the group. *Cost* refers to factors that inhibit or deter the enactment of the behavioral sequence, and the outcome for the individual is the difference between reward and cost.

Thus we are constantly making choices in our interactions and outcomes. These constitute trading relationships in which our rewards emerge from our own and others' behaviors. Rewards and costs are evaluated as above or below a comparison level which operates as the standard against which we assess the attractiveness of the relation.

Exchange theory represents the social interactionist viewpoint introduced in Chapter 1. A number of critics also perceive a behaviorist orientation in Homans because of his stress on reinforcement and a quantifiable determinism (Ekeh, 1974). A contrasting viewpoint in the social sciences is *functionalism,* which stresses the interrelations of underlying variables in social behavior rather than specific responses to specific stimuli. In the functionalist view, if the outcome of group interaction can be conceptualized in economic terms, then virtually any type of interpersonal interaction can be described in terms of exchange. On the whole, exchange theory focuses on the fact that many interactions can be rewarding, and to the extent that they are rewarding, they will continue. Other interactions which give rise to no reward or even punishment will cease. The theory suffers, however, if values like love, helping, or knowledge are conceptualized as a divisible, depletable pie which is cut up and distributed to the people involved in an interaction.

SUMMARY

Group performance can be superior to individual performance when the group is heterogeneous and there is some spontaneity of action. Various kinds of situations are relevant to group participation, such as the risky shift condition which involves the diffusion of responsibility or quasi-anonymity that the group offers. Individuals define and modify their needs and values in terms of the group setting.

The more cohesive the group, the greater the influence it can exert over individual members, and hence, the greater will be the group's ability to resist outside interference and influence. The term *group cohesiveness* encompasses a wide variety of explanations for the bonding which occurs among members of the group. Generally, there are two types of definitions of group cohesiveness or group attractiveness. One refers to an intangible group property such as atmosphere, group morale, or a feeling of belongingness. A more contemporary definition of group cohesiveness is the force that acts on individual members to remain in a particular group, or more generally, the attractiveness of the group for its members. In general, as the studies discussed in this chapter indicate, the attractiveness of the group for its members depends on the payoffs or rewards each member receives from belonging to the group.

Balance theory contributes to an understanding of interpersonal attraction. Symmetry in interpersonal associations is pleasant, but under some circumstances asymmetries and imbalances create tension and inspire efforts to restore balance. The theory of behavior exchange, to the extent that we can identify costs and rewards of behaviors, sentiments, and the like, provides some insight into the bargaining or exchange process fundamental to the interactions in groups.

Interpersonal attraction is the basis for the relationships between people which characterize group behavior. These relationships are derived in large part from the individuals' role behaviors within the group, which is the topic of the following chapter.

WORDS TO REMEMBER

Brainstorming.   Process by which inhibition in a group is counteracted by encouraging members to offer a maximum of ideas or suggestions, however wild or zany they may be.

Bureaucracy.   System of organization characterized by rigid rules, impersonalization, and hierarchical placement of personnel.

Cohesiveness.   The attribution of the group for its members, implying close interaction within the group and reluctance to depart from it.

Equity theory.   The hypothesis that a person refers to others in order to determine fairness and justice in interpersonal relations; relies on reciprocity norms, which specify that contributions and benefits should be traded with others on an equitable basis.

Exchange theory.   Decision-making principles based on costs and rewards, in management, games, and other interpersonal encounters such as love or marriage.

Functionalism.   Viewpoint which stresses the interrelation of variables, that is, how the function of a given behavior is interlaced with other behaviors; in particular, refers to exchange theory and the relation of cost and reward. Functionalism can be contrasted with *behaviorism,* which is oriented to specific responses to specific stimuli (see Chapter 5).

Groupthink.   A special case of conformity defined by Irving Janis. The illusion of infallibility within the group, or cohesiveness, inhibits critical judgment, and fear of criticizing the opinions of other members may restrict the consideration of alternatives in decision making.

Risky shift. The tendency in certain laboratory groups for subjects to make more daring decisions than they would alone or had made previously.

QUESTIONS FOR DISCUSSION

1. Define the concepts of brainstorming, information overload, risky shift, and nonintervention. Illustrate with examples from your own experience, if you can.

2. Discuss the relationship between reinforcement and group attraction.

3. What has group cohesiveness to do with job satisfaction and productivity?

4. What factors influence a person's desire to affiliate with strangers?

5. When does gift-giving have the greatest influence on attraction?

6. Are people who help other people or groups always well liked?

7. When does similarity enhance attraction? When does similarity breed contempt?

8. Frequently the most capable person or the most productive person in a group is less liked than persons of moderate capability. Why?

9. How would you promote the likability of a very powerful person or a person who has extraordinary capabilities?

10. How might a social psychologist analyze romantic love scientifically?

11. How do shared values enhance interpersonal liking?

12. How does balance theory differ from dissonance theory?

13. Describe exchange theory. How does it relate to other theories of interpersonal behavior?

14. How are behaviorism and functionalism relevant to group processes?

READINGS

Blankenship, R. L. (Ed.). *Colleagues in Organizations: The Social Construction of Professional Work.* New York: John Wiley & Sons, 1977.

Presents a number of studies of the professional in the process of decision making, bargaining, and the like.

Blau, P. M. *Exchange and Power in Social Life.* New York: John Wiley & Sons, 1964.

An illuminating presentation of exchange theory.

Ekey, P. P. *Social Exchange Theory.* Cambridge, Mass.: Harvard University Press, 1974.

A comparison of the Blau and Homans approaches.

Gergen, K. J., Greenberg, M. S., and Willis, R. H. (Eds.). *Social Exchange: Advances in Theory and Research.* New York: Plenum Press, 1980.

An examination of the subject in both the Homans and the Thibaut-Kelley traditions and its application to many issues, ranging from operant conditioning to the nature of sex roles.

Homans, G. C. *Social Behavior: Its Elementary Forms.* Rev. ed. New York: Harcourt, Brace Jovanovich, 1974.

A methodical conceptualization of exchange, well supported by psychological and social theory.

Kreeger, L. (Ed.). *The Large Group: Dynamics and Therapy.* Itasca, Ill.: F. E. Peacock Publishers, 1975.

Contributions to resolving tensions, especially the problem of identity, in organizations.

Rapoport, A. *Fights, Games, and Debates.* Ann Arbor: University of Michigan Press, 1960.

A renowned authority on gaming theory outlines in readable fashion the strategy and its implication for other areas, including international tensions.

Swingle, P. G. (Ed.). *Experiments in Social Psychology.* New York: Academic Press, 1969.

Experiments 4–7 focus on brainstorming, coalition formation, and game behavior.

Tedeschi, J. T., Schlenker, B. R., and Bonoma, T. V. *Conflict, Power and Games.* Chicago: Aldine Publishing Co., 1973.

Although not easy reading, the book is an excellent review of some critical research in this area.

Thibaut, J. W., and Kelley, H. H. *The Social Psychology of Groups.* New York: John Wiley & Sons, 1959.

A systematic approach to reward, cost, and other variables of social exchange, as well as models of tasks, norms, and roles.

Triandis, H. C. *Interpersonal Behavior.* Monterey, Calif.: Brooks/Cole Publishing Co., 1977.

One of the keenest examinations of interpersonal attraction, attribution, and the concept equity.

ROLE
BEHAVIOR

Every person assumes a number of roles in a lifetime or even in the course of a day, as Shakespeare recognized:

> All the world's a stage
> And all the men and women merely players;
> They have their exits and their entrances;
> And one man in his time plays many parts.

The concept of role signifies far more than a dramatic performance, however. The term *role* refers to the performance of a person occupying a particular position in a particular setting. Each person occupies a number of positions, such as student, employee, family member, friend, or club president, each of which represents a role and its subroles. The student role, for example, calls for subroles like going to class, studying for exams, choosing a major, and so forth. Each role includes an intricate set of behaviors, and it undergoes almost continual change as the person interacts with others.

This chapter introduces the study of role with a section which defines the anthropological-sociological view of roles, examines study of sex roles as an example, and defines the limits to this traditional definition. Then the dimensions of roles, including variables such as position and location, variations, and relation to self-identity and image are established. A social-psychological interpretation of role is proposed which points out its relation to norms, expectations, and consciousness of roles. The final section explores some of the factors in role conformity, deviance, and conflict.

THE CONCEPT OF ROLE

Role and *social role* have become familiar terms in social psychology, although there is some disagreement as to their definition, function, and scope. Certainly *role* refers to the patterning of an individual's behavior within the group or the larger society. At the same time, however, it can be considered a phase of personality in the sense that people learn their social roles as they learn attitudes, habits, and various behavior traits. Thus the concept of role has real possibilities in studying both the situational and predispositional factors in groups, or the reciprocal relation of personality factors and the sociocultural setting.

Roles can be studied experimentally, and their importance in group processes was indicated in several of the studies reported in the preceding chapters in Part III. Laboratory studies particularly indicate the significance of situational factors in defining roles. One experiment on patterns of role behavior involved informal group interaction in which members associated the names of fellow members with items in a list of behavior traits that had been derived from observation of the group (Cloyd, 1964). Over a series of 20 sessions, different patterns of role behaviors emerged.

Other researchers analyzed the role behavior of 52 business executives and engineers as they were involved in problem-solving group experiments (Moment & Zaleznik, 1963). They were interested in how the motivation and social background of individuals would affect their role performance in respect to: (1) the ways they behaved toward others; (2) the ways others behaved toward them, and (3) the ways others perceived and evaluated their behaviors. The role typology that emerged was composed of:

1. *Technical specialists,* who specialized in ideas but who were not perceived as being especially congenial in the group.
2. *Social specialists,* who were chosen to promote the congeniality of the group but whose ideas were not rated as being strong.
3. *Stars,* who were strong in both ideas and congeniality.
4. *Underchosen participants,* who were low in both ideas and congeniality.

Different role behaviors developed for each type. The technical specialists were comparatively quiet but tended to converse at length when they did speak up. They were highly oriented toward task achievement. The social specialists were primarily concerned with their relationships to others and to concrete tasks. The stars were the most active conversationalists and enjoyed social participation, especially the *process* of working with people, yet they were concerned with achievement. The underchosen were the most aggressive, hostile, and self-oriented of the four role types. Their interest in achievement was directed to concrete tasks. They experienced conflict in their affiliation and generally rejected close relations with others.

These roles were found to be associated with certain background factors. The technical specialists were generally younger and better educated. The stars were slightly older and were apt to be firstborn children from high-status families. The underchosen had experienced upward mobility and were relatively distant toward their original families and often toward their wives. Their role performance was handicapped by a high level of status anxiety.

The study of role behaviors can produce large amounts of similar information the social psychologist can use in trying to determine why people behave as they do in their relations with one another.

The Anthropological-Sociological View of Roles

Anthropologists use the concept of role in describing the behaviors of persons belonging to different age, sex, and occupational groups. Linton (1936) defined it as the dynamic aspect of status, or a special position in society. Thus role involves the performance of the rights and duties constituting a particular *status,* such as the seven age-sex groupings which exist in practically all societies: infant, boy, girl, adult man, adult woman, old man, old woman. Sociologists such as Talcott Parsons (1949) treat role from the standpoint of *social structure.* Role, Parsons said, is the concept linking the individual as a behaving entity to the social structure. Institutionalized roles such as those defined by age, sex, or occupation are the means by which varied human potentialities "dovetail into a single integrated system capable of meeting the situational exigencies with which the society and its members are faced." Organizations and societies demand a degree of stability in the roles assigned to their members; Katz and Kahn (1978) describe role behavior as referring to "the recurring actions of an individual appropriately interrelated with the repetitive activities of others so as to yield a predictable outcome" (p. 189).

This anthropological and sociological view of roles has brought out many important facets of the topic, such as the distinction between *ascribed* roles—those assigned automatically by society—and *achieved roles*—those an individual fits into through learning and experience. Ascribed roles, notably those pertaining to age and sex, are assigned largely on the basis of biological and physiological factors. Others, like that of nobleman or peasant, or upper- or lower-class status, are assigned on the basis of social inheritance or expected position in society. The intercultural similarities that have been found in age and sex roles testify to the presence of biological factors. Thus a child's role in any society is typically one of active play and exploration and an adult's is one of dignity and less muscular movement—both of which agree with known physiological conditions. While biological factors are involved, however, there are also cultural variables, as Margaret Mead (1935) pointed out long ago in regard to sex differences (see Chapter 2).

Studying Sex Roles

Sex, one of the most important role designations, can be used as an example of the kinds of variables that determine various types of role behaviors. Others, such as social class, were discussed in Chapter 3; the role of the aging portion of

Identity and role are easily stereotyped according to custom. Scottish kilts are not a secure index of either masculinity or femininity, for example. *Source:* British Tourist Authority.

the population will be discussed in Chapter 19, and racial or ethnic group belongingness is considered in Chapter 18.

Our clothes, occupations, tastes, values, hobbies, and speech, among other things, reflect the fundamental difference between male and female. The obvious biological differences between men and women are in part responsible for the numerous assumptions about psychological differences that have taken root. In Western culture, for example, women are traditionally considered to be emotional, intuitive, and talkative, whereas men are supposed to be logical and rational. In such comparisons women seldom are given the advantage, possibly because men have been culturally encouraged to make speeches, write books, and occupy the influential role positions.

In physical development boys are heavier and taller up to age 10, girls excel to age 15 to 16, and then boys forge ahead. However important glandular structure may be in sex development, environmental and psychological factors merge with the biological ones. Indeed, the same hormones are found in both male and female, even though the hormonal balance differs between the sexes. Moreover, a few persons suffer confusion not only about their sex roles but about their sex identity. When they feel they are trapped in the wrong body they may seek transsexual surgery to correct the condition.

Biological or Cultural Basis?

It is clear that differences in average height, weight, and strength of men and women are biological in origin, as are their rates of early childhood development and a few specific traits such as color blindness. But in regard to skills, attitudes, and personality differences, cultural or learning factors enter the picture. All societies have different sex roles, different patterns of expected behavior for boys and girls, for men and women. To some extent these roles are a result of parents' expectations about sex typing in socialization of the child, as described in Box 3–3 in Chapter 3. The ways boys and girls are socialized on the basis of these expectations directly affects the formation of their attitudes and values, as described in Box 14–1.

Over the years many studies have found sex differences in interests and attitudes, but the differences were not always statistically significant. There is much overlapping, and the range of individual differences is usually more striking than differences between the means of the two groups.

The physiological differences between the sexes have something to do with the occupational sex roles found in all cultures, but these undeniable differences are not necessarily or entirely the reason for sexual differentiation with respect to activities like cooking, engineering, art and decoration, mechanical work, and the like, as is often alleged. Some cultural influences were defined in Chapter 3, such as the parents' socialization of the child through the identification of appropriate behaviors (Luria & Rose, 1979). Influential cultural features include such *role signs* as type of costume and headgear, access to recreational outlets, degree of seclusiveness, and status positions (Banton, 1965).

The effects of sex differences on occupations have also been unclear and

Box 14–1
STOP THAT FIGHTING!

The power that viewing violence on TV has to stimulate aggressive behavior in children has been corroborated by L. D. Eron and associates, with some interesting sex-role connotations. In their early studies in the 1960s they found that viewing TV violence was correlated with substantial aggressive behavior in boys but had no effect or an inverse effect on girls. But in the 1970s, as girls began to be socialized the same way boys are, TV violence was found to encourage aggression in girls as well as boys.*

Not only were girls in the 1960s socialized to accept nonaggressive behavioral roles, but there were few aggressive female role models on television. Most of the women shown on violence-oriented programs were either victims of aggression or passive observers. Now girls are being socialized in ways to encourage their own aggressive behavior, and more aggressive female role models are being shown on the television screen.

Eron recommends that to control aggressive behavior, both boys and girls should be socialized the way girls traditionally had been, in order to develop socially positive qualities such as tenderness, sensitivity, nurturance, and cooperativeness in both sexes. Eron says, "The level of individual aggression in society will be reduced only when male adolescents and young adults, as a result of socialization, subscribe to the same standards of behavior as have been traditionally encouraged for women" (p. 251).

*L. D. Eron, "Prescription for Reduction of Aggression," *American Psychologist,* 1980, *35,* 244–252.

subject to some dispute. Menstruation is not considered to be as much of a handicap as it formerly was because of a more enlightened attitude toward it. G. H. Seward (1944) found that the menstrual cycle has little effect on the woman worker, although "the persistence of a code of menstrual invalidism" had contributed to absenteeism rates in industry. The effects that pregnancy and childbearing can have on a woman's work are obvious. In practically every society, primitive or civilized, some provision is made for lightening women's occupational labors at this time.

Women's childbearing function and endocrinal postmaternal drive are basic to their child-caring role (found in all cultures) and also related, though more indirectly, to their traditional domestic role. Nevertheless, there is no *necessary* connection between motherhood and gardening, cooking, decorating, house-cleaning, and the like. Indeed, in several cultures one or more of these duties are performed by the men, who, being physiologically more muscular and energetic, are suited to some of these tasks as well as they are to their typical roles of athlete and warrior.

Establishing a Balance between the Sexes

Both males and females must be secure in their own sex identity before there can be clearly defined, harmonious relations between the sexes (Josselyn, 1970). The adequacy of adult models, particularly the parent of the same sex, is important in the socialization of children if they are to acquire a sense of security about their own as well as the opposite sex. But parents who exemplify a rigid, strongly differentiated, traditional sex role impose a strain on their children's search for a mature sex identity in our rapidly changing world, as was noted in Chapter 3. For adolescents, experiences in the school, peer groups, and heterosexual and dating activities also have much to do with the kind of identification they make with both sexes. This drive for self-validation in dating and its involvements is critical in their establishment of an identity with their own sex, as well as in making a successful transition to adulthood.

With the rise of the women's rights movement has emerged an increasing awareness of the need to reduce the psychological barriers between the sexes (Seward & Seward, 1980). To a marked extent, sex roles have become blurred. New terms such as "androgyny" have appeared to indicate the desire of both men and women to assume characteristics of the other sex.

However, in most cultures there are many obstacles to a satisfactory balance between the sexes, principally because men are reluctant to give up their favored position. In Middle Eastern and Third World countries women typically have few or no choices, traditional sex roles are so strongly held. Nevertheless, middle- and upper-class women, particularly in the larger cities there, are beginning to assert themselves and choose careers along with—or even without—being homemakers.

In Western nations married women often must decide between an occupational role or the role of homemaker and child "carer." The choice may be difficult, but increasingly it is being dictated on purely economic grounds; in inflationary times many families have to have two incomes to maintain any standard of living. In these cases the woman's problem is not how to pursue a meaningful career but how to find work she can do which will fit in with her husband's career, her domestic obligations, and, most difficult, her children's needs for care. Many educated women are delaying having children until they become established in a career so they can later accept part-time positions or take periodic withdrawals from the world of work (Fogarty, Rapoport, & Rapoport, 1971).

Thus women, more than men, must plan their lives according to role patterns. Those who pursue careers—or even have undemanding jobs that bring money in to the household—continue to bear the major burden of housework and child care. Few nations have child-care facilities sufficient to meet the needs of the working mother; France and Sweden are exceptions, but the costs of these social programs are high. In Canada and the United States public facilities for child care are for the most part unsatisfactory or nonexistent.

Women's need and desire to enter the job market, as well as other social and economic developments—such as the ideological support of the women's movement, the availability of the pill as an aid to family planning, and the participation of both men and women in sports and other activities which formerly were considered suitable only for one or the other (not to mention the unisex trend in clothes and hairstyles)—all testify to changing attitudes toward the proper roles for men and women in society. The sharing of the roles of husband and wife has been validated, for example, by a study of Chicago suburban households (Mowrer, 1969). Such changes usually start with and are most evident among business and professional people who are well educated. It is significant that even the most militantly male or female colleges and universities became coeducational during the 1970s, with very few exceptions.

Aside from the economic incentive, men are gradually deferring to women's psychological need for careers. Turnabout cases are reported as newsworthy in the press, as when the husband of a newly appointed university president or ambassador follows his wife to her place of employment. In the shrinking academic job market a husband-wife team, both armed with doctorates, may share a single slot in university departments in which male dominance and nepotism have been abolished. Nonetheless, in many areas a degree of separateness is maintained by placing women in relatively low-level career slots (e.g., secretaries and nurses) in which their role is to assist men in performing the really important work (Safilios-Rothschild, 1977).

To what extent women's role will continue to be strengthened depends on the social climate in the years ahead. The change toward more equality seems to be a factor of age; one study revealed markedly less stereotyping of sex roles among the young than among the elderly (Albrecht, Bahr, & Chadwick, 1977).

The traditional domestic role for women received some support from the Republicans' refusal to back the Equal Rights Amendment in their 1980 national election platform. As the Reagan administration took form, the possibility of ratification of the amendment in the remaining states needed for adoption became dimmer. Some conservative groups who had helped put the Republicans in power in the White House and the Senate emphasized the need to combat the decline of the nuclear family—in which the wife supports the husband psychologically and he supports her and the children materially. But this point of view fails to recognize the fact that only 13 percent of households now consist of the ideal nuclear family, as shown in Figure 3–4 in Chapter 3.

Socioeconomic conditions or situational factors more than ideology, therefore, will be responsible for any continuing momentum in the movement for equal rights for women. The twofold goal remains: "bringing women into the world of work and bringing men into the 'world' of the home" (Huber, 1976).

Limitations of the Anthropological-Sociological Definition

As the section on the study of sex roles indicates, the conventional conception of role, in which roles are defined as the dynamic or functional aspects of a person's status and position in the social structure, needs to be modified in certain respects to make it more useful to social psychologists. The anthropological-sociological definition of roles often fails to take into account the variations in prescribed role behavior which occur in real life, for example. In Western culture, obedience is expected of children and self-restraint of clergymen. Yet depending on the personality of a particular child or minister and on the specific situation, considerable variation in these themes is permitted.

The orthodox conception of role also does not include *situational roles*—that is, coherent patterns of social behavior appropriate to a particular situation. This kind of role typically occurs in new or unstructured situations where some selection is possible. A person introduced into a new group may play the role of sophisticate, clinging vine, expert, or very important person.

Third, despite W. I. Thomas' early insistence on defining the situation, most treatments of role have only recently included a perceptual component. Since individuals vary, they perceive and interpret situations differently, which has much to do with determining their role behavior.

All these variables are suggested in the following definition by S. Stansfeld Sargent (1951): "A role is a pattern or type of social behavior which seems situationally appropriate to the person in terms of the demands and expectations of those in his or her group" (p. 360). These guidelines apply to the studies of roles by social psychologists reported in the section below titled "A Social-Psychological Interpretation of Role."

THE DIMENSIONS OF ROLES

Variables in the Nature of Roles

The significance of roles must be approached in the context of *role positions,* which can be thought of as locations in the role structure. The position of police officer, for example, implies various roles—directing traffic, protecting property, making arrests, and helping citizens, among other tasks. The position is relatively constant throughout the world, but the roles differ according to local or national cultures. It can make a difference whether there is a democratic climate or freedom from corruption, whether professional training is expected, and how the officer's status is perceived by citizens, for example.

There is also a *position network* (Yinger, 1965). In every position there are a number of counterpositions, such as those occupied by close relatives, fellow students, or teachers. These positions imply unique kinds of reciprocal role relationships; your roommate does not occupy the same position in relation to you as your partner in a laboratory experiment. Reciprocal roles can be either symmetrical or asymmetrical, depending on the equality of the positions. Between friends the tie is equalitarian, but between parents and children, or ministers and parishioners, the relationship is asymmetrical.

Sarbin and Allen (1968) have noted other variables in the nature of roles. One is the *role location* of the individual within the social structure. A person must choose, among several role options, the one that is most appropriate to the situation. This decision depends on the person's ability to identify with others who are relevant to the situation and to handle cues from them. People almost constantly engage in role perception in order to determine, for example, whether or not to take the aggressive role—to ask that girl or guy to a movie, to be a curve pusher on tomorrow's exam, or to try to nudge out a rival for the position of club president.

Once a person locates his or her role, or more specifically, identifies who occupies the other positions, it is necessary to determine the *role demands,* or the requirements of given roles. Discovering the boundaries of possible role behaviors and the norms in specific role situations can be a more complex process than simply discovering who the relevant peers are. The problems of role demands and relevant norms have been studied in experimental settings, as in a study of perceptual defense by Sarbin and Allen (1968). Role demands for this study were designed to include the "operation of modesty norms, communication norms, control-of-aggression norms, face-saving norms, norms designed to prevent embarrassment to others and reciprocity norms."

It is also necessary to develop appropriate *role skills* and learn how to arrive at more effective role behavior. These tap existing capacities but depend primarily on the perception and cognition of interpersonal situations and on the ability to handle them. Empathy and identification are especially germane to this process—that is, being able to "feel oneself into" the other person's thoughts and emotions.

Variations in Roles

Role expectations and behaviors can vary along axes ranging from required to prohibited, as shown in Figure 14–1. The horizontal and vertical central axes indicate the degree of obligation in roles. For instance, a husband is *required* to provide some economic contribution to the marriage, *expected* to help in household chores, has the *option* of accompanying his wife to church or the opera, and is *prohibited* from using physical force. Dominant and submissive describe the two ends of one continuum; authoritarian and anarchistic describe another. An authoritarian role requires individuals to control or to be controlled; an anarchistic role is beyond the limits of conventional society and therefore neither controls or is controlled. Other axes within given roles might be conceptualized—conscious versus unconscious, broad versus narrow, or diffuse versus specific in patterning of the role.

There are numerous other dimensions in which roles can vary, such as formality, breadth, specificity, permanence, and prestige. Roles can, for example, be *formal* or *informal.* The university registrar, the chairman of the board, or the clergyman officiating at a wedding operate within prescribed behaviors and in a rather formal manner. In contrast, social life at a snack bar, in over-the-fence chats between neighbors, or within the family is conducted with behaviors that are more informal and spontaneous. Informal and formal role behaviors often merge, however, especially in a society with rapidly changing interpersonal contacts and a minimum of barriers between different social groupings.

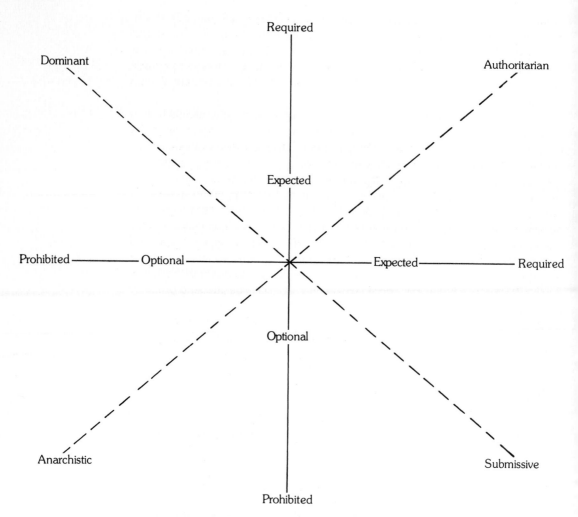

**Figure 14–1. Axes in Dominant-Submissive
and Authoritarian-Anarchistic Role Behaviors**

Source: Adapted from A. P. Hare, *Handbook of Small Group Research,* 2d ed. (New
York: Free Press, 1976), p. 133.

Another dimension of roles is their *breadth* or *extensiveness.* A minister plays
the role in all or practically all social contacts, though many variations on the
central theme are possible. A head of state usually conforms in public contacts to
the culturally prescribed role. Other roles are more variable: A young man may be
a leader in one group and a buffoon in another; a girl may act as a sophisticate in

only one small circle of acquaintances; a man may be bossy and dominate only in his office, never in his home or club.

Roles also differ in *specificity of patterning.* On official occasions or in ceremonial or ritualistic situations such as a formal wedding, a university graduation, or a dramatic performance, the acts and words are rather quite predetermined. Even in highly organized hierarchical relationships such as military life, however, some latitude is permitted, which is what makes one officer's method of issuing orders distinctive. In many roles, however, there is little or no prescription of specific behaviors, and conformity is demanded only to general norms or broad categories of "musts" and "must nots": A child must not be rude to or disobey his or her parents; a minister must not drink, swear, or go to burlesque shows; a doctor must treat all sick people to the best of his or her ability, and so on. Considerable variation is permitted, however, and outside such broad limitations behavior is left unregulated by the role.

Furthermore, roles shift in time, and as they do they often become more elaborate in detail. Although a fixed role model is a well-known characteristic of a bureaucratic setting (Kahn, et al., 1964), sooner or later the bureaucrat changes the norms or elaborates the details, at least to some degree.

For instance, in an analysis of a college housing and food service over a nine-month period, managers who had a high professional orientation (as measured by such criteria as joining a professional organization and subscribing to professional journals) became very active in communication, counseling, and planning. Managers without this professional orientation neither assumed these activities nor were pushed into them by their supervisors. Thus the role occupant often *makes* rather than *takes* the role (Haga, Graen, & Dansereau, 1974).

The *continuity and permanence* of roles also vary. While occupational roles are relatively permanent, they change over time, particularly in a changing society. Age roles last over a period of years: childhood, adolescence, adulthood, old age. Many other roles are transitory; an eligible bachelor, for example, has a role of relatively short duration. Other roles are occasional and last but a few hours or minutes, though they may recur in comparable social situations.

One dimension in which roles vary greatly is *importance and prestige.* The role of a friend entails far greater personal intimacy and evokes deeper emotional reactions than that of a casual acquaintance. The fulfillment of a family or professional role involves an enduring personality adjustment, as compared with such roles as those of visitor or neighbor.

The importance of roles varies according to their value to individuals and groups. Some could consider the role of worshiper, for example, to be the central one in life. One woman regards the mother-wife role as dominant; another does not. South Seas natives place less emphasis on occupational roles than do Americans. In the United States the relative ranking of roles varies greatly within subcultural groups. Some upper-class professionals might consider it square to work, marry, have children, attend church, and save for the future, while some blue-collar workers would value these activities and roles highly, or the reverse is possible.

The roles a person takes—or does not take—depend to a considerable extent

To some extent, personal appearance makes the role. The uniforms of the police officers make their function in this situation readily apparent. *Source:* © Theodore Anderson, 1981.

on class or caste membership and affiliation. In some groups not taking a traditional role can be quite unhealthy, such as an American male blue-collar worker rejecting the traditional dominant male role. Each subculture in a large and complex society has its own versions of honored and dishonored roles.

Self-Identity and Image

In the same way roles vary according to individuals and situations, individuals themselves vary in the extent to which they achieve coherence or integration of

Box 14–2
WILL THE REAL GEORGE APLEY PLEASE STAND UP?

You probably would not talk the same way to a fellow fraternity or sorority member and to a professor, and you would not behave the same way on a date as in an academic seminar. Everyone presents disparate roles to the world. George Apley, a character in a 1930s novel by J. P. Marquand, filled the roles expected of him when he wrote home from Paris.* His letter to his mother read:

> Dear Mother: No sooner did we arrive at the hotel after a very rough channel crossing than I found again what a very small place the world is. There in the dining room were Dr. and Mrs. Jessup from Mt. Vernon Street, and Jane Silby and her aunt from Commonwealth Avenue, and the Morrows from Brookline . . . Uncle Horatio and our driver had great difficulty over the fare, as Uncle Horatio does not believe in giving more than the usual ten percent fee extra. We are going with Dr. and Mrs. Jessup through the Louvre tomorrow, where I am looking forward to seeing the Mona Lisa.

But a letter to a classmate presented a different picture:

> Dear Mike: Well, here I am in Paris and I wish you were here too. I saw Wintie over in London and we split a bottle together in a Public House and talked about the Club. I have always heard how pretty the French girls were and I am disappointed. If you and I were to walk up Tremont Street we could see a dozen prettier ones. Uncle Horatio and Dr. Jessup and I have been out several evenings to "see the town." We have been to several shows. There is no doubt that the French are a very immoral lot, even when one does not understand everything that is said. They certainly seem to enjoy and thrive on immorality. Uncle Horatio is really quite a "sport" and once he has got Henrietta and Aunt Brent safely out of the way you would be surprised at some of his goings-on. Several evenings we have both of us been quite tight.

---

*John P. Marquand, *The Late George Apley* (Boston: Little, Brown, 1937).

their various roles. Most persons succeed in executing even divergent roles without becoming disorganized, and some have the capacity to reveal quite different aspects of their personality, each in an appropriate situation (see Box 14–2). If this is done skillfully, in accordance with situational demands, it may win approval, as with the gracious hostess or the adroit statesman. If, however, the changes in role are dramatized or are greater than the situations seem to warrant, the individual may be considered to have a chameleonlike personality or to be an insincere opportunist.

Peoples' roles must be understood in the light of their own patterns of hereditary and environmental influences. Children's first roles develop under the influence of their families, friends, neighborhoods, and communities. Biological forces also play a part, though always as mediated by the social milieu.

Knowledge of the important roles in any society is communicated to children by all their social contacts—in home, school, community; by parents, siblings, relatives, friends; over TV, on the radio, and in movies; through newspapers and magazines—especially the comics. Even more important, children learn through their own observation. Naturally their knowledge of roles and their functions differ according to their own social experience, which can affect their attitudes toward various roles and orient them toward some roles and away from others. Study of an individual's major roles, like the study of personality variables, depends on the person's entire life history. When abnormal or unusual inherited factors exist, such as deformity, disease, or glandular imbalance, they bulk large as role determinants. If no unusual physical factors are present, the causes of roles predominantly rest in social experience.

Roles are also related to the concept of *image*. Every U.S. president, for example, has evoked a unique image. Most people recall John F. Kennedy as a brilliant, energetic, affable, rather casual person, to whom public attention was pleasing. He established a high public image in a dramatically short time. Gerald Ford, following Richard Nixon and Watergate, started off with a very favorable image, which he facilitated by the modest quip, "Remember, I am a Ford, not a Lincoln!"

Although role and image overlap, they are not the same. To some degree the American president has had to define the role within certain precise expectations, as in performing given rituals or duties such as delivering a message to Congress, welcoming a foreign dignitary, and, most important, carrying out the executive role as defined by the Constitution. In many such functions the president's role behavior has been structured by his perception of the situation, the knowledge he brings to the problem, and his own definition of the presidential role. Examples are Harry Truman's firing of General Douglas MacArthur in 1951 for insubordination or Nixon's sacking of Archibald Cox as special prosecutor in the Watergate affair in 1973. Nixon also dared to open negotiations with Communist China, and Jimmy Carter gambled on securing peace in the Middle East by inviting Premier Begin and President Sadat to a summit conference at Camp David. Kennedy departed from the usual presidential role in making the White House a center for the arts, science, and intellectual interests.

Thus there are different nuances in the role of the U.S. presidency, depending on the occupant of the office. The leadership role also reflects the needs of the times. The cynicism following Watergate undoubtedly was instrumental in the election of Carter, who came from outside the Washington establishment. Yet when he adopted a rather fluid and "folksy" kind of leadership role, the electorate turned to Ronald Reagan and the more traditional image of a dominant leader who could manipulate legislative action and "talk turkey" to foreign governments. Every person, whether president, laborer, professional, or student, accepts and performs certain roles, either obligatory or optional, and these become a significant part of her or his personal identity.

A SOCIAL-PSYCHOLOGICAL INTERPRETATION
OF ROLE

In the perspective of the social psychologist, our prevailing roles are determined by the culture and the situation in which we find ourselves, but our own perceptions, motivations, values, attitudes, and emotions play a part in the way the role is enacted. This complexity of role relationships is seen in a study of ministers in Little Rock, Arkansas, in 1957, at the time of the original case of school desegregation (Campbell & Pettigrew, 1959). The ministers were found to be influenced in their role behavior by three systems:

1. The *self-reference system*—the behavior they would ideally prefer if no sanctions could be applied from external sources.
2. The *professional reference system*—their role obligation to urge integration, which was the position of the national church organization.
3. The *membership reference system*—dependence on their congregations for their position. All of the congregations were segregationist, and this meant considerable strain for ministers who were either active or passive integrationists. As a result their behavior was often frustrated and vacillating, and there was a certain degree of rationalization.

A few years later, during the social protests of the late 1960s, another study found Protestant ministers could be divided into conservatives who were not interested in social action and those who defined their profession as primarily one of ethics or who assumed a community problem-solving role (Nelson, Yokley, & Madron, 1973). This meant that their ideology was a better predictor of the ministerial role than were other variables.

Norms obviously are related to roles; in fact, roles have been defined as "shared norms concerning the behavior of certain persons in certain settings" (Jones & Gerard, 1967, p. 177). Men are constrained by different norms than women are, for example, but they share expectations about the behavior implied in each role. The relation of norms and roles is even clearer within a face-to-face group. A chart drawn up by Thibaut and Kelley (1959) to show how members did or did not adhere to group norms indicated that two persons assume the same role when their behavior in a given situation is controlled by the same norms.

Role Expectations

Role expectations and actual role performance can be similar or quite different. For example, a husband may expect his wife to follow a role model based on what he perceived in his mother or on the totality of images he has gained from his socialization, including the mass media and his dating experiences, but the wife has a different role definition for herself. Much of the shock felt by the American public over the Watergate scandal arose from the discrepancy between expected behavior in the presidential role and Nixon's actual behavior as disclosed by the investigation. Less than ten years later the Abscam investigations of 1980 and 1981, which revealed evidence of bribe taking by members of Congress, would be shrugged off by the public, who seemed to think that was about what could be expected.

The discrepancy between expectation and performance can be reduced in some situations; in marriage, for example, improved communication between wife and husband could remove or at least diminish the misunderstanding. However, the presidential role has a historic basis and is less flexible and unlikely to be modified very rapidly, despite many incidents of presidential behavior which have been inconsistent with the expectations of the public.

There is a high degree of agreement about some values, but a basic problem in many roles is their vagueness. According to Sarbin and Allen (1968), the lack of role clarity stems from three sources. One is the uncertainty about expectations, which often leads to low productivity and efficiency, whether at the workbench, in the classroom, or in the family setting. The second is a lack of consensus among occupants of complementary roles such as parents and adolescents, management and labor, or administrators and teachers. The third is incongruity between the person's expectations for his or her role and those held by various judges. For instance, the definition of the husband's conduct toward his wife is apt to be judged by relatives, friends, neighbors, or even the community at large.

Role clarity is further confused by contemporary social changes. The role of modern woman is inevitably changing, as noted above. The role of older persons also is undergoing change, as Chapter 19 will demonstrate.

Another complicating factor is the multiplicity and interrelatedness of roles. The position of wife might include the role of sexual companion, co-worker, wage earner, best friend and buddy, hostess, mother figure (to the husband), and arbiter of emotional tensions—as well as civic participant, neighbor, and social secretary. In addition there is a *role set* or the totality of complementary roles attached to a given position; the wife-mother for example, must interact with husband and children (Merton, 1957). Of course modifications occur as the partners work toward joint evaluations, and from these emerge norms which become binding upon both members. Role definitions may change, stabilize, or in some cases become extremely rigid (Borden, Gregg, & Grove, 1969).

Role expectations, according to Sarbin and Allen (1968), are collections of cognitions which range all the way from rudimentary, commonsense knowledge to specific rules and procedures, as in a bureaucratic framework. Role expectations may help two or more participants arrive at some consensus about their reciprocal roles and the appropriate norms. Failure to agree on these norms can result in dismay and confusion, and if one of the individuals has sufficient power, sanctions are applied. A third party may act as an arbiter in the role definition, especially if his or her own interest is involved (Goode, 1960a).

Consciousness of Roles

Most people would probably reject the notion that they are playing roles, fearing it smacks of insincerity. On the whole, people seem unconscious of the roles they play—even the more obvious sex, age, and professional or occupational roles. But each person gradually learns what is required in his or her position. Teacher and student, employer and employee, husband and wife would seldom stop to think about the appropriate interactional behavior, but it would never occur to most people to light up a cigarette in church or to tell a ribald story at a formal dinner. Such situations are clearly defined by our past experience, and the responses are made without conscious decision. In new or unusual circumstances, however, the situation must be interpreted or defined, and the role to be played may be consciously thought out.

In general, the higher the status or visibility of a role and the greater the power associated with it, the more likely we are to be conscious of it. A statesman, outstanding scholar, corporation head, or society leader is more likely to be aware of his or her role in the social order than a farmer, student, or housewife. Aside from variations in situations and in status, people show marked differences in self-awareness, including the ability to see themselves as others do and to be conscious of their roles. The levels of involvement in role behavior are defined in Box 14–3.

Our self–image, whether or not it is fully conscious, often includes some conception of our roles (see Chapter 4), because the self develops in a social matrix. Our social relationships—with parents, teachers, friends, and others—become crystallized into roles; indeed our self-image is based in large part on such roles, especially if they are conceptualized and we are considered, for example, a good child, a bright student, a loyal friend—or a clumsy oaf or dumbbell!

Because self-awareness provides a perspective for evaluating one's role behavior, it can be a means of social control. It has been shown, for example, that awareness of the self, derived principally from immediate feedback on test performance, can be a means of reducing cheating (Diener & Wallbom, 1976). Another study indicated that similar types of feedback data could substantially raise the performance level on a number of given tasks (Diener & Srull, 1979).

ROLE CONFORMITY, DEVIANCE, AND CONFLICT

Role expectations and performances sometimes pose inconsistencies, and role performance often falls short of social expectations, as noted above. But on the whole we accept our roles and conform, as Chapter 11 demonstrated. Role deviance inevitably leads to conflicts and strains.

Why Do People Conform?

Conformity, which was shown to be the principal effect of group interaction in Chapter 11, is really an aspect of role behavior. According to F. H. Allport's J-curve hypothesis of conforming behavior (1934), if this behavior is plotted on a curve it resembles an inverted letter *J*, as shown in Figure 14–2. This figure charts motorists' behavior at a corner with red lights and a policeman (in simpler times when traffic laws were not so strictly enforced and all traffic officers were police*men*). His studies found that nearly all motorists stopped for a red traffic light, in the same way that nearly all Catholics made the sign of the cross with a

Box 14-3
FROM NONINVOLVEMENT TO BEWITCHMENT

People differ in how deeply they become involved in their various roles and how they enact them. Efficiency would surely suffer if a person tried to fill every one of their roles with maximum effort. In effect, personal and social demands permit only a partial commitment to many roles.

To manage these multiple roles, people engage in them with varying levels of involvement. Theodore Sarbin and Vernon Allen have identified eight levels of role involvement in any culture.* They are:

Level zero: *Noninvolvement*—role expectations which exist only in potential, for instance, lapsed membership in an organization, which could become a role again if the membership is reactivated.

Level 1: *Casual role enactment*—a student relaxing between classes, a purchase at the supermarket or at the gas station—except when a shortage or the price of a commodity makes for a more studied role enactment.

Level 2: *Ritual acting*—a sales clerk perfunctorily smiling at a client or an actor giving a routine performance on stage.

Level 3: *Engrossed acting*—removing oneself from one's own identity and hurling oneself into a role. The modern theater offers less opportunity for such a display of emotion than the melodramas of the last century did.

Level 4: *Classical hypnotic role-taking*—experiencing sensory and motor changes and rigidly carrying out a number of posthypnotic suggestions.

Level 5: *Histrionic neurosis*—often identified as conversion hysteria; patients show some organic disorder in the absence of pathology. Several preliterate societies provide for the husband to enact the role of the wife during late pregnancy and birth. In this institution, called the *couvade,* the husband is expected to express acute pain.

Level 6: *Ecstasy*—trances, possession, and "swooning" are culturally approved types of ecstasy, itself a diagnostic term of early medical practitioners. This kind of role enactment is found in both modern cults and ancient rites.

Level 7: *Bewitchment*—as documented by anthropologists, persons who consider themselves the objects of sorcery and magic may exhibit an appropriate fate, including the role of a dying victim.

The last three dimensions exemplify the extremes of external role behavior, as most people seldom go beyond levels 1 and 2, and so much role behavior is rather bland. Nevertheless, people often are emotionally or internally involved in role decisions and enactments, such as the contrived management of an image on a date or attempts to make an impression on the boss.

_____

*T. R. Sarbin and V. L. Allen, "Role Theory," in G. Lindzey and E. Aronson (Eds.), *Handbook of Social Psychology,* Vol. 1 (Reading, Mass.: Addison-Wesley Publishing Co., 1968), pp. 488–567.

finger dipped in the holy water font on entering a church. Each of these acts exemplifies expected behavior, with some degree of punishment for noncompliance. State and local laws define the motorist's role quite clearly in terms of "must" and "must nots." A good Catholic knows exactly what behavior is expected in church and, though it is less clearly prescribed, the proper behavior outside church as well.

To a large extent role conformity is a product of socialization. In a study of 72 boys aged 10 to 16, Kohlberg (1964) outlined three levels in the development of moral judgments. At the first stage, a child operates mainly on a premoral level of conduct in which rules are obeyed simply in order to avoid punishment and to obtain rewards. Second, the child acquires conventional role conformity as a means of avoiding social disapproval. Third, the child begins to internalize a role of morality based on rational decisions as to what constitutes socially accepted behavior. These norms are conceived as the decisions of an impartial judge. Thus,

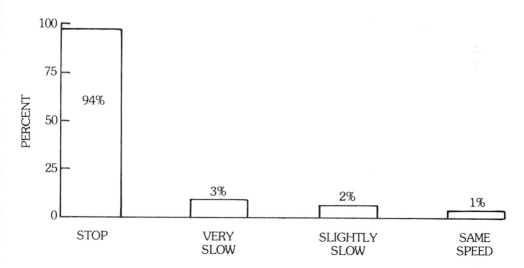

Figure 14–2. Conforming Behavior: Variations in Motorists' Behavior at Stoplight

Source: F. H. Allport, "The J-Curve Hypothesis of Conforming Behavior," *Journal of Social Psychology,* 1934, *5,* 141–183.

to cite an extreme case, John W. Hinckley, Jr., the disturbed youth who apparently sought instant fame by shooting Ronald Reagan and three others in March 1981, may have been disappointed in the public reaction to his deviant act. Rather than being considered unthinkable and profoundly shocking, as the assassination of John F. Kennedy had been less than 20 years previously, the attempt on the president's life seemed to be shrugged off by the public—although regretfully—as something that would have happened sooner or later.

Role-taking, then, is an inherent means of widening the sphere of morality (Kohlberg, 1969). Empathy, guilt, social approval, and disapproval are all based on the principles of reciprocity. In assuming the role of the other person, an individual acquires a sense of obligation. The reference group can be parents or peers, and conformity may be oriented either to socially adequate or inadequate models. The shocking results of the Milgram (1965) experiment on obedience and the simulated prison Zimbardo studied (Haney & Zimbardo, 1973), as described in Chapter 11, demonstrate how under conditions of stress individuals acquire unaccustomed roles.

The reasons why people conform and tend to avoid deviant behavior have been summarized by Blake and Davis (1964) as follows:

1. Internalization of norms. Norms are accepted by the individual as part of the socialization process, though of course with less than complete uniformity.
2. Desire for approval. The desire for social approval is a fundamental one in human behavior, supported by the status structure which encourages nondeviancy.
3. Deference to possible punishment for deviance. Peers, relatives, the people next door, or formal law enforcement agencies all can punish deviants.
4. Anticipation of security. Though conformity often brings little or no obvious reward, it seems safe and without risk.
5. Lack of opportunity for deviant behavior. Often the individual conforms because the environment presents little or no opportunity for deviance—in either a positive (e.g., upward mobility) direction or negative (e.g., delinquency).

A society sometimes permits liberalization or weakening of moral codes, so that, for example, tolerance of bribery or of racketeering is the norm—until public pressure becomes strong enough to change it (Cohen, 1965).

Role Conflict and Strain

The intimate relationship of roles and norms means that indecision and conflict in one are accompanied by problems in the other. Stouffer (1962) demonstrated this discrepancy in a study of student-projected role behaviors in regard to cheating. Subjects were asked on a questionnaire what they would do if they were serving as test proctors and found a student cheating. The choices of behavior ranged on a five-point scale from dismissing the cheater from the examination and reporting her or him, to completely ignoring the situation. The replies were different when the items referred to catching an ordinary student as opposed to a roommate-friend.

Stouffer also investigated other particularistic (loyalty to a friend) versus universalistic (absolute principles of justice) approaches to role behavior. Students were asked to indicate their role obligation (what they *should* do) and role performance (what they *would* do) in four different situations: (1) A friend testifying in favor of a driver in a trial regarding automobile speed at the time of an accident, (2) a drama critic writing a favorable review of a less than adequate play written by a friend, (3) an insurance doctor tempted to alter the findings of a friend's physical examination, and (4) a member of a board of directors who could save a friend from financial disaster by imparting secret information. Only 24 percent favored avoiding their obligations in the car accident, compared to 70 percent who chose the particularistic role for the board member. In several national samples (Colombia, Japan, the United States and Western Germany) studied by Williamson (1970), an acute generational difference was found. Older persons favored universalistic criteria, at least on a verbal level, whereas the younger leaned toward a particularistic approach.

Behavioral norms are usually subject to change, and the borderline between deviance and nondeviance is not always clear. In the prohibition era of the 1920s official norms in regard to drinking were rejected and eventually changed. A remarkable shift of norms was evident in the development in the 1960s of a middle-class drug subculture, when the traditional territory for drugs (notably marijuana) had been in cults and portions of the lower-class subculture (McGlothlin, 1975). By the 1970s marijuana had moved into the secondary schools, largely because of student norms which were ascribable to peer influence; that is, friends using the drug was a more important factor in the acceptance of this behavior than either the attitudes of the students themselves or the tolerance of the drug by their parents or other authorities (Andrews & Kandel, 1979). Thus acceptance of norms and consequent role behavior are a function of social approval within the subsociety in which one moves.

Role conflict, deviance, and inconsistencies typically produce *role strain* in the person, and various attempts are made to eliminate or reduce the tension. Military chaplains, for example, often had difficulty reconciling their role as an officer with their pastoral duties among enlisted personnel (Burchard, 1954). Some ways of resolving these conflicts were asking to be addressed as "Chaplain" rather than by rank, waiving the rule against fraternization between officers and enlisted men, and stating that chaplains have no command role, with the implication that they are not really officers. A different kind of role strain has been found in high school counselors, who are primarily oriented to psychological guidance of students and consequently have a strained relationship with teachers who are classroom or subject oriented. They also are frustrated in their role of vocational counselor by their awareness of the difficulties of matching students' abilities and goals with the demands of the employment world (Bredemeier & Bredemeier, 1978).

Goode (1960b) points to various means of reducing role strain, such as delegating certain aspects or segments of the role to another person; elimination of the role relationship through retirement, curtailment, or resignation; extension, or taking on more relations or duties so as to avoid conflicting ones; and erection of barriers, like using a secretary to ward off visitors.

Many role situations in large organizations are complex and ambiguous (see Box 14–4). An investigation of relationships in government agencies (Miles, 1977) found that professionals who were at a considerable distance from administrative levels or in in-between areas, or those with only conditional authority, so the decision-making authority rested elsewhere, were especially likely to experience role conflict. An obvious remedy was to bring together those who shared the decision making, in order to reduce the role stress.

Other studies of professional subcultures have indicated strain in such groups as university professors, some of whose conflicts are long-standing (Knapp, 1962). These include conflicts over loyalty to one's field of teaching or to the salary-paying institution; over interest in research or in teaching; over living in the intellectual world or pursuing an active social and community role. Another frustration experienced by many professors is lack of control over academic matters, especially in average or marginal universities (Lazarsfeld & Thielens, 1958). By the 1980s the role of the university professor in Western society seemed quite insecure. The student revolts of the late 1960s had divided many faculties between teachers who basically supported the students' aspirations and those who did not. Declining student enrollments, an oversupply of PhD's seeking jobs, erosion of the tenure system, and a financial crisis in the universities have further weakened their status. The move toward unionization of college teachers in many institutions is another complication of their professional role. It is not surprising that professors today have difficulty defining their identity vis-à-vis the needs of their students, their profession, the university administration, and the community.

Box 14–4
BEHIND THE FORMAL FACADE

Carefully drawn organizational charts of the positions in a hierarchy illustrate an ideal system, but they fail to show the informal role patterns that individual members define for themselves. These roles are usually segmental rather than complete, and together they make up the complex roles of many administrative positions. They are shifted as the role occupant's motive and the situation change and call for different approaches to problem solving. B. M. Gross has defined the various roles organization members may assume.*

Task, technique, and people oriented. Task-oriented members see their role as "getting the job done"; those who are technique-oriented show a bureaucratic conformity to rules; and the people-oriented cut through organizational rituals to meet the needs of individuals.

Nay-sayers and yea-sayers. The yes man has to be counterbalanced with a person who can say no. The man at the top is more likely to reject a suggestion than someone in the middle, but each organization develops its own style of prescribing roles. Variations of nay-sayers and yea-sayers are rule enforcers, rule evaders, and rule blinkers, who have individual approaches to the organizational operating procedure.

The involved and the detached. Ego involvement usually increases at the higher levels in the organizational structure. But at any level, some people voluntarily work overtime, make ingenious efforts to resolve crises, or pass up offers from another company.

Impersonals, personals, and charismatics. In most organizations there are bureaucrats, those who "blow their top," and the inspired leaders of other people.

There are also variants like regulars, deviants, and isolates who define their special relationships to the group and its values. There are newcomers and old-timers, climbers and stickers, cosmopolitans and locals; a person's role is determined by the loyalties—and rigidities—built over time, and by restlessness and the aspiration to move up or out. Other roles include builders and consolidators, thinkers and doers, grandstand players and behind-the-scenes operators. Each role is determined by the way a personality structure meets the challenge of the situation.

---

*B. M. Gross, *Organizations and Their Managing* (New York: Free Press, 1968), pp. 243–53. See also P. M. Blau, *The Dynamics of Democracy* (Chicago: University of Chicago Press, 1955).

SUMMARY

The concept of role is an aid in describing and interpreting social interaction, especially within clearly defined groups. As the social psychologist defines it, the concept allows for individual variation, stresses the perceptual factor and the reciprocal nature of the interaction, and includes situational roles. Most instances of role behavior involve both cultural and personal determinants, along with changing local circumstances. The social system or the structure of the specific situation is an inescapable reality that determines role portrayal.

On the whole, people are unconscious of their roles, although everyone learns many roles in the course of their socialization. The multiple roles a person occupies in an urban society often cause role conflict or strain, but conflict or at least incongruity among a person's roles not only creates tensions but may also inspire both comedy and pathos. Another critical area is role expectations. In order for people to establish sufficient clarity in the perception and execution of their roles they must identify the role demands and develop a set of skills for negotiating them.

The theory of roles focuses in part on a position network in which the person must work out the various parameters of role location. Much of the investigation of roles in this chapter is concerned with sex roles, the roles of executives and school administrators, or artificially devised role situations in a laboratory setting.

There is often only relative consensus on role behavior. Most people tend to conform, but the level of tolerance for deviance from norms varies with time and place, as witness the changing lifestyles of the last decade or two. Roles provide a situationally oriented approach to personality that supplements, and may help correct, the usual trait-oriented psychological approach. Much, but not all, social behavior has role character; role relationships are minimal in critical situations and in new and unstructured social groupings. The conspicuous roles of leaders and followers in the group setting are examined in the next chapter.

WORDS TO REMEMBER

Deviance. Behavior which falls short of the norms expected of a group member. The term may be thought of statistically as deviations from average performance or a standard, as in number of absences from work.

Internalization of norms. Socialization process by which norms and consequently roles are acquired.

Multiple roles. Numerous roles enacted by a single individual because of a plurality of positions—in family, work, school, etc. There are also subdivisions within these roles; the family role for a man may include husband, father, brother-in-law, wage-earner, counselor, etc.

Norms. Shared beliefs about standards of behavior that are expected of every person in a given group or society. Often they point to expected rather than actual behavior. Negative norms are often known as *sanctions.*

Position. Location of a person within the social order. When position is defined as relatively higher or lower, it is known as *status.*

Roles. Rights and obligations of a member of a given group, organization, or society; social behaviors as defined according to norms. Roles may be *expected* or *prescribed,* but as actually played by the person they are *enacted* roles. *Ascribed* roles are automatically assigned by society, and *achieved* roles are acquired by the individual. Roles are usually identified with a given position or status.

Role conflict. Incompatibility between roles, or conflicting demands imposed by the group or society on a person. *Role strain* refers to the inconsistencies within a given role.

QUESTIONS FOR DISCUSSION

1. Why are roles crucial to an understanding of our society?

2. Name some of the misperceptions or mythologies about sex roles. To what degree have these misunderstandings been corrected?

3. What are the implications of sex identity?

4. Compare some of the variables in the nature of roles, such as position, role location, and similar concepts.

5. Explain the major variations in roles. How would they be used to define your own role positions?

6. What is meant by situational roles? How do roles relate to the group setting?

7. How have Nixon, Carter, and Reagan defined the role of the U.S. presidency? (Or take two or three other leaders and make a similar comparison.)

8. How does the concept of role clarity fit in with the term *role expectations?*

9. Give an example of role conflict. How did Stouffer study this? How would you differentiate between role conflict and role strain?

10. Can you think of examples of informal roles in an organizational hierarchy in addition to those described by Gross (Box 14–4)? How well do these roles usually articulate with the formal structure?

READINGS

Banton, M. *Roles: An Introduction to the Study of Social Relations.* New York: Basic Books, 1965.

Considers the significance of roles from economic, historical, and sociological viewpoints and treats family, class, and professional aspects of the problem.

Gergen, K. J. *The Concept of Self.* New York: Holt, Rinehart & Winston, 1971.

A social psychologist presents an enlightening interpretation of the relation of role and the self.

Goffman, E. *Encounters: Two Studies in the Sociology of Interaction.* Indianapolis: Bobbs-Merrill Co., 1961.

Games-playing and a medical setting as two different milieus for the study of role behavior.

Gross, N., Mason, W., and McEachern, A. W. *Explorations in Role Analysis.* New York: John Wiley & Sons, 1958.

Classic case study of the school superintendent as a portrait of the bureaucratic role.

O'Kelly, C. G. *Women and Men in Society.* New York: Van Nostrand, 1980.

A cross-cultural, historical, and social-psychological introduction to gender roles.

Sarbin, T. R., and Allen, V. L. Role Theory. In G. Lindzey and E. Aronson (Eds.), *Handbook of Social Psychology* (Vol. 1). Reading, Mass.: Addison-Wesley Publishing Co., 1968.

A keenly analytical account of the social-psychological approach to role.

Seward, G. H., and Williamson, R. C. (Eds.) *Sex Roles in Changing Society*. New York: Random House, 1970.

Cross-national comparisons in a psychological, sociological, and historical framework.

Seward, J. P. and Seward, G. H. *Sex Differences: Mental and Temperamental*. Lexington, Mass.: Heath and Co., 1980.

An examination of the psychological and social aspects of gender identity and role behavior.

LEADERSHIP

Leaders and followers are essential behavioral roles in the group setting. Those who take the role of leader can influence the extent to which groups of all sizes and types will be effective in maintaining or changing the attitudes and behaviors of the followers.

The study of leadership may involve either the person or the situation. Both are essential, of course. But it is the interaction between the person and the situation that produces leaders, and this is difficult to disentangle and analyze. One way to approach the problem is by defining the many different types of leaders and situations within which leaders must act. In the final analysis, however, leadership is a process by which an individual exercises influence or control over other individuals. Understanding how such an influence is accomplished involves the concept of social power, which was introduced at the beginning of Part III in Chapter 11 and which is inherent in many of the personality and situational aspects of leadership.

The dimensions of leadership are first defined in this chapter in terms of the process of becoming a leader, the effects of leadership, and the functions of a leader. The next sections consider the two factors in interactional analysis of leadership—the traits of the person and the characteristics of the situation. The quality of leadership in the group setting then is examined in respect to participation, communication networks, transactions between leaders and followers, and leadership styles and climates.

DIMENSIONS OF LEADERSHIP

An appreciation of the different types of leadership can be arrived at by considering various aspects of the phenomenon—the process of becoming a leader, the effects of leadership, and the functions of a leader.

The Process of Becoming a Leader

The processes by which leaders come to positions of influence are one way to differentiate between types of leadership. The different forms indicate the nature and extent of a leader's influence and are helpful in reaching an understanding of why leaders behave the way they do.

Election

Elected leaders are able to maintain positions of influence only insofar as they can maintain the support of their constituents, or those who have elected them. When they fail to perform as expected or become unpopular, they run the risk of being voted out of office at the next election. Politicians therefore have learned to follow their ratings in polls of the electorate and other indicators of their political acceptance, to the extent that they may be more concerned with ingratiating themselves with their constituents than with their performance as leaders. (The role of the elected leader in the coercive models of linkage between public opinion and public policy is described in Chapter 16.)

This dependence on constituency support can be a source of both strength and weakness for an elected leader. Interest groups have discovered that if they organize they can become powerful enough to make elected representatives reflect their wishes in legislative action—or nonaction. Thus elected leaders can become responsible, if not subservient, to powerful special-interest groups and voting blocs such as racial, ethnic, or religious minorities; the antiabortionists; or the National Rifle Association, which opposes any form of gun control.

In small groups like clubs or business organizations, leadership positions are often determined by popularity rather than by ability or performance. Leaders work to ensure their popularity with a majority of the membership, and in this process they can make democratic organizations autocratic or even tyrannical if they ignore or suppress minorities by reflecting only the will of the majority.

Emergent Leadership

An emergent leader usually comes to prominence in highly unstructured situations or informed groups. When people get together to discuss what to do Friday night, how to raise money for a project, or how to cross a raging river, for example, one person usually seizes the initiative through force of suggestions or actions. We tend to follow individuals who have good ideas or at least are willing to do something. Emergent leaders, like elected leaders, depend on constituency support. When the group members no longer feel they are achieving their goals, new leaders will emerge, a process which is heightened in times of crisis. When a group's future or its goals are threatened, emergent leaders are usually replaced (see Box 15–1).

Box 15–1
LEADERSHIP: KNOWING WHAT TO DO IN A CRISIS

Crises in which group members face a common threat occur in all kinds of groups. Companies run into financial difficulties; national borders are threatened; sports teams have losing streaks; racial, ethnic, religious, and linguistic minority groups encounter discrimination; towns face natural disasters. The examples of groups in crisis are endless.

When groups experience crises the influence of their leaders tends to increase, according to a study by R. L. Hamblin.* If the leaders cannot produce solutions to crisis problems, they will be replaced with new leaders. In a laboratory situation devised to study groups in crisis, three-person groups played a kind of shuffleboard game in which they had to discover the rules for themselves. These college subjects were told they would be compared with teams of high-school students. After an initial period of successful play the rules were continuously changed so the experimental (crisis) groups could never win, while the control (noncrisis) groups went on earning their points.

Members were asked for suggestions, and each member was given an influence score every time a suggestion he or she made was tested out by the other group members. Then an influence ratio was calculated to show the relation of each member's influence scores to the average of the other members. An acceptance rate measured the proportion of suggestions accepted from each one. The study found that while the leader's influence ratio declined in the control groups, it remained steady over successive periods in the experimental groups. The leader's acceptance rate also remained higher in the crisis than in the noncrisis groups, and the crisis groups were almost three times as likely to replace their unsuccessful leaders.

---

* R. L. Hamblin, ''Leadership and Crises,'' *Sociometry*, 1958, *21*, 322–355.

Appointment

Another form of leadership is represented by the appointed leader. Early in your grade school experience the teacher probably left the room and appointed somebody to be a monitor. That person had a certain influence (probably punitive) which served as a basis for her or his leadership. In appointed leadership there must be a recognized source of authority from which the appointed leader gains influence. Military officers may appoint enlisted men to carry out certain leadership functions, or the president of a company may appoint a junior executive to serve as chairperson of a department. The members of the

An extraordinary case of authoritarian leadership ending in tragedy was the Jonestown massacre. (Here Jones appears at the time of his involvement in San Francisco politics prior to the exodus to Guinea.) *Source:* Top photo: Wide World Photos, Inc.; Bottom photo: United Press International, Inc.

U.S. president's cabinet are good examples of appointed leadership; the source of their authority clearly rests in the president, with the advice and consent of the Senate.

The kind of leadership demonstrated by persons who have been appointed to their positions will depend in part on their competence and other personal qualities. This was shown in a study by Read (1974) of high school students appointed or elected to a mock jury, where leadership was found to be clearly dependent on social skills such as persuasiveness.

Structural Leadership

Structural leadership is exercised by persons who possess sources of strength and happen to be in positions on which others must depend. Executives' secretaries, for example, who are first to receive all incoming and outgoing information, are frequently deferred to by both subordinates and equals because their control of the flow of information and access to the executive put them in a position of power. People in the right place at the right time and, more importantly, people with the right resources to meet crises have a greater probability of finding themselves in the leadership role.

Structural leadership can be the product of either an emergent or an enduring social structure. The Kennedys or Rockefellers or European members of the hereditary nobility naturally find themselves in positions of influence because of the structure of their society. In Great Britain, for example, many titled persons, in the spirit of *noblesse oblige,* serve in Parliament or hold other public offices. Whether they become notable leaders depends on their motivation, intelligence, empathy, and other personal qualities more than their positions in society, however.

Effects of Leadership

Leaders can be categorized on the basis of their effects on others, as well as on the source of their influence. Leaders can direct followers to self-destructive or socially harmful activities, or they can lead them to adopt positive, prosocial attitudes and behaviors. At one time or another, such diverse personalities as Jesus, Adolph Hitler, Albert Einstein, Joan of Arc, Joseph Stalin, Richard Nixon, Malcolm X, Billy Graham, Winston Churchill, Indira Gandhi, and Mao Tse-Tung have all been considered leaders by large numbers of people. It is difficult to see what if anything they have in common—except their visibility and ability to influence others.

Charismatic leadership, a concept originally suggested by Max Weber, is based on exceptional or supernatural powers like those attributed to Jesus, Mohammed, or Joan of Arc. Franklin D. Roosevelt's success in combating the Great Depression of the 1930s endowed him with something of a charismatic character. John F. Kennedy had somewhat the same attraction, which was heightened after his assassination. According to Zollschan and Friedman (1976), the charisma provides a kind of cathexis of emotional involvement between leader and follower. An example of the lengths to which a charismatic leader can induce followers to go is given in Box 15–2.

Like the king or queen of Great Britain, *the symbolic leader* has prestige but little power. A variation is the *institutional leader,* who fills a traditional or ceremonial role such as the president in certain dictatorships. *Experts* among artists, scientists, and certain other professional groups also enjoy an honored role.

Box 15–2
CHARISMATIC LEADERSHIP AND MASS DEATH

A macabre example of a charismatic leader was James Jones, leader of the ill-fated socioreligious cult known as the People's Temple, which eventually settled at Jonestown in Guyana. The background of this tragic episode is rooted in Jones's strange career as a religious leader, which began in Indiana and moved on to northern California, where he first chose the remote town of Ukiah to escape what he considered the pressures of an urban, commercial civilization and possible nuclear destruction. His ambition later led him to establish the People's Temple in 1971 at San Francisco, where he gathered followers for his mix of self-styled religion, charity, and urban politics. As protests grew over his authoritarian leadership and financial irregularities, he arranged in 1975 for the purchase of land in the jungle area of western Guyana, where he set up a communal society. His followers, largely blacks and a handful of liberal whites, were convinced that this commune was the alternative to the capitalist and militaristic society they knew in the United States.

It is not easy to understand the dynamics by which Jones convinced his adherents to give up their material assets and follow him to this self-contained, deprived community. Presumably he appealed to persons who had little stake in their own communities or who suffered from severe insecurity and anxiety and had a need for the reassurance and submissiveness that a dominant leader could offer.

His charismatic leadership became increasingly autocratic, and he turned to terrorist methods to keep the community intact as frustrations mounted.* Ties within the nuclear family were discouraged, contacts outside the community were forbidden, and any sign of disloyalty to the leadership was subject to various kinds of punishment. Jones himself became paranoid, and his megalomaniacal leanings were evident not only in ruthless interference in the private lives of his subjects but in incessant verbal control through communications broadcast on loudspeakers and a compulsion to record events on tape, including mock mass suicides.

The ultimate tragedy occurred when Congressman Leo Ryan made an inspection tour of the commune in November 1978 after receiving reports of violations of human rights. The possibility that he and his party would attempt to interfere was thwarted when, after a two-day visit to the camp, they returned to the airport, where a gunman murdered Ryan and several assistants and newsmen as they attempted to leave. That evening Jones informed all the members of the colony that the end of their ordeal in this world was at hand. To what degree the order to consume the Kool-Aid type of drink laced with cyanide met with resistance is not known, but Jones had even the final minutes recorded, and the tapes suggest that resistance was minimal. In the end, 913 persons, including Jones, died in this unique, apparently self-induced holocaust.

In retrospect, Jones represents a curious messiah. Although he thought himself a combination of Jesus, Buddha, and Lenin, he wished to be called Dad by his followers. When his dream for supremacy was threatened by outside forces he called on the faithful to follow him into death. In the same way, at the end of World War II on the eve of the Russians' entry into Berlin Hitler had instructed the German people to follow his suicidal example, and centuries ago Eleazar had inspired the isolated Israelites holding out against the Romans at Masada to take their own lives rather than submit to slavery. All three were extreme cases of charismatic leadership and all apparently had dedicated followerships, but for psychological and sociocultural reasons the process of disenchantment ran its course in different ways. An isolated colony, a complex nation, and a group of religious zealots would hardly support identical forms of charismatic leadership.

---

* Jean Baechler, "Mourir à Jonestown," *Archives of European Sociology,* 1979, *20,* 173–210.

This kind of leadership may be institutionalized through professional certification or by the granting of honors and awards such as the Nobel or Pulitzer prizes. *Intellectual leaders* or *theorists* have enormous influence on the ideological climate of their times. Examples are Galileo, Johann von Goethe, Charles Darwin, and Sigmund Freud, and, in the political area, Machiavelli, Thomas Jefferson, and Karl Marx.

An *administrative leader* has the ability to manage and get things done. The approach of this kind of leader may vary between authoritarianism and democracy as has been shown in many studies. The *bureaucrat* is a variation of the administrative type; this type of leadership stresses the division of tasks, services, and roles for the purpose of implementing production or attaining goals. Weber considered the bureaucratic model a sharp contrast to the charismatic one.

Agitators or *reformers* have great driving force, which may or may not be combined with charismatic attraction or administrative skill. Examples are as diverse as Martin Luther King, Jr., the Ayatollah Khomeini, and Phyllis Schlafly or Bella Abzug, who represent opposite views of the women's movement. Sometimes this kind of leadership is a function of the group or situation, and the leader just happens to be in the right place at the right time. Personality, ideology, and chance events may all be influential. *Elite leadership* is provided by a group or network of powerful persons, as in the interlocking directorships of large companies or the relations among government agencies. This concept is based on the idea that there is a small elite group in every community. Another form of elite leader is the *technocrat,* an expert in necessary technological know-how, as in information and decision-making systems.

Functions of a Leader

In many situations there are several leaders, each of whom exerts influence over the direction of a group as its members, its needs, or its operating conditions change. Only highly structured or autocratic groups have single, continuing leaders. Generally several members of a group exercise influence, according to the situation. In this respect *the essence of leadership is the behavior of individuals who work toward the development of a social structure for the purpose of goal attainment.* Our survey in this section on the functions of leaders focuses on how they *do* behave rather than on how they *should* behave. The results of some other studies on the relation of leadership style or climate to group effectiveness are reported in the final topic of this chapter.

R. M. Stogdill's *Handbook of Leadership* (1981) brought together the results of hundreds of research studies on leaders' behaviors. Some years ago Hemphill (1950) had postulated that nine types of leader behavior are relevant to effective direction of a group in the attainment of its goals. These nine dimensions of leadership include:

1. *Facilitating*—encouraging new ideas and practices.
2. *Membership*—interacting with members.
3. *Representation*—advancing and defending the group.
4. *Integration*—reducing conflict.
5. *Organization*—defining the leader's and the members' work.
6. *Domination*—restricting the work and decision making.
7. *Communication*—facilitating exchange of information.
8. *Recognition*—expressing approval or disapproval.
9. *Production*—setting levels of achievement.

From these dimensions survey questionnaires were constructed and administered to a large number of subjects, and statistical analysis revealed four principal dimensions of leadership (Halpin & Winer, 1952). Later Gibb (1969) described these four factors as follows:

1. *Consideration* (49.6%)—the extent to which the leader, while carrying out functions, is concerned about followers.
2. *Initiating structure* (33.6%)—the way in which the leader organizes and defines the production relationships of self and subordinates or fellow group members.
3. *Production emphasis* (9.8%)—the leader's way of motivating followers by emphasizing the job to be done or the group goal.

4. *Sensitivity or social awareness* (7.0%)—to be a socially acceptable individual in interactions with other group members, the leader must be sensitive to what goes on in the group and willing to accept changes in ways of doing things.

Other research supports the same types of categories. Blake and Mouton's managerial grid (1964), like Fiedler's (1967) contingency model to be discussed at the end of the chapter, distinguished between managerial types on the basis of the leader's emphasis on the person or the situation. The managerial grid, which has been used as a device in management training sessions, attempts to measure five different managerial attitudes with varying degrees of concern for people and concern for production. Blake and Mouton assumed that managerial styles can be plotted on a two-dimensional grid using these two attitudes as the coordinates, as shown in Figure 15–1. The pairs of numbers on the grid indicate, on a scale of 1 to 9, concern for production in the first number and concern for people in the second. Thus a 9,1 managerial style indicates high concern for production and low concern for people—an autocratic model. Blake and Mouton maintain that managers can be trained to approach a 9,9 team management executive style.

The five managerial styles shown on the grid are:

1. *Impoverished management* (1,1)—minimal concern for people or production coupled with minimum activity necessary to retain position.
2. *Task management* (9,1)—focus is completely on production; subordinates are simply another instrument of production.
3. *Country club management* (1,9)—focus is on keeping everyone friendly and jovial. Work will flow at an easy tempo if conflict is eliminated.
4. *Middle-of-the-road management* (5,5)—satisfactory (i.e., moderate) levels of production and human concern.
5. *Team management* (9,9)—high task achievement developed by integrating task and human requirements into a unified system.

FOCUS ON THE PERSON

Much of the early research on leadership was concerned with the study of personal traits, such as the ingenious attempt at analysis of presidential leadership described in Box 15–3. The presumption underlying this search is that leaders must have recognizable combinations of inherited or acquired characteristics. Trait theories of leadership, like the trait theory of personality described in Chapter 4, vary somewhat in their emphasis on situational factors in the determination of leadership. According to the *great person theory*, leaders are born with just the right combination of traits and characteristics to thrust them into leadership positions. Another viewpoint is that though one or two inherited traits such as intelligence might be necessary for leadership, most leadership behavior derives from learned or acquired skills or from being in the right situation at the right time.

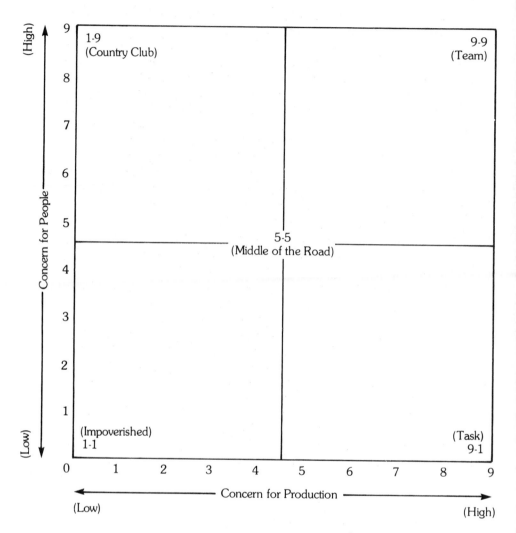

Figure 15–1. Leadership Styles in the Managerial Grid

Source: Adapted from Robert R. Blake and Jane S. Mouton, *The Managerial Grid* (Houston, Tex.: Gulf Publishing Co., 1964).

Box 15–3
THE ACTIVE-POSITIVE PRESIDENT

The promises a candidate for president of the United States makes in election campaigns usually do not indicate much about the performance to be expected in office. A better indicator could be the type of presidential leadership the candidate might develop.

James Barber views U.S. presidential leadership as being of four possible types: active-positive, active-negative, passive-positive, or passive-negative.* He maintains that a given personality structure shapes behavior in predictable ways. A president's personality is fused with the "power situation," along with the "climate of expectations" at the moment of entering the office. The "dynamic of the presidency" is the degree of sensitivity demonstrated in decision making. The president's style and ideology, therefore, are the end product of the president's experience, particularly in the early years. Most critical is the level of activity that can be mustered and whether the president appears to be comfortable with high political office.

The most favorable style is the *active-positive*. Presidents with this style enjoy the political process and actively seek orientation, flexibility, and growth toward personal and public goals. *Active-negative* types show ego needs, power-seeking, a drive for power, and (especially) a somewhat ambivalent self-image, usually because of a troubled childhood. The *passive-positive* types tend to be receptive, compliant, and other directed; low self-esteem may lead them to rely on the wants of others. *Passive-negative* presidents are in office because "they think they ought to be." Their stance is to withdraw, stressing vague principles or prohibitions and often producing a false moralism in the end.

These variations appeared even in the first four presidents, starting with Washington. In the 20th century, examples of an active-negative leadership style are Wilson's failure to compromise in "selling" the League of Nations to the Senate, Hoover's lack of initiative in fighting the depression, and Johnson's ruthless pursual of the war in Vietnam—to the point of being overwhelmed by the feeling that he had been rejected by the American people, and in effect he became a prisoner in the White House.†

Among passive-negative presidents are Coolidge and possibly Eisenhower, with Taft and Harding falling into the passive-positive mold—genial but ineffective. Franklin Roosevelt, Truman, and Kennedy, different as they were in style, were all active-positive. Barber would place Nixon as an active-negative and Carter as an active-positive.‡

More recently Barber has characterized presidential leadership as reflecting alternating climates of spontaneity and duress, so that the national mood calls for either vigorous leadership or a calming spirit. In one sequence, Theodore Roosevelt came on as a fighter, Harding as a soothing influence, Franklin Roosevelt as a champion for the little man.§ In this perspective, Carter's administration can clearly be seen as the calm between Nixon and Reagan.

---

* J. D. Barber, *The Presidential Character: Predicting Performance in the White House* (Englewood Cliffs, N.J.: Prentice-Hall, 1972).

† Doris Kearns, *Lyndon Johnson and the American Dream* (New York: Harper & Row, 1976). See the introduction to Box 9–1 in Chapter 9.

‡ *Time*, January 3, 1977, p. 17.

§ J. D. Barber, *The Pulse of Politics* (New York: W. W. Norton & Co., 1980).

Intelligence

All theorists agree that leaders tend to be above average in intelligence. This recognition dates back to Lewis Terman's influential, continuing *Genetic Studies of Genius,* whose original funding in 1922 enabled him to begin his longitudinal study of 1,500 children whom his Stanford-Binet Individual Intelligence Scale had identified at 140 IQ and above. Five volumes in the series were published between 1926 and 1959, and in the second of these C. M. Cox (1926) reported estimates of the IQs of some 300 historical personages, arrived at by applying mental test standards to their childhood behavior as reported in history and biography. She found a range of nearly 100 points; Copernicus was placed at 105, Cromwell at 110, Lincoln and Washington at 125, Leonardo, Napoleon, and Darwin at 135. The upper limits were reached by Goethe at 180 and John Stuart Mill at 190. The accuracy of these estimates is open to question, but in any event they suggest that leadership involves much more than intelligence.

While it can be assumed that leaders are generally more intelligent than nonleaders, the nature of the situation can have drastic effects on the extent to which intelligence and leadership are correlated. In some situations intelligence virtually assures leadership, whereas in others there is no relationship or perhaps even a negative one. In problem-solving groups, for example, leaders tend to have higher intelligence scores than nonleaders, but popular leaders have not been found to be more intelligent than the people who select them (Cattell & Stice, 1953). Stogdill (1981) concluded from nearly a score of studies that scholarship also has a positive relationship to leadership.

Social Status

Some early investigations studied the socioeconomic background of leaders. In Cox's (1926) study of eminent men and women she found the 52 percent came from noble or professional families and another 29 percent from semiprofessional, higher business, and gentry backgrounds. Only 5 percent came from families engaged in semiskilled or unskilled labor. Following up on J. M. Cattell's studies of American scientists, Visher (1947) reported on the occupational backgrounds of about 800 of the most prominent ones and found the following proportions of parental occupations: professions, 46 percent; business, 23 percent; farming, 22 percent; labor, 9 percent.

Somewhat later a study of jury deliberations in mock trials found a strong tendency to select as foremen people of relatively high status (Strodtbeck, James, & Hawkins, 1958). Compared to chance selection, proprietors and professionals, for example, were chosen almost twice as often, and laborers were elected only half as often. Status also determined the extent of participation in deliberations, with proprietors and professionals participating more than people with clerical occupations, who in turn participated more than skilled workers. Individuals with the lowest participation were the low-status jurors such as unskilled workers.

Other Characteristics

Early research on the personality traits of leaders found them to be high in self-confidence, dominance, extroversion, talkativeness, and general "adjustment." As noted above, Gibb (1969) found that leaders show consideration and have interpersonal sensitivity, as well as ability in initiating structure and assuring production. Certainly such studies have provided some worthwhile data, but in general the attempt to isolate traits associated with leadership has been rather sterile and disappointing (Cartwright & Zander, 1968). Sometimes investigation of a number of attributes is productive, as in Loye's (1977) study of two adult groups which showed a positive relationship between the attributes of activism and risk taking.

An ambitious approach to study of the relation between personality characteristics and leadership potential involved 2,157 California delegates to the presidential nominating conventions of both parties, many of whom had held party office or were aspiring to political careers (Constantini & Craik, 1980). They were mailed questionnaires and asked to respond to the Gough Adjective Check List (a list of 300 adjectives frequently used to describe persons on which respondents check those items they consider descriptive of themselves). These Republican leaders differed from their Democratic counterparts by having higher scores on personal adjustment, self-control, dominance, order, and endurance. Democrats were higher on change or spontaneity, exhibition or self-centeredness, and autonomy. The differences held for both males and females. With the large sample size, while the differences were statistically significant they were not overwhelming, and the results must be considered tentative because of the small rate of return (40 percent). Moreover, certain "personality styles" can hide inner feelings. The researchers noted that "on the Republican side, the conscientious and cautious dispositions, forged by firm psychological constraints, may entail a marked degree of inner denial and outer blandness. On the Democratic side, spontaneity and self-assurance may give way to inner vacillation and impulsive assertiveness" (p. 653).

THE PERSON-IN-SITUATION APPROACH

As Stogdill (1981) indicates, a person who is a leader in one situation is not necessarily a leader in other circumstances. It is not enough to study leader personality per se or to analyze social structure by itself. The two must be studied together, as in the relationship between a certain kind of person in a certain kind of situation. The style of a leader in a particular role position will be affected by peculiarities of the situation, as Box 15–4 demonstrates.

According to a study of the 20 largest corporations in the United States, leadership or executive ability is most often evaluated on the basis of various tests administered to those being considered for hiring or promotion (Byham, 1970). The tests frequently involve simulations of situations a candidate would face in a

Box 15-4
THE MANDATE PHENOMENON

An election landslide has an intoxicating effect on a U.S. president, according to Theodore White.* It produces a "delusion of omnipotence" which entices the president to take actions that would not be considered if the election had resulted in a mere plurality of the vote. Among the examples of presidents who obtained more than 60 percent of the popular vote (most elections are far closer) was Franklin Roosevelt's victory in 1936, which led him to attempt a Supreme Court packing plan that cost him considerable popularity. The 1964 Democratic victory led Lyndon Johnson into the disastrous war in Vietnam and a daring social action program. Richard Nixon's 1972 landslide victory convinced him of his invincibility and the need for rigid control of civil liberties, and only the Watergate scandal kept him from pursuing this goal. Most recently, Ronald Reagan's 1980 triumph at the polls gave credence to his efforts to transform campaign promises into national policy.

The *mandate phenomenon* was observed in the decisions of leaders in three laboratory groups.† The leader was arbitrarily assigned in one group, elected by a bare majority in a second, and unanimously elected in the third one. The groups' task was to identify and test the effects of physiological stimulation on group performance. The leader with a mandate (i.e., unanimously elected) took the riskiest solution—some noxious stimulation which promised an external reward.

Apparently leaders with a mandate consider their situations very secure. They may even feel they have something of the qualities of a charismatic leader because their self-esteem is heightened, and they anticipate less criticism from the group. If there is criticism they can say, "Don't blame me; you elected me unanimously." They also believe the group members expect them to show more self-assertiveness.

---

* T. H. White, *Breach of Faith: The Fall of Richard Nixon* (New York: Atheneum Publishers, 1975).
† Russell D. Clark, III, and Lee B. Sechrest, "The Mandate Phenomenon," *Journal of Personality and Social Psychology*, 1976, *34*, 1057–1061.

higher office. Executive capacity in such situations is indicated by the person's ability to delegate authority, promote new ideas, and cope with time pressures, among other characteristics such as insight and self-control. Although managerial ability is only one kind of leadership, the study suggests that individuals differ in their ability to exercise interpersonal skills in complex situations.

A beginning exercise in management training sessions probed these skills by having groups of about five people discuss the following problem:

You are the management of a firm employing 500 people. You have been instructed by the managing director to set up a supervisory training program. You are to consider the main difficulties which the scheme will have to overcome to get started, and, secondly, the course subjects to be included. You will not appoint a chairperson. You will not appoint a secretary.

As the group discussed the problem for about 20 minutes, some members focused on procedural matters while others directed their attention to the content of the discussion, offering suggestions or attempting to move the group toward consensus. Later the members identified those who had emerged as leaders. In line with research findings such as those of C. D. Ward (1968), the leaders turned out to be, in the main, male, older than the average of the group, taller, well-dressed, centrally or prominently located, and not minority group members.

Researchers into managerial problems have recognized that different situations require different forms of leadership. Requirements differ, for example, as a function of organizational level (Nealey & Fiedler, 1968), even within the same organization. In a particular organizational setting the leader may be described as having what Katz and Kahn (1978) label as an *influential increment,* or the expertise and legitimate power needed to resolve tensions and achieve higher levels of production.

Psychohistory

The interaction between personality and situational factors throughout the career of a personality is examined in psychohistory, a sort of combined psychoanalytical and biographical technique. Historians and psychoanalysts have provided a host of such portraits, from Moses and Leonardo da Vinci to Hitler and Lyndon B. Johnson. A good example is a study of the relationship between Woodrow Wilson and his closest adviser, Colonel House (George & George, 1976).

H. D. Lasswell (1948) and C. S. Bluemel (1948) pioneered the psycho-historical study of various leaders. Lasswell, a psychiatrically minded political scientist who used a psychopathological approach to study political leaders, traced many cases of political leadership to father or brother hatred, sex repression, feelings of guilt or inferiority, and the like. Bluemel saw clear psychiatric syndromes in various leaders. The obsessive-compulsive pattern was identified in Columbus, Charles Lindbergh, and Mahatma Gandhi and the aggressive character pattern in Oliver Cromwell and Stalin. According to Bluemel, Joan of Arc and Hitler were schizophrenic, and Napoleon was manic depressive.

The psychohistory approach to leadership research is related to the identification of traits (Mazzlish, 1972). Psychoanalysis, like history, searches the past for explanatory models of subsequent events. Some psychohistorians concentrate on prominent personalities of the past and try to explain their rise to prominence through examination of their works and biographies. Others attempt to explain present-day personalities such as Nixon, based on what is known about their past (see Box 15–5).

Box 15–5
RICHARD NIXON'S INNER HISTORY

Psychohistory is a useful vehicle for attempting to explain "the behavior of national figures, especially when this behavior fails to satisfy the expectations of the group." An example is an investigation of the personality development of former president Richard M. Nixon.*

Richard's father was strong-willed and argumentative; he had no great concern about what people thought of him. His mother was more approachable but probably more self-contained. Richard avoided conflict with his father by keeping his emotions under unflinching control, and this tendency helped prevent him from making close friends. "Most boys go through a mischievous period," his mother recalled, "Well, none of these things ever happened to Richard. He was very mature when he was five or six years old." He stoically accepted discipline; his father's spankings were suffered without a whimper. Nor did he fight physically with others boys—"his dad wouldn't have stood for it."

Among the childhood tasks he was assigned was mashing potatoes. His mother noted that among her sons he alone never left any lumps, and his whipping motion was unique: "Even in these days when I am visiting Richard and Pat in Washington, or when they visit me, he will take over the potato mashing. My feeling is that he actually enjoys it."

Similarly, his school record also demonstrates his compulsiveness. He was never late for class and always fastidious about his grooming. He remarked to a cousin that "he didn't like to ride the school bus, because the other children didn't smell good." "I have a fetish about disciplining myself," Nixon noted years later. Presumably this sense of autonomy had its roots in childhood, perhaps infancy. His strong commitment to law and order was not mere political role-playing. A Freudian interpretation might be that he never resolved the anal stage of development.

---

* M. Rogin and J. Iottier, "The Inner History of Richard Milhous Nixon," *Transaction, 9,* 1974, 20.

In general, psychohistory concentrates on parent-child and sibling relationships and other dynamics of the formative years as a way to "explain" later behavior. However, the controversy between those who lean to a personality theory in terms of traits, needs, and attitudes versus those who favor situational explanations of leadership is also found in psychohistory. Recognition of the relationship between person and situation, between leader and followers, is essential in this as in other aspects of the study of leadership.

INTERACTIONAL ANALYSIS OF
LEADERS AND GROUPS

As the studies of leadership personalities and situations described above have shown, neither alone can provide an adequate understanding of leadership. In this as in all other areas of social psychology, therefore, it is necessary to consider the relation between the person and the sociocultural setting. A group's leaders often are the essential factor in determining how effectively the group functions and whether it achieves or maintains the status of a cohesive social unit with acceptable goals. This final section in Part III considers how the interactions of leaders and followers affect the quality of leadership in the group setting: participation and willingness to take action, communication networks, the transactions between leaders and followers, and various leadership styles and climates.

Participation

Leaders generally have a high participation rate in groups. Morris and Hackman (1969) hypothesized that what distinguishes leaders from nonleaders when both are high in participation might be the former's emphasis on facilitative activities for the group which enhance its goal-directed behavior, whereas active participators who are not perceived as leaders emphasize activities which distract from the group's goal. While their research confirmed this, they concluded that "To a greater degree than was realized previously, leaders or nonleaders are distinguishable only by their overall rates of participation" (p. 361). Other researchers have also found that rate of participation is one of the principal determinants of perceived leadership (Kirscht, Lodahl, & Haire, 1959).

People who speak up in groups are given immediate reinforcement in terms of attention and, sometimes, agreement and support from other group members, because by speaking they reduce the tension felt by the group during periods of silence or tedious discussions. If leaders are to stay in positions of influence in long-standing groups, however, it is up to them to reinforce or reward the group. This can be accomplished in a number of different ways. The leader might help the group increase its productivity or hasten the attainment of desired goals, or the leader could demonstrate decisive action in times of crisis.

When Havron and McGrath (1961) studied army and air force crews in an attempt to determine the characteristics of leaders that are related to superior group performance, they found that intelligence and knowledge of the job, as well as accurate estimates of the intelligence, abilities, and attitudes of subordinates, were essential, but effective leaders also were willing to act in a variety of situations. This was shown in a clever test. During individual interviews with the leaders of effective and ineffective squads, the experimenter left the room on some pretext. Shortly after, a telephone across the room started to ring. Almost all of the effective squad leaders went over and answered the phone, most of them after only a few rings, but most of the ineffective squad leaders did not, even after 10 rings. Apparently, then, leaders demonstrate a willingness to act, and this, coupled with a knowledge of the task at hand, contributes to their effectiveness.

Ability to function in a crisis situation affects the image of a leader in various ways. In one experiment the leader who was cast in the role of martyr was rejected or devalued by the group (Lerner, 1965). Devaluation in this instance is in keeping with the *just-world principle* described in Chapter 6—the person who suffers misfortune is perceived as somehow deserving of that fate! In another kind of stress situation the leader who manages a safe exit was perceived as neither more nor less effective by the group. Elected leaders were viewed as more competent than appointed leaders, but the reverse judgment could be made when there was greater stress. Generally the leader tended to be seen as more competent as the stress was increased (Klein, 1976).

Communication Networks

The communication structure in a group figures heavily in the determination of leadership and has direct effects on group efficiency and performance. The one situational factor which has been consistently and reliably related to leadership, however, is centrality, or provision for communication links with the largest number of group members. Communication networks, which are conceptualizations of the various communication channels available among group members, provide a means of studying the range and freedom of the communication process in a group. (Figure 10–1 in Chapter 10 shows the various steps in this process.)

Most large organizations can produce an organization chart to identify the chain of command and the lines of authority and responsibility in the management structure, and often the chart also indicates the flow of communications. The official organization chart or the formal rules setting forth who communicates with whom and in what manner is not so important in an organization as the informal communication network that actually operates, however. The informal network which unofficially regulates communications among members has the same status as the informal groups discussed in Chapter 12 and the informal roles assumed by members, as described in Chapter 14. It provides the channels people actually use to communicate in the organization, rather than the routes communications are supposed to follow according to the organization's systems.

Researchers investigating the informal network have found, for example, that high-status individuals are likely to speak more than low-status persons in military group situations or in hospital and industrial settings, and communication tends to flow upward in a group in which there are considerable differences in status. Low-status people direct their communication to high-status people, and the high-status persons tend to talk to one another (A. R. Cohen, 1958; Riley et al., 1954).

Channels of communication in any organizational structure can be closed, one-way, or two-way. In many universities, for example, although there are telephones in the office of the president or chancellor of the university and in those of the junior faculty members, it would be considered quite out of order for a junior faculty member to initiate a call to the president. A call from the president's office to the faculty member, on the other hand, would be considered an acceptable use of the communication channels. Communication structures in organizations, therefore, are not necessarily determined by technology. Telephones may provide a link between two offices, but the persons in them recognize that this link is to be used only in specific ways.

The study of communication networks is an attempt to determine the effects of imposed structure on the problem-solving efficiency of groups. In addition, researchers are interested in the methods of problem-solving used by groups in different structures as well as the satisfaction of individual members in various positions within the communication network. Figure 15–2 illustrates various communication networks that have been studied in experimental situations. In these three-, four-, and five-person networks, the dots represent persons or positions, the lines represent communication channels, and the arrows indicate one-way channels. A line connecting two dots indicates that communication can flow in either direction, but an arrow at the end of a line indicates one-direction communication only. When no line connects the dots communication is prohibited.

A schematic system such as Figure 15–2 facilitates consideration of the implications of different group structures. An organization chart based on the notion of a hierarchical chain of command, for example, would appear as in Figure 15–3. A structure of this nature seems to indicate that the boss has the most responsibility, the boss's assistant has less, and the four subordinates have the least. The usual perception of such hierarchical systems is that the boss is in charge of the whole show, making the decisions and directing the activities. If the implications of this structure are considered in terms of who is actually in control, that is, who has control over the information networks, however, the hierarchical system is precisely the same as the five-person wheel shown in Figure 15–2. The difference is that three of the spokes have been arranged on the bottom and one has been put at the top. The person with the greatest control over the information network is the one right in the center—the boss's assistant. The reason is that any communication from the subordinates to the boss or from the boss to the subordinates must pass through the boss's assistant, who can change, exclude, distort, or be completely confused by the information. It is not unusual for executives to isolate themselves from the communication networks in an organization by relying on secretaries to fill the role positions between their own positions and those of their subordinates, as was noted in Chapter 14.

The major structural factor in most communication networks that have been studied is the degree of *centralization*. For simple tasks which require efficient collection of information, highly centralized networks are more efficient. When the task is complex and information must not only be collected but interpreted in some way, or there is a great risk of error, decentralized networks are better. They also have consistently been found to be more satisfying for members than highly centralized networks. Shaw (1964) found that individuals on the periphery of a centralized network who see themselves as simply relaying information to those who are actively involved in decision making tend to be more dissatisfied than those who believe they are part of the process (see Chapter 13).

One distinction of centralized information networks is their dependence on

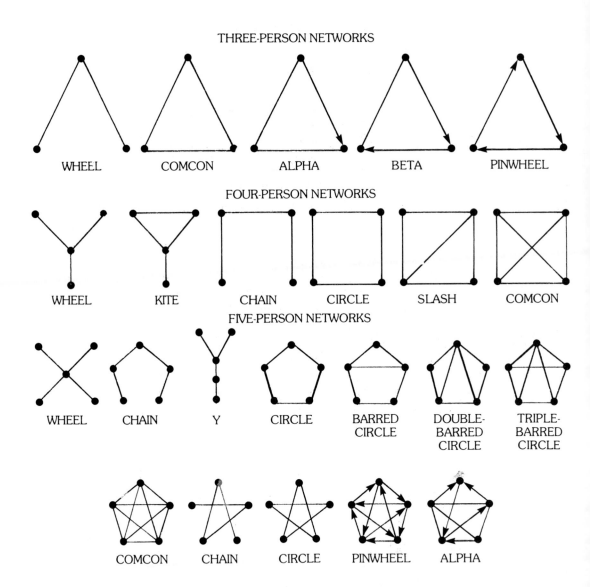

Figure 15-2. Types of Communication Networks

Source: M. E. Shaw, "Communication Networks," in Leonard Berkowitz (Ed.), *Advances in Experimental Social Psychology,* Vol. 1 (New York: Academic Press, 1964), p. 113.

Figure 15–3. Hierarchical Organizational Structure

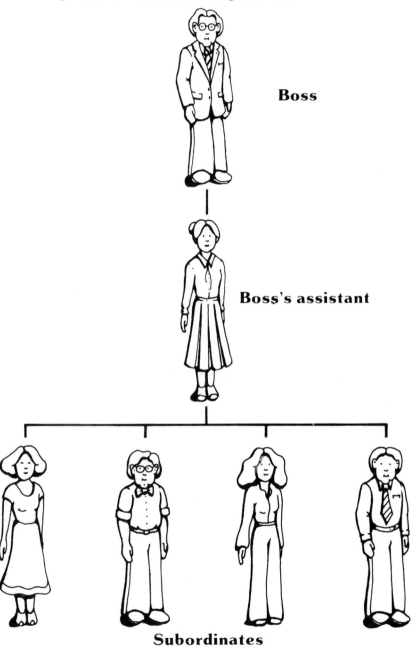

Boss

Boss's assistant

Subordinates

the concept of *saturation,* or the amount of information a particular cell or person can reasonably be expected to handle (Shaw, 1964). This is comparable to the idea of information overload introduced in Chapter 13. The efficiency of highly centralized groups is dependent on the competence of the most central person, and the more complex the task, the greater the probability of information overload or saturation for that person.

The communication structure of a group can affect its problem-solving efficiency, insight, leadership, members' morale and satisfaction, and retention and use of information. As a situational factor it also interacts with the individual characteristics of the persons in leadership positions. A highly centralized group will perform poorly if an incompetent person is placed in the most central position, whereas a decentralized group is less dependent on the leadership qualities of a single individual but requires these qualities in more members. The person in a central position may be there because of a personal drive toward dominance, but an ordinarily submissive member may be an active participant if given the opportunity to occupy a central position (Stogdill, 1981).

Leaders and Followers

Leadership is increasingly being proven to be a transaction between leaders and followers (Hollander & Julian, 1970). In one study which focused on the interactions among group members, subjects worked in groups of four on reasoning, mechanical assembly, and discussion tasks (Haythorn, 1953). Trained observers rated the following behavioral traits for each group member: aggressiveness, initiative, prestige, confidence, submissiveness, efficiency, sociability, insight, authoritarianism, individual solution, and leadership. The most interesting aspect of this research was the data on relationships among the members' traits. If one member of a group demonstrated aggressiveness, self-confidence, authoritarianism, or leadership, the other members would show less of these behaviors than they otherwise would. This study thus demonstrates the *compensatory* nature of the interactions among group members.

The compensatory principle is also supported by data which indicate that leaders and followers frequently exchange roles (Hollander, 1960). As Gibb (1969) pointed out, followership is an active role in the accomplishment of a group task. Active followers frequently initiate leadership acts, and it is important to understand that "good" followership generates much of the energy that is attributed to the leader. In fact, a fixation on the leader as the source or primary mover of groups may well represent a misattribution of causality, as described in Chapter 6.

In summarizing the important aspects of interaction theory, Gibb (1969) paid particular attention to leadership as a role behavior:

1. Groups are mechanisms for achieving individual satisfactions.
2. Any group is a system of interactions within which a structure emerges by the development of relatively stable expectations for the behavior of each member. Such expectations are an expression of each member's interactional relations with all other members and are, of course, determined by the other

members' perceptions of his personal attributes and his performance on earlier occasions.

3. This role differentiation is a characteristic of all groups, and some role patterns appear to be universal. However the nature of the group-task situation, the size of the group, and a great variety of other variables determine the role needs of the group-in-situation.

4. The association of a particular individual member with the performance of a role or pattern of roles is largely determined by the particular attributes of personality, ability, and skill which differentiate him perceptually from other members of the group.

5. Leadership is but one facet, though perhaps the most readily visible facet, of this larger process of role differentiation. Leadership is simply this concept applied to the situation obtaining in a group when the differentiation of roles results in one or some of the parties to the interaction influencing the actions of others in a shared approach to common or compatible goals.

6. Leadership, like any other role behavior, is a function of personal attributes and the social system in dynamic interaction. Both leadership structure and individual leader behavior are determined in large part by the nature of the organization in which they occur. Leadership structure is relative, also, to the population characteristics of the group or, in other words, to the attitudes and needs of the followers. (p. 270)

Leadership Styles and Climates

The leader-follower relationship is also apparent in the determination of leadership styles or climates. In one study, democratic and autocratic leaders (as determined by a leadership belief scale) were assigned democratic or autocratic subordinates and given the task of planning a travel itinerary (Crowe, Bochner, & Clark, 1972). Both types of leaders behaved democratically with democratic subordinates but autocratically with autocratic subordinates. This study indicates that the followers' influence can be strong enough to bring leaders to adopt a style opposite to their own preferred leadership style.

One problem with respect to leadership climates or styles within organizations is the congruence of managerial styles. The requirements for leadership tend to differ at different levels, so that the standards of leadership for superiors may be different from those for subordinates, and this can affect workers' productivity and satisfaction. The results of studies of this problem have been equivocal. In some instances congruent styles have been found to enhance satisfaction and performance (Hunt, Hill, & Reaser, 1973), but other investigators have found greater satisfaction where managerial styles are not the same across levels (Nealey & Fiedler, 1968).

The style of leadership often depends on the expectancies of the group. Certain groups prefer comparatively more directive leadership; university students in an introductory course, for example, preferred classes that were directively led as opposed to those that were permissively led (Wispe, 1951). Page and McGinnies (1959) reported that adult groups involved in discussions of a mental health film rated a directive leader significantly more favorably than a

The ultimate in charismatic leadership may be provided by the papacy. John Paul II has a special charisma as an "outsider," the first non-Italian Pope in four centuries. *Source:* United Nations/Photo by M. Jiminez.

nondirective leader. This finding was largely attributable to the reactions of those who participated least in the discussion, however.

Fiedler (1967) has offered a *contingency model* of leadership effectiveness. He maintains that the effectiveness of the particular leadership style depends on situational demands. The leader's ability to direct a group's activities is determined by "situational favorableness," which entails:

1. The group members' respect and liking for the leader.
2. The extent of legitimate power and authority provided by the position the leader holds.
3. The clarity of the structure of the task (i.e., is the procedure clear?).

Fiedler postulates that the leader's style may reflect either a task orientation or an interpersonal orientation. The results of many experiments have indicated that task-oriented leaders are more effective in either very favorable or very unfavorable situations, whereas interpersonally oriented leaders do better in groups of intermediate favorableness (Chemers & Skrzypek, 1972).

Clearly, then, an understanding of leadership requires an understanding of group dynamics and interactional analyses, as defined in Chapter 1. First it is necessary to understand the type of leader being considered: Is the person a charismatic leader with claims to divine powers and the ability to attract a great many followers, perhaps, or an emergent leader who has been able to deal with a crisis effectively? Then the nature of the group, the task to be accomplished, and the needs and goals of both the leader and the group members must all be considered.

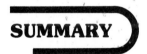

SUMMARY

The study of leadership, a conspicuous instance of role behavior, can be approached from a number of viewpoints. It can be classified by personal types or traits or by an analysis of the group structure or the situation, but the interactionist viewpoint, which considers the relation between the individual leader and the group, is distinctly favored by recent empirical studies.

Leader types range from the emergent to the appointed, the charismatic to the administrative, the person oriented to the production oriented. The type approach hardly offers explanatory concepts, but it does suggest an intriguing series of descriptions. Psychological studies of leader characteristics in terms of physical, mental (i.e. intelligence), and personality traits also have disclosed few significant differences between leaders and followers.

A number of studies have indicated the relation of group structures and leadership variables. Shifts in the group such as crises determine the type of leadership that is acceptable to the members. All leadership qualities must be evaluated in a situational context or task setting. The role of followers in the leader-follower relationship has been found to be quite important, and some evidence for a probabilistic theory of leadership in which leaders and followers shift roles has been presented.

A number of approaches to the study of leadership are described in this chapter. This acknowledges that there is both emergent and appointed or elected leadership, depending on the formality and other characteristics of the group. As in all the areas of social psychology considered in this text, the interaction between the individual and the sociocultural setting is considered the most important factor, combining the structural and trait or individual components of leadership.

Differences in style of leadership have been demonstrated by the various occupants of the office of the presidency of the United States, as described in Chapter 14. These men have brought differences in personality and ideology to the situations with which they have had to cope. To varying degrees, all leaders must know how to manage similar relationships between individuals and situations. The ability to direct collective behavior to achieve prosocial goals may ultimately prove to be the distinctive mark of a leader in today's society. This is the emphasis of the applications of social psychology described in Part IV.

WORDS TO REMEMBER

Charismatic leadership. Leadership based on personal characteristics of a leader endowed by followers with a *charisma* (vision), or a kind of magnetism. Washington, Lincoln, Franklin Roosevelt, Hitler, and, after his death, John Kennedy were among those who had such a mystique.

Communication structure or networks. Conceptualization of the variety of communication channels available as well as the range and freedom of communication in a group. Types of networks include the chain, circle, wheel, and Y.

Contingency model of leadership. Idea developed by F. E. Fiedler that the effectiveness of leadership depends on the situation. If the situation is moderately favorable, a people-oriented leader is more effective than a task-centered leader, but in situations that are either very favorable or unfavorable to leadership the task-centered leader is more effective.

Leadership climate. Kind of setting and quality of the power structure that favors a given type of leader or a certain *leadership style.*

Psychohistory. Method of studying leaders through the use of psychoanalytic and related techniques, biographies, diaries, and other accounts.

Social power. Ability to stimulate or enforce compliance, or at least consensus, in a group or society.

Trait theory. An approach to leadership as the product of specific traits, mental or physical, which are often considered to be inherent or inborn. Can be contrasted with the *situational approach* to leadership; the question is, does the person make history, or does history make the person?

QUESTIONS FOR DISCUSSION

1. Think of some of the leaders you have known in school or other settings and analyze why they were leaders. What dimensions of leadership have you observed in these leaders?

2. What is meant by emergent leadership? In what situations is it most likely to occur? How does it compare to appointed or structural leadership?

3. What kinds of caution should be observed in devising a typology of leadership? Suggest a typology based on some of the factors considered in this chapter.

4. Describe how leadership is thought of as a transaction. Give examples.

5. What specific traits, physical and mental, correlate with leadership? To what degree is intelligence a necessary trait in leaders?

6. In what respects can leadership be related to status factors? Is the basis for the elite theory of leadership a justifiable one?

7. How does the communication structure in a group affect the emergence of leadership?

8. What are the advantages and disadvantages of the psychohistorical approach to leadership?

9. How does Fiedler conceive of leadership effectiveness in terms of the situation?

10. Characterize the leadership styles of leaders you have met or studied.

READINGS

Bass, B. M. *Leadership, Psychology, and Organizational Behavior.* New York: Harper and Row Publishers, 1960.

An able exploration into the situational aspects of leadership, documented with over 1,100 references.

Downton, J. V., Jr. *Rebel Leadership.* New York: Free Press, 1973.

Charisma, commitment, and the transactional theory of leadership, illustrated by recent historical examples.

Hollander, E. P. *Leadership Dynamics.* New York: Free Press, 1978.

An authority on leadership analyzes its effectiveness and role in a variety of areas, from exchange theory to social change.

Jennings, H. H. *Leadership and Isolation* (2nd ed.) New York: Longmans Green, 1950.

Although somewhat dated, it remains a stimulating research study using the sociometric approach to the study of leadership.

Lassey, W. R. (Ed.). *Leadership and Social Change.* Iowa City, Iowa: University Associates Press, 1971.

A welcome collection of very readable articles on leadership in a wide range of settings.

Loye, D. *The Leadership Passion.* San Francisco: Jossey-Bass Publishers, 1977.

An absorbing account of tests and interviews with campus leaders, in an appropriate theoretical context.

Napier, R. W. and Gershenfeld, M. K. *Groups: Theory and Experience.* Boston: Houghton Mifflin Co., 1973.

Chapter 5 ably explores the psychological bases of leadership and power.

Stogdill, R. M. *Handbook of Leadership.* Rev. ed. (B. M. Bass, Ed.) New York: Free Press, 1981.

The most complete statement to date on the theories and dimensions of leadership.

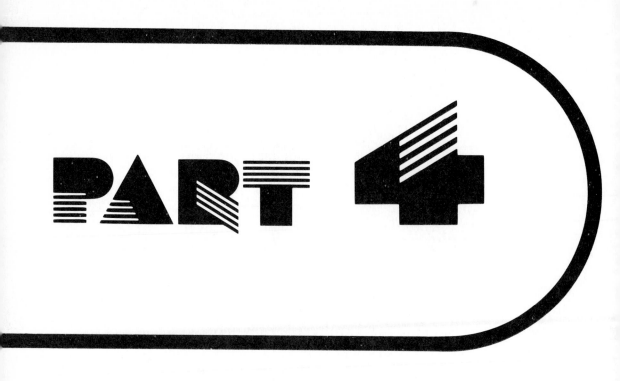

PART 4

The preceding parts of this text have shown how culture and the individual interact, how social behavior develops through the central processes of cognition and motivation, and how the group setting influences individual and group behavior. The exploration of the theory underlying these concepts, which comprise the heart of social psychology, has incorporated reports of numerous studies which have researched how these concepts can be applied to help us understand why people behave as they do in our society. Now Part IV focuses on how this understanding can form a basis for the formulation of plans to reduce the tensions and solve the problems that trouble responsible members of society today.

To set the stage for this consideration of applied social psychology, Chapter 16 explores the complex basis of collective behavior. Fad, fashion, crowds, rumor, and other collective responses particularly characterize 20th-century society. These somewhat standardized patterns of social behavior affect people's responses to emerging situations, and they often are responsible for public acceptance or rejection of ideas and innovations that could lead to solutions.

Chapter 17 is a broad view of the nature of social change, particularly as it is brought about by social relationships among individuals. Social movements, which combine characteristics of collective behavior and group structure, also are considered. They provide a vehicle for organized pressure and support for a particular change in the social order.

Applications of social psychology to two of the significant problem areas which have continued to gather force in the second half of the 20th century are examined in Chapter 18. It first considers the basis of racial and ethnic prejudice and discrimination and the implications of inequality for the social order. The age-old, agonizing, and increasingly urgent question of how to assure world peace is the second topic.

Chapter 19 shows how social psychology can suggest solutions to two other growing social problems: the environment and aging. Protection and conservation of the physical environment is a relatively new area of inquiry which has been incorporated in national public policy legislation. The status of the aged, and increasing portion of the population which in one sense represents another minority group, is another emerging area in which public concern may be translated into plans for social change. The social psychologist can contribute by extending the idea of socialization, which was considered in relation to children in Chapter 3, to cover individuals at the other end of the life cycle.

APPLIED
SOCIAL
PSYCHOLOGY

COLLECTIVE BEHAVIOR

Collective or mass behavior is a broad term for similar social behaviors by a large number of people. It may represent the ultimate example of the relation between the individual and the socioeconomic setting, since it emerges only (1) when the ordinary norms of behavior are ambiguous or threatened, (2) during periods of considerable social change or crisis, or (3) when people's fundamental motives or desires are blocked. Most manifestations of mass behavior are transitory and are not affected by the ordinary institutional processes. While collective behavior traditionally refers to relatively emotional and erratic behavior, recent research suggests that it is not as spontaneous or chaotic as it once appeared to be. This is borne out by evidence of nonviolent protests and full-scale riots which are carefully planned by special-interest groups as a means of achieving their goals. The politics of confrontation is encouraged by the unrelenting search for dramatic happenings by TV crews and press reporters.

At its broadest base collective behavior includes the varied patterns and functions of the crowd; the nature of rumor; audience reactions; shifts in public opinion; fashion, fads, and crazes; and protests, riots, and panics. The most dramatic examples of collective behavior include convulsive phenomena such as revivalist meetings, wartime rallies, or the flight of people from a burning building or other disaster, as well as mobs, riots, and panics.

The study of collective behavior has had a checkered history which falls within the scope of social psychology. Much of the impetus to establish the discipline came from theories which were highly impressionistic, such as those advanced by Gabriel Tarde and Gustave LeBon, whose ideas on imitation and suggestibility were described in Chapter 1. These were later synthesized in the first social psychology texts by William McDougall and Edward Ross, both of which appeared in 1908. The interest in collective behavior by sociologists and psychologists continued until the 1920s and 1930s and seemed to have run its course by the end of World War II. As fear of nuclear war stimulated interest in disaster research, however, and the confrontations of the late 1960s reawakened academic interest in riots and civil disobedience, the relevance of studying collective behavior again became apparent. Moreover, precise investigative methods which apply even to crisis situations had become available.

Concern for the basic problems of society is interwoven into the study of mass or collective behavior. Confrontations, protests, demonstrations, and a growing number of social movements (see Chapter 17) are emerging as attempts to resolve these issues. The widespread availability of the products of the mass communications media has served to make the public aware of these tensions and helped shape public opinion about people and events. The power of social influence and group pressure to shape people's attitudes and behaviors, in turn, was demonstrated in Chapter 11. The final link is to make public policy responsive to public opinion, so that a democratic government truly represents the will of the people.

A *political linkage* is Norman Luttbeg's (1981) term for "any means by which political leaders act in accordance with the wants, needs, and demands of the public in making government policy." He classifies these as "coercive models," by which the public can force representatives to obey its wishes by withholding political support, and "noncoercive models," which *reflect* public opinion (see Figure 16–1). Luttbeg's descriptions of these models bring together the concepts described in Part III—social influence, group pressure, membership, group norms, socialization and role behavior, and leadership.

The coercive models utilize elected leaders, as described in Chapter 15. The public can express its preferences by its vote in two of these models: The *rational-activist,* in which the vote directly influences the enactment of policy by leaders, and the *political parties,* in which the vote relays public preference to leaders via support for the platforms of political parties. In the third coercive model, *pressure groups,* membership in a special-interest group conveys the public's preference. The two noncoercive models depend on similar socialization of the public and its leaders. In the *belief-sharing or consensus* model, they share actual norms or preferences, and in the *role-playing* model the leader takes the role of delegate of the people: "Representatives vote what they believe to be the preferences of their followers and even anticipate public preferences because they think they should" (Luttbeg, 1981, p. 7).

The emphasis in this chapter is on the more dramatic types of collective behavior that emerge as a result of dissatisfaction or impatience with normal political processes. The relation between frustration and aggression, which was explored in Chapter 7, often applies in these circumstances. These are the types of behavior that have traditionally been considered collective in social psychology, as noted above. The chapter begins with a discussion of current theories of

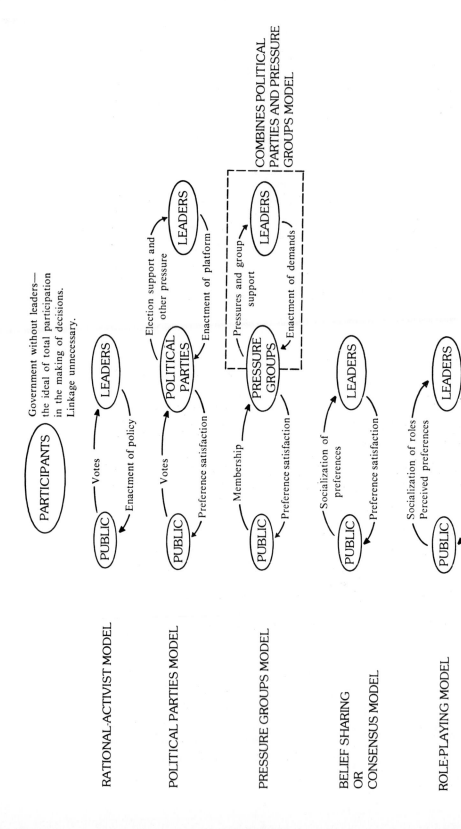

Figure 16-1. Linkages between Public Opinion and Public Policy

Source: Reprinted from Norman R. Luttbeg (Ed.), *Public Opinion and Public Policy* (Itasca, Ill.: F. E. Peacock, Publishers, 1981), p. 9.

collective behavior, followed by a section which defines the crowd, its aggressive manifestation, the mob, and crowd behavior such as the panic syndrome. Then it considers the nature of rumor as an unfounded type of communication which sets the stage for the various types of collective behavior. Fashions, fads, and crazes are described as cyclic types which surface in a diffuse crowd setting, and riots, protests, and terrorism are presented as the most erratic, destructive types.

THEORIES OF COLLECTIVE BEHAVIOR

The theoretical approaches to collective behavior have been of three general types, according to Ralph H. Turner (1964): contagion, convergence, and emergent norm. *Contagion,* the oldest approach, emphasizes feelings, attitudes and behaviors that are "communicated rapidly and accepted uncritically." Historically this was the accepted theory of crowd behavior, as expressed in the ideas of early theorists on suggestibility, imitation, and even instinct.

Convergence theory focuses on the influence of the group setting (as described in Part III) and the gathering of people with similar predispositions derived from their perceptions (Chapter 6), motivations (Chapter 7), and attitudes and values (Chapters 8 and 9). An example is the lynching mobs comprised of frustrated members of the lower socioeconomic class. Convergence theorists also have attempted to explain crowd behavior in terms of social learning mechanisms, like the approaches of Albert Bandura and of Neal Miller and John Dollard described in Chapter 5.

Emergent-norm theory takes into account the emergence of social norms in the crowd, as reported in the studies by Muzafer Sherif, Solomon Asch, and R. S. Crutchfield on conformity in the group setting described in Chapter 11. This approach emphasizes the lack of unanimity in many crowd situations and the passers-by who are marginally involved in them. For instance, in Nazi Germany of the 1930s storm troopers regularly attacked Jewish stores and their owners while onlookers passively stood by. Turner (1964) notes that convergence theory stresses "the continuity between normal *individual* behavior and crowd behavior," but emergent-norm theory points up "the continuity between normal *group* behavior and crowd behavior" (p. 392; italics added). Both are more in keeping with the scientific method of study than contagion theory.

Neil J. Smelser (1962) has proposed a theory of collective behavior in which the various types are interpreted in terms of six variables. He interprets craze and panic (which are discussed in later sections of this chapter), for example, in these terms (pp. 218–221):

1. *Structural conduciveness.* Certain institutionalized aspects of the sociocultural setting build in aberrant behaviors or at least make them permissible. Religious cults of a highly erratic nature have appeared periodically in our culture, for instance. The streaking craze, when nude males sprinted across campuses in the spring of 1974, would not have been conceivable without the general liberalization of sexual norms during the 1960s.

2. *Strain.*   Ambiguities and conflicts in the status quo can become strong needs for radical change in conventional behaviors. An economic boom occurs when individuals perceive no means of obtaining a satisfying profit on ordinary investments (as described later in Box 16–5). Political bandwagons can develop when there is no clear-cut preference for candidates, as in the last few days of the 1980 presidential campaign.

3. *Growth and spread of a generalized belief.*   Beliefs which identify the reason for the status quo and provide alternative responses to it (which are labeled either *wish-fulfilling* or *hysterical*) are primarily oriented either to norms or to values. The 1970s revival of occultism and interest in astrological signs as a determinant of personality was in part an irrational response to a series of social crises that were perceived by the public as insoluble.

4. *Precipitating factors.*   Some event must trigger the crisis situation. For instance, rumors of white violence to blacks on a bridge to Belle Isle on a warm Sunday evening precipitated the race riots in Detroit in 1943 (Lee & Humphrey, 1943).

5. *Mobilization of participants for action.*   This stage is more explicit and organized in social movements, to be discussed in the next chapter. But a race riot, for example, represents a mobilization stage like the formation of gangs or groups of individuals armed with Molotov cocktails or simply a password, like "Burn, Baby, Burn," as in the Watts upheaval in Los Angeles in 1965.

6. *Operation of social control.*   Various forms of social control prevent many potential collective behaviors from taking place, or, according to Smelser, they "minimize conduciveness and strain." These controls may be instituted through norms, leadership, or other mechanisms, but in most craze situations there is a virtual absence of them.

Smelser's systematic theory of collective behavior is useful in studying the causes and functions of various forms of this type of behavior and in understanding why they emerge. However, it has not been demonstrated that his generalizations can be applied to specific situations, and it is not clear whether crisis situations necessarily follow this model. It especially does not allow for the contingencies by which "given outcomes are more likely to occur than other outcomes" (Oberschall, 1973). The complex nature of collective behavior may in fact discourage the formulation of a definitive or universal theory. At best we are still in the hypothesis stage.

THE CROWD AND CROWD BEHAVIOR

Most social scientists distinguish between an audience and a crowd. The *audience* is a highly structured group, with a fairly definite educational or recreational purpose. Its members are oriented toward the speaker or performers

Symbols of law and order can inspire patriotic feelings and minimize possible disorder in a spectator crowd. *Source:* © Theodore Anderson, 1981.

and only incidentally toward each other. The chief characteristics of the audience are a specific purpose, a predetermined time and place of meeting, and a standard form of polarization and interaction (Young, 1956). Hence the audience is not an example of mass behavior as that term is commonly used.

The *crowd* is a less clearly organized group, though its members are in intimate contact and they sometimes have common interests and attitudes. Cantril (1941) defined a crowd as "a congregate group of individuals who have temporarily identified themselves with common values, and who are experiencing similar emotions." A street crowd may assemble around two young men having a fight or a policeman arresting a drunk, for example. The members of the crowd are interested in, or curious about, what is happening. They talk to each other, push forward to get a better view, offer comments and suggestions, make gestures, and generally register their approval or disapproval. In a word, the crowd situation is much more fluid than an audience, and the members interact far more with each other. In this typical *interstimulation,* the remarks and gestures of some crowd members stimulate similar behavior in others, which in turn facilitates further restless expression that may build up to a crescendo of excited action. This interstimulation often takes the form of what is referred to as *milling* before a stampede.

The Structure of the Crowd

There is some degree of standardization in the group form of crowds, as Wright (1978) found in analyzing a number of situations. He classified mass behavior according to two models: (1) task activities, which are specific to certain goals, such as parading or looting; and (2) crowd or adjunct activities, which provide background to the task and in which converging and (especially) milling are usually evident. Task activities generally have four phases: (1) focusing or locating the object, (2) converging on the object, (3) performing the task (delivering the protest, giving the beating, looting), and (4) divergence or scattering. Adjunct activities are usually less structured. Wright interprets mob action as a group phenomenon with a specific spatial pattern. The kind of task determines the size of the group, which varies in clusters of from one to four for crowds moving about or one to eight members engaged in talking.

A fundamental distinction among crowds is the degree of dispersion. The *diffuse crowd* is a potential grouping in which people with similar interests or characteristics are encouraged to act in similar ways by rumor and other volatile means of communication. The more usual crowd situation, however, is that of the *compact crowd,* which is characterized by heightened emotionality and has spatial properties such as boundaries as well as size and density (Milgram & Toch, 1969).

The usual pattern of a crowd, at least the spectator variety, is in the form of a *ring.* Even when the crowd is enlarged by successive layers, a circular shape is retained because there is a common focus of attention. The audience type of crowd, which is confined within an auditorium or other space, is, of course, an exception, as are hostile crowds which mill around. *Alignment* may characterize still another type of crowd behavior (Crouch, 1970). The alignment can be either parallel, as in a marching squad, or reciprocal, as in a speaker confronting an audience or two opposing groups or crowds.

Crowd boundaries may be more or less *permeable,* that is, the crowd may be open or closed (Canetti, 1963). A demonstration in favor of or opposing a policy may not allow participation by a person wearing the badge of the opposite side, for example. The *sharpness* of the boundaries depends on the focus and polarization of the crowd: It may have scattered, passive participants at the edges, or close ranks when threatened by police, or disperse again into the diffuse crowd it originally was. The *solvency* of boundaries concerns the degree to which one collectivity blends into another. Infiltration or "laminated crowds" may occur when antagonistic subgroups oppose each other; only the most highly polarized crowds discourage the interaction of clusters.

Crowds also vary according to the climate of feeling, the salience of the issue, and the emotional impact of the leader. They also can be measured by *size* and *density.* A large crowd is perceived as guaranteeing anonymity to the participants, although there are exceptions; a North Carolina judge once tried the individual members of a lynching mob, for example. Photographic techniques now permit the identification of crowd participants even at night, as in the Harlem riots in 1964. The surging effect of the crowd is in part a result of size. Density, or the sense of crowdedness, varied from 4 to 8 square feet per person when it was measured in several campus rallies. Density helps give the effect of solidarity (Canetti, 1963), but like size, it may or may not indicate the crowd's support for an issue or movement. Pedestrian traffic density was found to be higher at a prowar parade than at an antiwar parade during the Vietnam confrontation (W. R. Berkowitz, 1970), but other data seemed to indicate maximum intensity within the opposition group.

Personality and Situational Factors in Crowd Behavior

Attempts to explain crowd behavior have been undertaken by many social psychologists. One of the earliest was Le Bon, who observed that crowds are marked by suggestibility and loss of restraint. His idea was that a collective mind is formed by almost hypnotic contagion, which blots out the intellectual aptitudes and moral ideas of the individual. A theory more acceptable to social psychologists was advanced by F. H. Allport, who rejected interpretations of crowd behavior which direct attention to the crowd as a whole and overlook or minimize the significance of individual factors. He asserted that the driving force of spontaneous, moblike crowds rests in basic individual responses, not mere aggregation or manipulation by a leader; "The individual in the crowd behaves just as he would behave alone, *only more so*" (Allport, 1924).

Cantril (1941) suggested that there are three essential components of what has been called the *mob mind:*

1. Confusion of causal relationships; individuals jump at oversimplified explanations.
2. Restriction of the individual's world; immediate action may occur in terms of temporary, limited values, uninhibited by the usual cultural norms and values.
3. Identification with the situation; individuals lose themselves in the crowd or mob.

Interpretations of crowd and mob behavior suggest that neither a situational nor an individual or motivational theory is adequate by itself. Crowd behavior has several essential components, all of which play a part in the outcome. Four interrelated influences are described below:

1. *General atmosphere or setting.* Some social event has occurred—a child has been run over by a car, a family has been evicted, an explosion or fire has taken place. Or an event *is alleged to have occurred*—there are reports that a woman has been raped, a black youth has been beaten by a policeman, a child has been abandoned. Whether or not the event has occurred, the way it is

reported determines the way the situation is perceived and interpreted; that is, the report sets and interprets the psychological atmosphere.

2. *Motivational factors.* A person's drives, motives, emotions, and attitudes are important in respect to how the situation is perceived. Whether a black is accused of rape, a white shopkeeper is viewed as exploitative, or a group of Southern villagers decide a civil right should be ignored, each event is structured by the frustrations and needs of individuals, and violence is viewed as a means of seeking redress for grievances. Curiously, many of the same persons who in a mass setting would burn a building or carry out a lynching would emerge in a disaster situation as rescuers.

3. *Patterns of conformity.* The group influences described in Chapter 11 directly affect crowd behavior. Friendship clusters are especially relevant in the supposedly spontaneous outbursts following a football victory, or "the not-so-lonely crowd," as Aveni (1977) describes such settings. The interactions among the members of the crowd encourage groups norms to emerge, and the leader of the crowd brings them into sharper focus, as noted in Chapter 15. Participants identify themselves with the activity in progress—the lynching, destruction, or rescue attempts. Thus there is a general impression of conformity and solidarity, despite individual differences.

4. *The participant as decision maker.* The traditional notion is that a person in a crowd acts in a purely erratic manner, goaded by semiconscious or unconscious impulses and a tendency to follow the leader. The reality is somewhat different. Even in a crisis individuals must decide among given options, considering whether they will be held accountable for their actions—that is, whether they will be caught by the police or anyone will identify them later. In the My Lai incident during the Vietnam War, as a result of which Lieutenant William Calley was found guilty of ordering his company to shoot scores of Vietnamese civilians (see Box 18–2 in Chapter 18), the individual soldier had to evaluate the authoritative basis and permanence of Calley's order and specifically what would be the lesser of two evils for himself—to disobey the order (and in military life such failure to conform can have serious consequences) or to go against his usual norms and kill noncombatants.

Acting alone rather than in conformity with a crowd increases the cost of the activity. Each member of the crowd, like each player in the psychological games described in Chapter 12, seeks to gain maximum rewards, and, as Berk (1974) notes, in a crowd "the payoffs for various possible actions are *fundamentally dependent on the actions of others gathered at the scene*" (p. 69). Each player wants to win and must consider what the others are likely to do. A person's response may be cooperative or competitive, but the latter is probable in a panic situation. In the cooperative crowd the participant can maximize the reward by working with others; in the competitive situation receiving the payoff probably depends on eliminating or struggling against peers.

Indeed, a crisis can produce its own means of social control, as it did in the collective anxiety, grief, guilt feelings, and sense of participation which followed the assassination of President Kennedy. Zablocki (1976) defines a crisis as "any stage of high risk and high hopes" which calls for decisions to be reached under the urgency of time.

A study of observers and participants at 126 "protest events," particularly those associated with the Vietnam War, suggests that violence growing out of political protest should be viewed as "a set of dynamic events during which a developmental process occurs" (Kritzer, 1977). In these events the interaction or reciprocal behavior between protestors and the police is critical. The crowd may provoke the police into action, which then elicits a violent reaction from the crowd. If there are sufficiently strong norms against violence on either side, however, the provocation may fail. Differential perception of the episode by the two sides is relevant, and attempts to reconcile them may be a means of resolving the conflict, as was illustrated in Box 12–1 in Chapter 12.

In earlier theories of the crowd the behavior of people in crowds was depicted as highly uniform, and they were seen as suggestible, irrational, destructive, and lacking self-control. A more careful analysis of the crowd in both historical and contemporary perspectives by Crouch (1968) found some opposing tendencies. According to his view, crowd participants are suggestible to the degree that their value systems can accept outside influences, but they may also be countersuggestible, as laboratory demonstrations have indicated. When feats of magic are analyzed, for example, the irrationality of the crowd is found to be an extension of the individuals' cognitions of everyday life. In a crowd or in a voting booth people act on a variety of beliefs, such as a conviction that the stars control our destiny; acceptance of a conspiracy theory about a takeover of the government by big business, communists, or blacks; or adherence to the idea that a strong military establishment can assure peace.

Violence and destruction do occur in crowd settings, but so do they in real life. To LeBon, the French Revolution was the prototype of the unruly mob, but even in that holocaust there were trials before the guillotine fell. Self-control fails in a crowd not so much because individuals lose control of themselves—it is doubtful whether any individual is ever really autonomous—but because conventional controls break down.

An explanation of the anonymity and irrationality often found in crowd behavior can be gained from the research on *deindividuation,* such as the experiments of Philip Zimbardo on dehumanization in a prison setting described in Box 11–3 in Chapter 11. In another experiment Zimbardo (1970) placed subjects in two groups: in one they were anonymous and wore hoods similar to those worn by the Ku Klux Klan, and in the other they were identifiable. The deindividuated subjects showed greater aggressiveness in administering electric shocks to victims, whereas the control group (those in the individuation condition) were more restrained and even leaned backward to avoid giving excess shocks to others who had been portrayed as being obnoxious.

Diener et al. (1980) hypothesized that self-monitoring and self-regulation could be discouraged by manipulating environmental or laboratory conditions. He found that group size (but not group density) was negatively correlated with

Norms that inhibit crowd behaviors may be imposed on members of a group, such as West Point cadets. The type of crowd determines the extent to which social control operates, however; more freedom is allowed in a football stadium than on the parade ground. *Source:* © Theodore Anderson, 1981.

self-awareness, and self-awareness was reduced when subjects were with members of their own sex only. Deindividuation thus is related to the tendency to engage in aggressive or violent behaviors, as is documented in the history of the KKK, Nazi concentration camps, and mechanized warfare.

When Does a Crowd Become a Mob?

Smelser (1962) calls aggressive tendencies in a crowd a *hostile outburst* which generally occurs with some precipitating cause after the usual avenues of social control have failed to function. Often a hostile outburst takes the form of a kind of scapegoating, such as the patriotic rowdyism of hard-hat construction workers at peace rallies in some American cities during the 1962 Cuban missile crisis, which was in part an expression of frustration at this terrifying impasse in international affairs. Race riots are another example of deep-seated hostility which is usually sparked by some precipitating event. This observation dates back to the disastrous Chicago race riots of 1919, for which the stage was set by the large-scale migration of southern blacks into Chicago residential areas. The precipitating incident that triggered the mob activity was the use of a traditionally white bathing beach by a black person. More recently the economic and social disadvantages of blacks in large American cities have constituted a climate of frustration which is easily touched off by an incident such as the shooting or arrest of a black person by a white police officer.

Often crowd behavior is facilitated by the presence of a leader, sometimes a self-appointed leader from the group membership. This leader focuses and expresses the sentiments of the group and may harangue followers until the crowd becomes a mob intent on some kind of action, such as tearing down an opponent's goalposts, staging a protest march, or storming a jail and lynching a suspect.

Most treatments of crowd behavior are concerned with what Blumer (1946) calls the *acting crowd,* which is likely to have a leader and which often turns to aggressive behavior—that is, it becomes a *mob.* Brown (1954) classifies mobs as being of four types: (1) aggressive (a lynching or race riot), (2) escape (a panic), (3) acquisitive (a run on a bank), and (4) expressive (a revival meeting).

It is not unusual for a crowd to become a mob, since the structuring of the two situations is quite similar. One type of mob which appeared prior to the Civil War but has generally disappeared had lynching, or hanging a victim by mob action instead of judicial process, as its purpose. Cantril (1941) calls a lynching mob "a congregate group of individuals who feel strongly that certain of their values are threatened and whose attitudes direct them to kill or injure a human being" (p. 80). The typical lynching occurred in the South, had a black male for a victim, and was perpetrated by a mob of native whites, who usually escaped arrest or punishment. Ginzberg's (1962) history of lynchings reported that they occurred disproportionately in the summer, as did most of the ghetto riots of the 1960s. In an analysis of 102 instances of serious collective violence, sustained temperatures around 90° F. (the long, hot summer) were found to be a factor (Baron & Ransberger, 1978).

Exploring the psychological setting of lynching mobs, Cantril found strongly ingrained norms, notably the belief that blacks were inferior and had to be kept in their place. White Southerners were strongly ego involved with these beliefs or frames of reference and would act aggressively if they felt they were threatened. Violent behavior such as a lynching represents people's attempts to defend their status with an aggressive response to frustration. Lynchings had virtually disappeared as a phenomenon of American social life by 1940, although the resurgence in the late 1970s and early 1980s of ultraconservative fringe groups such as the Ku Klux Klan brought other violent attempts to intimidate blacks.

It is practically impossible to investigate mob behavior experimentally, but Meier, Mennenga, and Stoltz (1941) made an interesting attempt. They distributed news bulletins to one large group of college students and a fake newspaper extra to another, each of which told of a brutal kidnapping and murder. Then they determined who among the students would join the mob as participants, who would go along to assist, who would not participate, and who would try to deter the mob from violence. Of the total groups of students, 12 percent said they wanted to join the mob with the expectation of participating, and another 23 percent would go along to see what happened. The would-be participants were usually males, younger, more extroverted, less self-sufficient, and less frequently associated with a church than the nonparticipants. The great majority of the subjects thought the crime had actually occurred. The investigators concluded that:

> . . . in the crowd setting the individual will behave in accord with the dominance of previously established habits, attitudes, and behavior patterns, but . . . the action itself will be to some degree conditioned by the nature of the situation, since the response of participation or deterrence will be to some degree in accordance with the degree to which guilt is or is not completely established. (p. 524)

The Panic Syndrome

Like crowd behavior in general, panic is often described in terms of hysteria, irrationality, and a kind of stampeding response (see Box 16–1). It usually is a result of competition for something in short supply, whether an exit in a burning high rise or economic security in inflationary times. According to Lang and Lang (1961), panic refers "not to a particular kind of response, but to all the various collective responses that express demoralization." It is a collective retreat from group goals into privatization, and it often results from a breakdown of primary-group ties.

Some people can adapt to the panic syndrome in some circumstances, but the response is usually maladaptive. Lang and Lang (1961, pp. 92–93) have identified the following such responses:

1. Paralysis and immobility as a result of inaccurate perception and contradictory impulses toward action.
2. Psychoneurotic reactions which reduce efficiency in adapting to the situation.
3. Hyperactivity, combined with confused, random, or precipitate action.
4. Premature and rigid fixation on a given course of action, without awareness of other options.
5. Disorganization as each person attempts to escape from the threat without regard to the security of others.

Despite the lack of self-control in panic, a collective definition of the situation emerges (Turner & Killian, 1972). For instance, if the participants perceive a given exit as closed, their action is not irrational. They may define the situation very differently once they perceive the other alternatives.

There may or may not be a contagion of panic in the crowd. It is not certain whether the presence of others has a reassuring or a disturbing effect on the fears that arise when a threatening situation is recognized. The immediate effect of the

Box 16-1
AN INVASION FROM MARS

There have been so many theatrical versions of visits from outer space that a production about an invasion from Mars would hardly cause a ripple of interest today. But in 1938, a Mercury Theater radio broadcast by Orson Welles of a drama entitled "War of the Worlds" resulted in a panic that caused thousands of listeners to actually try to flee the invaders.

Hadley Cantril and associates did a follow-up study to determine the extent of the panic and what caused it.* They noted the unprecedented extent to which people in all walks of life became suddenly and intensely disturbed:

> Long before the broadcast was ended, people all over the United States were praying, crying, fleeing frantically to escape death from the Martians. Some ran to rescue loved ones. Others telephoned farewells or warnings, hurried to inform neighbors, sought information from newspapers or radio stations, summoned ambulances and police cars. At least six million people heard the broadcast. At least a million of them were frightened or disturbed. (p. 47)

The data furnished by Cantril point up several situational and personal factors to account for the panic. First, the drama was done with great realism, not only in terms of vocal expression but by the use of actual place-names and of persons who sounded authentic. Even more important was the fact that people tuning in late on the program assumed, naturally enough, that it was a news broadcast rather than fiction.

A significant emotional factor at the time was jitters about war—the Munich settlement had occurred only a few weeks before, and rumors of World War II were in the air. Many more predispositional factors were present in some but not all of the listeners. For example, some had implicit faith in news heard over the radio. Of those who attempted to check the validity of what they heard, some did it ineffectively, for instance, by looking out of the window, seeing traffic going by, and concluding "people were rushing away." A few were expecting the end of the world and decided this was it. Some persons who were more unstable became overly emotional and incapable of any rational action.

It is hardly strange that such dramatic reports in the form of an actual news broadcast, coupled with general and various specific personality factors, led to panic reactions. Furthermore, people lacked a frame of reference for dealing with such a weird event, as compared with an accident or fire. Believing the event was real, failing to verify it for various reasons, and knowing no means to deal with it, many thousands of people turned to prayer or hysterical flight.

---

* H. Cantril, H. Gaudet, and H. Herzog, *The Invasion from Mars* (Princeton, N.J.: Princeton University Press, 1940).

group may be to reassure the individual that the cues of danger are not serious. The sense of danger becomes greater for a person who finds out otherwise and resents having been misled.

Suggested methods of preventing mass panic have stressed the need to develop group discipline, and to promote leadership in the crisis, to distract attention from danger by directing the participants to other activities, and to dispel rumors with accurate, officially sanctioned reports.

THE NATURE OF RUMOR

A precipitating factor in crowd behavior, as noted in the preceding section, is the psychological atmosphere set by reports of a real or reputed occurrence. The way the event is reported determines the way concerned people will perceive and interpret it. Often the report takes the form of rumor, an unfounded communication which may be spread by word of mouth or reported in the press. When editors are not vigilant about reporting facts only, the report may be colored by the way it is presented or given credence by attributing it to an unidentified but presumably authoritative source.

Published or oral, rumor often provides the glue which binds individuals together into a crowd and justifies their actions. In their study of the psychology of rumor, G. W. Allport and L. J. Postman (1947) define the concept as a specific proposition or belief, passed along from person to person, usually by word of mouth, without reference to secure standards of evidence. The essentials of rumor are importance and ambiguity; that is, the amount of rumor in circulation varies with the importance of the subject to the individuals concerned and the ambiguity of the evidence. For example, during World War II people repeated such rumors as "I hear that out at Camp X they have so much meat they throw whole sides of fresh beef into the garbage." The meat shortage was of great importance to civilians, and they did not know the facts. Because the situation was ambiguous, the rumors circulated wildly.

Rumors serve to explain, justify, and provide meaning for the individual. Often the rumor is a projection of a person's own motivational and emotional state (see Box 16–2).

The Transmission of Rumor

Experimental studies were undertaken by Allport and Postman (1947) to discover the tendencies or processes influencing the content of rumor as it is communicated. One person was asked to look at a picture and describe it to a second, giving a dozen or so details. The second person then passed on the description to a third who had just entered the room, who then told it to a fourth, and so on. The version of the last person (usually the sixth or seventh) was then compared with the original picture.

The findings clearly showed several tendencies involved in the transmission of rumor or testimony. One of these is *leveling*—an increasing brevity and loss of detail. Another is the *sharpening* of certain details, such as retaining a certain word

---

Box 16–2
THE EXAGGERATED RUMORS ABOUT MRS. KING

A classic example of the spread of a rumor was provided by Karl Menninger.* In the following dialogue, he shows how the attitudes of the women are reflected in their interpretations of the message they hear and color the message as they pass it on.

Mrs. Adams to Mrs. Beck: Where is Mrs. King today? Is she ill?

Mrs. Beck to Mrs. Clark: Mrs. Adams wonders if Mrs. King may not be ill.

Mrs. Clark (who doesn't like Mrs. King) to Mrs. Davis (who does): I hear Mrs. King is ill. Not seriously, I hope?

Mrs. Davis to Mrs. Ellis: Mrs. Clark is saying that Mrs. King is seriously sick. I must go right over and see her.

Mrs. Ellis to Mrs. French: I guess Mrs. King is pretty sick. Mrs. Davis has just been called over.

Mrs. French to Mrs. Gregg: They say Mrs. King isn't expected to live. The relatives have been called to her bedside.

Mrs. Gregg to Mrs. Hudson: What's the latest news about Mrs. King? Is she dead?

Mrs. Hudson to Mrs. Ingham: What time did Mrs. King die?

Mrs. Ingham to Mrs. Jones: Are you going to Mrs. King's funeral? I hear she died yesterday.

Mrs. Jones to Mrs. King: I just learned of your death and funeral. Now, who started that?

Mrs. King: There are several who would be glad if it were true.

---

* Karl Menninger, *The Human Mind* (New York: Alfred A. Knopf, 1930), p. 282.

---

or idea through the whole series of communications. In one series the word *remonstrate* was passed on without change; in several series the detail of a flowerpot falling from a windowsill was consistently emphasized. A still more significant tendency influencing the communication of rumors is *assimilation,* that is, conformity to the habits, interests, wishes, and expectations of the subjects. In the interpretation of a picture of a black man and white man facing each other and talking while the white man holds an open razor, more than half the time the razor had moved into the black man's hand by the time of the final report—a clear instance of assimilation in line with a stereotyped expectancy.

Allport and Postman use the term *embedding process* to represent the threefold process of leveling, sharpening, and assimilation, defining it as "an effort to reduce the stimulus to a simple and meaningful structure that has adaptive significance for the individual in terms of his own interests and experience." Thus the actual words a person hears "become so embedded into his own dynamic mental life that the product is chiefly one of projection." Rumor suffers such serious distortion through this embedding process, they conclude, that "it is never under any circumstances a valid guide for belief or conduct."

Some studies of rumor formation question whether embedding occurs in real-life situations; it may be found in the classroom or laboratory setting because there is less opportunity to test reality there. An experimental situation provides few means of correcting the omissions or exaggerations that creep into the rumor process (Schachter & Burdick, 1955), however, and in the natural setting there are cues by which the distortion in rumor transition can be checked. In most crises, public authorities and eventually the mass media—radio, television, or the press—are anchorages in determining the plausibility of a situation. Thus rumor is subjected to some degree of reality testing. It is not altogether surprising that in a study of rumors observed in World War II by Caplow (1947), most rumors proved to be valid.

Functions of Rumors

A rumor may be considered a "manifestation of a shared perspective" (Lang & Lang, 1961). It is a means of communication when more legitimate media are unobtainable. Shibutani (1966) suggested that rumor follows a supply-and-demand curve; when the demand for news exceeds the supply made available through institutional channels, rumors are likely to result.

According to Rosnow and Fine (1976), a rumor passes through three stages:

1. *Birth.* The rumor emerges out of some need for fantasy, or as a means of "explaining" or arousing anxiety or fear, or in an aggressive urge.

2. *Adventure.* This is the circuitous route by which a rumor catches on. Wartime censorship favors rumor formation, as does disenchantment with official sources of information, as in the public's distrust of the Warren Commission report regarding the circumstances surrounding the assassination of President Kennedy in 1963.

3. *Death.* This is the final outcome; in reality most rumors have a brief life span, usually a few days to a few weeks. Disproof, irrelevance, or dissipation is the final outcome. But rumors can continue to circulate, as they still do concerning Kennedy's assassination. They also can reappear at cyclic intervals, like the legend on one midwestern campus that women students who combed their hair under the gingko tree by the light of the full moon would see their true loves!

Rumor develops when there is an unfilled demand for news, and the more threatening the situation the more desperate is the need to formulate an explanation. Rumor not only provides knowledge and aids decision making but can have some cathartic effect as a cognitive and expressive means by which people can relieve their anxieties. Thus, as Shibutani (1966) said, rumors can serve as both instruments and products in the development of emotional moods, and consequently they can play a major role in crowd behavior.

A different function of rumor is as a trial balloon. For instance, the White House "leaks" the names of possible candidates for the Supreme Court as a means of testing public reaction. All the names on the list may not represent valid candidates, but the public response indicates what kind of judge would be acceptable or unacceptable, and a more likely list of names follows. The political arena is one in which rumors are particularly fruitful, but business organizations also deliberately circulate rumors about possible changes in personnel policy, financing procedures, or expansion plans in order to sound out employees' opinions or public reactions.

No public agency can control the rumor process. The rumors about Richard Nixon's involvement in the Watergate bugging incident were fueled when official versions of events issued by the White House later were declared to be "inoperative," and Nixon's denials eventually had to be withdrawn. They spiraled into a national crisis when newspaper investigations and court testimony revealed a complex plot that the executive office had been aware of and had tried to cover up. In a functioning democracy both the judicial process and a free and active press are means of arriving at the truth of a matter, but their integrity and credibility must be guarded zealously if the public is to have confidence in them. The *Washington Post,* which won a Pulitzer Prize for meritorious public service for its investigative reporting on Watergate in 1973, had to return another prize for feature writing in 1981 when the reporter's confidential source turned out to be nonexistent and the story proved to be a fabrication.

Sometimes collective behavior is an expression of latent anxieties and prejudice. In the civil riots of the 1960s, rumor contributed to existing tensions as word spread through city ghettos of exploitation by shopkeepers and police harassment. In Tampa, Florida, the rumor circulated that a white officer had shot a black youth who had his arms up in the act of surrender, and the rumor became the spark that turned an incident into a major disturbance. In the disastrous riots of Detroit and Newark rumor complicated attempts to control events by police and community leaders (U.S. Riot Commission, 1968). The ghetto constitutes an isolated mass in which little opportunity for participation in the larger community exists, and so action can be triggered by almost any type of propaganda. The residents' mistrust of the news media leaves them more susceptible to informal sources of information. Thus, in various ways, rumor sets the stage for crowd behavior.

FASHIONS, FADS, AND CRAZES

The cyclic types of collective behavior—fashions, fads, crazes, and booms—occur in a diffuse crowd setting rather than in a focused, compact crowd—a distinction explained in a preceding section of this chapter. Fashion operates within a conventionalized setting, in contrast to fads and crazes, which are less predictable and controllable.

Fashion

Fashion has been described as being transitory, novel, and trivial, responding to people's fundamental need for change. Despite these connotations in terms of dress, however, fashion can involve more than superficial behaviors, as Lang and Lang (1961) point out. The end products of architectural and engineering designs are hardly trivial, though they do reflect trends in lifestyles such as saunas and condominiums. Even science often reflects fashion, as in the current revival of interest in collective behavior. Psychiatrists have periodically preferred certain modes of therapy; prefrontal lobotomies and insulin or electric shock were in vogue in the 1940s and early 1950s, until tranquilizers became more fashionable.

Status is important in determining fashion; the reward for adopting a new style early is prestige and status. According to Turner and Killian (1972), rapidly changing fashion "depends upon a society in which upward mobility and prestige striving are favorably valued. The rapid succession of styles becomes necessary when the higher social strata are not able to maintain a monopoly of the symbols of high status."

In 1937, when the Duchess of Windsor's wedding gown was considered the height of fashion, a copy moved from a prestige shop to cash and carry stores within a period of several weeks. Today, dress manufacturers look to the middle class to set styles, in order to attract a mass market. Conformity, the usual result of group pressure as defined in Chapter 11, may also be the fundamental motive underlying fashion, but it is now geared more to the standards of the middle class.

Students of fashion suggest that both the desire for conformity and the desire for recognition or prestige are motives for following fashion in the way people dress. Psychoanalysts say that fashion serves women, particularly, as a sublimated outlet for aggressive or exhibitionist tendencies, which are repressed in their socialization. Thorstein Veblen's 1920s theory of the leisure class suggested that because a well-dressed woman symbolized her husband's success and prestige, her fashionableness satisfied both husband and wife. Sherif and Cantril (1947) defined one of the chief functions of clothes as extending the self of the wearer, and in this sense, they said, many persons become strongly ego involved with fashion. Smelser (1962) saw excitability and ambiguity in the fashion situation—the anticipation of what the designer will create and to what degree it will be accepted. There is a certain amount of unpredictability about whether fashions will spread within and between communities. But commercial domination of the field and the manipulation of imagery by advertising and marketing experts has made fashion more a product of bureaucracy than the result of individual, spontaneous acceptance or rejection (Rosenblum, 1978).

Probably the most remarkable feature about fashion today is its volatility and variability. The tempo of fashion is rapid; U.S. car manufacturers, for example, changed designs almost yearly to capture the public fancy, until they became convinced of the overriding need to produce compact, fuel-efficient models (see Box 16–3). Women's hemlines follow the vagaries of fashion as variations are constantly introduced, meet with initial rejection, become accepted, and then are considered ripe for replacement. The voluminous "new look" which followed

Box 16–3
IMAGE MAKERS AND STYLE SETTERS

The focus of fashion in dress, automobiles, or any type of product is often the creation of an image. In a survey of university students, Orrin E. Klapp found various images associated with drivers who chose four different types of cars in 1972, before miles per gallon became the chief criterion for judging automobiles.* These choices were perceived as reflecting characteristics of the drivers, as follows:

Mustang—show-off, classy, practical.

Thunderbird—middle-aged, playboy, sophisticated.

Lincoln—successful professional or businessperson, middle-aged to older person with conservative tastes, somewhat of a snob.

Foreign sports car—youngish, nonconformist, speed fiend.

The Madison Avenue image-making approach has been applied to almost every form of behavior, including the selling—or the buying—of the U.S. president. Keeping abreast of fashion in products, personalities, politicians, or any commodity packaged for sale calls for a novel approach and a sense of the popular taste of the moment, as the image of what's in style undergoes constant change.

---

* O. E. Klapp, *Currents of Unrest: An Introduction to Collective Behavior* (New York: Holt, Rinehart & Winston, 1972), p. 313.

removal of restrictions on fabric use in World War II was replaced by the miniskirt, which men liked on women better than women did. Resistance was strong to an attempt to substitute the midi, or calf-length skirt, and it was tempered by the availability of an alternative—the pantsuit. Turner and Killian (1972) note that "The little-understood transformations, whereby the reluctant and the violently opposed imperceptibly sometimes come to acquire the very tastes which they initially resisted, offer one of the most potentially fruitful subjects for research on the operation of the diffuse crowd within the institutional structure of fashion" (p. 154).

The tolerance of men today in accepting varied clothing styles is further evidence of the volatility of fashion. New materials, designs, and colors, plus the social acceptance of tieless and coatless styles of dress, have given males a new fashion freedom—and opened up a rich market for the garment industry. The trend toward unisex fashions, or the breaking down of sexual differences in styles which was noted in the discussion of sex roles in Chapter 14, is another means of deemphasizing fashion conformity. Even the cosmetic industry has spread to men who want to keep looking young. Far from dying, however, fashion is moving in less predictable directions.

There are other indications that fashion is more than ever a relative concept which depends on the sociocultural setting. As noted above, the role of the upper-class as the arbiters of fashion has virtually disappeared. But the design of the Rolls Royce as the ultimate in automobile luxury has remained unchanged for decades, while styles in the lower price ranges have quickly succeeded one another. The goal now is to produce a fuel-efficient, economical, compact automobile which looks like a high-powered, expensive sports car. A primitive simplicity can even be the basis of fashion (Konig, 1973). The adoption of the anything-goes style of the hippies, which first appeared on campuses in the late 1960s, became a badge of those who ignored the dictates of society, for example. As most college students again turned to serious career preparation a decade later, the classic "preppie" look came back into favor.

Fads

The term *fad* typically represents a sporadic, short-term kind of fashion, the effects of which sometimes border on the cultist. A fad may be local or national in scope, but it is always temporary and unpredictable. What begins as a fad may end up as a fashion, custom, or hobby. Bobbed hair, blue jeans, and bingo all started as fads and continued in permanent forms, for example.

A distinction can be made between cultist and spasmodic types of fads. *Cultist* types include dietary regimens such as vegetarianism, health-oriented practices like nudism or jogging, semireligious observances like Yoga and Zen Buddhism, and consciousness-raising experiences like Esalen, Rolfing, and transcendental meditation. In these cases there is an ideology which suggests that following these practices can guarantee health, happiness, and a better way of life. One example of such a fad in the 1940s was the activationists, a group whose goal was uninhibited self-expression in athletics, dancing, art, and writing.

The *spasmodic* type of fad catches on and spreads like wildfire for a short time, then dies rapidly away. Often these are in the areas of dress or recreation, like jigsaw puzzles or miniature golf, which have survived on a limited scale after their heyday in the 1930s. Frisbees, skateboards, snowmobiles, hot tubs, and bellbottom trousers are other examples. Usually their rise—and fall—are more rapid than in the cultist type of fad, since often they have the advantage of commercial support.

Both cultist and spasmodic fads have special appeal for the young. Alienation can be a factor encouraging this adoption, particularly with the cultist types. A fad may even represent a kind of counterculture or rejection of the established norms, as when farmers' blue jeans became popular among middle- and upper-class urban youths. It also can represent co-optation of the norms of one class by another, as with the designer jeans favored by those who could afford them in the early eighties.

Box 16–4
HOW TO FIND A FAD AND GET RICH

If you could predict what direction the next fad to capture the public's interest would take, you might prosper like the popularizers of the hula hoop and the pet rock did. In our present state of knowledge, prediction about fads is shakier than in almost any other area of social psychology. Nevertheless, some guidelines to what makes a fad catch on can be suggested.

1. To be successful, a fad must seem *novel and new*. However, as revival of astrology and other pseudopsychological cults indicates, the term *novelty* applies anew to each generation. Old ideas are constantly being repackaged and presented as new ones.

2. Fads must be broadly *consistent with the times*. The Vietnam War was an appropriate time for popularization of the peace symbol—and the counterfad of displaying or wearing the American flag. As R. H. Turner and L. M. Killian note, "a person wearing the symbol could demonstrate a philosophy of opposition to all wars, selective opposition to the Vietnam war, a vague, selective preference for peace rather than war, or the temporary enjoyment of a currently popular piece of jewelry!"*

3. Fads must be *harmonious with widespread interest and motive patterns*. Zippers, which filled a need when they appeared in the early 1930s, are still needed. Nudist camps arrived about the same time and thrived for over 30 years, but they lost their vogue as the magazine centerfold portrait, erotic art and films, and a greater sexual freedom met some of the same needs.

4. A fad should be *newsworthy*, because dissemination is aided by publicity and advertising. The eventual nationwide popularity of the hula hoop or the frisbee was largely due to the role of the mass media in the diffusion process.

5. Our rapidly changing urban culture is congenial to the introduction of fads. *Novel stimuli* such as positive thinking, encounter groups, sports cars, or hard rock music are welcomed as a means of achieving status, conforming to the group, or taking part in the "new wave."

---

* R. H. Turner and L. M. Killian, *Collective Behavior,* rev. ed. (Englewood Cliffs, N.J.: Prentice-Hall, 1972), p. 141.

The spread of a fad is a complex process. The reasons skateboards became popular, only to be replaced by roller skates, are different from those that could explain the popularity of the peace symbol in the Vietnam War era. Most of the data are speculative, but a few cautious hypotheses about fads can be suggested (see Box 16–4).

The line between fads on the one hand and fashions, crazes, cults, and other phenomena of mass behavior on the other is hard to draw. What starts as a fad may remain as a fashion, hobby, sport, or custom. Short hair for women and longer hair for men, slacks, and cosmetics all started as fads.

Crazes

A craze is more intensive, more emotionally involved, and usually more extensive than a fad. Instead of centering about diet, clothing, or verbal expressions, crazes are feverish, all-consuming activities that spread like wildfire. The Christian crusades of the 12th and 13th centuries and the witch-hunting mania of the 16th and 17th centuries are good examples of widespread crazes. McCarthyism and the probing for communists and left-wingers during the early 1950s in the U.S. reached the proportions of a craze. Other examples are the chain-letter mania and the excessive enthusiasm for entertainers like Frank Sinatra, Elvis Presley, James Dean, the Beatles, or Janis Joplin. Among the more curious crazes was the dance marathon, which peaked during the depression years of the 1930s. Unscrupulous promoters exploited contestants who danced until they dropped on their feet in hopes of winning the prize money (Calabria, 1976). Not only did those events appeal to people's sadomasochistic urges, but they provided some degree of excitement in a drab world, and anyone with 15 cents for admission could observe others who were worse off than they were.

Smelser (1962) defines crazes as "mobilization for action based on a positive wish fulfillment belief." He considers them fundamental aspects of collective behavior, covering different spheres such as economics (speculative booms; see Box 16–5), politics (bandwagon effects), personal expression (fads and fashion), or religion (revivalism). An example was the use of yellow ribbons to show support for the American diplomatic hostages in Iran in 1980. The craze took on frenzied proportions during the welcome-home ceremonies in January 1981, when people tried to outdo one another in the size of the badges they wore and airport towers, buses, and even skyscrapers were wrapped in yellow banners.

One factor that has not received much attention in the study of crowd behavior, especially in crazes, is the social network underlying contagion. In one study, sociometric patterns were found to be relevant to the spread of a hysterical belief among workers at a textile plant (Kerckhoff & Back, 1968). In a medium-sized mill 62 persons, mostly women, complained of severe pain, nausea, and a rash over a period of several days. They were convinced the cause was an insect in a shipment of cloth from England, but when health officials were called in they found the victims were suffering from "nothing more than extreme anxiety" (p. 46). A number of strains were evident among those who were affected; they suffered from tensions on the job, including relations between labor and management and other interpersonal problems. They put in more overtime, were the sole breadwinners of their families, and had more children under six years old. The hysterical belief was readily accepted by these social isolates, who transmitted it to other isolates or semi-isolates. Less isolated workers assumed the belief less intensely, and so it tapered off.

Thus, it appears that the social network acts both as a conductor and a resistor

Box 16–5
THE BOOM AS AN ECONOMIC CRAZE

A boom nearly always takes the form of a "get-rich-quick" scheme that expands like a bubble, then bursts. In 17th century Holland there was a boom called the tulip mania, when interest in these flowers became so great that prices skyrocketed and everyone began to speculate. Single bulbs of choice kinds sold for hundreds of dollars, as fortunes were made and people from all walks of life thronged to the tulip markets in the cities of Holland. Within a few months, however, the bubble burst, and merchants found themselves holding on to bulbs nobody would buy.

In the United States there have been two major booms—the California gold rush of 1848–50 and the Florida land boom of the 1920s. News of the discovery of gold brought a tremendous migration of people to California that equaled the greatest population movements in world history. People also flocked to Florida when word went around that the area was beginning to boom and easy money could be made by investing in real estate. Between three and ten million went there in 1925, according to various estimates. Few could resist the temptation to put down a few thousand dollars as a binder on an expensive lot, with the hope of reselling it at a fabulous profit. The "bust" came in 1926.

The late 1970s saw another spurt in real estate prices in California. Even speculators were wondering when that bubble would burst.

Crazes and booms of the "get-rich-quick" sort are powered by acquisitive motives coupled with frustrations. A compound of "facts," publicity, and rumors helps people define the situation as a golden opportunity. They are more successful if the idea is new or unique in some way so others have not had a chance to become disillusioned.

at different phases in an epidemic. Unlike other kinds of diffusion, crazes seem to originate among the less integrated members of the population and spread to the more conservative establishment. In this respect the diffusion of a craze differs from that of scientific information, for example, where the more active members of the scientific community become the innovators (Coleman, Katz, & Menzel, 1957).

Crazes assume a variety of forms and can involve relatively few persons. Enthusiasts have pursued sightings of unidentified flying objects since the 1940s, for example. There are also crazes that appeal only to those who are highly disturbed or militant—like those involved in the hijackings that began in the late 1960s and the embassy takeovers beginning in the late 1970s. When they succeed to any extent, the same behaviors are reinforced in others who are motivated by a wish for notoriety or allegiance to unpopular or undisseminated ideas or values (Pitcher, Hamblin, & Miller, 1978).

PROTESTS, RIOTS, AND TERRORISM

The more erratic, destructive forms of collective behavior may seem to depart completely from conventional, institutionalized forms, but some measure of rationality is usually present in such mass episodes (Oberschall, 1973). Protests, demonstrations, riots, and even terrorism are usually directed at obtaining some political objective or group goal. As in all real-life settings, civil disturbances are affected by learning mechanisms, leader-follower relations, and emotional involvements. The urban riots of the 1960s were not merely irrational outbreaks against authority or even mass protests against the overcrowding that resulted from widespread migration of rural blacks into the cities, though this is often cited as a cause. Instead they were desperate attempts at political decision making, since blacks and others perceived the usual channels of communication and protest as being closed to them. Indeed, the burning of slums may be an effective way of communicating demands for better housing. (The black ghetto riots are considered further in the section on the civil rights movement in Chapter 17.)

Both professional and lay interpretations of the crowd have portrayed riots as emerging from the dregs of society. According to a study of French and English rebellions in the 18th and 19th centuries, however, it was the middle-class shopkeepers, artisans, and the like who originally attacked the status quo (Rude, 1964). The militant campus uprisings of the 1960s took place first at the more affluent colleges and universities, not the poorest. A profile of the urban rioters in Watts also demolishes the "riffraff" theory (D. O. Sears, 1969). Of the 15 percent of the area's residents who were directly involved and another 30 percent who were "close spectators," most were young males from a wide variety of backgrounds. The Detroit rioters had a similar profile; they were comparatively better educated, although, like most ghetto residents, they had not completed high school (U.S. Riot Commission, 1968).

The locale of mass protest in the United States has shifted toward institutional settings as organizational strains have developed between leaders and followers or public servants and citizens. In the late 1960s, for example, large universities like Berkeley and Columbia were charged with defeating their main purposes by fostering research more than teaching, accepting military contracts, and ignoring community needs (Denzin, 1968). When the students became alienated their frustrations were evidenced in acts of aggression such as seizing control of campus buildings, smashing windows, and defying authorities. Decisions by the administration to call in the police only served to splinter the university community further. Decision making by faculty and students got out of hand as it was caught in the entanglement of rioting, conflicting ideologies, and the organizational framework (Cantor, 1969).

Similarly, prison riots have broken out due to numerous causes such as inequities in the criminal justice system, overcrowding, and the failure of corrections authorities to open up communication channels, consider individual differences in prisoners, establish some system of self-government, or impose punishments fairly. Protests are launched against established government agencies by welfare rights activists, school board watchdogs, foes of public housing, and conservative groups who want a say in what types of literature are available in public libraries. In one way or another they all disturb the peace, whether by nonviolent means such as obstructing access to an agency's office or provocative actions such as throwing rocks or toppling fences. In larger institutional settings, new norms have been emerging among formerly disciplined public servants, as police officers and fire fighters have organized and labor strikes against airlines, the post office, and school systems have become acceptable. It is questionable whether the traditional analyses of crowd behavior are relevant in these organizational situations.

Protests, demonstrations, riots, and other more or less violent collective actions have become means of expressing disapproval or outrage about conditions which certain segments of society consider unacceptable. Those who seek to change the status quo are usually more active, but Establishment supporters also recognize the effectiveness of demonstrations such as book burnings in manipulating public opinion, especially when arrangements can be made to have the event covered by the media. The current view of the crowd has moved a long way from LeBon, whom Robert Merton (1960), a more contemporary social critic, considers to be "an apprehensive conservative, worried by the growth of the proletariat with its socialist orientation."

Terrorism: A Marginal Form of Collective Behavior

Terrorism, which can be defined as the use of violent tactics to produce a given end for a group of people, usually for a political goal (E. Evans, 1979), is a recurring phenomenon in the 1980s, but it is not a new one. The attacks in the United States during the 1830s on Catholic immigrants or the assassination of an Austrian archduke in 1914 which led to World War I are two very different examples of terrorism. Variations have abounded since the late 1960s in many parts of the world as grievances against the status quo and the struggle for national liberation have encouraged ingenious methods of violence. The constant presence of the mass media, particularly television, has increased the effectiveness of terrorism by providing the necessary publicity.

Four types of terrorism have been identified by Russell, Banker, and Miller (1979). One type emerges from nationalist or ethnic *separatist* groups like the Irish Republican Army or the Palestine Liberation Organization, whose ultimate goal is to create an autonomous state. Often these groups are headed by politically motivated persons who could emerge as national leaders, as the Ayatollah Khomeini did in Iran.

Another type of terrorism is represented by *ideological* movements—Marxist, Maoist, and anarchist, among others—which are committed to creating a new order. The neofascist organizations in Italy or the Weathermen in the United States of the Vietnam period are examples. Although primarily directed by middle-class intellectual leaders, these groups may use criminal elements in carrying out their tactics.

A third type is comprised of *nihilist* groups with less clear-cut goals, whose usual aim is to destroy a society. The Baader-Meinhof gang in Western Germany, the Red Brigade in Italy, or the Symbionese Liberation Army of the 1960s in the United States are examples. These organizations usually begin with specific ideological goals, but in the end the pattern of violence becomes simply destructive. They are very different in origin and character from the other types, but their nihilism can be demonstrated in outbreaks such as the urban ghetto riots during the 1960s, when the slogan "Burn, baby, burn!" inspired the destruction of entire neighborhoods (see Chapter 17).

In contrast to these highly organized forms of terrorism is the fourth type, the more spontaneous and *sporadic* kinds of terrorism such as airplane hijacking, kidnapping, or the taking of hostages. A sensational instance was the overpowering and detaining of U.S. embassy personnel in Tehran by militant Iranian students in 1979. Since this act primarily involved only indirect violence, it was not terrorism in the usual sense but more an expression of collective indignation at the traditional U.S. support of the Shah and a desire for some sort of revenge. The violation of established rights of protection for diplomatic representatives and the long-term deprivation of freedom suffered by the hostages put it in the category of terrorism, nevertheless.

Because most terrorism is sustained by tightly organized and often secret groups, the label of *collective behavior* may seem to be inappropriate. At times terrorism has the properties of a craze, however, and the size of some terrorist organizations and the diffusion of techniques across national boundaries are similar to certain aspects of mass behavior. Moreover, the ability of terrorism to inspire a public reaction, as in the solidarity emerging in the United States during the 14 months of the hostage situation in Iran, offers a dramatic example of collective behavior.

The motives or underlying causes for terrorism are inevitably complex. Since terrorist activity is frequently the outlet for the pent-up feelings of an exploited population, the frustration-aggression hypothesis is relevant. Of course, the question remains as to why some groups turn to this solution to alter what they perceive as an unacceptable situation, whereas others do not.

Outbreaks of violence are often precipitated by a given event, such as the entry of the Shah into the United States for medical treatment which apparently triggered the taking of the hostages in Iran, but the basic cause was 20 years of oppression by an autocratic state, coupled with the religious and ideological intensity of certain sectors in Iran.

The inability of Third World masses to achieve their ends is a critical factor in the resort to violence. More precisely, when capabilities and success in meeting goals fail to keep pace with rising expectations, a violent outlet for the resulting frustration is likely. Terrorism also represents a bargaining situation in which costs and risks must be measured according to anticipated benefits, as in the exchange theory described in Chapter 13. However differently expressed, terrorism provides a way for the disadvantaged to further their goals by obtaining publicity, polarizing society, disrupting international agreements or alliances, or simply harassing public authorities.

SUMMARY

Collective behavior refers to standardized or similar patterns of social behavior that are transitory in nature and usually result from suggestion. Crowds exemplify collective behavior in face-to-face situations; they are marked by localized attention, increased interstimulation, and individual identification with group norms and purposes. Interpretation of such behavior requires data as to how the members perceive the situation, their personality structures, and the interactional processes occurring within the group. There has been significant research in recent years on the structure of crowds, including boundaries as well as size and density.

Rumors are a form of unfounded communication which facilitates other types of collective behavior. They thrive where motivations and emotions are strong and facts are scarce. Study of the course of rumors reveals certain processes that direct and alter their content, notably leveling, sharpening, and assimilation. Panics are collective responses that express demoralization. Often the major determinant is not real danger but people's fears and emotional instabilities that lead them to misinterpret an event or a reported event and to communicate their "hysterical" reactions to others.

Some types of collective behavior occur outside rather than within face-to-face groups. Fashion, for example, is a sanctioned type of cyclical change found in certain areas of social behavior, such as those involving dress and design. People who follow the dictates of fashion seem to do so because of prestige and conformity motives. Fads resemble short-term fashions and may be of the cultist or spasmodic types. Though impossible to predict and difficult to interpret, a successful fad is characterized by novelty, consistency with the times, and harmony with widespread interests and needs. What starts as a fad sometimes endures as a fashion or custom. Crazes and booms are like intense fads, widely disseminated through rumor and publicity. The boom usually is stimulated by a get-rich-quick scheme.

It is a logical step from collective behavior to social change, the topic of the next chapter. Protests, riots, demonstrations, and other forms of collective behavior such as terrorism are often directed toward achieving these goals. The two topics are brought together in social movements, which are considered in the second part of the chapter.

WORDS TO REMEMBER

Collective behavior. Relatively spontaneous, unstructured, or erratic behavior, often induced by *interstimulation* or responses among participants, as opposed to more orderly institutional behavior. Examples are fads, rumor, and panic.

Contagion. Tendency within a crowd for feelings, attitudes, and actions to be rapidly and uncritically communicated. R. H. Turner calls this the *contagion theory* of crowd behavior. He also describes *convergence theory,* which maintains that crowds are made up of divergent persons who nonetheless have a shared predisposition, and *emergent-norm theory,* which emphasizes a focus that emerges within the crowd as passers-by are attracted to it and come to share its norms and attitudes.

Crowd. A temporary grouping or assemblage of persons, with fairly strong interstimulation. Crowds can be classified into various types, such as casual, acting, aggressive, escapist, or expressive.

Crowd mind. The collective consciousness of a crowd, as uniquely different from that of the individuals who compose it. This theory emphasizes the irrational and emotional components of crowd behavior. The term is basically equivalent to the *group mind* idea, which proposes that the mentality emerging from a group or collectivity exists beyond the individual nervous systems that compose the group. The theory is now discredited.

Deindividuation. A kind of anonymity caused by abnormal environmental conditions; self-consciousness is restricted, and the individual becomes submerged in the group or collectivity.

Fad. A type of collective behavior less patterned than *fashion* but not as erratic or emotionally driven as a *craze.*

Leveling. The tendency of rumor formation to create brevity by reducing detail, according to G. W. Allport and L. J. Postman. Other processes include *sharpening,* or focusing on a given theme, and *assimilation,* or blending the rumor into the value system of the individual or the society.

Mass behavior. Term roughly equivalent to collective behavior.

Mob. An unruly collectivity marked by milling and, usually, aggressive behavior.

Mobilization. In N. J. Smelser's theory, mobilization accounts for rumor, crazes, and other forms of collective behavior because of several factors, such as *structural conduciveness* (cultural features of a given society at a given time) and *strain* (the ambiguities and conflicts in the social order).

Panic. A type of withdrawal, often a collective, maladaptive response to fear or anxiety.

Rumor. Unverified report, usually circulated by word of mouth.

QUESTIONS FOR DISCUSSION

1. In what societal conditions does collective behavior develop?

2. In what respects can the Watergate episode be regarded as a type of collective behavior? What psychological mechanisms were involved in the public response to the war in Vietnam? Which ones were involved in the hostage situation in Iran and the official and public responses to it?

3. How does Smelser define the factors underlying collective behavior? To what extent is his theory a satisfactory one?

4. What types of collective behavior seem most relevant to episodes of mass behavior over the last 20 years?

5. How can crowds be structured spatially?

6. How have psychological explanations of crowd behavior changed since LeBon? What theories of social influence and group behavior can be applied in analyzing collective behavior?

7. What are the variables underlying rumor formation? How has rumor functioned in race riots?

8. State the meaning of the panic syndrome and describe how it might operate in a massive earthquake or an accident in a nuclear power plant.

9. What motives are involved in following the dictates of fashion?

10. How would you distinguish between a fad and a craze? Give some recent examples of these two kinds of collective behavior.

11. Describe the psychology underlying a boom.

12. Why was Orson Welles's imaginary invasion from Mars effective when it was broadcast?

READINGS

Brown, R. *Social Psychology*. New York: Free Press, 1965.
    Chapter 14 is an ingenious discussion of the subject, including Brown's theory of the payoff as a determinant of given forms of collective behavior.

Canetti, E. *Crowds and Power* (C. Stewart, trans.). New York: Viking Press, 1963.
    An analytic and historical approach to crowds and their manipulation.

Cantril, H. *The Psychology of Social Movements*. New York: John Wiley & Sons, 1941.

This classic work is especially valuable for its interpretation of lynching.

Festinger, L., Riecken, H. W., and Schachter, S. *When Prophecy Fails*. Minneapolis: University of Minnesota Press, 1956.

An investigation of several hypotheses regarding belief and rumor in a marginal religious cult whose leaders predicted a world disaster, yet salvation for the members.

Genevie, L. E. (Ed.). *Collective Behavior and Social Movements*. Itasca, Ill.: F. E. Peacock, Publishers, 1978.

A storehouse of historical, theoretical, and empirical studies.

Graham, H. D., and Gurr, T. R. (Eds). *Violence in America*. New York: New American Library, 1969.

Historical and cross-disciplinary analyses to the conflict and disorders as assembled for the National Commission on the Causes and Prevention of Violence.

Hoerder, D. *Crowd Action in Revolutionary Massachusetts, 1765–1780*. New York: Academic Press, 1977.

The introduction sets the tone for this scholarly work on collective behavior in changing colonial society.

Roloff, M. E. and Miller G. R. *Persuasion: New Directions in Theory and Research*. Beverly Hills, Calif.: Sage Publications, 1980.

Although oriented to the focus of Chapter 9, the analyses, which range from altered physiological states to political campaigns, are also relevant to collective behavior.

Rosnow, R. L., and Fine, G. A. *Rumor and Gossip: The Social Psychology of Hearsay*. New York: Elsevier, 1976.

An absorbing account of rumor formation with many examples offered from contemporary society.

Smelser, N. J. *Theory of Collective Behavior*. New York: Free Press, 1963.

A richly documented and impressive theorization of mass behavior. Chapters 6–8 provide absorbing reading.

Tilly, C. *From Mobilization to Revolution*. Reading, Mass.: Addison-Wesley Publishing Co., 1978.

A scholarly, theoretical analysis based on the problem of power mobilization and violence and their role in rebellion and social movements.

Turner, R. H., and Killian, L. M. *Collective Behavior*. Rev. ed. Englewood Cliffs, N.J., Prentice-Hall, 1972.

A comprehensive collection of materials specially relevant to crowds is given in Parts 1 and 2.

Wright, S. *Crowds and Riots: A Study in Social Organization*. Beverly Hills, Calif.: Sage Publications, 1978.

An examination of the form and function of the crowd, with reference to the role of group processes.

SOCIAL CHANGE AND SOCIAL MOVEMENTS

A principal focus of this text is how the data accumulated in research in social psychology can be applied to bring about change in human relationships. The study of perception, motivation, socialization, attitude formation, interpersonal attraction, and group influence is all to some extent oriented to the idea of solving social problems through changing people's attitudes and behaviors. The findings on cultural and social influences on personality, for example, have significance for parents, teachers, legislators, and administrators of schools and institutions, among others. Data on the effects of frustration on social behavior have serious implications for intergroup relations on local, national, and international levels.

This chapter turns specifically to applications as it considers the problems of social change, of how individuals and groups can be changed with the ultimate aim of improving the mental health and lifestyles of individuals, planned organizational interventions, and ethnic and international relations. At the outset we must note certain grave difficulties in making practical applications of the techniques and findings of social psychology. The field overlaps both psychology and all the various social sciences. It is tremendously complex; it involves all the variables the psychologist and psychiatrist must contend with, plus those that concern the anthropologist, sociologist, and political scientist. Social psychologists have often hesitated to offer their services in a problem-solving capacity because their research efforts do not always yield reliable results which can be predictably extended to the real world. Behavioral scientists also typically suffer from the cautiousness and timidity that characterize most academics.

The popularity of certain social scientists as television talk-show guests should provide them all with a greater sense of security and self-assurance. Even more reason is evidence of the widespread public interest in the concepts of social psychology as an aid to understanding events and personalities. *Time* magazine, for example, frequently includes a section titled "Behavior" with such stories as the "sad, baffling dependence" of mirror-image 37-year-old twins who speak and act in unison, responding to identical stimuli in identical ways (April 6, 1981). Many news stories in this and other publications take a social-psychological slant when the coverage of events includes attempts to explain them, as *Time* did in an April 13, 1981, feature on "Those Dangerous Loners" who become assassins. This story went back to John Wilkes Booth, who two years before he shot Abraham Lincoln declared it would be "a glorious opportunity for a man to immortalize himself."

The social psychologist is concerned with broad areas of human relationship which are riddled with tradition. Many vested interests operate to oppose new ideas, and the very persons who stand to benefit most from a proposed social change are often those who oppose it most vigorously. Thus the social psychologist has the added task of studying ways and means of convincing people that proposals based on principles of the discipline are desirable and feasible.

This chapter begins by considering how various behavioral scientists approach the concept of social change. Then the discussion turns to the relation of individuals and groups to change processes, with emphasis on attitudes, planned interventions, and group dynamics. The next part of the chapter is concerned with the characteristics, development, and organization and mobilization of social movements. A final section presents the civil rights movement as a case study of this type of social change.

THE SOCIAL SCIENTIST'S APPROACH TO CHANGE

Perhaps the most striking process in our contemporary culture is *change.* Every cultural pattern is continually being altered, and this, in turn, molds the personalities of those in it. In contrast to the world of material objects and technology, the world of values, attitudes, ideas, and behavior is essentially conservative. Nevertheless, there are periods of crisis and revolution when change hurtles on in almost uncontrolled fashion, to shape both ideas and overt behavior. Alvin Toffler based his answer to future shock, *The Third Wave* (1980), on a *revolutionary premise:* The upheavals of today are not chaotic or random but form a clearly discernible revolutionary pattern. The rapid changes taking place are cumulative, adding up to a major transformation in lifestyles and leading to a sane, desirable future in which the individual's intellect, imagination, and will are liberated.

It is the job of social scientists—particularly anthropologists, sociologists, and social psychologists—to interpret the phenomena of social change (see Box 17–1). They are concerned with the nature, causes, processes, and effects of changing social behavior, more or less apart from the individuals concerned. Their work is at a different level from that of psychologists, since their major unit is the

Box 17–1

BEHAVIORAL SCIENTISTS ORGANIZED FOR SOCIAL CHANGE

The Society for Psychological Study of Social Issues, which soon came to be known as SPSSI, was founded in 1936 on the thesis that every social problem (war, economic depression, crime, racial prejudice, labor conflict) has its roots in the mental processes of human beings, and social reformers should be aware of the need for scientific investigation of social issues. SPSSI's objectives, as stated in 1964, are:

> . . . to seek to obtain and disseminate to the public scientific knowledge regarding social change and other social processes by promoting and encouraging psychological research on significant theoretical and practical questions of social life and by promoting and encouraging the application of the findings of such psychological research to the problems of society.*

The Journal of Social Issues, founded in 1945, has published articles or whole issues on topics such as human behavior in disaster, anti-intellectualism in the United States, brainwashing, desegregation in the North and the South, impacts of studying abroad, new light on delinquency, the sexual renaissance in America, misperception and the Vietnam War, student activism, ghetto riots, new perspectives on women, environmental stress, and many more.

Encouraged by the contributions of SPSSI and aided by some of its members, a group of sociologists formed the Society for Study of Social Problems in 1951. Its aim is to promote research and teaching on significant problems of social life and to foster cooperation among persons and organizations applying scientific findings to the formulation of social policies.

These two organizations have done much to focus the interests of social and behavioral scientists in the areas of intergroup relations, social change, mental health, community problems, international relations, and human relations in general. They serve as a kind of gadfly or stimulant within the larger body of psychologists and sociologists to keep them interested in and focusing on major social issues and problems.

---

*The Society for Psychological Study of Social Issues, *Handbook for Officers and Committees* (Ann Arbor, Mich., 1964), p. 1.

group rather than the individual. Social psychologists, as we have noted, deal primarily with individuals in their social relationships.

The utility of the social-psychological approach depends in large part on how social change is conceptualized. This approach can contribute little to our understanding of the rise and fall of civilizations; on so broad a canvas, economic, geographical, political, and assorted historical determinants bulk as large as the psychological ones do. Social scientists, however, interpret social change as an altering of social relationships *within* a more or less clearly defined culture group. They are concerned with describing the social processes and influences producing social change; the social psychologist's interpretation, which is based primarily on the analysis of attitudes, draws on theirs and in turn supplements it, as we will demonstrate.

The lines of inquiry into social change have been defined by Allen (1971, pp. 44–46) in terms of two factors:

1. *Where and when?* The investigator must locate the specific arena of change—a geographic domain or an institution, the Tennessee Valley or a local high-school district. No less important is setting limits in space and time: where and when is the change occurring?

2. *What has changed?* The unit of change can be a material object, a value or attitude, a group or an organization. The unit may be small or great. The question may be whether automobile design is shifting to simpler lines, or whether the United States is moving toward a more equalitarian and democratic social environment. Will the nation return to a quasi-Victorian normative structure or continue to increase the frontiers of personal freedom?

Other approaches consider the effects of change on the social structure, at what levels social change can be conceptualized, and how change relates to stability.

Types of Change

A fundamental distinction can be made between planned and unplanned change (Bennis, 1961). Planned change implies mutual goal setting by groups and organizations which have the power to implement their goals. This was defined as the distinguishing mark of a social organization in Chapter 12, and the leader's role in achieving these goals was identified in Chapter 15. Undoubtedly most transformations in society, whether technological, ideational, or social, belong in this area of change. Planned change can be arrived at by democratic, or interactional, arrangements, as when individuals or groups work together in fairly spontaneous relationships, or it can be bureaucratic or rational in character. Social movements vary in the degree to which they represent relatively undisciplined aspects of collective behavior or are highly bureaucratic or organizational. Planned change also runs the gamut from being essentially democratic to totally autocratic, but a democratic society sometimes uses authoritarian means in demanding changes of individuals or groups, just as change occasionally can be on a reciprocal or nonauthoritarian basis in a totalitarian society.

One type of relatively unplanned change is directed primarily at socialization. Change can be effected, for example, through the parental relationship with the child; in this case, socialization is an almost individual affair. There is also the group-centered change found in the classroom. Like parents, educators are

The island of Sark in the English Channel represents an oasis of relative stability in a world of change. A fiefdom since the Middle Ages, it permits no auto traffic. Besides the reigning family, all the people are farmers or shopkeepers. *Source:* British Tourist Authority.

primarily concerned with socialization as a means of continuing the status quo, but they may wittingly or unwittingly bring about alterations in accepted norms or beliefs. In certain instances, socialization is directed toward change in a totally coercive way, as in the indoctrination process, brainwashing.

Another type of unplanned change is based on accidents of climate, a chance discovery, or other fortuitous events. This variety of change is beyond the control of individuals or societies. Earthquakes and illnesses fall into this classification; and for some participants war is an accident of fate. More and more, modern technology, in the natural or behavioral sciences as well as in engineering, is being committed to the task of bringing under control nearly all the phenomena that affect human beings.

Social change can also be considered in terms of a series of societal revolutions. The Neolithic and city-living revolutions took place well before the Christian era. After the Dark Ages there were the commercial revolution in banking and marketing, the communications revolution in printing, and the scientific revolution of Copernicus, Galileo, and Newton, which continued into the 19th and 20th centuries with Darwin, Freud, Einstein, and Keynes. Related developments were the industrial and democratic revolutions, the latter culminating in the liberation of former colonies in the 40s and 50s, a process which is still continuing. After World War II came the cybercultural revolution, symbolized by the social consequences of computerization. A recent possibility is an environmental revolution (Wolf, 1976). The social-psychological underpinnings of this movement are examined in Chapter 19.

Values in Stability and Change

The pattern of stability and change in a society is ultimately decided by groups of individuals or organizations. Usually change is propelled by elites (like the elite leaders described in Chapter 15), who in turn mobilize groups. First there must be an awareness of the need for change, and then development of a capability for mobilizing the media of change follows (Etzioni, 1968). Institutional opposition can be fatal, or a conflict may continue for decades—as was true in the battles of the American labor movement or the Anti-Saloon League. The American women's rights movement began in the 1840s, met some success nearly 80 years later with passage of the 19th amendment, which permitted women to vote, and was renewed in the 1960s as an effort to assure equal civil rights on a constitutional basis.

Social movements can be analyzed in the context of norms, values, and power. Fundamentally, social change proceeds as a conflict in values. As R. M. Williams(1971) points out, "values are constituents of dynamic systems because of their interconnectedness, their informational or directive effects and their capacity as carriers of psychological energy" (p. 129). These changes can be social, psychological, moral, or aesthetic, and they can represent either an inherent or an instrumental goal. Potentially, changes in values may involve the entire society. As different institutions compete in their goals and the means to reach them, both the elites and the public are the arbiters of how certain goals and values are to be integrated. Generally values change more slowly than norms or the institutions themselves. There is evidence that the values maintaining the direction of specific institutions tend to change only after the structure or the function of institutions has been altered.

In broad terms, the most salient values in our society relate to the concepts of freedom and equality, particularly as defined in the costs-and-rewards framework of exchange theory (see Chapter 13). These values also serve to promote a social system that is flexible in its provisions for reducing tensions. Western society is primarily committed to adjustability rather than rigidity, although the precise balance between stability and change varies.

TECHNOLOGICAL AND SOCIOCULTURAL FORCES AFFECTING CHANGE

Cultural changes are brought about by innovations, which may be either accidental or purposeful discoveries and inventions, or external forces in the environment. The number of discoveries and inventions occurring in any one culture is relatively small, however, and the comparatively rapid growth of human culture has depended on borrowing or diffusion.

This process involves a number of concepts. *Diffusion* refers to the transmission of traits from one culture to another. *Acculturation,* or borrowing (as defined in Chapter 2), refers to the modification of one culture by another through extensive contact. *Assimilation* suggests a more complete blending, as exemplified by immigrants who have resided long enough in a new land to learn its language and customs and to become integrated into the culture through intermarriage and economic participation. Acculturation and assimilation are two-way changes, while diffusion is fundamentally a one-way process. North American Indian tribes have taken over many Western ways, and they have given European-based cultures in North America place names, foods, pottery, and art forms. Likewise, assimilated immigrants have made linguistic, economic, artistic, and philosophical contributions to North American culture.

One of the most significant studies of change within a given society is Margaret Mead's (1956) report of her return visit in 1953 to the Manus, a tribe she had first studied in 1928. During her absence a number of innovations had occurred: the coming of missionaries with a humanitarian message; a particularly effective local leader, Paliau; the Australian program of self-government; and the presence of American and other service personnel during World War II. Originally a harsh, rigid, suspicious group, the Manus had become an optimistic, cooperative, friendly society. Mead suggested, therefore, that rapid total change may be preferable to a piecemeal transformation. Cultural discontinuities and maladjustments are less when the total structure is altered, rather than allowing reminders of the past to continue to forestall adjustments to new ideas.

The Role of Technology

Many behavioral scientists have identified the technology of a society as the greatest agent of social change. The material substructure provides the base on which a culture stands and can function. This is borne out in studies like the factor analysis by Heise, Lenski, and Wardwell (1976) which found links between technological factors such as animal husbandry, plant cultivation, and metallurgy on the one hand and institutional patterns like kinship and the marriage system on the other in a number of primitive societies. Innovations like the discovery of fire, the invention of the wheel, the introduction of agriculture, and the domestication of animals in effect constituted a cultural revolution that made possible the advanced societies of the ancient Near East. With some fluctuations, there has been progressive elaboration of the technology ever since.

Modern society has been especially identified with technological advances. Because of the rapid rate of change and invention, many ideological movements have been oriented to issues involving technology: damage to the physical environment, alienation and dehumanization of people by computers and other machines, and the dangers of nuclear fission, for example. The possibility of technological breakthroughs in many areas of life must always be taken into account (see Figure 17–1).

All societies are based on technology, which enters into such fundamental practical activities as producing food or building a house. Technology can be defined as "the complex of knowledge, methods and other resources used in making a particular kind of product or in creating a particular procedural system" (Hannay & McGinn, 1980).

The role of technology is forcibly presented in the acculturation problems of preliterate cultures. Sherif and Sherif (1956) studied some of the effects of international contacts and modern technology on isolated Turkish villages and found that the concepts of time, space, and distance had been Westernized to the extent that industrialization had occurred. The unit of measurement for distance depended upon the degree to which an individual used a vehicle or walked. For example, 50 kilometers might be expressed as: "You start early in the morning and reach there by sunset," or "You reach there (by the time) you work on crops of one dönüm (of land)." The more a village had changed the more possible was future change; that is, change was positively accelerated.

Another social scientist (Theodorson, 1953) questioned whether any so-called simple society can accept the machines of Western culture and reject its basic social behavior. Industrialization means that the individual's waking hours must predominantly be oriented to a factory system, with a consequent loss of time for the family and the village. Skills and achievement become more important than personal gratification or the retention of kinship ties. The best workers are chosen by industrialists, and they must produce under given conditions and at a specified place and time.

Modernization in Developing Areas

As developing nations have entered the industrial age, the history of modernization in the Third World has provided an interesting example of how the

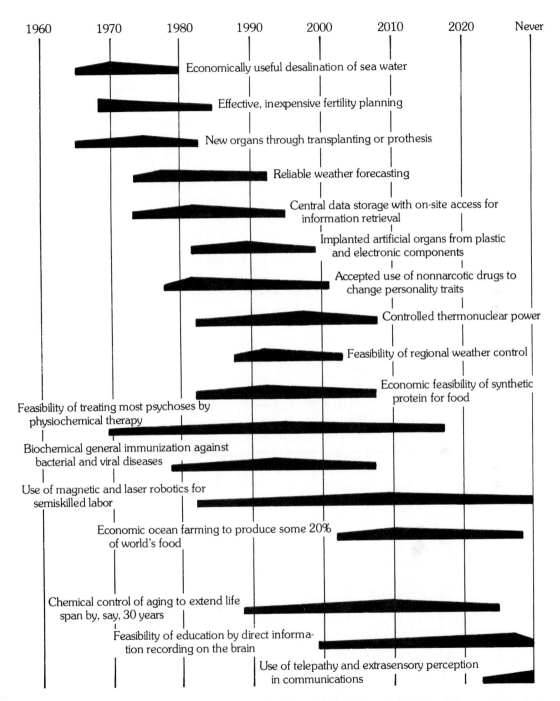

Figure 17-1. Conjectural Periods of Adoption of Inventions and Discoveries (High points on bars show the date suggested by most scientists when developments will take place, as corrected for more recent developments.)

Source: Adapted from O. Helmer, "Science," *Science Journal,* October 1967, p. 51.

processes of acculturation, assimilation, and diffusion operate. Whole continents are gradually emerging from feudalism, colonialism, and illiteracy, and over a billion people in parts of Latin America, Africa, the Middle East, and Southeast Asia now stand on the threshold of complete industrialization and urbanization. As they acquire a cash economy, educational skills, an urban lifestyle, and a means of democratic participation, the question is how the process of development can be accelerated without disturbing individual prerogatives or cultural integrity. Too often, change is promoted at the expense of those who carry on traditional practices—a craft, a language, a religious belief, or some expression of individualism.

The transfer of technology to the Third World has had both social and economic effects on the societies involved (Norman, 1981). In Brazil, for example, the economic growth has benefited only the upper 20 percent of the population. This results in not only social inequities but dwindling fuel reserves and potential disturbances of the ecology.

Modernization involves a shift from dependency on natural resources and traditional behavior patterns associated with a rural social order to industrial production for a world market, which calls for new standards of literacy, technical skills, incentives, and entrepreneurship. The transition from primary- to secondary-group relations (see Chapter 12), from a sacred to a secular society, and from particularistic to universalistic norms—all these are part of modernization.

Social-psychological factors are also relevant. Motivation, for example, which was examined in Chapter 7, is central to an understanding of any change in behavior. McClelland (1961) traced the need for achievement as a motive for economic development in both advanced and developing societies and found a relationship to various cultural supports, as well as to the family role structure (see Chapter 3), particularly the mother-son relationship. Achievement is related to several personality variables (see Chapter 4) and may have remarkably different outcomes for various individuals and subcultures.

Expanding on the psychological approach to change, Hagen (1962) suggested that personality change is necessary to development. He characterizes traditional and contemporary society in terms of the authoritarian and innovational personality variables, respectively. A change is made when a person in the traditional society loses faith in the status quo and develops a preference for an out-group or newly emerging order. The loss of esteem for the older social structure as a source of approval, which is described as "withdrawal of status respect," can lead to innovation, a revolutionary ideology, or some other critical approach.

Both McClelland and Hagen have tested their theories cross-culturally. Although the data in their studies are largely suggestive, the concepts have become springboards for other inquiries into the social psychology of social and economic development.

Other researchers have found that social change in developing areas rests on both the behavior of elites and the attitudes of the population as a whole. In interviews with urban samples in several countries (Colombia, Germany, Japan,

Spain and the United States), Williamson (1970) found that modernism is related to social and community participation, middle-class (rather than lower-class) belongingness, a sense of mobility, and future rather than past orientation. Most related to modernism in the attitudinal scale were: (1) low familism or kinship orientation, (2) cognitive flexibility, or an open versus a closed mind, (3) a minimal sense of hierarchy, or subordination to others, (4) acceptance of urban rather than rural norms, and (5) dissatisfaction with the status quo. Even more telling is the finding of Inkeles and Smith (1974) in six developing nations (Argentina, Chile, India, Israel, Nigeria, and East Pakistan) that education is the most powerful weapon in modernizing attitudes. Employment in a large-scale organization like a factory is almost equally strong.

Social psychologists also have been able to trace the direction of social change in developing areas. The process of change is affected by patterns of cooperation and competition, the individuals' relation to membership and reference groups (see Chapter 12), and the way the threat of change is handled (Macklin, 1969). A means must be found for directing individuals' motivations toward new norms and redefined institutional roles, including an attitude of public responsibility. At the same time, it is important to integrate modernism within the existing culture to minimize alienation, anxiety, and violence.

Patterns of Social Change

Studies of patterns of social change, or the complex dynamics of change over time, can provide answers to questions about universal trends, the effects of interrelated institutions, and the rate of change. Sociologists attempt to approach such problems statistically, using quantitative techniques like the sigmoid or *S-shaped curve,* which applies to social inventions that imitate the product life cycle of technological or commercial innovations. There is first a gradual public acceptance, then a rapid rise in adoptions until the maximum is reached, followed by a tapering off and sometimes death. This pattern holds true in such diverse areas as motor vehicle registrations and life expectancy tables. It has also been demonstrated in social-psychological research into such questions as the diffusion of messages in a limited period. Various other techniques for determining changes in attitudes, for example, were described in Chapter 9.

J. W. Berry's (1980) model of the sequence of sociocultural change, showing the relation of external and internal behavioral and cultural antecedents and consequences, is shown in Figure 17–2. For both society and the individual, there is a two-way flow between culture and behavior, a concept established in Chapter 2. Because many innovations are dysfunctional or disorganizing, there is also an almost constant two-way flow between the old and the new, so that both people's behavior and the culture undergo periodic revision. A perfect equilibrium between the traditional and innovative forces in a culture is seldom reached.

Equilibrium theory is one of two general theories which have been developed to interpret the relation of events to the underlying social system (B. Moore, 1955). In this theory, it is assumed that the inputs and outputs in a social system tend toward "a state of rest in which the conflicts and strains among the system's

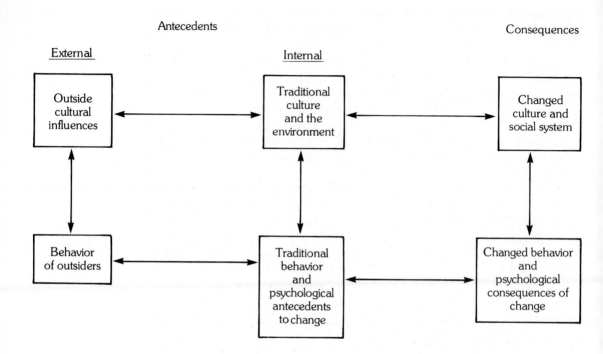

Antecedents ‎ Consequences

External ‎ Internal

Figure 17–2. Model of the Sequence of Sociocultural Change

Source: Adapted from J. W. Berry, "Social and Cultural Change," in Harry C. Triandis and Richard W. Brislin (Eds.), *Handbook of Cross-Cultural Psychology,* Vol. 5, *Social Psychology,* Boston: Allyn & Bacon, 1980, p. 216.

component parts are reduced to a minimum." The *process theory,* in contrast, emphasizes the evolutionary or cyclic trends in social systems. This is the theory of Pitirim Sorokin as well as Oswald Spengler and Arnold Toynbee, whose interest was in the philosophy of history and the rise and fall of civilizations. The two theories also can be combined, as in the optimality concept of the Italian economist and sociologist Vilfredo Pareto. Social dislocation or strain can lead to revolution when one or more parts of the cultural pattern are out of balance with the larger social order (see Parsons, 1951).

The equilibrium model is generally regarded as the appropriate one for understanding the functional interrelations of the social system and explaining social change, as somewhat similar to Heider's (1958) balance theory described in Chapter 13. W. E. Moore (1963) regards society as a *tension-management system,* a concept which recognizes that tensions are intrinsic within a society. Change itself is likely to be tension producing as well as tension reducing, since any social transformation, by its very nature, produces tensions. Yet in large part, successful change depends on the number of flexibilities present in the system.

The flexibility in the individual's response to role expectancies and relevant norms is shaped by groups and organizations, for example, as Chapter 14 demonstrated.

Forces of Change in Western Society

The great significance of technological developments in producing rapid social change in Western European and American societies was recognized many years ago by W. F. Ogburn (1922). The appearance of inventions and technological advances has accelerated during the past few hundred years, despite many obstacles erected as a result of fear, tradition, conservatism, or vested interests. The social effects of inventions like the automobile, radio, airplane, movies, TV, and the computer have been far-reaching. A number of social scientists have analyzed the intricate effects of specific inventions—the telephone, for example (de Sola Pool, 1977)—on modern society.

One problem in analyzing social change is to differentiate between innovations that merely impinge on the surface of a culture and those that affect the social structure. Developments like television or even popularization of paperback books have had an immense influence on the use of leisure time, the way we get information about the world, and the diffusion of ideas, but it is questionable that these changes have had the same kind of impact as, say, the invention of the computer. Beyond providing for the conquest of space or breakthroughs in medical technology such as artificial organs, the computer has produced a virtual social revolution. Its effects can be compared to the onset of industrialization nearly two centuries ago. In its simplest form it became available only in the 1950s, but its remarkable capacity for storing, compiling, and analyzing information has changed the scope of modern life (see Box 17–2). New generations of advanced computer design have given it a potential for control of the entire citizenry through such devices as a national data bank, which is particularly formidable when supplemented by electronic surveillance.

Social inventions also can have far-reaching effects on the social structure. An example is the U.S. social security system, which acknowledged the national obligation to care for the aged and the disabled, or at least to contribute to their care. The effects of this system are critical for the psychological well-being of millions of people.

Most discussions of social change fail to probe the effect of change on the social structure itself. Any number of changes affect our society, but the extent to which they restructure social values, goals, and relationships is a problem area for further research.

The Diffusion of Innovations

The norms of a society determine receptivity to innovation, and people's perceptual and attitudinal structures are highly significant in producing an awareness of the need for change. These concepts (which were introduced in Chapters 6, 7, and 9) help explain the rapid transformation of Japanese society after World War II. Not only were Japan's social institutions responsive to change,

Box 17–2
CYBERNETICS: COMMUNICATION AND CONTROL

Most computer applications to date have been in business and industry, where computerization serves three functions in the planning and automation of operations: (1) allocating resources and establishing priorities, (2) management control and implementation of policy, and (3) control over the assembly line.* The feedback process of the computer permits constant control of operations. And its automated memory has made it possible to shift the process to "feedforward," which provides a capability to anticipate problems and take corrective action.

Human events also can be treated in terms of behavioral systems based on the computer and other developments in communications engineering. A development of the 1950s, cybernetics, or the science of communication and control, has been studied in a number of group and organizational settings.† This technique is based on an analogy between the communication processes of humans and machines. It seeks to maintain an equilibrium in the behavioral system through adaptation achieved by the use of controlled feedback. As a controlling mechanism, it processes information by monitoring the results of its own actions with a *detector* subsystem and automatically changing its behavior with an *effector* subsystem in order to achieve a given task or goal.

In the cybernetics system, memory can be viewed as stored change accumulated from single inputs from related systems.‡ As a mechanism of social change cybernetics implies an equilibrium between the amounts of information load in the feedback channels and the lag in the reaction to such information. It is thus a problem-solving operation depending on a coordinated response to the information fed in. The most far-reaching effect of developments such as cybernetics in the computer revolution is automation. Communication, production, and distribution are among the phases of this mass operation. Although directed by engineers, the process of self-correction has reduced the role of the individual and the opportunity for creative rearrangement of the inputs and outputs.

---

*M. Greenberger, "The Computer in Organizations," in C. R. Walker (Ed.), *Technology, Industry and Man: The Age of Acceleration* (New York: McGraw-Hill Book Co., 1968, pp. 302–323.)

†Norbert Wiener, *Cybernetics* (Cambridge, Mass.: MIT Press, 1961).

‡R. A. Bauer, *Social Indicators* (Cambridge, Mass.: MIT Press, 1966).

but a specific program for change was supervised by the United States as an occupying power. Members of the U.S. armed forces also had close relations with the Japanese people, especially the women, which tended to bring the country's traditional norms into question.

Diffusion is primarily a form of communication which regulates the spread of "(1) the *innovation*, (2) which is *communicated* through certain channels (3) over *time* (4) among members of a *social system*" (Rogers & Shoemaker, 1971, p. 18). The description of the communication process in Chapter 10 showed how a message is sent via a specified medium to a receiver, who will be inclined to accept or reject it in accordance with her or his personality structure. An immunologist may meet with negative reactions in introducing a new vaccine, for example, although the resistance encountered would be paltry compared to that experienced by William Jenner in the 19th century when he tried to get people to accept the idea of being vaccinated with a small dose of cowpox in order to be immunized against smallpox. The acceptance of innovations in ideas and values is even more problematic. Several years ago when the Foundation for the Study of Democratic Institutions offered a revised Constitution of the United States, it was received with reactions ranging from skepticism to outright hostility. The barriers to new ideology can be almost insurmountable.

Within social systems the decisions to accept or reject changes are made by individuals or groups of individuals, as the next section will make clear. Rogers and Shoemaker (1971, p. 36) classified decisions about innovations according to four types:

1. *Optional*—the person is free to accept an innovation whatever the attitudes of others. A housewife can decide to use the birth-control pill, or a high-school teacher may be able to integrate rock music into the curriculum.
2. *Collective*—the community arrives at consensus. If a community fluoridates the drinking water, the individual has to go along.
3. *Authority*—an administrator or public official decrees a policy about a production process, rubbish collection, or dress code, for example. Individuals may object, but at the cost of some inconvenience or social criticism.
4. *Contingent*—the individual's decision depends on the setting or the facilities. A medical attendant can inject a patient with a drug only if the hospital has it available.

Genuine rather than perfunctory acceptance of an innovation is related to the individual's ego involvement in its consequences. Often a change comes before those concerned are psychologically or intellectually prepared for the event, as when a democratic system of government was forced on the German people following World War I, or complete autonomy was given to students in a few liberal colleges at the beginning of the 1970s.

The diffusion of innovations which represent a change in values is subject to severe risk. Unless the opinion leaders have an intimate relationship with the public, their campaigns for adoption are likely to meet with limited success. Decision making in this respect is slow, and a rapid rate of adoption can occur only in a controlled society or where power is concentrated in relatively few hands.

Certain factors predispose individuals or groups to accept or reject change (E.

M. Rogers, 1962), whether the innovation is hybridization methods for farmers, medical advances for physicians, or new reading techniques for school teachers and administrators. The difference is largely due to the stage of innovation—awareness, trial or evaluation, and adoption—at which the change will be accepted.

First there is a distinction between *cosmopolites,* who are important at the awareness stage, and *localites,* who become more important in the evaluation and adoption phases. Another factor is the time element: The awareness-to-trial period is generally longer than the trial-to-adoption period, which in part accounts for the sigmoid or S-shaped curve found in many instances of social change, as noted above. Timing considerations are important in the shape of the curve: The awareness-to-trial period is shorter for relatively earlier adopters than for later adopters, whereas the trial-to-adoption period is longer for earlier than for later adopters. All of these factors are influenced by the extent to which the innovation is perceived to be in congruence or harmony with the existing culture and social system. The communicability of the innovation also determines its diffusion.

There is also an important difference between early and late adopters. Early adopters are younger, have higher social status, and enjoy more opinion leadership. Innovators are usually perceived as deviants, both by themselves and society, and are more likely to be influenced by impersonal sources, whereas later adopters depend primarily on personal sources. These generalizations vary, of course, for the area of innovation. Nevertheless, it can be expected that the wealthier and more mobile farmer, the doctor who attends the most professional meetings, or the school system that has the highest budget per student will be most open to change.

Cultural diffusion and social change thus have mixed effects, and many developments can counteract or at least modify their undeniable benefits. Some observers maintain that the problems are due to the basic discontinuity between technology and society—the disparity between social science and natural or physical science, the difficulty of keeping up with technology in ethics, religion, social work, government, and other disciplines concerned with human relations. This is what Toffler (1970) defined as *future shock* and Erich Fromm (1962) was referring to when he called for the humanization of our technological society.

INDIVIDUALS AND GROUPS IN CHANGE EFFORTS

Changing Individuals' Attitudes

Whether or not the members of a society can adjust to changing conditions depends in large part on their attitudes toward change. In static societies, relatively few social changes occur over a period of several generations. People have no awareness or expectation of change and therefore no attitude toward it. In Western Europe and North America, however, technological, economic, and social changes have been accelerating in the last few hundred years. Attitudes toward change have naturally developed in these cultures, following the processes of attitude formation and change.

The Liberal-Conservative Continuum

In Western societies attitudes toward change tend to fall somewhere along a liberal-conservative continuum—somewhere between favoring and opposing change. Labels can be attached to points on the scale, as shown in Figure 17–3. Here *radical* signifies one who favors rapid or even violent social change; *liberal* (or *progressive*), one who favors gradual social change; *conservative,* one who supports the status quo; and *reactionary,* one who would go back to "the good old days."

Such a scheme is simple and roughly in harmony with common usage of the four terms employed, but it raises several important questions, such as whether generalized attitudes toward change exist. In the United States, for example, it seems that technological changes are welcomed. However, many who favor technical advances do not advocate, and may indeed oppose, the social changes they make necessary. Technological change also can pose serious problems, as the confrontations regarding the long-term safety of nuclear energy dramatically indicate.

A 50-year-old study of Muncie, Indiana (which Lynd and Lynd, 1929, called "Middletown"), found that people accepted changes in material things far more readily than in nonmaterial aspects of the culture, such as the school curriculum. A research team visiting the community a half century later (Caplow, 1980) found that, despite several decades of rapid change, people in that city still clung to an ideology of the past. Some young people, for example, participated in the drug culture yet affirmed their belief in Protestant values. Adaptability to change appears to be highly specific and seldom consistent. Even in the 1920s when divorce was strongly criticized, a sizable portion of the community's residents were divorced.

Even if the terms *reactionary, conservative, liberal,* and *radical* are limited to attitudes toward *social* change, their generality can still be questioned. People who welcomed social security when it was introduced abhorred later changes in manners and morals. Some who sense a danger of increasing social power vested in government favor such federal programs as simplified spelling and calendar reform, or changeover to the metric system. Some who oppose the liberalizing of divorce laws also oppose any form of world government. Inconsistencies in a person's various attitudes along the liberal-conservative continuum can lead to a state of cognitive schizophrenia, as Bem (1970) defines it (see Box 9–2 in Chapter 9).

Figure 17-3. The Liberal-Conservative Continuum

Empirical evidence as to the specificity or generality of attitudes toward change is needed. Of the many studies of conservatism-radicalism that have been done since the 1930s, most have found some degree of generality. The correlations are often low between attitudes in different areas, however, such as law, politics, social custom, religion, economics, and international relations.

In 1968 a British psychologist, Glenn D. Wilson, devised a *Conservatism Scale* to measure what he had found to be a general factor in attitudes. In applications of the scale he found high correlations between religious dogmatism, right-wing political orientation, intolerance of minority groups, preference for conventions, insistence on strict rules, and superstitious resistance to science.

There are some difficulties in defining conservatism or radicalism solely in terms of attitude toward social change. Should we use *radical* to describe a person who strives for change in the form of repealing income tax and social security legislation and a return to the days of unbridled individualism? Obviously, it is necessary to know something about people's underlying goals and values before their attitudes can be described accurately. Nonetheless, these terms will probably continue to be used to characterize personality trends and to predict the behavior of individuals and groups with reference to social change (see Box 17–3).

Box 17–3
THE NEW CONSERVATISM: SOCIAL CHANGE IN REVERSE

For more than a half century before the eighties, Americans had steadily been becoming more tolerant in their attitudes and values. Urbanization, the rise of secularism, increasing education were accompanied by a more personal freedom, as in sex behavior. There was more respect for civil rights, despite reversals such as the attacks of Senator Joseph McCarthy on political deviants during the early 1950s.

Samuel Stouffer documented the general shift toward liberalism in his study of the mid-1950s.* He predicted that increased education, together with generational shifts (younger people are more liberal than older people), would mean a continuing trend toward liberalism. To a certain extent this theory has been supported. Whereas in 1954 approximately 31 percent of the general public and 83 percent of community leaders were found to be generally tolerant, the percentages for 1973 were 54 and 83, respectively.† Moreover, from 1972 to 1976 surveys showed a gradual rise in tolerance for communists, socialists, atheists, and homosexuals, though the degree of toleration is related to the specific issue. Historic events affect attitudes toward a given issue; for instance, the number of Americans disapproving of government wiretaps nearly doubled between 1973 and 1975, a likely effect of Watergate.

A more recent national survey found this trend toward liberalism has apparently slowed down. In analyzing NORC (National Opinion Research Center) data collected between 1972 and 1978, James A. Davis found an irregular trend toward conservatism. On a number of issues, such as environmental protection, aid programs for blacks, improving educational innovations, and military spending, the younger and better educated were as conservative as older persons with less education.‡

Political behavior is inevitably related to this growing conservatism. In the 1964 presidential election roughly 40 percent of the electorate accepted the extreme conservatism of Barry Goldwater. The George Wallace candidacy for president in 1968 and Richard Nixon's landslide victory in 1972 are other examples. But overwhelming evidence of the growing tide of conservatism was provided in the successful primary campaign and eventual election of Ronald Reagan as president in 1980. Although the victory depended on many factors (not least of which was President Carter's failure to realize his aims for the economy), it was apparent that many voters were ready for a reversal of social change. The extent of social change had simply been too rapid; the power of the mass media, the "rights" of minorities such as women, blacks, or gays; the massive bureaucracy required by a welfare state—these and other developments were being forced on a public that was not ready to accept them. The 1980 reaction was abetted by prodigious funds made available by conservative groups to defeat candidates they regarded as too liberal and a militant attack on liberalism by fundamentalist religious movements such as the Moral Majority.

History will have to assess to what degree the election of Reagan reflected either the desire of Americans to reverse social innovations or a mandate to invigorate the economy. National politics have often been marked by swings of the pendulum from left to right—although probably within a more narrow orbit than in other Western nations like Italy or Chile. In the words of one observer: "Conservatism is being called the ideology of ideas just now because it is searching for new practical solutions to economic and social problems (sometimes so old that they merely look new)."§

---

*S. A. Stouffer, *Communism, Conformity, and Civil Liberties* (Garden City, N.Y.: Doubleday & Co., 1955).

†Clyde Z. Nunn, Harry J. Crockett, Jr., and J. Allen Williams, Jr., *Tolerance for Nonconformity* (San Francisco: Jossey-Bass Publishers, 1978), p. 168.

‡James A. Davis, "Conservative Weather in a Liberalizing Climate: Change in Selected NORC General Social Survey Items, 1972–78," *Social Forces*, 1980, 58, 1129–1158.
§L. Morrow, "To Revive Responsibility," *Time*, February 23, 1981, p. 74.

These attitudes come from the individual's socialization in various subgroups and various personality variables, such as sensitivity and empathy, acceptance or rejection of authority, and rigidity or flexibility. The social climate also is significant. Social scientists agree, for example, that the bloodshed and genocidal character of the war in Vietnam was the major factor underlying the campus violence of the late 1960s in the United States.

The Individual's Relation to Planned Intervention

Political processes are a beginning point in initiating social change. In planned interventions, which comprise the biggest proportion of all changes in a society, as noted at the beginning of the chapter, the problem is how to make the goal and the means of achieving it significant to individuals. As Renshon (1974) points out, political events are important to the degree that they are "felt to have an impact on the individual's social or physical life-space—his day-to-day existence" (p. 76). This climate of change appears to occur only in crisis periods, as when the Great Depression provided the socioeconomic setting for the revolutionary social legislation of the New Deal. Similarly, the American public's revulsion to the morass in Vietnam had an impact in redefining the role of the U.S. military in foreign policy, temporarily at least.

The reciprocal relation between the individual and the sociocultural setting, which has been developed throughout this text, is the basis of planned social intervention. It rests on the premise that social change depends on changing individuals' attitudes and behavior, and to change a traditional social practice or system the central processes of cognition and motivation in individuals must be changed. Doob (1968, pp. 45–56) suggests several basic influences in this process:

1. *Predispositions.*   People are more likely to accept a proposed change when it is not in conflict with traditional attitudes and values which have proven to be satisfactory. They tend to be aware of discrepancies which arise as a result of changes among their beliefs, attitudes, and values, and this in turn leads to additional change.

2. *Perceptions.*   People often accept a proposed change when it appears to offer advantages for the present and future. As people change the content of their beliefs and communications they begin to perceive events differently.

3. *Other persons.*   People are more inclined to accept a proposed change if it is introduced by persons whom they consider important and competent, especially if consultation has taken place. Also, they seek group ties with others who support an innovation.

4. *Personality traits.*   People are more likely to accept a proposed change when it is in harmony with the modal personality of their culture (see Chapter 2) or with a goal they desire. As they begin to change their attitudes they acquire new traits which represent basically different orientations. Among these may be deferred gratification, initiative, autonomy, self-confidence, and aggressiveness, especially among those who are strongly dissatisfied with the status quo.

5. *Learning.*   People accept an innovation when it involves demands whose components they have already acquired or are confident they can require. With the new learning the person develops new abilities and learns to adapt to novel situations.

How and what people learn can be a crucial aspect of their acceptance of social change, as demonstrated in Bandura's (1971) concept of modeling described in Chapter 5: If we observe another's actions and what happens is satisfactory, we will act in a similar fashion. Modeling is not always an effective means of learning, however. According to Kunkel (1977), it depends on "the relevance of other people's rewards to one's own deprivations, the characteristics of the model, one's relationship to the model, the perception that one's own consequences will be similar to the model's experiences, and—most important—the later opportunity to engage in the behavior one has observed" (p. 445). This concept of vicarious reinforcement, which advances the notion that "self-reinforcement or the internalized social norms" are a major part of people's cognition and motivation, may prove to be the most hopeful learning mechanism for a society.

Efforts to change individuals can take several approaches. Hornstein et al. (1971) describe four relevant models:

1. *Analytic*—resistance and transference therapy in the Freudian context.
2. *Social psychological*—the influence of other persons, or group dynamics.
3. *Behaviorist*—changes in the individual through the use of operant conditioning.
4. *Cognitive*—changes through rational-empirical knowledge, a recurrent theme from Socrates to present-day moralists.

Whatever the approach, the strategy of planned change must consider the feelings, attitudes, and values of the individuals it is aimed at influencing. Much of the research concerned with social change has been directed at examination of the attitudinal shifts involved in accepting or rejecting an innovation. Full expression of feelings and attitudes is desirable for persons undergoing any wholesale alteration of their environment. For instance, a mandated change in lifestyles such as interracial housing, employment, or schools would call for intensive ventilation, and for some individuals, psychotherapy would be ideal if it is practical in terms of time and money.

Change is an option for any society, but as changes depend on a restructuring of attitudes, important ones arrive slowly. Moreover, only attitudes that are enduring and generalized are likely to result in significant behavioral changes (Zimbardo & Ebbesen, 1970). Other means of attitudinal change such as role-playing (see Chapter 9) must also be considered in any design of social change.

Group Dynamics

Group dynamics, introduced in Chapter 12, is concerned with studying organizational processes, small or large, in order to produce changes in the roles and attitudes of group members (Lippitt, Watson, & Westley, 1957). Often it uncovers the need for a *change agent,* a person with a critical role in proposing and overseeing the adoption of a change aimed at specific individuals or groups, who are known as the *change target.*

The study of group dynamics has revealed the use of several kinds of strategies to facilitate change in different types of groups. Zaltman and Duncan (1977) describe four types of these strategies:

1. *Facilitative*—the target group is already aware of the problem and the necessity of remedial action and will consider external assistance as well as self-help.
2. *Reeducative*—the target group is still attempting to diagnose the need for change and exploring the available options.
3. *Persuasive*—strategies are aimed at areas of change in which considerable resistance is encountered; emphasis is often on the decision-making stage.
4. *Power*—strategies use some form of coercion. An example is the attempt in 1973 by Common Cause in California to reform campaign finances, lobbying, and other political practices with questionable ethics. When the legislature failed to make any effort to enact these reforms, Common Cause turned to the initiative and referendum process, which in California can result in binding legislation. The legislature eventually passed a partial version of the desired reforms.

In an organizational setting, the critical point at which to initiate change is often *when* and *where* stress develops. Those who occupy strategic roles in a social system may or may not recognize discontent and search for innovative solutions, such as the use of aides in a school or hospital to relieve tensions resulting from a heavy amount of routine work (Benne & Birnbaum, 1969).

Both the formal and informal structures in an organization (as defined in Chapter 12) must be brought into the planning operation; a change strategy is most effective when all relevant personnel are involved in the innovation. Likewise, change in a democratic social order tends to be more satisfying than in an authoritarian organization where it is imposed from above. Warren (1977) distinguishes among three kinds of change strategies:

1. *Cooperative*—little or no opposition is encountered, and all personnel are disposed to accept the change.
2. *Campaign*—opposition is moderate, and resistance can be minimized by compromise.
3. *Contest*—the opposition appears to be unalterable, and the approach is largely one of conflict. Individuals or groups desiring change may have to modify their plans in order to win over the opposition. The role of mediating agents or third parties is often critical.

The Role of the Change Agent

Many types of organizations rely on change agents to determine the most effective ways to bring about change. Typically they are social psychologists or other behavioral scientists who are brought in as consultants by organizations in business or industry or by government agencies. The relation between the change agent and the target group is more often than not one of mutual trust and understanding of, and commitment to, the organization's goals.

The first task of the change agent is to determine or devise an appropriate helping role in which to observe and work through the established behavior patterns of the target group. Among the other techniques the change agent uses are:

1. Helping individuals determine their own roles in the planned change.
2. Creating new group loyalties and goals.
3. Providing a group environment in which the agent can assume a strongly supportive or directive role.
4. Offering encouragement in what may become a painful transition for members of the organization or community.

These are the approaches used by members of the U.S. Peace Corps in community programs in developing areas.

The role of the change agent, according to Lippitt, Watson, and Westley (1957), consists of five parts: (1) development of a need for change, or unfreezing; (2) establishment of a change relationship; (3) working toward change, or moving; (4) generalization and stabilization of change, or freezing; and (5) achieving a terminal relationship. With appropriate variations, this sequence can be used to explore such problems as why worker morale is low, why relations with the public have deteriorated, or how to integrate blacks into a white neighborhood.

Often the most critical phase of the process for the change agent is diagnosis of the problem: learning to ask the most relevant questions, seeking information, participating as an observer in routine processes, and observing outside activities. During the change process the sense of mutuality in joint efforts and commitment will tend to alter goals and methods for both key personnel and the rank-and-file membership. Often resistances such as opposition from vested interests is also encountered, however, and the feeling of alienation is likely to be unsettling. Such blockages call for increased or altered media of communication and expanded efforts at group decision making.

SOCIAL MOVEMENTS

In one sense a social movement is a form of social change, but it is also a form of mass behavior in which rumor and a diffuse anxiety reaction, or even the panic syndrome, may be involved (see Chapter 16). Although social movements share many characteristics of collective behavior, their orientation to major social changes makes more permanent group structures necessary.

A social movement can be thought of as a social group of a particular kind—a group that is moving, dynamic, going somewhere (see Box 17–4). It is different from a club or professional association, or from an institutionalized group like the family, church, or school. Almost every social movement has a basis in the social needs of its members—the needs for security, affiliation and status, achievement and power, and integration and creativity, as defined in Chapter 7. Cameron (1966) noted that some people join a movement because of its plans and policies, and others do so because they like the people in it. Other people join movements

Fascism in Italy and National Socialism in Germany are the classic prototypes of a totalitarian social movement. They had all the trappings of an aggressive social movement: ceremonies, slogans, and uniforms; strict control of nearly all national institutions; explicit opposition to out-groups; one charismatic, authoritarian leadership. *Source:* Culver Pictures, Inc.

Box 17–4
PERPETUAL MOTION IN MOVEMENTS

Every social movement changes in time. In fact, by its very nature a movement cannot be static; it moves from vicissitude to victory to vicissitude. Some go up, some down. The options or stages in a social movement have been described by Roberta Ash Garner* as follows:

1. *Formalization*—usually the first stage, when a free-floating movement is shaped into a coherent organization.
2. *Suppression*—the application of sanctions against digressive individual behavior.
3. *Co–optation*—a structural process which involves moving personnel into elite positions. Both suppression and co-optation provide for a balanced ongoing structure, but both can be self-defeating.
4. *Goal displacement*—the initial goals of the movement (which were directed toward a given social change) may give way to the necessity of organizational maintenance or some kind of ideological change for the sake of popular support.
5. *Oligarchization*—an initially democratic movement breaks apart into a decision-making elite and a disaffected, remote rank and file.
6. *Conservatization*—a grass-roots, unoffensive outlook is assumed. Funding becomes the central focus, leadership is more professional, and decision making is centralized.
7. *Institutionalization*—full incorporation into the status quo and the mainstream of the society.
8. *Factionalization*—breaking up for reasons of personality or ideology or both.
9. *Goal realization*—the end of a movement when its basic goal is satisfied. The suffrage movement vanished once women had the vote, but the crusade for women's rights emerged nearly a half century later to pursue other goals.
10. *Becalming*—goal transformation may occur, but fundamentally the constituency for whom the movement developed is no longer relevant.

A movement assumes different forms as the social climate changes or fortuitous events take place. There are also other possibilities, such as *routinization of charisma,* when the aura around the leadership is lost or fatal mistakes are made.

A number of potential movements never reach the first stage of formalization, as in the case of defiance of Prohibition in the 1920s. Potential or unformed movements of today, like gay liberation, legalization of drugs, reform of marriage laws, or the rights of the aged, may or may not pass through these stages. Some notable movements of the past have died, such as the World Federalists movement which was born after World War II and subsided during the 1950's, apparently because the ideal of world government was too remote. Technocracy, the hope for a rational socioeconomic system, which surfaced in the change-oriented 1930s, also died.

---

*R. A. Garner, *Social Movements in America,* 2nd ed. (Chicago: Rand McNally & Co., 1977), pp. 13–16.

in a search for identity. In a period of great organizational complexity like the present one, some movements and cults, such as the rural commune, offer individuals a degree of personal significance (J. Wilson, 1973). This need for personal meaning and commitment also pervades a number of the religious cults which have appeared in recent years.

A social movement has been defined as a "large-scale, widespread, and continuing, elementary collective action in pursuit of an objective that affects and shapes the social order in some fundamental aspect" (Lang & Lang, 1961). The term is applied to vastly different episodes or phenomena, temperance and prohibition crusades and the civil rights movement in the United States, the emergence of Methodism in England in the 18th century, and the rise of fascism in Italy, agrarian reform in Latin America, and Castro's 26th of July movement in Cuba. Social movements should be distinguished from certain other types of collective behavior described in Chapter 16, such as *mass movements* like large-scale migrations or a gold rush; the *following* of a popular hero; or *cults,* which have restricted membership (Turner & Killian, 1972).

As the term is commonly used, social movements have several characteristics:

1. They are relatively new groupings, not yet institutionalized and often amorphous in character, at least in the early stages.
2. They aim to achieve some change in the status quo, usually by orderly, evolutionary steps rather than by revolution, at least in Western society.
3. Their goals are broad rather than narrow and typically involve both humanitarian and self-seeking ends.
4. The members demonstrate proselytizing zeal and crusading spirit.

As a form of collective behavior a social movement demonstrates less uniformity of action than traditional, more settled groups, but a movement is not necessarily homogeneous or united. As compared to more permanent organizations, social movements permit more emotional spontaneity, but the outlets are controlled by the movement. Generally their free and uninstitutionalized character sets movements off from other social phenomena. A social movement is different from a political party, for instance, even though at times, especially in the heat of an election, the boundary can become very thin.

In the later 19th and early 20th centuries, the temperance crusade against the drinking of all forms of alcohol became a social movement in the U.S. Spearheaded by able leaders and propagandists in the Women's Christian Temperance Union and the Anti-Saloon League, it eventually became influential enough to assure passage of the 18th Amendment to the U.S. Constitution (1919), which prohibited the manufacture and sale of alcoholic beverages. Its supporters, many of whom were religious people in small towns and on farms in the Midwest and South who saw "the demon rum" as the cause of sin, poverty, and corruption, expected that prohibition would bring the dawn of a better day. But after the amendment was passed the "drys" were on the defensive, and their membership dwindled when it became obvious that prohibition had hardly produced a utopian society. Its critics held prohibition accountable for condoning lawlessness because most citizens refused to obey the Volstead Act, which enforced the amendment, as well as for such effects as invasion of privacy by federal agents, corruption of government officials and police, and the growth of organized crime, which was financed by enormous bootlegging profits. The movement officially died when prohibition was repealed by passage of the 21st Amendment in 1933.

Types of Social Movements

There have been a number of classifications of social movements. One of these points up the difference between general and specific movements. *General movements* are on a large scale and may activate an entire nation, like National Socialism in Germany. They usually come in the wake of vast social changes, such as a revolution. *Specific movements* have more limited goals and appeal to a more restricted followership, being concerned with such causes as old-age pensions, limitations on drinking, or even vitamin-enriched foods. Frequently these movements direct their appeal to special-interest groups or some distinct part of the population, like a given age or sex group; the temperance and suffrage movements were mainly confined to women, for example. Class, geographic, or religious interests may also dictate the development of a movement. Christian Science is predominantly an expression of middle-class, urban women who found traditional Protestantism too confining for intellectual, health, and other reasons. The Grange was largely the outgrowth of dissatisfied small-scale farmers caught in the Panic of 1873.

Turner and Killian (1972) classify movements into three ideal types, oriented to values, power, or participation. In *value-oriented movements,* issues, goals, and reform are all-important, as in the abolition movement prior to the American Civil War or the World Federalists after World War II. *Power-oriented movements* are preoccupied with force and aggressive tactics, since they are concerned with social control, or changing the power structure of society. Frequently this type has a centralized form of leadership, and sometimes the leader personifies the movement, as with Hitler and National Socialism. In *participation-oriented movements* the members gain their greatest satisfaction from participation itself, as in the later phases of the Townsend movement, an old-age-pension movement of the 1930s. Probably all movements manifest these three orientations to some extent, but one or another may dominate, depending on the developmental phase of the movement as well as on its structure and function.

Smelser (1962) differentiates between norm-oriented and value-oriented movements. *Norm-oriented movements* are planned and operate within the basic norms of a society. Such social movements may be intended to change certain norms within society, but the basic social structure or system is not notably affected. Any type of norm may be subject to change—economic, educational, political, or religious. A norm-oriented movement may also run the gamut of the liberal-conservative continuum (see Figure 17–3 above), from radical to reactionary. Although such movements may exist on a limited scale, like a university student body that seeks to change the power structure of the institution, they cannot be considered social movements unless they find some degree of mass support.

Value-oriented movements are directed toward basic changes in society; values imply a deeper commitment to generalized beliefs than norms do. An example is the American Revolution, which was directed against the authority of the state. Even more far-reaching were the French and Russian revolutions, or the present-day nationalist movements against colonialism. American organizations continuing to fight the battle for racial integration, like NAACP and the Urban League, may be considered norm-oriented in that the basic values of the United States are not questioned, and agitation focuses on norms through which the value structure is mediated. In contrast, the Black Panthers rejected many of the values as well as the norms of Western society, and National Socialism in Germany called for basic changes in the political, economic, and social institutions of the nation.

The disparity of aims, values, and memberships in various social movements makes for a varied typology. In broad philosophical terms they can be classified as *rational* or *irrational*. In this sense, the World Federalists, the National Organization of Women, or Zero Population Growth can be compared with, say, the Ku Klux Klan or the American Nazi party—as widely divergent as these organizations are. However, it is difficult to find absolutely objective tests for evaluating the rationality of movements. Historically, movements that have been considered irrational are sometimes judged by later generations to be rational. Consequently the distinction between "normal" and "crackpot" is seldom clear-cut.

Probably all movements process reality to some degree, whether they can be considered rational or nonrational. Movements that are most suspect to disinterested observers try to isolate their members from the outside world. An example is the Reverend Sun Myung Moon's Unification Church, which aspires to be a politically oriented social movement and demands total resocialization of the individual member, who must give up all family ties and turn over all income to the group (I. L. Horowitz, 1978). Within a democracy a movement may be appraised in terms of the means it uses to achieve its goals, though the criteria are not always clear. In certain situations, for example, violence may be defended; some observers perceive a Marxist revolution as the only means of changing a decaying feudal order in some Latin American countries.

A distinction can also be made between *aggressive* and *defensive* movements. A social movement is aggressive in its struggle to change a policy or attain power, but once it has power it may shift its stand and defend the status quo. Organized labor struggled for its rights for more than a half century, but after World War II it became increasingly conservative. Usually a defensive movement engages in active political participation.

As a social movement, the struggle for women's rights began in the last century and reached its apex when suffrage was granted in 1920. After being dormant for over a generation, the movement began to assume broader dimensions in the 1960s. *Source:* Magnum Photos, Inc./Burt Glinn.

Sources of Development

The great variety of types of social movements described above suggests there is no simple explanation—such as discontent, frustration, or social disorganization—for the development of a movement. For one thing, many persons are not aware of their disadvantages, or if they do perceive some kind of social frustration they are unable to pinpoint the cause. There are other solutions than social movements, such as seeking medical aid for a drinking problem rather than joining Alcoholics Anonymous, or turning to religion in order to cure social evils. Social disorganization also is no guarantee that people will turn to movements to achieve reforms. Several revolutions, in fact, have erupted at times when conditions were improving, as in the American colonies and France in the late 18th century. When segments of a society are alienated, hopelessness and retreatism are more predictable than an organization and a plan of action that promises a solution.

Movements do not always receive support from the sectors they are likely to help. It is no accident that intellectuals frequently initiate plans for eliminating political or economic injustice. The Social Credit Party emerged in Canada during the early 1930s for the benefit of the working class, yet it received primarily middle-class support. In its early phase Senator Barry Goldwater's conservative movement in 1964 was supported largely by people with moderate incomes, not those in the highest or lowest brackets. Farmers were among the strongest advocates of this effort to return to the ideals of individualism. Similarly in France, the Poujade movement, which was directed to helping the economically disenfranchised, lacked support among the poor. The leaders of the Russian Revolution were nearly all from the white-collar intelligentsia. In mobilizing for social change, neither dissatisfaction nor anomie is sufficient to launch a movement, though either may serve as a prelude.

Often social movements (like collective behavior) can be seen in the framework of the frustration-aggression hypothesis. Whatever the merits of this theory, as Chapter 7 showed, it can be said that a frustrated individual or group is likely to turn to aggression, or, in some instances, to retreat. Frustration is widely interpreted as occurring when customary rewards are lacking, or when the obstacles to them are unreasonable, as when a greedy landlord demands such high rents that the means for other necessities are sharply curtailed (Berk, 1974). Relative deprivation is another kind of frustration; it has been demonstrated that people become frustrated when their expected level of consumption is not maintained. As shown in Figure 17–4, riots, revolutions, and social movements are initiated when the gap between expected and actual need satisfaction becomes intolerable. Another circumstance favoring these outcomes would be when the actual need satisfaction remains relatively constant but the expected need suddenly rises (in Figure 17–4 the upper line would bend upward and the lower line would continue as a straight line). Smelser's concept of structural strain, discussed in Chapter 16, is relevant here; it is the basis for most studies of social movements.

Shifts in status are related to certain kinds of political and economic

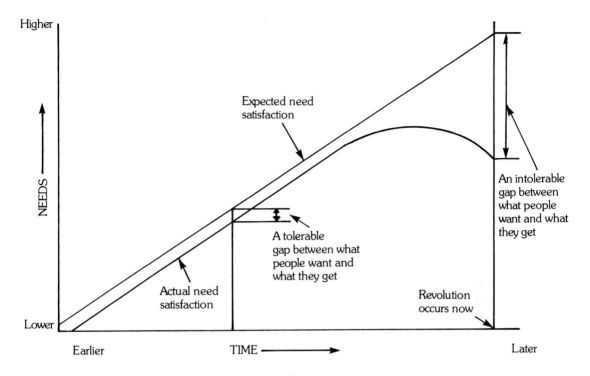

Figure 17–4. Social Crisis and Need Satisfaction

Source: J. C. Davies, "The J-Curve of Rising and Declining Satisfactions as a Cause of Some Great Revolutions and a Contained Rebellion," in H. D. Graham and T. R. Gurr (Eds.), *Violence in America* (New York: New American Library, 1969), p. 672.

movements. The Nazi movement was in part an outgrowth of status frustration, both because of the feeling of national impotence following the Versailles treaty and the impoverishment of the middle class through inflation. "Status politics" has often been linked with the radical right; in line with the concept of status consistency introduced in Chapter 3, a person who has lost status could be attracted to a movement aimed at restoring traditional values. With special reference to right-wingers, Rohter (1967) found that victims of status frustration fall into three categories:

1. The decliners—people in a changing society whose training and skills are no longer relevant.
2. The new arrivals—those whose mobility has been too rapid for the traditional

upper class to accept; consequently, radical rightism becomes a means of destroying the more urbane and liberal aristocracy.

3. The value keepers—those whose ideology rejects change.

Organization and Mobilization

For a social movement to be organized and attract people, there must be a broad base of support. An analysis of student movements found several factors were favorable to the accumulation of power, including the tendency of the established political elites to tolerate or accept counterelites (Shimbori, 1964). Another is the concentration of students in critical urban areas. Most Latin American universities are located in capitals or other politically sensitive cities, for example, and students there wield considerable political power.

The style of organization—that is, how relations are ordered within a movement and how conflicts and external contingencies are met—can also be pivotal. This style is affected by the degree of opposition the movement encounters; if it is totally rejected by the Establishment, an uncompromising stand usually results. Another determinant is the social position of the followers; one style is found in the moralistic and parliamentary climate of the middle class. Another style emerges in social movements where workers use "comrade" and the second-person informal address like *tu* or *du,* as pointed out in reference to the language of social status in Box 10–2 in Chapter 10.

The pattern of involvement in the movement is also important. A movement appeals to members because of the subculture it represents, the attitudes and values of members, or the type of leadership it has. The John Birch Society, for example, was one of the first to draw on the discontent among conservative Republicans and religious fundamentalists. This group depends more on administrative than charismatic leadership, and although the membership represents various occupational statuses, its grass-roots appeal is limited. Consequently, except for the conservative tide of the late 1940s and early 1950s, the movement made only minor inroads into the body politic. Since the 1980 national election it has been overshadowed by groups with wider appeal and more charismatic leaders, such as the Rev. Jerry Falwell's Moral Majority.

It has been claimed that recent social movements have benefited from the existence of mass societies. Supposedly, the takeover of Germany in the 1930s was easier because a mass society had been fashioned by industrialization and urbanization, but in reality Germany was a highly stratified segmented society. Hitler would hardly have succeeded in his power grab without the tight party organization that had been imposed on rural areas and small towns (Oberschall, 1973). In the United States a similar framework was fashioned by the Populist movement as it spread across the prairies in the last decades of the 19th century, when the society was individualistic and diverse. In contrast, black militants have had difficulty solidifying a reform movement within what is conventionally described as a mass society.

Often a mass society can be more accurately identified as open or *pluralist,* or a society in which various groups have the right to exist on equal terms or to jockey for power. Such a society often permits repressed elements to redress their grievances through such means as the farmer workers' movements which sprang up after World War II (Jenkins & Perrow, 1977). Migrant workers have long been submerged in the labor movements, and it was not until the 1960s that they were able to mobilize external resources in order to find satisfaction of some of their demands. In the tumult of that decade, the United Farm Workers, like other movements, could turn to the liberal establishment and political leaders in Washington and elsewhere for help. The social climate can be as critical as the organization or the leadership in the success of a movement.

In Oberschall's (1973) terms, mobilization depends on both the type of society (segmented or integrated) and the kinds of linkages between competing groups. People are more likely to enter conflict groups in a segmented (or pluralistic) society with a proliferation of organizations and considerable participation by members. In these cases, recruitment occurs on a bloc rather than an individual basis, which explains rapid mobilizations such as those of students in the Free Speech Movement at the University of California in 1964. Our pluralistic society also enabled Martin Luther King, Jr., to mobilize thousands of Southern blacks. In contrast, peasant movements in Latin America have had limited success in recruitment because of the hierarchical and integrated (i.e. controlled) nature of that social order. Movements in traditional rural societies are usually difficult to mobilize.

Allegiance to a cause is a complex psychological event. In addition to discontent or frustration, loneliness, conformity, status needs, or some other social motive may drive a person to join. For an insecure person an unpleasant incident involving a member of a minority group, or just seeing a black person in a Cadillac or hearing that a son wasn't accepted into medical school because of affirmative action, may be the trigger.

Recruitment and mobilization are essentially a matter of conversion, which to some extent is analogous to a religious experience. Indeed, in the past a lower-class person might seek a religious commitment in a Pentecostal sect as a means of resolving personal and social problems, or, more likely, search for a movement dedicated to solutions of problems such as crime, high taxes, inflation, unemployment, or restriction of liberties. Conversion can represent a drastic change in ideology, when rapidly changing situations in a person's experience prompt the shift (Milgram & Toch, 1969). This transformation occurs when the person moves away from a traditional frame of reference: a Roman Catholic becomes a Communist, or vice versa; a Rockefeller embraces the Democratic Party; or a jaded, upper-class university student joins the "Jesus people."

An intriguing aspect of the conversion phenomenon is the growth during the 1970s of exotic religious cults such as the Hare Krishna. An interview study of a related movement, the Nichiren Shoshu, suggests that the susceptibility of a person to this kind of cult is in part the individual's lack of moorings and social support. In this vacuum he or she is drawn into a new social network (Snow, Zurcher, & Ekland-Olson, 1980). It appears, then, that the success of some types of social movements depends on the vulnerability of alienated people in a mass society, as well as high pressure recruitment techniques.

Extreme cults and movements like the Hare Krishna aim for complete resocialization of members, but the process is not always smooth. *Source:* © Theodore Anderson, 1981.

Incipient and Ostensible Movements

Most (but not all) social movements have the following characteristics:

1. *Discontent with the status quo* that has become both intense and articulate.
2. *Effective leadership,* frequently centered in one leader who has charismatic properties, so followers can feel maximum identification.
3. A *plan of action* which includes a concrete and specific program for attainment of goals.
4. A *set of symbols,* ideology, slogans, music, ritual, or other paraphernalia for implementing the program.

Bittner (1963) suggests that a fifth point—complete commitment to the movement on the part of the members, including some perception of suffering as evidence of the individual's psychological involvement—could be added.

Social movements that exhibit only a few of these characteristics are generally known as *incipient movements.* Some remain in this incomplete condition for a number of months or years before assuming the shape of a vigorous, full-blown effort. The attempts of American blacks to achieve equality, or at least to end some of the more obvious discriminatory practices, remained in the incipient stage for over a generation; desegregation became a major social movement only after World War II. The large-scale entry of women into the labor force was necessary for women's liberation to become established as a movement (Huber, 1976).

An example of an incipient movement that has as yet only ambivalent support from the general public is public protest against the generation of nuclear power (Barkan, 1979). The protest was given visibility by the Three Mile Island generator disaster in 1979, when radiation was released, but it suffers from several structural defects. Most notable is its diversity of interests—there is indecision whether to attack the corporate structure or the threat of nuclear accidents. As with many movements there is also a question about the effectiveness of tactics like civil disobedience and disruptive action, and its decision making and leadership remain diffuse.

Some potential social movements never go beyond the incipient stage. Except for a few communities like San Francisco, the gay rights movement has not been based broadly enough to constitute a successful movement. The drive to eliminate smoking also has failed to attain the organizational momentum that once characterized the temperance movement, though the campaign against smoking as deviant behavior is being continually intensified (Markle & Troyer, 1979).

Other potential social movements remain as cults, as the lonely heart clubs did in the 1920s (see Box 17–5). Nudism almost became a social movement but had too limited a coterie. The swingers clubs of the 1970s also fell short of a movement, though various proposals to reshape marriage into a more flexible institution did have some acceptance.

There is also what Toch (1965) calls the *ostensible movement,* such as the promotional activity that focuses on a recreational pursuit like health spas, or the fan clubs built around celebrities of various sorts. Several movements of the past have focused on the charisma of a leader. When the Rev. M. J. Divine created the Kingdom of Father Divine, with himself as a deity, it became a movement that provided escapism for many blacks and a few whites during the 1930s and 1940s (S. Harris, 1953). Every few years there is evidence of the rise and fall into oblivion of such charismatic religious leaders. At times their followers may number in the millions, and then they dwindle to a few thousand or hundred. When a new leader comes to prominence and a new movement is on the rise, followers may flock to it out of curiosity, stay because of the excitement, and leave when a different new leader arrives.

CASE STUDY OF A MOVEMENT: CIVIL RIGHTS

The civil rights movement had its origin in the protests of blacks against their disadvantaged position in contemporary American society. The hallmark of the

Box 17–5
CULTS, NONMOVEMENTS, AND QUASI MOVEMENTS

In normal times, and even in periods of crisis, most Americans do not identify themselves with any movement. It is possible to escape from personal or social frustration through art, nature, fantasy, alcohol, drugs, or some variant of schizophrenia. But some people do elect to join cults or "nonmovements" that offer a group escape from the realities of the times. Ron E. Roberts and Robert M. Kloss define a collective nonmovement as "a social or collective solution to a problem which does not attempt to influence the labor or property relations of a given society."*

One nonmovement is the "Jesus people," who seek an intimate relationship with God in the hope of finding personal salvation rather than any solution to social problems. For them the sins of the world, like economic deprivation, racial tensions, or war, are simply matters of personal morality and are incidental to the ultimate religious values. This belief is in contradiction to the ideology of several established churches which not only frown on what they consider the irrational emotionalism of the "Jesus freaks" but take specific stands on social issues.

Other cults, such as transcendental meditation, Yoga, and Hare Krishna, have become stylish in middle-class circles, including some college campuses where, according to Roberts and Kloss, "awareness of the social situation has led to despair rather than action." Whatever the differences, these cults all have something in common with the beat generation of the 1950s and the Yippies of the late 1960s in their defiant break with the Establishment. Somewhat like this stance is black cultural nationalism, which has become absorbed in African customs, art, literature, and dress to help members regain a sense of identity.

Similar, yet dissimilar, are quasi movements like the Moral Rearmament of a generation ago. Its emphasis on personal happiness and success suggests some of the escapism in the more recent cults. Its theme of upper-class respectability and the tight leadership by Frank Buchman, together with the paraphernalia of a social movement, led to a wider following, however. The "born again" gospel of Billy Graham had lower-middle-class or grass-roots support and charismatic leaders, but it remained incipient for years and seemed to reach its peak in the Nixon administration.

Escape from the nation's and the world's ills can assume many forms—some have the mark of propriety, but others are more peripheral to the mainstream of American values. They apparently share a basic commodity, however; they all offer an alternative to a commitment to reform social institutions and reduce the inequities of the social order.

---

*R. E. Roberts and R. M. Kloss, *Social Movements: Between the Balcony and the Barricade* (St. Louis: C. V. Mosby Co., 1974), p. 41, 44.

movement over the years has been equality of opportunity, based on "the idea of removing barriers to upward mobility by eliminating discriminatory practices and substituting a posture of color-blind, scrupulous impartiality" (Rothman, 1977). The emphasis is on individual worth and ability; achieved status (based on the individual's performance) is valued over ascribed status (based on the relative position of the groups into which an individual is born). The thrust of the civil rights movement, according to Rothman (1977), has been "to eliminate group criteria for gaining status, because by such standards privilege has been conferred by tradition, rather than being achieved through mobility that comes from fair and open competition" (p. 41). The possibilities of achieving social mobility and status consistency, as described in Chapter 3, can directly affect people's attitudes and behaviors.

When doors began to be opened to blacks as a result of the Civil Rights Acts of 1964 and 1965, other groups such as Hispanics, welfare recipients, and women began to seek similar protection against discrimination. Other groups out of the mainstream, such as homosexuals, also have been able to improve their positions by asserting their rights under the law.

The genesis of black protest, and thus of the entire civil rights movement, was the formation of the National Association for the Advancement of Colored People (NAACP) in 1909 as an interracial organization concerned with making legal attacks on discriminatory practices. Action groups throughout the country became involved in a purposeful drive to reduce or eliminate prejudice against blacks. (Racial and ethnic discrimination are examined in the second half of Chapter 18.) The movement was given impetus when World War II reawakened public consciousness of democratic principles, and a number of social and economic changes, including urbanization, rising educational standards, and the end of traditional colonialism in several parts of the world helped provide a favorable social climate.

Blacks had made considerable progress during the war years, due in part to their contributions to the armed forces and military production, but except for occasional lip service to their cause and partial recognition of their rights, by 1955 they seemed to have reached a stalemate beyond which they were unlikely to progress further in a predominantly white society without some form of direct action. Their demands for equal treatment in jobs, housing, and other domains met with resistance, particularly in the Deep South, where a feudalistic social pattern was threatened. In response to the demands of blacks, white citizens' councils emerged to attempt to maintain the status prerogatives of whites.

Organizational Support

Although all black rights oranizations have not had precisely the same aims or used the same methods, most have advocated nonviolent revolution as the principal solution to the problem. To meet the appeal of the action-oriented organizations which emerged in the 1950s, the NAACP adopted a more militant program and the National Urban League, which originated in 1910, expanded its welfare programs for blacks. The Southern Christian Leadership Conference, centered in the work of Dr. Martin Luther King, Jr., was perhaps the most conspicuous of the newer organizations, but it suffered reverses after King's assassination in 1968.

The Congress of Racial Equality (CORE), founded in 1942, played an extremely important role in carrying out sit-ins, freedom rides, and other techniques of passive resistance. It had an elaborate program for training recruits in self-discipline to counter the sometimes violent resistance to desegregation efforts. Later the organization suffered from financial difficulties, and factions developed within the membership which questioned whether it had accomplished any more than tokenism and favored restricting membership to blacks (Meier & Rudwick, 1973). Other organizations like the Student Nonviolent Coordinating Committee (SNCC) made significant contributions to the nonviolent integration of places open to the public. A more militant approach to the problem was taken by black nationalist groups such as the Black Muslims (see Box 17–6).

Other groups have had a more local purpose, such as the Montgomery Improvement Association formed in 1956, with Dr. King as chairman, to support the Montgomery, Alabama, bus boycott. On December 1, 1955, Mrs. Rosa Parks refused to yield her seat to a white passenger, for which she was arrested and fined. When news of this arrest spread through the black community, a mass meeting was held at which resolutions calling for the end of segregation on Montgomery buses were adopted. Car pools were organized, a boycott of the city buses was instituted, and eventually King and other leaders were arrested. A Supreme Court ruling ended segregation on Montgomery buses in December 1956. The boycott was found to be a critical weapon in the desegregation process, and both the significance of the Montgomery victory to the cause and the efficacy of passive resistance were firmly established.

Although all these groups and organizations have not worked together, their combined force has helped their common cause assume the stature of a full-fledged social movement. The civil rights march on Washington in the summer of 1963 was evidence of the implications of the revolution, but it was the thousands of arrests and the dozens of killings associated with such places as Birmingham and Selma that dramatized the degree of involvement in the movement by numerous blacks and whites alike.

Past, Present, and Future

The civil rights movement moved through several different phases following World War II. First came the efforts of the federal government and some states to end discrimination in employment and housing. Some prominent black people were appointed to high positions, as when President Eisenhower named several black judges. The employment potential for blacks expanded somewhat during the relative prosperity of the Korean War economy. But in the early 1950s the popularity of Senator Joseph McCarthy's communist-hunting tactics forced all liberals into a defensive position which inhibited action in the interests of the integrationists.

The second phase began with the landmark 1954 school desegregation

Box 17–6
BLACK NATIONALISM

Blacks who could not accept the discipline demanded by Martin Luther King, Jr., and other proponents of passive resistance turned to more militant movements. One that saw some favor in the early years of the thrust for civil rights for blacks was the Black Muslims. This essentially religious organization, officially called the Nation of Islam, emerged in the 1930s with Elijah Muhammad playing the leading role. The order was dedicated to the end of white dominance in the world and called for a separate territory to be set aside for blacks.

The Black Muslims were originally separatists who advocated equal education but separate schools, with black children being taught by teachers of their own race, and who believed that intermarriage between races should be prohibited. They adhered strictly to the Koran's moral codes and sought to teach the religion of Islam without interference.

The movement appealed principally to lower-class urban blacks. Its rapid growth in the 1950s and 1960s to perhaps 100,000 members (although less than 1 percent of the total black population), demonstrated how frustration and anxiety can produce a highly emotional, nationalist type of movement.

Extremist attitudes among the members led not only to militant rejection of the white community but also to the development of in-group factions. A major schism between the adherents of Muhammad and the disciples of Malcolm X, who brought the group's message to a larger, more sophisticated audience, led to the latter's suspension from the church in 1963 and assassination two years later. Wallace Muhammad, who succeeded his father in 1975, called for radical changes—even welcoming whites.

_____

*Eric Lincoln, *The Black Muslims in America* (Boston: Beacon Press, 1973), pp. 153–154.

decision of the Supreme Court, which was noted in Chapter 3. This led both integrationists and segregationists to take a harder line, as evidenced by attempts to integrate the Little Rock, Arkansas, schools, and the Montgomery, Alabama, bus boycott described above.

The third phase was marked by the militancy of sit-ins and the voter registration drives by CORE and SNCC in the early 1960s. The 1963 march on Washington and passage of the Civil Rights Act of 1964 were critical episodes in this era. The urban riots in Watts, Detroit, Newark, and a score of other cities from 1964 to 1967 and the assassination of King in 1968 dramatized the cause of the blacks as never before, but it also brought fragmentation of both the leadership and the organizational base of the movement. By 1970 the movement seemed to

Sit-ins in the South during the early 1960s became a means of changing the legal status of blacks and affecting the attitudes of both blacks and whites. *Source:* Photo Researchers, Inc./Bruce Roberts.

have run its course and to be marking time until it could find a revitalized base of support.

Ability to move the black cause forward is basically an economic problem, dependent on the contingencies of prosperity or depression, both of which are complicated by inflation. In any economic condition, employment opportunities and incomes for blacks still lag behind those for whites. Despite general recognition of the need for unity, blacks also have failed to coalesce behind a common cause. Middle-class blacks may pledge their support to those of the lower class, even though they make deals with the white middle class, but the reason is apt to be to protect themselves from the threat of ghetto crime (Oberschall, 1973). In the United States, Southern black communities usually assert their demands for basic civil liberties, but in the North there are cleavages in the effort due to occupational, residential, and other subcultures.

One reason the civil rights movement ebbed despite the momentous gains of the crucial decade of 1954–64 is that its traditional allies became absorbed in another cause—the peace movement. College students and liberals who had enlisted in the civil rights cause shifted to the peace movement following escalation of the Vietnam War. The ghetto riots undoubtedly reflected the sense of frustration experienced by the blacks, who had achieved what they did by moving in the direction of civil disobedience. The only course seemed to be more direct action.

Analysis of the urban riots in 1964–67 (which were referred to in Chapter 16) clearly demonstrates the blacks' feeling of isolation and powerlessness; the channels of communication and protest had been closed. There is some research evidence that ghetto residents who felt most alienated from their environment had little hope for changing their positions, and consequently they were the most likely to turn to violence (Ransford, 1969). According to an intensive study of Watts rioters in Los Angeles in 1965, Northern-born black males were more vulnerable to a feeling of inadequacy and isolation from political processes than blacks who had been reared in the South. They also had been socialized toward more assertiveness, so that violence was an acceptable norm of behavior (Sears & McConahay, 1970).

Black militancy is often ascribed to feelings of *relative deprivation* (the disadvantages of blacks compared to the white majority) and *rising expectations* (the growing demands of blacks for a better lifestyle). In a study of the Miami and Cleveland black communities, these two factors were found to be important in determining militancy, but not as much as other specific variables (Abeles, 1976). For example, the more militant blacks were especially sensitive to the income gap between themselves and whites and to the disadvantages of better educated blacks compared to professional whites. The degree of residential segregation, which discourages interaction between the two races, also tended to heighten militancy, and relative deprivation appeared to have more effect on mobilizing leaders than followers.

As a result of failure to resolve the problems of leadership and organization, dissent among blacks has moved in several different directions. As blacks became less trusting of liberals and white leaders, breaks with the traditional white membership and leadership in NAACP and the Urban League became inevitable. At the same time, the black elite became more diversified. The clergy was no longer the major avenue to political power among blacks, as illustrated in the state legislature election victory of Julian Bond over a prominent Atlanta minister in 1965.

It is difficult to predict the future of the black revolution as one of the major social movements of this century in the United States. The lull would seem to be temporary, since the goals remain unfulfilled. Even though protest levels are well below those of the 1960s, university students of the 1980s are still concerned with issues in race and ethnic relations, such as the involvement of U.S. corporations in apartheid South Africa. For liberals the highest priority in the 1950s and early 1960s may have been civil rights, but other causes have come to occupy the minds and hearts of most Americans. The question is whether any of these—such as halting environmental deterioration, finding new energy sources, curbing overpopulation, instituting governmental reforms, or maintaining the right to dissent—can become as compelling as national goals as was the drive for equality among racial and ethnic groups during the Kennedy-Johnson years. In the scale of social movements, the civil rights offensive occupies a position somewhere between a reform and a revolution; as with most movements, control is its ultimate end (Lauer, 1976). To achieve this the movement continues, but society now perceives its goals as only one of several priorities. As the social climate has become more viably conservative (see Box 17–3 above), the lull has persisted.

SUMMARY

Social change, which brings the alteration of customs, values, institutions, and social behavior, is a concern of sociologists, anthropologists, and other behavioral scientists. The most prominent sociological interpretation emphasizes the cultural lag between rapid technological advances and slower social changes. Any question of social change deals with values, which differ greatly among societies and their various subcultures.

Social psychologists have been particularly interested in one aspect of the problem—attitudes toward social change, they have devised complex instruments to measure it and ways to study the important determinants of a person's attitude toward social change—influences from family, school, and community, intelligence and knowledge, age and stake in the status quo, and certain personality variables such as sensitivity or reverence for authority. Most individuals adjust to social changes without great strain, unless tremendous modification of behavior is called for or they have become exceedingly rigid. But technological and economic changes can produce insecurity and frustration, along with material improvement. Bringing about social changes through rational planning is made difficult by the forces of habit and tradition.

Certain agencies are beginning to focus on the problems of social change. Social psychology can offer society help in its efforts to discover principles of change and to work out practical techniques for producing it. One way is in the study of social movements as new, dynamic groupings of people who seek some change in the status quo. Their goals are both humanitarian and self-seeking, are usually broad in scope, and are proclaimed fervently by crusading members.

A distinction can be made between value-oriented, power-oriented, and participation-oriented movements. Presumably all movements grow out of discontent with social, political, or economic institutions, but all social dislocations do not give rise to movements. Leadership, organization, and timing are among the factors that account for a viable social movement. Successful leaders are often charismatic; indeed, some might be labeled pathological, like those in the Nazi movement in Germany.

A recent movement is the one for civil rights discussed in this chapter. Though widely different in their aims, membership, and methods, such movements can be traced to discontent and frustration, usually arising from some kind of cultural lag. One exception is the radical right, which appears to favor change in the direction of a return to the past. These movements exhibit various patterns of leadership and gain popular support when their programs harmonize with values which emerge from the constantly changing social and political climate.

Social movements are only one part of society's efforts to solve its problems, however. Some situations produce tensions which have troubled society for centuries, such as racial discrimination and war, which will be discussed in Chapter 18. Other problems have developed more recently as a result of social, economic, or political changes; and two of these will be discussed in Chapter 19: the environment and aging. Social psychology can contribute to both tension reduction and problem solution in society.

WORDS TO REMEMBER

Acculturation. Social and cultural changes resulting from prolonged contact between cultures.

Assimilation. Absorption or amalgamation of an individual or group into the society through social and economic participation, usually on an intergenerational basis.

Change agent. An individual who plays a critical role in the adoption of a given innovation.

Cultural change. Modification of cultural elements by spread (diffusion) from one culture to another or by invention within a culture.

Cultural lag. As defined by W. F. Ogburn, the tendency of parts of the culture to change at differential rates. Often the institutional or nonmaterial aspects of the culture change at a slower rate than the technological aspects do.

Cyclic behavior. The tendency of cultures to move in stages, as exemplified in various philosophies of history.

Diffusion. The borrowing or spread of traits from one culture to another, as contrasted to independent invention.

Innovation. The process by which several cultural traits are linked together to form a new cultural trait or complex. A more popular term is *invention,* which can be either technological or social.

Modernization. Set of changes in advanced economic or industrialized societies, as compared to the pattern in preliterate or underdeveloped areas.

Sigmoid or S curve. Pattern of social change in which one innovation is tentatively adopted by a relative few, undergoes rapid spread, and then tapers off.

Social change. Alterations in interpersonal behavior over time. The term can be compared to *societal change,* which refers to the most basic kind of change, as in institutional shifts. The two terms are used almost interchangeably, however, overlapping with *cultural change,* which refers to the nonpersonal aspects of pattern alterations.

Social movement. Large-scale action to achieve reform which may lead to dislocation within a society. It may be segmental or totalistic, aggressive or defensive, highly organized or fragmentary. An *incipient movement* is usually fragmentary.

Technology. Specialized knowledge directed to practical change and, in most societies, oriented to the making of a living.

QUESTIONS FOR DISCUSSION

1. What is the relation of values to the study of social change?

2. How do the different behavioral sciences approach the problem of change? Are these differing approaches justified, in your opinion?

3. What psychological factors are involved in modernization in developing nations? What is the direction of change in postindustrial societies?

4. How does the concept of achievement motivation relate to social change?

5. Compare the equilibrium and the process theories of social change. Can you suggest another alternative?

6. What factors might be involved in decision making about institutional change?

7. Describe the role of a change agent in a particular social setting.

8. Define a social movement and name its essential ingredients. Give some recent examples of movements and evaluate how well they have succeeded.

9. What conditions affect recruitment to a social movement?

10. How are rising expectations and relative deprivation related to the development and success of movements?

11. Compare the dynamics of the women's rights and prohibition movements, both of which involve constitutional amendments.

12. In the history of an actual or hypothetical movement, explain the options open to leaders.

13. Name some movements that became frustrated or failed to achieve what they hoped to attain. Name some that had indirect or unanticipated consequences.

14. Suggest a social movement to correct some current social problem. Define its goals and name groups in society who might be attracted to it.

READINGS

Barrett, H. G. *Innovation.* New York: McGraw-Hill Book Co., 1953.
> A penetrating analysis of the subject, largely from an anthropological and psychological viewpoint.

DeVos, G. A. (Ed.). *Responses to Change: Society, Culture, and Personality.* New York: D. Van Nostrand Co., 1976.
> Anthropologists and social psychologists contribute insights into contemporary cultures undergoing extensive change.

Genevie, L. E. *Collective Behavior and Social Movements.* Itasca, Ill.: F. E. Peacock Publishers, 1978.
> An interdisciplinary approach to a number of social movements.

Gerlach, L. P., and Hine, V. H. *People, Power, Change: Movements of Social Transformation.* Indianapolis: Bobbs-Merrill Co., 1970.
> Attitude formation in the pentecostal and black power movements.

Lang, K., and Lang, G. E. *Collective Dynamics.* New York: Thomas Y. Crowell Co., 1961.
> Chapters 16 and 17 ably present basic generalizations about social movements.

Nash, J., Dandler, J., and Hopkins, N. S. (Eds.). *Popular Change in Social Change.* The Hague, Mouton, 1975.
> Collection of papers on cooperatives and related reforms in the Third World.

Oberschall, A. *Social Conflict and Social Movements.* Englewood Cliffs, N.J.: Prentice-Hall, 1973.
> A penetrating analysis of the dynamics in 20th-century movements.

Teich, A. H. (Ed.). *Technology and Man's Future.* 3d ed. New York: St. Martin's Press, 1981.
> A series of essays on the impact of technology on both Western and the non-Western societies.

Warren, R. L. *Social Change and the Human Personality.* Chicago: Rand McNally & Co., 1977.
> A well-organized presentation of the kinds of change strategy.

Wilson, J. *Introduction to Social Movements.* New York: Basic Books, 1973.
> A provocative study of how discontent is mobilized and the problems of tactics, integration, and commitment.

Zaltman, G. (Ed.). *Processes and Phenomena of Social Change.* New York: John Wiley & Sons, 1973.
> Micro and macro approaches to social change from an interdisciplinary viewpoint.

Zaltman, G., & Duncan, R. *Strategies for Planned Change.* New York: John Wiley & Sons, 1977.
> Considers the problem of resistance to change and the relation of change agents and targets, with emphasis on different strategies.

18

ETHNIC DISCRIMINATION AND WAR

This text has brought together the results of research by behavioral scientists since the beginnings of the discipline of social psychology early in this century. The concepts and data presented have been liberally illustrated with references to problems that are routinely encountered in the family, at school, on the job, or in the polling booth. We have no illusions about offering any absolute guidelines for decision making, however, and we of course have been able to touch on only a few of the numerous problems of contemporary society. The final two chapters focus on four principal areas of current concern: discrimination, conflict and war, the environment, and aging. The emphasis is on how social psychology, through its study of the relations between individuals in groups, can contribute to society's efforts to reduce the tensions and anxiety these problems produce.

This chapter considers the ancient problem of racial and ethnic prejudice and discrimination, plus the more recent possibility that a sizable portion of the population and the environment will be destroyed by nuclear warfare. These problems have in common several of the social–psychological concepts introduced in Parts I through III. They both have their roots in conflicts between *in-groups and out-groups,* or majority and minority groups, as defined in Chapter 12. *Ethnocentrism,* which was defined in Chapter 8 as belief in the superiority of one's own group, has been used in several studies as synonymous with prejudice. The term applies to other groups in a nation or community as well as to other nations and leaders. The in-group is always supported and the out-group is always disfavored in some fashion.

The basis for many of the interpersonal perceptions, both within a community and in regard to various nations, is a *stereotype,* or an imaginal, attitudinal identification of the out-group, individually or collectively. As noted in Chapters 6 and 8, attitudes and opinions about others can become stereotypes when there is a perceived inconsistency among an individual's attitudes or between her or his attitudes and behavior, so only those cues about the perceived object that fit the person's preconceived opinion of it are recognized. The individual becomes comfortable with these stereotypes, and any disturbance to them is interpreted as an attack on his or her social foundations.

Studies of the authoritarian personality and aggressive attitudes and behaviors also are relevant to attempts to understand and determine the causes of both ethnic discrimination and war. The *frustration-aggression hypothesis,* introduced in Chapter 7, suggests that when a motive or attempt to satisfy a need is blocked, frustration results, and this can lead to aggression. Leonard Berkowitz and others have shown that while frustration does not always lead to aggression, under certain circumstances the probability of its occurrence will be enhanced. The *authoritarian personality*—a constellation of antidemocratic, intolerant tendencies—was related to ethnocentrism by T. W. Adorno, as reported in Chapter 8. Research on the concept has found a relation between neurotic tendencies such as anxiety states and authoritarian attitudes and behaviors.

RACIAL AND ETHNIC DISCRIMINATION

Racial and ethnic discrimination have a lengthy history and are found throughout the world. With its policy of apartheid, for example, the Union of South Africa has established the most complete set of racial boundaries among peoples: Europeans, Asians, Cape Colored, and Africans. Varying types and degrees of discrimination are found in the hostility between Arab and Jew, the ethnic minorities that the 16 republics of the Soviet Union represent, the struggle between the French and the English cultures in Canada, and the hierarchical social structure of Europeans *mestizos* and Indians in several Andean countries. Even in homogeneous societies prejudice is not unknown. A Swede looks down on a Lapp, and the Japanese oppose the *buraku.*

There is a subtle but important semantic distinction between the terms *prejudice* and *discrimination. Prejudice* is a negatively biased *attitude* toward a member of a minority group. *Discrimination* is actual *behavior* and refers to patterns of preference, or the acceptance of one individual or group rather than another. Generally the two are related, but an individual can practice one and not the other. A salesperson who is anti-Semitic will still be affable to a Jewish client, or a supervisor who has no personal prejudice against Mexicans may not hire them because of an unstated company policy. Despite personal reservations about the capabilities of black students, a college administrator may urge their enrollment because it is popular to do so by contemporary norms, or because an integrated student body is required for private or government financial support.

There are also distinctions between the terms *racial* and *ethnic. Racial* is an adjective describing a race of peoples, based on common observable physical traits that are transmitted by birth. *Ethnic* applies to both races and large groups of people classified according to common traits and customs. Thus racial discrimination is directed at members of races whose traits are inborn; ethnic discrimination adds the dimension of social custom. Ethnic prejudice can be directed at nationalities such as Polish or the Irish, as well as at racial minorities. Rothman (1977) points to the possibility that "The white nationality member, like his black, red, and brown counterpart, feels himself to be powerless and overshadowed, a disregarded, disadvantaged minority" (p. 240).

Racial Prejudice in the United States

In the United States racial and ethnic prejudice is one of the most critical issues confronting the nation. The sheer size of the racial minorities is striking: 27 million blacks; 14 million Mexican-Americans, Puerto Ricans, and other Spanish-speaking persons; over 1 million people of Asian background; and 812,000 American Indians. The largest group, the blacks, have traditionally been discriminated against by the dominant white population; they were slaves for nearly two centuries and remained in serfdom for over a generation after the Civil War. The need for workers during the two world wars encouraged blacks to migrate out of the South to the northern industrial centers, so that though about 90 percent of them lived in the rural South at the turn of the century, three fourths now are urban, and at least 50 per cent of the total black population lives in the North and West.

The section on the civil rights movement in Chapter 17 noted how the segregation of blacks in jobs, housing, schools, and the military service came into question in the late 1940s, as the nation became aware that it had fought a world war in support of freedoms abroad that were denied to a tenth of its own population. The federal government first desegregated the armed forces, and a 1954 supreme court decision, *Brown* v. *Board of Education*, ruled out "separate but equal" provisions for public education. Nevertheless, the pattern of a semicaste society remained in the South, and more subtle forms of discrimination continued in the North. The integration of blacks into a white society was a major point of confrontation during the 1960s. As action groups struggled on behalf of voter registration, desegregation of public facilities, and the equal opportunities in jobs and housing for blacks, they aroused deep hostility in sectors of the white society. In response, black separatism rather than integration became the goal of some militants. But though the black communty may be divided in its aims, it is uniformly determined to end the status of second-class citizenship for blacks in the United States.

Despite the advances of blacks in the postwar period, disproportionate numbers remain at the poverty level, live in substandard housing, receive limited educations, hold menial positions, and go unrepresented in government. There has also been little improvement in the submerged positions of other ethnics such as Hispanic Americans and American Indians. This system of stratification permits a large proportion of Americans to identify some out-group to which they can feel superior. The costs are high, not only in socioeconomic terms but in psychological consequences, as the first half of this chapter will demonstrate.

Like other Hispanics, Puerto Ricans often find themselves belonging to two different worlds. In recent years such groups have been encouraged to keep their ethnic identities. *Source:* © Theodore Anderson, 1981.

Patterns of Discrimination

A number of options are open in the way a society deals with ethnic differences. Simpson and Yinger (1972) have proposed a continuum of approaches to the problem, ranging from assimilation (forced or permitted) at one end to extermination at the other, with pluralism, legal protection of minorities, population transfer (peaceful or forced), and continued subjugation in between. All of these have actually been used at one time or another by various nations.

People have varying attitudes about the interactions with minorities they will accept or reject. For over a half century social psychologists have used the Social Distance Scale devised by Bogardus (1925) to study the acceptance or rejection of various out-groups, as described in Chapter 8. The hierarchy or preference among Americans for, say, Western Europeans as opposed to nonwhites has held firm, though the tolerance level for each group has risen (Bogardus, 1958). Many examples of studies of prejudiced attitudes toward racial and ethnic minorities were given in Chapters 8 and 9.

An extensive investigation of attitudes toward blacks, encompassing some 5,000 interviews conducted in 15 cities in the North, found a pattern of discrimination which varied according to the situations (Campbell & Schuman, 1968). Nearly all whites favored equal employment opportunities, yet only half accepted open housing. To the question of why blacks are in a disadvantaged position in housing, employment, or schooling, whites tended to answer that blacks lack drive. Younger and better educated whites were generally more perceptive and more favorable to integration. Black interviewees were more sensitive to the cues revealing prejudice but differed about whether they had been harmed by discrimination. Among both whites and blacks, individual definitions of the situation determined the amount of discrimination perceived or the degree to which an ethnic minority was favored or rejected.

A person's definition of the situation is derived in part from the norms of the group. In some situations overt expressions of prejudice are forbidden, but in others they are not. A black child who is tolerated as a peer in the classroom may not be welcome as a playmate. In New York and other cities a "five-o'clock anti-Semitism," whereby there is a friendly relationship on the job but a reluctance to mix socially after hours, has been noted. In Western society increased integration has led to more interaction between different ethnic groups (including interracial marriage), but in their daily lives most people still give little attention to members of other races. This pattern begins well before adulthood. In a study of students in 14 high schools in Pennsylvania, Williamson (1976) found that white students placed more social distance (in reference to with whom they would share a table, dance, go to a party or marry) between themselves and blacks and Puerto Ricans than these two minority groups placed between themselves and whites. Moreover, the movement toward an integrated society has resulted in polarized atttitudes toward out-groups which in some instances have led to mistrust and latent aggression. This has been borne out by experiments in elementary school and college classrooms (Donnerstein et al., 1972)

The degree of ethnocentrism within both the establishment and minority communities is related to the political climate. Kilson (1975) found that, ironically, blacks responded to the drift of whites with a more repressive neoconservatism, which was first signaled by the election of Richard Nixon in 1972, by deemphasizing their own militancy and antiwhite attitudes. Soon after the conservatives' victory in the 1980 national election (see Box 17–3 in Chapter 17), however, black leaders began to refer to the disenfranchisement of blacks and poor people.

Although blacks are more subject to discrimination than any other minorities, some in–groups always consider some out-groups—French Canadians, Orientals, Jews, or Italian-Americans, among others—as a source of competition for jobs and housing or as a target for their own deficiencies. Certain people's physical features or religion or even the sound of their names can be displeasing to other people. Well over half of the U.S. population must have felt the sting of prejudice—perhaps everyone except the WASPS, the dominant group of white Anglo-Saxon Protestants, and even some of these, like women, fat people, or liberals, are vulnerable. Indeed, the radical right is painfully conscious of the advances of immigrant groups who seem to have usurped the legitimate place of "real Americans." A clerk may feel threatened because a refugee from a Warsaw ghetto becomes first violinist in a symphony orchestra, or a waiter may resent a restaurant owner who was born in Greece.

The Source of Prejudice

The source of prejudice is in the individual's central processes of cognition and motivation which determine attitudes and behavior, as indicated in Part II. To analyze the structure of the problem, however, it is possible to trace the historical development of the patterns of subordination between ethnic groups. For instance, because of a different approach to color, a more positive attitude toward intermarriage, and a differing ethnic composition in the days of slavery, Brazil and the Caribbean have had relatively less discrimination than the United States (Hoetink, 1967). Another aspect of racial prejudice is economic, since an ethnic hierarchy allows some levels to be exploited as employees. Illegal aliens will accept menial jobs at substandard wages. Blacks offer a cheap source of temporary workers on the fringes of the labor market.

A crucial aspect of ethnic relations in which social psychologists can make significant contributions is in the area of attitudes, beliefs, and stereotypes. People's needs and wants are rationalized in a system of attitudes that justifies maintenance of the dominant position of the in-group. There is research evidence that these negative attitudes are still salient, although they have become less widespread. In one study (Brink & Harris, 1967), 52 percent of the respondents said they believed that blacks "smell different" (down from 60 percent in 1963), 50 percent thought that blacks had "looser morals" (55 percent in 1963), and 43 percent said blacks "want to live off a handout" (41 percent in 1963).

How Does a Child Become Prejudiced?

The stage at which the average child can be expected to have negative

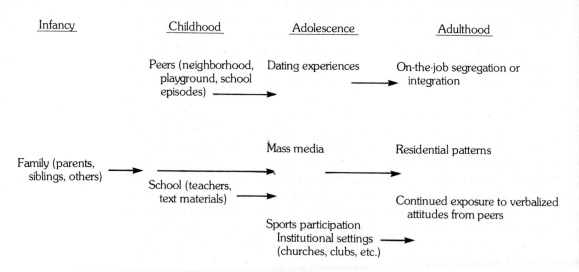

Figure 18–1. Development of Personal Attitudes toward Ethnic Groups

feelings toward members of other racial or ethnic groups has not been established in more than a generation of research studies. A person's experiences are only arbitrarily related to the periods in the life cycle, as shown in Figure 18–1. The influence of family, peers, schools, and other membership and reference groups usually endures throughout life, although specific beliefs and attitudes may vary from time to time.

In summarizing the research on how people become prejudiced, P. A. Katz (1976) takes the viewpoint that it emerges over the years through a complex process of perceptual and cognitive steps. He defines eight such steps, as follows:

1. *Early observation of racial cues.*   By the age of three the child is probably aware of different racial groups.

2. *Formation of rudimentary concepts.*   The child is exposed to a number of relationships which are verbalized in various ways, such as "Oh yes, that boy has darker skin because he is a Negro," accompanied by "And I don't want you to play with him." By age four children are able to arrange their cognitions in a way that is favorable or unfavorable to a member of an out-group.

3. *Conceptual differentiation.*   The child widens the opportunties to make differentiations: "He must be black even though his skin is light, because he has broad lips and curly black hair." The generalizations and differentiations receive feedback or reinforcement from peers or adults.

4. *Recognition of the irrevocability of cues.* The child learns that some statuses such as age change in time, but others such as race and sex are fixed.

5. *Consolidation of group concepts.* After age five, the child's ability to label and identify both positive and negative instances of relations is improved. In this consolidation process the perceptual and cognitive bases of attitudes are neatly attached to the concept of group membership—the "us" and the "them."

6. *Perceptual and affective elaboration.* The child continues to learn the precise and often fairly subtle cues accompanying racial classification, along with strong doses of evaluation. Thus the child learns that some races are emphatically better than others, and through the years a hierarchy of racial superiority and inferiority becomes clear.

7. *Cognitive development.* Once the feeling tone is established, there emerges a set of attitudes with specific content: "Chicanos are always late, can't be depended on, and are usually dirty."

8. *Attitude crystallization.* By late childhood the attitudes become further structured and seemingly automatic. There is little necessity to rethink them unless confronted with a totally new situation or the social environment is markedly changed.

Situational and Personality Factors

The process of attitude formation continues into adolescence and adulthood, often influenced by the situational setting (see Box 18–1). Studies show more selectivity in ethnic stereotypes and more individual differences among respondents recently, as compared to the years immediately following World War II (Ehrlich, 1962). Situational factors continue to influence stereotyping. Residential segregation, for instance, permits little or no contact between ethnic groups, but what contact there is is more positive than negative, and the quality of the interaction is variable (Amir, 1976). Perception also is a highly selective process. In a sample of college students, pictures of blacks were judged according to the situations in which they were perceived. A black walking in a ghetto (a stereotyped situation) was perceived differently from a black as a passenger on a yacht (nonstereotyped), even though overall prejudice was greater in the perception of a black as compared to a white (Riddleberger & Motz, 1957).

Severe prejudice is derived from deep psychological needs, however. To the classical bigot (Archie Bunker was a prototype), an out-group is a convenient scapegoat for one's own weaknesses and provides a means of externalizing inner conflicts. Antiracial feeling in some instances constitutes a form of paranoia, or what has often been identified as the psychology of the bigot, which is characterized by a peculiar proneness to projection and scapegoating. The frustration-aggression hypothesis has been widely applied as an explanation for

Box 18–1
PREJUDICE AND THE POLICE:
BLACK AND WHITE IN BLUE

A study of two randomly selected precincts of the police force in a major city showed shifts in attitudes among black and white police officers during the 18 months after entering the police academy.* As they went from the academy to their work routines they showed increasing negativism toward the opposite race. Both races thought preferential treatment was given to the other. Black officers became increasingly disenchanted with the police department and exhibited a stronger sense of black cohesiveness. Whites saw less need for a police-community relations unit.

A hedonistic orientation was observed in both black and white officers, as shown by a strong interest in "a comfortable life" and "pleasure." On the Rokeach instrumental value scales both samples indicated less interest in being "helpful" and "forgiving." At the time of graduation from the academy, both blacks and whites were more likely to perceive reports of police brutality as false or exaggerated than they had at the initial testing. But after graduation, blacks were more accepting than whites of the possibility of police harassment of citizens.

While it would be presumptuous to extend these findings beyond the sample in one city, the study does show how a stereotyped attitude can be strengthened by experiences in the workaday world.

*J. E. Teahan, " A Longitudinal Study of Attitude Shifts among Black and White Police Officers," *Journal of Social Issues,* 1975, *31,* 47–56.

scapegoating; for example, experimentally frustrated anti-Semitic students were found to behave in a more aggressive fashion toward both an obviously Jewish bystander and a nondesignated bystander, compared to nonfrustrated students (Berkowitz, 1959).

Survey studies have assessed the relationship between neurotic tendencies and prejudice (or ethnocentrism) as well as authoritarianism (Kirscht & Dillehay, 1967). In one study which used the F scale as a measure of authoritarianism (see Chapter 8), antiblack subjects showed higher F scores, even though status factors and religious participation were controlled (Martin & Westie, 1959). But all studies using the F scale have not found a consistent relationship between personality syndromes and prejudice. In a sample of whites in South Africa, an area of acute racial prejudice, the F scale elicited social conservatism more than a specific personality profile (Ray, 1980). Prejudice toward Africans seemed to be primarily a result of socialized or institutionalized attitudes. The responses reflected a perception of threat among the subjects, who felt vastly outnumbered by the Africans. Whatever the validity of this or other studies of the causes underlying ethnic attitudes, racial prejudice can be explained only by a set of complex variables.

Prejudice generally results from conformity to the sociocultural setting, in any case. Many people have negative attitudes toward blacks because they are socially rewarded for conformity to this standardized belief. Unlike true bigots, they vary in their adherence to norms that work against an ethnic minority. The public responds to the climate of opinion in the society. Following the death of President Kennedy a relatively tolerant attitude emerged. Later the tide of opinion turned again, as voters expressed their discontent over a number of social dislocations. The furor over attempts to integrate schools, for example, was reflected in votes for right-wing candidates which placed conservative Republicans in power in Washington in 1980.

Effects of Discrimination

Various minority groups differ in their degree of sensitivity to discrimination, because each group has its own historical and cultural background. Blacks experienced over two centuries of slavery, and now for more than a century have struggled to erase the stigma of having once been slaves. Spanish-Americans come from diverse backgrounds; Hispanics, for example, were in New Mexico well before the Anglos occupied the Eastern seaboard. Puerto Ricans are American citizens, essentially because of the "accident" of Spain's losing a war in 1898. Mexicans, most numerous of the immigrants, have moved into the United States (generally into areas that were Mexico before 1846) under a variety of conditions, usually to serve as cheap labor.

Thus nearly all minority groups have an inferior status, but it differs due to geographic, economic, and social factors. Nuances of the particular class position of each group determine the degree of access its members have to the privileges of society.

Each minority group has a range of sensitivity, and *labeling* is an index. By the late 1960s *black* became the accepted term for *Negro*, which had replaced *colored* several decades earlier. Each of these terms reflects changing status. Like blacks, Mexican-Americans have been subject to highly negative epithets. One that has come to be officially accepted is *Chicano,* although a survey in a number of Mexican communities showed it to have less pleasant connotations than *Mexican American* (Garcia, 1981).

There are also differences among minority groups in the background factors that cause distress. Both blacks and Mexican-Americans suffer from low incomes, but Mexicans have been less sensitive than blacks to the effects of low levels of education (Mirowsky & Ross, 1980). It appears that for those of Mexican origin, educational attainment has a relatively smaller effect on self-esteem. Group support provided by family and friendship networks seems to make Mexican-Americans less subject to the negative effects of limited schooling.

Cultural Conflict and Personality Adjustment

The effects of discrimination are worsened when personality conflicts develop because of a discrepancy between the norms and values of the minority culture and those of the in-group. Cultural conflicts (introduced in Chapter 3) have been particularly acute for American-born children of immigrant parents. Working against the parents' efforts to bring up their children in the ways of their homeland is the process whereby the children are assimilated into the dominant culture by peers, the school, and the community. Although this problem has lessened as immigration has declined, it persists for refugee groups such as the Vietnamese boat people in 1980 and both legitimate and illegal aliens with persistent cultural ties, like Mexican Americans and Puerto Ricans. The efforts of professionals to provide social services to the Spanish-speaking population often fall short because they have little understanding of the inner motives, language, family structure, and other institutions of this minority group (Padilla, Ruiz, & Alvarez, 1975).

The problem of cultural conflict and its effects on personality was studied by G. H. Seward (1972). One area where she found cultural conflict most acute is with the Jewish people, who have a heritage that is not readily acceptable in the prevailing culture. Among the mechanisms by which Jews attempt to resolve the conflicts they experience are *overconformity* or *rebellion,* the converse of overconformity. Other outlets include the rejection of both cultures, or the embracing of some extremist ideology or social movement such as atheism or communism. The development of a marginal culture is probably the most satisfactory method of solving the conflict. The tendency in some areas to fuse the Hanukkah and Christmas celebrations is an example.

Blacks who move from the rural South to cities of the North usually experience some cultural conflict because the folkways of their past are poorly adapted to the competitive, impersonal, rapidly moving nature of urban life. Inability to function in this milieu is one more factor in their drift into truancy and delinquency, as demonstrated by the unsuitability of the black dialect or nonstandard English in the business and social world which was noted in Chapter· 10. Socioeconomic status is probably a greater factor in this effect than cultural conflict, however (Willie et al., 1965).

For blacks, who have consistently been treated as inferiors, the conflict has been far more severe than for other minority groups. Middle-class blacks are caught in more personality conflict than blacks of the lower class (Frazier, 1957). Until the civil rights movement of the 1960s (see Chapter 17), upwardly mobile blacks turned to the white middle class for their models of respectability, social behavior, mobility, and even the type of housing selected. Complexion creams and hair straighteners were popular means of imitating the physical characteristics of the dominant ethnic group, as documented by advertisements in *Ebony* as late as the 1950s. All this changed with the opening wedge of the drive toward equality and the popularity of the Afro hairdo. Upwardly mobile blacks have in fact become conspicuous in the civil rights movement. The more militant

Denied access to equality in economic, educational, and other areas of American life, nonwhites confined to the ghetto may seek a variety of escapes. One example is the storefront church. *Source:* © Theodore Anderson, 1981.

organizations like the Black Muslims require their members to have some degree of economic security.

The discovery of racial pride and identity has been a major force in reducing anxiety and self-hatred among minorities. As Seward (1972) indicates:

> To alleviate frustrating conditions not only is good for society but would also be the best therapy for the individual. Members of minorities need to affirm their ingroup identity before they can assimilate the secondary identification with the mainstream culture. In such cases, every therapist knows that his first

task is to restore the individual to his own roots. Where there has been a rich cultural heritage conducive to group pride, as exemplified by La Raza for the Mexican American, there is strong leverage. In the case of the Negro American, on the other hand, whose heritage consisted of slavery and social rejection, identification with the despised ingroup has been unable to provide the boost in self-respect needed for emotional health. (pp. 81–82)

Improvements in personality adjustment for minority members must await fuller integration into American society. As mentioned in Chapter 3, a principal means of promoting this result is integration in the schools. A recent study of school desegregation (Rosenfield & Stephan, 1978) noted the positive effects of interethnic contact on the self-esteem of minority members. Low authoritarianism in parents and nonpunitive child-rearing practices also were correlated with positive racial attitudes. Moreover, children whose parents favored integration responded more warmly to ethnic minorities. This and a number of other studies suggest that despite the socioeconomic costs of integration, it can be of benefit to both blacks and whites.

As in other programs designed to improve intergroup relations, however, the ultimate success of school integration depends on changing people's attitudes. Experiencing personal contacts and acquiring and evaluating information can influence people to modify their neutral or negative attitudes about another ethnic group, but familiarity will not necessarily ensure unprejudiced attitudes toward it (see Chapter 9). The resolution of conflict in regard to ethnic discrimination and other social problems requires more comprehensive strategies.

CONFLICT AND ITS RESOLUTION

The problems associated with ethnic discrimination described in the preceding section suggest the potential presence of conflict in many intergroup relations. Indeed, conflict underpins numerous social processes. As the preceding discussion of motivation (in Chapter 7), group processes (in Chapter 12), and social change (in Chapter 17) has indicated, social conflict is not only inevitable but may even have a few desirable consequences. An example is the study reported in Box 13–1 in Chapter 13, which found that diversity of ethnocentric (prejudiced) attitudes enhanced perception and communication with a group.

Conflict has been classified in different ways. Dahrendorf (1959) made a fundamental distinction between *legitimate and routinized conflict,* as in labor-management relations or negotiations between government agencies or in the United Nations; and *illegitimate and uncontrolled conflict,* as in gang warfare or the border clashes of the Middle East. Conflict can also be thought of as homogeneous or heterogeneous. In *homogeneous conflict* the parties are of like character or involve the same institution, as in wars between nations or jurisdictional disputes between unions. In *heterogeneous conflict,* different organizational forms are involved, as in the struggle between church and state (Boulding, 1962).

Deutsch (1973) classified conflict as either *latent* or *manifest* and either *genuine* or *false.* Misinterpretation can lead to *displaced conflict,* as when two parties argue over an object or goal which is not the real cause of their conflict; a husband and wife may argue over money, for example, when their real problem is a deep-seated personality conflict. Conflict also can be *misattributed;* for instance, whites might accuse blacks of taking jobs to which they lay claim, but the basic problem is a weakness in an economic system which does not provide jobs for all. These different kinds of conflict are not mutually exclusive. A misattributed or displaced conflict can also be a latent one, or a displaced conflict can become a false one. The point is that conflict serves different purposes for different people.

Misattribution as a Source of Conflict

Misattribution of the adversary's motives and actions is frequently at the base of conflict (Horai, 1977). One party suspiciously attributes risks or dangers—real or imaginary— to others. This *labeling* process by which qualities are attributed to those with whom we disagree is probably universal. On an international scale, labeling can carry high risks. Both the United States and the Soviet Union periodically indulge in a guessing game based on a variety of behaviors, ranging from the public statements of leaders (see Box 6–4 in Chapter 6 on the mirror image) to an intricate web of espionage. Excuses and rationale are the stimulus for moves and countermoves. In 1965 President Johnson justified the U.S. intervention in the Dominican Republic with a commitment to a tight hemispheric defense against leftist ideology and leadership. Three years later the Soviet Union applied a similar rationale—regional security and ideological purity—to its intervention in Czechoslovakia. In 1981 a similar scenario was played out by the same two superpowers, as the United States justified military aid for the rightist regime in El Salvador and the Soviets continued to support the communists in Afghanistan.

Among the most dramatic shifts in attributional conflict was made by Egypt and Israel at the end of the 1970s. The change began with Anwar Sadat's visit to Jerusalem in 1977 and climaxed in the Camp David and Cairo accords reached during the following two years. The resolution of conflict was only partially successful, however, since both nations had different goals and definitions of security, and their acceptance of each other's values was qualified (Cohen & Azar, 1981). The interaction of the two nations' leaders resulted in an agreement that contained the scope of conflict rather than fundamentally changing the images and attitudes each nation had of the other.

Kriesberg (1973) views conflict as moving through a sequence of more or less predictable stages (Figure 18–2). All conflicts do not reach every stage, however. The sequence depends on the degree to which the conflict is conscious or unconscious and manifest or latent, as well as on the options open to each contestant. The awareness, escalation, deescalation, and termination processes all are modified by the outcome. The time dimension may be days or even years, with continual modification of the conflict as situations and protagonists change.

The Tactics of Bargaining

Groups with reward structures oriented to individual achievement, competition, or cooperation utilize differing strategies of bargaining, as noted in Chapter 12. The principles of games theory apply to large organizations, including

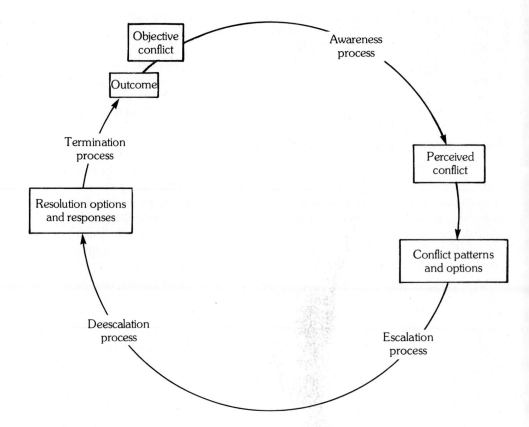

Figure 18–2. Cyclical Pattern of Conflict

Source: Adapted from Louis Kriesberg, *The Sociology of Social Conflicts* (Englewood Cliffs, N.J.: Prentice-Hall, Inc., 1973), p. 19.

nations, as well as to persons and small groups. Nations faced with the need to confront a common foe, for example, often form coalitions and attempt to resolve their differences.

Exchange theory (see Chapter 13) is concerned with the *comparison level* (CL), or the level of satisfaction a person feels with an outcome that has emerged from interaction with others (Thibaut & Kelley, 1959). With the CL as a standard, the individual weighs alternative outcomes, and the CL is usually revised upward when an outcome is favorable and downward for the reverse. The CL—whether a student's grade "cum," the process of mate selection, a prison riot, or negotiations between two rival states—determines the success of the undertaking and the degree of conflict resolution—or failure.

A basic concept in conflict and conflict reduction is the perception of *threat*.

Marriage, mobility in the pecking order, and diplomacy all have the potential of threat. Boulding (1977) defined war as the breakdown of a threat system. In a classic experiment, Deutsch and Krauss (1960) simulated a conflict situation entitled the Trucking game, in which two players imagine that each owns a trucking company. The profits the players can make depend on the number of deliveries on their trucks. The players are handed a road map indicating that each has two alternate routes, a lengthy, zigzag one or a shorter, relatively straight one. The latter route is of course preferable, but it is a one-lane road with a gate at each end. The gates can be controlled by neither player (no threat), one player (unilateral threat), or both players (bilateral threat). Cooperation was greatest when neither player had access to a gate, and conflict was greatest when both had access. Profit was possible only in the no-threat situation.

The parallels of the Trucking game to both interpersonal and international conflict are evident. Two persons pose a threat to each other when they both want the same job or role. Two nations bargain on the basis of threat: OPEC can cut off the supply of oil to the Western powers, which in turn can refuse to sell these countries arms or take steps to reduce their own dependence on foreign fuel. Since Western Europe, Japan, and other areas produce almost no petrochemical fuels, however, the exchange situation is hardly symmetrical. Moreover, the struggle to obtain oil from the Middle East has to be perceived in the context of the rivalries of the two superpowers, the survival of Israel, and a network of political and economic variables. As in many conflicts, therefore, the situation is often asymmetrical.

Threats usually involve *demands,* which may act as deterrents or escalators in the conflict situation (Milburn, 1977). Prior to Pearl Harbor, President Franklin Roosevelt had demanded that the Japanese limit their aggressive actions in China, and he subsequently froze their bank deposits. The 1979–81 diplomatic hostage situation in Iran also was marked by demands and counterdemands. Generally such threats vary in degree of credibility and ambiguity. Threats that are not believed by the adversary may be restated as specific acts of aggression in order to validate them.

Bargaining is the process whereby two or more parties try "to agree on what each shall give and take or perform and receive in a transaction between them" (Eldridge, 1979). Bargaining can be either tacit or explicit. Following Sadat's trip to Jerusalem in 1977, bargaining between Egypt and Israel became truly specific for the first time. Such concrete, tangible bargaining is usually more productive than the abstract or symbolic variety. Generally, too, tense situations are more conducive to successful negotiations than a relaxed atmosphere (Druckman & Mahoney, 1977). Cultural and personal styles are likewise relevant to the quality of outcome. During the 1970s the People's Republic of China moved from an adversary style of international relations, with total victory as the goal, to the Western pattern of settling for small gains as a means of arriving at agreement on larger issues.

Wehr (1979) advocates the *mapping* of conflict as the first step in its resolution. This technique can offer both an intervenor and the conflict parties insights into the origins, dynamics, and possible outcome of the conflict, with the understanding that the process is constantly undergoing change, and any map is subject to revision. Such a map should specify:

1. The background of the conflict.
2. Designation of the conflict parties, including both those directly and indirectly involved.
3. A definition of the specific issues.
4. Polarization, spiraling, and image formation.
5. Alternative solutions to the problem, including the potential for limiting the conflict and the possible intervention of neutral third parties.

The applicability of these maps of conflict depends on the desire of both sides to reach a nonviolent solution. Throughout history, in both the Western and non–Western world, violence has been the outcome of most deep conflicts. Forms of passive resistance or civil disobedience—as practiced by Mahatma Gandhi in India early in this century or the sit-down demonstrations in the civil rights movement of the 1960s—have occasionally succeeded as nonviolent means of settling conflicts, however. Boulding (1977) defines *civil disobedience* as "a counterthreat strategy to the threat system of an established order or government." It is regarded by some groups, notably the Quakers, or the Society of Friends, as the most viable way to end conflict.

While it would be unrealistic to expect such far-reaching conflicts as discrimination and war to be resolved by peaceful means in the near future, there are exceptions. Passive resistance might provide a possible solution to the Catholic-Protestant strife in Northern Ireland; for example, the opposing parties could be convinced of the futility of violence. Most hopeful of solution by this means are conflicts in which cultural differences are minimal and democratic processes rather than totalitarian regimes prevail.

WAR AND PEACE: A RECURRENT TRAUMA

On the domestic scene in the United States, the potential for conflict due to such conditions as urban stress, crime, and ethnic tensions is formidable. But an even greater threat in terms of survival of the human race is international violence. The United States has participated in four major wars in this century. Ever since it dropped the first atomic bombs on Hiroshima and Nagasaki in Japan in 1945, as a means to terminate World War II quickly, the shadow of a nuclear holocaust has threatened the world. The availability of nuclear weapons has intensified the search for an international organization or government with the power to ensure some kind of peace, a problem thinkers have grappled with since the time of Hugo Grotius in the 16th century.

As indicated in the consideration of conflict in the preceding section, social psychologists have been studying attitudes about peace and war for years (Kelman, 1965). This concern involves many areas of the discipline, ranging from

The tragedy of war has troubled Western thinkers since at least the 16th century, with the plans of Hugo Grotius for an international union. In his series "The Disasters of War" Goya depicted the savagery of the Napoleonic invasion of Spain. *Source:* Print Collection, Art, Prints and Photographs Division, The New York Public Library, Astor, Lenox and Tilden Foundations.

social motivation to the cultural basis of personality, from the processes of attitude change to game theory. While these approaches cannot be detached from those taken by other social scientists, they do shed light especially on the attitudes surrounding international tensions, the role of the military, and prospects for the peaceful resolution of conflict.

Scientists seem to cooperate better in helping win wars than in helping prevent them. An exception was the social psychologists of the 1930s who initiated research and education efforts devoted to achieving lasting peace. Collaborative efforts by members of the Society for Psychological Study of Social Issues bore fruit in a yearbook entitled *Human Nature and Enduring Peace,* which was published just before the close of World War II (Murphy, 1945). It included a section entitled "The Psychologists' Manifesto," which is a series of forthright statements about war and peace signed by over 2,000 members of the American Psychological Association.

The first of these statements considered the question: Is war inevitable—is man "instinctively" warlike? The answer was that war can be avoided—it is not innate but is built into people. No race, nation, or social group is inevitably warlike. The frustrations and conflicting interests which lie at the root of aggressive wars can be reduced and redirected by social engineering. People can realize their ambitions within the framework of human cooperation and can direct their aggressions against natural obstacles that thwart them in the attainment of their goals. Although we cannot give any final answer to what constitutes our genetic structure, there is evidence that the human beings are as cooperative and altruistic as they are competitive and aggressive (Campbell, 1972).

A few years later a group of eight internationally famous social scientists from six countries was brought together by the United Nations Economic and Social Council to consider the causes of nationalistic aggression and the conditions conducive to international understanding. Their statement began with this sentence: "To the best of our knowledge, there is no evidence to indicate that wars are necessary and inevitable consequences of 'human nature' as such" (American Association of University Professors, 1948).

Unfortunately, these theoretical labors of American social scientists had little political effect and did not prevent the nation from becoming involved for three years (1950–53) in the Korean War and for at least eight years (1965–73) in the Vietnam War. One poll of attitudes in 1976 showed that 74 percent of a large-scale American sample considered the "danger of war" to be among the nation's primary concerns (Watts & Free, 1976). By 1980, as a result of instability in the Middle East, the Soviet invasion of Afghanistan, and a breakdown in attempts to limit nuclear armament by the Soviet Union and the United States, statesmen and citizens alike were experiencing a sense of anxiety approaching feelings of doom.

Peace has had a tentative status in all parts of the world. In recent years civil war has raged in Africa and Northern Ireland; there have been armed conflicts between Arab countries and Israel, between India and Pakistan, and between El Salvador and Honduras; and violent outbreaks have occurred in other places such as the frontier between the Soviet Union and the People's Republic of China. The outlook for the future is no brighter, as Christians fight Christians, Israelis fight Moslems, Moslems fight Hindus, blacks fight whites, and so on.

Nationalism and Aggression

A basic cause of the wars of the past 200 years has been *nationalism,* or loyalty to one's own nation as a sort of super in-group. Nationalism has historical, cultural, economic, and psychological roots. From childhood to adulthood, most humans are indoctrinated in the home, at school, and by the mass media to adopt a set of ethnocentric attitudes about their national citizenship which can serve as a tremendous driving force.

Identification of the tendency of aggressiveness to find its way into violence as a means of settling disputes was foreshadowed in the discussion of aggression and modeling in Chapter 5 and the frustration-aggression hypothesis in Chapter 7. Those who exhibit unacceptable or deviant behavior are considered as threats to the social order and therefore fair game for punishment of a violent nature. During the Vietnam War, for example, 38 percent of a national male sample said they regarded student protest as a form of violence, and 50 percent said they felt that recourse to shooting was an acceptable means of handling campus disturbances (Blumenthal et al., 1972).

Readiness to use violence is shaped by the particular setting, however. An extreme example was the tragic killing of four Kent State University students by the Ohio National Guard on May 4, 1970. What appeared to be a wanton and meaningless episode can also be viewed as an outgrowth of the unrest and violence which characterized the Vietnam period (Stotland, 1978). The quality of the leadership and training of the guards was questionable; they lacked adequate instructions on how to maintain peace and had been provoked by students for several days preceding the killings (although it is significant that no guard had been hurt). Their inability to disperse the crowd left them with a feeling of incompetence and reduced their self-esteem, and their resort to violence may have been an attempt to restore their self-image (as described in Chapter 4). Fundamentally, this incomprehensible event illustrates the end result of intergroup conflict in a culture in which violence has been openly displayed. In the atmosphere of protest in the 1960s, numerous stimuli could trigger violent outbursts.

Research has shown a positive correlation betwen nationalistic attitudes and aggressive reaction patterns, suggesting that a combination of personality needs and ideological content determines a person's orientation to other nations. Christensen's (1959) study of a sample of Norwegian naval cadets, which found that aggressiveness was related to their tendency to approach conflict according to threat orientation, rather than problem orientation was reported in Chapter 8. Through the use of clinical tests he arrived at a *"latency hypothesis"* which assumes a positive relationship between nationalism and aggressive reaction patterns. Cognitive aspects also are an important consideration. It is a combination of personality factors and ideology that determines a person's orientation to the peoples of other nations.

Another aspect of nationalism is the stereotypes people have about others in out-groups. Cross-cultural studies have shown that these responses remain relatively constant over a long period. In a post–World War II cross-national survey of stereotypes about American, British, Chinese, French, and Russian people, Buchanan and Cantril (1954) made four generalizations about these attitudes in all eight countries surveyed:

1. There is a tendency to ascribe characteristics to certain peoples.
2. There is a uniform tendency among respondents of all countries to describe the Russians in the same terms, and somewhat less agreement on the Americans.
3. Stereotypes of one's own countrymen are invariably flattering.

4. The prevalence of complimentary over derogatory terms in a national stereotype is a good index of friendliness between nations.

Although national stereotypes are comparatively fixed, there are variations depending on historical events and the economic and psychological pressures that occur within a given nation or group. Americans changed their stereotypes of Germans, Russians, and Japanese before, during, and after World War II (Klineberg, 1964). Other examples of how stereotypes change in the interests of the dominant group were given in Chapter 2.

Stereotypes often become directed toward the leader of a nation. According to surveys—informal interviews in the Soviet Union and opinion polls in the United States—Russians and Americans alike think of each other in a more or less neutral fashion but believe that the people of the other nation have been misled by their leaders into taking a path of aggressiveness (Frank, 1967). (The mirror image which characterizes the reciprocal perceptions of Americans and Russians is described in Box 6–4 in Chapter 6.) During wartime, hatred of the enemy becomes focused on its leader—the Kaiser in World War I, Hitler in World War II, and Mao and Ho Chi Minh in the Vietnam War.

Another factor making for aggressive nationalism is the personal gain it represents for many individuals. It becomes a rallying cry for the political leader who tries to distract the public from unpleasant domestic realities by drawing attention to the threat of a foreign power. There are vested industrial interests which make profits from the manufacture of weapons, and military officers are able to further their own careers more rapidly in times of international crisis. The subculture of war can also affect civilian life. There were times during the Cold War when it was safer, careerwise, for a nuclear physicist to champion nationalist values rather than internationalist ideas.

Sociocultural Conditioning

Nationalism and warlike attitudes are produced through exposure to various forms of violence in comics, TV, and games, and in many subtle ways, the child learns how aggression and the military are valued in Western society. In the mid-1960s the availability of toys associated with violence took on the aspects of a fad (see Chapter 16). A study of the trade magazine *Toys and Novelties* showed that between 1964 and 1967 advertisements for war toys increased from 5 percent to nearly 15 percent (Andreas, 1969). Concerned citizens organized opposition to this trend, and with the growing unpopularity of the war in Southeast Asia, sales declined. Even so, violence-oriented toys still account for about an eighth of all toys sold in North America.

Ethnocentrism also is developed by cultural conditioning, through such means as parental remarks, formal education, peer groups, or the mass media. To admit the equality of another nation is seen as inviting disaster. In wartime, the situation is intensified by concern for members of the armed forces. This sense of sacrifice was a factor in the public's reluctance, after American withdrawal from Vietnam, to grant amnesty to those who had resisted the draft.

Psychological Bases of War

When a nation is economically insecure or seriously frustrated in attempts to gain power, its tensions can easily be directed into aggressive action. Observers of Germany, Italy, and Japan before World War II noted this sort of frustration, which could be exploited by dictators and funneled into preparations for war. Since World War II the sources of international tensions have been even more complex. The Arab-Israeli conflict, which became inevitable in 1948 when a UN partition plan divided Palestine into Arab and Jewish states, has political, economic, geographic, historical, and ideological overtones. Basically, however, both sides are deeply frustrated in their search for security; the state of Israel carries on relentless military actions to secure the borders of its expanding territory, and the Palestinians, who are in the role position the Jews occupied for 2,000 years—a people without a homeland—respond with terrorism. Similarly, the Protestant-Catholic civil strife in Northern Ireland, which is complicated by the presence of the British; the Chinese-Soviet conflict over communist ideology; and the India-Pakistan rivalry all represent the search for both psychological and material security, though other factors are also relevant. Even the quality of the confrontations between the United States and the Soviet Union has shifted with the rise of multiple bases of power, as the growing freedom of allies in the Eastern and Western blocs and the uncommitted, developing Third World nations complicate the uneasy peace.

Although some form of frustration is probably relevant to the causes of war, it should not be assumed that national frustrations automatically lead to armed conflict. The frustration-aggression hypothesis, as noted at the beginning of this chapter, is at best a tendency rather than a law. Primitive peoples and certain nations have suffered decades if not centuries of deprivation and frustration without attacking their neighbors. China was basically a pacifist nation until the Communists came to power in 1949. India has only recently demonstrated militaristic tendencies, apparently as a response to threats from neighbors to the North and East. Sweden was a highly aggressive nation in the 18th century but has been very reluctant to become involved in recent international conflicts. Germany has seemingly made a similar transition in the 20th century.

Certainly the nature of war has to be understood in the context of aggression and intergroup confict, which was discussed in Chapter 12. To some extent, hostility is the outcome of group solidarity which develops as a response to intergroup competition. There is a reciprocal effect between group cohesiveness (see Chapter 13) and intergroup rivalry, with ethnocentric feelings as a by-product (Deutsch, 1973). As with the ethnic minorities described earlier in this chapter, goals are blocked for given nations, and what is perceived as relative deprivation can become the basis of overt conflict.

The motivation for war can be considered as affecting both citizens and leaders, though at different levels of decision making. It also affects both men and women, though a sex bias operates here as in other areas. Both men and women have a capacity for aggressive behavior, but usually it is men who commit the violent crimes, fight the wars, and form the political elite. This distinction has its roots in the diverse socialization of boys and girls (see Chapter 3) and the persistence of the sex roles society considers appropriate (see Chapter 14). Eron's (1980) findings of a relation between an aggressive response to TV violence and the traditional socialization of boys, for example, were described in Box 14–1 in Chapter 14. There is evidence that males are not only stimulated by displays of violence on TV and movie screens but are also socialized to take aggressive action by active or vicarious participation in sports like football and hockey. Iglitzin (1978) suggests that these sports should be regulated in order to reduce their violence, although there is a question whether the American male might not be even more violent if he could not sublimate his aggressiveness on the field, diamond, or rink. There is no known relationship between military behavior and participation in contact sports, in any event.

Leadership is of course subject to various sensitive and acute pressures in its attempts to handle international tensions. In crisis situations leaders must act within a set of options based on their perception of threat, but no less important are an understanding of the psychological background, the ability to manipulate goals and the perception of clear or distorted images. As for the layman, the real world can be a different one for the leader and the opponent. Special kinds of isolation or bias are possible, as in the groupthink phenomenon described in Box 13–2 in Chapter 13, a kind of in-group situation which can result in injudicious decisions. This was responsible for the acceptance by President Kennedy and his cabinet of plans for the ill-fated Bay of Pigs excursion in 1961, but the failure of this attempt to invade Cuba may have given them a sense of caution that served them well in the Cuban missile crisis the next year. Bolstered by this triumph and his landslide electoral victory in 1964, President Johnson in turn came to have an enormous feeling of confidence and power which may have made him less critical of the judgments of military advisors who advocated the war in Southeast Asia. In the aftermath of Vietnam and Watergate, the time was ripe in 1976 for the election of President Carter, who had a much less grandiose concept of presidential power.

The Warfare State

From its founding until World War I, the United States remained essentially a nonmilitary state, although its armed forces took part in several declared wars and intermittent police actions against North American Indians and several Latin American conflicts. The all-out effort of World Wars I and II involved the entire population, however, and with the American-Soviet Cold War confrontations of the 1960s, the nation's consciousness of its role of world leadership was aroused. The military came to be viewed as a means of imposing a kind of Pax Americana on the world.

Even before involvement in the war in Southeast Asia, the Department of Defense had a budget accounting for over 50 percent of federal expenditures (as compared to 23 percent for domestic social welfare programs). If the space program is included, the Department of Defense was responsible for 54 percent of the total expenditures on research and development in the country. The U.S. Army or the Department of Defense issued more than 300 contracts to 88 universities between 1942 and 1971 for research on biological warfare, for example, an effort that was later abandoned. President Reagan's proposed budget for fiscal year 1982, the first in which he sought to put his promises to limit government spending into effect, was based on raising defense spending by $4.3 billion and decreasing nondefense spending such as social programs by $38.5 billion.

Are we justified in calling the United States a militarized society? In the drift of events in the 1960s, the military penetrated into many segments of national life as the country geared up for the war in Vietnam. But the war become intensely unpopular, and from the viewpoint of most observers it was a conflict that became progressively more futile. When promises of a speedy termination of the conflict were not fulfilled, the integrity of the administration and the military came into question, and a *credibility gap* developed which seriously undermined public confidence in the goverment. Yet for several years much of the nation, especially hard-hat construction workers, middle-class conservatives, and veterans' organizations, supported the official U.S. effort to prop up a questionable government in Saigon.

Beyond the specific effects of mass involvement in military operations, another psychological factor is the dehumanization which accompanies war, as Vietnam illustrates. Terrorist raids, defoliants, and computerized, unmanned bombing missions were "justified" to counteract the treachery of the enemy. The killing of an entire village population in the My Lai incident is only one symptom of the consequences of impersonal warfare (see Box 18–2). It is significant that when Lt. William Calley was found guilty in a court martial, many Americans could not accept the idea of his guilt. Many citizens granted that higher-level officers were hardly innocent of this annihilation, but they believed this junior-grade officer should not be punished because he was simply carrying out orders, a justification which was examined in relation to the conformity studies described in Chapter 11.

The feasibility of pushbutton warfare has also encouraged an attitude of impersonality and dehumanization. For the sergeant who sits at the control panel in the Strategic Air Command or the pilot who engages in precision or mass bombing, ethical considerations are even more frightening than in traditional conflicts. Bernard, Ottenberg, and Redl (1971) see *dehumanization* as a kind of self-protective maladaptation to several psychological factors: (1) increased emotional distance from other human beings; (2) a diminished sense of personal responsibility for the consequences of one's actions; (3) overinvolvement with procedural problems, to the detriment of human needs; (4) inability to oppose dominant group attitudes or pressures; and (5) a feeling of personal helplessness and estrangement. Several members of the crew of the Enola Gay, which dropped the first atomic bomb on Hiroshima, had severe psychiatric problems in later years, and the extent of personal disorganization suffered by veterans of the Vietnam War is still to emerge. For those in control of the atomic missile facilities the ultimate consequences of action will be different from those in older forms of warfare, since the degree and type of destruction are so awesome.

Because the entire population is subject to food blockades or bombing raids, modern warfare has had increasingly personal effects. What's more, the battlefield

Box 18–2
ON LOOKING THE OTHER WAY

Society seems to have an unlimited capacity for rationalizing evil. Until the humanitarian movement of the 19th century, only an occasional criticism was voiced. But revelations of the sadistic practices of modern warfare and terrorism have forced a public reaction which adopts various forms of rationalization. When Germans learned of the genocide policy of the Nazis, for example, many chose either to disbelieve or to deny the events—or they simply repressed the information.

The news of the My Lai incident, in which over 200 women and children in a Vietnamese village were massacred by U.S. troops in December 1968, evoked worldwide outrage. An analysis of public reaction in the United States, however, showed that a number of Americans resolved their uneasy feelings by denial, as expressed in comments like, "Our boys wouldn't do this; someone else is behind it"; or "Anything could happen—how do we know what's going on?" Another means of coping with the unacceptable information was the justification that a soldier in the field has no alternative: "What would their punishment have been if they had disobeyed?" or "Do they get shot if they don't shoot someone else?" Others explained the event as necessary military policy: "Had these civilians, these women, set traps for these people?"*

When Lieutenant William Calley, who was responsible for at least one of the companies participating in the carnage, was found guilty in a court-martial, the public response was ambivalent. Much of the protest was based on the idea that Calley was just a scapegoat for the superior officers, including generals, who had given the orders. There was also a feeling that Calley had a duty to follow orders whatever their consequences—the precise justification Adolf Eichmann had used in his defense for the crimes of Auschwitz.

It is hardly surprising that people attempt to rationalize their own defects, but when they also rationalize the crimes of others some fundamental questions about human motivation are raised. By the mid–1970s, Calley had been "whitewashed" in public opinion, which brings up the question of how long any society remembers amoral deeds perpetrated by its own members. The 1979–81 hostage-taking of U.S. embassy staff members by Iranian student-militants eventually raised the question of whether the Iranians would acknowledge the mistreatment and deprivation of freedom they inflicted on the hostages any more than the Americans would acknowledge U.S. support of the repressive regime of the Shah.

---

*Nevitt Sanford and Craig Comstock, *Sanctions for Evil* (San Francisco: Jossey-Bass, Publishers, 1971), pp. 63–67.

vividly enters the home through the TV screen, and it is not known at what point individuals can psychologically turn off this experience. In the violence in Vietnam, the length and remoteness of the conflict were factors, as was the government's rationalization of the aims and cost of the war. Once President Nixon withdrew a large share of the American fighting personnel, the war had even less saliency. Regardless of the casualty figures, the war became an event in a distant part of the world, involving mostly Asians. The economic advantages the war brought to several million wage earners in military support industries also could not be discounted.

It would be difficult to determine the degree to which the Vietnam War really was unpopular, or how Americans on the whole perceived the ethical issues that were implicit in the national debate about it. Only 40 percent of those interviewed in a national poll in the 1960s said they felt that citizens had a right to engage in peaceful demonstrations against the war, for example. To what extent did the informed public regard the war as a legitimate activity and rejection of the national war effort as illegitimate? The answer seems to be that until relatively late in the war, most citizens tended to accept official policy. Even after the Viet Cong occupied all of Vietnam in 1975, Americans were reluctant to consider the probability that this war had been in vain. In retrospect the war remains unpopular, but perhaps as much as anything because it is difficult to acknowledge as the only war the country ever lost.

Nuclear Deterrence versus the Arms Race

In the 1960s both the United States and the Soviet Union seemed to become aware of both the futility of the Cold War and the risks of nuclear disaster (Boskey & Willrich, 1970). When the nuclear test-ban treaty was signed in 1963, there was some hope of further detente between the two superpowers, but the situation in Southeast Asia discouraged these efforts. For surer methods of deterrence they turned to superweapons such as the intercontinental ballistic missiles (ICBMs); the U.S. MIRV system, for example, was designed to penetrate the Soviet ABM system. The policy of mutual deterrence, which relies on the availability to both sides of counterforce weapons—missiles with warheads—has flourished in an era of mutual suspicion and technological weapons innovation. A significant new phase in the nuclear arms race was the proposal by the United States to build the MX mobile missile system, in which 200 weapons, each armed with 10 nuclear warheads, would be constantly shuttled by huge trucks among 4,600 concrete shelters in Utah and Nevada.

The first Strategic Arms Limitations Talks (Salt I) agreement was signed in May 1972 by the U.S. president, Richard Nixon, and the Soviet general secretary, Leonid Brezhnev. When it expired Salt II was signed by the heads of the state in 1979, but it failed to get the required confirmation in the U.S. Senate. Nevertheless, the idea of limiting the numbers of weapons on both sides persisted, in recognition of the need for a mutual agreement to halt nuclear proliferation. An accord would not only have significant advantages for the two powers by lessening the need for military expenditures, but it would also help reduce tensions for all nations.

A major problem of the arms race since World War II has been the continuance of a *war psychology,* the condition that characterized Europe on the eve of two world wars. We exist in a global atmosphere in which each of the two major power blocs—with third and fourth blocs emerging in the less developed areas of the world, especially in mainland China and India—operates according to a policy of counterthreat and deterrence. Katz (1965) explains that this produces a somewhat unstable structure with the following characteristics:

1. The buildup of an elite group of military advisors whose frame of reference is overkill capacity, preventive war, and similar concepts.
2. The fostering of a military-industrial complex which gears the economy to war preparations, so that local as well as national groups become interested primarily in defense contracts.
3. The triggering of mechanisms for international destruction by what may be perceived as a hostile threat from an unfriendly nation.
4. The tendency of public opinion to equate national security with the nuclear striking power of the nation.

Pilisuk and Hayden (1965) have examined the question of the existence of a military-industrial complex which prevents peace. Deterrence and the arms race are staggering burdens, both psychologically and economically, and may even defeat their very purpose—the prevention of war.

Since deterrence is a medium of communication, it can be only partially effective, as has been shown in simulated conflict situations as well as in international events. The degree to which it is effective is limited by its threat ability (Boulding, 1978). It is arguable that possession of nuclear arms by the United States in the early postwar years, and by the Soviet Union and other powers later, prevented nuclear war. In the succession of crises in these years, both the superpowers were involving each other and their allies in actions that deterrence ought to have prevented. Except in unusual circumstances like the Cuban missile crisis of October 1962, deterrence does not prevent provocative actions by other nations, large or small. At best it provides a very uneasy road to travel.

The practice of deterrence has become all the more risky as the tempo of crises has increased. Moreover, low-level nuclear conflicts can be expected to merge as the group of nations with nuclear weapons becomes larger—probably growing to 20 by 1985. The two superpowers of the Cold War years have given way to multiple power centers and shifting coalitions, more like the decades before World War II than those immediately following it. In this escalation process there is the "mounting feeling of being threatened" (Smoke, 1977).

The tense atmosphere of the 1980s subjects both the public and its leaders to many cross-pressures. Because decision makers generally think the enemy has comparatively more options open to it, a crisis situation is all too likely to elicit hasty and risky actions, as Figure 18–3 illustrates. In this crisis environment the leaders are likely to experience intense cognitive dissonance (see Chapters 6 and 9), in which the possible courses of action constantly decrease. This is one reason

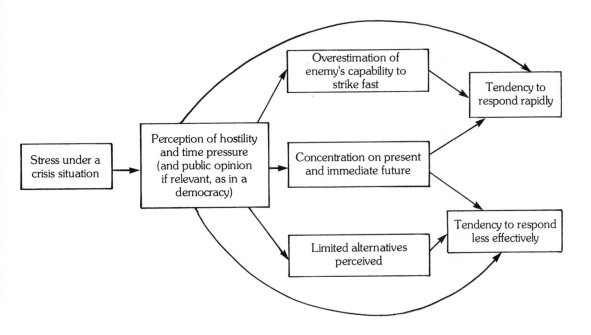

Figure 18–3. Crisis and Response in International Relations

Source: Adapted from O. R. Holsti, *Crisis, Escalation, War.* Montreal: McGill-Queens University Press, 1972, p. 122.

that the reduction of tensions by a SALT agreement is necessary, even if it permits only an agreement to disagree.

The problem can be placed in the context of game theory (see Chapter 12), in which international conflict would be seen as operating according to a zero-sum situation—whatever one wins, the other must lose. Game theory involves both conflict and neutral situations between the participants. As Box 12–3 in Chapter 12 demonstrated, international relations is analogous to Chicken; a nation must expose itself to the risk of failure or disaster in order to threaten its opponent. Even though the threat may be unilateral, punishment is always bilateral and involves both parties (Swingle, 1970a). The threat of nuclear disaster is overwhelming, compared to other considerations, but it is questionable to what extent the risk enters into the calculations of the protagonists.

Escalation and deescalation efforts can become caught in a series of rapidly moving events, as in the Cuban missile crisis. In fact, deescalation may be perceived by the other side as a trap. But in most crises of the Chicken type, usually the more rational opponent has no option but to back down. The question remains whether either side can provide brakes for the vehicle on the collision course a nuclear confrontation would take.

The sequence of events may—or may not—lead to an easing of tensions. Several months after Khrushchev backed down in the Cuban missile crisis, President Kennedy announced "a strategy of peace" which called for a reexamination of the arms race and an end to nuclear tests in the atmosphere. But Kennedy was reluctant to promote a true ban on armaments, fearing the charge of appeasement in the 1964 national election. The confrontation with communists in Vietnam discouraged further cooperation, and the standoff remained until the deescalation of the war under President Nixon and the signing of Salt I. President Carter emphasized limited reprisals, such as the withdrawal of U.S. athletes from the 1980 Winter Olympics in Moscow and an embargo on grain shipments to the U.S.S.R. following the Soviets' invasion of Afghanistan. President Reagan named a former general, Alexander Haig, as secretary of state and the announced goals of foreign policy were to stop Soviet expansionism and to expand American military might rapidly. Somehow the doves and hawks in both world powers move within the gyrations of national and international elites, guided by their perceptions of the shifting balance of security or insecurity.

Despite some progress in the reciprocal reduction of tensions, we are left with the possibility of a nuclear disaster. So far, none of the nations possessing nuclear weapons has dared to use them, though the outlines of an escalation strategy (Kahn, 1965) still guide military thinking. Cost alone may discourage some nations from becoming members of the "nuclear club," but the race for supremacy between the Soviet Union and the United States could hardly be perceived as other than expensive, dangerous, and futile.

The likelihood of a nuclear explosion, whether from accident or design, has a hypothetical probability of, say, 5 percent according to the Harvard biologist George Wald. This probability is far too high for any feeling of security. It is unlikely that the superpowers will dismantle their warheads, but the hope for peace or stability may lie in various other directions, from curriculum reforms to new kinds of international economics. The change in national climates that must accompany a movement toward international stability depends, above all, on the reshaping of people's perceptions and attitudes about one another.

Alternate Solutions to International Conflict

It would be inappropriate for a social psychology text to propose a ready-made plan whereby international conflicts might be resolved or eliminated, and behavioral scientists have made few definitive judgments in this area. But it would be detrimental if we ignored this problem. The urgency of the world situation calls for examining every possible alternative to the arms race as a means of settling disputes. This section examines why the nations encounter difficulties in international decision making and communication with other powers.

A fundamental barrier to creating a climate of peaceful and rational solution to international tensions is the reluctance of the public to consider alternatives and accept innovations. Many of the same people who supported the American involvement in Vietnam in the 1960s lost no time in condemning the Soviet invasion of Afghanistan in the 1980s—although both were cases of a major power intervening in an undeveloped nation. Public opinion is difficult to change, it prefers simplified alternatives, and its various positions are frequently inconsistent (Sawyer & Guetzkow, 1965).

Public opinion about war (see Box 18–3) can lead public policy, or follow it, as implied in the introduction to Chapter 16. Where social change is concerned, an established government policy can encourage public opinion to fall in line, as demonstrated by the improvements in ethnic relations since World War II. But public policy in international relations can meet more resistant attitudes, because people's *misperceptions* about other nations and their leaders are greater in times of heightened tension. In this generation the Arab-Israel conflict has represented this kind of selective inattention to the other side (R. K. White, 1977). The solutions to the problem that have been tried have come largely from outside influences, such as President's Carter's Camp David accords, as noted above. Sometimes, too, public opinion becomes set against public policy, as evidenced by the public's eventual rejection of the official government position on the Vietnam War.

Americans and Iranians, Russians and Chinese have images of each other, and often they bear little relationship to reality. Like the other products of interpersonal perception described in Chapter 6, *images* are perceptive and feeling states which can be either diffuse or fairly specific. They are in an intermediate position between attitudes and opinion, ranging from stereotypes to vague, fleeting feelings about an object or situation in a person's cognitive structure (see Chapter 8). They may refer to the self or be directed to quite distant objects such as the president, the leader of another nation, or the nation itself. We selectively organize our images about the other side—whether a political party, a nation, or its leader—and this process is accelerated in wartime.

Plans of Action

Plans for an international organization took on some reality with the founding of the World Court at the turn of the century and the League of Nations after World War I. The League's impotence became evident in the 1930s as Europe drifted toward World War II. The United Nations was given a more far-reaching organizational structure and wider representation when founded at the end of that war, yet the conflict of powers and superpowers continues. Despite the outstanding contributions of UN agencies, the reduction and control of international tensions is often left to other forces. Nonetheless, the world might well have been even more disturbed without the General Assembly's efforts during the 1970s to control the proliferation of nuclear weapons. A number of nations—and millions of people—have become convinced that nuclear arms is a no-win game (Sharp, 1978).

Other comprehensive plans for controlling peace have also been recommended. In the late 1940s the World Federalists pled their case for a federal state encompassing the entire world. Other plans center on widening the channels of communication, a gradualist policy of arms reduction, or a wholesale attack on poverty and illiteracy, together with economic and social development (Etzioni,

Box 18–3
PATRIOTISM, FEAR OF COMMUNISM, AND NUCLEAR WARFARE

Acceptance or rejection of the possibility of nuclear warfare depends to some extent on a person's age. A study of 477 adults in a large metropolitan area found that acceptance was greatest among those who were born before 1927 and who had received their political socialization during or before World War II.* Those who were born between 1927 and 1942 and who came of age during the Cold War were intermediate in their attitude about nuclear war. The most rejecting were the adults who were born between 1943 and 1949 and who reached early adulthood during the Vietnam War and other confrontations.

The same study found that the public's attitude toward war in general is increasingly reticent, but there is a relation between the attitudes of patriotism, fear of communism, and rejection of the possibility of nuclear war. Those who expressed less nationalistic attitudes and less unfavorable attitudes toward communism were the most likely to reject nuclear war. For instance, only 14 percent of the World War II generation reected nuclear war; when patriotism and fear of communism were low, the percentages of rejection were 54 and 49, respectively. For those labeled the *dissent generation* 36 percent rejected the nuclear approach; yet the rate rose to 50 percent when high patriotism or high fear of communism was expressed. In other words, opinions about patriotism and communism were more powerful influences than the generational difference.

*V. Jeffries, "Political Generations and the Acceptance or Rejection of Nuclear Warfare," *Journal of Social Issues*, 1974, *30*, 119–25.

1962). One plan that received considerable attention is Graduated Reciprocation in Tension Reduction (GRIT), proposed by Charles Osgood (1962) as "an alternative to war or surrender." Its basic assumption is that the United States (or some other nation) should take the initiative in a "peace offensive" by proposing to reduce arms or greatly increase cultural exchanges. These proposals must arise from "a sincere intent to reduce and control international tensions," must be announced publicly, and must include an explicit invitation to another nation to reciprocate. The reciprocal programs would use international agencies where possible and would be designed to reduce the imbalances between the have and have-not nations. The success of the plan in halting international conflicts has been limited by the priority of perceived threats over mutual trust. There is some evidence of its influence, however, as in President Kennedy's negotiations leading to the nuclear test ban in 1963.

Polarization over the Vietnam war had far-reaching effects for American society, including an increase in isolationist sentiment. *Source:* Wide World Photos, Inc.

As a program for reducing tension, managing conflict, and achieving mutually beneficial cooperation, GRIT strategy also has been applied in laboratory settings. Results of a Prisoner's Dilemma game (see Chapter 12), for example, showed that cooperative strategies could be worked out in a conflict situation (Lindskold & Collins, 1978).

The struggle to discover means of conflict reduction is taking place in a variety of settings—the research laboratory, labor relations, and international organizations, among others. The power blocs may find them indispensable in view of the possibility of a nuclear holocaust. But as long as nuclear weapons remain available, there will be anxiety that the safeguard system will break down. An error, accident, or a psychopath could always start a chain reaction that would bring on the apocalypse.

SUMMARY

The focus in this chapter has been on two particular problem areas. First is ethnic prejudice and discrimination and their causes, a problem that is not unique to any place or time. The barriers to full acceptance of minorities, not only in the United States but in other parts of the world, have cultural, economic, social, and psychological roots. Prejudice involves learning, perception, motivation, and problems of self-identity and group identity. It is expressed in the form of stereotypes, misperceptions, and negative attitudes, as preceding chapters have shown.

Considerable progress has been made in preventing discrimination in the United States since the 1950s, but the dislocations of blacks and Spanish-speaking Americans, as well as other minorities, remain. The stigmatization resulting from prejudice has had deep personality effects. They will persist until resocialization takes place within the large segments of the American public.

The second problem area is international tension. The behavioral scientist's interest in this question has increased enormously since World War II. As in other areas of research, social psychologists have cooperated with representatives of other disciplines to study the causes of international tensions and to explore means by which an enduring peace can be achieved. Among other channels they are exploring are stereotypes, techniques for changing nationalistic attitudes, and means of reducing and sublimating aggressiveness. The fruits of their efforts have not yet fully ripened, but there is a promise of greater achievement along these lines.

An understanding of both ethnic conflicts and international tensions can be enhanced by consideration of various kinds of conflict and means for its resolution. Misattribution complicates both domestic and international conflict, despite the social, economic, political, and military realities. Social psychologists have analyzed the use of threat and demands in the laboratory and their counterparts in international disputes. Bargaining can be either tacit or explicit, but the more specific the issues, the more likely a successful outcome. While conflict is most often resolved by violence, passive resistance or civil disobedience is perceived by many observers as a necessary alternative.

QUESTIONS FOR DISCUSSION

1. What constitutes a minority group?

2. Differentiate between prejudice and discrimination. What are their costs to society?

3. How is race scientifically defined? What is the difference betwen race and ethnicity?

4. How would you analyze the psychological causes of prejudice? How do they relate to social, economic, and other causes of prejudice?

5. How has prejudice affected the personality functioning of blacks or Spanish-speaking Americans?

6. What are the different ways conflict has been classified? Describe the more important of these distinctions.

7. How does bargaining involve the use of threat? Name some recent examples in domestic or international conflict.

8. What is meant by the *mapping* of conflict?

9. How have social psychologists been involved in research on international tensions?

10. Analyze various kinds of stereotypes that apply to interpersonal perception on the international scale.

11. How does society build aggressive and militaristic motives into individuals?

12. What is meant by the warfare state? Describe its psychological effects.

13. Give examples of decision making by various powers on military and foreign policy and show how they have affected nuclear arms proliferation.

14. Have any viable alternatives to mutual deterrence been developed? Describe recent efforts along this line.

WORDS TO REMEMBER

Cultural conditioning. The general learning experiences people acquire from their backgrounds, such as class and religion.

Discrimination. Overt behavior associated with prejudice or a negative attitude toward a given minority group.

Ethnic. Of or relating to a large group with similar traits and customs, based on national, religious, or racial origins.

Ethnocentrism. Strong and often irrational identification with one's own cultural group or nation.

Integration. The range of policies and practices designed to bring a given ethnic group into the in-group. The term implies a relatively complete sharing, compared to *desegregation*, which generally refers to the ending of segregation, or separatism in residence, education, employment, or other spheres of life.

Labeling. The attribution of stereotypes or unfavorable images to others or to ethnic groups, nations, or their members.

Nationalism. Ethnocentric attitudes favoring one's own nation at the expense of others.

Pluralism. The concept that all individuals or ethnic groups should have the right to practice their own customs, language, and lifestyles. It can be contrasted with the idea of standardization, homogeneity, or the *melting pot,* which characterized early immigration history in the United States.

Prejudice. A set of negative attitudes, generally directed toward a given group or individual.

Race. Statistical concept based on given physical traits (blood type, cranial dimensions, pigmentation, etc.). It has sometimes been confused with nationality, religion, or culture.

Stereotype. Categorization of a person or a group on the basis of inadequate data; usually a bias acquired through the early socialization process or from later personal experience.

Threat. Use of demands or scare tactics as a means of obtaining compliance or other advantage in bargaining.

Warfare state. Nation with a strong emphasis on military preparedness. It has especially characterized the two world power blocs, the Soviet Union and (at times, at least) the United States.

READINGS

Allport, G. W. *The Nature of Prejudice.* Reading, Mass.: Addison-Wesley Publishing Co., 1954.

An enduring classic on the historical and psychological aspects of the subject, including the remedial.

Ashmore, R. D. "Black and White in the 1970's," *Journal of Social Issues,* 1976, *32,*2. Several outstanding articles on the psychology of racial prejudice.

Blumenthal, M. D., et al. *Justifying Violence: Attitudes of American Men.* Ann Arbor, Mich:

Institute for Social Research, 1972.
A survey of the range of attitude hostility in a sizable national sample.

Crain, R. L., and Weisman, C. S. *Discrimination, Personality, and Achievement.* New York: Seminar Press, 1972.
An empirical study of the attitudes of northern blacks.

Eldridge, A. F. *Images of Conflict.* New York: St. Martin's Press, 1979.
An excellent, readable account of ethnic and international conflict, well documented with recent historical examples.

Farrar, L. L., Jr. (Ed.). *War: A Historical, Political and Social Study.* Santa Barbara, Cal.: ABC–Clio, 1978.
A collection of absorbing analyses, from religion to film.

Hraba, J. *American Ethnicity.* Itasca, Ill.: F. E. Peacock Publishers, 1979.
Psychological, sociological, and historical approaches to five ethnic groups: Chinese, Japanese, blacks, Mexicans, and native Americans.

Kelman, H. C. (Ed.). *International Behavior: A Social Psychological Analysis.* New York: Holt, Rinehart & Winston, 1965.
One of the more complete collections of studies on nationalism, international relations, decision making, and the underlying attitudes.

Martinez, J. L., Jr. (Ed.). *Chicano Psychology.* New York: Academic Press, 1977.
The contributions of behavioral scientists to defining the behavior of Mexican Americans.

Morgan, P. M. *Deterrence: A Conceptual Analysis.* Beverly Hills, Cal.: Sage Publications, 1977.
Political considerations in national decision making in this critical area.

Osgood, C. E. *An Alternative to War or Surrender.* Urbana: University of Illinois Press, 1962.
A psychologist's plan for the United States to assume the initiative in reducing or eliminating the arms race.

Simpson, G. E., and Yinger, J. M. *Racial and Cultural Minorities* (4th ed.). New York: Harper & Row, 1972.
Relatively complete statement on the historical, educational, economic, legal, and other institutional aspects of the problem.

Watson, P. (Ed.). *Psychology and Race.* Chicago: Aldine Publishing Co., 1973.
A collection of readings on the psychological bases of racial and national differences.

THE ENVIRONMENT AND AGING

This final chapter considers two areas of social concern which are likely to continue to grow in the future. Both of these are relatively new areas of concern as compared to the issues of Chapter 18—racial and international tensions—which have been a research focus for the better part of this century. The social psychology of the environment, which is concerned with the behavior of people in their physical setting, can suggest solutions to such problems as pollution, energy use, crowding, urban stress, and overpopulation. The social psychology of aging is concerned with the role of the growing number of older people in our society and their rights as a sort of underprivileged minority.

Because of their pervasive interest in interpersonal relations, social psychologists for years overlooked the importance of environmental conditions as determinants of people's attitudes and behaviors. The reciprocal relation between the individual and the sociocultural setting has been regarded as fundamental, as this text has consistently demonstrated, but the possibilities of conditioning the reactions of people as individuals and members of groups to their physical environments, and the effects of physical surroundings on the way people feel and act, have only recently been recognized. All individuals react to spatial features and other environmental stimuli such as the density of people, noise, pollution, or the aesthetics of physical structures. Like other citizens, social psychologists also are concerned about the deterioration of the natural environment and are seeking ways to apply their knowledge to encourage conservation of the resources of the planet. The concerns of environmentalists have become a leading arena of social protest, to the extent that they may be the basis for the next social revolution, as was noted in Chapter 17.

This focus on ecology is not altogether new. In the 1930s Kurt Lewin was stressing the importance of the environment, both its physical and psychological dimensions, in his field theory (see Chapter 1). The emphasis of earlier social scientists such as Charles H. Cooley, W. I. Thomas, and G. H. Mead, however, was on the interpersonal environment, and spatial factors, density, and environmental protection were given only passing attention. The first part of this chapter gives evidence of the growing interest of social psychology in this area.

The choice of aging as the final topic in this text is appropriate because it draws on almost every aspect of social psychology we have considered. It is an area of research to which the social psychologist can make a contribution. It illustrates the impact of culture on individuals; Americans treat the aged differently than most other societies do. The psychology of aging also is a product of socialization, or, more explicitly, resocialization. Aging is concerned with cognitive processes, especially attitude formation and change, both toward the aged and among the aged. And the roles of the elderly often change in a society; there is even some neutralization of sex roles in the later stages of life. Finally, the growing numbers of older people in the population have given rise to a new social movement or a new expression of collective behavior. The aged constitute one more minority group—one to which you too will some day belong if you live long enough—and the prospects for longer life are constantly improving.

THE SOCIAL PSYCHOLOGY OF THE ENVIRONMENT

Scientific study of the environment is concerned with *ecology*, the original meaning of which was derived from the study of the exchange of energy in plants and animals. The interrelationship of organisms and their environment is often referred to as an *ecosystem*, "a more or less closed system of reciprocal life patterns" between the flora and fauna in a given geographic area (Ramsay & Anderson, 1972). As the world has become more complex, ecology has come to include a wide range of reciprocal inputs between humans and their natural setting. In the broadest interpretation, environmental or ecological psychology can encompass almost any behavior of individuals which is determined by their physical or social setting.

Psychological Study of Environmental Problems

A number of fields of psychology as well as many other disciplines are involved in efforts to analyze, understand, and protect the ecology. The experimental psychologist's role in studying the physical environment has contributed important knowledge about the ecosystem. The social psychologist analyzes the environment from an overall perspective, examining the complex relations among various types of environments with the help of colleagues from specialties such as clinical, management, and industrial psychology. The principal concern is with the analysis of the attitudes and behaviors of people in their settings.

Similarly, the environmental psychologist attempts "to establish empirical and theoretical relationships between the behavior and experience of the person and his built environment" (Proshansky, 1976). The emphasis is on the absolute integrity of the relation between people and physical events. The person's awareness of belonging to a physical setting requires a response within that setting, so that the laboratory can never be an adequate substitute for real-life setting. In environmental psychology self-identity is seen as a fairly subtle process applying to questions of privacy, territoriality, aesthetic preference, and the like. Content is more critical than process, as the environmental psychologist focuses on specific places like schoolrooms, city streets, gardens, and hallways. The orientation of the research must consider time as well as space, and the total sociocultural setting cannot be ignored (see Box 19–1).

As the science of psychology has moved from the experimental study of individual behavior to a many-faceted discipline focused on individuals and groups in a variety of settings, psychologists have analyzed numerous aspects of the environment. Psychological study of the ecology includes the use of space and structures, the societal and institutional environment, and means of conserving scarce resources, among other topics. The problem of ecological deterioration brings into play many disciplines, primarily engineering and the natural sciences, but the question of how to change values and attitudes which are the basis of social change remains largely the task of the behavioral scientist.

The social psychologist's analysis of group and organizational behavior involves the significance of various regulatory mechanisms in interpersonal behavior such as supply and demand, rewards and punishments, public opinion, group pressure, and other forms of social power introduced in Chapter 11. The environment is approached in such terms as crowding, temperature, air pollution, noise levels, and the aesthetic of building design. Unlike ecology in the physical world, social ecology is colored by explicit value orientations, since it is concerned with the effective functioning of human beings (Insel & Moos, 1974).

Moos (1973, pp. 652–665) suggests six means of conceptualizing the human environment:

1. *Ecological dimensions*—the physical aspects that set limits or define the range of behaviors in which the human being can act—for instance, climate, topography, architectural design and structure.
2. *Organizational dimensions*—the influences of size, staffing quotas, salary levels, and the span of organizational control.
3. *Personal characteristics within the setting*—the character of the environment as determined by the socioeconomic background of the inhabitants—age, sex, status, group membership, abilities, and so on.
4. *Behavior settings*—the milieu in terms of social ecology.
5. *Reinforcement properties of the environment*—the degree to which persons change from one setting to another because of the learning experience and social reinforcement they receive in successive environments.

Box 19–1
PSYCHOLOGICAL MAPPING

One of the techniques psychologists use to study the environment is psychological mapping, which indicates the basis on which landmarks and distinctive physical features are recognized. Stanley Milgram, who studied the psychological mapping of city dwellers in New York and Paris, found the residents tended to identify landmarks and neighborhoods on the basis of the relation of spaces and buildings or cultural features, rather than socioeconomic importance.*

Using a representative sample of residents in all five boroughs in New York, he found that when scenes of that city were flashed on the screen, sites in Manhattan were recognized by 64 percent of the total sample, but less than 40 percent could recognize sites in Brooklyn or the Queens, and only 26 percent could identify locations in the Bronx and Staten Island. In locating a given building or complex in the right neighborhood or on the right street, the differences were even sharper.

These differences were due to the "unique configuration of spaces and buildings" in Manhattan, as in Columbus Circle and Rockefeller Center, as much as to the importance of these buildings as landmarks. Chinatown and Little Italy had distinct images because of their cultural features.

In the Paris sample, the findings were not very different. The historic monuments of central Paris were recognized proportionately more than outlying structures which could have more significance in the socioeconomic life of the residents. These findings are especially interesting in view of the claim of Parisians the *tourists* do not know the real Paris!

_____

* Stanley Milgram, *The Individual in a Social World* (Reading, Mass.: Addison-Wesley Publishing Co., 1977), pp. 54–90.

6. *Psychosocial dimensions and organizational climate*—the interchange between the person's experience and others, and how these perceptions of the environment change in time.

Thus social psychologists are concerned with the optimum functioning of both the environment and the people in it. Research focused on the work setting, educational climates, psychiatric wards, correctional institutions, neighborhoods, and the community can provide the information needed to study this relationship, with emphasis on how individuals perceive the different dimensions and how the environment can be changed to best advantage.

More than their European counterparts, central cities in the United States are perceived as environments of deterioration, disarray, and crowdedness. *Source:* © Theodore Anderson, 1981.

Social Change and Ecological Deterioration

Although in the broadest sense the psychologist is concerned with effecting change in all types of environments, the greatest concern at present is with human survival, despite the breakdown of the traditional social order. Overpopulation, air pollution, noise, and the depletion of the world's resources are major problems in this area. The social psychologist has a particular interest because more than half of the behavioral scientists in the world are citizens of a nation—the United States—which requires over a third of the earth's natural resources to provide for a population that represents a mere 6 percent of the world's total.

Though there has been much interest in the environment, the degree of commitment to ecological reform is difficult to measure. The public interest in ecology that emerged in the United States in the late 1960s may have been encouraged by the Nixon administration as a means of diverting the people's attention from the unpopular military involvement in Vietnam (Ridgeway, 1970).

Business, industry, and labor groups often seem to regard ecological concerns as merely inhibiting to their goals for production, profits, or jobs. Although the supplies of many indispensable, unrenewable resources are steadily shrinking, there is little concerted effort to make unpopular decisions about priorities. After the 1974 oil shortage no significant measure for conserving supplies was adopted, despite lip service to the reality of an energy crisis. Suggestions to conserve petroleum products by phasing out large cars or developing alternate sources of energy have been slow to be implemented—despite announcements that known petroleum reserves would be depleted within a generation. Even the severe 1979 shortages of gasoline were not regarded as requiring any immediate action.

Social psychologists, who have a commitment to the analysis of attitude formation and change (see Chapters 8 and 9), are investigating the reasons for the failure of the public and its leaders to come to grips with pollution of the atmosphere, oceans, and waterways; mineral depletion; overpopulation; and inefficient, unaesthetic land occupancy. A study of three samples—conservationists (Sierra Club members), college students, and non-college-trained adults—found an emotional involvement but considerable ignorance about these problems (Maloney & Ward, 1973). The Sierra Club members had the most complete knowledge; the general adult sample the least.

Lack of specific information about the ecology underlines the difficulty of finding solutions for environmental problems. Even public pressure on government representatives to take the necessary steps to slow down ecological destruction often is lethargic. The role of concerned psychologists in this respect is to develop ways to change the value structure of the public, so its consumption patterns conform to a more modest, more rational lifestyle. This would be evidence of a concern for the future, an orientation often suggested in studies of values (Kluckhohn & Strodtbeck, 1961).

Behavior Settings

Roger Barker formulated a unique approach to ecology with his conception of *behavior settings,* or the specific environments in which individuals interact. A store, a church social hall, a baseball field, or a school constitutes a setting with a self-regulatory quality of its own. The setting has a structure that is independent of the participants. The size, location, and tradition of the setting impose limits on how individuals can act within it; there are rules of the game—or norms—that hold, irrespective of the individual.

Moreover, each setting has an efficient or optimal number of participants. The demographic aspect of the setting is important because any enterprise can be under- or overpopulated. The size of an organization has a reciprocal influence on the social climate, and both affect the quality of the participation.

The study of a Kansas town (called "Midwest") by Barker and Wright (1954) which was introduced in Chapter 3 investigated the *territorial range* of different subgroups within the community—or the areas with which certain groups are identified. The territorial range for young children had an index of 60, and for adolescents it increased to 79. That is, children were present in 60 percent and adolescents in 79 percent of the community's behavior settings at one time or another.

Barker made a more recent comparative analysis of the significance of behavior in underpopulated Midwest and overpopulated Yoredale, an English community (Barker & Schoggen, 1973). On the whole, Yoredale, with its larger, more compact population, made greater and more efficient use of most of its behavior settings, and its inhabitants spent more time in private settings. In contrast, more of the behaviors of Midwest residents took place in public areas. Because of the smaller population of Midwest, more of its citizens were called on to enter a diversity of environments, and they had to be more versatile in the role positions they occupied.

Handling Personal Space

A fundamental factor in the way people respond to their physical surroundings is their sense of identity, autonomy, freedom, and control as they function in the sociocultural setting (see the sections on perception of causality and freedom in Chapter 6). According to Proshansky, Ittleson, and Rivlin (1970, pp. 173–183), a person's search for autonomy in her or his life space is based on three conceptions:

1. The human being is a thinking, goal-directed organism.
2. The satisfaction of needs depends on interaction with a physical environment.
3. As individuals organize their physical environments perceptually, they strive to maximize their freedom of choice.

We handle space in accordance with our socialization in certain spatial categories. According to Hall (1966), one of these is *fixed feature space*, the limits spatially imposed by walls or the arrangements of streets, squares, or blocks, or the precise functions assigned to a building or room. In Western culture, which is more rigid than non-Western cultures, spatial arrangements often tend to keep people apart. In *semifixed space*, features like walls and furniture can be moved about, as in settings like a sidewalk cafe or an open classroom. In this social setting, people are brought together. *Informal space* allows people to develop their own treatment of space.

Our self-identity (see Chapter 4) is arrived at in terms of a given spatial involvement. The ways we use space are determined by how we relate to other people, our images of spatial dimensions, cultural traditions, and the situation at hand. We each set up boundaries and resent any invasion of our spatial arena. Introverts, for example, like a comparatively greater distance between themselves and others (Sommer, 1969), and schizophrenics, because of their suspicions or reluctance to enter conversations, keep their distance from other patients in a mental hospital. Most people arrange their spatial boundaries by moving toward or away from the other person. The direction is especially important if motivation is sufficiently strong: You approach an attractive person of the opposite sex at an informal party, for example, and whether the other person moves toward or away from you provides a clue to the degree of mutual interest.

The culture and various subcultures also help determine how people use space (see Chapter 2). A Latin American likes to converse at close range, whereas an American or a German is more likely to stay at arm's length. Many observers have noted that Americans favor more spatial separation than Europeans do. Possibly this is because Americans are accustomed to larger territories, or perhaps they compensate for their casual, easy friendliness by seeking distance as a barrier. In the same way, formal relationships among Europeans allow them to be closer physically without overstepping bounds.

Usually the specific setting establishes the norms for the appropriate distance between ourselves and the other person. A cocktail party reduces interpersonal barriers not only because the room is crowded but because alcohol inhibits the need for a territorial shield. Theater managers report that people waiting in line for an R-rated film stand closer together than those waiting for a film rated G or PG.

Privacy

Animals set up territorial prerogatives; the human personality seeks both territoriality and privacy, or what is described in Box 4-1 in Chapter 4 as *the territories of the self.* According to Westin (1967), the search for privacy involves four dimensions:

1. *Solitude*—the state of privacy in which the person is protected from observation by others.
2. *Intimacy*—the quality of the setting which allows a strong interpersonal relationship to be realized by the members of a group—whether a married couple, a family, or a circle of friends.
3. *Anonymity*—the ability of the individual to maintain freedom from identification and surveillance.
4. *Reserve*—a relatively more complex relationship which allows people to conceal particular aspects of themselves and involves respect for the other person.

Thus privacy allows the individual to enter into a process of self-evaluation, and territoriality can provide a "means of establishing and maintaining a sense of personal identity" (Proshansky, Ittleson, & Rivlin, 1970). Territoriality appears to be a universal need which is found throughout much of the animal world; a number of species designate their territories by leaving odorous secretions. Human beings also have a sense of sovereignty over their domains, be it a seat in a theater, a home, or citizenship in a nation. In a critical situation the need for spatial identity can become very sensitive. In a laboratory study of 18 pairs of sailors who volunteered for the experiment and were divided into isolated and nonisolated samples, the isolated subjects had stronger preferences for a particular bed, chair, or specific location (Altman & Haythorn, 1967). Yet there were noticeable individual differences in both samples. Territorial needs seemed to increase for those who were less similar to their partners on traits like dominance and affiliation.

While the trend toward multiple dwellings in urban areas might imply more flexibility in regard to territorial demands, there is more concern with privacy now, in more crowded conditions, than was true for the frontiersman. The present enthusiasm for condominiums suggests that the need for isolation or privacy is subordinate to the advantages of being near one's work or a favored location like downtown or the beach. The preference for buying a condominium rather than renting an apartment also could signify a compromise between the freedom of a detached dwelling and the anonymity of the conventional apartment house. These shifts in consumer trends illustrate the compromises made in privacy and territoriality when faced with the realities of a crowded urban society.

Preferences and Aesthetics

Another determinant of how people use space is their sense of style or fashion (see Chapter 17) and their perceptual and aesthetic preferences. Our ideas about building design, room plan, furniture layout and the vistas we want to see from our windows or as we move along the streets, sidewalks, and roadways have both social and individual sources (Schorr, 1970). If there is no dining room, for example, a family is more likely to eat in the kitchen or family room than in the living room. This may be in line with cultural norms, or the family may prefer it for practical or aesthetic reasons. In a new Chilean housing project some families decided to move the furniture from their living rooms out into the hall so they could experience less distraction and more togetherness. Other cultures often crowd more objects and persons into a room than Americans customarily do.

In the larger environment, some like to look out on a public square and observe the movements of people; others would rather contemplate a quiet garden. A household's choice of where to live may include an apartment in the densely populated urban center, a detached house in an outlying neighborhood, or a house and lot in a suburban or rural area. These choices may be limited by considerations of finances or commuting time, and often they are decided on the basis of positions in the life cycle. Single living or the early years of marriage can favor the city, and the child-rearing years the suburbs, with an eventual return to the convenience of the city. Housing preferences are conditioned by many variables, and the research findings on these preferences are valuable for urban planners as well as for social scientists (see Box 19–2).

Preference for the central city and the development of high-rise housing may be favored by a shortage of fuels. The kind of structure that will be most appealing reflects a number of individual and situational factors, including reactions to height, density, type of construction, availability of service facilities, the interpersonal relationships fostered by the setting, and the presence or absence of children (Herrenkohl, 1972). Acceptance of the high rise can be influenced by the norms of density acceptable to urban planners; currently, 8 to 12 dwelling units per acre are considered as the maximum in planning new urban communities

A woman's search for identity and autonomy in the social setting can lead 'to symptoms of anomie and alienation, even in an attractive environment. *Source:* © Theodore Anderson, 1981.

(Whittick, 1974). Differences of national culture and of subcultures like class, age, sex, or marital status also help determine the acceptability of multiple or high-rise housing (Williamson, 1978, 1981).

As Western culture drifts toward the urban way of life, architects and engineers must be motivated to provide aesthetically pleasing designs and vistas, as well as functional uses of space. Contrast the images associated with a 19th-century industrial city such as Pittsburgh with those provided by planned communities like Washington, D.C., or Paris, or model cities like Reston, Virginia, or Columbia, Maryland: an unrelieved profile of concrete, utility poles, and billboards against a background of blighted shops and office buildings and substandard housing, compared to gracious public buildings and homes on tree-lined streets, with community squares, fountains, and park areas.

Some cities evoke images because of their historical and cultural associations, as well as their treatment of space. Others have a distinct visual or graphic form—San Francisco clinging to its hills surrounded by the ocean and bay, New York's vertical profile and varied ethnic neighborhoods. A city may have a kind of

Box 19–2
RESIDENTIAL CHOICE

If a family could choose a place to live regardless of convenience or financial considerations, it might consider the kind of neighborhood, amount of space the family wanted, and style of housing that offered the most companionship or privacy. These are among the questions social scientists have asked about residential choice.

William Michelson studied people in the urban environment and found certain influences on housing for various sociocultural groups. His findings, which may not hold for all societies and which must be judged within the context of the needs and realities confronting a particular household, include the following:

1. Intense, frequent association with a wide range of relatives thrives in areas in which many people have easy physical access to each other, but this lifestyle is diminished in areas of low density.
2. Active, traditionally masculine pastimes are part of home life only when the environment is structured to minimize the impingement of neighbors.
3. People with cosmopolitan lifestyles desire more physical separation from neighbors and place less emphasis on proximity to facilities and services than those whose interests are local.
4. Adults, before and after raising children (as well as those who are childless), frequently rate centrality (i.e., access to consumer goods and services) more highly than do families with growing children.
5. Completely random placement of working-class residents among middle-class neighbors results in their isolation rather than integration.
6. National and cultural values frequently transform the type and the use of urban spaces.
7. People who value convenience highly are likely to prefer more mixed land uses and small lot sizes. People who value individualism highly prefer larger lot sizes.
8. People associate private open space with active family pursuits, regardless of the size of the space.
9. High neighborhood densities seem more related to social pathologies than crowding within dwelling units, but this effect is mediated by personal and cultural factors.
10. The position and outlook of doors can determine interaction patterns.

---

* W. Michelson, *Man and His Urban Environment: A Sociological Approach* (Reading, Mass.: Addison-Wesley Publishing Co., 1970), pp. 193–95.

contrived focus, like the strip in Las Vegas, yet give the visitor a confused set of images in which "the difficult visual order of buildings and signs" is imposed on "the obvious order of street elements" (Venturi, Brown, & Izenour, 1973).

The more pressurized use of space and the need to provide adequate transportation in cities requires planners to look for ingenious means of offering aesthetic experiences. One consideration in the design of Boston's expressway system was presentation of a pleasant visual array of both nearby and distant objects—a difficult task in a city without a unified image or a central set of objects like Chicago's skyline on the lakefront (Appleyard, Lynch, & Myer, 1967). One objective in shaping the highways for the occupants of vehicles is to clarify the visual impression of the environment, although practical problems may prevent engineers from including these considerations. Urban planning of the future calls for anticipating perceptual needs. With the growth of metropolitan areas, structures designed for work, play, rest, or movement must communicate a sense of integrity to the urban dweller.

In considering aesthetics, a distinction can be made between space and landscape. According to Sonnenfeld (1966), *landscape* refers to the configuration of forms distributed in space, as well as the various images conveyed by color, movement, and other appeals to the senses which convey ideas of possible use or have emotional connotations. *Space* is more ambiguous; it has a connotation of openness or distance and properties like movement, isolation, or privacy. Any approach to the arrangement of space and landscape is arbitrary. There are no universal specifications, but in view of "diminishing space and depreciating landscape," as Sonnenfeld puts it, a good deal of innovation is necessary in order to take future interests into account. Cultural, social, and economic bases are all ineffective in classifying environmental preferences from the standpoint of spatial and landscape needs. Possibly a more useful differentiation could be made between the native and nonnative. The outsider is usually more adaptable to environmental change than the long-term resident, who is more rigid about accepting spatial and landscape changes.

Crowdedness and Urban Stress

The enormous growth of the world's population in recent years has been aptly described as an explosion. It was not until 1850 that world population reached 1 billion, but another billion had been added by 1930. It reached 3 billion in 1965 and had soared to 4 billion by 1976. This geometric rate of growth is likely to continue, and additional billions will be added even more frequently.

Worldwide, in the 1980s over 70 million people are being added to the population each year, despite several decades of birth control in developing nations, where the rate is highest. Even the most modest predictions place world population at 5.5 billion by the year 2000, less than a generation away. While it is difficult to make precise predictions, it can be surmised that the earth will remain a crowded—and largely undernourished—planet.

Much of the increased population is being concentrated in urban communities. Whereas in 1900 less than a third of the population of the United

States was urban, by 1980 over three fourths lived in metropolitan areas. This tendency toward urbanization also appears in developing regions such as Latin America and the Middle East. Most individuals are now living in concentrated groupings, though the densities of cities vary greatly. But density takes different forms. Even with 8 million inhabitants, greater Los Angeles cannot be described as having a dense population because the area is so large. There is enough space for most households to have separate dwellings, but then nearly 4 million cars must compete for space on the freeways and city streets. Thus there is a feeling of crowdedness in Los Angeles, despite the extent of the sprawling metropolitan area.

The psychological effects of crowding are not entirely clear, since it is difficult to isolate density from other negative influences such as poverty, substandard dwellings, inadequate recreational facilities, lack of police protection, and noise level. In an intensive study of a metropolitan area (Schmidt, Goldman, & Feimer, 1979), the perception of crowding was related to a multitude of factors: room density, awareness of noise, nearness to major traffic arteries and commercial areas, and, on the positive side, the availability of parks. Also relevant were the subjects' comparisons with other cities and their class and ethnic backgrounds. The factors underlying the feeling of crowdedness vary according to whether density is viewed in the context of the dwelling (see Box 19–3), the neighborhood, or the city as a totality.

Crowdedness can even be considered positive because it affords a sense of participation and excitement. But as noted in Chapter 4, more often the sense of crowding is interpreted as a violation of a person's territoriality or sense of privacy. Crowding appears when "the number of people an individual is in contact with is sufficient to prevent him from carrying out some specific behavior and thereby restricts his freedom of choice" (Proshansky, Ittelson, & Rivlin, 1970).

Experiments on the effects of crowding have not had altogether consistent results. In a now classic study, Calhoun (1962) found that when laboratory rats were allowed to breed freely (food supply and cleanliness were maintained in the cages), the eventual result was overpopulation. This was followed by competition, aggressiveness, disease, and, finally, a sudden drop in the size of the colony. Other studies of mammals have produced similar findings; the end product of crowding is a rise in infant mortality and, eventually, a decline in breeding. Crowding among human beings would seem to have the same effects, largely because of the other kinds of stress associated with crowdedness. Too many persons sharing limited quarters must experience some frustration, which may lead to aggression. Yet the effects vary with the cultural setting, and the feeling of crowdedness could be assumed more in a slum population in, say, Calcutta, than one in New York City.

Laboratory studies of human subjects under conditions of crowding or density have been inconclusive, in any event. When subjects were asked to perform various kinds of tasks such as crossing out numbers and forming words, along with more complicated mental problems in low- and high-density conditions, there was no significant difference (Freedman, Klevansky, & Ehrlich, 1971). The conclusion was that density is not "a simple negative, aversive stimulus." In another study the effects of density appeared to intensify the

Box 19–3
FEELING CROWDED

Some rooms or buildings seem more crowded than others, though they may have the same number of people in them. Andrew Baum has suggested that crowdedness may be dependent on how a person's options in social contacts are affected by architectural design.* To test this hypothesis, Baum and G. E. Davis conducted an investigation with first-year women students in a dormitory which offered three different living arrangements, with rooms off a short corridor, off a long corridor, or off a long corridor with intervening spaces.† Findings based on observation, questionnaires, and laboratory tests, pointed to a less crowded feeling along the short and broken corridors; residents there had less difficulty establishing social contacts, since they felt free about interacting with nearby residents and were more inclined to leave their doors open. Small groups were less likely to develop in the long-corridor setting, and the posture of these residents toward others was more withdrawn.

In another study Baum and Davis compared room colors and found that the darker tones with high visual complexity ("busy" wallpaper or a surplus of furnishings in the room) seem more crowded than light-colored rooms with a minimum of clutter.‡

These studies suggest that architectural planning can influence our orientation to other people. Reducing the size of residential groupings, for example, might prevent stress due to crowding.

_____

*A. Baum and S. Valins, *Architecture and Social Behavior,* Hillsdale, N.J.: Lawrence Erlbaum Associates, 1977.

†A. Baum and G. E. Davis, "Spatial and Social Aspects of Crowding Perception," *Environment and Behavior,* 1976, *8,* 527–544.

‡A. Baum and G. E. Davis, "Reducing the Stress of High-Density Living: An Architectural Intervention," *Journal of Personality and Social Psychology,* 1980, *38,* 471–481.

characteristic responses of individuals, especially as related to sex differences (Freedman et al., 1972). In a mock jury trial the men gave harsher sentences and the women more lenient ones. In a situation of high density, also, the men liked each other less and women liked each other more. Apparently men saw the situation of high density as threatening, but for women it was socially stimulating.

Griffitt and Veitch (1971) found negative effects on attitude and mood in the experimental group, which was subjected to conditions of high density (4 square feet per person) and temperature (93 degrees), compared to control groups tested at 73 degrees and 13 square feet per person. This finding was supported by an observation in the report of the National Advisory Commission on Civil Disorders (U.S. Riot Commission, 1968) that a number of the urban riots of the 1960s occurred when temperatures approached or surpassed 90 degrees—the "long, hot summer," as noted in Chapter 16.

The study of crowding, like most topics in social psychology, involves both situational and personality factors. Stokols (1976) distinguishes between *neutral,* or physical, and *personal,* or psychological, aspects. Some interpretations stress the concept of privacy or territoriality (discussed above), or the "selective control of access to oneself or to one's group" (Altman, 1975). According to Stockdale (1978), crowding is a function of the situation, but the cues indicating crowdedness may be *perceptual,* as in the visibility of many people, *associative-symbolic,* as in the image of tall buildings, *temporal,* as in the pressures of a full time schedule, or *sociocultural,* as in a society comprised of different types of people. A study of the reactions to various hypothetical situations (Taylor, 1981) found that subjects tended to perceive density according to two psychological dimensions: *social constraint,* when people are obliged to interact with others who are marginal to their own interests, as in a major airport the day before Thanksgiving, and *spatial constraint,* in which people's movements are constricted, as on a small dance floor.

In these situations it is the *perception* of the context that counts, however; we enjoy many crowded situations, such as a rock concert or cocktail party. Time, mood, and place all count, and the individual responds to a variety of needs by seeking out crowds.

Crowding has been found to have differential effects on behavior, including sex activity. Edwards and Booth (1977) found a crowded household had some negative influence on marital intercourse, largely because of the lack of privacy. They also found extramarital activity was higher when women experienced prolonged crowding; and (the most statistically significant finding) that when crowding was experienced both in childhood and adulthood, men under stress reported increased marital intercourse.

Crowding is related to other aspects of the environmental protection: air pollution, water pollution, the disposal of waste products (including nuclear wastes), and the decay of housing units, for example. The effects of noise have received increasing attention from psychologists; according to research findings, the effects vary according to source, frequency, regularity, and the noise threshold of the individual. Glass and Singer (1972) carried out a prolonged investigation of sensitivity to noise to both laboratory and real-life samples. The subjects reacted more negatively to unpredictable and uncontrollable noises, as shown by poorer scores in frustration tolerance (solving a series of puzzles for which no solution was possible) and in proofreading (correcting a manuscript). Some reticence about helping others also accompanied unpredictable noise. Relatively loud sounds (108 decibels for nine seconds per minute, for a period of 23 minutes) produced no significant effect on behavior; though they evoked stronger galvanic responses, there was no measurable influence on mental tasks.

In the social psychologist's approach to the environment, however, the study of crowding and urban stress, like other aspects of the relation between people

Environmental psychology has arisen from a myriad of interests, such as the problem of crowdedness in large areas of the world. *Source:* United Nations.

and their physical setting, must involve more than analysis of the nature and effects of physical stimuli. The social psychologist's concern with the environment is directed to discovering ways to bring about desired changes in the attitudes and behavior of individuals in their social relations with others.

This concern acknowledges the fact that people continually respond to the cues in their environment. Parr (1980) conceives of this relationship as the P (person) functioning in an E (environment), subject to a number of M (mediating variables—or the expectations and discrepancies found in the environment). There is an almost continual hope that P may be able to change E through his or her B (behavior). Most people—and particularly the elderly—are forced to contend with various limitations on how they can deal with the environment. The second part of this chapter deals with these and other problems faced by the aging in a constantly changing society.

THE SOCIAL PSYCHOLOGY OF AGING

The role of the aged in contemporary American society is becoming of greater interest as the average age of the population increases. In the preceding century only a relatively few people lived to the upper years; today 1 out of 10 people is over 65, and by the year 2000 1 out of 8 will belong to this group. Society is beginning to ask: How can the status of the elderly be raised? How can this period of the life cycle be made more meaningful and productive? What kinds of housing and social groupings would provide adequate social networks among older people?

To answer these and other questions, research centers on aging have been established throughout the country. The Andrus Gerontology Center of the University of Southern California may be the best known, but there are also centers at Duke University, the University of Chicago, the University of Michigan, and many others that are doing research on aging and training students in various functions for working with the aged. In scores of communities various programs also are being set up to aid older people, and organizations devoted to their interests are proliferating.

This new outlook stands in contrast to the traditional indifference of behavioral scientists toward the aging process. According to an analysis of research and textbooks in social psychology (Blank, 1979), until the late 1970s, the adjustment problems of middle and upper age were generally neglected. Now, as psychologists and sociologists are moving toward a life-span approach in their investigations of the dynamics of behavior (Blank, 1982), the problems of later life are receiving attention comparable to that traditionally devoted to developmental stages from infancy to early adulthood.

The Elderly as a Minority Group

The aged make up the fastest growing minority in North American society. If aging is considered to begin at 60, oldsters comprise about 16 percent of the U.S.

population, and they should represent between one fifth and one fourth by the year 2000. Life expectancy, which in 1900 was 47 years, has risen to almost 77 for women—the stronger sex, in terms of longevity. A 1977 Census Bureau report predicted a life expectancy in 2050 of 81 for women and just under 72 for men. At the beginning of the 1980s, a newly retired person of 62 or 65 could well have 15, 20, or even 25 years ahead. Medical progress, improvements in the environment, and encouragement of a better diet, more exercise, and social involvement for older people presage a further gradual increase in longevity.

The special interests of the aged as a minority group are being represented by an increasing number of advocacy groups which are seeking to establish the rights and meet the needs of older people (see Box 19–4). These include community agencies such as councils on aging, senior service centers, bureaus and commissions for the aging, and geriatric centers; local and regional groups; and national organizations. They depend on various sources for funding, including private contributions, foundation grants, and the support of local and federal governments. These agencies and organizations not only further the interests of older people, they also perform a great variety of services for them, from information and referral, through legal, tax, and psychological counseling, to provision for daily needs such as transportation, one good meal a day, home visits, and home maintenance and repair.

Difficulties can be anticipated as society attempts to adjust—socially, psychologically, economically, and politically—to a situation in which every fourth or fifth person is over 60. The interest in a youth culture in the 1970s (see Chapter 3) may well have shifted to concern with a culture of the aged by the 1990s. The transition could prove to be a great strain on our understanding and the fabric of our human arrangements.

The category of the aged actually can include anyone beyond the first stages of youth, as many middle-aged persons can testify. A man of 45 who loses his job in engineering may be told he is too old to qualify for training for personnel work, for example. Recently there have been efforts to help women who need or want to return to work or school once the children are grown.

Stereotypes or preconceived notions about aging abound in the United States, as they do in respect to other minority groups. The term *agism* has joined *racism* and *sexism* as an indicator of prejudice and discrimination against a portion of society. In the case of the elderly, however, it reflects a deep-seated uneasiness about a condition that will affect every person who lives long enough. The result has often been an attitude of distaste and revulsion toward growing old and becoming ill or disabled (Butler, 1969). Ironically, this negative view of aging is shared to some extent by the old themselves, who absorb these myths from the cultural pattern of their youth.

One index of the stereotyping of the elderly was provided by an analysis of cartoons in popular magazines by Sheppard (1981). A factor analysis found the humor had one of four dimensions. The one that appeared most frequently was *ineffectuality;* the elderly were portrayed as useless or in some way handicapped. Next was *disparagement,* or insulting or denying status to the aged, followed by

Box 19–4
ADVOCACY FOR THE AGED

A lifetime of observing how things work in society has prepared today's older people to recognize the value of joining together in organizations designed to further their special interests.

The National Retired Teachers Association, established in 1946 by a retired high school principal, Ethel Percy Andrus, first saw the need for group health insurance for older people. Success in this venture led to the founding of AARP (American Association of Retired Persons), open to all persons over 55. The appeal of lower-cost insurance and prescriptions and other benefits caused AARP membership to mushroom, but the greatest service the association may perform for its millions of members is its influence as an organized interest group with influence in Congress.

The National Council of Senior Citizens developed with strong labor support and devoted much effort to pressing for Medicare, increased social security benefits, and other reforms in national policy for treatment of the aging. It has several million members in affiliated clubs all over the country. The National Council on the Aging is primarily an organization of other organizations for the aging. It assists them with planning, gives technical aid, provides consultation and publishes informational and training materials, "devoted to a better life in the later years."

The most militant interest group is the Gray Panthers, founded by Maggie Kuhn, a retired church social worker. The Gray Panthers deplore the tendency for retired people to be put in "playpens for the old," where they while away their time playing bingo and shuffleboard. The members are dedicated to activist efforts to achieve social reform and social change.

obsolescence, or focusing on the decline of sexual interests, reduced mental functions, or outmoded values. Least frequently used was *isolation,* in which the ageds' loneliness and search for companionship were depicted. Of course humor can be directed to the aged, as to any age group, but these cartoons suggest that negative attitudes about the elderly are deeply engrained.

Myth and Reality about the Aged Personality

Like any stereotype, those about the elderly prevent the perceiver from seeing a particular older person as an individual with a certain background, personality, abilities, and potentialities. One way to eliminate this kind of biased thinking is to examine the myths and stereotypes about agism in the light of facts and figures.

Individual Differences

One underlying misapprehension is that chronological age is the proper criterion for judging aging and the index for problems of the elderly. This idea may stem from the biblical injunction that the age of man is three score and ten years, or from the U.S. choice of age 65 as the time to retire and start collecting social security and Medicare benefits. This reliance on the calendar, of course, overlooks the tremendous differences among people. Some individuals in their fifties and early sixties are debilitated, feeble, inadequate, and dispirited. Others in their seventies and eighties are lively, interested, productive, and motivated.

There is tremendous variability among the aging—probably more so than in any other age group. The conformity pressures of jobs are removed; and the individual is free to loaf or to keep busy, to socialize or to withdraw, to join community groups or to pursue private interests. As the gerontologist Ollie Randall (1977) put it:

> We hear much today of the new generation of the elderly—the "aging and the aged." This implies we are a group (which we are not) for the phrase attributes the same characteristics to all of us. We are perhaps the most individualistic people alive today . . . We are as different from one another as it is possible to be, even when we belong to the same family or the same culture.

Some persons manage very well the transitions from one stage to another in their development—from childhood to adolescence to maturity to retirement and old age (see Figure 19-1). There are no neat boundaries in the life cycle, the transitions between stages are gradual, and they are seldom the same for any two people. The earlier stages are intrapersonal, involving morality, competency, and mastery, but the last stage is interpersonal, and the commitment is to survival or self-protectiveness (Lowenthal, 1977).

The happiness or adjustment the person finds in the last stage varies greatly, depending on the kind of person he or she is. A study of retired teachers, for example, found them to be generally in good health, active, and satisfied. Many had worked full or part time after their retirement, and about half had done or were doing volunteer work, some of it devoted to helping the aged (Ingraham, 1974). Results of a survey of the attitudes of approximately 70,000 members of the American Association of Retired Persons published in a 1973 newsletter showed that large majorities reported satisfaction with their family arrangements and housing, and 80 percent or more of those in all income groups said they were happy with their independence and freedom from responsibility.

Mental Functions

Other confusions and myths are concerned with the elderly's intelligence and learning ability. The adage has it that you can't teach an old dog new tricks, and we speak glibly of the rigidity or lack of adaptability of old people. A great deal of research has been done in this area, and the consensus is that overall intelligence or learning ability undergoes a very gradual decline after about age 50. One authority concludes that this decline is part of aging, but the research shows it may

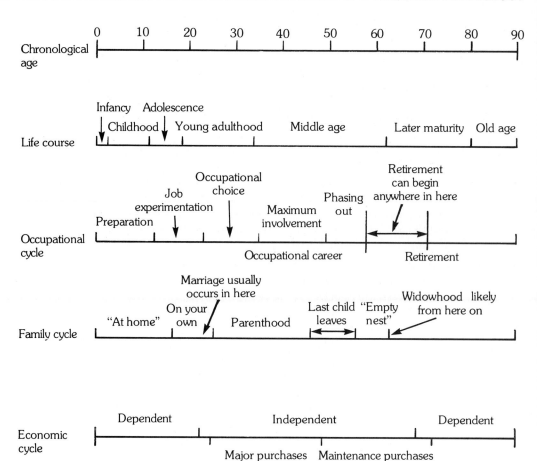

Figure 19–1. Relationships among Age, Life Cycle, and Family Cycle

Source: R. C. Atchley, *The Social Forces in Later Life,* 3d. ed. (Belmont, Cal.: Wadsworth Publishing Co., 1981), p. 91.

start later than has been thought, and it may be smaller and include fewer functions (Botwinick, 1977). The decline is hardly apparent before age 50 or 60. It is more noticeable in tests of *fluid intelligence* based on physiological functioning and involving speed, recent memory, perceptual-manipulative tasks, and nonverbal performance in general. Tests of *crystallized intelligence* on verbal skills such as vocabulary or word meaning, knowledge, or information declined very little or even showed an increase with age. These skills are learned from the culture.

A good deal has been written about the decline in various psychological abilities in old age, but a reasonable explanation is seldom given. What is passed off as lower intelligence in tests may be an excessive tendency among the aged to check their results (Botwinick, 1977), and response time tells little about overall cognitive ability. As long as the cerebral cortex, or brain, remains intact, cognitive skills slow down only if the person fails to keep up intellectual tasks, so self-stimulation is no longer taking place. Test results indicate that older people of above-average intelligence lose their ability more slowly than the less intelligent do (Schaie, 1975). Verbal abilities generally remain higher than psychomotor skills do.

Many tests have a built-in bias which operates to the disadvantage of the elderly—not unlike tests which compare minority-group students with those from the dominant white culture. Most intelligence tests contain items that are more appropriate to those who were recently educated, for example. The time dimension also differs for the old and the young, and older people tend to guess somewhat less than younger people do.

Severe mental decline seldom occurs before age 75, and new medical discoveries may prove to be a deterrent. Research on the cause and treatment of Alzheimer's disease, the most common form of mental impairment in old age, is expanding. Recent evidence suggests the disease, which affects the cells of the brain, may be caused by a slow-acting chemical disorder or virus. The rate and severity of decline vary with the individual, proceeding from loss of short-term memory and mild personality changes to confusion and disorientation. Identification of the disease and research on causes and cures hold promise that the present middle-aged population has a chance of escaping what used to be called *senility*.

While many older people are functioning as well as they did when they were young, the young of today function at a higher level than the young of 50 years ago. Warner Schaie (1975) puts it this way:

> Our studies strongly suggest that in the areas of intellectual abilities and skills, old people, in general, if they are reasonably healthy, have not declined, but rather have become obsolete. This conclusion might be viewed as a rather negative value judgment. That is not true at all, because obsolescence can be remedied by retraining, while deterioration would be irreversible. Indeed, if it can be shown that the real intellectual problem for older people is the fact that they are functioning at the level they attained in their younger days, but which is no longer appropriate for successful performance in contemporary society, it follows that we may be able to do something about this situation. (p. 120)

And something is being done, as shown by the large number of older people who are going back to school, attending regular classes or adult and extension programs or emeritus colleges. The Elderhostel movement also is bringing seniors to university campuses as students for short course sessions in many parts of the country.

Attitudes

According to the stereotype, the aged are less likely to choose alternatives involving risk. It has been thought that their responses in various kinds of mental and performance tests reveal anxiety or insecurity, possibly because they have a less stable self-image. This supposed reserve of the aged is being questioned, however, and research suggests that they have become more willing to take chances. When the risk is built into a task already chosen there is little age difference, but the elderly are less likely to assume a risky task in the first place (Okun & Elias, 1977).

The stereotype of ideological conservatism among the elderly also is subject to revision. Although they tend to vote more often than the young and vote more conservatively, this generalization must be qualified. The attitudes of the upper-age population, as with any sector, are conditioned by a number of factors. For instance, a survey of attitudes toward legalized abortion from 1965 to 1973 showed little difference by age of respondent (Cutler et al., 1980). Yet in a National Opinion Research Council survey of public opinion support of euthanasia, or mercy killing, the old were less favorable than the young were. This difference was more a factor of lower educational attainment and the preponderance of women in an old-age sample, however. In addition, nonwhites were unfavorable, partly because of their stronger religious convictions and lower educational levels, but the finding was also associated with greater opposition to any form of capital punishment (R. A. Ward, 1980).

In analyzing the degree of conservatism or liberalism in the ideologies of different generations, Bengstein and Cutler (1976) pointed to these competing hypotheses:

1. *Maturational.*   There is a trend toward increasing conservatism in values and attitudes over the life cycle.

2. *Generational.*   The period during which the individual enters a critical phase of the life cycle affects these attitudes. For instance, those who became adults during the period of the Great Depression retained a liberal position for a generation, but some shifted with the Republican tide of the 1950s.

3. *Historical.*   A given event such as a war, a major political upheaval, or the assassination of a president may have a strong effect, either temporary or permanent, on this ideology, which can cut across all ages.

Blank (1981) found generational differences in attitudes toward achievement and material satisfaction in a sample of young, middle-aged, and older persons. This is understandable because many of those now entering upper age finished their educations at the onset of the Great Depression of the 1930s. They were barely launched in their careers by the mid-1930s, only to be delayed by several years of military service in World War II, and so many of them never quite realized their life ambitions. A different kind of life cycle awaited those who were too young for World War II and too old (or saved by educational exemptions) for the Korean or Vietnam conflicts; a critical portion of their lifetime took place in prosperous times.

The Socioeconomic Setting

The United States officially acknowledged its concern with the aged in the 1930s, lagging behind Western Europe, notably Germany, which had ushered in various kinds of social security as early as the 1880s. It was the climate of the New Deal and the feverish support of the Townsend Plan, which proposed an automatic monthly pension of $200 for everyone over 60, that encouraged passage of the Social Security Act in 1935. At first the system protected only workers in industry and large organizations, but gradually it was extended to nearly all employees, including the self-employed. Eventually disadvantaged persons such as disabled workers, widows, and children also were given some types of coverage, and the system was extended in 1965 to provide some health protection for the aged with Medicare. Social security payments have been tied to the cost of living and gradually increased in order to combat the effects of inflation on retirees' income. The availability of private pension plans and individual retirement accounts (IRAs) to supplement social security payments has also become more widespread.

Despite these aids, the economic situation of the aged remains precarious. Social security was meant to supplement other income, yet two-thirds of all retirees are almost totally dependent on these monthly payments. Those who never qualified for social security—fortunately an ever-diminishing number—have it even worse. As a result, a third of those over 65 live in poverty. In the case of minorities such as blacks and Hispanic Americans, the combination of poverty and older age intensifies the stigma these people have been subjected to throughout their lives.

Most of the aged are more troubled by other problems than their economic position, however. Social isolation, health, and the frustrations of low status and lack of purpose mark the role of the aged in American society.

The Life Situation

From a demographic viewpoint, any stereotype of what constitutes the life situation of the aged would be misleading. Almost 14 out of 20 live in some kind of family setting, most often with a spouse. More than a fourth live alone, and the ratio increases with age as, sooner or later, death removes the marriage partner. One third of women over 65 live alone, and the number of men doing so increased from 13 percent in 1960 to 16 percent in 1970 (Carp, 1976). Generally the elderly do not live with their children; only 15 percent of the women and 7 percent of older men reported living with children or other relatives.

Contrary to a common belief, most elderly people remain in the area in which they spent their adult years, some in the neighborhood in which they were born. Only 8 percent have the desire and the means to spend the remainder of their lives in a location other than where they spent their middle age (Mathieu, 1976). Thousands of the aged have moved to the sun belt, which stretches from Florida to California, but states with the highest numbers of aged include Iowa and Nebraska, and even California has a lower ratio of the aged than most states.

About a sixth of the older people in the United States live in rural areas, which offer only minimal services, and a third live in the suburbs or retirement communities. The other half live in central cities, in a variety of housing units ranging from dilapidated hotels and rooming houses to single dwellings and apartment houses. Public housing has increasingly become an option in recent years.

Habitat and Housing

A fundamental question in providing housing for the elderly is how to create maximum flexibility in the environment and extend the number of available options. Both theorists and practitioners are attempting to plan living quarters in which older people can develop their own environment, based on their needs, interests, and capacities. Housing arrangements are limited by such needs as providing for personal mobility within the dwelling and ease in entering and leaving it.

The elderly react to their environment by cognitive appraisal, followed by various coping attempts, as shown in Figure 19–2. The intermittent or continuous

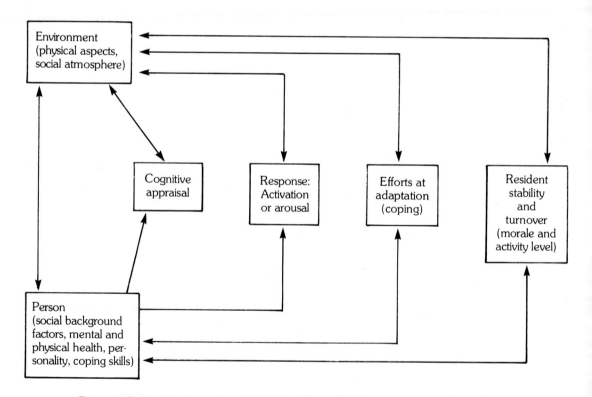

Figure 19–2.   Environmental and Personal Variables in Adjustment to the Environment by the Elderly

Source: Adapted from R. H. Moos, ''Specialized Living Environments for Older People: A Conceptual Framework for Evaluation,'' *Journal of Social Issues,* 1980, *36*:2, 75–94.

give-and-take between person and environment is colored by the images that are reflected from other contacts, personal and physical. A change in the physical environment can stimulate awareness or pride. After installation of a new carpet in their ward, for example, geriatric patients became more careful about their own physical appearance and offered more helping behavior to their fellow patients (Cheek, Maxwell, & Weisman, 1971).

The sources of coping depend on the kind of environment provided. In institutional settings, residents with a strong need for control adapt better to a structured or regulated setting. Others who are action oriented or desirous of independence tend to be frustrated by a physical environment that discourages freedom of movement. Physical barriers may be desirable from the viewpoint of the staff, or even for the safety of the residents, but can impede the development of personal autonomy. Only arbitrarily can responses be detached from behavioral outcomes (Moos, 1980).

A fundamental question is the kind of housing mix that would be most favorable to the adjustment of the aged. Despite the trend toward age-segregated housing, two thirds of the elderly prefer a mixed population (Lawton, 1976). The majority continue to live in their former residences, which usually assures some kind of age grading. Significant environmental considerations in housing for the elderly are the size and form of the structure, whether high or low rise, and how the rooms or apartments are arranged around communal facilities such as terraces, social rooms, or laundries. Degree of density, ranging from the multiple dwellings of the inner city to the single homes of a retirement community in a semirural environment, is another factor. Equally important is the degree of independence the housing provides. Atchley (1981) defines two types of elderly households: persons or couples living on an autonomous or semiautonomous basis (with occasional help such as Meals-on-Wheels), and those living in group or congregate housing. The latter type includes:

1. Those living in their own units and doing limited household work like cooking.
2. Retirement home residents, who take meals with the group but are able to care for their personal needs.
3. Patients in nursing homes, which provide total care.

As in all housing, preferred housing units for the elderly depend on architectural design. The placement of halls, doors, and windows may determine the occupants' awareness of the outside world, for example. One study found that leaving a door open is positively related to the amount of social interaction (Lawton, 1970). If the housing is age-integrated, the aged should have their own social facilities like a lounge or TV room, since social networks increase with the ratio of same-age residents. While it is advantageous for persons of various age levels to be aware of one another, socialization occurs most often among people of similar age.

Moving can be a crisis for the aged, since it frequently occurs as a result of

Of all the problems of the elderly, loneliness is reported to be the most acute.
Source: Little Brothers of the Poor/David L. Fisk.

some kind of disruption such as the death of a spouse, reduced ability to get around, or a changing neighborhood (Nelson & Winter, 1975). Often the decision to move is a reluctant one based on two contradictory situations: the rigidity of the aged to change, and their inability to cope with the present environment. It often has a positive outcome, however; Carp (1974) found that residents who moved to a more functional housing unit not only liked it better but were happier and more inclined to interact with others, as compared to a control group. Storandt, Wittels, and Botwinick (1975) and other studies have also validated the positive effects of new housing.

Community and Neighborhood

The importance of community ties for the aged depends on both individual and situational factors. The community may offer various kinds of services for the aged, such as welfare programs, clubs, voluntary associations, and consumer services. Federal, state, and local governments have markedly expanded their services to the aged, and a wide range of personal services is now provided by agencies which give information and make referrals for such services as telephone reassurance, job placement, and income counseling (Atchley, 1977).

In a reciprocal fashion, the elderly also offer services to the community (see Box 19–5). They vote and hold political offices, act as baby sitters, continue their employment or move on to new occupations. Older persons have organized a number of service programs in which they serve as volunteers in schools and hospitals or consultants to small businesses.

More fundamental than these situational factors, perhaps, is the approach to the community or neighborhood that is reflected in the imagery of the individual, and the way the older person perceives and defines it. The community and neighborhood may be the few blocks in which one can go on foot or a more extensive area in which relatives are visited, and for the most mobile and affluent the meaning of community is remarkably vast. In a still broader sense, the mass media can define the range of the community, depending on the availability and selection of local newspapers, radio or T.V. programs. For most of the aged, however, the community means the immediate neighborhood.

Community involvement, like most roles of the aged, is determined by the mental and physical resources of the individual. To some extent it hinges on the extent of the person's group ties and participation in voluntary organizations, which increase in middle and upper age (Kleemeier, 1961). Habits established early tend to persist. A person who is not integrated into the community by age 40 is hardly likely to be after 65. On the whole, voting, religious attendance, and joining voluntary associations become more common in the middle and later years. This shift to greater participation reflects greater leisure, an awareness that only so many years remain, and a preference for activities that do not pose the financial and physical costs of the more vigorous outlets of the young.

Even though the elderly may turn to the community for distraction in order to relieve loneliness, interactions with relatives and friends remain their primary interest. Poor health, financial problems, or lack of transportation can inhibit

Box 19–5
HELPING ONESELF AND HELPING OTHERS

Voluntary groups and government-sponsored programs have been built around the idea that the aged both enjoy and benefit from helping behavior. Voluntary organizations can achieve amazing results by giving seniors opportunities to provide for the welfare of their segment of society. An example is Ventura County, California, where Tony Lamb, a retired engineer, became Coordinator of Aging. Through cooperative action, a senior center was constructed in Thousand Oaks, skill banks were set up all over the county, and senior survival and advocacy courses were introduced in the community colleges. In addition to a hot meals program, a "nutrition-mobile" was procured to get food to people who couldn't get it themselves. Funds were raised for "senior survival services" for those in emergency situations. Lamb mentions these and other accomplishments in a realistic treatment of aging at the community level.*

Government-sponsored programs also have recognized that older people want to help. The Retired Senior Volunteer Program (RSVP) recruits over-60 volunteers to serve in local nonprofit institutions such as schools, libraries, social agencies, and boys' and girls' clubs. They are not paid but are reimbursed for travel and luncheon expenses. Foster Grandparents are paid to work 20 hours a week furnishing companionship and care for orphans and retarded children in institutions. The Service Corps of Retired Executives (SCORE) provides a means for retired businessmen and businesswomen to use their experience to advise and assist younger people starting their own businesses. A nutrition program, established by congressional action to provide one good hot meal a day to persons over 60, provides for meals served in schools, churches, and community centers, with volunteers providing many of the necessary services and the socializing which accompanies the meals at many locations.

---

*T. Lamb and D. Duffy, *The Retirement Threat* (Los Angeles, Cal.: J. P. Tarcher, 1977).

participation. Even organizations committed to senior citizens, like the Golden Age clubs or the American Association of Retired Persons, reach only a minority of the aged.

Role Positions and Changes

In a sense we return in our last years to the dependency state in which we began life; there are inevitable comparisons between childhood and old age in regard to mental ability, personal and social responsibility, and need for family support. As noted above, chronological age is seldom an adequate index for retirement or the other roles associated with the advanced years. Artists and professionals do not relinquish their creativity or careers at age 65 any more than a homemaker's role diminishes. The process of aging and its consequent change of roles depends on many factors, such as health, age of children, and drive, to mention only a few. Ideally, retirement would be a gradual process. Half-time employment for the late sixties or early seventies has been suggested as one way to achieve this.

The reduction of activities in the later years is usually identified as *disengagement,* or "an inevitable process in which many of the relationships between a person and other members of society are severed, and those remaining are altered in quality" (Cumming & Henry, 1961, p. 61). This process, of course, begins in middle age and is intensified in upper age. In a Kansas City study with a large sample of older people, life satisfactions generally were correlated with activity, but there were exceptions according to personality type—persons who are passive and dependent may function best at a low level of activity (Havighurst, Neugarten, & Tobin, 1968). Another study showed that as compared to 40-year-olds, 60-year-olds saw their environment as more complex and somewhat dangerous and the self as conforming to outer-world demands (Neugarten, 1973).

Both the individual and society are involved in disengagement, and the process can be slowed up or even reversed. When new interests are cultivated, the process might be better defined as *reengagement.* With the more dynamic approach to aging today, the term *disengagement* refers more appropriately to those over, say, 75 rather than to the recently retired. The original theory of disengagement has been only partially supported. In one sample studied, "action takers" were found to outnumber the passive (Guttmann, 1978). Thus the majority of the aged seem to make their own decisions, rather than permitting others to arrange their lives.

Level of Control

Social psychologists have also been investigating how morale among the elderly relates to levels of control, another aspect of the role process. One of the depressing aspects of aging is inability to exercise control over one's environment. Langer and Rodin (1976) attempted to reverse demoralization among residents of a nursing home by changing their mental set with observations such as: "You don't realize the influence you have over your own lives here." The experimental group was told of their rights to determine the arrangement of their rooms, how they spent their time, and where and how they would meet visitors. A control group was treated with the more traditional modes of passivity. It was apparent that the freedom to make choices gave the residents a sense of self-control, and attendants reported greater alertness and active participation in members of the experimental group.

The perception of control is in part determined by the interaction of the reference group (Schulz & Hanusa, 1980). The social experiences of the aged usually involve relatives and institutional personnel, who assume a protective and nonchallenging approach to the lives of the aged. The negative attitudes of the institutionalized elderly may be more a self-fulfilling prophecy than the inevitable effects of aging. In part this is an effect of the decision to be institutionalized and the temporarily disorganizing effects of entering the custodial situation. One study compared the results of a depression inventory between a young and an elderly sample and found that physical or health symptoms more than psychological factors accounted for the difference in depression scores (Zemore & Eames, 1979). In this context aging in itself is not necessarily a depressing experience.

Exchange Theory and Role Behavior

From one perspective the tendency toward withdrawal among the aged is attributable to a shift in the balance of forces. The role of the aged can be seen as a rebalancing of exchange relationships, as defined in Chapter 13 (Hendricks & Hendricks, 1977). The choice between disengagement and activity is a decision the individual has to make according to his or her perceptions of how to maximize rewards and minimize costs. Interaction between two or more individuals will be continued if they both think they will profit from it. Therefore the dependent partner must be able to reciprocate the reward, and the one who is less in need of services enjoys a power advantage.

Social activity among the aged is often lessened because of an exchange setting in which the ability of the older partner to reciprocate has been reduced (Dowd, 1975). Lack of power in the exchange relationship can force the elderly to comply with the wishes of the young and withdraw from society. Redefining the role of the aged in our society would result in greater participation, socially, economically, and recreationally, and make the aged stronger contenders in the power relationships with relatives and with other power centers in the community.

Family Relations

For the elderly the most frustrating aspect of aging, other than health, may be diminishing contact with the outside world. Loneliness is the most frequent complaint among those over 65, especially among widows (Lopata, 1973); the never married, in comparison, are better able to adjust to the isolation experienced in the later years (Gubrium, 1976).

Most older people have some contact with family members, however. Over 75 percent have at least one living child, and in one study four-fifths reported seeing one of their children within the past seven days (Adams, 1968). Usually the children (or sometimes nephews or nieces), who are generally in middle age themselves, determine the degree of involvement with the older generation. Daughters or daughters-in-law, more often than sons, decide on the rules. Several factors shape the responses of this middle generation: a feeling of emotional attachment and filial obligation, awareness that the same fate awaits them, and realistic hopes for inheritance. As the aged become more autonomous they expect relatively less attention from their children. In one study, parents who expected the most from their children had the lowest satisfaction in upper age (Seelbach & Sauer, 1977).

Grandparenthood.   Traditionally, this role has helped older people by providing a liaison with their own children which counteracts their feeling of uselessness. The meaning of grandparenthood reflects changes in society, however. When parents are married earlier they become grandparents sooner, often by the age of 50. As the birth rate has fallen and women have postponed childbearing, the stage of grandparenthood has come later.

Neugarten and Weinstein (1964) found the grandparent role is closest when the grandchildren are still in childhood. They found the role has five different styles:

1. *Formal or traditional*—grandparents who follow a culturally prescribed relationship, usually affectional and helpful.
2. *Fun seeker*—younger grandparents who want equalitarian ties with grandchildren.
3. *Surrogate*—grandparents who feel responsible for caring for grandchildren.
4. *Reservoir of family wisdom*—grandparents who take a directive role toward grandchildren.
5. *Distant figure*—like fun seekers, these grandparents are young, but they remain somewhat detached. Often they have not worked out a satisfactory relationship with their grandchildren either because of physical distance or strains with their own children, or they cannot accept the status of grandparent, possibly because it is a reminder of their own aging.

A recent study suggests that young adults who are primarily of blue-collar status perceive their grandparents as companions, or at the very least do not view them as necessarily remote and old-fashioned. Most of the subjects felt responsible for helping their grandparents in various ways (Robertson, 1976). More research on the grandparent role is in order as it continues to change.

Sex Roles

Disengagement and general adjustment to aging are related to sex roles, which were examined in Chapter 14. The stereotypes about traditional sex roles regard men's roles as instrumental or pragmatic and woman's as primarily expressive. In this sense retirement disrupts the role of the male more, not only because his formal career is at an end but because of the difficulty of finding adequate substitute roles. Women's overall functions have traditionally changed less dramatically; since household tasks such as cleaning and cooking continue. With the enormous increase of women in the job market since World War II and the women's rights movement, however, more women are experiencing an identity crisis on reaching the midsixties.

Some reversal of traditional sex roles occurs at entry into old age. According to Gutmann (1977), men "recapture the 'femininity' that was previously repressed in the service of productive instrumentality; and women generally become more domineering and independent" (p. 312). Traits are associated with the two sexes in part on the basis of the stage of life. Back (1974) found that in

Box 19–6

AGE AND SEX STATUS: A CROSS-CULTURAL NOTE

In most societies, the passing of the years brings on some degree of sex reversal.* The older men drift toward passivity and, especially in Asian culture, are encouraged to assume a more meditative role. Elderly Chinese, for instance, are expected to forego meat and sex and live a life of contemplation.† In Hindu culture, upper age means renunciation of worldly pursuits. Among the North American Plains Indians, an older male who can no longer compete with the young warriors has two options: he can become a "peace chief" or the "bad old man" who substitutes sorcery for the lost skill of a warrior.

In our society, too, the old are forced to give up to the young. Even more than in rural societies, males in an industrial order are apt to find their roles no longer meaningful in the upper years. Agricultural societies are less abrupt in cutting workers off. A number of studies have noted a cross-cultural tendency among females to seek "liberation" during upper age.‡ Women take a more active role in family tasks as the years progress. In our culture psychiatric and related problems like suicide become progressively worse for elderly men.

Sex-role reversal has a physical counterpart. In the very late years the basis of sex differences—endocrine processes—become inactive. In the end we are neutralized by nature itself.

_____

*D. Gutmann, "The Cross-Cultural Perspective: Notes toward a Comparative Psychology of Aging," in J. E. Birren and K. W. Schaie (Eds.), *Handbook of the Psychology of Aging* (New York: Van Nostrand Reinhold Co., 1977), pp. 302–326.

†P. Yap, "Aging in Underdeveloped Asian Countries." In C. Tibbitts and W. Donahue (Eds.), *Social and Psychological Aspects of Aging* (New York: Columbia University Press, 1962), pp. 442–453.

‡Gutmann, "Cross-Cultural Perspective," p. 309 f.

aging, men tend to rely more on external events and therefore become less comfortable, whereas women tend to rationalize their existence more. A certain degree of role flexibility is helpful in confronting change during the course of life (Sinnott, 1977). The blurring of male and female roles in the upper years is supported on a cross-cultural basis (see Box 19–6).

Retirement and Leisure

The traditional approach to retirement is to think of it as a time for well-earned rest. This appears to be intended as a message to retirees that they no longer enjoy the privilege of work and have been consigned to an indefinite period of leisure.

Because this idea violates the Protestant work ethic, many of the elderly have to be resocialized on how to use their leisure. Their success depends on a number of factors: health, economic situation, educational status, hobbies, and, of course, the possibility of continuing in their occupational roles.

Social status influences attitudes toward leisure and retirement. The executive may suffer from status deprivation when deference from underlings is no longer forthcoming. The blue-collar worker, who tends to retire earlier, usually makes the least preparation for this new phase of the life cycle and is poorly equipped to deal with leisure. Generally, middle-class people find retirement least difficult (Simpson, Back, & McKinney, 1966); only 3 percent of college-educated males reported a loss of status after retirement, as opposed to over a third of workers with less than a high school education (Strauss, Aldrich, & Lipman, 1976). Members of the middle class, which is accustomed to working with symbols, may be more able to rationalize their new status.

The transition to leisure after retirement begins well before, as the "intensity of expressive involvement" is slowly decreased (Gordon & Gaitz, 1976). We move from fairly vigorous activities like sports and dancing to more passive entertainment and participation. With age we make a more conscious effort to find a balance between relaxation and diversion, education and creativity.

Unquestionably the most absorbing pursuit of the aged, as for many of the young, is watching television. When a sample of persons over 65 was asked what they had done the day before, 70 percent reported watching television, and the next most popular activity (68 percent) was visiting with relatives and friends (Meyerson, 1961). The average viewing time was 3.9 hours per day. The type of programs enjoyed by the elderly was "concrete, nonfictional entertainment." Similarly, R. H. Davis (1975) found they liked variety shows, old-time music, quiz programs, and public affairs and had less interest in detective dramas, comedies, or love stories. Sponsors of course prefer programs that appeal to younger viewers because they have greater purchasing power. A content analysis found that less than 5 percent of the roles portrayed on the TV screen were of upper age, and, villainy, at least in male characters, is more often portrayed by older people (Aronoff, 1974). The "good guys" are usually the young characters.

The use of leisure is related to the person's perception of time. How we fill in our time has to do not only with our general adjustment but with how we relate to the past, present, and future. An older person in a particular situation may simply sit on the porch and watch the traffic pass by, become involved in watching TV programs, or enroll in evening school courses. Choices such as these depend on their basic orientation and whether or not they regard time as significant.

Increasing age does not necessarily mean indifference to the present and future. Selective memory, which tends to infuse events of the past with a warm glow, becomes more evident in the upper years, however. As we dwell on the past, the need to fill in present time with activities becomes less compelling. For most older people, some redefinition of time is almost inescapable. Many retirees are hardly aware of an increase in leisure. They claim that they were never so busy; and for them the choice of activity is determined by an awareness of only so much time left to do so many things they want to do.

Personality and Emotional Problems

For the elderly some degree of isolation is inevitable, sooner or later. The enforced withdrawal from career and child rearing has multiple causes and effects. The individual becomes conscious of a growing inability to retain ties with society. Energy, health, finance, or transportation problems may gradually restrict mobility, or there may be a lack of incentive or opportunity to retain old associations or make new ones.

In the first years after retirement, older people reorganize their lives through planning or trial and error. Eventually new interests emerge, such as church and volunteer groups and community programs for the aged, or former activities are renewed. Nevertheless, by the upper seventies or early eighties the problem of withdrawal is acute. Resources and strategies, both personal and situational, must be developed.

The individual's situation determines how great the feeling of loneliness or uselessness will be. A single person probably learns to cope with isolation better than one who has been widowed or divorced (Gubrium, 1976). Middle-status persons are better prepared for the later years by more adequate psychological and financial resources. For blue-collar workers time drags, but because the change from active to retired worker does not represent an overwhelming loss of status, the self or identity is less impaired.

Retired people gradually adopt a given role or personality structure. In a study of 87 men in the San Francisco area (Reichard, Livson, & Peterson, 1962) aged 55 to 84, five different personality patterns were discerned:

1. The *mature*—have a tendency toward flexibility, stability, and objectivity and accept age for what it is.
2. The *rocking chair*—are relaxed, passive and unstriving and accept a low profile; often they assume that women should be more active in old age.
3. The *armored*—are defensive, stable, conforming, and generally rigid in their response to life and other people.
4. The *angry*—are bitter, suspicious, and hostile, generally projecting their problems and frustrations unto others.
5. The *self-haters*—direct their hostility to themselves, may sink into depression.

An interrelationship of personality and role is evident. But personality, which is fundamentally structured by adulthood, is more basic than role in determining satisfaction. We draw on our ego strength as well as our experience in adapting to the later years. Thus the basic response to old age is partially crystallized in the middle years. The potential for aggressiveness, striving, or at least for adjustment comes from the self. However, aid from a number of private and public agencies can be mustered in order to avoid a passive-dependent response, or at least postpone this phase until the ninth and tenth decades of life. The probability of longer lifetimes, especially for women, is likely, but society must assure greater status for the aged.

The aged still face deep anxieties. Most older people do not fear death but accept its inevitability. (Younger people who think the old are afraid of dying are probably projecting their own unexpressed or repressed fears.) But oldsters do think of the future in terms of how much time they have left, and for some this becomes an obsession which causes much anxiety. Many complain that their energy levels and motivation are low, and they have lost interest in things that used to appeal to them. "Now that I've got the time," they say, "I really don't care to travel"—or to take courses, join social groups, do volunteer work, or learn to play bridge. It is easier for them to turn to alcohol or drugs (usually prescribed) or to spend their days in front of the TV set as an escape from their boredom and frustration. Or perhaps they find solace in moaning and complaining—and doing nothing constructive about it.

Many older people are able to cope with their problems without asking for help, but sometimes the strain is too great. The loss of relatives and friends, for example, can lead to depression, which might be avoided or reduced in intensity if the bereft individual would go through the process of mourning or bereavement to assimilate the loss. This is an area where a therapist or counselor could be of help. Older people are notoriously resistant to aid from "head doctors", however; apparently they regard any kind of proffered psychological help as a threat to their autonomy, and they generally prefer to battle it out themselves. Commendable as this may be, it often does not work. The suicide rate for older persons, particularly for males over 65, is the highest of all age categories (Butler & Lewis, 1977). Many programs provide therapeutic help for distressed seniors in an indirect and therefore more acceptable way (Sargent, 1980).

As the needs of the aged have developed in various areas, several distinct trends have emerged. Increasing interest in the topic of aging has brought a more realistic approach to it, including more willingness to discuss formerly taboo topics such as terminal illness and dying. More widespread preparation for retirement and activity planning for the retirement years have also been developed. There is pressure from older people for economic security in the face of continuing inflation as evidenced by demands for higher social security payments, rent supplements, or rent control; tax reductions or rebates; and reduced fares on public transportation, and lower-priced admission tickets. Opportunities are being sought for seniors to work part time or even full time, since mandatory retirement at 65 has ended.

In the face of the renewed drive to limit government expenditures in many countries, some goals have been sidetracked. These include demands for better medical coverage and other phases of health care, such as national health insurance or legislation, and funding for service programs, day activity centers, more emeritus college courses, and other enrichment activities.

SUMMARY

In recent years considerable interest in the physical environment has been sparked by several concerns—the depletion of sources of energy, increases in population, especially in the underdeveloped world, and the trend toward urban living. This has been accompanied by a growing inquiry into the notion of spatial relations.

The psychologist is concerned with the needs and definitions of space as structured by culture and personal characteristics. The massing of people—in educational institutions, prisons, or high-rise housing—is relevant to how the individual defines his or her environment. Among other concepts is Barker's study of behavior settings and the borderline between density and crowding, an area of research anticipated by animal psychologists. Also important are aesthetic needs and the distinction between landscape and space. Visual imagery plays a major role in our use of space.

Fundamental to the problem of crowding is the question of personal control and varied cognitions of space and time. Other areas of concern to psychologists are urban deterioration, environmental pollution, and the dwindling of the world's natural resources, such as air, water, and fuel.

This chapter has also considered the elderly as one more minority group, comparable to other minority categories such as race. Several stereotypes were examined to show their oversimplification of the later period of the life cycle. The degree of mental decline has been grossly exaggerated, for example.

A number of problems trouble the aged: economic dislocation, housing needs, detachment from the community. In all of these, behavior of the elderly differs greatly; for example, they vary in the extent of community services offered or received. The meaning of neighborhood and community differs from individual to individual.

One approach to aging is the question of role changes. The term *disengagement* has been used to refer to the gradual process of isolating and reducing activities, but research has only partially supported this concept. *Reengagement* would seem to be a more appropriate label for the shift in roles in the later years.

Personality problems and reduced social involvement are other concerns, but coping ability can be aided by preparation for retirement. It is probable, too, that society may become more innovative in providing therapy and other services for facilitating adjustment in the twilight years.

WORDS TO REMEMBER

Ageism. Prejudice or discrimination toward the elderly, largely attributable to stereotypes about the age level.

Anticipatory socialization. Acquisition of expectations and duties connected to a new role prior to actually assuming it. (See *resocialization.*)

Behavior setting. As defined by Roger Barker, the specific location (street, park, classroom) occupied by a person at a given time.

Cognitive mapping. Set of images a person has of a given area, such as a neighborhood, city, or vast region.

Density. Number of organisms or inhabitants per unit of space; can be characterized as low, medium, or high. As compared to density, *crowdedness* is a more subjective concept, or the conscious awareness of density, which can depend on various cues of noise, presence of tall buildings, etc.

Disengagement. Process by which people reduce their involvement with society. The theory was originally presented by E. Cumming and W. E. Henry and now appears to be most relevant to the period of later old age.

Ecology. Use by organisms of their environment, both physical and social.

Gerontology. The scientific study of aging from the viewpoint of various disciplines, such as medicine, psychology, and sociology.

Image. A person's cognitive representation of a specific location or landscape.

Landscape. Set or configuration of cues and images that the observer imposes on space.

Resocialization. Adult socialization, or the principle that every phase of life involves new learnings.

Territoriality. The delineation of space with which a person is identified.

Urban stress. Awareness of crowdedness from various cues in the city environment (visual, auditory, associative).

Voluntary associations. Organizations joined at various stages of life and in varying settings: clubs, lodges, civic and service organizations, and the like. Most notable for the elderly are the senior citizen centers.

QUESTIONS FOR DISCUSSION

1. What is meant by ecology? Define the ecosystem.

2. How does the psychologist define or measure territoriality and privacy?

3. How are housing and neighborhood preferences influenced by the individual and the group?

4. What are behavior settings? How do they apply to ecological needs?

5. What is the relationship between density and crowding? How are they different?

6. Analyze the varied factors underlying crowding. What solutions can be found for this problem in an urban society?

7. In what ways can the aged be thought of as a minority group? How does this group differ from other minorities?

8. What is myth and what is reality about the mental functions of the elderly?

9. What are the specific problems of the socioeconomic crisis of the aged? How are these problems being treated today?

10. How can the community be defined for those in the upper years? How does this definition differ from those for the other parts of the population?

11. What is meant by *disengagement?* What is its present status as an explanatory concept?

12. Characterize the social networks of the elderly. What type of contact do older people maintain with their families?

13. What types of grandparent roles are observable? In what ways might the grandparent role be in transition?

14. What specific personality syndromes have been found among the aged? What other individual differences might be found?

READINGS)

Atchley, R. C. *The Social Forces in Later Life.* 3d ed. Belmont, Calif.: Wadsworth Publishing Co., 1981.
A readable comprehensive text on the subject.

Bardo, J. W., and Hartman, J. *Urban Sociology.* Itasca, Ill.: F. E. Peacock Publishers, 1982.
Parts 2–4 are a well-organized analysis of ecological and social-psychological aspects about the city and the potential of urban planning.

Baum, A. *Human Responses to Crowding.* Hillsdale, N.J.: Lawrence Erlbaum Associates, 1978.
A number of careful investigations into the problem of density in college dormitories and other settings.

Blank, T. O. *A Social Psychology of Developing Adults.* New York: John Wiley & Sons, 1982.
An analysis of the life cycle and the concept of development with emphasis on the elderly, their personality, lifestyle, and attributions.

Crandall, R. C. *Gerontology: A Behavioral Science Approach.* Reading, Mass.: Addison-Wesley Publishing Co., 1980.
An insightful approach to the social and psychological aspects of aging.

Downs, R. M., and Stea, D. (Eds.). *Image and Environment: Cognitive Mapping and Spatial*

Behavior. Chicago: Aldine Publishing Co., 1973.

Selections drawn from a number of disciplines point to the imagery of cities, both in North America and abroad.

Glass, D. C., and Singer, J. E. *Urban Stress.* New York: Academic Press, 1972.

Series of experiments on the effect of noise and social stressors.

Handbook of Aging and the Social Sciences. (R. H. Binstock & E. Shanas, Eds.) New York: Ban Nostrand Reinhold Co., 1976.

Handbook of the Psychology of Aging. (J. E. Birren & K. W. Schaie, Eds.) New York: Van Nostrand Reinhold Co., 1977.

Both volumes offer a storehouse of research on the elderly.

Heimstra, N. W. *Environmental Psychology.* Monterey, Calif.: Brooks/Cole Publishing Co., 1974.

Highly readable, well-illustrated text on natural and built environments.

Hendricks, J., and Hendricks, C. D. *Aging in Mass Society.* Cambridge, Mass.: Winthrop Publishers, 1977.

Text which covers a variety of topics, including the aged in minority groups.

Ittelson, W. H., et al. *An Introduction to Environmental Psychology.* New York: Holt, Rinehart & Winston, 1974.

Very complete text on various types of interaction with the environment.

Lofland, L. H. *A World of Strangers: Order and Action in Urban Public Space.* New York: Basic Books, 1973.

A somewhat impressionistic but absorbing account of imagery in the city of the past and present.

Milgram, S. *The Individual in a Social World: Essays and Experiments.* Reading, Mass.: Addison-Wesley Publishing Co., 1977.

Part I examines the images of the urbanite, including study of psychological mapping of New York City and Paris.

Poon, L. W. (Ed.). *Aging in the 1980's: Psychological Issues.* Washington, D.C.: American Psychological Association, 1980.

Includes clinical issues, interpersonal relations, environmental issues, and general adjustment problems.

Sargent, S. S. (Ed.). *Nontraditional Therapy and Counseling with the Aging.* New York: Springer Publishing Co., 1980.

A number of authors discuss innovative therapeutic programs and approaches acceptable to older people.

Stokol, D. (Ed). *Perspectives on Environment and Behavior.* New York: Plenum Publishing Corp., 1977.

Series of penetrating statements on behavioral ecology, crowding, action research, and other problems.

REFERENCES

Abeles, R. P. Relative deprivation, rising expectations, and black militancy. *Journal of Social Issues,* 1976, *32*:2, 119–137.

Abelson, R. P. Simulation of social behavior. In G. Lindzey and E. Aronson (Eds.). *The handbook of social psychology* (Vol. 2). Reading, Mass.: Addison-Wesley, 1968.

Abelson, R. P., et al. (Eds.). *Theories of cognitive consistency: A sourcebook.* Chicago: Rand McNally, 1968.

Abrahamson, M., Mizruchi, E. H., & Hornung, C. A. *Stratification and mobility.* New York: Macmillan, 1976.

Adams, B. N. The middle-class adult and his widowed or still-married mother. *Social Problems,* 1968, *16,* 51–59.

Adorno, T. W., Frenkel-Brunswik, E., Levinson, D. J., & Sanford, R. N. *The authoritarian personality.* New York: Harper & Row, 1950.

Aiken, E. G. Changes in interpersonal descriptions accompanying the operant conditioning of verbal frequency in groups. *Journal of Verbal Learning and Verbal Behavior,* 1965, *4,* 243–247.

Albrecht, S. L., Bahr, H. M., & Chadwick, B. A. Public stereotyping of sex roles, personality characteristics and occupations. *Sociology and Social Research,* 1977, *61,* 223–240.

Alker, H. A. Is personality situationally consistent? *Journal of Personality,* 1972, *40,* 1–16.

Allen, F. R. *Socio-cultural dynamics: An introduction to social change.* New York: Macmillan, 1971.

Allen, V. L. Situational factors in conformity. In L. Berkowitz (Ed.), *Advances in experimental social psychology* (Vol. 2). New York: Academic Press, 1965.

Allen, W. L., & Crutchfield, R. S. Generalization of experimentally reinforced conformity. *Journal of Abnormal and Social Psychology,* 1963, *67,* 326–333.

Allport, F. H. *Social psychology.* Boston: Houghton Mifflin, 1924.

Allport, F. H. The influence of the group upon association and thought. *Journal of Experimental Psychology,* 1920, *3,* 159–182.

Allport, F. H. The J-curve hypothesis of conforming behavior. *Journal of Social Psychology,* 1934, *5,* 141–183.

Allport, G. W. Attitudes. In C. Murchison (Ed.), *Handbook of social psychology.* Worcester, Mass.: Clark University Press, 1935.

Allport, G. W. *Pattern and growth in personality.* New York: Holt, Rinehart & Winston, 1961.

Allport, G. W., & Cantril, H. Judging personality from voice. *Journal of Social Psychology,* 1934, *5,* 37–55.

Allport, G. W., & Postman, L. J. *The basic psychology of rumor.* New York: Holt, Rinehart & Winston, 1947.

Allport, G. W., & Ross, M. J. Personal religious orientation and prejudice. *Journal of Personality and Social Psychology,* 1967, *5,* 432–443.

Allport, G. W., Vernon, P. E., & Lindzey, G. *A study of values* (3rd ed.) Boston: Houghton Mifflin, 1960.

Allyn, J., & Festinger, L. The effectiveness of unanticipated persuasive communications. *Journal of Abnormal and Social Psychology,* 1961, *62,* 35–40.

Altman, I. *The environment and social behavior: Privacy, personal space, territory, and crowding.* Monterey, Calif.: Brooks/Cole, 1975.

Altman, I., & Haythorn, W. W. The ecology of isolated groups. *Behavioral Science,* 1967, *12,* 169–182.

Altman, I., & Taylor, D. A. *Social penetration: The development of interpersonal relationships.* New York: Holt, Rinehart & Winston, 1973.

American Association of University Professors. Tensions affecting international understanding. *Bulletin,* 1948, *34,* 546.

American Psychological Association. *APA ethical principles in the conduct of research with human participants.* Washington, D.C.: Author, 1973.

Amir, Y. The role of intergroup contact in change of prejudice and ethnic relations. In P. A. Katz (Ed.), *Toward the elimination of racism.* New York: Pergamon Press, 1976.

Anderson, N. Averaging versus adding as a stimulus-combination rule in impression formation. *Journal of Experimental Psychology,* 1965, *70,* 394–400.

Anderson, N. H. Ratings of likableness, meaninglessness, and likableness variances arranged in order of decreasing likableness. *Journal of Personality and Social Psychology,* 1968, *9,* 272–279.

Anderson, N. H., & Barrios, A. A. Primacy effects in personality impression formation. *Journal of Ab-*

normal and Social Psychology, 1961, 63, 346–350.

Andreas, C. R. War toys and the peace movement. Journal of Social Issues, 1969, 25, 83–100.

Andrews, K. H., & Kandel, D. B. Attitude and behavior: A specification of the cognitive consistency hypothesis. American Sociological Review, 1979, 44, 298–310.

Antonovsky, A. Social class, life expectancy and over-all mortality. Milbank Memorial Fund Quarterly, 1967, 14, 2.

Appleyard, D., Lynch, K., & Myer, J. R. The view from the road. In D. Lowenthal (Ed.), Environmental perception and behavior. Chicago: Department of Geography, University of Chicago, 1967.

Aronfreed, J. Conduct and conscience. New York: Academic Press, 1968.

Aronoff, C. Old age in prime time. Journal of Communication, 1974, 24, 86–87.

Aronoff, J. Psychological needs and cultural systems. Princeton, N.J.: Van Nostrand Reinhold, 1967.

Aronson, E. Dissonance theory: Progress and problems. In R. P. Abelson et al. (Eds.), Theories of cognitive consistency: A sourcebook. Chicago: Rand McNally, 1968.

Asch, S. E. Studies of independence and submission to group pressure: A minority of one against a unanimous majority. Psychological Monographs, 1956, 70.

Asch, S. E. Effects of group pressure upon modification and distortion of judgments. In E. E. Maccoby, T. M. Newcomb, & E. L. Hartley (Eds.), Readings in social psychology (3rd ed.). New York: Holt, Rinehart & Winston, 1958.

Atchley, R. C. The social forces in later life (3rd ed.). Belmont, Calif.: Wadsworth, 1980.

Atkinson, J. W. An introduction to motivation. Princeton, N.J.: Van Nostrand Reinhold, 1964.

Atkinson, J. W. Studying personality in the context of an advanced motivational psychology. American Psychologist, 1981, 36, 117–128.

Ausubel, D. P. Ego development and the personality disorders. New York: Grune & Stratton, 1952.

Aveni, A. F. The not-so-lonely crowd: Friendship groups in collective behavior. Sociometry, 1977, 40, 96–99.

Averill, J. R., DeWitt, G. W., & Zimmer, J. M. The self-attribution of emotion as a function of success and failure. Journal of Personality, 1978, 46, 323–347.

Azrin, N. H., Hutchinson, R. R., & Hake, D. F. Extinction-induced aggression. Journal of the Experimental Analysis of Behavior, 1966, 9, 191–204.

Back, K. W. Transition to aging and the self-image. In E. Palmore (Ed.), Normal aging (Vol. 2). Durham, N.C.: Duke University Press, 1974.

Baldwin, J. M. Social and ethical interpretations. New York: Macmillan, 1913.

Bales, R. F. Interaction process analysis. Chicago: The University of Chicago Press, 1950.

Bales, R. F. Task roles and social roles in problem-solving groups. In I. D. Steiner & M. Fishbein (Eds.), Current studies in social psychology. New York: Holt, Rinehart & Winston, 1965.

Baltzell, E. D. The Protestant establishment: Aristocracy and caste in America. New York: Random House, 1964.

Bandura, A. Principles of behavior modification. New York: Holt, Rinehart & Winston, 1969.

Bandura, A. The role of modeling processes in personality development. In W. W. Hartup and N. L. Smothergill (Eds.), The young child (Vol. 1). Washington, D.C.: National Association for the Education of Young Children, 1967.

Bandura, A. Psychological modeling. Chicago: Aldine-Atherton, 1971.

Bandura, A. Aggression: A social learning analysis. Englewood Cliffs, N.J.: Prentice-Hall, 1973.

Bandura, A. Behavior theory and the models of man. American Psychologist, 1974, 29, 859–869.

Bandura, A. Social learning theory. Englewood Cliffs, N.J.: Prentice-Hall, 1977.

Bandura, A., Ross, D., & Ross, S. Transmission of aggression through imitation of aggressive models. Journal of Abnormal and Social Psychology. 1961, 63, 575–582.

Bandura, A., Ross, D., & Ross, S. Imitation of film-mediated aggression models. Journal of Abnormal and Social Psychology, 1963, 66, 3–11.

Bandura, A., & Walters, R. H. Social learning and personality development. New York: Holt, Rinehart, & Winston, 1963.

Banton, M. Roles: An introduction to the study of social relations. New York: Basic Books, 1965.

Barber, B. Social stratification. New York: Harcourt Brace Jovanovich, 1957.

Barber, B. Social class differences in educational life chances. Teachers' College Record, 1961, 63, 108.

Barkan, S. E. Strategic, tactical and organizational dilemmas against nuclear power. *Social Problems,* 1979, *27,* 19–37.

Barker, R. G.,& Schoggen, P. *Qualities of community life.* San Francisco: Jossey-Bass, 1973.

Barker, R. G., & Wright, H. F. *The Midwest and its children.* New York: Harper & Row, 1954.

Barnett, M. A., & Bryan, J. H. Effects of competition with outcome feedback on children's helping behavior. *Developmental Psychology,* 1974, *10,* 838–842.

Barnouw, V. *Culture and personality* (Rev. ed.). Homewood, Ill.: Dorsey Press, 1973.

Baron, R. A. The reduction of human aggression: A field study of the influence of incompatible reactions. *Journal of Applied Social Psychology,* 1976, *6,* 260–274.

Baron, R. A., & Ransberger, V. M. Ambient temperature and the occurrence of collective violence: The "long, hot summer" revisited. *Journal of Personality and Social Psychology,* 1978, *36,* 351–360.

Bar-Tal, D. *Prosocial behavior: Theory and research.* Washington, D.C.: Hemisphere, 1976.

Becker, W. C. Consequences of different kinds of parental discipline. In M. L. Hoffman & L. N. Hoffman (Eds.), *Review of child development research* (Vol. 1). New York: Russell Sage Foundation, 1964.

Beeghley, L. *Social stratification in America: A critical analysis of theory and research.* Santa Monica, Calif.: Goodyear, 1978.

Bem, D. J. Self-perception: An alternative interpretation of cognitive dissonance phenomena. *Psychological Review,* 1967, *74,* 183–200.

Bem, D. J. *Beliefs, attitudes, and human affairs.* Belmont, Calif.: Brooks/Cole, 1970.

Bem, D. J. Self-perception theory. In L. Berkowitz (Ed.), *Advances in experimental social psychology* (Vol. 6). New York: Academic Press, 1972.

Bender, I. E., & Hastorf, A. H. On measuring general empathic ability (social sensitivity). *Journal of Abnormal and Social Psychology,* 1953, *48,* 503–506.

Benedict, R. *Patterns of culture.* Boston: Houghton Mifflin, 1934.

Bengston, V. L., & Cutler, N. E. Generations and intergenerational relations: Perspectives on age groups and social change. In R. H. Binstock & E. Shanas (Eds.), *Handbook of aging and the social sciences.* New York: Van Nostrand Reinhold, 1976.

Benne, K. D., & Birnbaum, M. Principles of changing. In W. G. Bennis, K. D. Benne, & R. Chin (Eds.), *The planning of change* (2nd ed.). New York: Holt, Rinehart & Winston, 1969.

Bennett, J. W. The interpretation of Pueblo culture: A question of values. In D. G. Haring (Ed.), *Personal character and cultural milieu* (3rd ed.). Syracuse, N.Y.: Syracuse University Press, 1956.

Bennis, W. G., A typology of change. In W. G. Bennis, K. D. Benne, & R. Chin (Eds.). *The planning of change.* New York: Holt, Rinehart & Winston, 1961.

Bentler, P. M., & Speckart, G. Attitudes "cause" behaviors: A structural equation analysis. *Journal of Personality and Social Psychology,* 1981, *40,* 226–238.

Berger, J., Fisek, M. H., Norman, R. Z., & Zelditch, M., Jr. *Status characteristics and social interaction.* New York: Elsevier, 1977.

Berk, R. A. *Collective behavior.* Dubuque, Iowa: William C. Brown, 1974.

Berkowitz, L. Anti-Semitism and the displacement of aggression. *Journal of Abnormal and Social Psychology,* 1959, *59,* 182–188.

Berkowitz, L. The concept of aggressive drive. In L. Berkowitz (Ed.), *Advances in experimental social psychology* (Vol. 2). New York: Academic Press, 1965.

Berkowitz, L. (Ed.). *Roots of aggression: A re-examination of the frustration-aggression hypothesis.* New York: Atherton Press, 1969. (a)

Berkowitz, L. Social motivation. In G. Lindzey and E. Aronson (Eds.), *Handbook of social psychology* (Vol. 3). Reading, Mass.: Addison-Wesley, 1969. (b)

Berkowitz, L., & Alioto, J. T. The meaning of an observed event as a determinant of its aggressive consequences. *Journal of Personality and Social Psychology,* 1973, *28,* 206–217.

Berkowitz, L., & Lepage, A. Weapons as aggression eliciting stimuli. *Journal of Personality and Social Psychology,* 1967, *7,* 202–207.

Berkowitz, W. R. Spectator responses at public war demonstration. *Journal of Personality and Social Psychology,* 1970, *14,* 305–11.

Bernard, V. W., Ottenberg, P. & Redl, F. Dehumanization: A composite psychological defense in relation to modern war. In R. Perrucci & M. Pilisuk

(Eds.). *The triple revolution emerging.* Boston: Little, Brown, 1971.

Bernstein, B. Social class, linguistic codes, and grammatical elements. *Language and Speech,* 1962, *5,* 221–240.

Bernstein, B. *Class, codes and control: Theoretical studies towards a sociology of language* (Vol. 1). London: Routledge & Kegan Paul, 1971.

Berry, J. W. Social and cultural change. In H. C. Triandis and R. W. Brislin (Eds.), *Handbook of cross-cultural psychology* (Vol. 5). Boston: Allyn & Bacon, 1980.

Berscheid, E. Opinion change and communicator-communicatee similarity and dissimilarity. *Journal of Personality and Social Psychology,* 1966, *4,* 670–680.

Berscheid, E., & Walster, E. Physical attractiveness. In L. Berkowitz (Ed.), *Advances in experimental social psychology* (Vol. 7). New York: Academic Press, 1974.

Bettelheim, B. Feral children and autistic children. *American Journal of Sociology,* 1959, *59,* 455–467.

Bindra, D. *Motivation: A systematic reinterpretation.* New York: Ronald Press, 1959.

Birdwhistell, R. L. Kinesics and communication. In E. Carpenter and M. McLuhan (Eds.), *Explorations in communication.* Boston: Beacon, 1960.

Bishop, C. A. Northern Algonkkan cannibalism and windigo psychosis. In T. R. Williams (Ed.), *Psychological anthropology.* The Hague: Mouton, 1975.

Bittner, E. Radicalism and the organization of radical movements. *American Sociological Review,* 1963, *28,* 928–940.

Blake, J., & Davis, K. Norms, values, and sanctions. In. R. E. L. Faris (Ed.), *Handbook of modern sociology.* Chicago: Rand McNally, 1964.

Blake, R. R., & Mouton, J. S. Reactions to intergroup competition under win-lose conditions. *Management Science,* 1961, *7,* 420–435.

Blake, R. R., & Mouton, J. S. *The managerial grid.* Houston: Gulf Publishing Co., 1964.

Blake, R. R., Mouton, J. S., & Hain, J. D. Social forces in petition signing. *Southwestern Social Science Quarterly,* 1956, *36,* 385–390.

Blank, T. O. Adulthood and aging in social psychology texts. *Teaching of Psychology,* 1979, *6,* 145–148.

Blank, T. O. Meaning and motivation in adult perceptions of causality. Paper presented at Eastern Psychological Association meeting, New York, April 23, 1981.

Blank, T. O. A *social psychology of developing adults.* New York: Wiley, 1982.

Blascovich, J., Ginsburg, G., & Veach, T. A pluralistic explanation of choice shifts on risk dimensions. *Journal of Personality and Social Psychology,* 1975, *31,* 442–429.

Blau, P. M. *Exchange and power in social life.* New York: Wiley, 1964.

Blau, P. M., & Duncan, O. D. *The American occupational structure.* New York: Wiley, 1967.

Bluemel, C. S. *War, politics and insanity.* Denver: World Press, 1948.

Blumberg, H. H. On being liked more than you like. *Journal of Personality and Social Psychology,* 1969, *11,* 121–128.

Blumenthal, M. D., et al. *Justifying violence: Attitudes of American men.* Ann Arbor, Mich.: Institute for Social Research, 1972.

Blumer, H. Collective behavior. In A. M. Lee (Ed.), *New outline of the principles of sociology.* New York: Barnes & Noble, 1946.

Blumer, H. Society as symbolic interaction. In J. G. G. Manis & B. N. Meltzer (Eds.), *Symbolic interaction: A reader in social psychology.* Boston: Allyn & Bacon, 1967.

Blumer, H. *Symbolic interactionism.* Englewood Cliffs, N.J.: Prentice-Hall, 1969.

Bogardus, E. S. Measuring social distance. *Journal of Applied Social Psychology,* 1925, *9,* 299–308.

Bogardus, E. S. Racial distance changes in the United States during the past thirty years. *Sociology and Social Research,* 1958, *42,* 127–135.

Boissevain, J., & Mitchell, J. C. (Eds.). *Network analysis: Studies in human interaction.* The Hague: Mouton, 1973.

Borden, G. A., Gregg, R. B., & Grove, T. G. *Speech behavior and human interaction.* Englewood Cliffs, N.J.: Prentice-Hall, 1969.

Boskey, B., & Willrich, M. *Nuclear proliferation: Prospects for control.* New York: Dunellen Co., 1970.

Botwinick, J. Intellectual abilities. In J. E. Birren and K. W. Schaie (Eds.), *Handbook of the psychology of aging.* New York: Van Nostrand Reinhold, 1977.

Boulding, K. E. *Conflict and defense: A general theory.* New York: Harper & Row, 1962.

Boulding, K. E. The power of nonconflict. *Journal of Social Issues,* 1977, *33*:1, 22–33.

Boulding, K. E. *Stable peace.* Austin: University of Texas Press, 1978.

Boulding, K. E. Science: Our common heritage. *Science,* 1980, *207*, 831–836.

Bourguignon, E. Psychological anthropology. In J. J. Honigmann (Ed.), *Handbook of social and cultural anthropology.* Chicago: Rand McNally, 1973.

Bowman, C. C. Loneliness and social change. *American Journal of Psychiatry,* 1955, *112*, 194–198.

Bramel, D. A dissonance theory approach to defensive projection. *Journal of Abnormal and Social Psychology,* 1962, *64*, 121–129.

Bredemeier, M. E., & Bredemeier, H. C. *Social forces in education.* Sherman Oaks, Calif.: Alfred, 1978.

Brehm, J. W. *Responses to loss of freedom: A theory of psychological reactance.* Morristown, N.J.: General Learning, 1972.

Brehm, J. W., & Cohen, A. R. *Explorations in cognitive dissonance.* New York: Wiley, 1962.

Brink, W., & Harris, L. *Black and white: A study of U.S. racial attitudes today.* New York: Simon & Schuster, 1967.

Brinton, J. E. Deriving an attitude scale from semantic differential data. *Public Opinion Quarterly,* 1961, *25*, 289–295.

Bronfenbrenner, U. The mirror image in Soviet-American relations. *Journal of Social Issues,* 1961, *17*, (3), 45–56.

Bronfenbrenner, U. The psychological costs of quality and inequality in education. *Child Development,* 1967, *38*, 909–925.

Brophy, I. N. The luxury of anti-Negro prejudice. *Public Opinion Quarterly,* 1946, *9*, 456–466.

Brown, R. *Social psychology.* New York: Free Press, 1965.

Brown, R. W. Mass phenomena. In G. Lindzey (Ed.), *Handbook of social psychology* (Vol. 2). Reading, Mass.: Addison-Wesley, 1954.

Bruner, J. S. Social psychology and perception. In E. E. Maccoby, T. M. Newcomb, & E. L. Hartley (Eds.), *Readings in social psychology* (3rd ed.). New York: Holt, Rinehart & Winston, 1958.

Bruner, J. S. *Beyond the information given: Studies in the psychology of knowing* (J. M. Anglin, Ed.). New York: Norton, 1973

Bruner, J. S., & Tagiuri, R. The perception of people. In G. Lindzey (Ed.), *Handbook of social psychology.* Cambridge, Mass.: Addison-Wesley, 1954.

Bryan, J. H., & Test, M. A. Models and helping: Naturalistic studies in aiding behavior. *Journal of Personality and Social Psychology,* 1967, *6*, 400–407.

Buchanan, W., & Cantril, H. *How nations see each other.* Urbana: University of Illinois Press, 1953.

Bulman, R. J., & Wortman, C. B. Attributions of blame and coping in the "real world": Severe accident victims react to their lot. *Journal of Personality and Social Psychology,* 1977, *35*, 351–363.

Burchard, W. W. Role conflicts of military chaplains. *American Sociological Review,* 1954, *19*, 528–535.

Burger, J. M., & Petty, R. E. The low-ball compliance technique: Task or person commitment? *Journal of Personality and Social Psychology,* 1981, *40*, 492–500.

Burgess, E. W. (Ed.). *Personality and the social group.* Chicago: University of Chicago Press, 1929.

Burgess, R. L., & Nielson, J. M. Distributive justice and the balance of power. In R. L. Hamblin and J. H. Kunkel (Eds.), *Behavioral theory in sociology: Essays in honor of George C. Homans.* New Brunswick, N.J.: Transaction Books, 1977, pp. 139–169.

Burnstein, E. Fear of failure, achievement motivation and aspiring to prestigeful occupations. *Journal of Abnormal and Social Psychology,* 1963, *67*, 189–193.

Burnstein, E., and Vinokur, A. Persuasive argumentation and social comparison as determinants of attitude polarization. *Journal of Experimental Social Psychology,* 1977, *13*, 315–332.

Burnstein, K. R. Classical conditioning: An evolutionary perspective. *Behaviorism,* 1977, *5*, 113–126.

Buss, A. R. The emerging field of the sociology of psychological knowledge. *American Psychologist,* 1975, *30*, 988–1002.

Butler, R. N. Age-ism: Another form of bigotry. *Gerontologist,* 1969, *9*, 243–246.

Butler, R. N., & Lewis, M. I. *Aging and mental health* (2nd ed.). St. Louis: Mosby, 1977.

Byham, W. Assessment centers for spotting future managers. *Harvard Business Review,* 1970, *48*, 150–167.

Byrne, P. Attitudes and attraction. In L. Berkowitz (Ed.), *Advances in experimental social psychology* (Vol. 4). New York: Academic Press, 1969.

Calabria, F. M. The dance marathon craze. *Journal of Popular Culture,* 1976, *10,* 54–69.

Calhoun, J. Population density and social pathology. *Scientific American,* 1962, *206,* 139–148.

Cameron, W. B. *Modern social movements.* New York: Random House, 1966.

Campbell, A., & Schuman, H. *Racial attitudes in fifteen American cities.* Ann Arbor: Institute for Social Research, University of Michigan, 1968.

Campbell, D. T. On the genetics of altruism and the counter-hedonic components in human culture. *Journal of Social Issues,* 1972, *28*:3, 21-37.

Campbell, E. Q., & Pettigrew, T. F. Racial and moral crisis: The role of the Little Rock ministers. *American Journal of Sociology,* 1959, *64,* 509–516.

Canetti, E. *Crowds and power* (C. Stewart, trans.). New York: Viking Press, 1963.

Cantor, N. F. *The age of protest: Dissent and rebellion in the twentieth century.* New York: Hawthorn Books, 1969.

Cantril, H. *Psychology of social movements.* New York: Wiley, 1941.

Caplow, T. Rumors in war. *Social Forces,* 1947, *25,* 298–302.

Caplow, T. Middletown fifty years later. *Contemporary Sociology,* 1980, *9,* 46–50.

Carlsmith, J. M., Ellsworth, P. C., & Aronson, E. *Methods of research in social psychology.* Reading, Mass.: Addison-Wesley, 1976.

Carlsmith, J. M., & Gross, A. E. Some effects of guilt on compliance. *Journal of Personality and Social Psychology,* 1969, *11,* 232–239.

Carp, F. M. Short-term and long-term prediction of adjustment to a new environment. *Gerontologist,* 1974, *29,* 444–453.

Carp, F. M. Housing and living environments of older people. In R. H. Binstock & E. Shanas (Eds.), *Handbook of aging and the social sciences.* New York: Van Nostrand Reinhold, 1976.

Carroll, J. B. *The study of language.* Cambridge, Mass.: Harvard University Press, 1953.

Carroll, J. B. *Language and thought.* Englewood Cliffs, N.J.: Prentice-Hall, 1964.

Cartwright, D. The nature of group cohesiveness. In D. Cartwright and A. Zander (Eds.), *Group dynamics* (3rd ed.). New York: Harper & Row, 1968.

Cartwright, D., & Zander, A. (Eds.). *Group dynamics* (3rd ed.). New York: Harper & Row, 1968.

Carver, C. S., & Humphries, C. Havana daydreaming: A study of self-consciousness and the negative reference group among Cuban Americans. *Journal of Personality and Social Psychology,* 1981, *40,* 545–552.

Cattell, R. B., & Dreger, R. M. (Eds.). *Handbook of modern personality theory.* Washington, D.C.: Hemisphere, 1977.

Cattell, R. B., & Stice, G. F. *The psychodynamics of small groups.* Urbana: University of Illinois, Laboratory of Personality Assessment and Group Behavior, 1953.

Caudill, W. Psychological characteristics of acculturated Wisconsin Ojibwa children. *American Anthropologist,* 1949, *51,* 409–427.

Chadwick, R. W. Power, social entrophy, and the concept of causation in social structure. Paper presented at the Albany Symposium on Power and Influence, State University of New York at Albany, October 1971.

Chafetz, J. S. *Masculine, feminine, or human? An overview of the sociology of the gender roles* (2nd ed.). Itasca, Ill.: F. E. Peacock, 1978.

Chaiken, S. Heuristic versus systematic information processing and the use of source versus message cues in persuasion. *Journal of Personality and Social Psychology,* 1980, *39,* 752–766.

Chalus, G. A. The mechanisms underlying attributive projection. *Journal of Personality,* 1978, *46,* 362–382.

Chapanis, N. P., & Chapanis, A. Cognitive dissonance: Five years later. *Psychological Bulletin,* 1964, *61,* 1–22.

Cheek, F., Maxwell, R., & Weisman, R. Carpeting the ward: An exploratory study in environmental psychiatry. *Mental Hygiene,* 1971, *55,* 109–118.

Chemers, M. M., & Skrzypek, G. J. An experimental test of the contingency model of leadership effectiveness. *Journal of Personality and Social Psychology,* 1972, *24,* 172–177.

Cherry, F., & Byrne, D. Authoritarianism. In T. Blass (Ed.), *Personality variables in social behavior.* Hillsdale, N.J.: Erlbaum, 1977.

Chomsky, N. The general properties of language. In C. H. Millikan & F. L. Darley (Eds.), *Brain mechanisms underlying speech and language.* New York: Grune & Stratton, 1967.

Christensen, B. *Attitudes toward foreign affairs as a function of personality.* Oslo: Oslo University Press, 1959.

Church, J. *Language and the discovery of reality.* New York: Random House, 1961.

Cialdini, R. B., Cacioppo, J. T., Basset, R., & Miller, J. A. 'Low-ball' procedure for producing compliance: Commitment then cost. *Journal of Personality and Social Psychology,* 1978, *36,* 463–476.

Cialdini, R. B., Levy, A., Herman, C. P., & Evenbeck, S. Attitudinal politics: The strategy of moderation. *Journal of Personality and Social Psychology,* 1973, *25,* 100–108.

Cicourel, A. V. *Cognitive sociology: Language and meaning in social interaction.* New York: Free Press, 1974.

Clark, R. D., III, Crockett, W. H., & Archer, R. L. Risk-as-value hypothesis: The relationship between perception of self, others, and the risky shift. *Journal of Personality and Social Psychology.* 1971, *19,* 425–429.

Clore, G. L. Reinforcement and affect in attraction. In S. Duck (Ed.), *Theory and practice in interpersonal attraction.* New York: Academic Press, 1977.

Clore, G. L., & Keffery, C. M. Emotional role playing, attitude change, and attraction toward a disabled person. *Journal of Personality and Social Psychology,* 1972, *23,* 105–111.

Cloyd, J. S. Patterns of role behavior in informal interaction. *Sociometry,* 1964, *27,* 161–173.

Cohen, A. K. The sociology of the deviant act: Anomie theory and beyond. *American Sociological Review,* 1965, *30,* 5–14.

Cohen, A. K., & Hodges, H. M., Jr. Characteristics of the lower blue-collar class. *Social Problems,* 1963, *10,* 303–308.

Cohen, A. R. Upward communication in experimentally created hierarchies. *Human Relations,* 1958, *11,* 41–53.

Cohen, A. R. Some implications of self-esteem for social influence. In C. I. Hovland & I. L. Janis (Eds.), *Personality and persuasibility.* New Haven: Yale University Press, 1959.

Cohen, A. R. *Attitude change and social influence.* New York: Basic Books, 1964.

Cohen, A. R. Some implications of self-esteem for social influence. In C. Gordon and K. J. Gergen (Eds.). *The self in social interaction* (Vol. 1). New York: Wiley, 1968.

Cohen, S. Environmental load and the allocation of attention. In A. Baum, J. E. Singer, & S. Valins (Eds.), *Advances in environmental research.* Hillsdale, N.J.: Erlbaum, 1978.

Cohen, S., Evans, G. W., Krantz, D. S., & Stokols, D. Physiological, motivational, and cognitive effects of aircraft noise on children. *American Pyschologist,* 1980, *35,* 231–243.

Cohen, S. P., & Azar, E. E. From war to peace: The transition between Egypt and Israel. *Journal of Conflict Resolution,* 1981, *25,* 87–114.

Cohn, W. Social status and ambivalence. *American Sociological Review,* 1960, *25,* 508–513.

Coleman, J., Campbell, F., Hobson, C., McPartland, J., Mood, A., Weinfeld, F., & York, R. *Equality of educational opportunity.* Washington, D.C.: U.S. Office of Education, 1966.

Coleman, J. S., Katz, E., & Menzel, H. The diffusion of an innovation among physicians. *Sociometry,* 1957, *20,* 253–270.

Coleman, J. S., Kelley, S. D., & Moore, J. *Trends in school desegregation, 1968–1973.* Washington, D.C.: Urban Institute, 1975.

Coleman, R. P., & Neugarten, B. L. *Social status in the city.* San Francisco: Jossey-Bass, 1971.

Coleman, R. P., & Rainwater, L. *Social standing in America: New dimensions of class.* New York: Basic Books, 1978.

Constantini, E., & Craik, K. H. Personality and politicians: California party leaders, 1960–1976. *Journal of Personality and Social Psychology,* 1980, *38,* 641–661.

Cooley, C. H. *Social organization.* New York: Scribner's, 1909.

Cooley, C. H. *Human nature and the social order.* New York: Free Press, 1956. (Originally published, 1902).

Cooper, H. M. Statistically combining independent studies: A meta-analysis of sex differences in conformity research. *Journal of Personality and Social Psychology,* 1979, *37,* 131–146.

Corsi, J. R. Terrorism as a desperate game: Fear, bargaining, and communication in the terrorist event. *Journal of Conflict Resolution,* 1981, *25,* 47–85.

Corwin, R. G., & Schmidt, M. Teachers in inner-city schools. In A. Lightfoot (Ed.), *Inquiries into the social foundations of education.* Chicago: Rand McNally, 1972.

Cox, C. M. Early mental traits of 300 geniuses. In L. M. Terman et al. (Eds.), *Genetic studies of genius* (Vol. 2). Stanford, Calif.: Stanford University Press, 1926.

Cox, D. F., & Bauer, R. A. Self-confidence and persuasibility in women. *Public Opinion Quarterly,* 1964, *28,* 454–466.

Crain, R. L. School integration and the academic achievement of Negroes. *Sociology of Education,* 1971, *44,* 1–26.

Crano, W. D. Primacy versus recency in retention of information and opinion change. *Journal of Social Psychology,* 1977, *101,* 87–96.

Crano, W. D., & Cooper, R. E. Examination of Newcomb's extension of structural balance theory. *Journal of Personality and Social Psychology,* 1973, *27,* 344–353.

Crouch, C. J. Collective behavior: An examination of some stereotypes. *Social Problems,* 1968, *15,* 310–322.

Crouch, C. J. Dimensions of association in collective behavior episodes. *Sociometry,* 1970, *33,* 457–471.

Crowe, B. J., Bochner, S., & Clark, A. W. The effects of subordinates' behavior on managerial style. *Human Relations,* 1972, *25,* 215–237.

Crutchfield, R. S. Conformity and character. *American Psychologist,* 1955, *10,* 191–198.

Cryns, A. G. Public letter writing in response to campus unrest and prison riots. *Journal of Personality and Social Psychology,* 1975, *31,* 516–521.

Cumming, E., & Henry, W. E. *Growing old: The process of disengagement.* New York: Basic Books, 1961.

Cutler, S. J., et al. Age and conservatism: Cohort changes in attitudes about legalized abortion. *Journal of Gerontology,* 1980, *35,* 115–123.

Dahl, R. The concept of power. *Behavioral Science,* 1957, *2,* 202–203.

Dahrendorf, R. *Class and class conflict in industrial society.* Stanford, Calif.: Stanford University Press, 1959.

D'Andrade, R. Anthropological studies of dreams. In F. L. K. Hsu (Ed.), *Psychological anthropology.* Homewood, Ill.: Dorsey Press, 1961.

Davis, A. Child training and social class. In R. Barker, J. S. Kounin, & H. F. Wright (Eds.), *Child behavior and development* (1st ed.). New York: McGraw-Hill, 1943.

Davis, A., & Havighurst, R. J. Social class and color differences in child-rearing. *American Sociological Review,* 1946, *11,* 698–710.

Davis, J. D. Effects of communication about interpersonal process on the evolution of self-disclosure in dyads. *Journal of Personality and Social Psychology,* 1977, *35,* 31–37.

Davis, R. H. Television communication and the elderly. In D. S. Woodruff & J. E. Birren (Eds.), *Aging: Scientific perspectives and social issues.* New York: Van Nostrand Reinhold, 1975.

Davitz, J. R., & Davitz, L. The communication of feelings by content-free speech. *Journal of Communication,* 1959, *9,* 110–117.

De Charms, R. *Personal causation: The internal affective determinants of behavior* (New York: Academic Press, 1968.

DeFleur, M. L., & Westie, F. R. Verbal attitudes and overt acts: An experiment on the salience of attitudes. *American Sociological Review,* 1958, *23,* 667–673.

DeFronzo, J. Religion and humanitarianism in Eysenck's T dimension and left-right political orientation. *Journal of Personality and Social Psychology,* 1972, *21,* 265–269.

Dember, W. N. *Psychology of perception.* New York: Holt, Rinehart & Winston, 1960.

Dennis, W. *The Hopi child.* New York: Appleton-Century-Crofts, 1940.

Denzin, N. K. Collective behavior in total institutions. *Social Problems,* 1968, *15,* 353–365.

De Rivera, J. (Ed.). *Field theory as human-science: Contributions of Lewin's Berlin group.* New York: Gardner Press, 1976.

De Sola Pool, I. *The social impact of the telephone.* Cambridge, Mass.: MIT Press, 1977.

Deutsch, J. M., & Gerard, H. A study of normative and informational social influence upon individual judgment. *Journal of Abnormal and Social Psychology,* 1955, *51,* 629–636.

Deutsch, M. An experimental study of the effects of cooperation and competition upon group process. *Human Relations,* 1949, *2,* 196–231.

Deutsch, M. The interpretation of praise and criticism as a function of their social context. *Journal of Abnormal and Social Psychology,* 1961, *62,* 391–400.

Deutsch, M. *The resolution of conflict.* New Haven, Conn.: Yale University Press, 1973.

Deutsch, M., & Krauss, R. M. The effect of threat upon interpersonal bargaining. *Journal of Abnormal and Social Psychology,* 1960, *61,* 181–189.

Deutsch, M., and Krauss, R. M. *Theories in social psychology.* New York: Basic Books, 1965.

De Villiers, J. G., & De Villiers, P. A. *Language*

acquisition. Cambridge, Mass.: Harvard University Press, 1978.

DeVito, J. A. *The interpersonal communication book.* New York: Harper & Row, 1976.

DeVos, G. A., & Hippler, A. A. Cultural psychology: Comparative studies of human behavior. In G. Lindzey and E. Aronson (Eds.), *Handbook of social psychology* (2nd ed.). Reading, Mass.: Addison-Wesley, 1969.

Diener, E., Lusk, R., DeFour, D., & Flax, R. Deindividuation: Effects of group size, density, number of observers, and group member similarity on self-consciousness and disinhibited behavior. *Journal of Personality and Social Psychology,* 1980, *39,* 449–459.

Diener, E., & T. K. Srull. Self-awareness, psychological perspective, and self-reinforcement in relation to personal and social standards. *Journal of Personality and Social Psychology,* 1979, *37,* 413–423.

Diener, E. & Wallbom, M. Effects of self-awareness on antinormative behavior. *Journal of Research in Personality,* 1976, *10,* 107–111.

Dion, K. L. Cohesiveness as a determinant of ingroup-outgroup bias. *Journal of Personality and Social Psychology,* 1973, *28,* 163–171.

Dion, K., Berscheid, E., & Walster, E. What is beautiful is good. *Journal of Personality and Social Psychology,* 1972, *24,* 285–290.

Dodd, S. C. On classifying human values: A step in the prediction of human valuing. *American Sociological Review,* 1951, *16,* 645–653.

Dodd, S. C., & Griffiths, K. S. The logarithmic relation of social distance and intensity. *Journal of Social Psychology,* 1958, *48,* 91–101.

Dollard, J. W., Doob, L. W., Miller, N. E., Mowrer, O. H., & Sears, R. R. *Frustration and aggression.* New Haven, Conn.: Yale University Press, 1939.

Dollard, J., & Miller, N. E. *Personality and psychotherapy.* New York: McGraw-Hill, 1950.

Donnerstein, E. Aggressive erotica and violence against women. *Journal of Personality and Social Psychology,* 1980, *39,* 269–277.

Donnerstein, E., Donnerstein, M., Simon, S., & Ditrichs, R. Variables in interracial aggression: Anonymity, expected retaliation, and a riot. *Journal of Personality and Social Psychology,* 1972, *22,* 236–245.

Doob, L. W. The behavior of attitudes. *Psychological Review,* 1947, *54,* 135–156.

Doob, L. W. *Becoming more civilized: A psychological exploration.* New Haven: Yale University Press, 1960.

Doob, L. W. *Communication in Africa: A search for boundaries.* New Haven: Yale University Press, 1961.

Doob, L. W. Psychological aspects of planned developmental change. In A. Gallaher, Jr. (Ed.), *Perspectives in developmental change.* Lexington: University of Kentucky Press, 1968.

Dowd, J. J. Aging as exchange: A preface to theory. *Journal of Gerontology,* 1975, *30,* 584–594.

Dozier, E. P. Rio Grande Pueblos. In E. H. Spicer (Ed.), *Perspectives in American Indian culture change.* Chicago: University of Chicago Press, 1961.

Druckman, D., & Mahoney, R. Processes and consequences of international negotiations. *Journal of Social Issues,* 1977, *33*:1, 60–87.

Drury, D. W., McCarthy, J. D. The social psychology of name change: Reflections on a serendipitous discovery. *Social Psychology Quarterly,* 1980, *43,* 310–320.

Duncan, B. L. Differential social perception and attribution of intergroup violence: Testing the lower limits of stereotyping of blacks. *Journal of Personality and Social Psychology,* 1976, *34,* 590–598.

Dunnette, M. D., Campbell, J., & Jaastad, K. The effect of group participation on brainstorming effectiveness for two industrial samples. *Journal of Applied Psychology,* 1963, *9,* 345–358.

Durkheim, E. *The elementary forms of religious life* (J. W. Swain, trans.). New York: Macmillan, 1915.

Eagly, A. H. Sex differences in influenceability. *Psychological Bulletin,* 1978, *85,* 86–116.

Eagly, A. H., Wood, W., & Fishbaugh, L. Sex differences in conformity: Surveillance by the group as a determinant of male nonconformity. *Journal of Personality and Social Psychology,* 1981, *40,* 384–394.

Edwards, A. L. Four dimensions in political stereotypes. *Journal of Abnormal and Social Psychology,* 1940, *35,* 566–572.

Edwards, A. L. *Techniques of attitude scale construction.* New York: Appleton-Century-Crofts, 1957.

Edwards, A. L., & Kenney, K. C. A comparison of the

Thurstone and Likert techniques. *Journal of Applied Psychology*, 1946, *30*, 72–83.

Edwards, A. L., & Kilpatrick, F. P. A technique for the construction of attitude scales. *Journal of Applied Psychology*, 1948, *32*, 374–384.

Edwards, J. N., & Booth, A. Crowding and human sexual behavior. *Social Forces*, 1977, *55*, 791–806.

Efron, D., & Foley, J. P., Jr. Gestural behavior and social setting. In T. M. Newcomb & E. L. Hartley (Eds.), *Readings in social psychology*. New York: Holt, Rinehart & Winston, 1947.

Eggan, D. The general problem of Hopi adjustment. In C. Kluckhohn and H. A. Murray (Eds.), *Personality in nature, society and culture*. New York: Knopf, 1953.

Ehrlich, H. J. Stereotyping and Negro-Jewish stereotypes. *Social Forces*, 1962, *41*, 171–176.

Ehrlich, H. J. *The social psychology of prejudice.* New York: Wiley, 1973.

Ekeh, P. P. *Social exchange theory: The two traditions.* Cambridge, Mass.: Harvard University Press, 1974.

Ekman, P. Facial expression. In A. W. Siegman & S. Feldstein (Eds.), *Nonverbal behavior and communication.* Hillsdale, N.J.: Erlbaum, 1978.

Ekman, P., & Friesen, W. V. Constants across culture in the face and emotion. *Journal of Personality and Social Psychology*, 1971, *17*, 124–129.

Eldridge, A. F. *Images of conflict.* New York: St. Martin's Press, 1979.

Ellis, A. *Humanistic psychotherapy: The rational emotive approach.* New York: Julian Press, 1973.

Ellsworth, P., & Carlsmith, J. Effects of eye contact and verbal content on affective response to a dyadic interation. *Journal of Personality and Social Psychology*, 1968, *10*, 15–20.

Elms, A. C. The crisis of confidence in social psychology. *American Psychologist*, 1975, *30*, 967–976.

Epstein, S. The stability of behavior: I. On predicting most of the people much of the time. *Journal of Personality and Social Psychology*, 1979, *37*, 1097–1126.

Erde, E. L. *Philosophy and psycholinguistics.* The Hague: Mouton, 1973.

Erikson, E. H. *Childhood and society.* New York: Norton, 1950.

Erikson, E. H. *Identity: Youth and crisis.* New York: Norton, 1968.

Erlanger, H. S. Social class and corporal punishment in childrearing: A reassessment. *American Sociological Review*, 1974, *39*, 68–85.

Eron, L. D. Prescription for reduction of aggression. *American Psychologist*, 1980, *35*, 244–252.

Ettinger, R. F., Norwicki, S., & Nelson, D. A. Interpersonal attraction and the approval motive. *Journal of Personality and Social Psychology*, 1970, *4*, 95–99.

Etzioni, A. *The hard way to peace: A new strategy.* New York: Crowell-Collier, 1962.

Etzioni, A. *The active society.* New York: Free Press, 1968.

Evans, E. *Calling a truce to terror.* Westport, Conn.: Greenwood Press, 1979.

Evans, R. I. Personal values as factors in anti-semitism. *Journal of Abnormal and Social Psychology*, 1952, *47*, 749–756.

Eysenck, H. J. *The psychology of politics.* London: Routledge & Kegan Paul, 1954.

Farber, M. L. The problem of national character: A methodological analysis. In N. J. Smelser & W. T. Smelser (Eds.), *Personality and social systems.* New York: Wiley, 1963.

Farley, R. Racial integration in the public schools, 1967–72. *Sociological Focus*, January 1975, pp. 3–26.

Fast, J. *Body language.* New York: Pocket Books, 1972.

Feather, N. T. Cognitive dissonance, sensitivity, and evaluation. *Journal of Abnormal and Social Psychology*, 1963, *66*, 157–163.

Feather, N. T. The relationship of expectation of success to need achievement and text anxiety. *Journal of Personality and Social Psychology*, 1965, *1*, 118–126.

Feld, S. C. Longitudinal study of the origins of achievement strivings. *Journal of Personality and Social Psychology*, 1967, *7*, 408–414.

Feldman, J. M. Stimulus characteristics and subject prejudice as determinants of stereotype attribution. *Journal of Personality and Social Psychology*, 1972, *21*, 333–340.

Felson, R., & Bohrnstedt, G. Are the good beautiful or the beautiful good? *Social Psychology Quarterly*, 1979, *42*, 386–392.

Festinger, L. Social psychology and group process. In C. P. Stone & Q. McNemar (Eds.), *Annual review of psychology* (Vol. 6), Stanford, Calif.: Stanford University Press, 1955.

Festinger, L. *The theory of cognitive dissonance.* New York: Harper & Row, 1957.

Festinger, L. *Conflict decision and dissonance* Stanford, Calif.: Stanford University Press, 1964.

Festinger, L., & Carlsmith, J. M. Cognitive consequences of forced compliance. *Journal of Abnormal and Social Psychology,* 1959, *58,* 203–210.

Festinger, L., Schachter, S., & Back, K. *Social pressures and informal groups: A study of human factors in housing.* New York: Harpers, 1950.

Fiedler, F. E. *A theory of leadership effectiveness.* New York: McGraw-Hill, 1967.

Fiedler, F. E. Effect of intergroup competition on group membership adjustment. *Personnel Psychology, 1970, 20,* 30–44.

Fishbein, M., & Ajzen, I. *Belief, attitude, intention and behavior.* Reading, Mass.: Addison-Wesley, 1975.

Fisher, S., & Lubin, A. Distance as a determinant of influence in a two-personal serial interaction situation. *Journal of Abnormal and Social Psychology, 1958, 56,* 230–288.

Fishman, J. A. *Language in sociocultural change.* Stanford, Calif.: Stanford University Press, 1972.

Fitch, G. Effects of self-esteem, perceived performance, and choice on causal attributions. *Journal of Personality and Social Psychology, 1970, 16,* 311–315.

Fleming, J. D. The state of the apes. *Psychology Today,* January 1974, p. 31 ff.

Flowers, M. L. A laboratory test of some implications of Janis's groupthink hypothesis. *Journal of Personality and Social Psychology, 1977, 35,* 888–896.

Fogarty, M. P., Rapoport, R., & Rapoport, R. N. *Sex, career and family.* London: Allen & Unwin, 1971.

Fogelson, R. D. Psychological theories of windigo "psychosis" and a preliminary application of a models approach. In M. E. Spiro (Ed.), *Context and meaning in cultural anthropology.* New York: Free Press, 1965.

Frank, J. D. The face of the enemy. In *Change: Readings in society and human behavior.* Del Mar, Calif.: CRM Books, 1967.

Frazier, F. *Black bourgeoisie.* New York: Free Press, 1957.

Freedman, J. L., & Fraser, S. C. Compliance without pressure: The foot-in-the-door technique. *Journal of Personality and Social Psychology, 1966, 4,* 195–202.

Freedman, J. L., Klevansky, S., & Ehrlich, P. R. The effect of crowding on human task performance. *Journal of Applied Social Psychology, 1971, 1:1,* 7–25.

Freedman, J. L., Levy, A. S., Buchanan, R. W., & Price, J. Crowding and human aggressiveness. *Journal of Experimental Social Psychology, 1972,* 528–548.

French, Jr., J. R. P., & Snyder, R. Leadership and interpersonal power. In D. Cartwright (Ed.), *Studies in social power.* Ann Arbor, Michigan: Institute of Social Research, 1959.

Friedrich, K. L., & Stein, A. H. Aggressive and prosocial television programs and the natural behavior of pre-school children. *Monographs of the Society for Research in Child Development.* 1973, *38,* No. 151.

Fromm, E. *The sane society.* New York: Holt, Rinehart & Winston, 1955.

Fromm, E. *The revolution of hope: Toward a humanized technology.* New York: Harper & Row, 1968.

Gage, N. L., & Cronbach, L. Conceptual and methodological problems in interpersonal perception. *Psychological Reviews,* 1955, *62,* 411–422.

Gamson, W. A. An experimental test of a theory of coalition formation. *American Sociological Review,* 1961, *26,* 565–574.

Gans, H. J. The "equality" revolution. In P. Blumberg (Ed.), *The impact of social class: A book of readings.* New York: Crowell, 1972.

Garcia, J. A. Yo soy Mexicano: Self-identity and sociodemographic correlates. *Social Science Quarterly,* 1981, *62,* 88–98.

Gardner, H. A., & Gardner, B. T. Teaching sign language to a chimpanzee. *Science,* 1969, *165,* 664–672.

Gardner, J. W. *Introduction to psycholinguistics: A survey of theory and research problems.* Englewood Cliffs, N.J.: Prentice-Hall, 1954.

Gaugler, E. A., & Zalkind, S. S. Dimensions of civil liberties and personality: Relationships for measures of tolerance and complexity. *Journal of Social Issues,* 1975, *31:2,* 93–110.

Gazda, G. M., & Corsini, R. J. (Eds.), *Theories of learning.* Itasca, Ill.: F. E. Peacock, 1980.

Geertz, C. *The interpretation of cultures.* New York: Basic Books, 1973.

George, A. L., & George, J. L. *Woodrow Wilson and*

Colonel House: A research note. In G. M. Kren & L. H. Rappoport (Eds.), *Varieties of psychohistory.* New York: Springer, 1976.

Gerard, H. B., Conolley, E. S., & Wilhelmy, R. A. Compliance, justification, and cognitive change. In L. Berkowitz (Ed.), *Advances in experimental social psychology* (Vol. 7). New York: Academic Press, 1974.

Gerard, H. B., Wilhelmy, R. A., & Conolley, E. S. Conformity and group size. *Journal of Personality and Social Psychology,* 1968, *8,* 79–82.

Gergen, K. J. *The concept of self.* New York: Holt, Rinehart & Winston, 1971.

Gergen, K. J. The codification of research ethics: Views of a doubting Thomas. *American Psychologist,* 1973, *28,* 907–12.

Gergen, K. J. Toward generative theory. *Journal of Personality and Social Psychology,* 1978, *36,* 1344–1360.

Gergen, K. J. Toward intellectual audacity in social psychology. In R. Gilmour and S. Duck (Eds.), *The development of social psychology.* London: Academic Press, 1980.

Gergen, K. J., Diebold, P., Seipel, M., & Gresser, C. Obligation, resource differences and reactions to beneficient actions. In K. J. Gergen (Ed.), *The psychology of behavior exchange.* Reading, Mass.: Addison-Wesley, 1969.

Gibb, C. A. Leadership. In G. Lindzey and E. Aronson (Eds.), *The handbook of social psychology* (Vol. 4). Reading, Mass.: Addison-Wesley, 1969.

Gibson, J. J. The implications of learning theory for social psychology. In J. G. Miller (Ed.), *Experiments in social process.* New York: McGraw-Hill, 1950.

Gilmore, J. P., & Zigler, E. Birth order and social reinforcer effectiveness in children. *Child Development,* 1964, *25,* 193–200.

Ginzberg, R. *100 years of lynching.* New York: Lancer Books, 1962.

Girodo, M. and Wood, D. Talking yourself out of pain: The importance of believing that you can. *Cognitive Therapy and Research,* 1979, *3,* 23-33.

Glaser, B. G., & Strauss, A. L. *Status passage.* Chicago: Aldine-Atherton, 1971.

Glass, D. C., & Singer, J. E. *Urban stress: Experiments on noise and social stressors.* New York: Academic Press, 1972.

Glass, D. C., Singer, J. E., & Friedman, I. N. Psychic cost of adaptation to an environmental stressor.

Journal of Personality and Social Psychology, 1969, *12,* 200–210.

Goethals, G. R., & Zanna, M. P. The role of social comparison in choice shifts. *Journal of Personality and Social Psychology,* 1979, *37,* 1469-1476.

Goetzkow, H. A decade of life with the inter-nation simulation. In R. M. Stogdill (Ed.), *The process of model building in the behavioral sciences.* Columbus: Ohio State University Press, 1970.

Goffman, E. *The presentation of self in everyday life.* New York: Doubleday, 1959.

Goffman, I. W. Status consistency and preference for change in power distribution. *American Sociological Review,* 1957, *22,* 281–288.

Goldstein, K. *The organism: A holistic approach to biology derived from pathological data in man.* New York: American Book, 1939.

Gollin, E. S. Forming impressions of personality. *Journal of Personality,* 1954, *23,* 65–76.

Good, L. R., & Nelson, D. A. Effects of person-group and intragroup attitude similarity on perceived group attractiveness and cohesiveness. *Psychonomic Science,* 1971, *25,* 215–217.

Goode, W. J. Norm commitment and conformity to role-status obligations. *American Journal of Sociology,* 1960a, *66,* 246–258.

Goode, W. J. A theory of role strain. *American Sociological Review,* 1960b, 25, 483–496.

Gordon, C., & Gaitz, C. M. Leisure and lives: Personal expressivity across the life span. In R. H. Binstock & E. Shanas (Eds.), *Handbook of aging and the social sciences.* New York: Van Nostrand Reinhold, 1976.

Gordon, E., & Cohn, F. Effect of fantasy arousal of affiliation drive on doll play aggression. *Journal of Abnormal and Social Psychology,* 1963, *66,* 301–307.

Gorsuch, R. L., & Cattell, R. B. Personality and socio-ethical values: The structure of self and superego. In R. B. Cattell & R. M. Dreger (Eds.), *Handbook of modem personality theory.* Washington, D.C.: Hemisphere, 1977.

Gottlieb, D. Poor youth: A study in forced alienation. *Journal of Social Issues,* 1969, *25,* 91–120.

Graham, W. K. Acceptance of ideas generated through individual and group brainstorming. *Journal of Social Psychology,* 1977, *101,* 231–234.

Graziano, W., Brothen, T. and Berscheid, E. Height and attraction: Do men and women see eye-to-eye? *Journal of Personality,* 1978, *46,* 128–145.

Greenblat, C.S., & Duke, R. D. *Gaming-simulation:*

Rationale, design, and applications. New York: Wiley, 1975.

Grey, A. L. *Class and personality in society.* New York: Atherton, 1969.

Griffitt, W., & Veitch, R. Hot and crowded: Influence of population density and temperature on interpersonal affective behavior. *Journal of Personality and Social Psychology,* 1971, *17,* 92–97.

Grinder, R. E. Distinctiveness and thrust in American youth culture. *Journal of Social Issues,* 1969, *25,* 7–19.

Gruder, C. L., Cook, T. D., Hennigan, K. M., Flay, B. R., & Halamaj, J. Empirical tests of the absolute sleeper effect predicted from the discounting cue hypothesis. *Journal of Personality and Social Psychology,* 1978, *36,* 1061–1074.

Gubrium, J. F. Being single in old age. In J. F. Gubrium (Ed.), *Time, roles and self in old age.* New York: Behavioral Publications, 1976.

Guthrie, E. R. *The psychology of learning* (Rev. ed.). New York: Harper & Row, 1952.

Gutmann, D. The cross-cultural perspective: Notes toward a comparative psychology of aging. In J. E. Birren & K. W. Schaie (Eds.), *Handbook of the psychology of aging.* New York: Van Nostrand Reinhold, 1977.

Guttman, L. A basis for scaling qualitative data. *American Sociological Review,* 1944, *9,* 139–150.

Haga, W. J., Graen, G., and Dansereau, F. Professionalism and role making in a service organization: A longitudinal investigation. *American Sociological Review,* 1974, *39,* 122–133.

Hagen, E. E. *On the theory of social change.* Homewood, Ill.: Dorsey, 1962.

Hahn, E. Chimpanzees and language. *The New Yorker,* December 11, 1971, p. 54 ff.

Hall, E. T. *The silent language.* Garden City, N.Y.: Doubleday, 1959.

Hall, E. T. *The hidden dimension.* Garden City, N.Y.: Doubleday, 1966.

Hall, E. T., & Hall, M. R. The sounds of silence. In V. P. Clark, P. A. Escholz, & A. F. Rosa (Eds.), *Language: Introductory readings.* New York: St. Martin's Press, 1972.

Hall, J. A., & Braunwald, K. G. Gender cues in conversations. *Journal of Personality and Social Psychology,* 1981, *40,* 99–110.

Hall, J. F. *Psychology of motivation.* Philadelphia: Lippincott, 1961.

Hallowell, A. I. *Culture and experience.* Philadelphia: University of Pennsylvania Press, 1955.

Halpin, A. W., & Winer, B. J. *The leadership behavior of the airplane commander.* Columbus: Ohio State University Research Foundation, 1952.

Hamachek, D. E. *Encounters with the self.* New York: Holt, Rinehart & Winston, 1971.

Hamilton, D. L., & Bishop, G. D. Attitudinal and behavioral effects of initial integration of white suburban neighborhoods. *Journal of Social Issues,* 1976, *32:*2, 47–67.

Hamilton, D. L., & Rose, T. L. Illusory correlation and the maintenance of stereotypic beliefs. *Journal of Personality and Social Psychology,* 1980, *39,* 832–845.

Hamilton, R. F. The marginal middle class: A reconsideration. *American Sociological Review,* 1966, *31,* 192–199.

Hammond, K. Measuring attitudes by error choice: An indirect method. *Journal of Abnormal and Social Psychology,* 1948, *43,* 38–48.

Hampden-Turner, C. *Radical man.* Garden City, N. Y.: Doubleday, 1971.

Hampden-Turner, C. *From poverty to dignity: A strategy for poor Americans.* Garden City, N.Y.: Doubleday, 1974.

Haney, C., & Zimbardo, P. G. Social roles and role-playing: Observations from the Stanford prison study. *Behavioral and Social Science Teacher,* 1973, 1, 25–45.

Hannay, N. B., & McGinn, R. E. The anatomy of modern technology. *Daedalus,* 1980, *1091,* 25–54.

Hare, A. P., & Bales, R. F. Seating position and small group interaction. *Sociometry,* 1963, *26,* 480–486.

Harlow, H. F. The nature of love. *American Psychologist,* 1958, *13,* 673–685.

Harlow, H. F. The heterosexual affectional system in monkeys. *American Psychologist,* 1962, *17,* 1–9.

Harré, R., & Secord, P. F. *The explanation of social behavior.* Totowa, N.J.: Rowman & Littlefield, 1972.

Harris, M. *Culture, people, nature* (3rd ed.) New York: Harper & Row, 1980.

Harris, S. *Father Divine: Holy husband.* New York: Doubleday, 1953.

Hastorf, A. H., Schneider, D. J., & Polefka, J. *Person perception.* Reading, Mass: Addison-Wesley, 1970.

Hauser, R. M., Dickinson, P. J., Travis, J. P., & Koffel, J. N. Structural changes in occupational mobility among men in the United States. *American Sociological Review,* 1975, *40,* 585–598.

Hauser, S. T. *Black and white identity formation.* New York: Wiley-Interscience, 1971.

Havighurst, R. J., & Neugarten, B. L. *Society and education.* Boston: Allyn & Bacon, 1975.

Havighurst, R. J., Neugarten, B. L., & Tobin, S. S. *Disengagement and patterns of aging.* In B. L. Neugarten (Ed.), *Middle age and aging.* Chicago: University of Chicago Press, 1968.

Havron, M. D., & McGruder, J. E. The contribution of the leader to the effectiveness of small military groups. In L. Petrullo & B. M. Bass (Eds.) *Leadership and interpersonal behavior.* New York: Holt, Rinehart & Winston, 1961.

Hawkins, J., Weisberg, C., and Ray, D. L. Marital communication style and social class. *Journal of Marriage and the Family,* 1977, *39,* 479–490.

Hayakawa, S. I. *Language in thought and action.* New York: Harcourt, Brace & World, 1941.

Hayes, C. *The ape in our house.* New York: Harper & Row, 1951.

Haythorn, W. The influence of the individual member on the characteristics of small groups. *Journal of Abnormal and Social Psychology,* 1953, 48, 276–284.

Heberlein, T. A., & Black, J. S. Attitudinal specificity and the prediction of behavior in a field setting. *Journal of Personality and Social Psychology,* 1976, *33,* 474–479.

Heffernan, W. J. *Introduction to social welfare policy: Power, scarcity and common human needs.* Itasca, Ill.: F. E. Peacock, 1979.

Heider, F. *The psychology of interpersonal relations.* New York: Wiley, 1958.

Heise, D., Lenski, G., and Wardwell, J. Further notes on technology and the moral order. *Social Forces,* 1976, *55,* 316–337.

Hemphill, J. K. *Leader behavior description.* Columbus: Ohio State University Personnel Research Board, 1950.

Hendricks, J., & Hendricks, D. *Aging in mass society: Myths and realities.* Cambridge, Mass.: Winthrop, 1977.

Herrenkohl, R. C. Social-psychological implications of tall buildings and design. *Proceedings of the International Conference on the Planning and Design of Tall Buildings.* Bethlehem, Pa.: Lehigh University, 1972.

Hewitt, D., & Rule, B. G. Conceptual structure and deprivation effects on self-concept change. *Sociometry,* 1968, *31,* 386–394.

Hilgard, E. R., & Bower, G. H. *Theories of learning* (4th ed.) Englewood Cliffs, N.J.: Prentice-Hall, 1975.

Ho, H. Z., Foch, T. T., & Plomin, R. Developmental stability of the relative influence of genes and the environment on specific cognitive abilities during childhood. *Developmental Psychology,* 1980, *16,* 340-346.

Hodge, R. W. Social integration, psychological well-being, and their socioeconomic correlates. In E. O. Laumann (Ed.), *Social stratification: Research and theory for the 1970's.* Indianapolis: Bobbs-Merrill, 1970.

Hoetink, H. *The two variants in Caribbean race relations: A contribution to the sociology of segmented societies.* London: Oxford University Press, 1967.

Hoffman, L. R. Group problem solving. In L. Berkowitz (Ed.), *Advances in experimental social psychology* (Vol. 2). New York: Academic Press, 1965.

Hoffman, M. L. Moral internalization: Current theory and research. In B. Berkowitz (Ed.), *Advances in experimental social psychology.* New York: Academic Press, 1977.

Hoffman, M. L. Is altruism part of human nature? *Journal of Personality and Social Psychology,* 1981, *40,* 121–137.

Hollander, E. P. Interpersonal exposure time as a determinant of the predictive utility of peer ratings. *Psychological Reports,* 1956, 445–448.

Hollander, E. P. Competence and conformity in the acceptance of influence. *Journal of Abnormal and Social Psychology,* 1960, *61,* 365–369.

Hollander, E. P., & Julian, J. W. Studies in leader legitimacy, influence and innovation. In L. Berkowitz (Ed.), *Advances in experimental social psychology* (Vol. 5). New York: Academic Press, 1970.

Hollander, E. P., & Webb, W. B. Leadership, followership and friendship: An analysis of peer nominations. *Journal of Abnormal and Social Psychology,* 1955, *50,* 163–167.

Hollingshead, A. B. *Elmtown's youth.* New York: Wiley, 1949.

Holmes, D. S. Debriefing after psychological experiments. *American Psychologist*, 1976, *3*, 858–875.

Holtzman, W. H., Diaz-Guerrero, R., & Swartz, J. D. *Personality development in two cultures.* Austin: University of Texas Press, 1975.

Homans, G. C. *The human group.* Harcourt, Brace & World, 1950.

Homans, G. C. *Social behavior in its elementary form.* New York: Harcourt, Brace, 1961.

Homans, G. C. *Social behavior: Its elementary forms* (2nd ed.). New York: Harcourt, Brace, 1974.

Honigmann, J. J. *Culture and personality.* New York: Harper & Row, 1954.

Honigmann, J. J. *The world of man.* New York: Harper & Row, 1959.

Honigmann, J. J. *Personality in culture.* New York: Harper & Row, 1967.

Honigmann, J. J. Psychological anthropology: Trends, accomplishments, and future tasks. In T. R. Williams (Ed.), *Psychological anthropology.* The Hague: Mouton, 1975.

Honigmann, J. J. *The development of anthropological ideas.* Homewood, Ill.: Dorsey, 1976.

Horai, J. Attributional conflict. *Journal of Social Issues,* 1977, *33*:1, 88–100.

Horner, M. S. The measurement and behavioral implications of fear of success in women. In J. W. Atkinson & J. O. Raynor, *Motivation and achievement.* New York: Wiley, 1974.

Horney, K. *The neurotic personality of our time.* New York: Norton, 1937.

Hornstein, H. A. et al. *Social intervention: A behavioral science approach.* New York: Free Press, 1971.

Hornung, C. A. Social status, status inconsistency and psychological stress. *American Sociological Review,* 1977, *42*, 623–638.

Horowitz, I. L. (Ed.) *Science, sin, and scholarship: The politics of Reverend Moon and the Unification Church.* Cambridge, Mass.: MIT Press, 1978.

Horowitz, M. Hostility and its management in classroom groups. In W. H. Charters, Jr., & N. L. Gage (Eds.), *Readings in the social psychology of education.* Boston: Allyn & Bacon, 1963.

Hovland, C. I. (Ed.). *The order of presentation in persuasion.* New Haven: Yale University Press, 1957.

Hovland, C. I., & Janis, I. L. *Personality and persuasibility.* New Haven, Conn.: Yale University Press, 1959.

Hovland, C. I., Lumsdaine, A. A., & Sheffield, F. D. *Experiments on mass communication.* Princeton, N.J.: Princeton University Press, 1959.

Hovland, C. I., & Mandell, W. An experimental comparison of conclusion-drawing by the communicator and by the audience. *Journal of Abnormal and Social Psychology,* 1952, *47*, 581–588.

Hsu, F. L. K. *Clan, caste, and club.* New York: Van Nostrand Reinhold, 1963.

Hsu, F. L. K. Role, affect and anthropology. *American Anthropologist,* 1977, *79*, 805–808.

Huber, J. Toward a sociotechnological theory of the women's movement. *Social Problems,* 1976, *23*, 371–388.

Hulett, J. E., Jr. Review of *Communication and social order* by H. D. Duncan. *Communication Review,* 1962, *7*, 458–468.

Hunt, J. G., Hill, J. W., & Reaser, J. M. Correlates of leadership behavior at two managerial levels in a mental institution. *Journal of Applied Social Psychology,* 1973, *3*, 174–185.

Hunt, M. *Sexual behavior in the 1970's.* Chicago: Playboy Press, 1974.

Hyman, H. H. The psychology of status. *Archives of Psychology,* 1942 (No. 269).

Iglitzin, L. B. War, sex, sports, and masculinity. In L. L. Farrar, Jr. (Ed.), *War: A historical, political and social study.* Santa Barbara, Calif.: ABC–Clio, 1978.

Ingraham, M. H. *My purpose holds: Reactions and experiences in retirement of TIAA-CREF annuitants.* New York: Winchell, 1974.

Inkeles, A., & Levinson, D. J. National character: The study of modal personality and sociocultural systems. In G. Lindzey & E. Aronson (Eds.), *The handbook of social psychology* (Vol. 4). Reading, Mass.: Addison-Wesley, 1969.

Inkeles, A., & Smith, D. H. *Becoming modern: Individual change in six developing countries.* Cambridge, Mass.: Harvard University Press, 1974.

Insel, P. M., & Moos, R. H. Psychological environments: Expanding the scope of human ecology. *American Psychologist,* 1974, *29*, 179–188.

Ittelson, W., & Slack, C. The perception of persons as visual objects. In R. Tagiuri & L. Petrullo (Eds.), *Person perception and interpersonal behavior.* Stanford, Calif.: Stanford University Press, 1958.

Jackson, E. Status consistency and symptoms of stress. *American Sociological Review,* 1962, *27,* 469–480.

Jackson, J. M. & Latané, B. All alone in front of all those people: Stage fright as a function of number and type of co-performers and audience. *Journal of Personality and Social Psychology,* 1981, *40,* 73–85.

Jackson, P. W. *Life in classrooms.* New York: Holt, Rinehart & Winston, 1968.

James, W. A study of the expression of bodily posture. *Journal of General Psychology,* 1932, *7,* 405–436.

Janis, I. L., *Victims of groupthink: A psychological study of foreign policy decisions and fiascoes.* Boston: Houghton Mifflin, 1972.

Janis, I. L., & Feshbach, S. Effects of fear-arousing communications. *Journal of Abnormal and Social Psychology,* 1953, *48,* 78–92.

Janis, I. L., & Field, P. B. Sex differences and personality factors related to persuasibility. In C. I. Hovland & I. L. Janis (Eds.), *Personality and persuasibility.* New Haven: Yale University Press, 1959.

Janis, I. L., & Mann, L. Effectiveness of emotional role-playing in modifying smoking habits and attitudes. *Journal of Experimental Research in Personality,* 1965, *1,* 84–90.

Janis, I. L., & Terwilliger, R. F. An experimental study of psychological resistances to fear-arousing communications. *Journal of Abnormal and Social Psychology,* 1962, *65,* 403–410.

Jencks, C. *Inequality: A reassessment of the effect of family and schooling in America.* New York: Basic Books, 1972.

Jenkins, J. C., & Perrow, C. Insurgency of the powerless: Farm worker movement. *American Sociological Review,* 1977, *42,* 249–268.

Johnson, J. A., Hogan, R., Zonderman, A. B., Callens, C., & Rogolsky, S. Moral judgment, personality, and attitudes toward authority. *Journal of Personality and Social Psychology,* 1981, *40,* 370–373.

Jones, E. E., & deCharms, R. Changes in social perception as a function of the personal relevance of behavior. In E. E. Maccoby, T. M. Newcomb, & E. L. Hartley (Eds.), *Readings in social psychology* (3rd ed.). New York: Holt, Rinehart & Winston, 1958. (a)

Jones, E. E., & deCharms, R. The organizing function of interaction roles in person perception. *Journal of Abnormal and Social Psychology,* 1958, *57,* 155–164. (b)

Jones, E. E., & Gerard, H. G. *Foundations of social psychology.* New York: Wiley, 1967.

Jones, E. E., & Nisbett, R. E. *The actor and observer: Divergent perceptions of the causes of behavior.* New York: General Learning, 1971.

Jones, E. E., & Thibaut, J. W. Interaction goals as bases of inference in interpersonal perception. In R. Tagiuri & L. Petrullo (Eds.), *Person perception and interpersonal behavior.* Stanford, Calif.: Stanford University Press, 1958.

Josselyn, I. M. Sexual identities in the life cycle. In G. H. Seward & R. C. Williamson (Eds.), *Sex roles in changing society.* New York: Random House, 1970.

Jourard, S. M. *Self-disclosure: An experimental analysis of the transparent self.* New York: Wiley-Interscience, 1971.

Judd, C. M., & Kulik, J. A. Schematic effects of social attitudes on information processing and recall. *Journal of Personality and Social Psychology,* 1980, *38,* 569–578.

Kahn, H. *On escalation.* New York: Praeger, 1965.

Kahn, R., Wolfe, D. M., Quinn, R. P., Snoek, J., Rosenthal, R. A. *Organizational stress.* New York: Wiley, 1964.

Kamin, L. J. *The science and politics of I.Q.* Hillsdale, N.J.: Erlbaum, 1974.

Kardiner, A. *Psychological frontiers of society.* New York: Columbia University Press, 1945.

Karpf, F. B. *American social psychology.* New York: Russell & Russell, 1972.

Katz, D. The functional approach to the study of attitudes. *Public Opinion Quarterly,* 1960, *24,* 163–204.

Katz, D. Nationalism and strategies of international conflict resolution. In H. C. Kelman (Ed.), *International behavior: A social-psychological analysis.* New York: Holt, Rinehart & Winston, 1965.

Katz, D., & Kahn, R. L. *The social psychology of organizations.* New York: Wiley, 1978.

Katz, D., & Stotland, E. A preliminary statement to a theory of attitude structure and change. In S. Koch (Ed.), *Psychology: A study of a science* (Vol. 3). New York: McGraw-Hill, 1959.

Katz, I., & Cohen, M. The effects of training Negroes

upon cooperative problem solving in biracial teams. *Journal of Abnormal and Social Psychology,* 1962, *64,* 319–325.

Katz, P. A. The acquisition of racial attitudes in children. In P. A. Katz (Ed.), *Toward the elimination of racism.* New York: Pergamon Press, 1976.

Kelley, H. H. Attribution theory in social psychology. In D. D. Levine (Ed.), *Nebraska Symposium on Motivation.* Lincoln: University of Nebraska Press, 1967.

Kelley, H. H. *Attribution and social interaction.* Morristown, N.J.: General Learning, 1971.

Kelley, H. H. Causal schemata and the attribution process. In E. E. Jones et al. (Eds.), *Attribution: Perceiving the causes of behavior.* Morristown, N.J.: General Learning, 1972.

Kelley, H. H. The process of causal attribution. *American Psychologist,* 1973, *28,* 107–129.

Kelley, H. H., & Volkart, E. H. The resistance to change of group anchored attitudes. *American Sociological Review,* 1952, *17,* 453–465.

Kelley, J. Causal chain models for the socioeconomic career. *American Sociological Review,* 1973, *38,* 481–493.

Kelman, H. C. Compliance, identification and internalization: Three processes of attitude change. *Journal of Conflict Resolution,* 1958, *2,* 51–60.

Kelman, H. C. Processes of opinion change. *Public Opinion Quarterly,* 1961, *25,* 57–78.

Kelman, H. C. *International behavior: A social psychological analysis.* New York: Holt, Rinehart & Winston, 1965.

Kelman, H. C. *A time to speak: On human values and social research.* San Francisco: Jossey-Bass, 1968.

Kelman, H. C., & Eagly, A. H. Attitude toward the communicator, perception of communication content, and attitude change. *Journal of Personality and Social Psychology,* 1965, *1,* 63–78.

Kelman, H. C., & Hovland, C. I. Reinstatement of the communicator in delayed measurement of opinion change. *Journal of Abnormal and Social Psychology,* 1953, *48,* 327–335.

Keniston, K. *The uncommitted: Alienated youth in American society.* New York: Harcourt Brace Jovanovich, 1960.

Keniston, K. The sources of student dissent. *Journal of Social Issues,* 1967, *23,* 108–116.

Kerckhoff, A. C., & Back, K. W. *The June bug: A study of hysterical contagion.* New York: Appleton-Century-Crofts, 1968.

Kessler, R. C., & Cleary, P. D. Social class and psychological distress. *American Sociological Review,* 1980, *45,* 463–478.

Kidder, L. H., Selltiz, D., Wrightman, L. S. & Cook, S. W. *Research methods in social relations* (4th ed.). New York: Holt, Rinehart & Winston, 1976.

Kiesler, C. A. Conformity and commitment. In E. Aronson & R. Helmreich (Eds.), *Social psychology.* New York: Van Nostrand, 1973.

Kiesler, S. B. Research funding for psychology. *American Psychologist,* 1977, *32,* 23–32.

Kilson, M. Blacks and neo-ethnicity in American political life. In N. Glazer & D. P. Moynihan (Eds.), *Ethnicity: Theory and experience.* Cambridge, Mass.: Harvard University Press, 1975.

Kimble, G. A., Garmezy, N., & Zigler, E. *Principles of general psychology* (4th ed.). New York: Ronald Press, 1974.

Kinsey, A. C., Pomeroy, W. B., & Martin, C. E. *Sexual behavior in the human male.* Philadelphia: W. B. Saunders, 1948.

Kirscht, J. P., & Dillehay, R. C. *Dimensions of authoritarianism: A review of research and theory.* Lexington: University of Kentucky Press, 1967.

Kirscht, J. P., Lodahl, T. M., & Haire, M. Some factors in the selection of leaders by members of small groups. *Journal of Abnormal and Social Psychology,* 1959, *58,* 406–408.

Kleemeier, R. W. *Aging and leisure.* New York: Columbia University Press, 1961.

Klein, A. L. Changes in leadership appraisal as a function of the stress of a simulated panic situation. *Journal of Personality and Social Psychology,* 1976, *34,* 1143–1154.

Klineberg, O. *Social psychology* (Rev. ed.). New York: Holt, Rinehart & Winston, 1954.

Klineberg, O. *The human dimension in international relations.* New York: Holt, Rinehart, & Winston, 1964.

Kluckhohn, C. Values and value-orientations in the theory of action. In T. Parsons & E. A. Shils (Eds.), *Toward a general theory of action.* Cambridge, Mass.: Harvard University Press, 1951.

Kluckhohn, F. R., & Strodtbeck, F. L. *Variations in value orientation.* New York: Harper & Row, 1961.

Knapp, R. W. Pressure in the colleges: The professor. *Life,* January 1965.

Kohlberg, L. Development of moral character and moral ideology. In M. L. Hoffman & L. W.

Hoffman (Eds.), *Review of child development research* (Vol. 1). New York: Russell Sage, 1964.

Kohlberg, L. Stage and sequence: The cognitive-developmental approach to socialization. In D. A. Goalin (Ed.), *Handbook of socialization theory and research*. Chicago: Rand McNally, 1969.

Kohn, M. L. Social class and parent-child relationships: An interpretation. *American Journal of Sociology*, 1963, *68,* 471–480.

Kohn, M. L. *Class and conformity: A study of values.* Homewood, Ill.: Dorsey, 1969.

Komarovsky, M. *Blue-collar marriage.* New York: Random House, 1962.

Komorita, S. S., & Chertkoff, J. M. A bargaining theory of coalition formation. *Psychological Review*, 1973, *80,* 149–162.

Konig, R. *A la mode: On the social psychology of fashion.* New York: Seabury Press, 1973.

Korzybski, A. *Science and sanity.* Lancaster, Pa.: Science Press, 1933.

Krauss, R. M., Geller, V., & Olson, C. Modalities and cues in the detection of deception. Paper presented at the meeting of the American Psychological Association, Washington, D.C., 1976.

Krech, D., Crutchfield, R. S., & Ballachey, E. L. *Individual in society: A textbook of social psychology.* New York: McGraw-Hill, 1962.

Kriesberg, L. *The sociology of social conflicts.* Englewood Cliffs, N.J.: Prentice-Hall, 1973.

Kritzer, H. M. Political protest and political violence: A nonrecursive causal model. *Social Forces*, 1977, *55,* 630–640.

Kroeber, A. L. *Anthropology* (Rev. ed.). New York: Harcourt, Brace & World, 1948.

Kunkel, J. H. The behavioral perspective of social dynamics. In R. L. Hamblin & J. H. Kunkel (Eds.), *Behavioral theory in sociology: Essays in honor of George C. Homans.* New Brunswick, N.J.: Transaction, 1977.

Kutner, B., Wilkings, C., & Yarrow, P. R. Verbal attitudes and overt behavior involving racial prejudice. *Journal of Abnormal and Social Psychology*, 1952, *47,* 649–652.

Kuznicki, J. T., & Greenfield, N. Vicarious and direct reinforcement: An experimental evaluation. *Journal of Social Psychology*, 1977, *101,* 103–111.

LaBarre, W. *Personality from a psychoanalytic viewpoint.* In E. Norbeck, D. Price-Williams, & W. M. McCord (Eds.), *The study of personality.* New York: Holt, Rinehart, & Winston, 1968.

Labov, W. The logic of non-standard English. In F. Williams (Ed.), *Language and poverty: Perspectives on a theme.* Chicago: Markham, 1970. (a)

Labov, W. *The study of nonstandard English.* New York: National Council of Teachers, 1970. (b)

Lamphere, L. The long-term study among the Navaho. In G. M. Foster el al. (Eds.), *Long-term field research in social anthropology.* New York: Academic Press, 1979.

Landes, R. The abnormal among the Ojibwa Indians. *Journal of Abnormal and Social Psychology*, 1938, *33,* 14–33.

Lang, K., & Lang, G. E. *Collective dynamics.* New York: Crowell, 1961.

Langer, E. J. The illusion of control. *Journal of Personality and Social Psychology*, 1975, *32,* 311–328.

Langer, E. J., & Rodin, J. The effects of choice and enhanced personal responsibility for the aged: A field experiment in an institutional setting. *Journal of Personality and Social Psychology*, 1976, *34,* 191–198.

LaPalombara, L. E. *An introduction to grammar: Traditional, structural, transformational.* New York: Winthrop, 1976.

LaPiere, R. T. Attitudes vs. actions. *Social Forces*, 1934, *14,* 230–237.

Lasswell, H. D. *Power and personality.* New York: Norton, 1948.

Lasswell, T. E. *Class and stratum.* New York: Houghton Mifflin, 1965.

Latané, B., & Darley, J. M. Social determinants of bystander intervention in emergencies. In J. R. Macaulay and L. Berkowitz (Eds.), *Altruism and helping behavior.* New York: Academic Press, 1970. (a)

Latané, B., & Darley, J. M. *The unresponsive bystander: Why doesn't he help?* New York: Appleton-Century-Crofts, 1970. (b)

Latané, B., Williams, K., & Harkins, S. Many hands make light the work: The causes and consequences of social loafing. *Journal of Personality and Social Psychology*, 1979, *37,* 822–832.

Lauer, R. H. *Social movements and social change.* Carbondale: Southern Illinois University Press, 1976.

Lauer, R. H., & Thomas, R. A comparative analysis of the consequences of change. *Human Relations*, 1976, *29,* 239–248.

Lawton, M. P. Assessment, integration, and environments for the elderly. *Gerontologist,* 1970, *10,* 38–46.

Lawton, M. P. The relative impact of congregate and traditional housing on elderly tenants. *Gerontologist,* 1976, *16,* 237–242.

Lazarsfeld, P. F. *Latent structure analysis.* New York: Bureau of Applied Social Research, Columbia University, 1957.

Lazarsfeld, P. F., & Thielens, W., Jr. *The academic mind.* New York: Free Press, 1958.

Leach, E. *Culture and communication.* London: Cambridge University Press, 1976.

LeBon, G. *The crowd.* London: George Allen & Unwin, 1917.

Lecky, P. *Self-consistency: A theory of personality.* New York: Island Press, 1945.

Lee, A. M., & Humphrey, N. D. *Race riot.* New York: Holt, Rinehart & Winston, 1943.

Lee, D. D. A primitive system of values. *Philosophy of Science,* 1940, *7,* 355–365.

Lee, J. A. *The colors of love: An exploration of the ways of loving.* Don Mills, Ontario: New Press, 1976.

Lee, J. A. Forbidden colors of love: Patterns of gay love. In P. J. Stein (Ed.), *Single life: Unmarried adults in social context.* New York: St. Martin's Press, 1981.

Leeper, R. W. Some need developments in the motivational theory of emotions. In D. Levine (Ed.), *Nebraska Symposium on Motivation.* Lincoln: University of Nebraska Press, 1965.

Lefcourt, H. M. The function of the illusions of control and freedom. *American Psychologist,* 1973, *28,* 417–426.

Lenski, G. E. *Power and privilege.* New York: McGraw-Hill, 1966.

Lerner, M. J. The effect of responsibility and choice on a partner's attractiveness following failure. *Journal of Personality,* 1965, *33,* 178–187.

Lerner, M. J. "Just world" research and the attribution process: Looking back and ahead. Unpublished manuscript, University of Waterloo, 1975.

Lerner, M. J. Respectable bigotry. In M. Friedman (Ed.), *Overcoming middle-class rage.* Philadelphia: Westminister, 1971.

Leventhal, H. Findings and theory in the study of fear communications. In L. Berkowitz (Ed.), *Advances in experimental social psychology* (Vol. 5). New York: Academic Press, 1970.

Levin, P. F., & Isen, A. M. Further studies on the effect of feeling good on helping. *Sociometry,* 1975, *38,* 141–147.

Levine, R., Chein, I., & Murphy, G. The relation of the intensity of a need to the amount of perceptual distortion. *Journal of Psychology,* 1942, *13,* 282–293.

Lewin, K. Group decision and social change. In H. Proshansky and B. Beidenberg (Eds.), *Basic studies in social psychology.* New York: Holt, Rinehart & Winston, 1965.

Lewin, K. *A dynamic theory of personality.* New York: McGraw-Hill, 1935.

Lewin, K. *Field theory as human-science* (J. de Rivera, Ed.). New York: Gardner Press, 1976.

Lewin, K. *Resolving social conflicts: Selected papers on group dynamics.* G. W. Lewin (Ed.). New York: Harper & Row, 1948.

Lewis, J. D. A social behaviorist interpretation of the Meadian "I." *American Journal of Sociology,* 1979, *85,* 261–287.

Lidz, T. The adolescent and his family. In G. Caplan and S. Lebovici (Eds.), *Adolescence: Psychological perspectives.* New York: Basic Books, 1969.

Lieberman, D. A. Behaviorism and the mind: A (limited) call for a return to introspection. *American Psychologist,* 1979, *34,* 319–333.

Lifton, R. J. Psychological effects of the atomic bomb in Hiroshima: The theme of death. *Daedalus,* 1963, *92,* 462–497.

Lightfoot, A. The potency of social class in determining educational inequities. In A. Lightfoot (Ed.), *Inquiries into the social foundations of education.* Chicago: Rand McNally, 1972.

Likert, R. A technique for the measurement of attitudes. *Archives of Psychology,* 1932, No. 140.

Limber, J. Language in child and chimp? *American Psychologist,* 1977, *32,* 280–295.

Lindskold, S., & Collins, M. G. Inducing cooperation by groups and individuals. *Journal of Conflict Resolution,* 1978, *22,* 679–690.

Lindzey, G., & Byrne, D. Measurement of social choice and interpersonal attractiveness. In G. Lindzey & E. Aronson (Eds.), *Handbook of social psychology* (2nd ed.; Vol. 2). Reading, Mass.: Addison-Wesley, 1968.

Linn, L. S. Verbal attitudes and overt behavior: A study of racial discrimination. *American Sociological Review,* 1965, *29,* 353–364.

Linton, R. *The study of man.* New York: Appleton-Century-Crofts, 1936.

Linton, R., & Kardiner, A. *Psychological frontiers of society.* New York: Columbia University Press, 1945.

Lippitt, R., Watson, J., & Westley, B. *The dynamics of planned change.* New York: Harcourt, Brace & World, 1957.

Lippmann, W. *Public opinion.* New York: Harcourt, Brace & World, 1922.

Litman, T. J. Self-conception and physical rehabilitation. In A. M. Rose (Ed.), *Human behavior and social processes: An interactionist approach.* Boston: Houghton Mifflin, 1962.

Locksley, A., Borgida, E., Brekke, N., & Hepburn, C. Sex stereotypes and social judgment. *Journal of Personality and Social Psychology,* 1980, *39,* 821–831.

Loewenberg, P. The psychohistorical origins of the Nazi youth cohort. In G. M. Kren & L. H. Rappoport (Eds.), *Varieties of psychohistory.* New York: Springer, 1976.

Loflin, M. D., & Winogrond, I. R. A culture as a set of beliefs. *Current Anthropology,* 1976, *17,* 723–725.

Lopata, H. Z. *Widowhood in an American city.* Cambridge, Mass.: Schenkman, 1973.

Lopreato, J., & Hazelrigg, L. E. *Class, conflict, and mobility.* San Francisco: Chandler Publishing Co., 1972.

Lowen, A. *Physical dynamics of character structure.* New York: Grune & Stratton, 1958.

Lowenthal, M. F. Toward a sociological theory of change in adulthood and old age. In J. E. Birren & K. W. Schaie (Eds.), *Handbook of psychology of aging.* New York: Van Nostrand Reinhold, 1977.

Loye, D. *The leadership passion.* San Francisco: Jossey-Bass, 1977.

Luchins, A. S. Primacy-recency in impression formation. In C. I. Hovland (Ed.), *The order of presentation in persuasion* (Vol. 1). New Haven, Conn.: Yale University Press, 1957.

Luchins, A. S., & Luchins, E. M. On conformity with judgments of a majority or an authority. *Journal of Social Psychology,* 1961, *53,* 308–316.

Lundberg, M. J. *The incomplete adult: Social class constraints on personality development.* Westport, Conn.: Greenwood Press, 1974.

Luria, Z., & Rose, M. D. *Psychology of human sexuality.* New York: Wiley, 1979.

Luttbeg, N. L. (Ed.). *Public opinion and public policy* (4th ed.). Itasca, Ill.: F. E. Peacock, 1981.

Lyman, S. M., & Scott, M. B. *A sociology of the absurd.* New York: Appleton-Century-Crofts, 1970.

Lynd, R. S., & Lynd, H. M. *Middletown.* New York: Harcourt Brace, 1929.

Maccoby, N. The great debate of 1960. In D. Krech, R. S. Crutchfield, & E. L. Ballachey (Eds.), *Individual in society.* New York: McGraw-Hill, 1962.

Macklin, D. B. A social psychological approach to modernization. In C. Morse et al., *Modernization by design.* Ithaca, N.Y.: Cornell University Press, 1969.

Maddox, G. L., Back, K. W., & Liederman, V. R. Overweight as social deviance and disability. *Journal of Health and Social Behavior,* 1968, *4,* 287–298.

Madigan, L. *The American Indian relocation program.* New York: Association on American Indian Affairs, 1956.

Maier, S. F., & Seligman, M. E. P. Learned helplessness: Theory and evidence. *Journal of Experimental Psychology: General,* 1976, *105,* 3–46.

Malinowski, M. *A scientific theory of culture and other essays.* Chapel Hill: University of North Carolina Press, 1944.

Maloney, M. P., & Ward, M. P. Ecology: Let's hear from the people: An objective scale for the measurement of ecological attitudes and knowledge. *American Psychologist,* 1973, *28,* 583–591.

Mann, L., & Janis, I. L. A follow-up study of the long-term effects of emotional role playing. *Journal of Personality and Social Psychology,* 1968, *8,* 339–342.

Maples, M. F., & Webster, J. M. Thorndike's connectionism. In G. M. Gazda and R. J. Corsini (Eds.), *Theories of learning.* Itasca, Ill.: F. E. Peacock, 1980.

Markle, G. E., & Troyer, R. J. Smoke gets in your eyes: Cigarette smoking as deviant behavior. *Social Problems,* 1979, *26,* 611–625.

Marlowe, D., & Gergen, K. J. Personality and social interaction. In G. Lindzey and E. Aronson (Eds.), *Handbook of social psychology* (Vol. 3). Reading, Mass.: Addison-Wesley, 1969.

Marsh, R. M. The explanation of occupational prestige hierarchies. *Social Forces,* 1971, *50,* 214–222.

Martin, J., & Westie, F. The tolerant personality.

American Sociological Review, 1959, *24,* 521–528.

Mashman, R. C. The effect of physical attractiveness on the perception of attitude similarity. *Journal of Social Psychology,* 1978, *106,* 103–110.

Maslow, A. H. *Motivation and personality.* New York: Harper & Row, 1954.

Maslow, A. H. *Toward a psychology of being.* Princeton, N.J.: Van Nostrand Reinhold, 1962.

Massarik, F., Tannenbaum, R., Kahane, M., & Weschler, I. Sociometric choice and organizational effectiveness: A multi-relational approach. In J. L. Moreno et al. (Eds.), *The sociometry reader.* New York: Free Press, 1960.

Mathieu, J. T. Housing preferences and satisfactions. In M. P. Lawton, R. B. Newcomer, & T. O. Byerts (Eds.), *Community planning for an aging society.* Stroudsburg, Pa.: Dowden, Hutchinson & Ross, 1976.

Mayo, C., & LaFrance, M. *Evaluating research in prosocial behavior.* Monterey, Calif.: Brooks/Cole, 1977.

Mazzlish, B. *In search of Nixon.* New York: Basic Books, 1972.

McCauley, C., Stitt, C. L., Woods, K., and Lipton, D. Group shift to caution at the race track. *Journal of Experimental Social Psychology,* 1973, *9,* 80–86.

McClelland, D. C. *Personality.* New York: William Sloane Associates, 1951.

McClelland, D. C. *The achieving society.* New York: Van Nostrand Reinhold, 1961.

McClelland, D. C. *Power: The inner experience.* New York: Irvington, 1975.

McClelland, D. C. Managing motivation to expand human freedom. *American Psychologist,* 1978, *33,* 201–210.

McClosky, H., & Schaar, J. H. Psychological dimensions of anomie. *American Sociological Review,* 1965, *30,* 14–40.

McGinnies, E., & Altman, I. Discussion as a function of attitudes and content of a persuasive communication. *Journal of Applied Psychology,* 1959, *43,* 53–59.

McGlothlin, W. H. Sociocultural factors in marihuana use in the United States. In V. Rubin (Ed.), *Cannabis and culture.* The Hague: Mouton, 1975.

McGuire, W. J. Inducing resistance to persuasion: Some contemporary approaches. In L. Berkowitz (Ed.), *Advances in experimental social psychology* (Vol. 1). New York: Academic Press, 1964.

McGuire, W. J. The nature of attitudes and attitude change. In G. Lindzey & E. Aronson (Eds.), *Handbook of social psychology* (Vol. 3, 2nd ed.). Reading, Mass.: Addison-Wesley, 1969.

McGuire, W. J. The yin and yang of progress in social psychology: Seven koan. *Journal of Personality and Social Psychology,* 1973, *26,* 446–456.

Mead, G. H. *Mind, self and society.* Chicago: University of Chicago Press, 1934.

Mead, M. *Coming of age in Samoa.* New York: Morrow, 1928.

Mead, M. *Growing up in New Guinea.* New York: Morrow, 1930.

Mead, M. *Sex and temperament in three primitive societies.* New York: Morrow, 1935.

Mead, M. *Male and female: A study of the sexes in a changing world.* New York: Dell. 1949.

Mead, M. *New lives for old.* New York: Morrow, 1956.

Medea, A., & Thompson, K. *Against rape.* New York: Farrar, Straus & Giroux, 1974.

Meddin, J. Chimpanzees, symbols, and the reflective self. *Social Psychology Quarterly,* 1979, *42,* 99–109.

Meenes, M. A comparison of racial stereotypes. *Journal of Social Psychology,* 1943, *17,* 327–336.

Mehan, H., & Wood, H. *The reality of ethnomethodology.* New York: Wiley, 1975.

Meier, A., & Rudwick, E. *CORE: A study of the civil rights movement, 1942–1968.* New York: Oxford University Press, 1973.

Meier, N. C., Mennenga, G. H., & Stoltz, H. J. An experimental approach to the study of mob behavior. *Journal of Abnormal and Social Psychology,* 1941, *36,* 506–534.

Menzel, H., & Katz, E. Social relations and innovation in the medical profession: The epidemiology of a new drug. *Public Opinion Quarterly,* 1955, *19,* 337–352.

Menyuk, P. *The acquisition and development of language.* Englewood Cliffs, N.J.: Prentice-Hall, 1971.

Merton, R. K. The role set. *British Journal of Sociology,* 1957, *8,* 106–120.

Merton, R. K. Introduction. In G. Le Bon, *Psychology of crowds.* New York: Viking Press, 1960.

Meyerson, R. An examination of commercial entertainment. In R. W. Kleemeier (Ed.), *Aging and leisure.* New York: Oxford University Press, 1961.

Michener, H. A., Fleishman, J. A., & Vaske, J. J. A

test of the bargaining theory of coalition formation in four-person groups. *Journal of Personality and Social Psychology,* 1976, *34,* 1114–1126.

Milburn, T. W. The nature of threat. *Journal of Social Issues,* 1977, *33:*1, 126–139.

Miles, R. H. Role-set configuration as a predictor of role conflict and ambiguity in complex organizations. *Sociometry,* 1977, *40,* 21–34.

Milgram, S. Behavioral study of obedience. *Journal of Abnormal and Social Psychology,* 1963, *67,* 371-378.

Milgram, S. Some conditions of obedience and disobedience to authority. *Human Relations,* 1965, *18,* 57–75.

Milgram, S., & Toch, H. Collective behavior: Crowds and social movements. In G. Lindzey and E. Aronson (Eds.), *The handbook of social psychology* (Vol. 4). Reading, Mass.: Addison-Wesley, 1969.

Miller, D. R., & Swanson, G. E. *The changing American parent.* New York: Wiley, 1958.

Miller, G. A., & McNeill, D. Psycholinguistics. In G. Lindzey & E. Aronson (Eds.), *The handbook of social psychology* (Vol. 3). Reading, Mass.: Addison-Wesley, 1969.

Miller, N., & Campbell, D. T. Recency and primacy in persuasion as a function of the timing of speeches and measurements. *Journal of Abnormal and Social Psychology,* 1959, *59,* 1–9.

Miller, N. E., & Dollard, J. *Social learning and imitation.* New Haven: Yale University Press, 1941.

Miller, N. E., et al. Graphic communication in the crisis of education. *Audio-visual Communication Review,* 1957, 5(3).

Miller, N., Maruyama, G., Beaber, R. J., & Valone, K. Speed of speech and persuasion. *Journal of Personality and Social Psychology,* 1976, *34,* 615–624.

Miller, S. M. Comparative social mobility. *Current Sociology,* 1960, *9,* 1–89.

Mills, J., & Harvey, J. Opinion change as a function of when information about the communicator is received and whether he is attractive or expert. *Journal of Personality and Social Psychology,* 1972, *21,* 52–55.

Mills, J., & Mintz, P. M. Effects of unexplained arousal on affiliation. *Journal of Personality and Social Psychology,* 1972, *24,* 11–14.

Mirowsky, J., II, & Ross, C. E. Minority status, ethnic culture, and distress: A comparison of blacks, whites, Mexicans, and Mexican Americans. *American Journal of Sociology,* 1980, *86,* 479–495.

Mischel, W. *Introduction to personality* (2nd ed.). New York: Holt, Rinehart & Winston, 1976.

Moede, W. *Experimentalle Massenpsychologie.* Leipzig: Hirzel, 1920.

Moment, D., & Zaleznik, A. *Role development and interpersonal competence.* Cambridge, Mass.: Harvard University, Graduate School of Business Administration, 1963.

Moore, B., Jr. Sociological theory and contemporary politics. *American Journal of Sociology,* 1955, *61,* 107–115.

Moore, W. E. *Social change.* Englewood Cliffs, N. J.: Prentice-Hall, 1963.

Moos, R. H. Conceptualizations of human environments. *American Psychologist,* 1973, *28,* 652–665.

Moos, R. H. Specialized living environments for older people: A conceptual framework for evaluation. *Journal of Social Issues,* 1980, *36:*2, 75–94.

Moreno, J. L. *Who shall survive?* Beacon, N. Y.: Beacon House, 1953. (Originally published, 1934).

Morgan, C. T. The physiological theory of drive. In S. Koch (Ed.), *Psychology: A study of a science* (Vol. 1). New York: McGraw-Hill, 1959.

Morris, C. G., & Hackman, J. R. Behavioral correlates of perceived leadership. *Journal of Personality and Social Psychology,* 1969, *13,* 350–361.

Morrow, L. The great kissing epidemic. *Time,* February 7, 1977, pp. 66–67.

Morse, S. J., & Gergen, K. J. Material aid and social attraction. *Journal of Applied Social Psychology,* 1971, *1,* 150–162.

Morton, J. What could possibly be innate? In J. Morton (Ed.), *Biological and social factors in psycholinguistics.* London: Logos Press, 1971.

Mowrer, E. R. The differentiation of husband and wife roles. *Journal of Marriage and the Family,* 1969, *31,* 534–540.

Murphy, G. (Ed.). *Human nature and enduring peace.* Boston: Houghton Mifflin, 1945.

Murray, H. A. *Explorations in personality.* Fair Lawn, N.J.: Oxford University Press, 1938.

Naftolin, D. H., Ware, J. E., & Donnelly, F. A. The Doctor Fox Lecture: A paradigm of educational seduction. *Journal of Medical Education,* 1973, *48,* 630–635.

Nation, J. R., & Massad, P. Persistence training: A partial reinforcement procedure for reversing learned helplessness and depression. *Journal of Experimental Psychology: General,* 1978, *107,* 436–451.

Nealey, S. M., & Fiedler, F. E. Leadership functions of middle managers. *Psychological Bulletin,* 1968, *70,* 313–329.

Nellis, W., & Graziano, C. Weaseling in the tube room. In J. P. Spradley & M. A. Rynkiewich (Eds.), *The Nacirema: Readings on American culture.* Boston: Little, Brown, 1975.

Nelson, H. M., Yokley, R. L., & Madron, T. W. Ministerial roles and social actionist stance: Protestant clergy and protest in the sixties. *American Sociological Review,* 1973, *38,* 375–386.

Nelson, L. M., & Winter, M. Life disruption, independence, satisfaction and the consideration of moving. *Gerontologist,* 1975, *15,* 160–164.

Nemeth, C. Group dynamics and legal decision-making. In L. E. Abt & I. R. Stuart (Eds.), *Social psychology and discretionary law.* New York: Van Nostrand, 1979.

Neugarten, B. L. Personality change in late life: A developmental perspective. In C. Eisdorfer & M. P. Lawton (Eds.), *The psychology of adult development and aging.* Washington, D.C.: American Psychological Association, 1973.

Neugarten, B. L., & Weinstein, K. K. The changing American grandparent. *Journal of Marriage and the Family,* 1964, *26,* 199–204.

Newcomb, T. M. *Social psychology.* New York: Holt, Rinehart & Winston, 1950.

Newcomb, T. M. *Personality and social change* (2nd ed.). New York: Holt, Rinehart & Winston, 1957.

Newcomb, T. M. Attitude development as function of reference groups: The Bennington study. In E. E. Maccoby, T. M. Newcomb, & E. L. Hartley (Eds.), *Readings in social psychology* (3rd ed.). New York: Holt, Rinehart & Winston, 1958.

Newcomb, T. M. *The acquaintance process.* New York: Holt, Rinehart & Winston, 1961.

Newcomb, T. M. Interpersonal balance. In R. Abelson, E. Aronson, W. McGuire, T. Newcomb, M. Rosenberg, & P. Tannenbaum (Eds.), *Theories of cognitive consistency: A sourcebook.* Chicago: Rand McNally, 1968.

Newcomb, T. M., The acquaintance process: Looking mainly backward. *Journal of Personality and Social Psychology,* 1978, *36,* 1075–1083.

Newcomb, T. M., Koenig, K. E., Flacks, R., & Warwich, D. P. *Persistence and change: Bennington College and its students after twenty-five years.* New York: Wiley, 1967.

Newcomb, T. M., & Svehla, G. Intra-family relationships in attitude. *Sociometry,* 1937, *1,* 180–205.

Newcomb, T. M., Turner, R. H., & Converse, P. E. *Social psychology: The study of human interaction.* New York: Holt, Rinehart & Winston, 1965.

Nisbett, R., & Schachter, S. Cognitive manipulation of pain. *Journal of Experimental Social Psychology,* 1966, *2,* 227–236.

Nisbett, R. E., & Wilson, T. D. Telling more than we can know: Verbal reports on mental processes. *Psychological Review,* 1977, *84,* 231-259.

Norman, C. Soft technologies, hard choices. In A. H. Teich (Ed.), *Technology and man's future* (3rd ed.). New York: St. Martin's Press, 1981.

Notarius, C. I., & Levenson, R. W. Expressive tendencies and physiological response to stress. *Journal of Personality and Social Psychology,* 1979, *37,* 1204–1210.

Notz, W. W. Work motivation and the negative effects of extrinsic rewards. *American Psychologist,* 1975, *30,* 884–891.

Oberschall, A. *Social conflict and social movements.* Englewood Cliffs, N.J.: Prentice-Hill, 1973.

Ogburn, W. F. *Social change.* New York: Viking, 1922.

Okun, M. A., & Elias, C. S. Cautiousness in adulthood as a function of age and payoff structure. *Journal of Gerontology,* 1977, *32,* 451–455.

Olmedo, E. L. Acculturation: A psychometric perspective. *American Psychologist,* 1979, *34,* 1061–1070.

Olofsky, J. L., Marcia, J. E., & Lesser, I. M. Ego identity status and the intimacy versus isolation crisis of young adulthood. *Journal of Personality and Social Psychology,* 1973, *27,* 211–219.

Oppenheimer, R. Analogy in science. *American Psychologist,* 1956, *11,* 134.

Orenstein, A., & Phillips, W. R. F. *Understanding social research.* Boston: Allyn & Bacon, 1978.

Osborn, A. F. *Applied imagination* (3rd ed.). New York: Scribners, 1963.

Osgood, C. E. *An alternative to war or surrender.* Urbana: University of Illinois Press, 1962.

Osgood, C. E., & Sebeck, T. A. *Psycholinguistics.* Bloomington: Indiana University Press, 1965.

Osgood, C. E., Suci, C. J., & Tannenbaum, P. H. *The measurement of meaning.* Urbana, Ill.: University of Illinois Press, 1957.

Osgood, C. E., & Tannenbaum, P. H. The principle of congruity in the prediction of attitude change. *Psychological Review,* 1955, *62,* 42–55.

Padilla, A. M., Ruiz, R. A., & Alvarez, R. Community mental health services for the Spanish-speaking/surnamed population. *American Psychologist,* 1975, *30,* 892–905.

Page, R. H., & McGinnies, E. Comparison of two styles of leadership in small group discussion. *Journal of Applied Psychology,* 1959, *43,* 240–245.

Palermo, D. S. *The psychology of language.* Glenview: Ill.: Scott, Foresman, 1978.

Parr, J. The interaction of persons and living environments. In L. W. Poon (Ed.), *Aging in the 1980's.* Washington, D.C.: American Psychological Association, 1980.

Parsons, T. Systematic theory in sociology. In *Essays in sociological theory.* New York: Free Press, 1949.

Parsons, T. *The social system.* New York: Free Press, 1951.

Payne, S., Summers, D. A., & Stewart, T. R. Value differences across three generations. *Sociometry,* 1973, *36,* 20–30.

Pei, M. *Invitation to linguistics.* New York: Doubleday, 1965.

Pepitone. A. Attributions of causality, social attitudes, and cognitive matching process. In R. Tagiuri & L. Petrullo (Eds.), *Person perception and interpersonal behavior.* Stanford, Calif.: Stanford University Press, 1958.

Pepitone, A. *Attraction and hostility.* New York: Atherton Press, 1964.

Pepitone, A. Toward a normative and comparative biocultural social psychology. *Journal of Social Psychology,* 1976, *34,* 641–653.

Pepitone, A., & Reichling, G. Group cohesiveness and the expression of hostility. *Human Relations,* 1955, *8,* 327–337.

Persell, C. H. *Education and equality.* New York: Free Press, 1977.

Peters, P. W. *A class divided.* New York: Doubleday, 1971.

Piliavin, I. M., Rodin, U., & Pilivian, J. Is good Samaritanism an underground phenomenon? *Journal of Personality and Social Psychology,* 1969, *13,* 289–299.

Pilisuk, M., & Hayden, T. Is there a military industrial complex which prevents peace? *Journal of Social Issues,* 1965, *21*:3, 67–117.

Pitcher, B. L., Hamblin, R. L., & Miller, J. L. Diffusion of collective violence. *American Sociological Review,* 1978, *43,* 23–35.

Pool, J. Coalition formation in small groups with incomplete communication networks. *Journal of Personality and Social Psychology,* 1976, *34,* 82–91.

Porter, L. W., & Lawler, E. E. Properties of organization structure in relation to job attitudes and job behavior. *Psychological Bulletin,* 1965, *64,* 23–51.

Postman, L., Bruner, K. S., & McGinnies, E. Personal values as selective factors in perception. *Journal of Abnormal and Social Psychology,* 1948, *43,* 142-154.

Powell, F. A. Open- and closed-mindedness and the ability to differentiate source and message. *Journal of Abnormal and Social Psychology,* 1962, *65,* 61–66.

Preiss, J. J. Self and role in medical education. In C. Gordon & K. J. Gergen (Eds.), *The self in social interaction* (Vol. 1). New York: Wiley, 1968.

Premack, D. The education of Sarah. *Psychology Today,* September 1970, p. 54 ff.

Proshansky, H. A projective method for the study of attitudes. *Journal of Abnormal and Social Psychology,* 1943, *38,* 393–395.

Proshansky, H. M. Environmental psychology and the real world. *American Psychologist,* 1976, *31,* 303–310.

Proshansky, H. M., Ittelson, W. H., & Rivlin, L. G. Freedom of choice and behavior in a physical setting. In H. M. Proshansky, W. N. Ittelson, & L. G. Rivlin (Eds.), *Environmental psychology: Man and his physical setting.* New York: Holt, Rinehart & Winston, 1970.

Pryor, J. B., and Kriss, M. The cognitive dynamics of salience in the attribution process. *Journal of Personality and Social Psychology,* 1977, *35,* 49–55.

Raimy, V. C. Self-reference in counseling interviews. *Journal of Consulting Psychologists,* 1948, *12,* 153–163.

Ramsay, J., & Anderson, C. *Managing the environment.* New York: Basic Books, 1972.

Randall, O. Aging in America today. *Gerontologist,* 1977, *17,* 6–11.

Ransford, H. E. Isolation, powerlessness, and violence: A study of attitudes and participation in the Watts riot. In A. D. Grimshaw (Ed.), *Racial violence in the United States.* Chicago: Aldine, 1969.

Raven, B. H., & Kruglanski, A. W. Conflict and power. In P. G. Swingle (Ed.), *The structure of conflict.* New York: Academic Press, 1970.

Ray, J. J. Racism and authoritarianism among white South Africans. *Journal of Social Psychology,* 1980, *110,* 29–37.

Raynor, J. O. Relationships between achievement-related motives, future orientation, and academic performance. *Journal of Personality and Social Psychology,* 1970, *15,* 28–33.

Read, P. B. Source of authority and the legitimation of leadership in small groups. *Sociometry,* 1974, *37,* 123–142.

Regan, D. T., & Fazio, R. On the consistency between attitude and behavior: Look to the method of attitude formation. *Journal of Experimental Social Psychology,* 1977, *13,* 28–45.

Richard, S., Livson, S. F., & Petersen, P. G. *Aging and personality.* New York: Wiley, 1962.

Reik, T. *A psychologist looks at love.* New York: Holt, Rinehart & Winston, 1944.

Reiss, I. L. *Family systems in America* (3rd ed.) New York: Holt, Rinehart & Winston, 1980.

Renshon, S. A. *Psychological needs and political behavior.* New York: Free Press, 1974.

Rethlingshafer, D. *Motivation as related to personality.* New York: McGraw-Hill, 1963.

Reynolds, G. S. *A primer of operant conditioning.* Glenview, Ill.: Scott, Foresman, 1968.

Rice, S. A. Stereotypes: A source of error in judging human character. *Journal of Personality Research,* 1926, *5,* 267–276.

Rich, H. E. The effect of college on political awareness and knowledge. *Youth and Society,* 1976, *8,* 67–80.

Riddleberger, A. B., & Motz, A. B. Prejudice and perception. *American Journal of Sociology,* 1957, *42,* 498–503.

Ridgeway, J. *The politics of ecology.* New York: Dutton, 1970.

Riley, M. W., Cohn, R., Toby, J., & Riley, J. W. Interpersonal orientations in small groups: A consideration of the questionnaire approach. *American Sociological Review,* 1954, *15,* 445–460.

Robertson, J. F. Significance of grandparents: Perceptions of young adult grandchildren. *Gerontologist,* 1976, *16,* 136–140.

Robinson, J. P., Rusk, J. G., & Head, K. B. Criteria for the construction and evaluation of attitude scales. In *Measures of political attitudes.* Ann Arbor, Mich.: Institute for Social Research, 1968.

Rock, I. *An introduction to perception.* New York: Macmillan, 1975.

Rodman, H., & Grams, P. Family and delinquency. In President's Commission on Law Enforcement and Administration of Justice: *Task Force Report on Juvenile Delinquency and Youth Crime.* Washington, D.C.: U.S. Government Printing Office, 1967.

Roethlisberger, F. J., & Dickson, W. J. *Management and the worker.* Cambridge, Mass.: Harvard University Press, 1939.

Rogers, C. M., & Wrightsman, L. S. Attitudes toward children's rights: Nurturance or self-determination. *Journal of Social Issues,* 1978, *34:*2, 59–68.

Rogers, C. R. *Counseling and psychotherapy.* Boston: Houghton Mifflin, 1942.

Rogers, C. R. *Client-centered therapy.* Boston: Houghton Mifflin, 1951.

Rogers, C. R. Some new challenges. *American Psychologist,* 1973, *28,* 379.

Rogers, E. M. *The diffusion of innovations.* New York: Free Press, 1962.

Rogers, E. M., & Shoemaker, F. *Communication of innovations: A cross-cultural approach* (2nd ed.). New York: Free Press, 1971.

Rogers, R. W., & Newborn, C. R. Fear appeals and attitude change: Effects of threat's noxiousness, probability of occurrence, and the efficacy of coping responses. *Journal of Personality and Social Psychology,* 1976, *34,* 54–61.

Rohter, I. S. The righteous rightists. *Transaction,* 1967, *4,* 27–35.

Rokeach, M. *The open and closed mind.* New York: Basic Books, 1960.

Rokeach, M. *Beliefs, attitudes and values: A theory of organization and change.* San Francisco: Jossey-Bass, 1972.

Romer, D. Internalization versus identification in the laboratory: A causal analysis of attitude change. *Journal of Personality and Social Psychology,* 1979, *37,* 2171–2180.

Rosenbaum, M. The effect of stimulus and background factors on the volunteering response. *Journal of Abnormal and Social Psychology*, 1956, *43*, 118–121.

Rosenberg, L. A. Group size, prior experience, and conformity. *Journal of Abnormal and Social Psychology*, 1961, *2*, 436–437.

Rosenberg, M. *Conceiving the self*. New York: Basic Books, 1979.

Rosenberg, M. J. When dissonance fails: On eliminating evaluation apprehension from attitude measurement. *Journal of Personality and Social Psychology*, 1965, *1*, 28–42.

Rosenberg, M. J. A structural theory of attitudes. *Public Opinion Quarterly*, 1960, *24*, 319–340.

Rosenblum, B. Style as social process. *American Sociological Review*, 1978, *43*, 422-438.

Rosenfield, D., & Stephan, W. G. Sex differences in attributions for sex-typed tasks. *Journal of Personality*, 1978, *46*, 244–259.

Rosenhan, D. L. On being sane in insane places. *Science*, 1973, *179*, 250–258.

Rosenhan, D. L., Underwood, B., & Moore, B. Affect moderates self-gratification and altruism. *Journal of Personality and Social Psychology*, 1974, *30*, 546–552.

Rosenkrantz, P., & Crockett, W. Some factors influencing the assimilation of disparate information in impression formation. *Journal of Personality and Social Psychology*, 1965, *2*, 397–402.

Rosnow, R. L., & Fine, G. A. *Rumor and gossip: The social psychology of hearsay*. New York: Elsevier, 1976.

Ross, A. S. C. U and non-U: An essay in sociological linguistics. In M. Steinmann, Jr. (Ed.), *New rhetorics*. New York: Scribner's, 1967.

Rosten, L. *The joys of Yiddish*. New York: Pocket Books, 1970.

Rothman, J. *Issues in race and ethnic relations: Theory, research and action*. Itasca, Ill.: F. E. Peacock, 1977.

Rotter, J. B. Generalized expectancies for internal versus external control of reinforcement. *Psychological Monographs*, 1966, *80* (1, Whole No. 609).

Rotter, J. B., Chance, J. E., & Phares, E. J. *Applications of social learning: A learning theory of personality*. New York: Holt, Rinehart & Winston, 1972.

Rubin, Z. Measurement of romantic love. *Journal of Personality and Social Psychology*, 1970, *16*, 265–273.

Rubin, Z. *Liking and loving: An invitation to social psychology*. New York: Holt, Rinehart & Winston, 1973.

Rude, F. *The crowd in history, 1739–1848*. New York: Wiley, 1964.

Ruesch, J., & Kees, W. *Nonverbal communication*. Berkeley: University of California Press, 1956.

Russell, C. A., Banker, Jr., L. J., & Miller, B. H. Out-inventing the terrorist. In Y. Alexander, D. Carlton, & P. Wilkinson (Eds.), *Terrorism: Theory and practice*. Boulder, Colo.: Westview Press, 1979.

Ryan, E. B., & Carranza, M. A. Evaluative reactions of adolescents toward speakers of standard English and Mexican American accented English. *Journal of Personality and Social Psychology*, 1975, *31*, 855–863.

Safilios-Rothschild, C. *Love, sex, and sex roles*. Englewood Cliffs, N.J.: Prentice-Hall, 1977.

Sakurai, M. M. Small group cohesiveness and detrimental conformity, *Sociometry*, 1975, *38*, 340–357.

Salazar, J. M., & Marin, G. National stereotypes as a function of conflict and territorial proximity: A test of the mirror image hypothesis. *Journal of Social Psychology*, 1977, *101*, 13–19.

Sampson, E. E. Commentary. In R. M. Latta (Chair), Integrating psychological and sociological social psychology, symposium presented at the Eastern Psychological Association meetings, Hartford, Conn., 1980.

Sanders, G. S., & Baron, R. S. Is social comparison irrelevant for producing choice shifts? *Journal of Experimental Social Psychology*, 1977, *13*, 303–314.

Sanford, F. H. The follower's role in leadership phenomena. In G. E. Swanson, T. M. Newcomb, & E. L. Hartley (Eds.), *Readings in social psychology*. New York: Holt, Rinehart & Winston, 1952.

Sanford, N. *Issues in personality theory*. San Francisco: Jossey-Bass, 1970.

Sapir, E. *Language: An introduction to the study of speech*. New York: Harcourt, Brace & World, 1921.

Sarbin, T. R. Role theory. In G. Lindzey (Ed.), *Handbook of social psychology* (Vol. 1). Reading, Mass.: Addison-Wesley, 1954.

Sarbin, T. R., & Allen, V. L. Role theory. In G. Lindzey & E. Aronson (Eds.), *Handbook of social psychology* (2nd ed.), Vol. 3. Reading, Mass.: Addison-Wesley, 1968.

Sargent, S. S. Conceptions of role and ego in contemporary psychology. In J. H. Rohrer & M. Sherif (Eds.), *Social psychology at the crossroads.* New York: Harper & Row, 1951.

Sargent, S. S. Class and class consciousness in a California town. *Social Problems,* 1953, *1,* 22–27.

Sargent, S. S. Assessing community attitudes and social relations. In M. Sherif and M. O. Wilson (Eds.), *Emerging problems in social psychology.* Norman: University of Oklahoma Press, 1957.

Sargent, S. S. (Ed.) *Nontraditional therapy and counseling with the aging.* New York: Springer, 1980.

Sargent, S. S., & Smith, M. W. (Eds.), *Culture and personality.* New York: Wenner-Gren Foundation for Anthropological Research, 1949, 1974.

Sarnoff, I. *Personality dynamics and development.* New York: Wiley, 1962.

Sarnoff, I., & Zimbardo, P. Anxiety, fear and social affiliation. *Journal of Abnormal and Social Psychology,* 1961, *62,* 356–363.

Sawyer, J., & Guetzkow, H. Bargaining and negotiation in international relations. In H. C. Kelman (Ed.), *International behavior.* New York: Holt, Rinehart & Winston, 1965.

Scanzoni, J. H. *Opportunity and the family.* New York: Free Press, 1970.

Schachter, S. Deviation, rejection and communication. *Journal of Abnormal and Social Psychology,* 1951, *46,* 190–207.

Schachter, S. *The psychology of affiliation.* Stanford, Calif.: Stanford University Press, 1959.

Schachter, S. *Emotion, obesity, and crime.* New York: Academic Press, 1971.

Schachter, S., & Burdick, H. A field experiment on rumor transmission and distortion. *Journal of Abnormal and Social Psychology,* 1955, *50,* 363–371.

Schachter, S., Ellerton, N., McBride, D., & Gregory, D. An experimental study of cohesiveness and productivity. *Human Relations,* 1951, *4,* 229–238.

Schaie, K. W. Age changes in adult intelligence. In D. S. Woodruff & J. E. Birren (Eds.), *Aging: Scientific perspectives and social issues.* New York: Van Nostrand Reinhold, 1975.

Scheier, M. F., Fenigstein, A., & Buss, A. H. Self-awareness and physical aggression. *Journal of Experimental Social Psychology,* 1974, *10,* 264–273.

Schein, E. H. *Coercive persuasion.* New York: Norton, 1961.

Schmidt, D. E., Goldman, R. D., & Feimer, N. R. Perceptions of crowding: Predicting at the residence, neighborhood, and city levels. *Environment and Behavior,* 1979, *11,* 105–130.

Schorr, A. L. Housing and its effects. In H. M. Proshansky, W. H. Ittelson, & L. G. Rivlin, (Eds.), *Environmental psychology.* New York: Holt, Rinehart & Winston, 1970.

Schrieke, B. *Alien Americans.* New York: Viking Press, 1936.

Schuck, J., & Pisor, K. Evaluating an aggression experiment by the use of simulating subjects. *Journal of Personality and Social Psychology,* 1974, *29,* 181–186.

Schulz, R., & Hanusa, B. H. Experimental social gerontology. A social psychological perspective. *Journal of Social Issues,* 1980, *36:2,* 1980.

Scimecca, J. A. *Education and society.* New York: Holt, Rinehart & Winston, 1980.

Scroggs, G. F. *Sex, status and solidarity: Attributions for nonmutual touch.* Paper presented at the meeting of the Eastern Psychological Association, Hartford, Conn., 1980.

Sears, D. O. The paradox of de facto selective exposure without preferences for supportive information. In R. Abelson, E. Aronson, W. McGuire, T. Newcomb, M. Rosenberg, & P. Tannenbaum (Eds.), *Theories of cognitive consistency: A source book.* Chicago: Rand McNally, 1968.

Sears, D. O. Participation in the Los Angeles riot. *Social Problems,* 1969, *17,* 3–20.

Sears, D. O. *Positivity biases in evaluations of public figures.* Paper presented at the annual meeting of the American Psychological Association, Washington, D.C., 1976.

Sears, D. O., & McConahay, J. B. Racial socialization, comparison levels and the Watts riot. *Journal of Social Issues,* 1970, *26,* 121–140.

Sears, R. R. Some child-rearing antecedents of aggression and dependency in young children. *Genetic Psychology Monographs,* 1953, *47,* 135–234.

Sears, R. R., Maccoby, E. E., & Levin, H. *Patterns of child rearing.* New York: Harper & Row, 1957.

Secord, P. Facial features and inference processes in interpersonal perception. In R. Tagiuri & L. Petrullo (Eds.), *Personal perception and interpersonal behavior.* Stanford, Calif.: Stanford University Press, 1958.

Seelbach, W. C., & Sauer, W. J. Filial responsibility expectations and morale among aged parents. *Gerontologist,* 1977, *17,* 491–499.

Seward, G. H. Psychological effects of the menstrual cycle on women workers. *Psychological Bulletin,* 1944, *41,* 99.

Seward, G. H. *Psychotherapy and culture conflict* (2nd ed.). New York: Ronald Press, 1972.

Seward, J. P. The structure of functional autonomy. *American Psychologist,* 1963, *18,* 703–710.

Seward, J. P., & Seward, G. H. *Sex differences: Mental and temperamental.* Lexington, Mass.: Heath, 1980.

Shaffer, L. F., & Shoben, E. J. *Psychology of adjustment* (2nd ed.). Boston: Houghton Mifflin, 1956.

Shannon, C. E. Prediction and entropy of printed English. *Bell System Technical Journal,* 1951, *30,* 50–64.

Sharp, J. M. O. (Ed.). *Opportunities for disarmament.* Washington, D.C.: Carnegie Endowment for International Peace, 1978.

Shaw, M. E. Communication networks. In L. Berkowitz (Ed.), *Advances in experimental social psychology* (Vol. 1). New York: Academic Press, 1964.

Shaw, M. E. *Group dynamics: The psychology of small group behavior* (2nd ed.). New York: McGraw-Hill, 1976.

Shaw, M. E., & Costanzo, P. R. *Theories of social psychology.* New York: McGraw-Hill, 1970.

Sheppard, A. Response to cartoons and attitudes toward aging. *Journal of Gerontology,* 1981, *36,* 122–126.

Sherif, C. W., Sherif, M., & Neberhall, R. E. *Attitude and attitude change: The social judgment approach.* Philadelphia: Saunders, 1965.

Sherif, M. A study of some social factors in perception. *Archives of Psychology,* 1935, *187.*

Sherif, M., & Cantril, H. *Psychology of ego-involvements.* New York: Wiley, 1947.

Sherif, M., Harvey, O. J., White, B. J., Hood, W. R., & Sherif, C. W. *Intergroup conflict and cooperation: The Robbers Cave experiment.* Norman: Institute of Group Relations, University of Oklahoma, 1961.

Sherif, M., & Sherif, C. W. *Groups in harmony and tension.* New York: Harper & Row, 1953.

Sherif, M., & Sherif, C. W. *An outline of social psychology* (Rev. ed.). New York: Harper & Row, 1956.

Sherif, M., & Sherif, C. W. *Reference groups.* New York: Harper & Row, 1964.

Sherif, M., & Sherif, C. W. *Social psychology.* New York: Harper & Row, 1969.

Sherif, M., White, B. J., & Harvey, O. J. Status in experimentally produced groups. *American Journal of Sociology,* 1955, *60,* 370–379.

Shevrin, H., & Dickman, S. The psychological unconscious. *American Psychologist,* 1980, *35,* 421–434.

Shibutani, T. *Improvised news: A sociological study of rumor.* Indianapolis: Bobbs-Merrill, 1966.

Shils, E. A., & Janowitz, M. Cohesion and disintegration of the Wehrmacht in World War II. *Public Opinion Quarterly,* 1948, *12,* 280–315.

Shimbori, M. Zengakuren: A Japanese case study of student political movement. *Sociology of Education,* 1964, *37,* 229–253.

Shuter, R. A study of nonverbal communication among Jews and Protestants. *Journal of Social Psychology,* 1979, *109,* 31–41.

Silverman, L. H. The reports on my death are greatly exaggerated. *American Psychologist,* 1976, *31,* 621-637.

Simmel, G. *The sociology of George Simmel* (K. H. Wolff, Ed. and trans.). New York: Free Press, 1950. (Originally published, 1908).

Simmons, R. G., & Rosenberg, M. Functions of children's perceptions of the stratification system. *American Sociological Review,* 1971, *36,* 235–249.

Simpson, G. E., & Yinger, J. M. *Racial and cultural minorities* (4th ed.). New York: Harper & Row, 1972.

Simpson, I. H., Back, K. W., McKinney, J. C. Continuity of work and retirement activities, and self-evaluation. In I. H. Simpson & J. C. McKinney (Eds.), *Social aspects of aging.* Durham, N.C.: Duke University Press, 1966.

Singh, J. A. L., & Zingg, R. M. *Wolf child and feral man.* New York: Harper & Row, 1942.

Sinnott, J. D. Sex-role inconstancy, biology, and successful aging. *Gerontologist,* 1977, *17,* 459–463.

Skinner, B. F. *Science and human behavior.* New York: Macmillan, 1955.

Skinner, B. F. *Verbal behavior.* New York: Appleton-Century-Crofts, 1957.

Skinner, B. F. *Beyond freedom and dignity.* New York: Bantam, 1971.

Skinner, B. F. *About behaviorism.* New York:

Vintage Books, 1974.

Slobodin, R. Some social functions of Kutchin anxiety. *American Anthropologist,* 1960, *60,* 122–133.

Sly, D. F., & Pol, L. G. The demographic context of school segregation and desegregation. *Social Forces,* 1978, *56,* 1072–1086.

Smelser, N. J. *A theory of collective behavior.* New York: Free Press, 1962.

Smith, C. S. *Adolescence.* London: Longmans, Green, 1968.

Smith, M. B. *Humanizing social psychology.* San Francisco: Jossey-Bass, 1974.

Smith, P. C., and Curnow, R. "Arousal hypothesis" and the effect of music on purchasing behavior. *Journal of Applied Psychology,* 1966, *50,* 225–256.

Smith, R. E., & Campbell, A. L. Social anxiety and strain toward symmetry in dyadic attraction. *Journal of Personality and Social Psychology,* 1973, *28,* 101–107.

Smith, R. G. *Speech-communication: Theory and methods.* New York: Harper & Row, 1970.

Smoke, R. *War: Controlling escalation.* Cambridge, Mass. Harvard University Press, 1977.

Snow, D. A. Zurcher, L. A., Jr., & Ekland-Olson, S. Social networks and social movements: A microstructural approach to differential recruitment. *American Sociological Review,* 1980, *45,* 787–801.

Snyder, M. Self-monitoring processes. In L. Berkowitz (Ed.), *Advances in experimental social psychology* (Vol. 12). New York: Academic Press, 1979.

Sommer, R. *Personal space: The behavioral basis of design.* Englewood Cliffs, N.J.: Prentice-Hall, 1969.

Sonnenfeld, J. Variable values in space and landscape: An inquiry into the nature of environmental necessity. *Journal of Social Issues,* 1966, *22,* 71–82.

Sorenson, E. R. *The edge of the forest: Land, childhood and change in a New Guinea protoagricultural society.* Washington, D.C.: Smithsonian Institution Press, 1976.

Spiro, M. E. Culture and personality: The natural history of a false dichotomy. In A. D. Ullman (Ed.), *Sociocultural foundations of personality.* Boston: Houghton Mifflin, 1965.

Spiro, M. E. Whatever happened to the id? *American Anthropologist,* 1979, *81,* 5–7.

Spitz, R. A. Hospitalism. *Psychoanalytical study of the child,* 1945, *1,* 53–74.

Spranger, E. *Types of men.* Halle: Max Niemeyer, 1928.

Springborn, B. A. *Some determinants and consequences of the locus of evaluation in small group problem solving.* Unpublished doctoral dissertation, University of Michigan, 1963.

Staats, A. W. *Social behaviorism.* Homewood, Ill.: Dorsey, 1975.

Stagner, R. *Psychology of personality,* 3rd. ed. New York: McGraw-Hill, 1961.

Steiner, I. D., & Vannoy, J. S. Personality correlates of two types of conformity behavior. *Journal of Personality and Social Psychology,* 1966, *4,* 307–315.

Stockdale, J. E. Crowding: Determinants and effects. In L. Berkowitz (Ed.), *Advances in experimental social psychology* (Vol. 11). New York: Academic Press, 1978.

Stogdill, R. M. (B. M. Bass, Ed.), *Handbook of leadership.* Rev. ed. New York: Free Press, 1981.

Stokols, D. The experience of crowding in primary and secondary environments. *Environment and Behavior,* 1976, *8,* 49–85.

Stone, G. P. Appearance and the self. In A. M. Rose (Ed.), *Human behavior and social processes: An interactionist approach.* Boston: Houghton Mifflin, 1962.

Storandt, M. I., Wittels, I., & Botwinick, J. Predictors of a dimension of well-being in the relocated healthy aged. *Journal of Gerontology,* 1975, *30,* 97–102.

Storms, M. D., & Nisbett, R. E. Insomnia and the attribution process. *Journal of Personality and Social Psychology,* 1970, *16,* 319–328.

Stotland, E. Self-esteem, competence, and violence: Psychological aspects of the Kent State killings. In L. L. Farrar, Jr. (Ed.). *War: A historical, political and social study.* Santa Barbara, Calif.: ABC-Clio, 1978.

Stotland, E., et al. *Empathy, fantasy, and helping.* Beverly Hills, Calif.: Sage Publications, 1978.

Stotland, E., & Dunn, R. E. Identification "oppositeness," authoritarianism, self-esteem, and birth order. *Psychological Monographs,* 1962, *76* (No. 528).

Stouffer, S. A. *Social research to test ideas.* New York: Free Press, 1962.

Strauss, A. Mirrors and masks: Transformations of identity. In A. M. Rose (Ed.), *Human behavior and social processes.* Boston: Houghton Mifflin, 1962.

Stricker, L. J., Messick, S., & Jackson, D. N. Suspicion of deception: Implications for conformity research. *Journal of Personality and Social Psychology,* 1967, *5,* 379–389.

Strodtbeck, F. L., James, R. M., & Hawkins, R. M. Social status in jury deliberations. In E. E. Maccoby, T. M. Newcomb, and E. L. Hartley (Eds.), *Readings in social psychology* (3rd ed.). New York: Holt, Rinehart, & Winston, 1958.

Stryker, S. Developments in "two social psychologies": Toward an appreciation of mutual relevance. *Sociometry,* 1977, *40,* 145–160.

Stryker, S. Social psychology: Trends, assessment, and prognosis. *American Behavioral Scientist,* 1981, *24,* 386–406.

Swanson, G. E. Mead and Freud: Their relevance for social psychology. *Sociometry,* 1961, *24,* 319–339.

Swensen, C. H., Jr. *Introduction to interpersonal relations.* Glenview, Ill.: Scott, Foresman, 1973.

Swingle, P. G. Effects of the emotional relationships between protagonists in a two-person game. *Journal of Personality and Social Psychology,* 1966, *4,* 270–279.

Swingle, P. G. Dangerous games. In P. G. Swingle (Ed.), *The structure of conflict.* New York: Academic Press, 1970, pp. 235–276. (a)

Swingle, P. G. Exploitative behavior in non-zero sum games. *Journal of Personality and Social Psychology,* 1970, *16,* 121–133. (b)

Swingle, P. G. Motivational properties of performance feedback. *Psychonomic Science,* 1970, *18,* 73–75. (c)

Swingle, P. G. (Ed.). *Social psychology in natural settings.* Chicago: Aldine-Atherton, 1973.

Swingle, P. G. *The management of power.* Hillsdale, N. J.: Erlbaum, 1976.

Swingle, P. G. Damned if we do—Damned if we don't. In L. H. Strickland (Ed.), *Soviet and Western perspectives in social psychology.* Oxford: Pergamon, 1979.

Symonds, P. M. *The ego and the self.* New York: Appleton-Century-Crofts, 1951.

Szasz, T. S. *The manufacture of madness.* New York: Harper & Row, 1970.

Tagiuri, R. Person perception. In G. Lindzey & E. Aronson (Eds.), *Handbook of social psychology* (2nd ed., Vol. 3). Reading, Mass.: Addison-Wesley, 1969.

Taguiri, R., Bruner, J. S., & Blake, R. R. On the relation between feelings and perception of feelings among members of small groups. In E. E. Maccoby, T. M. Newcomb, & E. L. Hartley (Eds.), *Readings in social psychology* (3rd ed.). New York: Holt, Rinehart & Winston, 1958.

Tagiuri, R., & Kogan, N. Personal preference and the attribution of influence in small groups. *Journal of Personality,* 1960, *28,* 257–265.

Tajfel, H. Social and cultural factors in perception. In G. Lindzey & E. Aronson (Eds.), *Handbook of social psychology* (Vol. 3). Reading, Mass.: Addison-Wesley, 1969.

Tajfel, H. Experiments in intergroup discrimination. *Scientific American,* 1970, *223,* 96–102.

Tannenbaum, A. S. (Ed.). *Control in organizations.* New York: McGraw-Hill, 1968.

Tarde, G. *The laws of imitation* (E. C. Parsons, trans.). New York: Holt, Rinehart, & Winston, 1903.

Taulbee, E. S., & Wright, H. W. A psycho-social behavioral model for therapeutic intervention. In C. D. Spielberger (Ed.), *Current topics in clinical and community psychology.* New York: Academic Press, 1971.

Taylor, R. B. Perception of density. *Environment and Behavior,* 1981, *13,* 3–21.

Taylor, S. E., & Fiske, S. T. Salience, attention and attribution: Top of the head phenomena. In L. Berkowitz (Ed.), *Advances in experimental social psychology* (Vol. 11). New York: Academic Press, 1978.

Taylor, S. E., & Koivumaki, J. H. The perception of self and others: Acquaintanceship, affect and actor-observer differences. *Journal of Personality and Social Psychology,* 1976, *33,* 403–408.

Taylor, S. E., & Mettee, D. R. When similarity breeds contempt. *Journal of Personality and Social Psychology,* 1971, *20,* 75–81.

Taylor, S. P., & Pisano, R. Physical aggression as a function of frustration and physical attack. *Journal of Social Psychology,* 1971, *84,* 261–267.

Tedeschi, J. T., Schlenker, B. R., & Bonoma, T. Cognitive dissonance: Private ratiocination or public spectacle? *American Psychologist,* 1971, *26,* 685–695.

Tedeschi, J. T., Schlenker, B. R., & Bonoma, T. *Conflict power and games.* Chicago: Aldine-Atherton, 1975.

Terhune, K. W. The effects of personality in cooperation and conflict. In P. G. Swingle (Ed.),

The structure of conflict. New York: Academic Press, 1970.

Terrace, H. The linguistic capacity of apes. Paper presented at the Eastern Psychological Association meetings, Hartford, Conn., 1980.

Tesser, A., & Conlee, M. C. Some effects of time and thought on attitude polarization. *Journal of Personality and Social Psychology,* 1975, *31,* 262–270.

Theodorson, G. A. Acceptance of industrialization and its attendant consequences for the social patterns of non-Western societies. *American Sociological Review,* 1953, *18,* 477–483.

Thibaut, J. W., & Kelley, H. H. *The social psychology of groups.* New York: Wiley, 1959.

Thibaut, J. W., & Riecken, H. W. Some determinants and consequences of the perception of social causality. *Journal of Personality,* 1955, *24,* 113–133.

Thistlethwaite, D. L., deHaan, H., & Kamenetsky, J. The effects of "directive" and "nondirective" communication procedures on attitudes. *Journal of Abnormal and Social Psychology,* 1955, *51,* 107–113.

Thomas, W. I. *Primitive behavior.* New York: McGraw-Hill, 1936.

Thompson, D. F., & Meltzer, L. Communication of emotional intent by facial expression. *Journal of Abnormal and Social Psychology,* 1964, *68,* 129–135.

Thompson, L. *Culture in crisis.* New York: Harper & Row, 1950.

Thompson, L. *The secret of culture: Nine community studies.* New York: Random House, 1969.

Thompson, L., & Joseph, A. *The Hopi way.* Chicago: University of Chicago Press, 1947.

Thompson, W. C., Cowan, C. L., & Rosenhan, D. L. Focus of attention mediates the impact of negative affect on altruism. *Journal of Personality and Social Psychology,* 1980, *38,* 291–300.

Thorndike, E. L. *Animal intelligence.* New York: Macmillan, 1911.

Thurstone, L. L., & Chave, E. J. *The measurement of attitudes.* Chicago: University of Chicago Press, 1929.

Tiryakin, E. The existential self and the person. In C. Gordon & K. J. Gergen (Eds.), *The self in social interaction* (Vol. 1). New York: Wiley, 1968.

Tittle, C. R., & Villemez, W. J. Social class and criminality. *Social Forces,* 1977, *56,* 474–502.

Toch, H. *The social psychology of social movements.* Indianapolis: Bobbs-Merrill, 1965.

Toffler, A. *Future shock.* New York: Random House, 1970.

Toffler, Alvin. *The third wave.* New York: William Morrow & Co., 1980.

Tolman, E. C. *Purposive behavior in animals and men.* New York: Appleton-Century-Crofts, 1932.

Tolman, E. C. *Drives toward war.* New York: Appleton-Century-Crofts, 1942.

Tolman, E. C. A psychological model. In T. Parsons & E. A. Shils (Eds.), *Toward a general theory of action.* Cambridge, Mass.: Harvard University Press, 1951.

Triandis, H. C. *Interpersonal behavior.* Monterey, Calif.: Brooks/Cole, 1977.

Triplett, N. The dynamogenic factors in pacemaking and competition. *American Journal of Psychology,* 1898, *4,* 507–533.

Triplett, N. The psychology of conjuring deceptions. *American Journal of Psychology,* 1900, *11,* 439–510.

Turner, R. H. Collective behavior. In R. E. L. Faris (Ed.), *Handbook of modern sociology.* Chicago: Rand McNally, 1964.

Turner, R. H., & Killian, L. M. *Collective behavior.* Rev. ed. Englewood Cliffs, N.J.: Prentice-Hall, 1972.

Tur-Sinai, N. H. The origin of language. In R. N. Anshen (Ed.), *Language: An enquiry into its meaning and function.* New York: Harper & Row, 1957.

U.S. Riot Commission. *Report of the National Advisory Commission on Civil Disorders.* New York: Bantam Books, 1968.

Ulrich, R. E., & Mountjoy, P. T. *The experimental basis of social behavior.* New York: Appleton-Century-Crofts, 1972.

Underwood, B. J. The language repertoire and some problems in verbal learning. In S. Rosenberg (Ed.), *Directions in psycholinguistics.* New York: Macmillan, 1965.

Valins, S. Cognitive effects of false heart-rate feedback. *Journal of Personality and Social Psychology,* 1966, *4,* 400–408.

Vanneman, R. The occupational composition of American social classes: Results from cluster analysis. *American Journal of Sociology,* 1977, *82,* 783–807.

Vanneman, R., & Pampel, F. C. The American

perception of class and status. *American Sociological Review,* 1977, *42,* 422–437.

Venturi, R., Brown, D. S., & Izenour, S. Learning from Las Vegas. In W. H. Ittelson (Ed.), *Environment and cognition.* New York: Seminar Press, 1973.

Vernon, M. D. *Human motivation.* Cambridge: Cambridge University Press, 1969.

Veroff, J., Depner, C., Kulka, R., & Douvan, E. Comparison of American motives: 1957 versus 1976. *Journal of Personality and Social Psychology,* 1980, *39,* 1249–1262.

Verplanck, W. S. Since learned behavior is innate, and vice versa, what now? *Psychological Review,* 1955, *62,* 139–144.

Videbeck, R. Self-conception and the reaction of others. *Sociometry,* 1960, *23,* 351–359.

Visher, S. S. Scientists starred, 1903–1943. In *American men of science.* Baltimore: Johns Hopkins Press, 1947.

Walker, E. L., & Heyns, R. W. *An anatomy for conformity.* Englewood Cliffs, N.J.: Prentice-Hall, 1962.

Walster, E., Walster, G. W., & Berscheid, E. *Equity: Theory and research.* Boston: Allyn & Bacon, 1978.

Walters, R. Implication of laboratory studies of aggression for the control and regulation of violence. *Annals of the American Academy of Political and Social Science,* 1966, *364,* 60–72.

Waly, P., & Cook, S. W. Effect of attitude on judgments of plausibility. *Journal of Personality and Social Psychology,* 1965, *2,* 745–749.

Ward, C. D. Seating arrangement and leadership emergence in small discussion groups. *Journal of Social Psychology,* 1968, *74,* 83–90.

Ward, R. A. Age and acceptance of euthanasia. *Journal of Gerontology,* 1980, *35,* 421–431.

Warner, W. L., & Lunt, P. S. *The social life of a modern community.* New Haven: Yale University Press, 1941.

Warr, P. Inference magnitude, range and evaluative direction as factors affecting relative importance of cues in impression formation. *Journal of Personality and Social Psychology,* 1974, *30,* 192–197.

Warren, R. L. *Social change and human purpose.* Chicago: Rand McNally, 1977.

Wassermann, J. *Caspar Hauser: Enigma of a century.* Bauvelt, N.Y.: Steiner Publications, 1973.

Watson, R. K., Sr. *The history of psychology and the behavioral sciences.* New York: Springer, 1977.

Watts, W., & Free, L. A. Nationalism, not isolationism. *Foreign Policy,* 1976, No. 24, 3–26.

Weber, M. *Essays in sociology* (H. A. Gerth & C. W. Mills, trans.). Fair Lawn, N.J.: Oxford University Press, 1946.

Wehr, P. *Conflict resolution.* Boulder, Colo.: Westview Press, 1979.

Weick, K. E. Systematic observational methods. In G. Lindzey & E. Aronson (Eds.), *The handbook of social psychology* (2nd ed., Vol. 2). Reading, Mass.: Addison-Wesley, 1968.

Weiner, B. *Theories of motivation.* Chicago: Markham, 1972.

Wertheimer, M. Gestalt theory of learning. In G. M. Gazda & R. J. Corsini (Eds.), *Theories of learning.* Itasca, Ill.: F. E. Peacock, 1980.

West, S. G., Whitney, G., & Schnedler, R. Helping motorists in distress: The effects of sex, race and neighborhood. *Journal of Personality and Social Psychology,* 1975, *31,* 691–698.

Westergaard, J. H. The withering away of class: A contemporary myth. In P. Anderson & R. Blackburn (Eds.), *Toward socialism.* Ithaca, N.Y.: Cornell University Press, 1966.

Westin, A. F. *Privacy and freedom,* New York: Atheneum, 1967.

Weyant, J. M. Effect of mood states, costs and benefits on helping. *Journal of Personality and Social Psychology,* 1978, *36,* 1169–1176.

White, R. K. Misperception in the Arab-Israeli conflict. *Journal of Social Issues,* 1977, *33*:1, 190–221.

Whiting, J. W. M. Methods and problems in cross cultural research. In G. Lindzey & E. Aronson (Eds.), *The handbook of social psychology* (Vol. 2). Reading, Mass.: Addison-Wesley, 1968.

Whittaker, J. O. Attitude change and communication-attitude discrepancy. *Journal of Social Psychology,* 1965, *65,* 141–147.

Whittick, A. (Ed.). *Encyclopedia of urban planning.* New York: McGraw-Hill, 1974.

Whorf, B. L. *Collected papers on metalinguistics.* Washington, D.C.: U.S. Government Printing Office, 1952.

Whorf, B. L. *Language, thought and reality.* New York: Wiley, 1956.

Wicklund, R. A. Objective self-awareness. In L. Berkowitz (Ed.), *Advances in experimental social psychology* (Vol. 8). New York: Academic Press, 1975.

Wicklund, R. A., & Duval, S. Opinion change and performance facilitation as a result of objective self-awareness. *Journal of Experimental Social Psychology,* 1971, *7,* 319–342.

Wiley, N. The ethnic mobility trap and stratification theory. *Social Problems,* 1967, *15,* 147–159.

Williams, K., Harkins, S., & Latané, B. Identifiability as a deterrent to social loafing: Two cheering experiments. *Journal of Personality and Social Psychology,* 1981, *40,* 303–311.

Williams, R. M. *American society: A sociological interpretation* (3rd ed.). New York: Knopf, 1970.

Williams, R. M. Jr. Change and stability in values and value systems. In B. Barber & A. Inkeles (Eds.), *Stability and social change.* Boston: Little, Brown, 1971.

Williams, T. R. *Psychological anthropology.* The Hague: Mouton, 1975.

Williamson, R. C. Dating, courtship and the "ideal mate": Some relevant subcultural variables. *Family Life Coordinator,* 1965, *14,* 137–143.

Williamson, R. C. Modernism and related attitudes: An international comparison among university students. *International Journal of Comparative Sociology,* 1970, *11,* 130–145.

Williamson, R. C. *Marriage and family relations* (Rev. ed.). New York: Wiley, 1972.

Williamson, R. C. Social distance and ethnicity: Some subcultural factors among high school students. *Urban Education,* 1976, *11,* 295–312.

Williamson, R. C. Orientation to change in advanced and developing societies: A cross-national sample. In L. L. Adler (Ed.), *Issues in cross-cultural research. Annals of the New York Academy of Sciences,* 1977, *285,* 565–580. (a)

Williamson, R. C. Variables in adjustment and life goals among high school students. *Adolescence,* 1977, *12,* 213–225. (b)

Williamson, R. C. Socialization in the high rise: A cross-national comparison. *Ekistics,* 1978, *45,* 122–130.

Williamson, R. C. Adjustment to the high rise: Variables in a German sample. *Environment and Behavior,* 1981, *13,* 289-310.

Williamson, R. C., & Van Eerde, J. A. "Subcultural" factors in the survival of secondary languages: A cross-national sample. *International Journal of the Sociology of Language,* 1980, *25,* 59–83.

Willie, C. V., et al. Race and delinquency. *Phylon,* 1965, *26,* 240–246.

Wilmot, W. W. *Dyadic communication: A transac-tional perspective.* Reading, Mass.: Addison-Wesley, 1975.

Wilson, J. *Introduction to social movements.* New York: Basic Books, 1973.

Wilson, P. R. Perceptual distortion of height as a function of ascribed academic status. *Journal of Social Psychology,* 1968, *74,* 97–102.

Wilson, S. *Informal groups: An introduction.* Englewood Cliffs, N.J.: Prentice-Hall, 1978.

Winterbottom, M. R. The relation of need for achievement to learning experiences in independence and mastery. In J. W. Atkinson (Ed.), *Motives in fantasy, action and society.* New York: Van Nostrand Reinhold, 1958.

Wish, M., D'Andrade, R. G., & Goodnow, J. E., II. Dimensions of interpersonal communication: Correspondences between structure for speech acts and bipolar scales. *Journal of Personality and Social Psychology,* 1980, *39,* 848–860.

Wispe, L. G. Evaluation section teaching methods in the introductory course. *Journal of Educational Research,* 1951, *45,* 161–186.

Woelfel, J. C. Political attitudes: Sources for white American youth. *Youth and Society,* 1978, *9,* 433–452.

Wolf, C. P. The structure of societal revolutions. In G. K. Zollschan and W. Hirsch (Eds.), *Social change.* New York: Schenkman, 1976.

Wong, R. *Motivation: A biobehavioral analysis of consummatory activities.* New York: Macmillan, 1976.

Wood, W., & Eagly, A. H. Stages in the analysis of persuasive messages: The role of causal attributions and message comprehension. *Journal of Personality and Social Psychology,* 1981, *40,* 246–259.

Wortman, C. B. Causal attributions and personal control. In J. H. Harvey, W. J. Ickes, & R. F. Kidd (Eds.), *New directions in attribution research* (Vol. 1). Hillsdale, N.J.: Erlbaum, 1976.

Wright, J. D., & Wright, S. R. Social class and parental values for children: A partial replication and extension of the Kohn thesis. *American Sociological Review,* 1976, *41,* 527–537.

Wright, S. *Crowds and riots: A study in social organization.* Beverly Hills, Calif.: Sage Publications, 1978.

Wyer, R. S., Jr. *Cognitive organization and change: An informative processing approach.* New York: Wiley, 1974.

Wylie, R. C. The present status of self theory. In E. F.

Borgatta & W. W. Lambert (Eds.), *Handbook of personality theory and research.* Chicago: Rand McNally, 1968.

Yinger, J. M. *Toward a field theory of behavior.* New York: McGraw-Hill, 1965.

Yinon, Y., & Bizman, A. Noise, success and failure as determinants of helping behavior. *Personality and Social Psychology Bulletin,* 1980, *6,* 125–130.

Young, K. *Social psychology* (3rd ed.). New York: Appleton-Century-Crofts, 1956.

Zablocki, B. The use of crisis as a mechanism of social control. In G. K. Zollschan & W. Hirsch (Eds.), *Social change.* New York: Schenkman, 1976.

Zajonc, R. B. *Social psychology: An experimental approach.* Belmont, Calif.: Wadsworth, 1966.

Zalkind, S. S., Gaugler, E. A., & Schwartz, R. M. Civil liberties attitudes and personality measures: Some exploratory research. *Journal of Social Issues,* 1975, *31*:2, 77–91.

Zemore, R., & Eames, N. Psychic and somatic symptoms of depression among young adults, institutionalized aged and noninstitutionalized aged. *Journal of Gerontology,* 1979, *34,* 716–722.

Zigler, E., & Child, I. L. *Socialization and personality development.* Reading, Mass.: Addison-Wesley, 1973.

Ziller, R. C. The alienation syndrome: A triadic pattern of self-other orientation. *Sociometry,* 1969, *32,* 298.

Zillman, D. *Decay of arousal: Implications for aggression.* Paper presented at the meeting of the Eastern Psychological Association, Hartford, Conn., 1980.

Zimbardo, P. G. *The cognitive control of motivation: Consequences of choice and dissonance.* Glenview, Ill: Scott Foresman, 1969.

Zimbardo, P. G. The human choice: Individuation, reason, and order versus deindividuation, impulse, and chaos. In W. J. Arnold & D. Levine (Eds.), *Nebraska Symposium on Motivation, 1969.* Lincoln: University of Nebraska Press, 1970.

Zimbardo, P. G., Cohen, A. R., Wesienberg, M., Dwarkin, L., & Firestone, I. The control of experimental pain. In P. G. Zimbardo (Ed.). *The cognitive control of motivation.* Glenview, Ill: Scott Foresman, 1969.

Zimbardo, P., & Ebbesen, E. B. *Influencing attitudes and changing behavior.* Reading, Mass.: Addison-Wesley, 1970.

Zollschan, G. K., & Friedman, W. Leadership and social change. In G. K. Zollschan & W. Hirsch (Eds.), *Social change.* New York: Wiley, 1976.

NAME INDEX

SUBJECT INDEX

The page numbers in heavy print indicate the definition of the term in the Glossary ("Words to Remember") at the end of each chapter.

Social Psychology was typeset at Parthenon Press, Nashville, Tennessee, printed and bound by Haddon Craftsmen, Scranton, Pennsylvania. The cover and internal design was by John D. Firestone & Associates, Inc., Canal Winchester, Ohio. The typeface is Souvenir with Sinaloa display.